The American Polity

The People and Their Government

THIRD EDITION

The American Polity

Polity THIRD EDITION

The People and Their Government

Everett Carll Ladd

University of Connecticut
The Roper Center for Public Opinion Research

W · W · Norton & Company

New York   London

Published simultaneously in Canada by Penguin Books Canada Ltd., 2801
John Street, Markham, Ontario L3R 1B4.

PRINTED IN THE UNITED STATES OF AMERICA.
Acknowledgments and copyrights appear on pages B23–B24, which constitute a continuation of the copyright page.

Cover photograph: Steve Liss / *Time* Magazine

Library of Congress Cataloging-in-Publication Data
Ladd, Everett Carll.
    The American polity: the people and their government /
Everett Carll Ladd.—3rd ed.
        p. cm.
    1. United States—Politics and government. I. Title.
JK274.L23   1989
320.973—dc19   88-12562

ISBN 0-393-95787-X

W. W. Norton & Company, Inc., 500 Fifth Avenue, New York, N. Y. 10110

W. W. Norton & Company Ltd., 37 Great Russell Street, London WC1B
3NU
1 2 3 4 5 6 7 8 9 0

For My Family

We begin our public affections in our families.
No cold relation is a zealous citizen.
                                —Edmund Burke

Contents

Part 2 Political Beliefs and Practice

Part 3 Governance

Preface

The American political parade is marching along faster than ever these days, and texts on government and politics have to hustle lest they get left far behind, unable to view the action. The decision reached shortly after the first edition was published in 1985 to revise the text substantially every two years is in large part a necessary response to the quickened pace of change in a nation and a world shrunk by satellite communication, computer networks, and jet air travel. For better and for worse, we have become more occupied with current political developments, and more insistent that our political illustrations and examples be chosen from them.

Revisions of an American government textbook must also be tailored to the schedule of our national elections—which are a recurring watershed. While our institutions show great stability and continuity, the conduct of government and the course of public policy reflect the biennial shift in the partisan balance that elections produce. Voting in years divisible by four gets the most attention, of course, because it decides who will occupy the White House as well as all 435 members of the U.S. House of Representatives and a third of the Senate. The 1988 election was certain as well to have an additional, special result—the assumption of power by a new administration. After 8 years in office, the Reagan administration was going to end on January 20, 1989, with the inauguration of a new president.

The assumption of power by a new administration is always a momentous event in the American system. In one sense the transition to the Bush administration in 1989 has been less abrupt than others historically because, while presidents were changing, the party in power was remaining the same. When Republican Reagan passes the baton to Republican Bush, it will be the first time since the Coolidge–Hoover transition in 1929 that a retiring incumbent is succeeded by a member of his own party. (Perhaps this parallel is not the most propitious). I am writing now and until early spring a new chapter that will examine the transition and first hundred days of George Bush's administration. (This chapter will be bound into every student copy for courses in fall 1989 and beyond; instructors will receive their advance copy of the chapter in late spring.)

Also, for the third edition, I have added two new chapters. The first, The American System of Divided Government (chapter 5), incorporates material that appeared in chapters 10 (Separation of Powers) and 11 (Federalism) of the second edition. Many faculty using the text have told me that they would like to see a coherent review of both separation of powers and federalism *preceding* the discussion of the institutions of national government—Congress, the presidency, the executive branch, and the judiciary—that comprises chapters 6 through 9. I thought they were right when I began this revision; now I am certain their advice was sound. I am also confident that students will find the integration of federalism and separation of powers in one chapter a more powerful introduction to what is the most striking feature of American government—the extent to which political responsibility is divided.

I have added a *wholly* new chapter (chapter 18), State Government and Public Policy. Students learn in chapter 5 that states have a large formal place in the structure of American government. Now they will see as well that state involvement extends throughout the processes of deciding what government will and will not do: the making of public policy. The role of the states in policy formation is a key one in our system; through the new chapter 18 it is more extensively and explicitly recognized in *The American Polity*.

Throughout, the third edition has been extensively updated: new material on the 1988 campaign and election, of course; new discussions, from the 1988 Trade Act to the INF Treaty, to make clear the changing problems and policies that dominate our attention as we enter the last decade of the twentieth century; new case studies, like President Reagan's attempt to appoint Robert Bork to the Supreme Court, to give a contemporary statement to familiar subjects; a thorough-going revision of tables and charts to make sure students are given the most up-to-date economic statistics, public opinion polling data, information on governmental performance, and the like.

Adding so much new material to a new edition could, however, cause a problem with the length of the text. Like others who teach the American government course, I sometimes yearn for a more concise text presentation. So, by combining two second-edition chapters on the Constitution and democracy into one chapter, streamlining other chapters, and eliminating sections that are not pertinent to politics of the 1990s, I have for the third edition reduced the overall length of *The American Polity*. (I might also note that for those who desire a less expensive though identical version for their students, a low-priced paperback edition is now available.)

As I call attention to our many efforts to make *The American Polity* the freshest possible introduction to our politics, institutions, and policies, I want to affirm the position that guided the first two editions and is undiminished here: For all of the change, *continuity* remains the big story in American political life. Historical experience must be melded with contemporary material if students are to be properly introduced to a polity that almost defines Alphonse Karr's aphorism: "Plus ça change, plus c'est la même chose."

APPROACHING THE STUDY OF AMERICAN GOVERNMENT

Students reading this text have already acquired information on the study of American government and politics from discussions with family and friends, in high school classes, through television, newspapers and magazines, and more. But the subject is a big one, and the ways of examining it vary enormously. In writing *The American Polity* I have assumed a readership aware of a familiar subject yet often unclear how the pieces fit together, how the system works. This audience needs a text that provides the store of basic common information about the polity required for further study and for informed citizenship: detailed information on American political beliefs and values, the primary institutions of government, the form and substance of political participation by individuals and groups, and the major policy commitments and choices the United States has made. But students also need greater depth and unity in a subject all too often studied piecemeal. This depth is achieved by providing as backdrops three different perspectives: societal, historical, and cross national.

Societal perspective. Social science has carved up the study of social experience into discrete segments, divided among disciplines like political science, economics, and sociology. This is unavoidable, but society is not so compartmentalized. Those parts of American society that we label "government" influence and in turn are influenced by all of the other parts—components involving the economy; systems of social and cultural values; education and technology; the ethnic, racial, and religious group composition of the population; and many others. The first section of the text looks closely at aspects of American society that are especially important in defining the environment for the country's government, politics, and public policy. In the remaining chapters I keep returning to the many concrete links between the polity and the larger society of which it is a part.

Historical perspective. As I noted above, with so much to discuss about the practice of American government today, the influence of the past can easily be shortchanged. Historical perspective is essential, for two somewhat different reasons. First, contemporary institutions and practices did not suddenly emerge full grown. We understand them better—whether it is the presidency, political parties, or American welfare policy—by seeing the course they have taken. To ignore the past is to deprive ourselves of an immense amount of comparative experience.

Second, there have been powerful continuities in American political experience. With the drafting of the U.S. Constitution in 1787 and its ratification a year later, a set of political institutions consistent with the country's political beliefs were put in place (see chapters 3 and 4). The persistence of the primary political institutions—the Constitution, the presidency, Congress, the judiciary, the sharing of power by the federal and state governments—over the last two centuries is an extraordinary feature of American political experience. In the text I frequently draw examples from earlier eras in American life to make more concrete that important continuities are everywhere evident in our political system, even in the face of great social and economic change.

Cross-national perspective. Some of the responses the United States has given to enduring problems of policy and governance closely resemble those made by Great Britain, France, West Germany, and the other major industrial democracies. But the American system also reflects its own distinctive institutional arrangements and policy choices. By providing cross-national comparison throughout, I have tried to present our own system in a rounder, more complete, and accurate way.

THE PLAN OF THE BOOK

As we have seen, the third edition contains many changes, but the basic organization of the book remains intact. The first two parts of *The American Polity* survey the setting for American political life. Part 1 examines the social setting, including the country's social origins and development, present-day economic trends, and such diverse social attributes of the populace as their ethnic backgrounds and educational attainments. Part 2 looks at the central beliefs and values of Americans: the country's ideological tradition, derived from classical liberalism; the expression of this ideology in the basic law, the Constitution; our commitment to and practice of a particular type of democratic government.

We move in Part 3 to a detailed consideration of the principal institutions and arrangements of national government. These include the distinctly American form of governmental interaction, built around *separation of powers, checks and balances,* and *federalism;* it also includes the Congress, the presidency and the executive branch, and the federal courts.

From the organization of government in Part 3, we turn in Part 4 to public opinion, political parties, voting and elections, interest groups, and communications media—the means by which groups participate in politics and government. People do not participate in a political vacuum, but in and through the setting their governmental institutions establish. The American system of dispersed power, accruing from separation of powers and federalism, gives interest groups many diverse points of governmental access through which to advance their goals.

Part 5, the last section of the text, is devoted to American public policy in five major sectors: civil liberties and civil rights, political economy, public welfare, the role of the states in making public policy, and defense and foreign policy. Like every other political system, the American polity ultimately expresses itself in the character of the policy choices it makes.

Lastly, on the text, I call this book *The American Polity.* With the same Greek root as the word politics, polity is a more succinct way of saying political system, and the two expressions are used interchangeably throughout this book. But there is reason beyond stylistic convenience for calling this an inquiry into the American polity. The greatest writer on politics in all of antiquity, and one of the most profound theorists of all time, was the Athenian philosopher Aristotle (384 to 322 B.C.). The first to write systematically on democracy as a system of government, Aristotle distinguished between two basic forms of democracy: One involved direct rule by the people, which he thought carried with it great threats to personal liberty and minority rights; the other was based on constitutionalism and the guarantee of individual rights, which he thought held promise of being the best of all government. Aristotle called the latter πολιτεια, or politeia, translated as polity or constitutional government.[1]

The American system of government is a polity in Aristotle's sense of the term: a particular type of democracy established on the principles of constitutionalism and representation, with safeguards for minority rights. It deserves to be studied as a whole, as something more than a collection of separate institutions and processes. It is in the meshing of diverse political activities and the interplay of people and their government that we most clearly see what is distinctive about our polity.

---

[1] *The Politics of Aristotle,* H. Rackham, trans. (Cambridge, MA: Harvard University Press, 1977), pp. 206–7.

THE LADD REPORTS AND LADD UPDATES

Daily newspapers like the *New York Times*, the *Los Angeles Times*, and the *Christian Science Monitor*, the broadcast networks, and weekly magazines of governmental affairs such as *Congressional Quarterly* and *National Journal* help us follow the ever-changing course of political events. But the perspective of a political science text, going beyond the headlines and analyzing the dynamics of American society and government, is also important. So for the third edition I will continue to write more extensive *Ladd Reports*, as well as briefer commentaries, the *Ladd Updates*, as the political occasions arise. The publisher will continue to make these available without charge to all students by request of instructors who are using *The American Polity* in their classrooms.

THE STUDY GUIDE AND INSTRUCTOR'S MANUAL

The *Study Guide* for *The American Polity* has been revised thoughtfully and imaginatively by David B. Magleby of Brigham Young University. Margaret Kenski of Pima Community College and Henry Kenski of the University of Arizona have expertly developed the combined *Instructor's Manual and Test-Item File* to reflect third edition changes.

ACKNOWLEDGMENTS

The third edition of *The American Polity* benefited from use by teachers and students at numerous universities, colleges, and community colleges, a broad and representative proving ground for a basic American government text. Fellow teachers of the introductory American government classes who have used *The American Polity* have provided me with constructive criticism that I have done my best to follow. My own classes of Political Science 173 at the University of Connecticut have continued to be a wonderful source for what works, and what doesn't work, in introducing students to American government and politics.

   This preface gives me a chance to acknowledge the help of faculty who gave me written assessments of the previous edition:

John Adams
   Millsaps College
Joseph M. Bristow
   County College of Morris
Ronald J. Busch
   Cleveland State University

Vernon Coleman
   The George Washington University
James S. Fleming
   Rochester Institute of Technology

Adrienne Fulco
Trinity College
Arthur B. Gunlicks
University of Richmond
Calvin Jillson
University of Colorado
Walter J. Jones
Memphis State University
Sarah Weiner Keidan
Oakland Community College
James W. Lindeen
The University of Toledo
Joseph R. Marbach
Temple University
Jack K. Masson
The University of Alberta
William D. McCarty
Norton & McCarty, P.A.

Wayne V. McIntosh
The University of Maryland
Christine Ridout
University of Lowell
John W. Sanderson
La Grange College
Joseph F. Schuster
*Eastern Washington
University*
Thaddeus J. Tecza
*University of Colorado,
Boulder*
Shirley Warshaw
Gettysburg University
Mikel L. Wyckoff
Northern Illinois University

I want to add a note of special thanks to George Cole of the University of Connecticut, John White of the Catholic University, and Ralph Bastedo of Furman University, for their many helpful suggestions for the new edition.

Burns W. Roper, chairman of the Roper polling organization, and Richard J. Cattani, editor of the *Christian Science Monitor,* have been sources of guidance and inspiration in a great many personal and professional regards. Working closely with my friends at *Public Opinion* magazine during the past seven years has also taught me much—besides being great fun. Seymour Martin Lipset and Ben J. Wattenberg have been coeditors throughout. David R. Gergen was the first managing editor. William Schambra was the magazine's first deputy managing editor, a position now held by Victoria A. Sacket. Nicola L. Furland and Graham Hueber have been assistant editors. I said in the preface to the second edition that I owe a debt to the current managing editor of *Public Opinion,* Karlyn H. Keene, that almost rivals the one run up by the Reagan administration. That is still true, as both have climbed. Her honesty, support, and unfailing good judgment have made this a better book.

My colleagues at the University of Connecticut have been extraordinarily tolerant and forbearing. Ranking high in these regards, as in helpfulness, are W. Wayne Shannon, G. Donald Ferree, Jr., Marily Potter, John Benson, Lois Timms-Ferrara, Anne-Marie Mercure, and John Barry. Ranking even higher, because her position put her so directly in the line of fire, is my research assistant, Marianne Simonoff. Her care and diligence have been invaluable throughout the project. I am pleased to be able to express here special thanks and deep appreciation to my administrative assistant, Lynn A. Zayachkiwsky. Yet I am afraid that these words are but a pale, too-feeble recognition of the consistently exemplary quality of her work.

Sometime in 1968, I had the great good fortune of meeting Donald S. Lamm. He was then a college editor at W. W. Norton, and from our discussions came my commitment to write a history of the U.S. party system—published two years later by Norton as *American Political Parties: Social Change and Political Response*. I have worked with him on a number of books since then, and the collaboration has been the most important of my professional life. Now as president of Norton, he has had a big hand in delivering *The American Polity*. As always, his support was valuable and his friendship invaluable. My many other Norton associations have been strong and positive. Donald Fusting has been my editor through all three editions of this text; my respect for his work has continued to deepen. Nancy Palmquist again did a wonderful job copyediting the entire manuscript. She and Ruth Dworkin deserve enormous credit for handling professionally and expeditiously the production of the book, especially the late-arriving November '88 election-related manuscript that might otherwise have resulted in a later publication date. Ben Gamit is responsible for the book's attractive layout, Elizabeth Garrigue for cover illustration selection, Hugh O'Neill for turning that selection into an appealing cover, and Rachel Lee for tying up a number of loose ends.

First things last: *The American Polity* is dedicated to my father and the memory of my mother, my wife Cynthia and our children Benjamin, Melissa, Corina and Carll, to Carll's wife Elizabeth Lovejoy Ladd and their newborn son Ryan Carll, and Corina's husband Gerald Moran.

Storrs, Connecticut
December 1988

Part 1

American
Society

Chapter 1

The American Polity: Continuity and Change

On May 9, 1831, a twenty-six-year-old French aristocrat completed an arduous voyage to the New World by setting foot in the seaport town of Newport, Rhode Island, where his New York–bound ship had been forced by an unobliging wind. Alexis Charles Henri Clerel de Tocqueville had come ostensibly to study American prisons in order to advise his government on penal reform. But Tocqueville's real intention was to examine "in detail and as scientifically as possible, all the mechanisms of that vast American society which everyone talks of and no one knows." Nine months later, on February 20, 1832, having crisscrossed the United States and interviewed hundreds of Americans—including President Andrew Jackson—Tocqueville sailed for home. It was not until a year and a half later, in the fall of 1833, that Tocqueville began in earnest to write his book. Working quickly, he finished one volume of his study in just a year. In January 1835, that first volume of *De la Democratie en Amerique* was published in Paris. It was immediately acclaimed a masterpiece not only in France but also in Great Britain and the United States. Now, more than 150 years later, it still lays fair claim to being considered the best book ever written about American society and politics.[1]

Tocqueville set out to accomplish two objectives that relate to the study of American government in our own time, and he largely suc-

---

[1] *Democracy in America* is available in several fine English translations and editions. The original Henry Reeve translation, as revised by Francis Bowen, and later further corrected by Phillips Bradley, has been published in paperback in two volumes (New York: Vintage Books, 1958). A one-volume paperback edition contains most of the essential material (New York: New American Library; first published, 1956). For a valuable description of Alexis de Tocqueville, his journey, and his ideas, see George Wilson Pierson, *Tocqueville in America* (Garden City, N.Y.: Doubleday/Anchor Books abridgement, 1959; first published as *Tocqueville and Beaumont in America*, 1938).

ceeded: to see the system as a whole, and to see where it was headed and why.

To see the system as a whole. Tocqueville believed that one could not understand a country's government by looking just at its governmental institutions. There was a strong interaction among (1) the beliefs and values of a people, (2) their social institutions, and (3) their political system. He thought, for example, that the religious beliefs and institutions the Puritans had brought with them to New England contributed much to the vigorous democratic practice that took root long before independence was achieved from the British Crown. The Puritans thought that every individual should have a knowledge of Scripture, which meant that everyone should be able to read—so they pioneered in establishing a compulsory system of public education. This helped make citizens more aware and better able to involve themselves in community life. Believing that each individual was equal in the eyes of God, the Puritans proposed rules, compacts, and institutions that gave each person a voice in affairs such as government. Such beliefs were "not merely a religious doctrine, but ... corresponded in many points with the most absolute democratic and republican theories," Tocqueville wrote. In New England "a democracy more perfect than antiquity had dared to dream of started in full size and panoply from the midst of an ancient feudal society."[2]

The early Americans and democracy

This was just one of many linkages involving beliefs, social institutions, and governmental arrangements that Tocqueville described in *Democracy in America*. We cannot understand today's American government and politics unless we recognize that ideas and values, economic perspectives and institutions, the social makeup of the population as defined by ethnicity, education, income, and all such dimensions of American society constantly impinge upon the country's political life.

American society and government

To see where we are headed and why. Tocqueville lived at a time when Western society was caught up in extraordinary change. The old order based on the principle of aristocracy—in which social position was determined by birth, and a small hereditary elite enjoyed a great disproportion of wealth, social status, and political power—was coming under attack and being replaced, with varying rates of speed from one country to another. The newly ascendant principles were: (1) individualism, (2) social equality, and (3) political democracy. *Individualism* involves the idea that society is built around the individual and is obliged to provide him with such rights as life, liberty, and a full chance to pursue happiness. It also carries with it an emphasis on individual responsibility, and the belief that society advances best

Individualism in society

[2] Tocqueville, *Democracy in America* (Vintage Books edition), vol. 1, p. 37.

Alexis de Tocqueville

Social equality and
political democracy

Democracy in America

by encouraging individual achievement. Tocqueville saw the tide of individualism rising throughout the West.

Tocqueville also believed that the increase of *social equality* was irresistible. The aristocracy to which he belonged in France had been humbled by the cry of *égalité* during the French Revolution (begun in 1789); similar currents were sweeping all of Europe. "The gradual development of the principle of equality is, therefore, a providential fact. It has all the chief characteristics of such a fact: it is universal, it is lasting, it constantly eludes all human interference, and all events as well as all men contribute to its progress."[3] Social arrangements rooted in the idea that some groups have a permanent claim to superior status, which was the basis of aristocratic society, were collapsing and would never be reestablished. *Political democracy* followed naturally from individualism and social equality. If societies were giving greater recognition to the claims of individuals who had equal rights and deserved an equal chance to work and achieve, political institutions providing for popular sovereignty or rule by the people would have to be devised and extended.

The world Tocqueville knew was beset by changes that forced societies to come to terms with the great ideas of individualism, equality, and democracy. It was a revolutionary era. Where would it end? The young Frenchman felt that "there is a country in the world where the great social revolution which I am speaking of seems to have nearly reached its natural limits." He meant America. So he came here

[3] Ibid., p. 6.

America has long offered opportunity to people from other lands—witness this eighteenth-century "Help Wanted in America" advertisement.

in order to discern its natural consequences and to find out, if possible, the means of rendering it profitable to mankind. I confess that in America I sought more than America; I sought there the image of democracy itself, with its inclinations, its character, its prejudices, and its passions, in order to learn what we have to fear or to hope from its progress.[4]

Still, Tocqueville really did not believe that the progress of individualism, equality, and democracy was going to be the same elsewhere as in the United States. The success of these ideas in America was unique because it was so free of conflict. The revolutionary impact of the ideas occurred

Uniqueness of American democracy

with ease and simplicity; say rather that this country is reaping the fruits of the democratic revolution which we [in Europe] are undergoing, without having had the revolution itself. The emigrants who colonized the shores of America in the beginning of the seventeenth century somehow

[4]Ibid., p. 15.

separated the democratic principle from all the principles which it had to contend with in the old communities of Europe, and transplanted it alone to the New World.[5]

America was founded on revolutionary ideas; but the speed with which these ideas triumphed had in a sense left America a conservative nation, one that throughout history would seek to maintain and extend values established at its birth rather than pursue new ones.

Continuity

The political ideals that dominated American life in Tocqueville's day remain ascendant in our own time. They continue to shape the approach of many of the most important political and social movements.

Individualism. The United States is still distinguished by strong currents of individualism. Over the years, the precise claims that individuals make have changed, and so have our views concerning whose rights are insufficiently recognized. Today, for example, the movement for women's rights is stronger and more politically active than in the past. The women's movement is wide-ranging, with a variety of different goals, but underlying it is the basic idea that women are individuals whose claims to the opportunity to achieve personal fulfillment and happiness are the equal of men's. Individualism frames,

Individualism

[5] Ibid., p. 14.

too, the terms or boundaries of many of the sharpest political disputes in the contemporary United States. What are the rights of individuals accused of crimes, and what measures should law enforcement officials and courts take to ensure them? How are these rights to be balanced against the rights and interests of the rest of the population? Or, in another area, to what extent should abortion be left as a matter of individual choice, rather than proscribed by law? No polity has done more than the U.S. polity to put the individual at the pinnacle of things—or argued more about which individual rights need greater emphasis.

Equality. In the same way, the egalitarianism that Tocqueville found in early America continues to distinguish the United States in the 1980s. The public's ideal of equality has consistently asserted that each individual must be given an opportunity to strive and to achieve according to his or her efforts and ability, without regard to the individual's social background. It is an ideal that insists on *equality of*

President Abraham Lincoln guided the Union through the Civil War, a war of states' rights and of equality.

opportunity—although emphatically not on *equality of result*. If some individuals work harder or are more able, they should, in the American sense of equality, be permitted to enjoy their rewards. During the Great Depression in the 1930s, public opinion pollsters asked a sample of the populace whether they thought government should impose

limits on how much money people could earn. Even with economic hardship widespread and tensions high, the majority of the populace rejected the idea of income limits. Even the poorest Americans said no to it. This same response is given by Americans today.

The goal of equal opportunity for everyone is, even with the greatest effort, impossible to achieve fully. And the United States at times has not made the effort at all. The denial of equality of opportunity to black Americans is the most flagrant instance where we mocked our ideal. But if it has been denied far more than we like to acknowledge, the goal of equal opportunity is nonetheless a powerful force in our national experience. It underlies the many laws national and state governments have enacted to bar discrimination by race, religion, sex, and other such attributes extraneous to individual effort and performance. And it helps account for the enormous positive commitment the United States has made to education, including bringing higher education within the reach of a larger proportion of the population than in any other country. We see the provision of educational opportunity as a primary means by which individuals of diverse backgrounds are given a chance to compete more effectively in social and economic life.

Democracy. The third principle that Tocqueville saw shaping the American political system also remains in place: Government should rest on the foundation of majority rule. Over the years, the precise machinery through which citizens choose their political leaders and democratic government functions has changed in a number of ways, some far from inconsequential. But the commitment to political democracy has remained vital. One aspect of this vitality is a general recognition that the democratic ideal is never fully or finally realized. Throughout U.S. history, there have been recurring movements committed to "political reform," which in virtually all instances has meant trying to make the democratic system operate in closer accord with certain ideal standards.

As we will see in the chapters that follow, debate continues today about what steps should be taken to increase the rate of voter turnout in American elections. Issues of campaign finance—including the increasing cost of electioneering, where the money now comes from and where it should come from—are lively ones. Reforming the political parties so that they can better perform their representative functions is under continuous debate, especially with regard to the presidential nomination process. Congressional reform—involving such matters as the organization and powers of committees and subcommittees, and the influence of interest groups in the legislative process—is seen by many to be critical. The role of the Supreme Court and the rest of the federal judiciary in making public policy prompts heated debate about the proper distribution of power and responsibility among the three branches of government.

Table 1.1
Eras in American Social and Political Development

Sociopolitical period	Approximate time span	Sociopolitical period	Approximate time span
Rural republic	1780s–1850s	Industrializing nation	1860s–1910s

A rural and localized society; land-owning farmers are the dominant economic group; government's role is highly limited and centered at the state and local levels.

An urbanizing society of increasing scale; there is rapid growth of industry and commerce, leading to the ascendancy of corporate business; government's role involves the promotion of industrialization and, subsequently, its regulation.

The fact that the ideas and ideals of individualism, equality, and democracy still form the underpinnings of the American system and frame the terms of the political debate imparts an extraordinary continuity to our political life. As historian Henry Steele Commager remarked, "Circumstances change profoundly, but the character of the American people has not changed greatly or the nature of the principles of conduct, public and private, to which they subscribe."[6]

SOCIAL CHANGE OFTEN DRIVES POLITICAL CHANGE

Sociopolitical periods For all the persistence of governmental institutions and underlying values, American society has been far from static. Evolving from a small farming nation settled on the eastern edge of the North American continent to a highly developed nation spanning the continent and exerting great influence on world affairs, the United States has packed into its two hundred years since independence massive changes in technology, economic life, demographic makeup, and more. With these changes, every American political institution has grown and evolved. Not every piece of social change has had a major impact on

[6]Henry Steele Commager, *Living Ideas in America* (New York: Harper and Brothers,1951), p. xviii.

Table 1.1 (continued)
Eras in American Social and Political Development

Sociopolitical period	Approximate time span	Sociopolitical period	Approximate time span
Industrial state	1920s–1950s	Postindustrial society	1960s–present

A mature urban, industrial society; complex, integrated industrial economy requiring central management; organized labor becomes a major economic and political interest group, power shifts to the national government, and government's role is greatly expanded.

A society of advanced technology, built on a heavy commitment to science and education; the service sector of the economy expands greatly, while manufacturing proportionally declines; older economic interests, including organized labor, lose influence; the proper management of government's role in the political economy becomes the primary domestic issue.

government and politics, of course, but the accumulated changes have. The components of a social setting are subject to many new developments starting at different times and proceeding at different rates; these changes finally merge to produce a new setting distinct from the preceding one. The idea of a **sociopolitical period** refers to the persistence of underlying social and economic relationships, and their accompanying demands on government, over a span of time. The United States has seen four great sociopolitical periods, each defined not by the passing of years but by the changing of society (Table 1.1). We are mainly interested here in the last of these, the period in which we are living, but we can better understand the present by seeing the process of change through which American society and government have arrived at it.[7]

The rural republic. During the first great social and political period, from the time the Constitution was drafted and ratified in the late 1780s to just before the beginning of the Civil War, the United States

[7] These developments are discussed at length in Everett C. Ladd, *American Political Parties: Social Change and Political Response* (New York: Norton, 1970).

An agricultural economy

was a pre-industrial society: Land-owning farmers were the dominant group, economically and politically. In 1800 more than four out of every five Americans who worked were farmers, and fifty years later farmers still comprised about two-thirds of the labor force. In 1839, agriculture accounted for nearly 70 percent of the total value of the commodity output of the U.S. economy. Since most people worked in jobs that required little formal or theoretical training, education could be limited to what was required for literacy. Besides, this preindustrial society could not afford to sustain any substantial portion of its productive-age population in "nonproductive" schooling. The U.S. educational system was a primary-school system: Of the 3.5 million pupils enrolled in 1850, only 20,000 were in grades nine and above; less than 1 percent of the population were high-school graduates; and the degrees awarded by all institutions of higher education numbered fewer than 3,000.

The economic activities we identify as "business"—banking, trade, manufacturing—were limited; big business simply did not exist. The Northeast was the center of the country's nascent commerce and manufacturing; in 1850 it accounted for three-fourths of the United States's manufacturing employment, concentrated in industries such as cotton and woolen goods, men's clothing, and shoes.[8] The West of this first period was the "Old West," what we now know as the North Central states. Its economy was mostly agricultural, and wheat and corn were the most important crops.

The South and cotton growing

The American South underwent major social and economic changes in the first half of the nineteenth century. In 1800 it was a land of small farmers. Their egalitarianism was much more characteristic of the South than was privileged life of the great planters and their slave-based agriculture in areas like tidewater Virginia. But in the early nineteenth century the South's cotton culture became a highly prosperous and expanding enterprise, and slavery an entrenched institution. The most important causes of this transformation were Eli Whitney's invention of the cotton gin, a machine for cleaning cotton; the opening up of extremely rich soil perfectly suited for the cotton culture in Georgia, Alabama, and Mississippi; and, with the peace and renewal of trade that followed the Napoleonic wars in Europe, an enormous market for raw cotton to be used in textile manufacturing. The South produced only 73,000 bales of cotton in 1800, but more than 525,000 bales in 1825, 2.1 million in 1850, and 4.4 million in 1861.[9] The extension of the plantation system made southern society much more highly stratified and increased inequalities of income. Power came to rest with the planter class. The net effect of these

[8] Douglass C. North, *The Economic Growth of the United States, 1790–1860* (New York: Norton, 1966), pp. 115–60.
[9] U.S. Bureau of the Census, *Historical Statistics of the United States: Colonial Times to 1970* (Washington, D.C.: Government Printing Office, 1975), p. 518.

changes was to set the South further apart from the rest of the country; differences in political culture, modest at the turn of the century, had become a chasm on the eve of the Civil War.

In 1790, 95 percent of all Americans lived on farms or in small villages; the biggest city, Philadelphia, had less than 50,000 inhabitants. Even by 1850, 85 Americans in every 100 were still rural dwellers. This population was scattered over an area that grew through annexations from just under a million square miles in 1790 to 3 million at mid-century. People and goods moved through this vast expanse by waterways, and on land by animal and on foot. There were no railroads until 1830, and in 1850 only the beginnings of the vast railroad network soon to be developed. In communications the first telegraph service (between Baltimore and Washington) did not begin until 1844. There was no integrated national economy, no national media of communication; Maine and South Carolina were separated by weeks of arduous travel.

Transportation and communication

In this highly localized society, "states' rights" had a basic legitimacy that most of us now cannot easily recognize. A large federal government just was not needed in this independent farming society. Federal spending averaged only two dollars per capita each year from the turn of the century through the 1850s. Most governing occurred at the state and local level.

The industrializing nation. In the years from the Civil War in 1865 up to the 1920s, the United States became the leading industrial nation, with about one-third of the world's total manufacturing capacity. In the 1860s a clear majority of American workers were in agriculture; but the agricultural labor force began a precipitous relative decline as manufacturing and commerce expanded. By 1920 only about one out of every four workers engaged in farming. Between 1870 and 1920, the number of workers in trade and finance jumped from 830,000 to 8.5 million; in transportation and other public utilities from 640,000 to 4.2 million; and in manufacturing from 2.3 million to 10.9 million.

Growth and centralization

The population of the United States tripled between 1870 and 1920, reaching 106 million. During this period the great cities we know today were built. By 1900, New York City's population had climbed to over 3 million, and New York had taken its place as one of the world's great metropolises. In place of small family farms producing food only for local areas, big corporations drew resources from throughout the country and the world, and serviced national markets. This was the half-century in which all the major electronic media except television developed. Telephones first came into use in the 1870s, and by 1920 13.3 million of them were in use in the country. A new transportation network was established, centered on the railroad and the motor car, and the physical mobility of the population was vastly extended. The productive capacities of the economy were enormously expanded by industrialization. Between 1870 and 1920 the gross national product (GNP) of the United States—measuring the value of all goods and services produced—increased in real terms by roughly 800 percent.[10]

Expansion of government

The increases of scale and interdependence that took place in the second period spurred the expansion of government. Regulation for working conditions had made little sense when most Americans were independent farmers; it was a different matter when millions entered the ranks of factory labor. Pure food and drug legislation did not seem imperative when most people lived on farms and consumed what they produced; the call for such regulation became increasingly insistent with the impersonality of big cities and big business corporations. The industrializing society required much higher investments in education than its agricultural predecessor had; total public expenditures for education grew from just $90 million in 1875 to $558 million in 1913 and $2.2 billion in 1927. The expansion of government services took place mostly at the state and local level; federal expenditures were only moderately higher in the 1870–1920 period (apart from World War I) than they had been before the Civil War, and what increase did take place was largely accounted for by defense, veterans' pensions, and interest on the debt.

The industrial state. The Great Depression, which began in 1929, did not so much create as abruptly signal the emergence of a new socio-political setting, the third decisive one in American history. It shifted national attention from one set of concerns to another with unaccustomed speed. Long before the Depression there had been recognition that the further industrial development proceeded and the bigger and more integrated the economy became, the more central economic management and regulation the country would require and the more governmental protection individuals would need. Overall, though, in 1929 the response in American political thought and governmental institutions lagged behind the requirements of the new setting.

The rise and fall of the business elite

Political power in the United States was redistributed after 1929. In the half-century of rapid industrialization, businessmen had acquired enormous political influence. They had come to be seen as the architects of prosperity. The country was engaged in a great enterprise, and they were the instruments for its betterment. Then, almost overnight, with the Depression, instead of cheers there were boos and catcalls. Instead of being the custodians of American prosperity, the builders of the American dream, they were presiding over

[10] These data are from *Historical Statistics of the United States*, p. 231. Describing the increase as 800 percent in *real* terms means controlling for the effects of price changes. In this case, the purchasing power of the dollar in 1929 was used as the base for recalculating the GNP for each year in the span between 1869 and 1931.

Franklin D. Roosevelt signs into law the Social Security Act of 1935, marking a major shift toward greater governmental responsibility in the lives of Americans.

an economic system in unparalleled collapse and appeared powerless to effect a remedy.

Organized labor was one of the principal new claimants for power and recognition in the industrial state. Industrialization had created a large urban working class; but for it to assume real political power it needed effective organization. This was achieved in the ten years after 1935. In the early 1930s just over 10 percent of the nonagricultural work force belonged to labor unions. The general encouragement to unionization given by the administration of Franklin D. Roosevelt, legislation enacted by Congress, and the vigorous initiatives of a new generation of labor leaders produced a surge in membership, which brought it to about 35 percent of the nonagricultural labor force just after World War II. Labor leaders acquired much more economic and political influence than they ever had before.

Rise of organized labor

Prompted by the economic collapse of the 1930s, and more generally by the increased demands of an urban and industrial society, government took on new responsibilities. In 1913 total spending by the national, state, and local governments had been about $33 per person. That figure jumped to $130 per person in 1936, $375 in 1948, and $837 in 1960. Inflation accounted for some of this increase, but much of it was real and reflected government's assumption of a big role in public welfare and economic management. And, responding to the greater integration and interdependence of the society and the national character of many of its problems, the federal government's share of public spending rose above the combined total of the states and municipalities after World War II, the first time this had occurred when the country was at peace. Federal spending has exceeded state and local spending every year since.

New governmental responsibilities

Technology, industrial age and postindustrial, has altered the nature of work and production.

Postindustrial society. Today we read about how American politics is changing. By the late 1960s and 1970s, a great variety of changes had come together to define yet another social era, the fourth in the country's history: the postindustrial society. Since American society now differs significantly from that of the New Deal industrial era, the polity could scarcely have remained static.

In the next chapter we review the key transformations that have ushered in the new postindustrial setting and shaped it. And throughout this text we discuss government and politics against the backdrop of the contemporary society—its needs and resources, its group composition and interests, and its social organization.

FOR FURTHER STUDY

Everett C. Ladd, *American Political Parties: Social Change and Political Response* (New York: Norton, 1970). Analyzes changes in American political parties and politics against the backdrop of basic changes occurring in American society.

Seymour Martin Lipset, *The First New Nation* (New York: Doubleday, 1963). A classic study of the social origins and development of the United States by a distinguished political sociologist.

Clinton Rossiter, *Seedtime of the Republic* (New York: Harcourt, Brace, Jovanovich, 1953). A thoughtful, highly readable history of American social and political experience in the colonial and revolutionary periods, stressing the development of American political thought.

Alexis de Tocqueville, *Democracy in America* (New York: Vintage Books, 1959), in two volumes. Also available in other excellent editions, abridged and unabridged. A brilliant interpretation of the underlying dynamics of American society and government, written and first published in the 1830s by Tocqueville, a young French aristocrat who had toured the United States during Andrew Jackson's presidency.

U.S. Bureau of the Census, *Historical Statistics of the United States: Colonial Times to 1970*, Parts 1 and 2 (Washington, DC: Government Printing Office, 1975). An extremely useful historical reference work in two volumes, containing comprehensive census data on diverse aspects of American life dating back to the first census of 1790.

Chapter 2

Postindustrial Society

What is this present-day sociopolitical setting in the United States, which many observers have labeled **postindustrial?** Its advances in technology have expanded national wealth and increased public expectations not just for private-sector consumption but also for government-provided services. Its demands for research and knowledge have fueled extraordinary increases in higher education and in professional and service occupations, which in turn have changed the makeup of the country's political interests and interest groups. For instance, labor unions now have as members more teachers than steelworkers, more government employees than autoworkers.

A vast national communications system has been erected, with television and the other electronic media at the center. These new forms of mass communication have greatly changed our leisure-time activities, of course, but they have also changed our politics. There is more news coverage these days than even two decades ago. One sign of this increase was the creation in June 1980 of a new cable network, Cable News Network (CNN), reporting news twenty-four hours a day. In April 1988, CNN was received by just over 50 percent of all households in the United States.

But much more is involved than increased news coverage by electronic media. Christopher J. Matthews, the principal assistant to House Speaker Thomas P. O'Neill, Jr., until O'Neill's retirement in December 1986, argues that "at a dizzying pace, the TV news networks have absorbed many of the democratic functions traditionally held by political parties: the elevation of key public issues, the promotions of new leaders, the division of executive and legislative authority, and the constitution of political opposition." The parties have not found any means of reversing these developments, which have profound implications for representative government. "Today," Matthews writes, "network executives make these decisions ... on a rational mix of 'news judgment' and commercial savvy. For better or worse, the nation's dogged two-party system has been challenged by a three-network system that runs at much higher voltage and delivers at a speed approaching light itself."[1]

Before looking further at the ramifications of the postindustrial era, let's sort out further the main characteristics of this period.

CONTEMPORARY AMERICA: A POSTINDUSTRIAL SOCIETY

The term "postindustrial society" was first introduced by sociologist Daniel Bell.[2] He contrasted this era with the preceding era, writing that "industrial society is the coordination of machines and men for the production of goods." Postindustrial society is "organized around knowledge."[3] The key developments defining the postindustrial era are "the exponential growth and branching of science, the rise of a new intellectual technology, the creation of systematic research through R & D [research and development] budgets, and ... the codification of theoretical knowledge."[4] Other observers have reached similar conclusions.

Postindustrialism: five key developments

Throughout this book, "postindustrial society" refers specifically to the cumulative result of five key developments or sources of social change.

(1) Advanced technology. Postindustrial America is a society built upon advanced technology. Technology itself is not a recent phenomenon, but technology built primarily upon abstract and theoretical knowledge *is* new.

(2) The knowledge base. This technology requires an unprecedented commitment to science and education. And it permits an unprecedentedly large proportion of the populace to engage in intellectual rather than manual labor.

(3) Occupations: The service economy. The occupational makeup of the work force in the postindustrial setting differs from that of the

[1]Christopher J. Matthews, "Boss Tube," *The New Republic*, December 16, 1985, p. 15.
[2]Bell has noted that the term actually appeared earlier than his first usage of it, with a quite different meaning, in an essay that David Riesman wrote on "Leisure and Work in Postindustrial Society," printed in the compendium *Mass Leisure* (Glencoe, Ill: Free Press, 1958). Bell's most important treatment of postindustrialism may be found in his book *The Coming of Postindustrial Society* (New York: Basic Books, 1973).
[3]Bell, *Coming of Postindustrial Society*, p. 20.
[4]Ibid., p. 44.

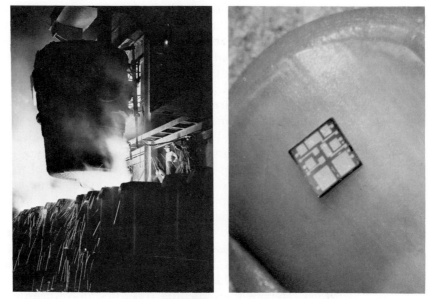

Products of two eras: for the industrial age, it was heavy industry, here, steel; for the postindustrial era, it is the computer industry, here, a microchip so small that a dozen could rest on a thumbnail.

industrial era and earlier times. The white-collar and service sectors grow. Bureaucracy becomes the distinctive work setting.

(4) Mass affluence. Postindustrial America is an affluent society, one where the increase in national wealth, built on technological innovation, has been so substantial as to move a large proportion, though by no means all, of the populace beyond active concern with matters of subsistence.

(5) New class relationships. The character of social classes and their relationships in the postindustrial era are very different from previous eras. Increased wealth and education, together with a new occupational mix, produce a new class structure.

Let's look more closely at each of these components to better understand recent changes that have altered not just the economy and social relations but also the setting for American political life.

ADVANCED TECHNOLOGY

Technology

Technology is commonly defined as the application of knowledge for practical ends. In this general sense the United States has made serious use of technology from its very inception. In the nineteenth century, knowledge about electricity and steam engines was applied with an extraordinary practical impact in manufacturing, transportation, and communication. The country was criss-crossed with rail, telephone, and telegraph lines, and heavy industries like coal and steel were developed. All this contributed to exceptionally large increases in industrial productivity. Manufacturing output climbed by about 1200 percent in the half-century following the Civil War.[5]

From tinkerers to industries

Almost all of the major industries that grew up in the nineteenth and early twentieth centuries—including steel, electric power, the automobile, and the telephone—were "mainly the creation of inventors, inspired and talented tinkerers who were indifferent to science and the fundamental laws underlying their investigations."[6] William Darrah Kelley and Sir Henry Bessemer developed the oxidation process that made it possible to mass-produce steel—even though they were unaware of the emerging science of metallurgy. Thomas Alva Edison did his major work on something he vaguely referred to as "etheric sparks," which resulted in the electric light and otherwise sparked the first electronic revolution—even though he was not sympathetic to the theoretical research being done on electromagnetism.

Applying theoretical knowledge

What distinguishes the technology of postindustrial society is a change in the character of innovation: the sustained application of *theoretical* knowledge for practical ends. Most of the worlds that lay before the "talented tinkerers" have been conquered. Since World War II technological progress has been based directly and explicitly on theoretical knowledge—and thus on the work of the scientific community. From chemicals to computers, from military hardware to agriculture, from genetic engineering to superconductors, the dependence on science is now generally acknowledged.

Science Comes of Age

Industry, science, and education

One indication of this dependence is the extent to which business corporations have tied themselves to science and higher education. New industrial complexes have grown up around leading research universities. The development of the computer industry in the "Silicon Valley" near Stanford University in California, and on "Route 128" near the Massachusetts Institute of Technology (MIT), are the most dramatic instances. Many of the leading corporations have become major employers of scientific talent. International Business Machines (IBM), the largest computer manufacturer, employed about 2500 Ph.D.s in 1984. Bell Laboratories, a unit of American Telephone and Telegraph (AT&T), employed over 2600 in 1985; and DuPont, the chemical giant, had over 3400 men and women with doctorates on its payroll in the United States alone in 1986—a larger number than employed at most research universities. And this does not account for the hundreds more Ph.D.s employed by DuPont's foreign subsidi-

---

[5]Based on an index of manufacturing production developed by Edwin Frickey, *Production in the United States, 1860–1914* (Cambridge, Mass: Harvard University Press, 1947). The index is reprinted in U.S. Bureau of the Census, *Historical Statistics of the United States: Colonial Times to 1970*, Part 2, p. 667.
[6]Bell, *Coming of Postindustrial Society*, p. 20.

aries, or for the three hundred or so M.D.s and J.D.s also on DuPont's payroll.

Research and
development (R&D)

There has been a vast increase in the economic resources committed to **research and development** (R&D). The age of the great inventors like Alexander Graham Bell and Thomas Alva Edison, and the gifted implementors of technology like Henry Ford, is in many ways an attractive, even romantic one, involving as it did the solitary individual working with very modest resources in his own garage or tiny laboratory. The practice in postindustrial America contrasts greatly with James Conant's recollection that during World War I, as president of the American Chemical Society, he offered the services of the society to Newton D. Baker (then Secretary of War) only to be told that those services would not be needed because the War Department already had a chemist! Conant also described a board headed by Edison, created to help the Navy during World War I, on which Edison placed one physicist because, as he told President Woodrow Wilson, "we ought to have one mathematician fellow in case we have to calculate something out."[7]

However romantic that earlier industrial era seems, it is gone forever. Technological innovation now requires large commitments of resources. Economist John Kenneth Galbraith notes that it cost just $28,500 to produce the first Ford in 1903, compared to $60 million to engineer and tool up for the production of the first Mustang in 1964. And two decades later, it cost Ford $3 billion to produce the first Taurus.

R&D

The growth of R&D

In 1940, all branches of the national government spent just $74 million for research and development. Two decades later, federal R&D expenditures had climbed to $8.7 billion; and in 1987 the national government's R&D spending was over $61 billion. (See Table 2.1.)

Table 2.1
Research and Development Expenditures since the 1940s (in millions of dollars)

| | Industrial ⟶ Postindustrial | | | | | |
	1940	1950	1960	1970	1980	1987
All R&D expenditures (government and private)			13,730	26,134	60,222	124,250
Federal government expenditures for R&D	74	1,093	8,746	14,896	29,555	61,350

Source: 1940–50: U.S. Bureau of the Census, *Historical Statistics of the United States: Colonial Times to 1957*, p. 613. 1960: Idem, *Historical Statistics of the United States: Colonial Times to 1970, Part I*, p. 965. 1970–82: Idem, *Statistical Abstract of the United States*, 1988, p. 557.

[7]James Bryant Conant, *Modern Science and Modern Man* (New York: Columbia University Press, 1952), pp. 8–9.

The private sector in the United States expended another $63 billion for R&D in 1987, for a total R&D commitment of over $124 billion.

Even when the effects of inflation are taken into account, one finds a growth in R&D from World War II to the present so great as to change the essential character of scientific and technological innovation in the postindustrial age.

THE KNOWLEDGE BASE

Advanced technology, derived from theoretical knowledge, requires a large cadre of scientists and engineers for its continuation and a highly trained and educated labor force for its use. At the same time, by developing machinery to do work once assigned to manual labor and by increasing productivity and national wealth so massively, it has permitted an unprecedented proportion of the population to engage in educational and other intellectual activities.

The American Education Explosion

The knowledge society

We see the essential character of the *knowledge society* in the United States's commitment to education since World War II. In 1940 just 5 percent of the population age 25 and older had graduated from college. But by 1986 the proportion was over 19 percent. As Figure 2.1 shows, in the last decade and a half alone the formal educational attainment of the American population has extended dramatically.

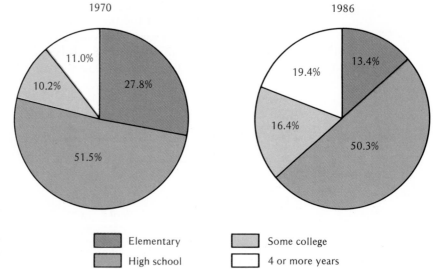

Educational Attainment in America, 1970 and 1986 (percentages are of those 25 years of age and older)

Source: U.S. Bureau of the Census, *Statistical Abstract of the United States*, 1979, p. 145; idem, 1988, p. 126.

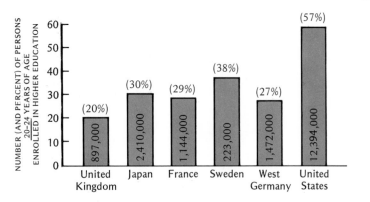

Figure 2.2
**Levels of Higher Educa-
tion in Leading Indus-
trial Nations**

Source: World Bank, *World Development Report, 1984* (New York: Oxford University Press, 1987), p. 263. United Nations Education, Scientific, and Cultural Organization (UNESCO), *Statistical Digest* (Paris: UNESCO, 1986), pp. 148, 206, 267, 270, 274, 306, 310. The data are for 1983–84.

In 1970, about 28 percent of those 25 years and older had only elementary school training; in 1986, that proportion had been more than cut in half, dropping to just 13 percent. The proportion with at least some college training climbed from about 21 percent to 36 percent.

College enrollments in the U.S. and abroad

Not only are these figures extraordinary by comparison to earlier periods in U.S. history, but they are also impressive when compared to other countries—even the most advanced nations. In 1983–84, when 12.4 million Americans attended higher education institutions, only 1.5 million West Germans, 1.1 million French, and 900,000 British citizens were enrolled in comparable schools in their respective countries. Those nations have much smaller total populations than the United States, of course, but as Figure 2.2 shows, the percentage of young Americans attending college—about 57 percent in 1983—dwarfs higher education enrollments in any other industrial nation.

Soaring Expenditures for Education

America's commitment to education has been costly. In 1930, we spent roughly $3.4 billion for education, from elementary school through college, public and private. Expenditures climbed only modestly through 1950—but at this point they took off. By 1987, as shown in Figure 2.3, spending for education in the United States had reached $282 billion, $112 billion for higher education and $170 billion for elementary and secondary training.

Public support for educational spending

Americans have borne these heavy financial obligations to education with little complaint. In 1987, the General Social Survey conducted by the National Opinion Research Center asked a cross-section of the public whether they thought we were, as a nation, spending too much, too little, or about the right amount on education. Sixty-

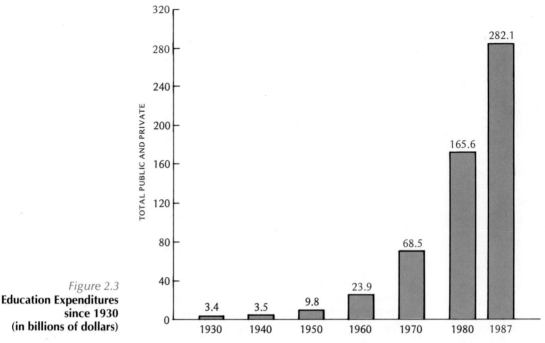

Source: 1930–50: U.S. Bureau of the Census, *Historical Statistics of the United States: Colonial Times to 1970, Part I,* pp. 373–74, 375, 384. 1960–87: Idem, *Statistical Abstract of the United States 1988,* p. 119.

six percent said we were *not spending enough*—this at a time when national expenditures for education were about $280 billion a year! Only 5 percent responded that too much was being expended, while 29 percent said expenditures were at approximately the right level.

Vigorous arguments continue on important issues facing the American educational system: Are teachers' salaries high enough? Are educational standards high enough? Should parents be given vouchers, paid for with tax dollars, that they can use to pay for private as well as public primary and secondary schooling for their children? Some critics argue that at present the nation's schools are not doing enough to teach basic skills, or not enough to prepare young people for tomorrow's jobs. But if the search for excellence and equity in American education is complicated and unending, there seems to be no doubt that the public recognizes education's immense role in our postindustrial society and is prepared to support it.

OCCUPATIONS: THE SERVICE ECONOMY

In 1790, the first American decennial census found 95 percent of the total work force engaged in agricultural pursuits. As late as 1860, on

Industrialism: from the farm to the factory

the eve of the Civil War, a large majority of the work force (roughly three-fifths) was still in agriculture—compared to about one-fifth in non-farm manual labor jobs and one-fifth in various white-collar and service positions. The rapid industrialization of the late nineteenth and early twentieth centuries changed this ratio dramatically. Millions of Americans left farms and rural areas for factories and the cities. Between 1860 and 1920, the number of Americans engaged in non-farm blue-collar jobs jumped from 2 million to 17 million and neared what was to be its all-time high as a proportion of the total labor force.

Rise of the white-collar worker

After World War II, with the further introduction of machinery into agriculture, the proportion of farmers in the labor force continued to drop—*but so did the proportion of blue-collar workers.* Between 1950 and 1980, the American labor force increased by about 30 million. This was entirely accounted for by the white-collar and service sector, which climbed from about 28 million in 1950 to 64 million in 1980. The rapid expansion in the blue-collar and manufacturing work force had been a prime indicator of the growth of the industrial society. The explosion in the number of white-collar and service workers is a distinctive sign of postindustrialism. When in 1956 the number of white-collar workers outnumbered blue-collar workers, it was the first time in the United States or anywhere in the world that the balance had thus shifted.

Services, Services

One problem in referring to the growth in the number of "white-collar and service" workers is that the category covers so much ground. It includes those who work as household servants; persons in other personal services such as the operators of beauty shops and retail stores; those in business services like banking and real estate; individuals employed in transportation, communication, and utilities; and those in health, education, research, and government.

Classifying jobs by sector

One way to bring the current mix of occupations into sharper focus is to classify all jobs by the "industry sector" into which each falls. The U.S. Bureau of Labor Statistics (BLS) identifies nine such sectors. Four of them might be thought of as "things producing": agriculture, mining, construction, and manufacturing. The shares of the total labor force employed by two of these sectors—agriculture and manufacturing—have continued to get smaller, in large part as a result of enormous increases in per-worker productivity. The proportion in agriculture dropped from 4.4 to 2.9 percent from 1970 to 1986, while the proportion in manufacturing declined from 26.4 to 19.1 percent.

The other five sectors that BLS identifies are all in some sense "services producing," but the range of services is extremely broad: communication and transportation; wholesale and retail trade; finance,

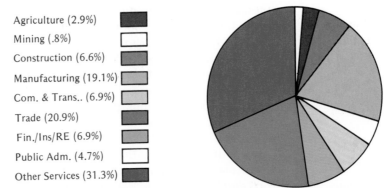

Agriculture (2.9%)
Mining (.8%)
Construction (6.6%)
Manufacturing (19.1%)
Com. & Trans.. (6.9%)
Trade (20.9%)

Figure 2.4
Employment by Industry Sector, 1986 (in percent)

Fin./Ins/RE (6.9%)
Public Adm. (4.7%)
Other Services (31.3%)

Source: U.S. Bureau of the Census, *Statistical Abstract of the United States,* 1988, p. 379.

insurance, and real estate; public administration; and a large residual category of other services including computer and data processing, entertainment and recreation, health and education. As Figure 2.4 shows, about 70 percent of all American workers were in one or another of these service industries.

Professional and Technical Employment

Growth of professional and technical jobs

The ranks of those employed in professional and technical jobs (teachers, scientists, computer programmers, engineers, etc.) have expanded twice as fast as the entire work force. In 1950 about 4.5 million people held professional and technical service positions; by 1980 the total had climbed to almost 16 million—a gain of more than 350 percent. The number of engineers rose from 363 thousand to 1.4 million over these three decades; lawyers from 182 to 502 thousand (most of this since 1970); teachers from 1.1 to 4.3 million. Along with this overall growth have come significant shifts in the sex composition of many of the professions. Only 6,000 women were lawyers in 1950 (3 percent of the total in this profession), and only 12,000 physicians (6 percent). By 1986 over 118,000 women were lawyers (18 percent of all lawyers), and over 85,000 were physicians (18 percent).

Bureaucracy

A farmer plowing his field typified the work setting of the agricultural society. The factory assembly line was the distinctive setting for the industrial society. Bureaucracy is the predominant work setting for the postindustrial era. The term "bureaucracy" has long had unfavorable connotations, suggesting large, unresponsive, cumbersome administrative units that deal impersonally with those who turn to them for services. "I tried to get action, but that bureaucracy just won't move." "You have to file six copies of everything, and wait at least six months for an answer." But bureaucracy as originally conceived meant something very different. The influential German sociologist Max Weber (1864–1920) identified it with "rationalized administration."[8] The management of organizations was advanced, Weber argued, by introducing knowledge of administrative techniques and practice, by striving for impartiality in the administration of services, and by the general recourse to rationality (rather than subjectivity or personal whim) in organizational management. In this sense, bureaucracy was a great advance over earlier forms of administration.

Bureaucracy: rationalized administration

Today, the principles of rationalized administration have been applied across most large institutions in the United States, from government agencies to large business corporations. The tremendous growth of these bureaucracies has made them, for better or worse, the occupational homes of millions of American workers.

Growth of bureaucracies

INCREASES IN NATIONAL WEALTH

Throughout human history, people have had to struggle with subsistence needs: taking in enough calories to sustain life, having clothing warm enough to protect against the elements, acquiring basic housing or shelter. Even in more fortunate times and countries where most of the population did not face actual hunger or starvation, the margin over subsistence was always worryingly thin. There might be enough food today, but one could not forget that, as a result of natural disasters, crop failures, or illness, there might not be enough food tomorrow.

Against this backdrop, the economic experience of the contemporary United States is a truly radical one. For the United States is a wealthy society in a world that has been dominated by scarcity. The affluence Americans enjoy accrues from a number of conditions, but primarily from the extensive application of technology to economic production. Achieving the present level of national wealth is probably the single most dramatic accomplishment of the postindustrial era.

Affluence in America

Poverty and Affluence

Some people resist, even resent, the description of the United States as an affluent society, because to them it suggests a lack of sensitivity

[8]See, for example, Max Weber, *Economy and Society*, edited by Guenther Roth and Claus Wittich (New York: Bedminster Press, 1968). Weber's work was composed between 1913 and 1914.

Even in the midst of the wealth of contemporary America, poverty remains a pressing problem.

Poverty in America

Poverty: a relative
condition

to the continued presence of poverty. Surely the affluent society is not one where everyone is wealthy and poverty has been abolished. In the United States in the 1980s, millions of people—just how many is hard to estimate—experience some literal economic deprivation, such as inadequacy of diet or substandard housing. Government statistical data for 1986 showed about 32 million people living below the poverty line—just under 14 percent of the total population.[9]

Furthermore, poverty is not just an absolute condition: An important meaning of being poor is having considerably less than most other people. We think of ourselves as deprived when our standard of living is well below the level which has been established as the norm for the society—even if our diet is good, we have enough clothing, and our needs for shelter are met. Of course our economic expectations rise with what we see around us. Poverty is in part a relative condition.

[9]These data are from U.S. Bureau of the Census, *Statistical Abstract of the United States, 1988,* p. 434.

What Affluence Means

As a description of the condition of a society, **affluence** means something quite precise and limited: It is a situation in which a decisive majority of the population of a country does not face problems related to the struggle for subsistence, where economic privation is a concern of the few rather than the many. In the quarter-century after World War II, the United States did not abolish poverty or satisfy all economic wants, but it did reach a status where most people did not have to worry about the most basic economic needs.

Affluence and economic need

As late as the end of World War II a majority of the American public had incomes that provided them with only a very narrow margin over subsistence. The median family income in 1947 was just $3,000, and 81 percent of all families earned less than $5,000. Although the dollar would buy more in those days than it will now, these Americans had little left over when essential food, clothing, and shelter were taken care of. Their economic world was bounded by subsistence-type needs.

A Quarter-Century of Growth

Between 1947 and 1973, median family income doubled in real (inflation-controlled) terms. More individual family purchasing power was acquired in this quarter-century than in all preceding years of American history combined. When we remember, too, that at the close of World War II the United States was already a wealthy country by any historical or cross-national comparative standard, the extent of this revolutionary economic change is more sharply etched.

This big jump in wealth permitted Americans to become huge consumers. Since World War II we have consumed twice as much fossil fuel (mostly oil and gasoline) as we had in all of the preceding years of the nation's existence (a fact that clearly attests to major changes in styles of living, just as it helps explain why an energy crisis developed in the 1970s). The *increase of six million* in college and university enrollment between 1947 and 1973 is *four times the total enrollment in 1940*. Expenditures for toys climbed 500 percent in this quarter-century, those for cosmetics by 550 percent. Personal spending for recreation increased 500 percent.

American consumerism

An entire range of consumer goods previously limited to a small elite—if at all available—have come within the grasp of a large segment of the population. In 1947, at the start of the television age, less than one-tenth of one percent of U.S. families owned TV sets. But in 1987, 98 percent of all families had television, and at least some of the 2 percent who didn't were "conscientious objectors"—they thought the typical fare was too awful to watch. Fifty percent of all households had two or more motor vehicles. Cereals no longer suffice by being nourishing; they must excite the imagination with delightful shapes, colors, and sounds. Cat foods compete with extravagant claims as to which best titillates the palate of discerning felines. Americans in 1986 owned over 10 million outboard motors and over 14 million recreational boats. About 11.5 million Americans traveled abroad that year. In matters large and small, sensible and foolish, the range of consumption has been greatly extended in the postindustrial era.

Growth in per capita GNP

In the 1970s and 1980s, aspects of America's economic performance have caused widespread concern: two bouts with high inflation, the successful penetration of American markets by foreign imports such as Japanese automobiles, periods of sluggish overall growth. The 1978–82 span was the worst time. The real gross national product of the country—adjusted for the effects of inflation—was basically static over these years. Still, the overall real growth of the U.S. economy in recent years looks pretty good by historical comparisons. We have a full century of data on *real per capita* GNP growth—covering the bulk of America's experience as an industrial nation (see Figure 2.5). The three decades best for growth were 1900–10 (29 percent), 1940–50 (36 percent), and 1960–70 (32 percent). Next best percent is the span since 1970. Real per capita GNP climbed by 22 percent in the 1970s, and in the first seven years of the 1980s it rose an additional 14 percent. Taken together, the years since 1960 have almost certainly been the best period of sustained economic expansion in American history.

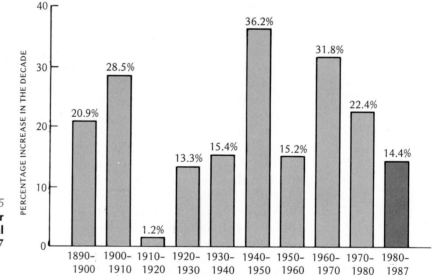

Figure 2.5
Growth in Real Per Capita Gross National Product, 1890–1987

Source: U.S. Bureau of the Census, *Historical Statistics of the United States, Colonial Times to 1970*, p. 224; Council of Economic Advisers, *Economic Indicators*, November, 1981, p. 2, and March, 1988, p. 2. Data for 1980–87 cover only the first seven years of the 1980s.

Income in the United States and Abroad

World leader in per capita GNP

If the affluence of the United States today is evident when compared to the country's past, it is equally clear when compared to the experience of other countries. According to calculations made by the Organization for Economic Cooperation and Development (OECD), the United States enjoys a substantial economic edge (measured in terms of the purchasing power of per capita GNP) over all of the other advanced democracies, Japan included. Between 1970 and the mid-1980s, Japan's economy grew somewhat faster than the U.S. economy, but the U.S. economy grew a lot and retained a significant lead in real per capita GNP (Table 2.2). Until recently, it was not possible to compare national income reliably even for countries like the United States and Great Britain; now the OECD measures give a good general picture. Data still are not available that would permit accurate comparisons of income in the economically advanced democracies to

Table 2.2
National Income Comparisons, 1970–86
(per capita gross national product, expressed in
purchasing power parities)

	1970	1986
United States	4,826	17,324
Denmark	3,795	13,030
West Germany	3,644	12,741
Japan	2,884	12,339
France	3,414	12,218
Netherlands	3,594	11,809
United Kingdom	3,291	11,498
Italy	2,866	11,406
Belgium	3,334	11,276
Austria	2,866	11,254
Spain	2,198	8,065
Ireland	2,033	6,903
Greece	1,629	6,224
Portugal	1,266	5,868

Source: OECD, *National Accounts,* vol. 1, Main Aggregates, 1960–86 (Paris: OECD, 1986), p. 145. The methodology used by the OECD in deriving the above data involves valuing the goods and services sold in different countries in a common set of international prices. The OECD calls this "purchasing power parities (PPP)." PPPs are international price indexes linking the price levels of different countries. They show how many units of currency are needed in one country to buy the same amount of goods and services that one unit of currency will buy in the other country: for example, how many French francs are needed to buy in France what one U.S. dollar will buy within the United States.

that in communist or Third World countries. The best data we have suggest that the per capita GNP of the Soviet Union is less than half that of the United States, Mexico's just one-eighth as great, India's and China's even lower.

The wealth or, more generally, the economic resources of a nation have implications that extend beyond immediate matters of living standards. The relative wealth of the United States and the continuing growth of its economy clearly seem to have lessened class tensions and buttressed popular support for national institutions. The huge size and rapid expansion of the American economy since World War II have sustained the major role the country has played in world affairs. Politicians sometimes speak of the need to make hard policy choices between "guns" and "butter"—between federal spending for defense on the one hand and domestic social programs on the other. But, in fact, the wealth of the United States in its postindustrial era has reduced, though not removed, the tensions in these choices. The country has expanded *both* its military spending and its domestic social spending.

Social and political effects of national wealth

CLASS RELATIONSHIPS

The concept of **social class** denotes status deriving from the amount of income received as well as the sources of this income: interest earnings from inherited wealth, ownership of a farm, a factory job, and so on. The concept also refers to the social and cultural outlooks that result from income status. For Karl Marx, capitalists were a social class not just because they had relatively large amounts of wealth, but also because of how they derived their money—from their ownership of private industry—and because they shared common interests and outlooks.

The concept of social class

America's class divisions historically have been relatively weak. Social norms and interests commonly described as middle class have been the common property of many disparate economic groups. In particular, the American working class has never had the coherence and self-consciousness found historically in Europe. And socialism, which developed as a working-class ideology, has always been weak in America (see chapter 3).

Weak class divisions

Working-Class Consciousness

Still, the United States has not been totally without a politically self-conscious and organized working class. The industrial era—especially the time of Franklin Roosevelt's presidency (1933–45)—stands as its high-water mark. Under the new or greatly expanded government programs of the Roosevelt administration, known as the New

Deal, working-class Americans received important recognition and support: national legislation guaranteeing the right to organize and bargain collectively; minimum wage legislation; social security benefits; various guarantees of occupational health and safety, and of the general humaneness of working conditions. Legislation securing these benefits was not directed exclusively toward urban factory workers, but this group was a principal claimant and beneficiary.

The New Deal and the rise of labor unions

During the New Deal the labor union movement gained strength. The political climate that followed the outbreak of the Great Depression in 1929—including the general encouragement of unionism given by the Roosevelt administration, new supportive legislation, and the vigorous initiatives of a new generation of labor leaders—produced a surge in union membership, from 3.5 million in 1931 to 10 million on the eve of World War II, to more than 14 million when the war ended. This was the heroic age of American labor.

The changing character of the labor movement

In the late 1940s and 1950s, however, union membership as a proportion of the nonagricultural labor force leveled out, and in the 1960s and 1970s it actually declined. In 1955, 33 percent of all workers in nonagricultural pursuits were unionized; in 1980, the proportion was down to 25 percent and by 1988 it was well under 20 percent. Not only has the American labor movement come to represent a declining proportion of workers, but the sectors where it holds the greatest promise of expansion lie outside the traditional industrial, blue-collar sector. Government employees have been a big growth area in recent years. Between 1968 and 1988 the membership of the American Federation of State, County, and Municipal Employees (AFSCME) grew from about 360,000 to 1.1 million. The American Federation of Teachers (AFT) quadrupled in this time span—from 165,000 to 665,000 members.

Economic Gains

If the traditional working class—urban, blue-collar, and trade union—has lost ground numerically, it has also become an established class in contrast to its new claimant status of the New Deal era. Most of the urban working class of the 1930s were economic have-nots; if not poor, they were right on the margin. As such, they supported government-directed efforts to change the economic order. The trade union movement organized this have-not working class and pushed effectively for its economic betterment and security.

Labor's shifting status

Over the ensuing decades, unions have achieved many of their objectives through collective bargaining, aided greatly by the overall growth of the American economy. The unionized labor force has moved up the socioeconomic ladder. In 1985, according to data from eight national surveys taken by the Gallup Organization, 78 percent of union families—those in which at least one of the principal wage-earners belonged to a labor union—owned their home rather than rented it. Home ownership has long been considered one indicator, even if only a rough one, of middle-class status. Only about 20 percent of union members had less than a high-school education, and 15 percent were college graduates. Just 8 percent of these union families reported incomes of $10,000—the income position of 22 percent of all non-union families. At the same time, 42 percent of union households, compared to 30 percent of nonunion households, had incomes of $30,000 a year or more. Both relatively and absolutely, the unionized work force has dramatically improved its economic position since the 1950s—just as its position in the 1950s represented a big gain over that of the Depression years.[10]

Middle Class, Even Conservative

The political consequences of drawing a large portion of the working class—especially that represented by labor unions—into what is for all practical purposes lower-middle-class status have been noted for some time now. "The fire has gone out in labor's belly," suggested journalist Stewart Alsop in 1967, because trade unions were no longer representing have-nots. Alsop recalled Franklin Roosevelt's packing Cadillac Square in Detroit with a half-million cheering workers in an October 1936 rally. He contrasted this to the mere 30,000 who turned out for Democratic President Lyndon Johnson in 1964, when Johnson was at his most popular and his Republican opponent, Barry Goldwater, gave labor its clearest target in many moons. Why then the poor turnout? "The workers who crowded shoulder to shoulder into Cadillac Square to hear Franklin Roosevelt regarded themselves as 'little guys' or 'working stiffs.' . . . The poor, and those who regarded themselves as poor, were in those days a clear majority of the population."[11] Alsop went on to point out that the typical trade unionist in 1964 was simply much better off, absolutely and relatively, than his counterpart had been twenty-five or thirty years earlier. He was more inclined to go boating or camping than participate in solidarity rallies; and he no longer sustained the drive for social change.

George Meany, president of the AFL-CIO from 1952 until his death in 1980, spoke insightfully of the transformation of labor's place in the postindustrial era. In a 1969 interview with the *New York Times*, Meany appeared willing to accept both "middle class" and "conservative" as descriptions of the membership of the labor movement:

"The fire has gone out in labor's belly"

George Meany and labor's conservatism

[10]The data presented here are derived from Gallup surveys taken nationally between January and June, 1985. Combining a number of surveys gives a larger composite sample size—here, about 12,000 cases—which in turn makes possible a more reliable picture of the economic positions of union and nonunion families. Survey data have to be used because no comparable census information is available.
[11]Stewart Alsop, "Can Anyone Beat LBJ?" *Saturday Evening Post*, May 1967, p. 28.

Huge rallies like this one in Cadillac Square, Detroit, marked a high point in the labor movement in the 1930s.

Labor, to some extent, has become middle class. When you have no property, you don't have anything, you have nothing to lose by these radical actions. But when you become a person who has a home and has property, to some extent you become conservative. And I would say to that extent, labor has become conservative.[12]

A working class that in many ways is middle class and conservative is a distinctive feature of postindustrialism.

New Class Groupings

A new middle class

Another key development affecting class structure has emerged from the extraordinary expansion of higher education since World War II. Most people in the burgeoning college stratum don't fit into the traditional class groupings. They are hardly in working-class jobs: Only six percent hold manual-labor positions of any sort. But neither are they, for the most part, business men and women. Just 26 percent of

[12]"Excerpts from Interview with Meany on Status of Labor Movement," *New York Times,* August 31, 1969.

them are managers or administrators of any kind. Nearly 60 percent of college graduates hold professional and technical jobs.[13] Such positions can be classified as middle class, but it is hard to fit them into traditional theories of class and politics. The vast expansion of the college-trained population has fueled a broad transformation of the upper middle class in the United States, from a business-defined and inclined posture to one shaped by intellectual experiences and values. Some observers see large elements of the college-trained population taking on the properties of an *intelligentsia:* a social class whose occupational roles, status, and outlook all spring from its involvement in the application of trained intelligence.

A "new class" of professionals

The first person to refer to segments of the growing stratum of college-trained professionals as a "new class" was economist John Kenneth Galbraith, in his 1958 book, *The Affluent Society.* In 1967 author/ lawyer David Bazelon advanced the concept of a new class by offering an ingenious explanation of its social dynamics.

> The education of the New Class member—an electronics engineer or a systems research analyst with a Ph.D. in sociology or a physicist working for the RAND Corporation or an economist dealing with manpower programs in the Department of Labor—is an application of training to *think ahead.* . . . So it strikes me as distinctly possible that *all* the education of *all* the members of the New Class has a common denominator—namely to plan something.

Since government is "the primary planning agency," new class "planners" look to government much more than does the older business class.[14] More generally, the new class and business are seen as political competitors, not allies.

Scholars are still not in agreement that a new class based on knowledge, intellectual activity, trained intelligence, and/or planning really does exist; and they certainly do not agree as to the precise political position of such a social group. Nonetheless, an expanding body of research by political scientists and sociologists does give substantial support to the idea that the class makeup and politics of contemporary America have been altered substantially by the dramatic growth in higher education, professional occupations, and scientific and other intellectual activity.[15]

---

[13]These data are derived from three large surveys of the American public conducted in 1984 and 1985 by the National Opinion Research Center of the University of Chicago (NORC). This ongoing series is known as the *General Social Survey.*

[14]David T. Bazelon, *Power in America: The Politics of the New Class* (New York: New American Library, 1967), p. 331.

[15]See Everett Ladd, *Pursuing the New Class: Social Theory and Survey Data,* in B. Bruce-Briggs (ed.), *The New Class?* (New Brunswick, N.J.: Transaction Books, 1979), pp. 101–22; and Alvin W. Gouldner, *The Future of Intellectuals and the Rise of the New Class* (New York: Seabury, 1979).

Kaluzny

Two sides of contemporary immigration: citizenship being conferred in ceremonies held July 4, 1986, and a person entering the country illegally being arrested by Immigration and Naturalization Service border guards.

ETHNOCULTURAL MAKEUP OF THE UNITED STATES

As throughout its history, the United States today is unusually diverse ethnically and religiously. This diversity has continually exerted great influence on national life. It has, for example, been the source of social conflict. Securing full citizenship and rights for all the ethnocultural groups that form the American nation was a real challenge a century ago, and still is in our own day.

The United States is a nation built on immigration. Between 1820 and 1980, more than 50 million immigrants decided to make the United States their home. The greatest wave of immigration took place between 1900 and 1924, when 17.3 million people moved to America—by far the largest migration in any quarter-century in human history. Now in the 1980s the United States is again experiencing a large immigration, this one from Latin American countries, especially Mexico. The story of American ethnic diversity is still being written.

Present Ethnic Makeup

A heterogeneous populace

Figure 2.6 shows how heterogeneous the American populace is. While people of English, Scottish, and Welsh background are still the largest ethnic group in the United States, they are now a distinct minority of the population. In 1980, in a country of 226.5 million, 83 percent were whites, 12 percent blacks, and 5 percent of other backgrounds. Hispanic Americans—6 percent of the population, or more than 13 million people—are not a racial group; a majority classify themselves as whites in Census surveys, but a large minority now describe themselves as "other" (not blacks or whites) when asked their racial identity.

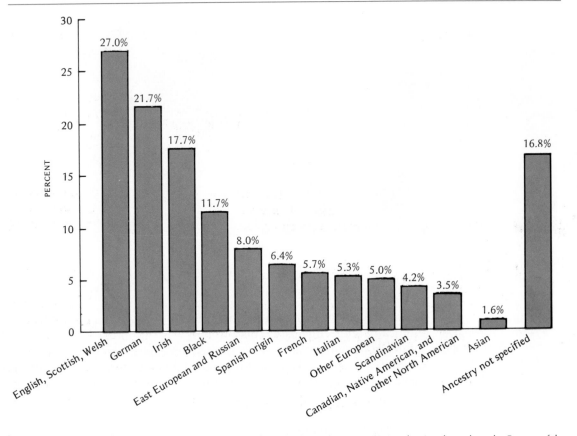

Figure 2.6
Ancestry of the American Population*

*Expressed as a percent of the total population, 1980. In releasing these data, the Bureau of the Census noted that "since multiple ancestry responses are classified in each applicable group, the sum of the ancestry groups is greater than the total number of persons."

Source: U.S. Bureau of the Census, 1980 Census of the Population, *Ancestry of the Population by State, 1980,* April 1983, pp. 1–3, 10, 12–14, 16, 22, 28; for "Black" and "Spanish origin," idem, *Statistical Abstract of the United States,* 1986, p. 29.

Religion

The American populace is now roughly 63 percent Protestant, 26 percent Catholic, 2 percent Jewish, and 2 percent of other religions, while 7 percent have no religious preference (see Figure 2.7). Among Protestants, Baptists are by far the largest group, making up about 21 percent of the entire population.

Religious beliefs and values remain important to Americans. It used to be thought that when countries become highly developed economically, when large proportions of their populations are college-trained— when they enter their postindustrial eras—the forces of secularization strengthen and religious commitments weaken. The present-day United States confounds this view. There has been some decline in

Importance of religious beliefs

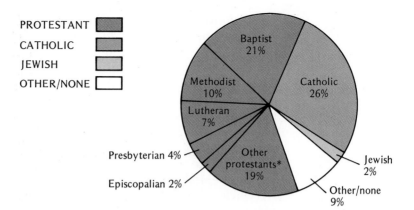

PROTESTANT
CATHOLIC
JEWISH
OTHER/NONE

Figure 2.7
**Religious Affiliation
(percent of populace)**

*"Other protestants" includes other, no denomination given, or a nondenominational church.
Source: General Social Surveys, 1985, 1986, and 1987 combined; National Opinion Research Center, University of Chicago.

church attendance, but Americans still show strong religious attachments. The proportion of the public stating that their religious beliefs are important to them is much higher in the United States than in any other of the highly developed countries. We discuss these findings as part of a more detailed review of American public opinion and values in chapter 10.

Socioeconomic Differences

Many Americans take pride in the ethnic and religious diversity of their country. But they also want a unity in the diversity, part of which involves equality of group access to income, education, and jobs. What is the present performance in this regard?

"The melting pot"

Within white America, historic ethnic-group differences in socioeconomic standing have been greatly reduced in recent years. Surveys taken by the University of Chicago's National Opinion Research Center (NORC) show that groups such as Irish Catholics—who in the past were widely subject to discrimination—have advanced greatly in the post–World War II years. The fabled melting pot has eliminated many of the old ethnic differences in socioeconomic status.

Black and Hispanic economic status

Blacks and Hispanics, however, are still in inferior economic positions. The median income for all white families in 1986 was about $30,800, but only $17,600 for black families and $20,000 for Hispanics. Even here, though, some movement is occurring. Among married-couple families, where both husband and wife are in the paid labor force, the median income for whites was $39,000 in 1986, for blacks $32,000, and for Hispanics $30,100—a significant difference, but one markedly reduced from what had prevailed earlier.[16]

[16]The *median income* of a group of families is the income exactly in the middle of the range: half of all families earn more; half less.

Race and religion in presidential voting

The political cleavage between Protestants and Catholics was a dominant one historically. John F. Kennedy's election as president in 1960, the first Roman Catholic to hold that office, was symbolically important in this context: it signaled the closing of a once great divide. When will a black man or woman be elected president, with comparable symbolism and meaning for American racial experience? National attitudes have changed significantly in this area, making the prospect far less remote than it was even a decade ago. Jesse Jackson's candidacy for the Democratic presidential nomination in 1988 galvanized the black community. His strong run—a second place finish behind Michael Dukakis—would not have been possible without overwhelming black support. Still, Jackson earned the respect of many white voters as well, and he tripled his proportion of the vote of white Democrats in the 1988 primaries from what he had won in his first race four years earlier. Jackson's highest percentage of the white vote in 1988 came in Wisconsin, where network exit polls showed him garnering 23 percent of the vote.

REGIONALISM

The regions of the United States still differ economically—for example, corn and wheat production are concentrated in the Midwest.

The major geographic areas of the United States have been fed by different streams of immigration, have experienced contrasting economic development, had differing needs, and frequently have been at odds politically. For every generation of Americans up through the 1950s, the Northeast was the "establishment" region. It was seen as the great center of industrial wealth—and was attacked by populist movements in the South and West. By the 1970s, however, some said that things had been turned around. We no longer had the imperial

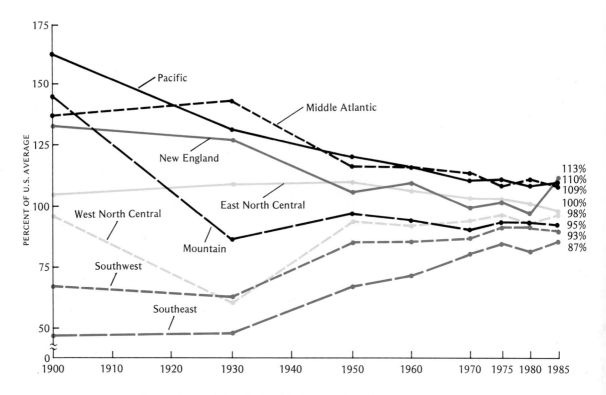

PERCENT OF U.S. AVERAGE

Pacific

Middle Atlantic

New England

East North Central

West North Central

Mountain

Southwest

Southeast

113%
110%
109%
100%
98%
95%
93%
87%

1900 1910 1920 1930 1940 1950 1960 1970 1975 1980 1985

Figure 2.8
America:
A Regional Review,
1900–85

Source: Regional Growth: Historical Perspective. Advisory Commission on Intergovernmental Relations, June 1980, p. 11. 1985 figures supplied by ACIR.

Northeast; the region was described as a troubled Frostbelt, in a state of decline as it lost people, jobs, and political influence. The South was no longer victimized; it had been redefined as the buoyant Sunbelt. Seemingly, winter-time temperatures had become the decisive features of American regionalism.

This trendy interpretation, however, had the story somewhat twisted. The main economic development was not Frostbelt decline so much
Convergence of
Frostbelt and Sunbelt
as the steady convergence of the regions' economic status. As Figure 2.8 shows, the various sections of the United States were vastly unequal at the turn of the century—hardly a desirable situation in terms of national unity. Over the last half-century in the United States, though, per capita income by region has become much more uniform. The Sunbelt states of the South have improved their position vis-à-vis the Northeast and Midwest, but this improvement must be understood as a reduction of the South's historic economic lag. The southern Sunbelt is still the least affluent part of the country and its population has the nation's lowest education levels.

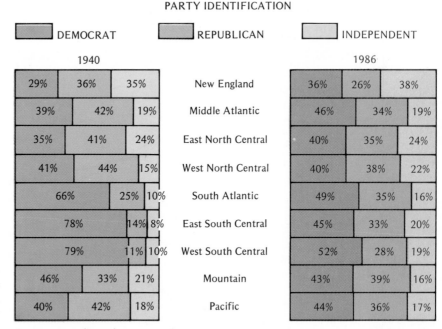

PARTY IDENTIFICATION

DEMOCRAT   REPUBLICAN   INDEPENDENT

1940			Region	1986		
29%	36%	35%	New England	36%	26%	38%
39%	42%	19%	Middle Atlantic	46%	34%	19%
35%	41%	24%	East North Central	40%	35%	24%
41%	44%	15%	West North Central	40%	38%	22%
66%	25%	10%	South Atlantic	49%	35%	16%
78%	14%	8%	East South Central	45%	33%	20%
79%	11%	10%	West South Central	52%	28%	19%
46%	33%	21%	Mountain	43%	39%	16%
40%	42%	18%	Pacific	44%	36%	17%

Figure 2.9
Regions Become More Similar, Party Identification

Question: In politics, do you consider yourself a Republican, Socialist, Independent, or Democrat?
Note: "Other" category which included Socialist calculated out for comparison purposes.
Source: Survey by the Gallup Organization July 21–28, 1940.
Question: Regardless of how you voted today, in politics today do you consider yourself a Democrat, Republican, Independent or something else?
Note: Sample = 17,620 voters.
Source: Survey by ABC News, November 4, 1986.

Social and Political Regionalism

Regional convergence in social and political attitudes

In social and political terms, America's regions have also come closer together. Racial attitudes in the southern states still differ from those elsewhere in the country, but not nearly as much as they did three and four decades ago. Sectional differences in party loyalties are now much smaller than they used to be. The trend in political attitudes is toward regional convergence (Figure 2.9). Regional variations are not going to disappear. Especially on such social questions as abortion, sexual norms, and the role of women, and in aspects of race relations, they remain striking. Note in the data presented in Figure 2.10 a general bicoastal liberalism, with New England, the Middle Atlantic, and the Pacific states the most socially liberal, and the South and Midwest more conservative. Overall, though, American regionalism has lost a lot of its historic divisiveness, as the regions have become more alike socially, economically, and politically.

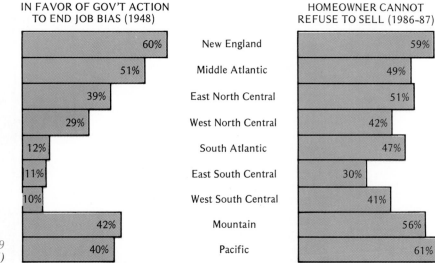

IN FAVOR OF GOV'T ACTION TO END JOB BIAS (1948)		HOMEOWNER CANNOT REFUSE TO SELL (1986–87)
60%	New England	59%
51%	Middle Atlantic	49%
39%	East North Central	51%
29%	West North Central	42%
12%	South Atlantic	47%
11%	East South Central	30%
10%	West South Central	41%
42%	Mountain	56%
40%	Pacific	61%

Figure 2.9 (continued)

Question: One of Truman's proposals concerns employment practices. How far do you yourself think the federal government should go in requiring employers to hire people without regard to their race, religion, color, or nationality? The percentages shown here are responses for federal government going all the way to end job bias.
Source: Survey by the Gallup Organization, March 5–10, 1948
Question: Suppose there is a community-wide vote on the general housing issue. There are two possible laws to vote on: One law says that a homeowner can decide for himself whom to sell his house to, even if he prefers not to sell to Blacks, The second law says that a homeowner cannot refuse to sell to someone because of their race or color. Which law would you vote for? (White response, 1986–87.)
Source: Survey by the National Opinion Research Center, 1986 and 1987.

OPPORTUNITY AND MOBILITY

The Horatio Alger story

The sense that the United States has extended opportunities for individual advancement has figured prominently in the nation's experience. Millions of immigrants moved here seeking a better life. The idea that any person can work his or her way up in wealth and status is central to the country's self-image or conception. We see this in American folklore. The name of one nineteenth-century writer of stories for young people has become synonymous with the idea that anyone, no matter how poor, can get ahead through hard work and perseverance. Horatio Alger, who was born in Revere, Massachusetts, in 1832, wrote more than 130 novels which proclaimed the land of boundless opportunity theme. Today we speak of those who rise spectacularly in social position through personal initiatives as living an Horatio Alger story.

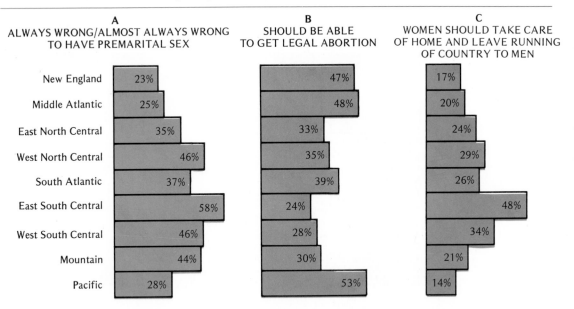

	A ALWAYS WRONG/ALMOST ALWAYS WRONG TO HAVE PREMARITAL SEX	B SHOULD BE ABLE TO GET LEGAL ABORTION	C WOMEN SHOULD TAKE CARE OF HOME AND LEAVE RUNNING OF COUNTRY TO MEN
New England	23%	47%	17%
Middle Atlantic	25%	48%	20%
East North Central	35%	33%	24%
West North Central	46%	35%	29%
South Atlantic	37%	39%	26%
East South Central	58%	24%	48%
West South Central	46%	28%	34%
Mountain	44%	30%	21%
Pacific	28%	53%	14%

Bicoastal Liberalism

A. *Question:* There's been a lot of discussion about the way morals and attitudes about sex are changing in this country. If a man and a woman have sex relations before marriage, do you think it is always wrong, almost always wrong, wrong only sometimes, or not wrong at all?
Source: Surveys by the National Opinion Research Center, 1985 and 1986.
B. *Question:* Please tell me whether or not *you* think it should be possible for a pregnant woman to obtain a *legal* abortion if . . . the woman wants it for any reason?
Source: Surveys by the National Opinion Research Center, 1985 and 1987.
C. *Question:* Do you agree or disagree with this statement: Women should take care of running their homes and leave running the country up to men?
Source: Surveys by the National Opinion Research Center, 1985 and 1986.

> "There's hope for you Dick if you'll try." "Nobody ever talked to me so before," said Dick. "They just called me Ragged Dick, and told me I'd grow up to be a vagabone (boys who are better educated need not be surprised at Dick's blunders) and come to the gallows."
> "Telling you so won't make it turn out so Dick. If you'll try to be somebody, and grow up into a respectable member of society you will. You may not become rich—it isn't everybody that becomes rich, you know—but you can obtain a good position, and be respected."[17]

Public opinion and the American Dream

How valid is the claim that the American social system has offered unusual opportunities for individual advancement? We know that a great many Americans believe the claim is true and have stuck with this belief through some rocky times. In 1939, when the United States was still gripped by the effects of the Great Depression, pollster Elmo Roper asked a cross-section of Americans whether they believed "that the great age of economic opportunity and expansion in the U.S. is over, or that American industry can create a comparable expansion

[17]Horatio Alger, *Ragged Dick* (New York: Collier, 1962), p. 75.

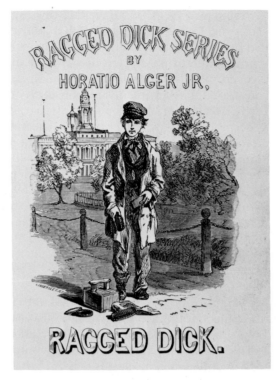

and opportunity in the future." Seventy-two percent thought the opportunity was still there, compared to 13 percent who said it was over and 15 percent who were unsure. Sixty-six percent of those *unemployed* said the opportunity remained.[18] This sense of opportunity persists. A January 1985 poll taken by ABC News and the *Washington Post* asked whether "it is true in this country that if you work hard, eventually you will get ahead." Seventy-two percent said it was true, including majorities of every economic stratum.[19]

"The Reluctant Bride"

Public opinion on government's responsibility

Because they believe they have substantial opportunity to improve their positions and are individually responsible for doing so, Americans have been less inclined than citizens of most other industrial nations to turn to government for the kinds of programs and assistance often referred to as "the welfare state." The United States has been, in the words of University of Chicago social scientist Tom W. Smith, "the reluctant bride of the welfare state, instituting national programs later than most countries . . . and spending a lower share

[18]Survey by Elmo Roper and Associates for *Fortune* magazine, September 1939.
[19]Survey by ABC News and the *Washington Post*, January 11–16, 1985.

of its national income on social welfare than most. . . ."[20] Drawing on data from the United States and a number of European countries collected under the International Social Survey Program (ISSP), Smith shows how different Americans are in their attitudes on individual versus governmental responsibility. Only 36 percent of Americans said they considered it government's responsibility to "reduce income differences between the rich and poor," compared to 72 percent of Austrians, 63 percent of West Germans, 81 percent of Italians, and 70 percent of the British. Thirty-three percent in the United States maintained that it was government's responsibility to "provide a job for everyone who wants one," as against 81 percent in Austria, 80 percent in Germany, 88 percent in Italy, and 69 percent in Great Britain.[21] We examine the consequences of such attitudinal differences in chapter 17, which provides a detailed assessment of American welfare policies.

Social Mobility

Another way to approach the question of individual opportunity is to examine objective data on social mobility. Mobility may be measured by comparing a person's present income, educational, or occupational position with that of his or her parents. An individual is upwardly mobile when his status is higher than that of his parents.

Upward mobility

Throughout much of history, social mobility was limited. In most aristocratic societies, as a rule, people stayed in the social and economic rank to which they were born, and they worked in the same jobs as their parents. Economic and technological developments of the last two centuries have, though, greatly extended opportunities for upward mobility in countries around the world. Mobility has been especially pronounced in the United States.

Educational and social mobility

In Table 2.3 individuals are located first by the amount of education they have received and then by the educational experience of their fathers. An exceptionally large proportion has been upwardly mobile educationally. Among those who today are college graduates, only 33 percent come from families where the father was a college graduate. Two-thirds have more education than their fathers. Of high school graduates, only 11 percent come from families where the father had more than a high school education, while 58 percent are from families where he had less schooling. These data reflect the fact that for each succeeding generation in this century, and especially since World War II, the amount of available education has risen sharply.

[20]Tom W. Smith, "The Polls: The Welfare State in Cross-National Perspective," *Public Opinion Quarterly*, Fall 1987, p. 406.
[21]The ISSP surveys cited here were conducted in each of the countries mentioned in 1985, except for the Austrian survey, which was done in 1986.

Table 2.3
Educational Mobility
(row percentages)

| | Father's education | | | |
Respondent's education	Less than high school graduate	High school graduate	Some college	College graduate
Less than high school graduate	83	13	3	2
High school graduate	58	30	6	5
Some college	40	31	14	15
College graduate	27	27	12	33

Source: General Social Surveys, 1985, 1986 and 1987; The National Opinion Research Center, University of Chicago.

Note: Respondents were asked 2 questions: 1. How much schooling did they have: a. less than high school graduate? b. high school graduate? c. some college? d. college graduate? 2. How much schooling did their fathers have: a.? b.? c.? d.?

Of the respondents who said that they themselves had had less than high school graduate training, 83 percent had fathers (read across) who had less than high school graduate training; 13 percent had fathers who were high school graduates; 3 percent had fathers with some college; and only 2 percent had fathers who were college graduates. Of the respondents who said they were high school graduates, 58 percent had fathers (read across) with less than a high school education; 30 percent had fathers who were high school graduates; 6 percent had fathers with some college; and 5 percent had fathers who graduated from college.

The old nautical expression, "a rising tide lifts all boats," captures this experience. The educational tide has continued to rise and it has lifted a great many people with it.

A similar relationship can be seen when individuals' current occupational status is compared to that of their fathers. Parents' social position certainly has some influence on what positions their children come to hold. Many people, though, achieve positions different from those of their parents, and often they manage to move *up* the ladder. Thus the objective data seem to square with people's perceptions that they have a good chance to advance through their own initiatives.

Inequality

Still, if mobility and opportunity are real, they co-exist with a great deal of income inequality. The gap between winners and losers in America's mobility race remains a wide one. The fifth of all families with the highest incomes in 1986 received 44 percent of all earnings, while the lowest-paid fifth received only 15 percent of national income. Together, the top 40 percent of all families gained over two-thirds of earnings, while the bottom 40 percent received under one-sixth of national income (Figure 2.11).

The degree of income inequality seems to have diminished from the

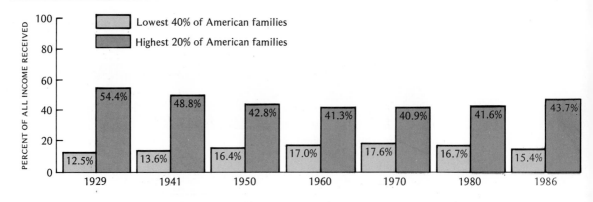

Figure 2.11
Income Distribution since 1929 (percent of all money income received by lowest 40% and highest 20% of American families)

Source: 1929–41: U.S. Bureau of the Census, *Historical Statistics of the U.S.: Colonial Times to 1957*, p. 166. 1950–70: idem, *Historical Statistics of the U.S.: Colonial Times to 1970*, p. 293, 1980: idem, *Current Population Reports*, series P-60, No. 154, p. 5, August 1986; 1986: idem, *Statistical Abstract of the United States*, 1988, p. 428.

1930s through the 1960s, even as the amount of income available overall greatly expanded. In 1929, the richest fifth of families received 54 percent of all income; the proportion subsequently declined significantly, reaching a low of 41 percent in 1965–70. Various social welfare programs, described in Chapter 17, contributed to this income redistribution. Recent data suggest, however, that the amount of income equality has been increasing—very slightly in the 1970s and then a bit more in the 1980s. The argument over the impact of Reagan administration programs is discussed in Chapters 16 and 17.

Socioeconomic Determinism?

Among diet-conscious Americans one sometimes hears, "You are what you eat." Nutrition certainly affects our health and well-being. We know, however, that many other things help make us what we are. The setting for politics is formed partly by key economic and demographic characteristics. Even so, American political life is not simply a product of such factors. They are only one part of our political environment. In the next section our focus shifts to another part: the political beliefs of Americans, and the ways these beliefs have been expressed in the nation's governmental institutions.

SUMMARY

Postindustrialism is a term, first introduced by sociologist Daniel Bell, that is now commonly used to describe central features of recent social change in the United States and other developed countries. The United States has gradually emerged into its postindustrial era over the last quarter-century.

The postindustrial setting is distinguished by five interrelated developments.

1. It displays extraordinary technological advances which, for the first time, accrue primarily from the systematic applications of science.

2. It requires great commitments to the knowledge base. This is especially evident in the rising proportion of the population receiving college training and the big outlays for education at all levels.

3. Postindustrialism is characterized by the predominant place of the service sector, compared to agriculture and manufacturing. In the United States and other advanced countries, white-collar positions have come to far outnumber blue-collar positions.

4. The achievements of science and technology have produced a level of national wealth in the United States that surpasses that of the earlier industrial era as dramatically as the industrial era surpassed the economic attainments of the agricultural setting.

5. Finally, social class composition and political behavior in postindustrial America differ from what they were in the preceding period. In particular, the working-class base for trade union activity has eroded, and union members have become more conservative politically. The growing college-trained population scrambles earlier assumptions about class makeup and interests.

Many social and political changes have occurred as the United States entered the postindustrial era. Nonetheless, in other important regards, contemporary American society is distinguished by the persistence of familiar features.

For example, the ethnic and religious diversity of the United States is an old story. Key to the American political experience has been the task of building a new national identity out of many disparate traditions. Inevitably, ethnic conflict has been prominent in the United States, as the country has moved from one ethnic frontier to another. The split between Protestants and Catholics was once a deep one, but it has long since lost its force. The groups making up white America have become more alike in socioeconomic position and political outlook. In our own time, the oldest of the ethnic cleavages in the country—between whites and blacks—has defined the frontier of ethnic change.

Regional interests and culture have been important parts of the setting for American politics. The greatest political division in U.S. history involved the drastically different sectional interests of North and South. Today, regional differences are still substantial in our society. In economic position and social outlook, though, the regions are less dissimilar now than ever before in U.S. history—this despite the hype about the Frostbelt and the Sunbelt.

American social makeup has been influenced by the amount of social mobility that has occurred. Many people experience movement up and down the social ladder. Class lines are fluid, not fixed. The belief is widely held in the United States that opportunity to move ahead is present, if one makes the effort, and this belief is shared by those with low incomes as well as the wealthy. The legitimacy of the political system is thus enhanced.

FOR FURTHER STUDY

Daniel Bell, *The Coming of Postindustrial Society* (New York: Basic Books, 1973). The most comprehensive account of the social and economic changes encompassed by the concept of postindustrialism, written by a distinguished political sociologist.

Greg J. Duncan *et al.*, eds., *Five Thousand American Families: Patterns of Economic Progress* (Ann Arbor, Mich.: Institute for Social Research, 1983), Volume 10. A massive, ongoing multivolume study of the economic experience of Americans.

John Kenneth Galbraith, *The New Industrial State*, 3rd revised ed. (Boston: Houghton-Mifflin, 1978). A leading interpreter of American economic experience discusses changes in the composition and mode of operation of large institutions, governmental and private sector alike, in the United States.

David Riesman, Nathan Glaser, and Ruel Denny, *The Lonely Crowd* (New Haven, CT: Yale University Press, 1950). An early, classic interpretation of changes in social relationships, centering especially on individualism, in the United States after World War II.

* * * *

Organization for Economic Cooperation and Development (OECD), *National Accounts, Volume I: Main Aggregates, 1960–1984* (Paris: OECD, 1986). An annual aggregating of economic statistics for twenty-five countries, covering a span of over two decades. An excellent reference for cross-national comparisons.

U.S. Bureau of the Census, *Statistical Abstract of the United States* (Washington, DC: U.S. Government Printing Office, published annually). Like *Historical Statistics*, this publication (latest edition, 1989) is a superb reference work; it contains current and recent historical information on such topics as population, vital statistics, education, geography and the environment, elections, federal, state, and local finances and employment, national defense, social insurance and human services, employment, income, banking, agriculture, manufacturing, and commerce.

Part 2

Political Beliefs and Practice

Chapter 3

The American Ideology

On Sunday morning, January 4, 1914, American automaker Henry Ford sat in his office in Highland Park, Michigan, with three other Ford Motor Company executives. Ford had called the meeting to discuss employee wages for the coming year. His company's minimum wage was then $2 a day, an amount in line with what American industry was paying. This rate was much lower than present wages, but not as much lower as it appears, because a dollar bought so much more then—a loaf of bread, a bar of Ivory soap, and a pound of sugar each cost about 8 cents, a bed sheet 35 cents, a pair of women's pumps $3.35, and a nine-day all-expense-paid cruise to Bermuda just $46.

Henry Ford told his colleagues that he wanted to raise the minimum wage significantly; he had various calculations of what the company could afford posted on an old blackboard in the office. Charles Sorensen was one executive present with Ford that cold January morning, and years later he wrote a detailed account of the meeting:

> Mr. Ford . . . had me transfer figures from the profits column to labor costs—two million, three million, four million dollars. With that daily wage figures rose from minimum of $2 to $2.50 and $3. Ed Martin [another executive present] protested. . . . While I stood at the blackboard, John Lee [the fourth Ford executive in the office] commented upon every entry and soon became pretty nasty. It was plain he wasn't trying to understand the idea and thought he might sabotage it by ridiculing it. This didn't sit well with Mr. Ford, who kept telling me to put more figures down—$3.50, $3.75, $4.00, $4.25, and a quarter of a dollar more, then another quarter.
>
> At the end of about four hours, Mr. Ford stepped up to the blackboard. "Stop!" he said. "Stop it, Charlie; it's all settled. Five dollars a day minimum pay and at once."[1]

[1] Charles E. Sorenson, *My Forty Years with Ford* (New York: Norton, 1956), p. 139.

Ford's historic wage
increase

Real wages at Ford increased 150 percent company-wide that day. Henry Ford took arguably the most dramatic step in the entire history of American industry without any pressure from workers; the company was not even unionized. He made his decision over the protests of his fellow Ford executives, who thought it would bankrupt the company. And after word of the pay raise had reverberated across the country and around the world, Ford was denounced by many other business leaders, who believed massive harm would result to all of American business from this "dangerous precedent." Even more startling, as Ford raised wages, he lowered the price of his car, the Model T. Priced at $850 in 1908, the Model T sold at steadily reduced rates until, in 1926, it cost just $295. Why did Ford do it?

Henry Ford offered his own explanation.

> It ought to be the employer's ambition, as leader, to pay better wages than any similar line of business. . . . The best wages that have up to date ever been paid are not nearly as high as they ought to be. . . . We made the change [the $5 day] not merely because we wanted to pay higher wages and thought we could pay them. We wanted to pay these wages so that the business would be on a lasting foundation. We were not distributing anything—we were building for the future.[2]

CAPITALISM, DEMOCRACY, AND THE AMERICAN IDEOLOGY

What Ford did proved to be good business. As prices dropped and wages rose—together with dramatic productivity increases through innovating assembly-line procedures—American workers were able to buy many more cars, Ford cars included. But the $5 day was not just an imaginative economic calculation. Ford took his dramatic step on January 4, 1914, because he believed that it was the responsibility of American business to "abolish poverty."

In implementing the $5 day, Ford was acting out—with unusual force and insight—an ideology that he shared with millions of his countrymen. He believed in the idea of **democratic capitalism.** America's private-property-based economy existed for something more than making businessmen rich; it existed to make possible an ever-higher standard of living for the general population. It was capitalism committed to democratic and egalitarian ends.

Democratic capitalism

"The idea that everybody can become a capitalist," wrote Leon Samson, a brilliant young American socialist, in 1935, "is an American conception of capitalism. It is [also] a socialist conception of capitalism. Capitalism is, in theory, and in Europe, for the capitalists. . . ." In America, though, it has highly democratic and equalitarian ele-

[2]Henry Ford, in collaboration with Samuel Crowther, *My Life and Work* (Garden City, N.Y.: Doubleday, 1923), pp. 117–30, *passim.*

For years Norman Rockwell's cover illustrations for the Saturday Evening Post *depicted one aspect of what it was to be American.*

Printed by permission of the Estate of Norman Rockwell. Copyright © 1954 Estate of Norman Rockwell.

ments, Samson argued, in trying to explain why socialism had failed to make inroads in the United States.

American capitalism and socialism

Nowhere is capitalism so well advanced [as in the United States]. But one must be careful to distinguish between the development of American capitalism and the *development of the American as capitalist*. For, if one were to examine the underlying aspirations of the American, his real sentiments and moods, it would not be difficult to discover in him trends of the soul that, far from being the traditionally capitalistic trends, are on the contrary tinged with every variety of socialism. Thus, for example, so unmistakable an American as [former President Herbert] Hoover from time to time unburdens himself of the belief that it is the destiny of the American system to abolish poverty. Now, Hoover may not know it but when he talks this way he is simply talking socialism. To "abolish poverty" is a time-honored socialist aim. Who has ever heard a responsible spokesman of European capitalism announce that it is the aim of, let us say, the French or the English "system" to "abolish poverty"?[3]

Henry Ford's decision in 1914 to raise his company's minimum wage from \$2 to \$5, without any immediate pressure to do so, was unusual, even heretical, in the general context of capitalist beliefs and behav-

[3] Leon Samson, "Americanism as Surrogate Socialism," in John H. M. Laslett and Seymour Martin Lipset, eds., *Failure of a Dream?* (Garden City, N.Y.: Anchor Press / Doubleday, 1974), p. 437. Taken from a chapter in Samson's *Toward a United Front* (New York: Farrar and Rinehart, 1935).

ior. It was consistent, however, with democratic capitalism—and more generally with the political ideology on which the United States was built.

THE ROLE OF IDEOLOGY

American politics is sometimes described as nonideological. In one sense this is valid: *conflict among competing ideological traditions* has been rare in the United States, for reasons we describe later in this chapter. But American politics is highly ideological in another sense: it is shaped and informed, even dominated, by a distinctive set of political beliefs.

Ideology

An *ideology* may be defined as a set of political beliefs and values that are constrained, or tied together. Like a quilt, an ideology is more than the sum of its patches; it is the patches bound together in a specified and ordered arrangement. An ideology isn't just a random collection of beliefs but rather a coherent view of the world. It provides answers to such questions as how government should be organized and power distributed, and what goals the society should try to realize.

Political Socialization

Political socialization

As we grow up, participate in assessing the nation's history and politics in school and with our families, listen to news programs on television, and read books, we are introduced to the underlying political beliefs and values of our society. This is called **political socialization.** Through it, we absorb bits and pieces of the political ideology.

Informal ideologies

Many citizens do not spend a lot of time examining political ideas. Political scientist Philip Converse showed over two decades ago that most people absorb only portions of formal ideologies. Their beliefs and preferences are organized loosely, sometimes even illogically.[4] Similarly, in his study of the political beliefs of a group of working-class Americans, Robert E. Lane noted that their views were characterized by "loosely structured and unreflective statements."[5]

There is a big difference between the formal coherence of American ideology, as it gets set forth in books, and the more disjointed political outlook of the average citizen. But even so the links are there. People often do not know precisely where their underlying values come from, so general is the process by which they are introduced to these views. But they are, nonetheless, guided and oriented by the prevail-

[4] Philip Converse, "The Nature of Belief Systems in Mass Publics," in David Apter, ed., *Ideology and Discontent* (New York: Free Press, 1964), pp. 206–61.
[5] Robert E. Lane, *Political Ideology: Why the American Common Man Believes What He Does* (New York: Free Press, 1962).

"Where there's smoke, there's money."
Drawing by Joe Mirachi; © 1985 The New Yorker Magazine, Inc.

ing political ideology. It seeps in through all sorts of openings, and informs the way they view the world.

ROOTS: CLASSICAL LIBERALISM

Classical liberalism

American political ideology has its roots in a body of political ideas that developed in Europe in the seventeenth and eighteenth centuries—the time when the American colonies were being settled. The European "parent" ideology was known as **liberalism.** It is now often called **classical liberalism,** to distinguish it from narrower usages of the terms **liberal** and **conservative** in everyday discussion (such as "I am liberal on the question of abortion, but conservative on government spending."). Elements of classical liberalism were brought to the United States by the early settlers, and through books by European liberal theorists (such as the seventeenth-century English philosopher, John Locke), which were well known in the colonies. Liberalism found fertile soil in America.

Six elements of American ideology

Six interrelated beliefs or commitments form the core of classical liberalism. (1) **Individualism** is the idea that societies and polities exist to fulfill the rights of each individual to "Life, Liberty and the pursuit of Happiness." (2) In order to realize their rights fully, individuals must have **freedom,** the opportunity to make their own choices with a minimum of restraint. (3) Systems of hereditary privilege are rejected by classical liberalism, in the name of **equality.** The intrinsic worth of each person should be seen as equal. (4) One set of goods that all individuals must be permitted to hold are defined by the term *private property.* By acquiring private property, people fulfill deep needs. Private property is a primary way individuals define themselves, protect themselves, and locate their own niche in society. (5) Government should reflect some measure of *popular choice,* rather than be dominated by a hereditary ruling class, the aristocracy. (6) The reach of governmental power must also be tightly circumscribed. For individuals to be strong and their rights protected, *limited government* must be achieved.

European Origins of Classical Liberalism

We can better understand classical liberalism by exploring briefly how it emerged in Europe in the seventeenth and eighteenth centuries. Liberalism developed as a protest against the then-dominant values, institutions, and class arrangements of *aristocratic society.* Aristocratic values defended legal and social inequality, special rights, privileges, and obligations of social classes, and arbitrary government as the proper and unalterable nature of things. Each social class had a fixed place in society and had duties and obligations which it had to meet for the well-being of the whole. In the corporal (relating to the human body) analogies so common to ideological defenses of monarchy and aristocracy in Europe, the relationship of the nobility and the peasantry was likened by theorists to that of head and limb. What nonsense it would be to speak of the *equality* of the two! They were naturally different in their abilities, and each had its proper place and function. As the head decides for the human body, so the monarchy and the aristocracy did for the society. Political ideology in every aristocratic society justified permanent subordinate status for most of the populace and their complete exclusion from decision-making.

> European aristocratic society

The ascending middle classes, whose numbers and influence were greatly expanded by the commercial and scientific development that began in seventeenth-century Europe, challenged the aristocratic system. Central to their challenge was a wide-ranging attack on the moral and intellectual foundation of aristocracy. New conceptions developed, for example, of how the human mind functions. The brain was seen as a machine—much like that conceived in the scientific thought of the great seventeenth-century English theorist Sir Isaac Newton. Ideas come from the senses. The job of the brain is to organize the many impressions brought to it. If the brain's input (the sensations from the individual's environment) can be controlled, then the output (the way a person thinks and acts, the type of person he is) can be determined.

> The middle-class challenge to aristocracy

Philosophers then took the argument one step further. The human brain, as a type of Newtonian machine, is approximately the same

Philosophical basis of liberalism

for all men. The outputs are different only because the inputs vary. John Locke described the brain at birth as an "empty cabinet," a "white paper . . . void of all characters, without any ideas."[6] This is heady stuff. People are approximately equal in natural capabilities; they differ in performance only because the environments of some are less good. How, then, can the permanent privilege of the monarchy and the nobility be justified? Aristocrats are simply people blessed with better environments. The intellectual basis of individualism emerged in part from a view of man that attributed his performance to his environment.

Economic expansion and individualism

The great economic expansion made possible by the commercial revolution of the sixteenth and seventeenth centuries and, a century later, by the industrial revolution, also encouraged individualism. It did so by creating material output great enough to offer people the promise that life could be something more than a struggle for survival. When most people had no prospect of living beyond bare subsistence, no matter how available resources were distributed, they acquiesced to extensive privileges for the few, from which they and their children were formally and permanently excluded. In societies of great scarcity, if any culture is to flourish, it is only by arbitrarily granting privilege to a few. Let the pie dramatically expand—precisely what economic and technological developments began to achieve in the seventeenth and eighteenth centuries—and people outside the hereditary privileged classes will step forward to claim their share. They will come to feel that life here and now owes them something more than perpetual wretchedness.

New social groupings

There was a continuing interaction between events and ideas. The economic stirring of trade, banking, and industry in the seventeenth and eighteenth centuries created new expectations. Masses of people came to believe that they could change the way they lived and channeled their energies into improving their day-to-day existence. Society became more secularized, and man came to view himself as a sovereign being with rights, not merely duties.

Expansion of the middle class

Society became more heterogeneous as economic development produced new social groups. An entrepreneurial middle class existed before the seventeenth century, but now there was a tremendous expansion of this middle class and a proliferation of specialized professional groups. Having arrived at positions of economic importance in the new order, operating from new centers of power which the economy had generated, confident in their ability to understand the world and participate in it, told by the new ideology that there was no tenable basis for the continuing privilege of the old hereditary ruling class, the middle classes launched their demands for sweeping changes in the character and makeup of the society.

[6] John Locke, *Essay Concerning Human Understanding* (Oxford: Oxford University Press, 1894; first published, 1689).

Enter America

The United States was born at the juncture of the revolutionary changes in economic life, science, and political thinking that nurtured liberalism and its sweeping innovations. Liberalism was not made in America; it developed in Europe and was brought to America by the colonists. What made America different from Europe—profoundly different—was the speed with which liberalism got established here and the extent to which it was modified by American conditions.

Absence of class conflict

In Europe, the aristocratic social structure had been long in existence and was not easily eradicated. For example, those who made the French Revolution in 1789 and the years following never won a complete victory. They succeeded in greatly weakening the aristocracy's grip, of course, but much of the old society survived. Liberalism took root—but as the ideology of one class, the middle class, within a larger society. In the United States, however, the middle class was able to develop without the class awareness and conflict thrust upon its counterparts in Europe. America was formed as what historian Louis Hartz called a "fragment society": a piece of seventeenth- and eighteenth-century Europe was broken off and transplanted here. The middle-class fragment, separate from the motherland, flourished in the New World without having to confront its natural ideological and class enemies. "A part detaches itself from the whole, the whole fails to renew itself, and the part develops without inhibition."[7]

Classic liberalism in America

In contrast to the European experience, liberal political ideas and values were not seen in America as the distinct property of one class—an entrepreneurial middle class—but rather as the common property of all citizens. Classical liberalism was thus transformed. It became simply "Americanism," the American ideology. Louis Hartz has described this development nicely:

> There has never been a "liberal movement" or a real "liberal party" in America: We have only had the American Way of Life, a nationalist articulation of John Locke which usually does not know that Locke himself is involved. . . . Ironically, "liberalism" is a stranger in the land of its greatest realization and fulfillment.[8]

American capitalism

As liberal political ideals were recast as a national ideology, they necessarily were subject to a whole host of additional changes. Both classical liberalism and the American ideology stress the importance of private property and individuals' property rights. But the ideal of a private-property-based economy seems very different when it is added that all citizens *should* have the opportunity to acquire prop-

---

[7] Louis Hartz, *The Founding of New Societies* (New York: Harcourt, Brace, 1964), p. 9; idem., *The Liberal Tradition in America* (New York: Harcourt, Brace, 1955).

[8] Hartz, *Liberal Tradition*, p. 11.

erty and otherwise advance economically, than when it is claimed that property rights are the perquisite of one social class. Leon Samson had this in mind when he insisted that "the idea that everybody can become a capitalist is an American conception of capitalism."

Building a nation on an ideology. There were political disagreements aplenty among those who created the new American government in the late eighteenth century. But these disagreements were *within* tight boundaries, because of the breadth of the agreement across the young country in the central political values we have been describing. Indeed, it was the broad popular commitment to this ideology that created among the mostly British settlers in eighteenth-century America a sense of being members of a new American nation. Subsequently, adherence to the ideology constituted a bond of common identity and citizenship among the diverse peoples who emigrated to the United States in the nineteenth and in our own century.

America founded on a creed

Many nations are established on a common ethnic heritage. But the United States is a nation of immigrants, coming from many ethnic traditions. For it to develop its own unity and identity some other type of cement was needed. Ideology provided it. G. K. Chesterton, a distinguished writer and English visitor to the United States in the 1920s, noted that much is made of the great American experiment

> of a democracy of diverse races, which has been compared to a melting pot. But even that metaphor implies that the pot itself is of a certain shape and a certain substance; a pretty solid substance. The melting pot

must not melt. *America is the only nation in the world that is founded on a creed.* That creed is set forth with dogmatic and even theological lucidity in the Declaration of Independence; perhaps the only piece of practical politics that is also theoretical politics and also great literature.[9]

The Legacy of the American Ideology

The ideas of classical liberalism—with their emphasis on the rights of individuals to political freedom, limited government and self-government, private property, and social and economic opportunity—are set forth in the great documents of American political life: the Declaration of Independence, the Constitution, and such speeches as Lincoln's Gettysburg and Second Inaugural addresses. How much have these ideas really shaped American social and political behavior?

In all societies, ideas taken most seriously have sometimes been ignored or flouted. This is not to make excuses for American short-comings. We can hardly forget that a number of the men who signed the Declaration of Independence, with its bold insistence that all people are created equal, were themselves owners of slaves. Slavery is, of course, a powerful denial of the ideal of individual rights and equality. Yet it survived and even expanded its hold, until it was finally ended by the Civil War (1861–65). And pervasive racial discrimination was permitted long after slavery as such was abolished.

Has America been true to its ideology?

It is one thing to recognize that the United States has at times fallen far short of the highest ideals professed by its ideology, something else to insist that these shortcomings make the ideology's claims mere sham. If one insists that a set of beliefs *always* be adhered to before we should take its claims seriously, one ends up dismissing every one of them. Where is the Christian nation that has lived up to the religion's highest claims? America's ideological commitments, including the emphasis on individual rights, have had great impact on the nation's social and political life, even though the dictates of these ideas have sometimes been ignored.

AMERICAN IDEOLOGICAL BLINDSPOTS

In many ways the deficiencies of American ideology are outgrowths of its strength. The ideology stresses the equality of individuals and the legitimacy of their respective claims for a chance at the good life. Throughout U.S. history, deprived groups—ethnic and religious minorities and women, among them—have effectively used these values in their fight for equality and recognition. The strength of the ideology, together with the extent to which American national identity has been built around it, has provided a means of entry into full

[9]Gilbert Keith Chesterton, *What I Saw in America* (New York: Dodd, Mead, 1922), pp. 7–8.

citizenship for millions of immigrants. American political values have often opened rather than closed doors to those previously on the outside.

A certain intolerance. The very strength and unity of the ideology, however, carries with it the basis for a special American form of intolerance. Historian Garry Wills has observed that if there is an American idea, to really be an American "one must adopt this idea wholeheartedly, proclaim it, prove one's devotion to it." There has never been a legislative committee on "un-French activities," or one on "un-English affairs." But the strength of the American creed has allowed the formation of the House of Representatives Committee on Un-American Activities, and this committee's general intolerance in the 1940s and 1950s of dissenting ideas.[10] "Now a creed," G. K. Chesterton observed, "is at once the broadest and the narrowest thing in the world."[11] The American creed, on which national identity was established, has attracted and been open to people from all over the globe. It is at the same time narrow in its insistence that citizenship *must* be based upon adherence to certain political values.

American insularity. "Can a people 'born equal,'" Louis Hartz asks at the close of his study of the American liberal tradition, "ever understand peoples elsewhere that have to become so? ... Can it ever

Adherence to an American creed

Two views of the American sense of national identity. At left, Lee Iococca at the Statue of Liberty as the torch was being repaired (photo © 1984 by Peter B. Kaplan).

"But enough about my unique brand of Americanism. Tell me about your unique brand of Americanism."

Drawing by Richter; © 1984 The New Yorker Magazine, Inc.

[10] Garry Wills, *Inventing America* (New York: Vintage Books, 1978), p. xxii.
[11] Chesterton, *What I Saw in America*, p. 7.

In the 1950s, the extreme anti-communist campaign led by U.S. Senator Joseph R. McCarthy showed a disregard for civil liberties.

An insular nation

understand itself?"[12] The American ideological world has been insular. At the outset, it was cut off from the conflicts of the European countries. Over the last two centuries, when countries around the world have been struggling to overthrow aristocratic institutions and traditions, the United States has found itself sympathetic—yet removed from their experiences and problems. One result of this is the common tendency of American conservatives and liberals alike to moralize about the shortcomings of other countries or governments. We often seem to feel a bit self-righteous: "We were able to overcome those problems; why can't they?"

Why No Socialism?

Socialism's evolution in the West

The dominance in the United States of a distinct political ideology has precluded certain political solutions and ordained others. This underlying bias shows clearly in America's approach to economic questions. Throughout the Western world, modern economic development—with its historic shift from agricultural to industrial economies—has been full of painful stress and disruptions. Working class movements evolved in the nineteenth century, with ideologies that are some variant of socialism—protesting the privilege and power of business and the upper classes and calling for workers' control of the means of production. The United States stands as a striking exception. Socialism has never been strong here. No socialist movement here has ever had serious prospect of winning national power. The electoral high-watermark of the American Socialist party came in 1912, when Eugene Victor Debs picked up 900,000 popular votes for presi-

[12]Hartz, *Liberal Tradition*, p. 309.

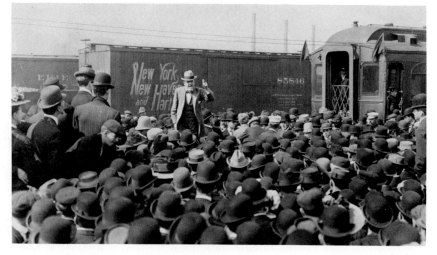

American socialist Eugene V. Debs campaigning in 1912.

dent, just *six percent* of the total vote. No socialist candidate has ever carried a single state in a national election.

Why no socialism in the United States? In part, because the intense *individualism* derived from liberalism has been resistant to the *collectivism* central to all forms of socialism. We noted in Chapter 2 that many Americans see themselves individually responsible for their positions and are less inclined than their counterparts in other industrial countries to turn to government. Socialism is apt to flourish when large numbers of people believe that they won't find a satisfactory life unless government weighs in to meet their collective needs. The *egalitarianism* of the American ideology has also held back the development of socialism. Leon Samson argued that Americanism is "substitutive socialism." A great appeal of socialism throughout the world has been its emphasis on equality, on the equal merit or worth of each person, an emphasis shared by the American creed. The American aversion to class rigidity, the impatience with class snobbery, the insistence that a good society is one where people are judged on the basis of what they do rather than on family pedigrees—all these reflect egalitarianism.

American egalitarianism

THE FOUNDATION OF AMERICAN POLITICAL INSTITUTIONS

The ascendancy of the liberal ideology in the United States has had profound influence on American politics. This influence has been strongest in molding the country's political institutions and providing their rationale and legitimacy.

We will develop this point in the next chapter, in discussing the origins of the U.S. Constitution, its longevity, and the type of democracy it ordains. Our political system owes its strength in large part to the faithfulness with which it articulates a dominating national ideology. That ideology and the governmental order go hand in hand; the latter institutionalizes the central assumptions of the former.

SUMMARY

Americans have strong feelings of national identity and unity. In contrast to other countries whose sense of ethnic identity is highly developed, the United States has achieved its national unity without ethnic commonality.

The American nation has been built on a political belief system or ideology. This ideology had its origins in the social frustrations and political interests of the rising middle classes of seventeenth- and eighteenth-century Europe. Known as classical liberalism, the ideas were brought to the New World by the middle-class fragment that settled here. And they were enlarged and transformed by American social conditions.

As it has developed in the United States, liberalism stresses an individualistic rather than a collectivist view of society: *individual rights*, including *political freedom* and *private property rights; equality of opportunity;* and *limited, democratic government.* It has been espoused by groups across the social spectrum, rather than remaining the ideology of one social class. Individuals have at times argued that America has denied them their rights under the liberal creed, but few have attacked the legitimacy of the creed itself.

Institutions established under the American ideology, such as the Constitution and a private-property-based economy, have drawn strength from its dominant hold on national thought.

FOR FURTHER STUDY

Robert N. Bellah, et al, *Habits of the Heart: Individualism and Commitment in American Life* (Berkeley, Ca: University of California Press, 1985). An important new examination of American individualism that is highly critical of recent developments within it.

Gilbert K. Chesterton, *What I Saw in America* (New York: Dodd, Mead, 1922). An insightful interpretation of American political ideology, written by a distinguished British writer and intellectual.

Louis Hartz, *The Liberal Tradition in America* (New York: Harcourt, Brace and Co., 1955). The most important interpretation by an American political scientist of how the conditions under which the United States was founded have continued to shape American political thought.

John Locke, *Second Treatise of Civil Government: An Essay Concerning the True Original Extent,* and *End of Civil Government* in Peter Laslett, ed., *Two Treatises of Government* (New York: New American Library, 1965; essay originally published, 1690). An essay by a major figure in the development of liberal thought in the seventeenth century, that influenced the conceptions of government of the American founders.

Leon Samson, "Americanism as Surrogate Socialism," in Samson, *Toward a United Front* (New York: Farrar and Rinehart, 1935). A brilliant account by a young American socialist, explaining why socialism was unable to develop in the United States as it had in other industrial countries.

Chapter 4

The Constitution and American Democracy

The United States Constitution was written by fifty-five men, representing twelve of thirteen states, who met in constitutional convention in Philadelphia during the spring and summer of 1787. By mid-1788, the new Constitution had been ratified, replacing the Articles of Confederation as the law of the land. A new president and Congress took office under the Constitution in the spring of 1789.

For 200 years in unbroken succession the United States has been governed under a single basic law. In the same span of time France has been governed by ten separate and distinct constitutional orders, including five different republics, two empires, one monarchy, one plebiscitary dictatorship, and one puppet dictatorship installed at Vichy during World War II. The United States has had but one constitution and, created under it, one set of governing institutions. Built on America's ideological foundation, the Constitution owes its remarkable staying power to the continuing dominance of liberal ideas.

But it is not just the basic constitutional form that has survived. So, too, has the spirit, the animating assumptions. The American Constitution of the 1980s and 1990s is in all essential regards the Constitution of 1787. American democracy today bears the deep imprint of the founders' design.

The founders believed that concentrated governmental power was a prime threat to individual liberty, so they dispersed power across a number of separate and independent governmental institutions—at the national level, Congress, the presidency, and the federal courts. They gave each of these the means of checking and balancing the others. Today, some wonder if the founders did too good a job in this regard. They worry that separation of powers, especially involving the executive and the legislature, leaves our national government unable to act coherently on a number of pressing national problems.

We will look at these issues in detail in the chapters ahead, especially in chapter 5.

The debate over what our democracy requires is as lively as ever. If Americans have learned anything in their two hundred years of experience with democratic government, it is that democracy is wonderfully rewarding, always very demanding, and at times frustratingly difficult to achieve satisfactorily. The great British prime minister Winston Churchill once remarked that "democracy is the worst form of government . . . except for all the others." This backhand defense of democracy may well be the most profound defense. The work of the founders of the American system should be judged not by whether it realizes all of its ideals but by the practical yardstick of how its performance compares to that of other systems.

Preference for limited, democratic government is, as we noted in chapter 3, a key part of the American ideology; and the U.S. Constitution has provided a set of such democratic institutions. For many Americans, then, the question of whether democracy is the best form of government involves little debate: "Government by the people" is good, or at least preferable to all other forms of government. Yet if this view seems natural and unassailable to most Americans, it is far from universally accepted. Throughout history most of the world's population have been governed under arrangements decidedly not democratic. Most political theories have defended other constitutional arrangements. Even apart from the argument over the general desirability of democracy, many observers insist that the government of the United States is flawed by democratic standards.

Behind these arguments lies a basic question: What does democracy as a political theory really encompass? Since the idea of democratic government goes back 2400 years, to the Greek city-state of Athens, we might think that the question of democracy's meaning would have long since been resolved to everyone's satisfaction. It has not, however. Later in this chapter we will take a close look at various conceptions of democracy, especially those common in the United States. We will trace the concept from its Greek origins, through the thinking of the framers of the U.S. Constitution, to present-day perspectives on what democratic government means or requires, and we will discuss different views on the quality of America's democratic performance.

We begin, though, by looking closely at the origins of the document that underlies and animates our democratic system: the Constitution. Three related questions need to be answered if we are to understand American constitutional experience and assess properly its legacy. How did the Constitution come to be written, approved, and implemented in the form we know today? Who were the men most responsible for the Constitution and what were their primary political objectives? What are the essential characteristics of the type of government that the Constitution establishes?

Government by the people

Democracy's evolving tradition

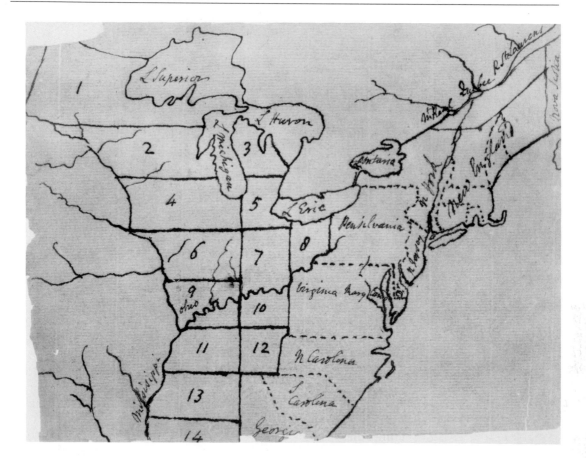

An early map of the nation including the original states and some proposals for new states drawn by Thomas Jefferson.

FROM IDEOLOGY TO GOVERNMENT

In the eighteenth and nineteenth centuries, many Americans came to believe that their country had a "Manifest Destiny." As sociologist Daniel Bell has put it, "not just the idea that a nation had the right to define its own fate, but the conviction of a special virtue of the American people different from anything known in Europe or even, hitherto, in this history of the world."[1] Clinton Rossiter has noted that this belief in a special national place and mission was held by virtually all of the leading American political figures of the "revolutionary generation."[2]

Americans of the late eighteenth century lived, John Adams wrote,

[1] Daniel Bell, "The End of American Exceptionalism," *The Public Interest*, Fall 1975, p. 199.
[2] Clinton Rossiter, *Alexander Hamilton and the Constitution* (New York: Harcourt, Brace, 1964), p. 17.

Thomas Jefferson's draft of the Declaration of Independence.

in "a time when the greatest law givers of antiquity would have wished to live"; they had before them an opportunity to "establish the wisest and happiest government that human wisdom can contrive."[3] From this sense of unique opportunity flowed a sense of unusual responsibility. "We . . . decide forever the fate of Republican government," James Madison told the Constitutional Convention on June 26, 1787.

American exceptionalism

Where did this highly developed and widely shared view of America as an exceptional society come from? The founders of new institutions often harbor high aspirations. But most members of the revolutionary generation believed deeply that the United States was to be, in the words of Isaiah, "a city . . . set on a hill," "a light unto the nations," beckoning through its attainments and example. The United States was established on a large, open territory that was only lightly populated by its original inhabitants, the Indian peoples. There were vistas and promises of a seemingly endless frontier. An abun-

"A city set on a hill"

[3] C. F. Adams, ed., *The Works of John Adams* (Boston, 1956), vol. IV, p. 200.

dance of rich land made the United States prosperous at the very outset. The ideal of a populace of independent property owners was readily attained. Americans were starting afresh, set apart from European nations.

American optimism did not wholly depend on such material good fortune. The American ideology sustained optimism in offering a blueprint for a new and successful society. It specified ideals that were considered at once worthy and attainable. The Constitution embodied the extraordinary breadth of attachment Americans of the 1780s felt to the liberal ideology and their belief that, if only appropriate institutions were put in place, they could maintain national political unity.

Constitution as an embodiment of liberal ideology

Separating Ourselves from Britain

Declaration of Independence

On July 2, 1776, the Continental Congress—representing thirteen North American colonies—approved a motion that had been introduced by Richard Henry Lee of Virginia about a month earlier: "That these united colonies are, and of right ought to be free and independent states." Assisted by Benjamin Franklin and John Adams, Thomas Jefferson expanded the resolution into the famous Declaration of Independence that was adopted on July 4. The Declaration powerfully affirmed the liberal ideal of individual rights made familiar by John Locke and advanced by a century and a half of American experience. (The text of the Declaration of Independence is reprinted in the Appendix to this book.)

Signing the Declaration of Independence, painting by John Trumbull.

The War for Independence, which began in 1775, was not decided until October 19, 1781, when the British General Charles Cornwallis surrendered his army to General George Washington. With their military band playing "The World Turned Upside Down," 7,000 British troops marched out of Yorktown, Virginia, and laid down their arms. Preliminary articles of peace were signed a year later, on November 30, 1782, and the final treaties were signed in Paris on September 3, 1783. America's *ideological* independence had been achieved long before 1783, however, and was framed around a national commitment to liberal values.

The Articles of Confederation

On July 12, 1776, a committee of the Continental Congress brought in a draft of a proposed constitution. After more than a year of arguing about such questions as how war expenses should be apportioned and voting power allocated among the states, the Congress finally approved the document on November 17, 1777, and submitted it to the thirteen state legislatures for consideration. The **Articles of Confederation,** as this first national constitution was called, were approved by all thirteen states except Maryland by 1779; Maryland ratified the Articles in 1781.

The Articles of Confederation faithfully reflected American political values of the time. They provided for a national government founded on republican principles—the idea that governmental institutions should be responsive to the will of the people—and distinguished by a commitment to individual liberty achieved through dispersed and limited governmental power. But in some basic structural regards, the government of the Articles of Confederation was flawed.

The main deficiency stemmed from the states' position as fully sovereign entities that merely ceded certain limited powers to the national government. The sovereign character and equality of the thirteen states was reflected in the manner of their representation in the Continental Congress. Each state, whatever its size, had only one vote; this was cast by delegates appointed by the state legislature. The states were supposed to contribute to the common expenses of the nation—for example, the costs of maintaining a national army—according to the value of their lands. But the national government lacked any means to compel state compliance, and it was always teetering on the brink of bankruptcy.

The impotence of the Continental Congress left the United States singularly ill-equipped to protect its own national interests in dealing with other countries. For instance, the Congress had printed paper money to meet the costs of the war with England. Near the war's end, this currency had become virtually worthless in the absence of a

(margin notes:)

War for Independence

Articles of Confederation

Weaknesses of the Articles

Continental Congress under the Articles

national taxing power. The Congress was forced to beg money and supplies from France. After the war, the Congress had to borrow money from bankers in Holland. When it turned to the states for funds as provided in the Articles, or when it sought the power to levy a 5 percent tariff on imports, the states turned this "beggar nation" down. In order to impose a tariff, the unanimous approval of the states was required; in 1781 and again in 1783, at least one state refused.

Since the Congress did not have the power to levy taxes and could not force the states to use their authority to tax as provided in Article VIII, it was unable to raise enough money for the common defense or general welfare of the United States. Even Revolutionary War debts could not be paid, including salaries owed for military service. Army officers encamped themselves at Newburg, New York, in 1783 and threatened mutiny to force the Congress to pay their long-overdue wages. This financial weakness also contributed to the Congress's inability to protect the trans-Alleghany wilderness region. It could not support troops to defend settlers from Indian attacks, nor could it prevent the British and Spanish governments from establishing settlements in these lands.

Inability to raise money

Along with its own financial weakness, the Congress had to contend with states issuing their own currencies. Article IX granted the Congress "sole and exclusive right and power of regulating the alloy and value of coin struck by their own authority or by that of the respective states. . . ." But this did not stop states from issuing money. Debtor and creditor factions in various states engaged in bitter struggles. Some states passed laws forcing acceptance of devalued paper currency at its face value; others deferred the collection of debts and prohibited courts from issuing judgments for debts. A former Army captain, Daniel Shays, led a group of armed Massachusetts farmers in an insurrection in 1786, attempting to prevent the county courts from sitting in judgment on debts. The whole system of monetary exchange was in chaos.

State currencies

Under the Articles of Confederation, the national government was little more than an aspiration. The claim of Article II, that "each state retain its sovereignty, freedom, and independence," was the reality. The provision of Article III that the states "hereby severally enter in a firm league of friendship with each other" fairly described the governmental order.

THE MOVE TO A STRONG NATIONAL GOVERNMENT

As a statement of republican principles embodying an ideal of popular government, the Articles of Confederation were admirable. As a constitution for a workable national government, they were a decided failure. Dissatisfaction with the Articles was not distributed evenly across the populace. American nationalists such as George Washington and Alexander Hamilton were the most profoundly troubled. Merchants in seaport towns felt the weakness of the Articles more acutely than did farmers in the heartlands. Not surprisingly, then, those philosophically committed to the idea of a strong, unified nation, encouraged by mercantile interests, took the lead in efforts to modify the Articles to provide for a stronger national government.

Common national values

Still, most Americans shared a sense of nation, built around their common political values. Thomas Paine was reflecting this general sentiment when he wrote in his first publication after the peace with Great Britain had been secured, "I ever feel myself hurt when I hear the Union, the great palladium of our liberty and safety, the least irreverently spoken of. . . . Our citizenship in the United States is our national character. Our citizenship in any particular state is only our local distinction."[4] Such views strengthened the hand of the most advanced nationalists, like Washington and Hamilton, who at the time were often called "Continentalists."

Liberalism as a barrier to change

The biggest barrier to constitutional change grew out of liberalism itself. Americans were suspicious of anything that suggested concentrated governmental power. The Articles of Confederation, whatever their deficiencies, did not create a tyrannical government. Those favoring a new constitutional arrangement had to convince a majority of their fellow citizens that the new government would not be too strong.

Three Who Made a Revolution

George Washington, James Madison, Alexander Hamilton

While many people contributed to the new Constitution, three men played the leading roles: George Washington and James Madison of Virginia, and Alexander Hamilton of New York. Of the three, Washington's involvement was the least intensive and direct, but perhaps the most important. His prestige, as the general who led the fight for independence, was enormous, and his character inspired confidence. The most decisive single factor in the implementation of the Constitution of 1787 was George Washington's total commitment to it. Washington gave essential legitimacy to the effort.

Madison and Hamilton furnished much of the energy and practical political imagination needed for constitutional reform. As early as September 3, 1780, from Washington's camp at Liberty Pole (now Englewood), New Jersey, Hamilton penned a long letter to James

[4]Thomas Paine, *Thoughts on the Peace, and the Probable Advantages Thereof, Common Sense*, Philadelphia, April 19, 1783; in William M. Vander Weyde, ed., *The Life and Works of Thomas Paine* (New Rochelle, N.Y.: Thomas Paine National Historical Association, 1925), p. 245.

Alexander Hamilton, James Madison, and George Washington.

Duane (a member of the New York delegation in the Continental Congress, which included delegates from all the states) indicting the Confederation as "neither fit for war or peace." He proposed correcting the "want of method and energy in administration" by instituting departments with single heads and giving the Congress "complete sovereignty in all that relates to war, peace, trade, finance, and to the management of foreign affairs."[5] Note the urgency of the call sounded by this 24-year-old statesman:

> The Convention [to reform the national government] should assemble the first of November next. The sooner the better. Our disorders are too violent to admit of a common or lingering remedy. . . . I require them to be vested with plenipotentiary authority that the business may suffer no delay in the execution and may in reality come into effect.

Hamilton pressed his case over the next seven years. So did James Madison. The two worked in concert in 1782–83 when both were delegates to the Continental Congress. In 1786, they again joined talents and energies at the Annapolis convention, called to discuss the economic difficulties of the states and to "consider how far a uniform system in their commercial regulations may be necessary to their common interest and their permanent harmony." The convention in turn delivered a call to the Congress to appoint delegates "to meet at Philadelphia on the second Monday in May next [1787] to take into Consideration the situation of the United States; to devise such further Provisions as shall appear to them necessary to render the Con-

The Annapolis
Convention

---

[5] Harold C. Syrett and Jacob E. Cooke, eds., *The Papers of Alexander Hamilton* (New York and London, 1961), vol. 2, p. 407.

stitution of the Federal Government adequate to exigencies of the Union; and to report such an Act for that purpose to the United States in Congress Assembled. . . ."[6] The Annapolis convention was a joint triumph for Hamilton and Madison.

Philadelphia, 1787

On May 25, 1787, with 29 men from nine states having arrived at the State House in Philadelphia, the constitutional convention officially opened. By unanimous vote, George Washington was chosen as its president. When it adjourned four months later, the convention had drafted the Constitution of the United States as we know it today.

Delegates to the Convention

The men assembled in Philadelphia were distinguished by extraordinary intellect and achievement. Even Thomas Jefferson called the delegates "demigods"—he himself was representing the new nation in France at the time, and he later took issue with some aspects of the convention's work. For one thing, the delegates were quite young. Their average age was lower than John F. Kennedy's when he was inaugurated as America's youngest president at age 43. The average age of the 1787 delegates was 42; but, despite their comparative youth, they were both mature and accomplished.

That the delegates shared general beliefs and objectives contributed enormously to their success. Classical liberals, their thinking was infused with new political ideas developed by seventeenth- and eighteenth-century European philosophers. The work of the English theorist John Locke (1632–1704) and the French philosopher Montesquieu (1689–1755) were well known to the delegates—the former for his emphasis on individual rights, the latter for his discussion of separation of powers—and influenced the writing of the Constitution.

THE MAKING OF THE CONSTITUTION

The assigned task of the convention was to revise the Articles of Confederation. But the delegates quickly decided to go beyond their instructions. They would establish an entirely new constitution. On May 30 they voted that "a *national* Government ought to be established," and they proceeded to work out its details.

A democratic federal government

The delegates agreed at the outset that there should be a *federal* system, composed of state governments and a national government with limited but constitutionally secure powers. While they differed in their assessments of *democracy*, they agreed that ordinary citizens should play a large role in choosing those who would administer their

[6] Max Farrand, *The Framers of the Constitution of the United States* (New Haven: Yale University Press, 1913), p. 10.

Washington presiding at the signing of the Constitution, painting by Thomas Rossiter.

affairs. The delegates believed that ordinary people were capable of actions both sublime and dangerous. A proper constitution should create a setting that would blunt the latter and encourage the former. The delegates shared the liberal distrust of concentrated power, and they created a constitution that would prevent such concentration and thus avoid tyranny.

Alexander Hamilton was a delegate, but his role in the convention's deliberations was relatively modest. The contributions of Oliver Ellsworth and Roger Sherman of Connecticut, Benjamin Franklin and James Wilson of Pennsylvania, and George Washington as the convention's presiding officer and unquestioned moral leader were much greater.

Madison's role

The decisive intellectual work was done by Madison. His influence and arguments were everywhere: in the convention debates, in the compromises struck, in the very language of the Constitution. Referring strictly to the work of the Philadelphia convention—rather than to activities leading up to it or those that followed in securing ratification and implementation—James Madison must be seen as the father of the Constitution.

Powers invested in the national government

The critical question of what powers should be granted to the central government prompted little argument. The national government should be able to levy taxes and regulate both interstate and foreign commerce. It should be able to raise and maintain an army and a navy. Concurrently, the states must be stripped of their powers to issue money, make treaties, and tax imports. Power had to be shifted from the states to the central government.

Over who should control the new government the delegates argued

Representation: the
Great Compromise

fiercely. The larger states pushed for representation in the national legislature based on population; the smaller states, understandably, wanted to maintain the old system of equal state representation. The *Virginia Plan*, proposed by the larger states, was drafted by Madison and presented to the convention by Edmund Randolph, Virginia's governor. The small states backed the *New Jersey Plan*, written by William Paterson, a former New Jersey attorney general. In mid-July the delegates reached what is known as the *Great Compromise*. Seats in the lower house of the legislature—the House of Representatives—were allocated according to population and filled by popular vote; seats in the upper house—the Senate—were allocated two to each state regardless of size, and filled by vote of the state legislature.

Slavery: the three-
fifths compromise

Slavery posed another important argument over control and representation. Southern delegates favored including slaves in the population base that would determine representation in the House of Representatives (although they had no thought of permitting the slaves to vote). In the *three-fifths compromise*, the delegates agreed that "three-fifths of all other Persons" (slaves) would be counted for taxation and representation. Final resolution of the slave trade issue was put off for two decades by the constitutional clause (Article I, section 9) that prevented Congress from outlawing the slave trade until 1808.

Bicameral legislature

Having struck these compromises, the delegates easily resolved their remaining differences. And, on September 17, 1787, they assembled to affix their signatures to the new Constitution. They had provided for a national government with a *bicameral* or two-house legislature, an executive branch headed by a president with broad powers, and a national judiciary consisting of a Supreme Court and such "inferior courts" as Congress might decide to create.

Key Provisions

Checks and balances

The most distinctive feature of the document crafted in Philadelphia is its unremitting attention to the problem of power. The Constitution established a federal system in which authority would be divided between the national and state governments. The formal responsibilities of each would be extensive. Power was then further divided among the three branches of the national government; each was given its own base of authority. An elaborate system of **checks and balances** was established, giving each branch the means to restrain the other two.

Separation of powers had long been provided for in aristocratic societies among the monarchy, nobility, clergy, and "the commons"—the latter including the rural gentry and urban middle classes. In eighteenth-century England the king had powers distinct and separate from the rest of the nobility—which was represented in the upper chamber of Parliament, the House of Lords—and from the middle classes, which had a base through representation in the lower chamber, the House of Commons.

Separation of powers

In this aristocratic model, **separation of powers** reflected the divergent claims of the several power centers of the society. But in America after independence, there was no monarchy or aristocracy; here was a middle-class society where "the commons" was very near the whole of the social order. The classical liberal commitment to a separation of powers expressed itself in a system of independent branches of government each intended to represent the interests of the general public. The president was expected to serve this common interest; so was Congress. The power of "the commons" itself was to be divided, lest any popular impulse or greedy faction threaten individual claims and minority rights.

The veto

In the American Constitution, every basic grant of authority is carefully limited. The president is commander-in-chief of the armed forces, but it is Congress's power to declare war and "to raise and support armies." The president has broad appointive powers, but his appointments require "the advice and consent" of the Senate. Congress has the sole constitutional responsibility for enacting all legislation, but the president has a veto over such acts, a veto that can be overridden only by a two-thirds vote of each house. All legislation must be approved in identical form by both houses of the legislature. Never before or since has so sustained an effort been made to provide for governmental authority at once vigorous and checked. The new government would be strong enough to establish a setting where individual initiatives could flourish, and checked enough so that individual rights would not be violated. The Constitution of the United States is the crowning political testament to these claims of the liberal creed.

Factions or special interests

James Madison expounded on the liberal theory of power in *Federalist Papers* 10 and 51, written in late 1787.[7] (See the Appendix for *Federalist Papers* 10 and 51.) As Madison saw it, special interests necessarily abound in free societies. He called them **factions.** "Liberty is to faction," he wrote "what air is to fire. . . ." To abolish liberty because it permits the expression of narrow, selfish interests would be as great a folly as "to wish the annihilation of air, which is essential to animal life, because it imparts to fire its destructive agency."

The answer to this dilemma, Madison insisted, was to prevent any individual or interest, or governmental institution, from gaining too

[7] *The Federalist Papers* is a series of 85 papers written in late 1787 by Madison, Alexander Hamilton, and John Jay, a colleague of Hamilton's from New York, who was to become the first chief justice of the Supreme Court. Their purpose was to help persuade New York to ratify the Constitution. A very convenient edition of *The Federalist Papers* is that edited by Clinton Rossiter (New York: New American Library, 1961). All references following to *The Federalist Papers* are to this edition. *Papers* 10 and 51 are reprinted in the Appendix to this book (pp. A21–A28).

much power. In *Federalist Paper* 51, Madison gave the classic liberal answer—the American constitutional power—to the problem of power.

Madison's answer to factions

> But the great security against a gradual concentration [of power] . . . consists in giving to those who administer each department the necessary constitutional means and personal motives to resist encroachment of the others. . . . *Ambition must be made to counteract ambition.* The interest of the man must be connected with the constitutional rights of the place. It may be a reflection on human nature that such devices should be necessary to control the abuses of government. But what is government itself but the greatest of all reflections on human nature? If men were angels, no government would be necessary. If angels were to govern men, neither external or internal controls on government would be necessary. In framing the government which is to be administered by men over men, the great difficulty lies in this: You must first enable the government to control the governed; and in the next place oblige it to control itself.[8]

Ratification

The framers of the Constitution required their handiwork to be ratified by special state conventions. They may have been motivated in this by a desire to bypass the state legislatures, where many members might resent the reductions being made in state authority. But the legislatures could still have blocked ratification by refusing to call for state conventions. Only Rhode Island did so.

Federalists versus anti-Federalists

The summoning of state ratification conventions prompted a vigorous national debate between those who favored the Constitution—called Federalists since they were endorsing a strong federal union—and their opponents known as anti-Federalists. The anti-Federalists feared that the new national government would prove too strong and would endanger the country's hard-earned liberty. Ultimately, they charged, America would become a single consolidated governmental unit. Article VI of the Constitution, which provided that "this Constitution, and the laws of the United States which shall be made in pursuance thereof . . . shall be the supreme law of the land . . ." seemed to many anti-Federalists to make inevitable the submergence of the state legislatures and the supremacy of the Congress. Not too much should be made of this split. A leading expert on this subject, Cecelia M. Kenyon, concluded that

> the factors that united the Federalists and anti-Federalists were stronger than those that divided them. . . . There was a general agreement that liberty and certain other related rights and interests of the individual were the proper ends of government; that consent was the only legitimate source of political authority; that the only form of government proper and feasible for Americans was republican; that republican governments . . . should be limited in the exercise of their powers, and by written fun-

---

[8] Ibid., p. 322. Emphasis added.

damental laws or constitutions; that there should be some kind and degree of union among the separate states.[9]

The move to
ratification

In most states the Federalists won easily; remarkable, considering the magnitude of the constitutional change being proposed. Delaware acted first, ratifying the Constitution unanimously on December 7, 1787. A few days later, Pennsylvania followed suit by a two-to-one majority. New Jersey gave unanimous approval on December 18, as did Georgia on January 2, 1788. The vote in Connecticut on January 9, 1788, was 128 to 40 in favor of the Constitution. The Massachusetts vote was the first close one. Delegates approved the Constitution by just 187 to 168 in early February 1788. Maryland endorsed the Constitution overwhelmingly in April, as did South Carolina in May. When New Hampshire ratified on June 21, by a close vote of 57 to 47, the Constitution had received the requisite endorsement of nine of the thirteen states. Virginia followed, also by a close vote, approving the Constitution on June 25.

Final ratification

Three states remained outside the new national union, but only one—New York—was of critical importance, for it was one of the big states, and it separated New England from the states to the South. Opposition in that pivotal state was strong and well-organized, and the anti-Federalist faction won 46 of the 65 seats to its convention. Alexander Hamilton was a member of the Federalist minority, however, and his energies on behalf of the Constitution give us a fascinating example of how much effective leadership can mean. Hamilton pleaded, cajoled, and compromised; and more importantly, he offered an intellectually imposing defense of the Federalist position. Through his labors, and aided by the fact that New York looked like a person standing on the pier while the schooner—here, the new government—was sailing away, the New York convention finally voted in favor of ratification on July 26, 1788, by a 30 to 27 margin. The new government was launched—though North Carolina did not ratify until November 1789 and Rhode Island withheld consent to the Constitution until May 1790.[10]

PUTTING THE NEW INSTITUTIONS IN PLACE

Washington elected
first president

Legislative elections were held in January and February, 1789. By early April enough Congressmen had completed the journey to New York, the temporary capital, for the government to commence operation. The ballots of the presidential electors were counted in the Senate on April 6. George Washington was the unanimous choice for

[9]Cecelia M. Kenyon, xcvii-xcviii.
[10]The story of Hamilton's momentous role in the New York ratifying convention is ably told in Rossiter's *Alexander Hamilton and the Constitution.*

president and, receiving 34 electoral votes, John Adams became vice president. Washington took his oath of office in Federal Hall in New York on April 30, 1789. Fewer than 24 months had elapsed between the convening of the convention in Philadelphia and Washington's inauguration as president under the new Constitution. It had been an extraordinary march along the road of nation building, and the pace did not slow over the next three years. The task of implementing the new system was as demanding as its writing and ratification had been. (See Box 4.1.)

Hamilton, Madison, and Washington again provided the primary leadership. In George Washington the new nation had a president at once strong and cautious. His personal sensitivity to criticism and his high sense of responsibility made him especially careful that no

Washington and the presidency

Box 4.1

George Washington Is Inaugurated as the Country's First President: A Contemporary Account

The first president of the United States of America, George Washington, took his oath of office, as provided by the new Constitution, on April 30, 1789. The following account of Washington's arrival in New York (the first capital) for his inauguration, from the *Connecticut Courant* of May 4, 1789, gives us a sense of just how momentous the event was for many Americans of that time:

[NEW YORK, April 25.]Thursday last, between 2 and 3 o'clock p.m. the Most Illustrious PRESIDENT of the UNITED STATES arrived in this city. . . .

It is impossible to do justice in an attempt to describe the Scene exhibited on his Excellency's approach to the city. Innumerable multitudes thronged the shores, the wharves, and the shipping—waiting with pleasing anticipation his arrival. His Catholic Majesty's Sloop of War, the *Calviston*—the ship *North Carolina*, (Mr. Dohrman's) and other vessels, were dressed, manned, and highly decorated. His Excellency's Barge was accompanied by Several other Barges, in one of which were the Hon. the Board of Treasury—the Minister of Foreign Affairs— and the Secretary of War—besides a long train of vessels and boats from New-Jersey and New-York. As he passed the *Calviston* they fired a salute of 13 guns—The Ship *North Carolina*, and the *Battery*, also welcomed his approach with the same number. . . .

The Procession moved through Queen Street to the House prepared for the reception of the President—from whence he was conducted, without form, to the Governor's where his Excellency dined.

serious error be made that might unsettle the new government. "The eyes of Argos are upon me," he once complained, "and no slip will pass unnoticed."[11] In the eight years of his presidency, no action was more consequential or salutary than his last one: his decision to step down voluntarily after two terms in office. Of all the monuments to successful democratic nation-building, none is more impressive than that of Washington walking away, gladly handing over the responsibilities of office.

James Madison became leader of the House of Representatives, and Alexander Hamilton was first secretary of the Treasury. Through Madison's leadership, Congress had by September 1789 created the

[11] Washington's reference was to the 100-eyed guardian of Io, ancestor of the people of Argos, Greece; the legend is in Homer's *The Iliad* and *The Odyssey*.

This great occasion arrested the publick attention beyond all powers of description—the hand of industry was suspended—and the various pleasures of the capital were concentered to a single enjoyment—All ranks and professions expressed their feelings, in loud acclamations, and with rapture hailed the arrival of the FATHER OF HIS COUNTRY. . . .

The Scene on Thursday last was sublimely great—beyond any descriptive powers of the pen to do justice to—How universal—and how laudable the curiosity—How *sincere*—and, how *expressive* the sentiments of respect and veneration!—All Ranks appeared to feel the force of an expression, that was reiterated among the crowd . . . "WELL, HE DESERVES IT ALL!"

The spontaneous essations of gratitude to the illustrious WASHINGTON, exhibited by all ranks of people, in a thousand various indications of the sublime principle, are the highest reward that virtue enjoys, next to a conscious approbation which always precedes such undissembled testimonials of publick affection.

Many persons who were in the crowd, on Thursday, were heard to say, that they should now die contented—nothing being wanted to complete their happiness, previous to this auspicious period, but the sight of the Saviour of his Country.

Some persons, advanced in years, who hardly expected to see the illustrious President of the States, till they should meet him in Heaven, were in the concourse on Thursday, and could hardly restrain their impatience at being in a measure deprived of the high gratification, by the eagerness of the multitudes of children and young people, who probably might long enjoy the blessings.

The Bill of Rights

State, Treasury, and War departments, and had passed the Judiciary Act, which established thirteen federal district courts and three circuit courts of appeal. The number of Supreme Court justices was set at six, and Washington named John Jay the first chief justice. Again under Madison's leadership, Congress prepared a dozen amendments, ten of which were ratified, guaranteeing what he called the "great rights of mankind." Known since as the **Bill of Rights,** these amendments affirmed the right of trial by jury, barred compelling individuals to testify against themselves in criminal cases, forbade unreasonable searches and seizures, and required that no one "be deprived of life, liberty, or property, without due process of law." The most notable provision was in the first amendment: Congress could make no law infringing freedom of speech, the press, or religion (see Box 4.2).

Secretary of the Treasury Alexander Hamilton

Hamilton's works were equally notable. As secretary of the Treasury for five years—the second most powerful man in American government—he advanced his consuming commitment to a strong national government. Hamilton was a gifted executive and planner. Recognizing that the new country needed capital to develop its untapped resources, he sought to persuade investors to commit their funds in America. His *Report on the Public Credit* set forth a program

---

Box 4.2
The Bill of Rights

On December 15, 1791, the first ten amendments to the Constitution were ratified. We know them as the Bill of Rights.

Amendment 1: The rights of religion, speech, and assembly.
Amendment 2: The right to bear arms.
Amendment 3: Quartering of soldiers.
Amendment 4: The right to be secure against "unreasonable searches and seizures."
Amendment 5: The right to "due process of law" (including protection against double jeopardy and self-incrimination).
Amendment 6: The right to a speedy trial by an impartial jury.
Amendment 7: The right to a jury trial in common law cases.
Amendment 8: Prohibition of excessive bail and "cruel and unusual punishment."
Amendment 9: The rights of the people are not limited to those enumerated above.
Amendment 10: Powers not delegated to the federal government by the Constitution, or specifically prohibited to the states, are reserved to the states and the people.

securing congressional approval for funding the existing public debt at the face value of the certificates. The nation's credit could not be secured, he reasoned, unless investors were convinced that the government would honor all obligations in full.

Hamilton then proposed that Congress charter a national bank to serve as an instrument for collecting and spending tax revenues, and to provide bank notes, which would serve as a badly needed medium of exchange. Congress approved the Bank of the United States, but Washington was urged to veto the legislation by Thomas Jefferson, his secretary of state, and by James Madison, who was a trusted adviser as well. But, Hamilton argued, the provision of Article I, Section 8, giving Congress the authority to pass all laws which shall be "necessary and proper" to carrying out the specific powers enumerated elsewhere in the article must be interpreted broadly. Washington accepted Hamilton's argument and signed the bill. In 1819, the Supreme Court was to explicitly sanction Hamilton's broad construction of the "necessary and proper" clause.

Establishment of a national bank

Hamilton rushed ahead. In December 1791 he submitted his *Report on Manufactures,* a bold plan for stimulating American mercantile and industrial development by setting up government tariffs, subsidies, and awards to encourage American manufacturing. While the report as a whole was pigeonholed by Congress, a number of specific tariffs that Hamilton recommended were enacted in 1792.

Hamilton's Report on Manufactures

By the end of 1792, the new government had been firmly established. The American Constitution continues to be a living, evolving instrument that receives definition from precedent and practice; a total of 26 constitutional amendments now exist. But the decisive steps of constitutional nation building had been taken and implemented, and the major articles of the Constitution are as strongly in force today as in the last years of the eighteenth century.

The Constitution was not a perfect instrument for securing liberty through the machinery of representative democracy. Its most decisive weakness was its failure to ban slavery. Still, the Constitution drafted in 1787 has achieved what Washington hoped for when he said it was to "raise a standard to which the wise and the honest can repair."

In his letter of September 17, 1787, by which he transmitted the Constitution to Congress for its consideration, Washington penned these words:

A workable Constitution

> That it will meet the full and entire approbation of every State is not perhaps to be expected; but each will doubtless consider, that had her interests alone been consulted, the consequences might have been particularly disagreeable or injurious to others; that it is liable to as few exceptions as could reasonably have been expected, we hope and believe; that it may promote the lasting welfare of that country so dear to all of us, and secure her freedom and happiness, is our most ardent wish.

THE CONSTITUTION AND DEMOCRACY

Liberty and democracy

Political scientist Martin Diamond has discussed the two central values that occupied the revolutionary generation—*liberty* and *democracy*—and how they were treated in the two great documents of the revolutionary era, the Declaration of Independence and the Constitution. The Declaration, Diamond argued, was a bold statement of a principle. It set forth the primacy of liberty as the comprehensive good, the objective against which all political administrations and activity had to be measured.[12] The Constitution set forth the means for the attainment of liberty, a form of government which "had to prove itself adequately instrumental to the securing of liberty." In this pursuit, the Constitution "opted for democracy . . . embodying the bold and unprecedented decision to achieve, in so large a country as this, a free society *under the democratic form of government.*"[13]

Democracy

Democracy derives from two Greek roots: *demos*, meaning the people, and *kratis*, meaning authority. During the fifth century B.C., the Greeks, particularly the Athenians, used the term to refer to government by the many, as contrasted to government by the few (oligarchy), or by one person (monarchy). In his famous "Funeral Oration," the Athenian statesman Pericles (495–429 B.C.) declared that "our [Athens's] constitution is named a democracy, because it is in the hands not of the few, but of the many." This idea that ultimate political authority should rest with the general public remains central to all conceptions of democracy.

Within this general understanding, however, a number of different conceptions of democracy can be found. The term itself has been used with sharply different meanings—which naturally poses problems for students seeking to learn about the subject. We need to locate the American conception of democracy in the broader historical context.

Aristotle's Idea of Democracy

Three forms of government

The first great political theorist to treat democracy coherently as a system of government was the Athenian philosopher Aristotle (384–322 B.C.). He argued that there were three general forms of government—kingship, aristocracy, and constitutional government or "polity"—and three others that were corruptions of the three proper forms: "tyranny corresponding to kingship, oligarchy to aristocracy, and democracy to constitutional government. . . . Tyranny is monarchy ruling in the interest of the monarch, oligarchy government in the interest of the rich, democracy government in the interest of the poor,

[12] Martin Diamond, "The Declaration and the Constitution: Liberty, Democracy and the Founders," *The Public Interest* (Fall 1975), pp. 46–47.
[13] Ibid.

The great Greek philosopher, Aristotle (right), with his famous teacher, Plato.

and none of these forms governs with regard to the profit of the community."[14] In Aristotle's view there were broad interests to be served (what we would call national or public interests). Any regime was degraded when it ignored these interests and instead advanced the selfish claims of one segment of society.

Especially important to our study is the distinction Aristotle made between "democracy" and "constitutional government"; he defined democracy as the perverted form. He was not opposed to popular sovereignty, to regimes based on the consent and participation of the many. He objected only to extreme direct democracy, which lacked a

Democracy versus constitutional government

[14]*Aristotle in Twenty-Three Volumes, XXI Politics,* H. Rackham, trans. (London: Heinemann, 1977), Book III, p. 207.

legal structure for protecting minority rights and interests. In short, he defended what we today know as constitutional democracy: majority rule tempered by basic laws that uphold the ideal of the public interest and protect individual and minority rights.

Aristotle anticipated a question that has occupied many contemporary students of government: What social conditions are necessary for constitutional democracy to flourish? Such a government simply is not possible, he felt, in most social settings. It is impossible when a small elite has great economic privilege while the vast majority has virtually nothing. "Where some own a very great deal of property and others none . . . there comes about either an extreme democracy or an unmixed oligarchy, or a tyranny may result from both of the two extremes, for tyranny springs from both democracy and oligarchy of the most unbridled kind. . . ."[15] Either the few will be successful in preserving their extreme privilege, by resorting to tyrannical rule, or the resentful many will deny minority rights in advancing their claims. What is necessary for constitutional democracy is a large middle class and a fairly even distribution of property.

Importance of a large middle class

> It is clear therefore that the political community administered by the middle class is the best, and that it is possible for those states to be well governed that are of the kind in which the middle class is numerous . . . for by throwing in its weight it sways the balance and prevents the opposite extremes from coming into existence.[16]

An Idea a Long Time Coming

Aristotle's assessment of democracy in the *Politics* has remarkable range and prescience. And like the experience of his native Athens with a limited form of democratic government, Aristotle's thinking was far in advance of the historical period in which it occurred. One would have to wait two thousand years—until Europe and America in the late seventeenth and eighteenth centuries—to find sustained philosophic inquiry that advanced beyond Aristotle's contribution, and the first successful implementation of democratic ideals.

As we saw in chapter 3 social and economic changes that began in seventeenth-century Europe nurtured a new set of political ideas and a new view of people and their rights that we know as classical liberalism. The keystone of liberalism is the high value it places on the rights and freedoms of the individual. Democratic government is the natural political expression of liberal individualism, for only democracy gives individuals the power to govern themselves. Once social conditions were such that individualism would flourish, democracy became a practical possibility.

Liberalism: the right of the individual

[15] Ibid., p. 331.
[16] Ibid.

The United States had no monopoly on such social conditions—and no monopoly on governments giving recognition to the claims of individuals. In Britain limits were increasingly placed on the powers of the monarchy and aristocracy in the eighteenth and nineteenth centuries, while at the same time the powers of representatives in Parliament grew. But the requisite social conditions emerged faster and more fully in eighteenth-century America, and so in response did democratic government.

Madison's Idea of Democracy

The work of the founders of the new American government of 1787 was a major step in both the theory and practice of democracy. The unique opportunity to establish a national government based on democratic principles in an environment so generally supportive of the enterprise, but with so little precedent in the experience of other countries, forced the founders to confront fundamental issues of democratic theory. In prior examinations of democratic theory, from Aristotle to John Locke to French philosopher Jean-Jacques Rousseau (1712–88), one critical element had been missing: close attention to the practical governmental mechanisms through which constitutional democracy could protect minority rights and achieve social balance. In 1787 the idea of constitutional democracy was a familiar one, but the actual articulation of the institutions of representative democracy was still in its infancy. The plan for representative institutions developed in *The Federalist Papers* is an important advance in democratic theory.

A plan for democratic institutions

Madison and Hamilton carried over the basic Aristotlean distinction between democracy and polity, though they referred to the latter as "republicanism." Like Aristotle, the authors of *The Federalist Papers* professed fear of democracy, and understood the term to mean unrestrained government prone to mob rule, disrespectful of minority rights, and incapable of realizing the national interest.

The Federalist Papers argues the case for **republicanism:** as James Madison wrote in *Federalist Paper* 10, "a government in which the scheme of representation takes place. . . ." The people are sovereign, but they cannot and should not govern directly. Representative institutions like legislatures need to be established within a governmental structure of clearly defined and dispersed powers. Through separation of powers and checks and balances, minority rights receive protection, and narrow interests opposed to the general public good are curbed. The framers thought, for example, that some majority passion might sweep through the legislature a law contrary to the basic rights and interests of some minority. But they felt that such checks on the legislative power as the president's veto and the judiciary's power to review and interpret the laws in light of constitutional

Republicanism

requirements lessened the chance that minority rights would actually be abused. Through this elaborate process of checks and balances, the public would still remain the ultimate source of all political authority.

The representative democracy that the framers of the Constitution sought gave equal weight to *popular sovereignty* and *individual rights*. The former required the selection of political leaders through regularly-held free elections. The latter required mechanisms to stop anyone, even popular majorities, from infringing upon certain rights of citizenship such as those set forth in the Bill of Rights.

Balancing popular sovereignty and individual rights

MAJORITY RULE VERSUS MINORITY RIGHTS

The American idea of democracy is a system of government equally committed to majority rule and the protection of minority rights. In many instances these two different commitments do not conflict with one another. But sometimes they do. For example, school segregation as practiced before *Brown* v. *Board of Education of Topeka*—the landmark desegregation decision handed down by the U.S. Supreme Court in 1954—seems often to have had majority backing. If we conclude that such segregation denied the claims of American democracy, it is because we believe that majority rule itself is undemocratic when it opposes essential individual rights.

The problem of majority rule

But which rights are so essential as to be off-limits even to majority will? American constitutional law, as it has developed in decisions of the Supreme Court, addresses this question, and we will examine what the Court has said in chapters 9 and 15. But there has never been full agreement among experts in constitutional law, or the public at large, on where the democratic requirement of majority rule must be suspended because the democratic requirement of respect for individual rights requires it.

Prayer in Public Schools

The often heated argument over school prayer is a good case in point. Various individuals and groups long opposed what was the common practice of opening the school day with the recitation of a prayer. They argued that it violated the right to full religious freedom guaranteed by the First Amendment to the Constitution. Some students were not in sympathy with the particular religious beliefs expressed by the prayer, and the government (in the form of public school officials) was abridging their freedom of religious choice.

In 1962 the Supreme Court agreed with the challenge to the constitutionality of prayer in public schools, in the case of *Engel* v. *Vitale*. The New York State Board of Regents had recommended to school

The public school classroom has been a battleground for those who debate school prayer and, more recently during the 1988 presidential election, for those who debate requiring the reciting of the Pledge of Allegiance.

Engel v. Vitale

districts that they adopt a specific nondenominational prayer, to be repeated voluntarily by students at the beginning of each school day. The prayer read: "Almighty God, we acknowledge our dependence upon Thee, and we beg Thy blessings upon us, our parents, our teachers and our country." The school board of the New York community of New Hyde Park adopted this prayer, but it was challenged by the parents of ten pupils in the district. These parents claimed that the prayer was contrary to their religous beliefs and ran counter to the "establishment" clause of the First Amendment: "Congress [and, by application, the states] shall make no law respecting an establishment of religion. . . ."

The school prayer controversy and individual rights

Writing for the Supreme Court's majority, Justice Hugo Black ruled that the "constitutional prohibition against laws respecting an establishment of religion must at least mean that in this country it is no part of the business of government to compose official prayers for any group of American people to recite as a part of a religious program carried on by the government." The majority had violated a constitutional guarantee of individual religious freedom. In subsequent cases the Court extended its ruling—for example, by prohibiting the recitation of the Lord's Prayer or other verses from the Bible.

These Court decisions generated strong opposition. Critics argued that the constitutional ban on laws "respecting an establishment of religion" was not meant and should not now be construed to prevent citizens in various communities from deciding that they would like to have a brief prayer at the start of the school day, in which anyone who wanted could choose not to participate. They insisted that school prayer did not abridge a basic constitutional right, and hence the preferences of the majority should be followed.

Public opinion and school prayer

Public opinion surveys have consistently shown decisive majorities in favor of prayer in schools and in favor of an amendment to the Constitution to overturn the Court's rulings. According to a September 1987 survey taken by CBS News and the *New York Times,* 71 percent favored "an amendment to the Constitution that would permit organized prayer to be said in the public schools." Also in September 1987, a poll by ABC News and the *Washington Post* posed a question that began by noting that "the United States Supreme Court has ruled that no state or local government may require the reading of the Lord's Prayer or Bible verses in public schools." The Court has high standing among Americans, and many people are inclined to back positions that they have been told represent Court rulings. Here, however, 62 percent of those interviewed said they *disapproved* the Supreme Court's position on prayer in the schools.

Proposed school prayer amendment

The efforts to amend the Constitution to permit school prayer first came to a vote in 1966. A majority of U.S. senators voted for such an amendment—but not the two-thirds majority required. Article V of the Constitution contains this provision designed to make it hard for a majority to make changes in the country's basic law: Congress can propose amendments to the Constitution only by two-thirds majorities of both houses; the amendments must then be ratified by at least three-fourths of the states before taking effect. In 1984 another attempt was made to enact a school prayer amendment, and again the major battle was fought in the Senate. The proposed amendment read:

> Nothing in this Constitution shall be construed to prohibit individual or group prayer in public schools or other public institutions. No person shall be required by the United States or any state to participate in prayer. Neither the United States nor any state shall compose the words or any prayer to be said in public schools. (Senate Joint Resolution 73)

Lobbying efforts

In the debate that ensued, lobbying was intense on both sides. Conservative religious groups worked hard for the amendment, and the Reagan administration supported them. The pro-amendment efforts were led in the Senate by Republican Majority Leader Howard Baker, who argued that "our purpose here is to render the state a neutral party in the exercise of religion rather than have the state compel or forbid that exercise." Most of the mainline religious groups—including Methodists, Episcopalians, Lutherans, and Jews—opposed the amendment. Lowell Weicker (Republican of Connecticut) led the fight against the amendment. He maintained that children holding minority religious views would feel uncomfortable participating in a prayer alien to their beliefs and stigmatized if they refused to participate.

The vote in the Senate on March 20, 1984, was a tough one for many senators. Not only did the polls show large majorities in favor of the amendment, but calls and letters from constituents strongly urged enactment. At the same time, senators were sensitive to the rights of minority religious groups. Arlen Specter (Republican of Pennsylvania), who is Jewish, recalled his own experiences as a boy attending elementary school in Wichita, Kansas: how uncomfortable he had felt when Christian prayers were recited at the start of each school day. In the end the Senate decided that school prayer was a case where the claims of minority rights outweighed majority choice. It voted for the amendment 56 to 44—eleven votes short of the two-thirds majority the Constitution requires for constitutional change.

Senate vote on school prayer

The next chapter in the argument over school prayer was written by the U.S. Supreme Court. In *Wallace* v. *Jaffree* (1985), the Court struck down as unconstitutional, by a 6-3 margin, an Alabama statute authorizing a one-minute period of silence in all public schools for "meditation or voluntary prayer." Writing for the majority, Justice John Paul Stevens ruled that Alabama's "endorsement . . . of prayer activities at the beginning of each school day is not consistent with the established principle that the government must pursue a course of complete neutrality toward religion." But in his sharp dissenting opinion, Warren Burger (chief justice from 1969 to 1986) insisted that "to suggest that a moment-of-silence statute that includes the word "prayer" unconstitutionally endorses religion . . . manifests not neutrality but hostility toward religion."

Wallace v. *Jaffree*

Both constitutional litigation and legislative debate on school prayer are continuing, reflecting the deep divisions among Americans on the issue. Despite strong public backing for a constitutional amendment permitting school prayer, many in Congress continue to believe that minority rights require a wall between church and state (here the public schools) that is high and firm. A school prayer amendment has not received the necessary two-thirds support in either the House or Senate.

DIRECT DEMOCRACY VERSUS REPRESENTATIVE DEMOCRACY

Though the framers opted for representative democracy, aspects of the idea of direct democracy have continued to find support in the United States. In the contemporary context, those who advocate more direct democracy want the people to vote or otherwise express themselves directly on major questions of government and policy. Many Americans believe that an extension of direct participation makes the country's democracy purer or more complete. Responding to these views, the United States government has incorporated some of the institutions and practices of direct democracy.

Toward Purer Democracy: The Direct Primary

Progressivism

In the early twentieth century, a new political movement known as **progressivism** gained great strength in many parts of the United States and advanced an ambitious program of political change. The Progressives included in their ranks men and women from all classes and sections of the country, but they were especially strong among the growing professional middle classes of the urban Northeast and Midwest. The latter believed that the big-city political party "machines" of the day were often corrupt, beholden to special interests, unenlightened. To purify this "boss-dominated" system, Progressives argued that the people must be given more power to rule directly.

Progressive Hiram Johnson campaigning in 1922.

One key reform urged by the Progressives was the **direct primary,** whereby the choice of party nominees is made by rank-and-file party

supporters in primary elections, not by party leaders through party conventions and caucuses. The Progressives enjoyed great success in this effort; direct primaries became the dominant instrument for choosing candidates in most parts of the country.

The Referendum and the Initiative

The Progressives also criticized the legislatures of their day as dominated by special interests—railroads, big corporations, and construction companies wanting contracts for roads and public buildings. They urged that the general public be permitted to vote directly on legislation through **referenda** and **initiatives.** In a referendum, a legislative body certifies a question for presentation to the public in a general ballot; in an initiative the public, through petitions signed by requisite numbers of voters, requires that policies be put to popular vote. Under the aegis of the Progressives, the referendum and the initiative were widely adopted. South Dakota (1898) was the first state to provide for the initiative.

The referendum

At the local level, referendum democracy flourishes; several thousand measures are presented each year to the voters in school districts, cities, and counties. The public votes directly on appropriations for school buildings, fluoridation of community water supplies, and the siting of waste disposal facilities. In the November 1986 elections, political scientist Austin Ranney found "at least one referendum measure appeared on the ballots in 43 states, for a total of 226 propositions."[17] A measure that would have permitted voter registration by mail was rejected by Massachusetts voters. Residents in Florida, Idaho, Kansas, Montana, and South Dakota voted to allow lotteries in their states, but North Dakotans said no to a state lottery. Residents in Kansas agreed to the sale of liquor by the drink. Voters in California decided that new taxes must be approved by a two-thirds vote of local governing bodies and by majorities of voters as well—a "make it hard for them to do it" proposition.

The problems of "pure" democracy

There is no simple answer to the question of whether the United States now strikes a proper balance between the direct and representative dimensions of democracy. Yet many agree that democracy in a complex society makes heavy demands on such intermediary institutions as political parties and legislatures, and on their leadership. Such institutions cannot be bypassed too frequently and still have the capacity to perform the functions we expect of them as vital intermediaries. While democracy cannot exist if the wishes of the general public are not freely and fully expressed and ultimately followed, succumbing too frequently to temptations to bypass representative institutions—bypass parties through direct primaries, for example,

[17] Austin Ranney, "Referendums and Initiatives, 1984," *Public Opinion*, December / January 1985, pp. 15–17.

and legislatures through the initiative—may weaken these institutions to the point where they can no longer work effectively. In chapter 13 we discuss this point with specific reference to the American party system.

Size and Representative Institutions

The town meeting

The earliest American institution for direct democracy, the New England town meeting, has declined greatly in practical governing importance. In the town meeting, all adult residents who choose to do so assemble at an appointed time and through majority vote enact a budget and rules bearing on town affairs. When communities were small and much of what government did was concentrated at the local level—as in New England of the seventeenth and eighteenth centuries—the town meeting's direct democracy was an important and practical part of the American system. Today, however, much of government decision-making involves units so large and issues so complex that the idea of all interested citizens assembling to decide them has become impossible. Town meetings are still held in New England, and citizens assemble in communities in all parts of the country to discuss local issues, but representative institutions like school boards and city councils have become necessary instruments of local government.

HOW DEMOCRATIC IS AMERICAN DEMOCRACY?

Beard's view of the framers' motives

A debate goes on today over just how democratic American democracy actually is. A book appeared in 1913 that for a time greatly influenced many people's thinking about the Constitution. It was Charles A. Beard's *An Economic Interpretation of the Constitution of the United States.* Beard argued that, rather than a document written by public-spirited men for the protection of "life, liberty, and the pursuit of happiness," the Constitution represented the assertion of economic interests of banking, manufacturing, and commerce. Furthermore, he maintained that, instead of extending democracy, the Constitution was imposed to rein in the majority. The Constitution was depicted as the product of a cabal of self-serving "plutocrats" who were fearful of the democratic impulses unleashed after the Revolutionary War. It had to be made to serve popular ends later on under the democratic leadership of leaders like Andrew Jackson, who was president from 1829 to 1837.

Was this view of the Constitution's founders justified? Beard's interpretation has been strongly criticized and largely discredited recently, especially by the work of historians R. E. Brown and Forrest

MacDonald.[18] Most scholars now hold a view similar to the prevailing view of nineteenth-century America: while the framers were not above self-interest, they were by no means a narrow, undemocratic economic elite. As historian John Garraty concludes in a recent work, "the closest thing to a general spirit at Philadelphia was a public spirit. To call men like Washington, Franklin, and Madison self-seeking would be utterly absurd."[19]

Rebuttals to Beard's interpretation

For a nation to be called a democracy, ordinary citizens must have real political power. Not only must they be able to vote, but they must be able to exercise ultimate authority over the big decisions of their country's political life. What are these big decisions? How can we know whether the people ultimately make them, or whether political elites—individuals and groups with disproportionate political resources—manage to assume the decisive decision-making roles? The concept of power is one of the most complex that political science contends with. Yet for all the analytic difficulties the concept poses, how power is distributed is a matter of great importance to democratic government. At some point power concentrates so substantially in the hands of political elites as to make a mockery of any claim to popular sovereignty. Some observers argue that this has happened in the United States. Others, while denying that this point has been reached, still see extensive power in the hands of elites as a serious problem in American democracy.

Power and democracy

Concentration of Resources

Various developments over the last century and a half have produced major concentrations of resources. There were no great fortunes in the United States a hundred and fifty years ago, but now there are enormous accumulations of wealth. Economic units—whether farms, banks, or factories—were generally very small in the 1830s; in the 1980s we have huge national and multinational corporations. The great consolidation of newspapers and magazines into large units that has occurred over the last century had not even begun in the 1830s, and the age of concentrated electronic communication had not even been imagined.

In the 1830s the primary political unit was the local government; now it is the national government. The hundreds to few thousands of citizens in a typical town a century and a half ago had a measure of direct control over government that is simply unattainable in today's far more complex and centralized nation-state.

[18] See R. E. Brown, *Charles Beard and the Constitution* (Princeton, N.J.: Princeton University Press, 1956); and Forrest MacDonald, *We the People: The Economic Origins of the Constitution* (Chicago: University of Chicago Press, 1976).
[19] John A. Garraty, *The American Nation*, 4th ed. (New York: Harper and Row, 1979), p. 123.

The debate continues on the extent of the media's influence.

Economic power and politics

How have these developments affected political power? Consider the case of an individual who has acquired millions of dollars in personal property as well as the presidency of a big business corporation. If he chooses, he may contribute large sums of money to candidates for elective office. His wealth, and the economic power derived from his position in business, give him a measure of access to political leaders far beyond that of most citizens. A telephone call to a politician from this wealthy corporate leader is likely to have a much greater impact on policy deliberations than one from the average voter.

Access to resources

But there are many types of politically important resources other than great wealth. Consider the position of an anchorman for one of the network's evening news programs. He is seen nightly by an audience in the range of 20 to 30 million persons; thus he has communications resources beyond any historic precedent. Political leaders in Congress, the executive office, and state capitals around the country are certainly aware of his capacity to take political messages into millions of households. How likely is it that the anchorman's influence in American political life is roughly equivalent to that of the average citizen?

Many others enjoy disproportionate resources. A president of a big university has more resources than the average student at his or her institution. The head of a major labor union has resources dwarfing those of the typical unionist. The point seems beyond dispute: Politically relevant resources are unevenly distributed; and the economic and technological developments discussed in chapters 1 and 2 have on balance led to greater concentrations.

What are the implications for democracy of such inequalities? As political scientist Robert Dahl has put it, "In a political system where nearly every adult may vote but where knowledge, wealth, social position, access to officials and other resources are unequally distributed, who actually governs?"[20]

Power Elites

No mature theory of American politics questions that there are **elites:** groups of people who possess disproportionately large amounts of scarce resources and hence power. The fact of disproportionate resources in the hands of special-interest groups requires the constant attention of all who are committed to democratic government. President Dwight Eisenhower, a conservative Republican who had been commander-in-chief of allied forces in Europe during World War II—and who was hardly unfriendly to either business or the military—in 1961 warned his fellow citizens to be vigilant against "unwarranted influence . . . by the military-industrial complex."[21] After World War II, as we discuss in chapter 18, a high level of defense spending became a permanent part of American national government, and interests such as defense contractors and military officials became active and influential lobbyists for their special concerns. Eisenhower saw the dangers this collection of strong, well-organized interests posed for democratic decision making in the vital area of defense and foreign policy.

The military-industrial complex

Some commentators go well beyond these widely shared concerns and perceptions, however, to the highly debated conclusion that the concentration of power in the hands of elites precludes real democracy in the United States. An extreme case is the argument of contemporary Marxist theorists. Their starting point is the proposition Karl Marx advanced in much of his work in the last century: Power in any society is derived from economic arrangements, and in any capitalist society like the United States the government "is nothing more than a committee for the administration of the consolidated affairs of the bourgeois class as a whole."[22] Building on this perspective, political scientist Michael Parenti states that

Marxist critique of capitalism

> our government represents the privileged few rather than the needy many and . . . elections, political parties and the right to speak out are seldom

[20] Robert Dahl, *Who Governs?* (New Haven, Conn.: Yale University Press, 1961), p. 1.
[21] Eisenhower's "Farewell Address," January 17, 1961.
[22] Ryazanoff, ed., *The Communist Manifesto of Karl Marx and Friedrich Engels* (New York: Russell and Russell, 1963), p. 28.

effective measures against the influence of corporate wealth. The laws of our polity operate chiefly with undemocratic effect . . . because they are written principally to protect the haves against the claims of the have-nots. . . . Democracy for the few . . . is not a product of the venality of office holders as such but a reflection of how the resources of power are distributed within the entire politico-economic system.[23]

The triangle of power: business, military, and political leadership

This view is not confined to Marxist scholars. In *The Power Elite,* sociologist C. Wright Mills maintained that America is run by a narrow group of people drawn from three central institutions: leaders of major private business corporations, the heads of the armed services and the defense establishment, and the political leadership of the executive branch of government.[24] For most of American history these units were relatively small and feeble, but after World War II they grew enormously. By the late 1950s, Mills asserted, there was no longer

> on the one hand, an economy, and on the other hand, a political order containing a military establishment unimportant to politics and to moneymaking. There is a political economy linked in a thousand ways with military institutions and decisions. . . . If there is government intervention in the corporate economy, so is there corporate intervention in the governmental process. In the structural sense, this triangle of power is the source of the interlocking directorate that is most important for the historical structure of the present.[25]

Mills's power elite is composed not of isolated groups and individuals but rather of people who have common interests and act together coherently to dominate policy on the major issues of national life.

The Liberal Democratic Rebuttal

Constitutional limits on power of elites

Is there a coherent, interacting elite that makes most of the big decisions in the United States, leaving popular sovereignty but an aspiration? Most political scientists don't think so; neither does the general public. The liberal rebuttal to the charge of elite rule must begin with the work of the Constitution's framers, because that work has defined the American system. Those who drafted the Constitution assumed that some interests would inevitably be stronger than others. The task of a properly arranged constitutional democracy, James Madison argued in *Federalist Papers* 10 and 51, was to put limits on what these interests could achieve. He believed that he and his fellow constitution makers had provided sufficient barriers to any power elite: a large, diverse nation of many contending interests, with government power divided first between the national and state units, and then further divided between legislature, executive, and judiciary. Behind

[23] Michael Parenti, *Democracy for the Few* (New York: St. Martin's Press, 1974), p. 2.
[24] C. Wright Mills, *The Power Elite* (New York: Oxford University Press, 1959).
[25] Ibid., pp. 7–8. Emphasis added.

Free elections—the cornerstone of democracy.

Operation Big Vote
REGISTER TO VOTE HERE
Sponsored by New York Federation of Urban Organizations

all of this were the people, able to choose their leaders in free elections and thereby to set the general course of public policy.

Pluralism

Fragmentation of power

Most contemporary political observers in the United States think that Madison has been proved right. Political power in the United States is highly fragmented, as interest groups contend within a government structure of dispersed authority. Public policy is the outcome of a highly involved pattern of political bargaining among constantly shifting interest alignments. Sometimes this perspective is called "pluralist," because it identifies a plurality of competing power centers. The predominant perspective among political scientists is that power is so dispersed at the national level, among the many committees and subcommittees of Congress, federal executive agencies, interest groups, and others, that overall public policy suffers a serious lack of coherence.[26] The current preoccupation with the fragmentation of the policy process runs almost diametrically against the idea of a coherent power elite able to control public policy.

To see this argument in action, consider the area of military spending, which was one of Mills's prime examples of a power elite. Big

[26]Chapters 5–8 develop these arguments.

defense contractors certainly interact closely with Defense Department officials and influential congressmen. Typically, though, they do not cooperate but instead fight it out with one another to secure contracts—as when United Technologies Corporation and General Electric battle for contracts to build new jet engines for Air Force planes.

On such foreign policy issues as the United States's role in Central America or the Middle East, political elites are often sharply divided. For example, some urge a stronger military response to movements in Central America that are seen as threatening U.S. interests and regional stability; others argue equally strongly that more economic aid to combat poverty, not arms, is the answer. Each faction among the contending elites tries to persuade the public of the rightness of its approach. In these policy debates, it is very hard to see the hand of one strong power elite.

None of this claims that American democracy does not confront continuing problems stemming from the presence of large concentrations of resources in a few hands. The whole area of money in politics involves one set of such problems. Various individuals and organizations—including businessmen and large corporations—have extensive financial resources; they also have strong interests in the decisions legislatures and executive agencies make. They try to advance their interests by lobbying, and by making contributions to the campaigns of candidates who support their views or who are in key positions to decide future questions. Through the vehicle of political action committees (PACs), millions of dollars of interest-group money are contributed to campaigns each election year. In chapters 11 and 12 we discuss the role of PACs, the legislation regulating them, and the larger issue of how American elections are, and should be, financed.

The United States in the early nineteenth century abounded in what we might call "natural equalities." Great fortunes, for the most part, had not yet been built. The size of audience that one could reach by a speech was limited to how far the unamplified human voice could carry. Big bureaucracies, big military establishments, big corporations, simply did not exist. We shouldn't romanticize this era as a time without problems; there were many, some that dwarf those of our own day. But the fact is that the idea of democracy was somewhat easier to envision and implement in that age before bigness, concentration, and scale. Today we have to work harder to maintain the ideal of popular choice or rule that is far-reaching and robust. But we still have important resources for doing so, and elections are one of them.

Elections and Popular Sovereignty

Critics of American democracy seem consistently insensitive to the role played by popular elections as the decisive instruments for

---

Some examples undercutting the power-elite theory

Political action committees, money, and political campaigns

choosing the president, members of Congress, governors, state legislators, mayors, and other political officials. Since the 1960s—when it was finally guaranteed to black Americans—voting has been open to the entire adult populace. While there is concern that voter turnout has not been higher, electoral decision-making is certainly majoritarian. In the presidential election of 1984, 92 million people voted: 53 percent of those of voting age, and 80 percent of those registered to vote.

Critics have attacked American electioneering and the choice of leaders it provides as mere sham, saying that the Republicans and Democrats are so alike ("Tweedledum and Tweedledee") that voters do not have a real choice of leaders. But this criticism lacks a convincing base. Scores of widely different political parties—Communist, Socialist, Libertarian, and many others—have offered themselves to the American electorate over the past century. If the Democrats and Republicans have won most contests, this seems to reflect general voter satisfaction with the choices that these two parties have offered the public.

Voter turnout and the two-party system

SUMMARY

The Articles of Confederation were the first constitution of the new American nation. Ratified in 1779, the Articles were consistent with the prevailing American belief in limited, popular government. But the central government they established was so weak that it could not meet economic or foreign policy needs, or fulfill the emerging sense of nation.

George Washington, James Madison, and Alexander Hamilton gave leadership to the forces seeking to strengthen, or replace, the Articles of Confederation. Their efforts and those of other like-minded politicians culminated in the constitutional convention that met at Philadelphia in the spring and summer of 1787 and drafted a new Constitution for the United States of America. Ratification was completed in 1788 when New York, the last big state to approve, narrowly voted its endorsement.

The Constitution reflected the basic impulses of the American ideology. Government was to be at once vigorous and restrained. It was to create a climate where individual initiative could flourish and national identity could be expressed, while being so checked and balanced that it could not threaten individual rights.

Authority was divided between national and state governments; and within the former, among the executive, legislative, and judicial branches which were at once independent and mutually dependent. Ambition, as Madison had put it in *Federalist Paper* 51, was made to counteract ambition.

The first conception of democracy was in Athens in the fifth century B.C.: government by the many rather than by the few. Aristotle enlarged this concept by combining two distinct elements: popular sovereignty and minority rights. Aristotle chose to call a system that successfully combined these elements a constitutional government or polity. Democracy meant an unrestrained direct democracy or mob rule. The framers of the American Constitution incorporated much of Aristotle's thinking. But they went even further in their specification of a system of carefully engineered representative institutions. What we now call a constitutional or representative democracy the framers called a republic.

Democracy in America is sometimes called liberal democracy. It places equal emphasis on realizing popular sovereignty and protecting individual and minority rights. These two objectives are sometimes in conflict, when majorities take actions that minorities think violate certain of their essential rights as citizens.

The American constitutional tradition holds that majority rule must be superseded in cases where majority actions infringe essential rights of citizenship, such as those articulated in the Bill of Rights. But as the country's experience in the area of civil rights shows, the most fundamental of minority rights have sometimes been denied nonetheless. And thoughtful people necessarily disagree on just which rights or interests are so essential as to be off-limits to majority choice or action.

One criticism of American democracy holds that power is so concentrated in the hands of certain elites as to make impossible the meaningful exercise of popular sovereignty. Defenders of American liberal democratic performance contend, in rebuttal, that the Madisonian system has generally succeeded in preventing great concentrations of power. They agree that some individuals and groups have more of such politically important resources as money, but they argue that the common pattern finds these elites in competition with each other for general public support. Elections give the public an important resource for determining national leadership and basic policy direction.

FOR FURTHER STUDY

Aristotle's *Politics*, Book 3, Volume XXI, of *Aristotle in Twenty-Three Volumes*, H. Rackham, trans. (London: Heinemann, 1977). A brilliant interpretation of political institutions and experience, including the first systematic writing on democracy, by perhaps the greatest of all political philosophers.

Ernest Barker, *Reflections on Government* (New York: Oxford University Press, 1958; first published, 1942). A rich, subtle defense of democracy by a distinguished British theorist, written during the profound totalitarian challenge to democracy that culminated in World War II.

Robert A. Dahl, *Dilemmas of Pluralist Democracy* (New Haven, Conn.: Yale University Press, 1983). The latest interpretation of the problems of pluralism by a distinguished American political scientist and theorist.

Martin Diamond, "The Declaration and the Constitution: Liberty, Democracy and the Founders," *The Public Interest*, Fall 1975. A brilliant essay by a political theorist explaining the relationship between the Declaration of Independence and the Constitution, and the ideals and approaches they articulate.

Anthony Downs, *An Economic Theory of Democracy* (New York: Harper and Row, 1957). A major interpretation of democracy drawing upon economic models and exchanges.

Alexander Hamilton, James Madison, John Jay, *The Federalist Papers*, edited by Clinton Rossiter (New York: New American Library, 1961; first published, 1787–88 in New York newspapers). Perhaps the most important work ever written on the nature of the American governmental system and the ideas underlying it; authored by three leading proponents of the Constitution in the ratification debate in New York.

G. Wright Mills, *The Power Elite* (New York: Oxford University Press, 1959). Perhaps still the best known and most provocative statement of the view that a unified "power elite" makes the key decisions in the United States.

Clinton Rossiter, *Alexander Hamilton and the Constitution* (New York: Harcourt, Brace, 1964). A description of the immense role Alexander Hamilton played in the events leading up to and following the ratification of the Constitution of the United States.

Garry Wills, *Explaining America: The Federalist* (Garden City, NY: Doubleday, 1981). A useful analysis of the central ideas expressed in *The Federalist Papers* and the objectives of their authors.

Chapter 5

The American System of Divided Government

We have seen how American ideology, emphasizing as it does the rights and claims of individuals, has sought to check and limit government. For the individual to be strong, government must be restrained. How to handle the problem of power is a central concern of all serious theories of government. The historic American answer to this problem is to divide power, so that no unit of government or political interest has too much.

James Madison provided a classic statement of this position in *Federalist Paper* 51, where he argued that the Constitution had solved the problem of power through the mechanism of a "compound republic." In it, "the power surrendered by the people is first divided between two distinct governments"—national and state—"and then the portion alloted to each [is] subdivided among distinct and separate departments." Those who administer each unit are given "the necessary constitutional means and personal motives to resist encroachments of the others. . . . Ambition must be made to counteract ambition." If men were angels, Madison argued, no government would be needed, while "if angels were to govern men, neither external nor internal controls on government would be necessary." But, human nature being what it is, an elaborate system of checks is essential, lest power get concentrated and abused.

Federalism is the term we now use to describe what Madison referred to as the division of power "between two distinct governments." In our federal system, both the national government and the states have their own constitutionally guaranteed positions and responsibilities. The national government is our main concern in this text, but the states also have large spheres of action and influence. In chapter 19 we look more closely at the role that the states—described by Supreme Court Justice Louis Brandeis as "laboratories of democracy"—play in making American public policy.

At the national level, the Constitution divides power among three independent branches: executive, legislative, and judicial. We call this division the **separation of powers.** The way executive and legislative power is handled is especially important—and here the American system is highly unusual as compared to other democracies. First, it formally divides the two by having the president and Congress elected for separate terms, the tenure in office and powers of each untouchable by the other. Then it requires these determinedly independent institutions to work together in a complex power sharing before anything can be done in any area of public policy.

We will be examining more specific aspects of the separation of powers throughout this text and especially in chapters 6–9. Here, our objective is to get an overview of the workings of separation of powers and federalism as the two main components of a larger American system—inspired by the ideology set forth in the Constitution—of divided government.

The Capitol building in Washington, D.C., where the Senate and House initiate and debate bills, react to the president's legislative initiatives, and are sometimes overruled by the U.S. Supreme Court.

SEPARATION OF POWERS

Madison argued in *Federalist Paper* 47 that "no political truth is certainly of greater intrinsic value . . . [than that] the accumulation of all powers, legislative, executive, and judiciary, in the same hands, whether of one, a few, or many, and whether hereditary, self-appointed, or elective, *may justly be pronounced the very definition of tyranny*" (italics added). The Constitution that he and his colleagues had finished drafting in Philadelphia only months before went to great length to preclude any such "accumulation."

First, it made the three branches formally separate and distinct. The tenure in office of the officials of each cannot be determined by the others. The president is elected by the people of the fifty states and serves out his four-year term without any intervention by another branch—except in the highly unlikely event of his being formally impeached by the House of Representatives and then convicted by the Senate for "high crimes and misdemeanors." Congress is also separately elected by the people: House members serve two-year terms and senators six-year terms that cannot be altered either by the president or the courts. Federal court judges—including justices of the U.S. Supreme Court—are appointed by the president with the "advice and consent" of the Senate for life terms, but removal is possible only through the rarely used procedure of impeachment and conviction by both houses of Congress.

Three distinct branches of government

Second, President and Congress share power in virtually every sphere of national government action, and the federal courts are also important participants. Article I of the Constitution gives Congress the authority to pass all laws, but the president may veto them. If he vetoes a bill, it must be passed again by two-thirds majorities in both the House and Senate to take effect. The president and his executive branch subordinates administer the laws, but here they in turn are subject to legislative "oversight" (see chapter 6, pp. 195-96). Disagreement over the meaning of legislation and how it should be applied may be brought to the courts for their resolution, and the Supreme Court has the final power to strike down acts of Congress and state legislatures, if it finds them in violation of the Constitution.

Division of power and authority

The president is commander-in-chief of the U.S. armed forces, but Congress has the power to declare war and, much more important in giving it a loud voice on defense issues, has the responsibility for appropriating every cent of the money spent by the armed forces for personnel and weapons. The president has the constitutional authority to negotiate treaties with foreign governments—as the Reagan administration did in 1987–88 with the U.S.-Soviet treaty curbing intermediate nuclear forces (INF)—but these treaties do not take effect until the Senate gives its approval by at least a two-thirds majority.

SEPARATION OF POWERS IN CONFLICT: HISTORIC RIVALRIES

From formal constitutional provisions like these, through which the three branches of the national government are given independent grants of authority and checks over one another, an elaborate informal system of interactions emerged which has given full meaning to the separation of powers. Again and again throughout American history, the branches have clashed as they have been forced to share power and responsibility in the same policy areas. Clashes between president and Congress are especially common, because their interaction is so extensive.

The Reach of "Advice and Consent"

Struggle over authority for dismissing executive officials

In 1789, the very first year of government under the new Constitution, President George Washington and members of Congress clashed over provisions of a bill, introduced by James Madison, calling for the establishment of an executive department of state. At issue was a clause in the bill giving the president the *sole right to remove from office* persons appointed by him (with the consent of the Senate) to this department. The bill's opponents argued that if the Senate's approval was required for appointments, it should also be required for dismissals. Washington and Madison maintained that without the power to dismiss subordinates, the president would be unable to carry out his constitutional duty to see that the laws are "faithfully executed" (Article II, Section 3). After six days of debate, the House finally passed the bill, by a narrow margin of 29–22. A tie occurred in the Senate, broken finally by the favorable vote of Vice President Adams. Present-day separation of powers would almost certainly work differently had Washington lost this early battle and subsequent presidents were forced to get the Senate's consent to their removing cabinet members and other high-ranking executive branch officials. The president's position would undoubtedly now be weaker than it in fact is—in relation both to Congress and his executive-branch subordinates.

Lincoln and Congressional Republicans

Lincoln's "10% plan"

Some of the most celebrated struggles between the president and Congress took place between Abraham Lincoln and Republican leaders in the Senate, against the backdrop of the Civil War. Lincoln and Senate Republicans clashed repeatedly over whose ideas would prevail on how to prosecute the war and the kind of peace to be secured. One notable example occurred in December 1863 when the president issued a proclamation establishing rules for readmission of confederate states to the union. The proclamation specified that when a number of citizens in a confederate state equal to at least *one-tenth* the number who had voted in the prewar 1860 presidential elections took an oath of loyalty to the Constitution and the Union, they could form a government and receive recognition. Tennessee, Louisiana, and Arkansas reorganized in 1864 under Lincoln's "10% plan," went to Washington, and sought to claim seats in Congress for their representatives.

The Wade-Davis bill

Radical Republicans in Congress—so-called because of their commitment to a radical, sweeping reconstruction of the postwar South—were incensed at what they regarded as usurpation of legislative authority by the president. Senator Benjamin Wade (R-Ohio) authored a bill vastly more restrictive than Lincoln's, requiring an oath of loyalty by 50 percent of the white population, and those charged with treason in connection with the war denied the vote. Known as the Wade-Davis measure, it also called for emancipation by congressional enactment. In defending his legislation Senator Wade made the following claims:

> The Executive ought not to be permitted to handle this great question to his own liking. It does not belong, under the Constitution, to the President to prescribe the rule. It belongs to us. The President undertook to fix a rule upon which he would admit these States back into the Union. It was not upon any principle of republicanism, because he prescribed the rule to be that when one tenth of the population would take a certain oath, they might come in as States. When we consider that in the light of American principle, to say the least of it it was absurd. . . . Until majorities can be found loyal and trustworthy for State government, they must be governed by a stronger hand.

Although the Wade-Davis bill was passed by both houses on July 2 shortly before Congress was to adjourn, Lincoln chose to ignore it. When a president refuses to sign a bill and Congress is in adjournment, the measure does not become law. (This provision of Article I, Section 7, is sometimes known as the "pocket veto.") Congress did succeed, however, in voting down recognition of Lincoln's new governments and the war ended with the issue unresolved.

Wilson and the League of Nations

Control over the making of treaties

One of the most dramatic confrontations between the president and Congress occurred in this century at the conclusion of World War I. President Woodrow Wilson tangled with a group of Republican senators, led by Henry Cabot Lodge, Senate foreign relations chairman, over ratification of the Versailles Peace Treaty and League of Nations Covenant Wilson had helped craft. Article II, Section 2, of the Constitution clearly states that treaty-making powers belong to the president. But the "advice and consent" of the Senate is also required, by at least a two-thirds majority. The Senate is far from a passive partner in this process.

As the ratification argument went on, neither Wilson nor Lodge would budge from their respective positions: Lodge felt that the Senate had the right to amend the treaty, even to the point of giving Congress the sole authority to vote for U.S. withdrawal from the League of Nations. Wilson felt that Congress had no right to make approval of the treaty contingent on any "reservations." There would have been enough votes among Democrats and moderate Republicans in the Senate to meet the two-thirds requirement for passage. But Wilson, ill and resentful of Lodge and his determination to undermine the League, ordered his own Democratic supporters in the Senate to vote against *any* amended version of the treaty. The result, predictably, was defeat for the treaty, and confusion and disillusion among America's allies who had looked for active U.S. involvement in the League of Nations—predecessor to the United Nations.

Wilson against Lodge

The INF Treaty, 1988

The interactions between the president and Congress need not be acrimonious. The invitation to clash is always present given the separation of powers, but so is the invitation to cooperate. In May 1988, the Senate voted on another treaty—the INF agreement that President Reagan had negotiated with the Soviet government. Not only did the Senate give its approval by an overwhelming 93–5 vote, but leaders of both parties went to some length to expedite the ratification vote so that the president would have the full approval in hand when he met in Moscow at the end of the month with Soviet leader Mikhail Gorbachev. An appreciative Reagan invited Senate majority leader Robert Byrd (D-W. Va.) and minority leader Robert Dole (R-Kansas) to join him in Moscow for the formal ceremonies in which the two governments exchanged the ratified instruments. They both accepted.

Cooperation between president and Congress

Byrd told a press conference before boarding an Air Force Boeing 707 from the presidential fleet that Reagan's invitation "underlines the nature of the American system, a system which has the separation of powers and a system in which both the executive and the U.S. Senate work together."

SEPARATION OF POWERS IN ACTION: THE MAKING OF THE BUDGET

Very often the end result of the workings of separation of powers is neither acrimony and stalemate nor a love fest, but rather a lot of hard bargaining between determinedly independent branches. The annual process of shaping a budget for the federal government provides us with an excellent view of separation of powers—the distinctive cast it gives to policy formation in the United States and the special obstacles it imposes. Under any institutional arrangement, the task of adjusting the contending claims made on a trillion-dollar budget by many hundreds of groups and interests would be formidable. Under American institutions, the task is complex and almost always frustrating.

The key effect of separation of powers is an *enormous expansion of the number of officials with formal constitutional and practical political roles in policy decisions like those involving budget size and priorities.* In most democracies, after an election is held, only a few officials have any direct say in policy making. In the United States, the number is huge. These independent political actors include the president and his executive branch officials, Republican and Democratic leaders of the House and Senate, majorities on various committees in both houses, and, when Congress is closely divided on a question, literally

Figure 5.1

Actors in the Budget-Making Process in the United States

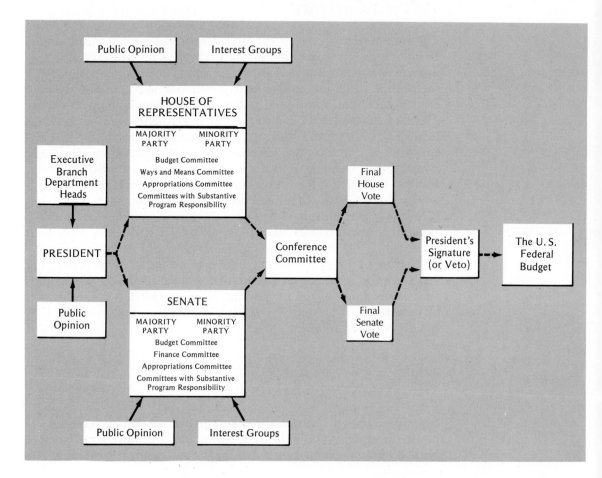

each member of Congress. So large a group inevitably displays diverse perspectives, interests, political needs, and ambitions, making agreement difficult and compromise the continuing imperative.

The making of the budget for FY (fiscal year) 1986 provides a good case study of the elaborate bargaining and compromise necessary to resolve any big policy question. Figure 5.1 sketches the line of authority in shaping the U.S. federal budget.

Act 1: The President Proposes. On February 4, 1985, Ronald Reagan sent his 1986 budget to Capitol Hill. The president's budget message was only about 3,000 words; it summarized his views on the state of the American economy and set out his main budgetary goals. But accompanying the message were five volumes of detailed budget data and proposals, covering every agency and unit of the federal government, developed for the administration over the preceding months by the Office of Management and Budget (chapter 7, p. 228). The president proposed to raise overall government spending only slightly, but to continue the trend of the four previous years with expenditures shifted proportionately from domestic programs to national defense. He called for outlays of $974 billion and anticipated revenues of just $794 billion, leaving the estimated deficit at a whopping $180 billion for FY 1986.

Before the president could make these proposals, much work had to be done. His administration had to adjust the competing claims for resources made by the various executive agencies. The president has final authority over them—but this doesn't mean departments like Defense, Health and Human Services, and Agriculture see eye to eye on how funds should be allocated.

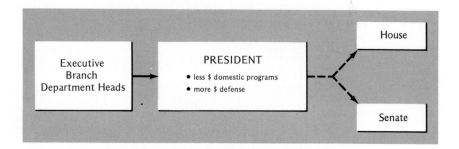

Act 2: Congress Reacts. The president's budget proposals were exactly that: *presidential proposals.* In formal, legal terms, they were nothing more than suggestions by the executive branch to a fiercely independent and much-divided legislature—to be taken seriously because the president was popular, because he could veto any congressional action he considered unacceptable, and because the budgetary arithmetic

that underlay them was often unavoidable—but suggestions nonetheless, to be dispensed with freely whenever Congress so chose. In the case of the 1986 budget, Congress didn't much like the president's suggestions. No one liked the $180 billion deficit it contained. Democrats were especially unhappy about the president's continuing emphasis on military spending. They charged that the domestic program cuts he had proposed would hurt the middle-class—citing in particular his plans to eliminate the Small Business Administration, to axe the subsidy for Amtrak, and to reduce student aid.

Act 3: House Democrats' Uncertain Call. With their large majority in the House of Representatives and on all of its committees involved in the budget process—the Budget and Appropriations committees, and the committees with substantive jurisdiction over the various program areas—the Democrats were assured a large role in shaping the 1986 budget. Nothing was going to happen without significant Democratic support. Such is the weakness of party discipline in Congress, however, and the extent of divergent views within each party, that House Democrats could not simply pass their own budgetary program. Except in the most general sense—their normal opposition to Reagan's initiatives and their belief that he was going too far in slashing domestic spending—they really didn't have a program. In his first term, especially in 1981, Reagan had managed to bring enough conservative southern Democrats (the so-called "Boll Weevils") over to his side to create, together with the Republicans, a fragile House majority in support of his administration's budget approach. In 1986 he was unable to do this—in part because the Democrats' House majority was 20 seats greater than it had been in 1981, and in part because most of the cuts that conservative Democrats could readily support had already been made. Still, the Democrats had to move

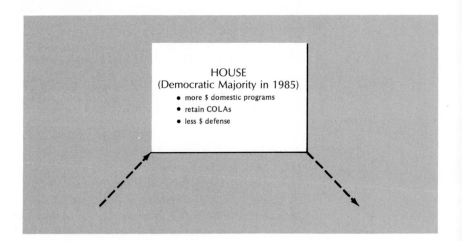

HOUSE
(Democratic Majority in 1985)
- more $ domestic programs
- retain COLAs
- less $ defense

cautiously to accommodate their various factions. In addition, many Democrats had come to believe that they would suffer politically if they continued to allow Ronald Reagan to claim plausibly that only the Republicans were serious about curbing government's growth. This left them trying both to prove themselves better budget cutters and still protect the domestic programs with which they had long been identified. Uncertainty reigned.

Act 4: Senate Republicans Scramble . . . and Scramble. Since the Republicans occupied the White House and had a Senate majority (53–47), the walls were somewhat lower on the executive/Senate side of separation of powers than on the executive/House side. The Senate leadership and the administration wanted to cooperate. One manifestation of this desire was the creation in March 1985 of a working group to resolve differences between the Reagan and the Senate GOP ideas. The working group included David Stockman, who was then Reagan's director of the Office of Management and Budget; White House Chief of Staff Donald Regan; the administration's chief of congressional liaison, Max L. Friedersdorf; and National Security Adviser Robert McFarlane. McFarlane was included because defense spending issues loomed large in the budget deliberations. The Republican Senate team included Majority Leader Robert Dole (Kansas); Budget committee members William Armstrong (Colorado), and Slade Gorton (Washington); Appropriations Committee Chair Mark Hatfield (Oregon); Armed Services Committee Chair Barry Goldwater (Arizona); Finance Committee Chair Robert Packwood (Oregon); Majority Whip Alan Simpson (Wyoming); GOP Conference Chair John Chaffee (Rhode Island); and the senator reputed to have the closest personal ties to Ronald Reagan, Paul Laxalt (Nevada).

However much they wanted to pull together, though, the administration and the Senate Republicans disagreed on some important budget issues. Moreover, Senate Republicans differed among themselves. On March 14, the GOP-controlled Senate budget committee had approved by straight party vote a fiscal 1986 budget resolution. Calling for defense cuts, this resolution brought Republican senators into conflict with their popular party leader in the White House. And specifying as it did a one-year elimination of the Social Security cost-of-living increase, the resolution left a lot of GOP senators feeling politically isolated and exposed—especially those up for re-election in 1986.

On April 4, the Republican Senate leadership reached a preliminary agreement on the budget, but this package quickly came apart on the Senate floor. The Republicans tried to hold their narrow 53-member majority together on behalf of the entire budget but couldn't manage it, especially with Senate Democrats trying to create as many politically unpopular votes for the Republicans as they could—like forcing them to go on record for cutting Social Security cost-of-living adjustments (COLAs). The president went on national television on April 24, urging support for the Senate/administration budget plan, but most senators did not report any strong public response. Senate Republican efforts to put together a fiscal 1986 budget continued to founder on intraparty differences over domestic and defense spending priorities.

Act 5: Senate Republicans Agree . . . Barely. On May 10, 1985, after months of effort, the Republicans finally got a budget resolution through the Senate. The vote was 50–49, with all but four Republicans voting "aye" and all but one Democrat "no." Republicans Alfonse D'Amato (New York), Paula Hawkins (Florida), Arlen Specter (Pennsylvania), and Charles McC. Mathias, Jr. (Maryland) were the four to vote against their party's position; all had terms expiring in 1986. Edward Zorinsky (Nebraska) was the sole Democratic dissenter. Backed by the president, the budget resolution would have eliminated the 1986 Social Security COLA, held defense spending to the rate of inflation, and eliminated thirteen domestic programs. The one-vote Republican margin was achieved only by rousing Republican Senator Pete Wilson (California) from a hospital bed where he was recuperating from an appendectomy; these heroics produced a 49–49 tie, which Vice President George Bush broke. (As presiding officer in the Senate, the vice president can vote only when a Senate vote ends in a tie.)

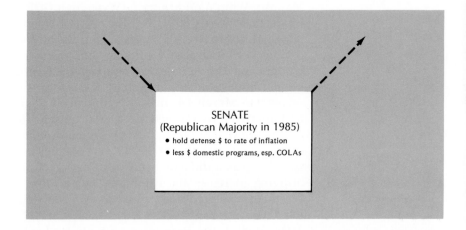

SENATE
(Republican Majority in 1985)
• hold defense $ to rate of inflation
• less $ domestic programs, esp. COLAs

Act 6: House Democrats Pass Their Budget Resolution. A week after the Senate acted, the House Budget committee approved a budget resolution that promised the same amount of deficit reduction as the Senate's resolution but went about doing so quite differently. The committee's action, subsequently approved by the entire House, was widely seen as a tribute to the skills of Budget Committee Chair William Gray (D-Pennsylvania), who nursed through a package acceptable to most Democrats. It provided less spending for defense and more for social programs than did the Senate plans, eliminated just one domestic program, and retained the 1986 Social Security COLA.

Act 7: On to Conference. When the House and Senate pass a measure in different forms, a conference committee is established to try to resolve the differences and report a common measure back to both houses for final action. The conference committee on the budget resolution, which included Republicans and Democrats from each chamber as usual, quickly fell into wrangling and mutual recrimination. Members expressed extreme pessimism. "I just don't see how we're going to get a budget," said Senator Pete Domenici (R-New Mexico), chair of the Senate Budget Committee. House and Senate negotiators disbanded in anger on June 25, deeply split on whether Social Security recipients should get a COLA in 1986; they reconvened on June 27 but remained deadlocked.

Act 8: "Ron" and "Tip" Agree . . . and Senate Republicans Are Furious. After a month in which all efforts to break the conference committee impasse had failed, President Reagan and House Speaker Thomas P. O'Neill, Jr., finally struck a deal. They agreed that the Senate should give up its insistence on eliminating the 1986 Social Security cost-of-living increase, and the House should accept the Senate's increase in defense spending. Senate Republicans felt they had been wronged—by their Republican leader, no less. They had gone out on a limb in their willingness to "touch" the politically untouchable, Social Security, for what they considered an essential national interest: reducing the huge deficit. And, as they saw it, the president had let them down by embracing the Democrat's position on Social Security. For his part, Reagan believed his bargain restored badly needed defense funding; furthermore, he was never comfortable about an approach to deficit

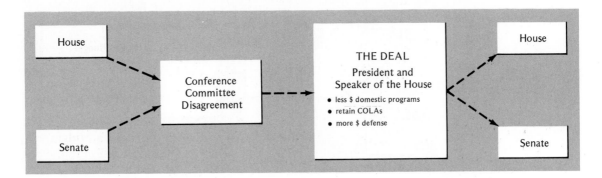

reduction that involved curbing Social Security increases. House Republicans tended to side with the president, against their Senate colleagues.

Act 9: The House / Senate Split. Even after the president and the Speaker had cut their deal, the troops remained divided. On Social Security COLAs the split between House and Senate was sharper than that between Democrats and Republicans. House Democrats and Republicans alike wanted to let the Social Security increase go through; all of them up for re-election in 1986, they apparently feared voters' wrath if they agreed to cuts. On the Senate side, many Democrats and Republicans were inclined to include Social Security cuts in a larger package of spending reductions—believing that nothing meaningful could be done to cut the deficit unless everything was put on the table.

Act 10: Agreement on a Budget Resolution. Finally, after seven months of wrangling, Congress adopted on August 1 a fiscal 1986 budget resolution. It called for some cuts in the growth of federal programs—though not nearly enough to prevent a massive federal deficit. It included neither major tax increases nor reductions in Social Security COLAs—though many members believed both were needed. It provided for a small increase in defense spending, just what was needed to compensate for inflation. It was an "LCD" budget: one that found the "lowest common denominator" in the contrasting proposals of Republicans and Democrats in the House and Senate, and the Reagan administration. Its great political virtue was that it made everyone somewhat unhappy: No one was able to declare a victory for his or her position. The budget resolution was dominated by compromises—unavoidable because no side could impose its own plan. In all these ingredients, the budget resolution enacted for FY 1986 reflected the dispersion of authority that separation of powers has made a routine part of policy formation in the United States.

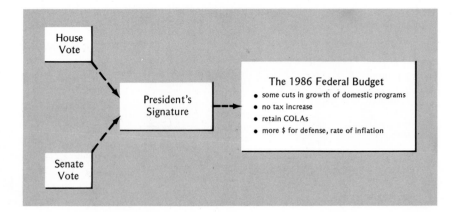

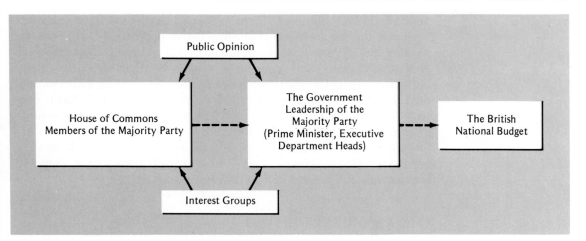

Figure 5.2
Actors in the Budget-Making Process in Great Britain

Policy Making in Britain

Comparison of how the budget gets formed in Great Britain and in the United States helps us to see how having a large number of people with a direct hand in the decision—the distinctive feature of separation of powers—transforms the entire process. (See Figure 5.2.) In both countries elected officials with direct authority over policy must respond to strong currents in public opinion—public attitudes, for example, on whether the growth in spending for social welfare programs should be curbed or should continue to increase. And in both countries interest groups lobby, seeking to influence policy decisions. Here, however, the similarity ends.

In Great Britain, public opinion and interest-group pressure are directed at a small, disciplined, tightly organized group of officials: the leaders of the majority party in the House of Commons who, as the prime minister and the secretaries of the various executive departments, constitute the government of the day. (The British legislature does have an upper chamber, the House of Lords, but over the years the powers of this nonelective assembly have been greatly cut back and its role made purely consultative.) The 650 members of the House of Commons, Britain's equivalent to U.S. senators and representatives, do hold formal authority over the budget, and all other matters of public policy, but party leaders exercise tight discipline over these legislators—as is the case in most parliamentary systems. As we will see in Chapter 6, the cabinet holds its executive authority because it enjoys the support of a majority in the lower house. At first glance this might seem likely to make the government weak and individual legislators strong—since whenever a majority of the legislators so decide they can bring the government down and constitute a

The majority party heads the executive

new one. In fact, however, the requirement that the government must maintain the regular support of a legislative majority if it is to remain in office has led to a host of mechanisms and traditions through which party leaders can exert strong discipline over their legislative members. So long as the party leaders are themselves reasonably united on a course of action, they are almost certain to exercise reliable control over their legislative majority. This means that, voting strictly on party lines, the House of Commons will enact any budget the cabinet agrees upon. If the prime minister and the other key leaders of her party come together on any course of legislative action, they will see the measure passed just as they have drafted it.

THE CASE FOR REFORM

The above account of the 1986 budget resolution is long—but it still vastly understates the complex task of setting a budget for the United States. Under the 1974 Congressional Budget and Impoundment Control Act, Congress is supposed to enact annually by May 15 a resolution setting nonbinding targets for spending and taxes to guide authorizing and appropriations committees in preparing their bills. It was this resolution—just one part of the total budget-setting process—that was finally completed on August 1, two and a half months late and to almost no one's satisfaction.

Developing public policy in the United States is a very messy process, thanks to separation of powers. It is not necessarily bad or unjustifiable, but it *is* frustrating. So many independent actors have a piece of the action. Is there a better way?

For the last one hundred years, some have argued that the end product of separation of powers is sufficiently flawed as to make necessary basic constitutional reform. One early critic put it this way:

Criticisms of separation of powers

As at present constituted, the federal government lacks strength because its powers are divided, lacks promptness because its authorities are multiplied, lacks wieldiness because its processes are roundabout, lacks efficiency because its responsibility is indistinct and its actions without competent direction. It is a government in which every officer may talk about every other officer's duty without having to render strict account for not doing his own, and in which the masters are held in check and offered contradiction by the servants. . . . Talk is not sobered by any necessity imposed upon those who utter it to suit their actions to their words. There is no day of reckoning for words spoken. The speakers of a congressional majority may, without risk of incurring ridicule or discredit, condemn what their own committees are doing; and the spokesmen of a minority may urge what contrary courses they please with a well-grounded assurance that what they say will be forgotten before they can be called upon to put it into practice. Nobody stands sponsor for the policy of the government. A dozen men originate it; a dozen compromises twist and alter it; a dozen offices whose names are scarcely known outside of Washington put it into execution.[1]

These searing criticisms, all centering about separation of powers, were made by a young political scientist over one hundred years ago. Their author, Woodrow Wilson, was to go on to be president of Princeton University, governor of New Jersey, and president of the United States (1913–21). If the style with which Wilson expressed his criticisms has a nineteenth-century ring to it, the substance of the criticisms seems to us distinctly contemporary. Wilson's intellectual successors now make many of the same charges.

Today's critics of separation of powers argue that it does awful damage to *political accountability.* Who is to be held responsible for policy when so many different officials, each independent of the other, in Congress and in the executive branch, have some hand in the action, yet no one has a controlling hand? Our huge federal deficits are a case in point. The president says he is distressed by their size, congressional Democrats and Republicans similarly proclaim their opposition to big deficits and their determination to bring them under control. In fact, almost no one anywhere in the executive or legislative branches defends the sustained high deficits of the 1980s. Still, they have persisted.

Congressional Democrats blamed Ronald Reagan for the deficits, arguing that his refusal to accept tax increases and his support for increased defense spending are responsible. The Reagan administration blamed the Democrats in particular and, to some degree, Congress in general for being too inclined to respond favorably to interest-group demands for spending programs, without regard to the fact that such programs must ultimately be paid for. To some considerable extent, everyone was right: Congress and the president shared responsibility for the high deficits. And, critics would argue, the system is also responsible: It permits lots of different officials to influence the shape of the budget without giving any one official formal authority such that he or she can really be held accountable for the end product.

The second major criticism of separation of powers is that it *hamstrings the chief executive.* He may win a huge majority in the presidential balloting but he isn't given the means to really form a government. He always has to go hat in hand to Congress—a Congress that about half the time since World War II has been controlled by the opposition party. Lloyd Cutler, who was counselor to President Jimmy Carter, notes that in 1979 the British Conservative party won a majority of some 30 to 40 seats in Parliament, and Conserva-

Margin notes:
Problem of political accountability

Who is to blame?

Hamstringing the chief executive

---

[1] Woodrow Wilson, *Congressional Government: A Study in American Politics* (Baltimore, MD: The Johns Hopkins University Press, 1981; first published, 1885), pp. 206–7.

tive Leader Margaret Thatcher thus became prime minister. Thatcher had, Cutler observed, "a very radical program, one that [could] make fundamental changes in the economy, social fabric, and foreign policy of the United Kingdom." Though there was reason for real doubt about whether this program could in fact achieve its objectives,

> there is not the slightest doubt that she will be able to legislate her entire program, including any modifications she makes to meet new problems. In a parliamentary system, it is the duty of each majority member of the legislature to vote for each element of the government's program, and the government possesses the means to punish members if they do not. In a very real sense, each member's political and electoral future is tied to the fate of the government his majority has formed. Politically speaking, he lives or dies by whether that government lives or dies.[2]

As a high-ranking Carter aide, Lloyd Cutler looked upon Thatcher's position with more than a little envy.

Comparing our system with Great Britain's

> President Carter's party has a much larger majority in both houses of Congress than [does] . . . Prime Minister Thatcher. But this comfortable majority does not even begin to assure that President Carter or any other president can rely on that majority to vote for each element of his program. No member of that majority has the constitutional duty or the practical political need to vote for each element of the president's program. Neither the president nor the leaders of the legislative majority have the means to punish him if he does not. In the famous phrase of Joe Jacobs, the fight manager, "it's every many for theirself."[3]

Policy incoherence

The third criticism of separation of powers is that it makes it virtually impossible for American government to frame the kind of *coherent, integrated approaches to complex policies* that the modern era demands. The policy incoherence bred of separation of powers was one thing in 1793, when the federal government did very little and could take a long time to do what it did—something quite different today when the national government spends a billion dollars a year, and operates a variety of programs that influence the course of the national economy, affect every citizen, and have a real responsibility for international peace and security. Critics insist that we now need to be able to form a government that can come up with coherent programs, see these through into law, and be held fully accountable politically for their success or failure.

Proposals for Change

From the young Woodrow Wilson to present-day commentators, critics of separation of powers have looked longingly at parliamentary

---

[2] Lloyd N. Cutler, "To Form a Government," *Foreign Affairs*, Spring 1980, p. 129.
[3] Ibid, pp. 129–30.

government, especially the form of parliamentarianism that evolved in Great Britain. An election is held and one party wins the majority of legislative seats. That party's leadership becomes the government. The prime minister is hardly a dictator; her authority is entirely dependent upon her party's legislative majority, and a new election must be held within five years. Moreover, she shares governmental power with the other leaders of her party. Nonetheless, the prime minister and cabinet, assured of a legislative majority, and generally possessing the means of disciplining recalcitrant members into supporting party programs, can develop policies while being assured that they will actually become law. Critics of separation of powers might not want to see the United States emulate Great Britain in many ways, but for the most part they would like to see it emulate British parliamentarianism.

No one argues, however, that the United States should abolish its present constitutional system and replace it with a full-fledged parliamentary system. Simple political realism accounts for much of the reluctance to urge so momentous a shift. Since the chances of it happening are literally zero, what would be gained by urging it, even if it seemed desirable? But more than this is involved. Like other analysts, critics of separation of powers in the United States recognize that our system has been in place for two hundred years and thus is an integral part of the national political tradition. No successful reform can ignore the traditions of the country for which it is being prescribed. Consequently, those who would like to see separation of powers changed have sought means of doing so that don't make too dramatic a break from the existing system.

In reviewing various proposals for reform, Lloyd Cutler has argued that "the most one can hope for is a set of modest changes that would make our structure work somewhat more in the manner of a parliamentary system, with somewhat less separation between the executive and the legislature than now exists."[4] One proposal calls for a constitutional amendment providing that, in presidential years, voters in each congressional district would be required to elect a trio of candidates *as a team:* president, vice president, and member of the House of Representatives. The idea here is to tie together the political fortunes of each party's presidential and congressional candidates. By constitutional necessity, were this proposal enacted, they would all stand or fall together.

A second proposal would amend the Constitution to permit (or require) the president to choose fifty percent of his cabinet from among his party's members in the House and Senate. These appointees would retain their congressional seats while in the cabinet. Article I, Section 6, of the Constitution states that "no person holding an office under

Margin notes:

Reforming within our existing system

Proposal to elect candidates as a team

Cabinet members chosen from House and Senate

[4]Ibid., p. 139.

the United States shall be a member of either house [of Congress] during his continuance in office." This would have to be repealed. The idea behind this proposed change is to create a greater sense of cooperation and intimacy between the executive and the legislature and add to their sense of shared responsibility for policy.

A third proposal would amend the Constitution to give the president power to dissolve Congress and call for new *congressional* elections. The president could exercise this only once in his term—to avoid any possibility that a president's dissatisfaction with congressional performance would lead him to send it back to the voters again and again, producing serious instability. The objective of this proposal would be to add a new means of breaking serious impasses between president and Congress; the president could make the case that he needs a Congress more supportive of his policies and let the voters decide whether they want to choose new congressmen.

Calling for a new Congress

A fourth proposal has called for constitutional change permitting an extraordinary majority (perhaps two-thirds) of both houses of Congress to declare "no confidence" in the president and call for new *presidential* elections.

"No confidence" vote

There are problems with many of these reform proposals. Consider, for example, the last one cited, that Congress be able to declare "no confidence" in the president. This would graft a common parliamentary device onto a system that would remain essentially nonparliamentary. The vote of no confidence is a standard means in parliamentary systems for bringing down a government. A vote on a particular bill is declared one that represents a formal test of whether the government continues to enjoy majority support. If the government (which is to say, the cabinet) loses the vote, it must resign. This is entirely natural and appropriate in the parliamentary tradition—where the very legitimacy of the executive is defined in terms of its enjoying majority support in the legislature. But in the American tradition, the strength and legitimacy of the executive is dependent not on its enjoying a congressional majority, but on its having been elected by popular vote expressed through a majority in the electoral college, and thereby entrusted with "the executive Power" of the United States.

SUPPORT FOR SEPARATION OF POWERS

A famous flap occurred in 1937 over President Franklin D. Roosevelt's attempt to curb the independence of a recalcitrant Supreme Court. The Court had invalidated a number of key New Deal measures, and Roosevelt, just off a huge victory in the 1936 elections, decided he had a mandate to change things. He proposed that the president be given power to appoint a new Supreme Court justice, up to a total of

FDR and Court packing

There was a lot of editorial and public comment on FDR's court-packing plan of 1936.

five, for every sitting justice who reached 70 years of age and didn't retire. This would increase the efficiency of the Court, the president argued, adding younger justices to pick up the workload. Everyone knew, of course, that Roosevelt's real intent was to get five additional appointments immediately; he would certainly have used these openings to "pack" the Court with judges who would agree with him on the basic constitutional propriety of New Deal actions.

Congress refused to go along with the president's proposal. The proposal was decisively beaten in a Senate controlled by the Democrats by a huge margin of 76 to 16 over the Republicans. Even without his court-packing plan, the president soon attained his judicial objectives, in part through shifts in the "swing votes" of two sitting justices and in part through the normal processes of retirements and new appointments. Today, most students of the Court, including those strongly supportive of Roosevelt's New Deal, think the president was wrong in trying to use his huge electoral margin to change the constitutional balance. That a president as popular as FDR would lose on this issue in the spring and summer of 1937 is impressive testimony to the strength of the American commitment to separation of powers, a commitment based in part on the view that even very popular and able officials can at times be wrong.

Congress vetoes president's plans

Historian Arthur Schlesinger, Jr., has argued that the key problem facing modern public policy in the United States isn't that we have in hand a set of wonderful solutions that we can't enact because of the fracturings produced by separation of powers.

Our problem—let's face it—is that we do not know what to do. . . . If we don't know what ought to be done, efficient management of a poor program is a dubious accomplishment—as the experience of 1981 demonstrates. [Schlesinger was critical of various economic proposals that the Reagan administration urged and that Congress did in fact enact.] What is the great advantage of acting with decision and dispatch when you don't know what you're doing?[5]

Schlesinger goes on to argue that

when the country is not sure what ought to be done, it may be that delay, debate, and further consideration are not a bad idea. And if our leadership is sure what to do, it must in our democracy educate the rest—and that is not a bad idea either. . . . I believe that in the main our Constitution has worked pretty well. It has insured discussion when we have lacked consensus and has permitted action when a majority can be convinced that the action is right.

Many would make the same general point a little more softly: Granted, there are cases where the net effect of separation of powers is to make it *harder*—not *impossible*—to implement sensible programs; there are also a great many other cases where separation of powers has helped block action that would have been unwise—unwise in part because it lacked a popular mandate. The indecision and compromise on the federal budget that we described above reflected a national uncertainty and lack of concensus on what should be done. At a minimum, it is far from clear that, overall, the United States has been badly served by the division of authority, the sharing of responsibility, and the slowing of action that separation of powers encourages.

Blocking unwise action

The Historical Record

Ability to act when the course is clear

The picture that constitutional reformers paint of American government as a helpless giant, unable to act coherently in the face of severe challenges, is itself highly questionable. Over the last half-century the United States Congress has passed, and the president has signed into law, an enormous amount of legislation dealing with public problems. It is very hard to accept the argument that our government has been persistently unable to act. When it hasn't acted very coherently, as with the deficit, the failure may reflect less the impact of separation of powers than lack of agreement in either party on what should be done, given the variety of contending economic and political objectives. Reformers seem to overstate the incapacities for action in the American system—and the coherence of policy and programs that results from the working of parliamentary democracies like West Germany, Italy, and Great Britain.

[5] Arthur Schlesinger, Jr., "Leave the Constitution Alone," in Donald L. Robinson, ed., *Reforming American Government* (New York: Norton, 1980), p. 53.

A Responsive System

The president: the repository of executive power

Even with separation of powers, the American president is hardly a feeble chief executive. He does find it relatively hard to move Congress in desired directions—compared to political chief executives and their parliaments in other democracies. But his standing as the repository, alone, of the executive power of the United States gives him extraordinary visibility and legitimacy that are counterbalancing assets. Winston Churchill made this point to Franklin Roosevelt in a wartime conversation. "You, Mr. President," Churchill remarked, "are concerned to what extent you can act without the approval of Congress. You don't worry about your cabinet. On the other hand, I never worry about Parliament, but I continuously have to consult and have the support of my cabinet."[6] The president is far more the master of his cabinet departments, whose heads are clearly subordinate to him constitutionally, than the British prime minister is of her government, where cabinet secretaries are party leaders occupying positions whose constitutional status is similar to, not subordinate to, that of the prime minister.

Power of Congress

At the same time, separation of powers has made the American Congress the most powerful legislature in the world. It cannot be treated merely as a rubber stamp, as in fact parliaments so often are, given the workings of strong party discipline. Congress is an active and vital representative body. When, in off-year elections, Americans return to Congress majorities less receptive to a president's programs than were those of the preceding congressional term, they are expressing themselves on the course of American policy in a manner that has real policy impact. The independence of Congress, in short, is democratic: It further empowers the public. And when the public is uncertain about what is to be done, separation of powers and a strong, independent Congress allow them to express that uncertainty—for instance, by electing a president from one party and a congressional majority from another.

FEDERALISM

The American commitment to limited, divided government has sustained a dispersion of national governmental authority that has few parallels elsewhere in the world. The same commitment is evident in our country's federal system, in which the power to govern is constitutionally assigned both to the central government and to the governments of the fifty states. Within a complex and continually evolving

---

[6]Winston Churchill, as quoted by Schlesinger, "Leave the Constitution Alone," p. 51.

set of constraints, the national and state governments share some functions and exercise others independently. Sorting out where the proper responsibilities of the national level leave off and where those of the state level begin, and keeping intergovernmental relations reasonably smooth and productive, have always been demanding tasks in the American federal system, and "boundary disputes" have been common.

Federalism and the historical record

The future of American federalism has sometimes seemed bleak. At the time of the Civil War, the question was whether a national federal union could and would endure. More recently the question has been whether the states can or should play an important role in the American governmental scene. Commenting on what many thought was the states' poor performance in responding to the economic crisis that beset the country during the Great Depression, political scientist Luther Gulick asserted that "the American state is finished. I do not predict that the states will go, but affirm that they have gone."[7] Today, some argue that the dispersion of power and decentralization inherent in federalism are anachronistic, given the interdependence of the society and the national character of so many of its problems in the post-industrial era.

Endurance of federalism

Each time it has been counted out, however, the federal system has recovered and shown its strength and resiliency. It remains one of America's most striking political inventions. Political scientist Samuel Beer noted that "at Philadelphia in 1787, it is generally recognized, the Americans invented federalism. . . ."[8] Martin Diamond called it "the most important contribution made by the American founders to the art of government. . . ."[9] And in an eloquent opinion penned in 1971, Supreme Court Justice Hugo Black asserted that " 'our federalism' occupies a highly important place in our nation's history and its future. . . ."[10]

The Constitutional Base of American Federalism

Federalism: a uniquely American form of government

In developing federalism, the American framers could draw on some earlier political thought. In the seventeenth century, German theorists who dealt with questions of law and government were especially interested in arrangements through which the territories making up the German Empire could retain their separate existence while the Empire would be able to perform its appropriate central functions. But this German thought and governmental practice were so remote from the American experience of the eighteenth century that it is

[7] Luther H. Gulick, "Reorganization of the State," *Civil Engineering*, August 1983, p. 420.
[8] Samuel H. Beer, "Federalism, Nationalism, and Democracy in America," *American Political Science Review* 72 (1978):11.
[9] Martin Diamond, *'The Federalist* on Federalism: 'Neither a National Nor a Federal Constitution, But a Composition of Both,' " *Yale Law Journal* 86, 6 (May 1977):1273.
[10] *Younger v. Harris*, 401 U.S. 37 (1971).

doubtful they actually exerted much influence. English and French schools of political philosophy, on which the framers drew so heavily, wholly ignored issues of federalism. A new governmental form really was invented at Philadelphia in 1787, in response to two inescapable elements of American political thought of the time: There should be a strong national union under a government with substantial authority, and the states should continue to have major political roles and power. American federalism has since proved attractive to other nations and their constitution makers. Today, approximately twenty countries have federal systems.[11]

American federalism has been highly dynamic and changing. But the Constitution clearly spells out its basic structure. Constitutional provisions on federalism can be usefully divided into five categories: those relating to the powers of the states, the powers of the national government, restrictions on states, federal guarantees to states, and interstate relations.

Powers of the States

Selection of Senate and president

Article I, section 3, of the Constitution establishes the upper house of the national legislature, the Senate, as the federal chamber. Seats are apportioned to represent the states as equal units. Each has two U.S. senators (California with 24.7 million residents in 1982 and Alaska with just 438,000). Today this is the only instance in American legislative representation where districts of unequal size are still sanctioned, as constitutionally they must be. *Article II, section 1,* delineates a state role in the selection of the president. Each state chooses, in a manner determined by its legislature, a number of presidential electors equal to the number of senators and representatives the state has in the U.S. Congress.

Amending the Constitution

Article V provides for a formal state role in amending the Constitution, by establishing two different procedures, both of which involve state governments directly. In the first, after Congress by a two-thirds vote has proposed amendments to the Constitution, the amendments are submitted to the state legislatures; at least three-fourths of the legislatures must ratify them before they can take effect. In the second, which has never been tried but often discussed, legislatures of two-thirds of the states may call for a convention to propose amendments. As in the first procedure, the amendments would still have to be ratified by three-fourths of the state legislatures (or state conventions) before becoming law.

[11] According to Daniel Elazar, 18 countries have federal forms of government: Argentina, Australia, Austria, Brazil, Canada, Czechoslovakia, the Federal Republic of Germany, India, Malaysia, Mexico, Nigeria, Pakistan, Switzerland, the United States, the Soviet Union, the United Arab Emirates, Venezuela, and Yugoslavia. See Daniel Elazar, "State Constitutional Design in the United States and Other Federal Systems," *Publius: The Journal of Federalism* 12 (Winter 1982):8.

The Tenth Amendment

Probably the most discussed constitutional provision relating to the powers of the states is in the *Tenth Amendment:* "The powers not delegated to the United States by the Constitution, nor prohibited by it to the States, are reserved to the States respectively, or to the people." The Supreme Court has given different constructions to these words at different times in U.S. history. For much of the nineteenth and into the early twentieth century, the Court interpreted the amendment as an important statement of states' rights and residual powers. From the 1930s through the 1960s, however, the Court generally backed assertions of national authority and gave the Tenth Amendment little weight. For example, in the landmark case of *United States v. Darby* (1941), it broadly construed Congress's powers under the commerce clause of Article I, and dismissed the Tenth Amendment as but stating "a truism that all is retained which has not been surrendered." Over the last decade the Court has seemed unsure how much weight it wanted to place on the Tenth Amendment. Its most dramatic ruling came in *National League of Cities v. Usery* (1976), when it struck down the amendments to the Fair Labor Standards Act that Congress had enacted two years earlier. These amendments extended to state and local government employees federal minimum-wage and maximum-hour requirements that previously had been applied only to employees engaged in interstate commerce. In the majority opinion, Justice William Rehnquist argued that

> This Court has never doubted that there are limits upon the power of Congress to override state sovereignty. . . . One undoubted attribute of state sovereignty is the states' power to determine the wages which shall be paid to those whom they employ to carry out their governmental functions.

Continuing issues involving the Tenth Amendment

Just nine years later, however, a closely divided Court (5–4) overruled its *Usery* decision, in *Garcia v. San Antonio Metropolitan Transit Authority* (1985). At immediate issue in this case was whether the San Antonio transit authority, a governmental entity of the state of Texas, was bound to pay its employees according to federal-government-set minimum-wage and maximum-hour legislation. In the majority opinion overturning *Usery*, Justice Harry Blackmun argued in effect that the courts should be extremely reluctant to intervene in a political argument between the states and Congress over the extent of the latter's legislative powers. Dissenting, Justice Lewis Powell, Jr., criticized the majority for promulgating a new doctrine, that federal officials "are the sole judges of the limits of their own power." *Usery* went one way, *Garcia* went the other way; both decisions were 5–4, decided differently because one Justice (Blackmun) switched sides. The issue of what the Tenth Amendment requires is still far from settled.

Powers of the National Government

The most formidable statement of the powers of the national government comes in *Article I, section 8*. After a long enumeration of what Congress can do—borrow money, raise armies, declare war, regulate commerce, advance science and the arts—section 8 declares that "the Congress shall have power . . . to make all laws which shall be necessary and proper for carrying into execution the foregoing powers, and all other powers vested by this Constitution in the government of the United States, or in any department or officer thereof." This sweeping grant has supported a generally expanding set of federal government functions and responsibilities. *Article VI* establishes the Constitution and the laws made under it as "the supreme law of the land," and requires state judges to uphold these provisions, "anything in the Constitution or Laws of any State to the Contrary notwithstanding."

The reach of Congress's power

Restrictions on States

The Constitution in a number of instances tells the states things they cannot do. The biggest set of prohibitions comes in *Article I, section 10*. No state can make treaties with foreign countries, issue currency, grant titles of nobility, or pass any "bill of attainder," "ex post facto law," or any law "impairing the obligation of contracts"; and without the consent of Congress no state can tax imports or exports or keep military forces in time of peace.

Five amendments to the Constitution, all enacted after the Civil War, add other important prohibitions on state action. The *Thirteenth Amendment* was directed against the southern states and forbade slavery. Coming on its heels and also passed with the South in mind, but with language that has had much broader applicability, the *Fourteenth Amendment* asserts that no state "shall abridge the privileges or immunities of citizens of the United States; nor shall any State deprive any person of life, liberty, or property, without due process of law; nor deny to any person within its jurisdiction the equal protection of the laws." As we will see in chapter 9, a stream of important Supreme Court cases have arisen under these expansive terms.

Limits to states' powers

The *Fifteenth Amendment* requires that no state deny to its citizens the right to vote "on account of race, color, or previous condition of servitude." In the *Nineteenth Amendment*, ratified in 1920, states were prohibited from denying the vote on the basis of sex. And the *Twenty-sixth Amendment*, which became law in 1971, brought the legal voting age down to 18 all across the country by stipulating that the right of citizens who are 18 years or older to vote shall not be denied by any state "on account of age."

Federal Guarantees to States

Constitutional guarantees

States are given a number of guarantees under the Constitution. According to *Article I, section 8*, all taxes that Congress levies must be uniform in their rates and other provisions for all states; no state may be taxed discriminatorily. *Article IV, section 3*, provides that no new state shall be brought into the Union from territory of one or more existing states without the express consent of the concerned state legislatures as well as the approval of Congress. In *Article IV, section 4*, the national government guarantees each state a republican form of government, protection against invasion, and, when the state requests it, federal assistance against domestic violence. Presidents have mobilized the National Guard and even used regular army troops to maintain calm and order in the states. *Article V* stipulates that the Constitution cannot be amended to deprive states of equal representation in the U.S. Senate.

Interstate Relations

The last of the constitutional provisions on federalism bears on the relations of one state to another. *Article IV, section 1*, stipulates that "full faith and credit" shall be given by every state to the laws and actions of every other state. The next section of this article provides that a state is bound to apprehend and extradite a person formally accused or convicted of violating the felony laws (those covering more serious crimes) of another state. It also asserts that each state shall grant the "privileges and immunities" given its own citizens to those of every other state—a provision presumably inserted to ensure that a resident of, say, Virginia would not be discriminated against by the police or other governmental officials when traveling or doing business in New York or South Carolina. This may seem quaint today, but it was a natural enough concern in 1787.

This is the federal framework that the Constitution establishes. Both the national government and those of the states are given expansive governmental mandates. Both are told there are things they cannot do. The national government is pledged to assure the states some basic protections, and the states in turn to honor each other's laws. This structure has been broad enough to permit a great deal of change in federal–state relations, but precise enough to maintain federalism over two centuries of extraordinary social and political transformations.

EVOLUTION OF AMERICAN FEDERALISM

We can safely say that the founders would not be at all surprised by the operation of separation of powers today. The national government does much more at present than it did 200 years ago, of course, and all three branches now play larger roles. But the *relationship* of the three branches, the way they must share power, has changed very little.

This is not so with federalism. The relationship of the national and state governments has shifted dramatically at various points in U.S. history. The constitutional form of federalism is unchanged but its practice has been transformed.

The Early Years of States' Rights

Most of what was done by American government in the country's early years was accomplished at the state and local level. Education was exclusively a local affair, and law enforcement very nearly so. The federal government played a significant role in national defense, of course. In domestic affairs it promoted such internal improvements as building roads and canals needed to move people and goods around the nation. But that was about all. Before the Civil War the states were clearly the dominant actors in most domestic affairs.

Nullification

States were understandably jealous of their prerogatives, and elaborate formulations of states' rights flourished. One example is the doctrine of **nullification,** whose main proponent was South Carolinian John C. Calhoun. Calhoun held that the Union was composed of *sovereign states* that did not surrender sovereignty upon entering it. As a condition of its sovereignty, a state retained the right to review the actions and laws of the central government and, if need be, to declare them "null and void." The ultimate extension of the idea of state sovereignty, of course, was the assertion of the right of *secession*.

President Jefferson Davis (seated facing) General Robert E. Lee, and the Cabinet of the Confederate States of America.

Secession

If a state believed the demands of the Union were incompatible with its own interests and sovereignty, according to those who advocated the right of secession, it could pull out of the Union altogether. In 1861, eleven southern states exercised what they saw as their right to secede, and the American Civil War began.

National assertions

In an environment where states' rights had broad appeal, one of the most consistent advocates of a broader national role was John Marshall, chief justice of the Supreme Court from 1801 to 1835. Marshall managed to win some victories for his nationalist perspective; his ruling in *McCulloch* v. *Maryland* (1819) is the most celebrated.

McCulloch v. Maryland

In 1791 Congress created the Bank of the United States to hold and dispense federal funds and perform other monetary functions. Though the Constitution says nothing explicitly about Congress's power to create corporations like the bank, the bank's constitutionality was not contested in the courts before its charter expired in 1811. A second bank was chartered in 1816, but it proved politically unpopular, partly because it competed with state banks. Maryland passed legislation imposing a heavy tax on bank notes issued by the Bank of the United States. McCulloch, a cashier of the bank's Baltimore branch, issued notes without paying the required tax, thus setting the case in motion.

The "necessary and proper" clause

In the opinion of the Court, the Constitution and the laws enacted under it by the government of the United States form the supreme law of the land and cannot be infringed or countermanded by any state. Among the powers enumerated in Article I, section 8, there was no mention of establishing a bank or creating any other corporation. But neither was there anything prohibiting such action. The Constitution, Marshall insisted, clearly provided for a variety of actions not expressly mentioned when it stipulated at the end of section 8 that Congress shall be able to enact "all laws which shall be necessary and proper for carrying into execution the foregoing powers. . . ." Establishing a national bank was a legitimate congressional act under the "necessary and proper" clause.

> We admit, as all must admit, that the powers of the government are limited, and that its limits are not to be transcended. But we think the sound construction of the Constitution must allow to the national legislature that discretion, with respect to the means by which the powers it confers are to be carried into execution, which will enable that body to perform the high duties assigned to it. . . . Let the end be legitimate, let it be within the scope of the Constitution, and all means are appropriate, which are plainly adapted to that end, which are not prohibited, but consist with the letter and spirit of the Constitution, are constitutional. . . .[12]

[12] *McCulloch* v. *Maryland*, 17 U.S. 316 (1819).

Despite such ringing language, however, Judge Henry Friendly noted, "the use made of these powers through the first century of our history under the Constitution was restrained."[13]

The Civil War and Its Aftermath

Decline of extreme states' rights

The Civil War was a momentous event in the life of the country. Few political institutions came out of the ordeal unchanged; federalism was no exception. After the war the federal union was put back together again with most prewar elements intact. But in one striking shift, extreme states' rights doctrines like nullification and secession had been scuttled once and for all by the Confederate Army's surrender at Appomattox Courthouse on April 9, 1865. Since then, politicians have from time to time insisted upon their states' sovereign right to pursue certain interests against federal standards—as many southern politicians did when confronted by new civil rights laws and rulings in the 1950s and 1960s. But after 1865, few Americans took seriously the idea that a state could declare national government acts "null and void" or withdraw from the Union.

Effects of new technology

Changes in technology and the economy led to an expansion of the national government's role. One was the transformation of the country beginning in the second half of the nineteenth century under the impetus of developments in technology and the economy. The U.S. shifted from a rural, localized country to an industrial, interconnected society. Between 1870 and 1920, America's population tripled, reaching 106 million. The great cities were built—in this half-century New York grew from 942,292 to 5,620,048, Chicago from 298,977 to 2,701,705. Huge industrial and financial institutions were established. In place of an economy of small family farms producing foodstuffs for immediate areas, there was one dominated by big corporations drawing resources from the entire country (indeed, the world) and servicing national markets. A new communications technology made reports of activity in one sector the immediate property of the entire nation. This was the half-century in which all major electronic media except television were developed. The number of telephones in the United States grew from 3,000 in 1876 to 340,000 in 1885, 4.1 million in 1905, and 13.3 million in 1920. A new transportation network was established, centered on the railroad and the motorcar. Miles of railroad track in operation increased from 8,800 in 1850 to 82,000 in 1880 and to 406,000 in 1920.

Regulatory legislation

With all these forces increasing the scale of enterprises and drawing the parts of the country closer together, demands for greater national government involvement became more insistent. The new federal regulatory legislation of the late nineteenth and early twen-

[13]Henry J. Friendly, "Federalism: A Forward," *Yale Law Journal* 86 (May 1977):1020.

tieth centuries, discussed in chapter 8, was one result. Pure food and drug legislation, for example, didn't seem important when most people lived on farms and consumed largely what they produced; but it became necessary in an age of large cities and big impersonal corporations.

This new national economic regulation was, however, only the first stirring, a hint of things to come. Federal spending remained modest. Outside of defense, veterans' pensions, and interest on the national debt, spending rose very little. Most governmental expenditures were still at the state and local levels.

The New Deal Years

"If the War between the States was a watershed," Judge Friendly observed, "the New Deal was a tidal wave."[14] Signs of major federal expansion were first evident in the years immediately following World War I. In 1926, with Calvin Coolidge, a conservative Republican, in the White House, federal per capita spending was nearly four times as high as a decade earlier under Woodrow Wilson, a progressive Democrat. The level of governmental activity in the United States has always reflected the demands of the social setting much more than the specific programs of the incumbent administration. The big jump in spending after World War I came because the country was entering a new sociopolitical era, one that posed much greater demands on national programs. Urban, industrial society required more governmental regulation and public assistance than the rural, localized, agricultural society that preceded it.

Extending national government functions

Under President Franklin D. Roosevelt after 1933, the managerial and welfare functions of the national government were greatly extended. New regulatory bodies such as the Securities and Exchange Commission (SEC) were established to watch over sectors of the economy—in the case of the SEC, to protect investors and the stock market through orderly procedures in securities exchange. The national government also intervened on behalf of groups that found it hard to compete without assistance. For example, the National Labor Relations Act (the Wagner Act) was passed in 1935 to aid trade unions by making it unlawful for an employer to interfere with workers' rights to organize and bargain collectively.

Welfare and prosperity

The national government also assumed welfare functions previously handled informally through private channels, by state and local agencies, or not at all. In 1934 Roosevelt told Congress that the American people demanded "some safeguard against misfortunes which cannot be wholly eliminated in this man-made world of ours." And in 1935 the Social Security Act was passed. Two of the most impor-

[14]Ibid., p. 1023.

Federal grants to the states for highway construction were one of the earliest grant programs and remain a major one.

tant new national programs encompassed by the Social Security legislation were unemployment compensation and retirement benefits. More generally, the national government declared that henceforth it would be responsible for smoothing out business cycles, preventing excessive unemployment, promoting economic growth—in short, for maintaining and extending prosperity.

In response to all these new functions, federal expenditures again increased sharply. Between 1925 and 1941, federal per capita spending jumped 400 percent. And, reflecting a pronounced tilt toward the national government, combined state and local spending dropped below federal spending during World War II and stayed below it when peace returned—for the first time in American history.

FEDERALISM IN THE POSTINDUSTRIAL ERA

The term **cooperative federalism** describes the enlarged federal role and heightened intergovernmental sharing of responsibilities that had evolved by the middle of the twentieth century. The arrangements

Cooperative
federalism

and assumptions of cooperative federalism were themselves rapidly transformed, however, by a host of new centralizing movements. And once more, technology was a principal cause. Throughout American history, technological development has brought society closer together, making its members more interdependent; thus government has had to play a bigger role. In the postindustrial era, as we noted in chapter 1, advances in communications, particularly television, have made it possible for Americans in northern Maine, in the industrial heartland of the Midwest, in the rural South, and in the suburban sprawl of southern California, to hear the same news, watch the same entertainment programs, see the same products advertised, and in general share in a remarkably national cultural life. Further integration of the economy has exerted similar centralizing pressures. In response, studies of public opinion and popular culture have shown that state and regional variations in outlook have diminished and a more uniform national pattern has emerged.[15]

National Rights

Expanding national
rights and
responsibilities

Another factor affecting American federalism has been an enlarged sense of national rights and responsibilities. Beginning in the 1950s, strong assertions of the rights and claims of national citizenship successfully challenged the racial discrimination that was the South's historical legacy. By the 1960s national opinion had moved to the point where major changes in race relations were required. Of course, the traditions and institutions that had consigned black Americans to second-class citizenship throughout the southern states were not produced by federalism. But the nature of a federal system, which gives considerable latitude to the states in policy choice, permitted discriminatory racial practices to be perpetuated with the force of state law. The attack on segregation became, in a sense, an attack on federalism. When southern governors like Orval Faubus in Arkansas and George Wallace in Alabama proclaimed their states' rights to continue to discriminate against blacks, they helped undermine the claim to legitimacy of the larger concept of states' rights that underlies federalism itself. Writing about federalism in 1975, William Riker observed that in the century after the Civil War

> the main beneficiaries have undoubtedly been southern whites, who could use their power to control state governments to make policy on blacks

[15]The Roper Center for Public Opinion Research has made extensive comparisons of state and regional differences in opinion and values documenting the weakening of regional variations. See *Public Opinion*, February/March 1983, pp. 21–33; see too pp. 41–44 of this text. This is not to suggest that American social and political attitudes are now homogeneous from coast to coast. Significant differences growing out of contrasting historical experience, ethnic makeup, and economic interests of the states and regions persist. But over the last two decades the movement has been toward more nationally uniform outlooks.

In 1963, Governor George Wallace defied the federal government ruling that blacks must be allowed to enroll in the state university, and blocked entrance to the University of Alabama.

that negated the national policy. . . . Clearly . . . in the United States, the main effect of federalism since the Civil War has been to perpetuate racism.[16]

States' Rights under Attack

The erosion of state power

Even if Riker erred in so sweeping an indictment, the lessons of the 1950s and 1960s seemed to be that the people talking the loudest about the importance of states' rights were those who took issue with the basic American value of equality. Surely this validated the expansion of national governmental authority and initiative not just in race relations but across the broad spectrum of public policy. As the claims of national citizenship have grown stronger, and the practical role of the national government has been greatly enlarged, the states have been left in an awkward position. Just what is their role and legitimacy? If the states are not sovereign but simply administrative units of the national government with changing roles in an evolving political process, why should one worry about pushing them aside if national approaches seem more productive? "Federalism came to be seen as a passing phase in the developmental process . . ."[17] The governmental enterprises of the fifty states, with their 13.7 million full-time employees (in 1985) and myriad departments and functions could scarcely be ignored. But prevailing theory could and did accord them a fairly feeble, largely administrative status.

[16] William Riker, "Federalism," in *Handbook of Political Science*, vol. 5, Fred I. Greenstein and Nelson W. Polsby, eds. (Reading, Mass.: Addison-Wesley, 1975), p. 154.
[17] David R. Beam, Timothy J. Conlin, and David B. Walker, "Government in Three Dimensions: Implications of a Changing Federalism for Political Science," paper presented at the 1982 annual meeting of the American Political Science Association, Denver, Colo., September 2–5, 1982.

A Tide of National Legislation

Civil rights and national legislation

The volume of new national legislation testified to the erosion of the states' position. One big thrust came in civil rights, but change was by no means confined to this area. Extensive new federal legislation was enacted on behalf of public safety and well-being, utilizing the "commerce" power: Article I, section 8, of the Constitution gives Congress power "to regulate Commerce" among the several states. . . ." Probably the most far-reaching new statute was the Occupational Safety and Health Act (OSHA) of 1970. Other legislation included the national Traffic and Motor Vehicle Safety Act of 1966, the Highway Safety Act of 1966, the Natural Gas Pipeline Safety Act of 1968, the Federal Coal Mine Health and Safety Act of 1969, the Port and Waterways Safety Act of 1972, the Federal Railroad Safety Act of 1970, the Consumer Product Safety Act of 1972, the Motor Vehicle and School Bus Safety Amendments of 1974, and the Highway Safety Act of 1976.[18] These laws provided national standards and enforcement in the various areas their titles suggest.

New areas of governmental concern

In other policy areas the legislative surge was also strong. Protection of borrowers and consumers was extended by the Consumer Credit Protection Act of 1968, the Fair Credit Billing Act of 1974, the Real Estate Settlement Procedures Act of 1974, the Equal Credit Opportunity Act of 1974, the Home Mortgage Disclosure Act of 1975, and the Consumer Leasing Act of 1976. Another major series of laws was enacted placing the national government firmly behind efforts to protect the environment. Notable here were the National Environmental Policy Act of 1969, the Water Quality Improvement Act of 1970, the Clean Air Amendments of 1970, the Noise Control Act of 1972, the Federal Environmental Pesticide Act of 1972, and the Deep Water Port Act of 1974. The list goes on and on in almost every sector of public policy. The change was not incremental; it was a massive increase that qualitatively altered the national government's role. Let the end be legitimate, Congress was saying, and legislation on almost any conceivable subject is permitted, even required.

Supreme Court decisions bolstered national power

Growth of national power was further enhanced by a series of Supreme Court decisions—in their own way as consequential as the new legislation. In a long series of cases, the Court selectively incorporated key provisions of the first eight amendments to the Constitution within the due process clause of the Fourteenth Amendment, thus making them applicable to the states. (See chapter 15 for a full discussion of selective incorporation.) Following *Monroe* v. *Pape* (1961), the long-ignored civil rights acts of the Civil War Reconstruction period were employed not only to prevent racial discrimination but to address

---

[18] For a fine review of these many interventions by the national government and their impact on the federal system, see Friendly, "Federalism: A Foreword," pp. 1025–27.

Medicaid, which provides health care to the poor, is financed by federal matching grants to the states.

many other alleged denials of constitutional rights: for example, those involving inmates of state prisons.

> In carrying out this mission, federal courts have felt authorized to take on an enormous degree of supervision of the operations of state prisons and mental institutions and to impose affirmative obligations on the states. One federal court, in an effort to obtain minority representation, has ordered the complete remodeling of a city government.[19]

Grants-in-Aid

In some cases the national government addresses problems by authorizing its agencies to spend money directly to deal with them. In many instances, however, reflecting the large presence of the states and municipalities in the American governing system, federal funds are given to states and municipalities in the form of *federal grants-in-aid*, with various stipulations on how they are to be spent.

The growth of federal grant programs

Before the Great Depression, Congress made grant funds available to the states for only a few clearly national functions such as building "post roads"—so called because the original rationale for a roadway system connecting all parts of the country was to service a national postal service mandated by the Constitution. During the Depression, a variety of new grant programs were added to cover additional services including welfare, employment assistance, public health care,

[19]Ibid, p. 1028. The case involving city government to which Friendly refers is *Bolden* v. *City of Mobile*, 423 F. Supp. 384 (1976).

public housing, and school lunches. From the end of World War II until the 1960s, still other programs were established providing grants for airports, hospitals, urban renewal, and library services. When John F. Kennedy took office in 1961, some forty-four federal grant programs were in place.

Extensive new grant programs were enacted in the 1960s and 1970s. Congress passed legislation through which revenues raised nationally were made available to states and cities to clean up the environment, provide health benefits for the elderly poor, make loans and grants to college students, establish or enlarge urban transportation systems, combat crime, get rid of slums, and extend a host of other services.

Major increases in federal grants

Some authorities conclude that about 500 federal grant programs were providing aid to state and local governments when Ronald Reagan took office in January 1981; others put the total even higher. Calculations made by the Office of Management and Budget (OMB) show 361 grant programs in 1981. The complexity of much of the legislation, and the fact that it is possible to count different program activities in different ways, account for the discrepancy in estimates. But it is clear that a huge increase in federal grants-in-aid had occurred in the preceding quarter-century. In 1955, federal grants totaled approximately $3.2 billion and provided about 10 percent of the total amount expended by state and local governments. A decade later, these grants had risen to $11 billion and accounted for 15 percent of state and local expenditures. By 1980, federal grants to state and local governments had reached $91 billion and were providing 26 percent of all funds spent by states and municipalities. In the 20 years between 1957 and 1977, grants-in-aid doubled in real terms—that is, controlling for inflation—every five years and increased overall by an extraordinary 700 percent.[20]

The Reagan Reversal

The steady growth of federal grants to the states over the late 1950s, 1960s, and 1970s was halted by the Reagan administration in the 1980s. Seeking curbs on domestic spending, the administration cut back on what it considered unnecessary grants-in-aid. Many smaller grant programs were eliminated and others were consolidated. Total spending under federal grants leveled out in terms of actual dollars and fell substantially both as a percentage of the gross national product and as a proportion of all state and local government spending. In 1978 26.8 percent of state and local expenditures were supported by federal grants; by 1987 the proportion had dropped almost nine points to 18 percent.

Cuts in grant programs

[20] G. R. Stephens and G. W. Olsen, *Pass-Through Federal Aid and Interlevel Finance in the American Federal System, 1957–1977,* vol. 1, a report prepared for the National Science Foundation, Washington, D.C., August 1979.

A cartoonist's view of Reagan administration efforts to shift some social programs to the states.

"IT'S FROM THE WHITE HOUSE... THEY'VE RUN OUT OF ROOM!"

Excluding the major entitlement programs of health and income security, such as Medicaid and Aid to Families with Dependent Children (AFDC), federal grants to state and local governments have fallen even more dramatically than the above data would suggest. Figure 5.3 shows that federal grants outside the entitlement program areas were actually cut in half between 1980 and 1987, measured in dollars of constant 1980 purchasing power.

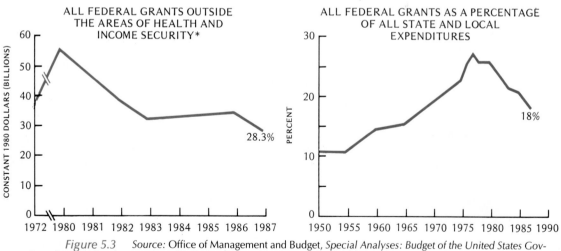

Figure 5.3
Trends of Federal Grants-in-aid

Source: Office of Management and Budget, *Special Analyses: Budget of the United States Government, FY 1989*, p. H-20; *Congressional Quarterly Weekly Report*, February 20, 1988, p. 329 (data adapted from federal budgets, fiscal years 1982–89, *Special Analyses H*).
* Included here are grants for natural resources, transportation, community development, education, employment and training, social services, and general revenue sharing, adjusted by the GNP deflators.

Many state officials have had a decidedly mixed reaction to these cuts. "There's a schizophrenia out there," said Raymond Scheppach, director of the National Governors' Association. "Some governors would like the federal government out of things. But that depends on whether they have to raise taxes to compensate."[21] In other words, the flow of federal grants has been a vehicle for increased federal control; many state officials are happy to see the source of this control reduced. At the same time, they liked one feature of the federal support—that it came to them without any need to raise taxes.

Concern over Reagan administration cuts

THE FUTURE OF FEDERALISM

The states still play an imposing role in American governmental relations, one bequeathed them by the Constitution and reinforced by centuries of practical governmental experience. The place of the states is enhanced, too, by their considerable political muscle. As Samuel Beer noted, in a country with 80,000 governments embracing 500,000 elected persons, there is a built-in powerful intergovernmental lobby on behalf of federalism.[22] Thousands of state and local government officials have an active interest in keeping their units of government active and viable.

Political muscle of the states

At the same time, as we have seen, the states have seen their role and *de facto* constitutional position diminished significantly over the past half-century. The end result has been that a host of "boundary disputes" have gone against the states. When a disagreement has arisen on whether a decision should be made by the national government or by the states, the trend has been toward the national government's favor. A couple of examples make this development clearer. Neither may seem very momentous individually—but they become important as part of a larger pattern. The first involves the setting of speed limits on the nation's highways; the second is the reach of the federal government's taxing powers.

The 55 Mile Per Hour Battle

Automobiles didn't exist in 1789, of course; they didn't appear on the scene until over a hundred years later. Early Americans did, however, confront many situations where public order, health, and safety required the use of government's policing authority. Who would exercise this authority—the states or the national government? In the American federal system, the answer was the states and their local

---

[21] Quoted in "Deficit Limits Reagan's Options in 1989 Budget," *Congressional Quarterly*, February 20, 1988, pp. 328–29.

[22] Samuel H. Beer, "The Adoption of General Revenue Sharing: A Case Study in Public Sector Politics," *Public Policy* 24 (Spring 1976):129.

Causing lengthy waits at the gas pumps, the Arab oil embargo was a major factor in the federal government's decision to conserve fuel by imposing the 55 mile per hour speed limit.

administrative units, towns and counties. These functions were not seen requiring national action—in the way, say, that coining money, declaring war, and regulating commerce with other countries were considered national functions.

When autos did appear in large numbers early in the twentieth century, and laws regulating their use on the country's roads became necessary to protect the general well-being of drivers of autos as well as horse-drawn carriages, pedestrians, and property, the laws were enacted by the states under their well-established police powers. No one even thought of it being otherwise. This continues in our own time. The terms under which we get and maintain our driver's licenses, register our motor vehicles, and operate these vehicles on the highways are determined by state law and vary from state to state. When we are arrested for exceeding posted speed limits, it is by state police, county sheriffs, or municipal police, not by law enforcement officials of the federal government. And we are required to appear in state or municipal courts, not in federal courts. Setting speed limits is a state function.

As in so many areas of American federalism, however, the states' position here has been eroded. Might there be occasions when highway speed limits would have some national purpose and be subject to congressional action? In 1973 and 1974 just such an occasion appeared. Amid the first round of big price increases and fuel shortages caused by the Arab oil embargo, Congress passed legislation to lower the maximum highway speed limit to 55 miles per hour—in the national interest of encouraging fuel conservation, as 55 mph was considered the most fuel-efficient driving speed.

Even at the time, when the nation saw energy problems at near-

Congress passes speed limit legislation

crisis proportions, some members of Congress objected to the national government's intruding into what was basically a state responsibility. Senator Carl T. Curtis (R-Nebraska) argued: "The states are irritated now about all the requirements placed on them, and if they do not comply their federal funds are in jeopardy. That sort of coercion is not the right way to do it."[23] This and other such arguments were brushed aside. The mood in Congress and among the general public was: Do something. We have a serious national problem.

The vehicle for congressional action is interesting. Congress did not believe it could pass a law directly setting highway speeds in Vermont, Minnesota, Arizona, and the other 47 states; passing such a law was the clearly established province of the states. What Congress did was mandate that *the states themselves* pass the new speed limit. What if the states refused? In 1973 each state was receiving a substantial portion of its highway construction and maintenance funds from federal grants, money for which came partly from distribution of federal gasoline tax revenue. Congress said to the states, "Setting highway speed limits is your business, but if you don't reduce the limit to 55 miles per hour on all roads we will cut your federal highway grant funds." The states complied. Here again is a key element in the evolution of federal–state relations in the twentieth century: the use of federal leverage to impose uniform responses to what are seen as national problems.

Federal / state relations over speed limits

By 1986, conditions relating to energy were very different from the time of the Arab oil embargo. OPEC's clout had diminished as an oil surplus replaced the earlier shortage. Oil prices were falling and energy conservation no longer seemed the compelling national need that it did in 1973. It was generally recognized that the 55 mph limit had reduced highway fatalities, but the public was less convinced of the necessity of the limit. Monitoring of highway speeds showed more and more of the driving public exceeding 55 mph—and more and more states weakly enforcing their official limits. In Montana, for instance, a driver cited for traveling 70 mph on an interstate highway during daylight hours could expect to be punished by nothing more than a fine of $5. Throughout the west a *de facto* state rebellion against the 55 mile speed limit was in progress.

Rethinking the 55 mph national speed limit

Facing this political pressure, Congress in effect struck a deal with the states. In 1987 it permitted them, if they chose, to raise the speed limit to 65 mph on *rural* interstate highways—those outside congested areas. Later in the year Congress also allowed the states to raise the speed limit to 65 mph on rural highways, primarily state turnpikes, that met the same design standards as interstate highways. It's important to note, however, that while the states finally got most of what they wanted, Congress is now firmly established as the

Congress and states negotiate new limits

[23]Quoted in "Senate Approves Heavier Trucks, Lower Speeds," *Congressional Quarterly*, September 14, 1974, p. 2451.

arbiter of highway speed limits. The states had to petition Congress *to permit them* to raise the speed limit—even on what are purely state roads, out of the federal interstate system.

Federal Power of Taxation

A Supreme Court decision handed down in April 1988 provides another vivid reminder of how the states' position in the American constitutional scheme, though still large, is suffering a kind of intellectual erosion. In *South Carolina* v. *Baker,* the Court upheld the constitutionality of a federal law that removed the federal tax exemption for interest on state and local bonds issued in non-registered form—sometimes called bearer bonds. The immediate issue was narrow and technical, involving a minor tax provision passed by Congress in 1982. But the majority opinion reached beyond the technical issue, overruling a major 1895 precedent as it held that the Constitution does not protect state and local governments against federal taxation of the interest received by holders of their bonds.

South Carolina v. *Baker*

Writing for the majority, Justice William J. Brennan, Jr., ruled that the states must look to the "national political process" for protection against federal taxation, and not to judicial enforcement of federalism principles long thought to be embodied in the Tenth Amendment and other provisions of the Constitution. The states have the right to try to persuade Congress not to tax the interest on their bonds; they do not have constitutional protection against that taxation.

Opinions of the Court

In a dissenting opinion, Justice Sandra Day O'Connor criticized the majority for "overruling a precedent that it has honored for nearly a hundred years. . . . Henceforth the ability of state and local governments to finance their activities will depend in part on whether Congress *voluntarily abstains* from tapping this permissible source of additional tax revenue" (emphasis added). State and local government groups reacted to the majority ruling with alarm. Alan Beals, director of the National League of Cities, charged that the Court's ruling "is tantamount to a decree of unconstitutional surrender imposed on state and local governments by the national government they created 200 years ago. We do not accept this butchery of the Constitution. . . ."

Adapting American federalism to the social and political requirements of the approaching twenty-first century will present a continuing challenge. There is a compelling case for national responses to problems that are increasingly national, if not global. There is also an impressive case for maintaining federalism's vitality.

The link between federalism and the maintenance of freedom can be traced back to the *Federalist Papers*. We have seen that Madison and Hamilton integrated the principle of separation of powers with the idea of federalism to produce what they believed would be a watertight defense of freedom. Other countries such as Great Britain have achieved high levels of political and social freedom without such dispersion of governmental authority. But many Americans still hold to the classical liberal belief that divided power as promoted by federalism helps guard against any unit of the government becoming too strong.

Multilevel government serving local needs

A related defense of federalism is the idea that the diverse needs of a heterogeneous population scattered over a big territory can best be served by a multilevel government. While various public opinion studies of recent years have shown that many citizens have a greater awareness of national officials and programs than of the state and local counterparts, the public still finds the system of semi-autonomous states useful to articulate local needs and interests. Even the strongest proponents of national citizenship agree that there are some areas where local choice should prevail. Few voices are heard, for example, on behalf of a national school system.

States as "laboratories of federalism"

There seems to be merit in a governmental system that gives states room to experiment with programs reflecting their contrasting needs and interests. Many states pioneered social programs long before the national government acted on them. The state of New York introduced minimum-wage, maximum-hour, and child-labor legislation decades before it was achieved nationally. If describing them as "laboratories of federalism" seems extravagant, the states have in fact experimented productively with many programs and policies. "It is one of the happy incidents of the federal system," Supreme Court Justice Louis Brandeis wrote in 1932, "that a single courageous state may, if its citizens choose, serve as a laboratory, and try novel experiments without risk to the rest of the country."[24]

Future of states' role

Two centuries after the drafting of the Constitution, federalism remains an important component of the larger American system of divided power. Yet the position of the states is somewhat ambiguous. Politically they remain vitally important participants. In one sense their political independence has been enhanced in the 1980s by a reversal of what had been a long trend toward greater state reliance upon federal grants-in-aid. As noted, a variety of developments in the Reagan years—including large federal budget deficits—have cut the flow of federal funds to the states—and cut them dramatically outside health and income support. If "he who pays the piper calls the tune," the proportional cuts in federal payments for state programs should buttress the states' political autonomy.

At the same time, there has been no reversal of the long-term weakening of the idea of state sovereignty. Over the last half-century "boundary disputes" between the federal government and the states have been settled mostly in the former's favor. Today it is the intel-

[24]*New State Ice Co. v. Liebmann*, 285 U.S. 262, 311 (1932), Justice Brandeis dissenting.

lectual case for independent spheres of state action, not the case for broad spheres of national government responsibility, that needs careful tending.

SUMMARY

The American constitutional system differs from that of most other democracies by providing for an elaborate division of governmental power. It does this principally through *separation of powers* and *federalism.* In a parliamentary system like Great Britain's, no separation of executive and legislature exists: The government or cabinet, which performs executive functions, is made up of the leaders of the party (or coalition) that has a majority in the legislature. The government holds office only so long as it can command a legislative majority and can secure legislative approval for all of its major programs.

The principal effect of American separation of powers is a great expansion of the number of officials with formal roles in all policy decisions. The very size and independence of this group—which includes the president and other executive branch officials, Republican and Democratic leaders of the House and Senate, majorities on various committees in both chambers, and often each individual member of Congress—ensures that the policy-making process will be fractious, decentralized, and dominated by a continuing need for compromise.

Various critics have long urged constitutional change to limit separation of powers. A century ago, Woodrow Wilson criticized the system as unacceptably dispersing power and responsibility across the executive and legislative branches. Today's reformers, including former Carter aide Lloyd Cutler, make the same charges. They also stress what they consider to be the special problems that separation of powers poses in an age of big government and complex, fast-moving problems.

Opponents of the proposed reforms deny that any major constitutional change is the answer. They defend separation of powers as providing constitutional means of blocking unwise and precipitate action. They stress that the picture painted of U.S. government as hamstrung and unable to act coherently is overdone. And they insist that separation of powers has contributed notably to maintaining Congress as a powerful and responsive representative institution.

Federalism was invented by the framers of the U.S. Constitution in 1787 to meet two contrasting objectives to which many Americans were committed: achieving a strong national union and preserving the states as important political units. *Federalism* is a system of government in which formal authority is shared by the national and the state governments. Today, about 20 countries have some form of federal system.

Federalism has a detailed and explicit base in provisions of the U.S. Constitution. Various articles and amendments specify the powers of the states and of the national government, impose restrictions on the states and extend guarantees to them, and treat interstate relations.

As American society has evolved, so has the federal system. In the localized society of the early nineteenth century, the states were the most important governmental units, and doctrines of states' rights flourished—including extreme ones like those proclaiming the right of nullification and secession.

After the Civil War established the permanence of the federal union, and as industrialization and technological development tied the country closer together and made it more interdependent, the role of the national government gradually expanded. Each subsequent stage of socioeconomic development produced greater political centralization.

At the end of the 1980s the states retain important roles in the American system of divided government. Their dependence upon Washington for funding has actually declined over the past decade, as the federal budget deficit and Reagan administration pressure have brought about reductions in grants-in-aid. Still, the federal government now enjoys an ascendancy in American constitutional theory that would have been unthinkable in earlier periods of the country's history.

FOR FURTHER STUDY

James Bryce, *The American Commonwealth* (New York: Macmillan, 1916), 2 volumes. The classic account of American institutions, including the separation of powers, written by a distinguished English theorist.

Martin Diamond, "The Federalist on Federalism: Neither a National Nor a Federal Constitution, But a Composition of Both," *Yale Law Journal* 86 (1977). A classic essay on the nature of American federalism by a theorist profoundly sympathetic to it.

Daniel J. Elazar, *American Federalism: A View from the States*, 3rd ed. (New York: Harper and Row, 1984). Perhaps the best general treatment of the historical development and present operations of the American federal system.

Henry J. Friendly, "Federalism: A Foreward," *Yale Law Journal* 86 (1977). A brilliant review of developments in American law affecting the operations of the federal system.

Morton Grodzins, *The American System* (New Brunswick, NJ: Transaction Books, 1983; edition revised by Daniel J. Elazar). An updating of Grodzins's classic analysis of American federalism.

Donald L. Robinson, *"To the Best of My Ability"* (New York: W. W. Norton, 1986). A lucid account of the historical development of separation of powers and a penetrating criticism of contemporary problems derived therefrom.

Woodrow Wilson, *Congressional Government: A Study in American Politics* (Baltimore, MD: The Johns Hopkins University Press, 1981; first published, 1885). A classical account of American national government in the late nineteenth century, lamenting the dispersion of power and the lack of political accountability.

Part 3

Governance

Chapter 6

Congress

It was not by chance that the framers devoted the first article of the U.S. Constitution to Congress. They expected the legislature to be the strongest branch of the new government. They also considered it the most important branch, because representative democracy simply could not exist in the absence of an autonomous legislature able to enact laws and be accountable ultimately to the people. Much has happened over the past two centuries to alter the operations of Congress and its place in the American governmental system. Today few would consider it the dominant branch. The role of the president and the executive branch has become too great for that. But Congress is still in the middle of the policy process.

Article I, Section 8, of the Constitution enumerates the powers of Congress. "The Congress shall have Power," Section 8 begins, "to lay and collect Taxes . . . to pay the Debts and provide for the common Defense and general Welfare of the United States. . . ." The section then continues its expansive list of Congress's powers, including:

To regulate Commerce with foreign Nations, and among the several States . . .;

To coin Money [and] regulate the Value thereof . . .; To establish post Offices and post Roads;

To declare war . . .;

To raise and support Armies . . . [and] to provide and maintain a Navy. . . .

The last clause of Section 8 contains the most sweeping grant of legislative power: "To make all Laws which shall be necessary and proper for carrying into Execution the foregoing Powers, and all other Powers vested by this Constitution in the Government of the United States. . . ." Known as the *"**necessary and proper**"* clause, this grant has been deemed sufficient over the last half-century to support any legislative commitment that Congress has wanted to make.

THE 1988 TRADE BILL: CONGRESS IN ACTION

No single piece of legislation can illustrate all of the complex workings of our national legislature and how the legislature fits into our larger system of divided government. But work on one recent bill, a massive effort to change and codify U.S. trade policy, gives us a good general introduction to Congress in action.

The late 1980s have seen a wide-ranging debate over America's economic position in the world community—and what should be done about it. In the face of a large gap between what this country imports and what it sells abroad—the trade deficit—global "competitiveness" emerged as a prime Washington buzzword. Proposals for action have run from improving education to providing assistance to industries struggling to regain their world position, from measures to lower barriers to U.S. sales in other countries to restricting foreign products coming into this country.

The need for global competitiveness

Against this backdrop, Congress began a drive early in 1987 for comprehensive trade legislation. Republican and Democratic differences on how to proceed had blocked legislation in the preceding (99th) Congress, and this time members in both parties sought compromises that would avoid another such partisan stand-off. On February 5, 1987, Lloyd Bentsen (D-Texas), chairman of the Senate Finance Committee, which has jurisdiction over key elements of trade legislation, introduced a bill with strong bipartisan support. Eighteen months later, Michael Dukakis was to choose Bentsen as his vice-presidential running mate, citing the senator's role in the trade legislation as one factor that led to his selection. The bill Bentsen introduced in February 1987 was co-sponsored by 56 senators—31 Democrats and 25 Republicans—among them majority leader Robert Byrd (D-W.Va.) and minority leader Robert Dole (R-Kan.). It contained a variety of different provisions that would:

Senate Finance Committee introduces trade legislation

- extend the president's authority to negotiate international trade agreements but require him to consult more with Congress on these matters;

- establish expedited congressional procedures for considering trade agreements;

- increase eligibility for assistance to workers who have lost their jobs as a result of foreign competition, and fund this program by levying a new customs duty on commercial imports of up to 1 percent of their value;

The U.S. Capitol in Washington, D.C.— Senate chamber on left, House chamber on right.

- enable industries injured by foreign competition to get relief more easily. Increased tariffs on imports were one form this might take, quota limits on imports another;

- require that the president take retaliatory action against nations determined to have engaged in unfair trade practices with the United States, unless he can stipulate that the retaliation would harm the American economy;

- tighten laws against "dumping," the sale in the United States by foreign producers of goods below cost in efforts to increase their market share and harm American producers;

- create in the White House a new council to coordinate U.S. trade policy.

Reagan administration submits revised proposal

The Reagan administration was unhappy with a number of these provisions, even though they had substantial support among congressional Republicans. Part of the administration's unhappiness involved the ongoing "turf" battles between the executive and legislative branches under the separation of powers. The administration didn't like Congress telling it in the proposed trade legislation that it had to take retaliatory action against unfair competition; it argued that the president and his trade advisers should have the discretion to move in the manner they considered most effective in situations that are often of great complexity. Apart from this, the president insisted that freer trade, not more barriers, was the proper goal, and that means relying on retaliatory barriers were likely only to prompt other countries to take more such actions themselves. The administration sent its own proposals to Capitol Hill—among them measures to make U.S. businesses more competitive and to stimulate technological development by spending more for scientific and high-tech research.

The U.S. has a two-house national legislature. Both the House of Representatives and the Senate must pass trade measures—and all other measures—before they can be sent to the president for his signature to become law. The Democrats had a majority in both the House and Senate, but the two chambers had some different ideas on what the final trade bill should be like. And, as we will see, the Reagan administration's position had stronger support in the Senate.

The key committee on the House side is Ways and Means—the revenue committee, just as Finance is the Senate's revenue committee. In the winter of 1987, Ways and Means chairman Dan Rostenkowski (D-Ill.) began to unveil the outlines of his own trade proposals. He said that he, too, was seeking compromise. "I'm not trying to write legislation to please Lane Kirkland," Rostenkowski said. "I'm trying to write legislation that will be signed by the president." Kirkland is president of the country's principal labor federation, the AFL-CIO; like many other labor leaders, he was advocating strong restrictions on imports—a position diametrically opposed to the administration's strong free-trade stance. Still, Rostenkowski supported the goals of an amendment to the previous year's trade bill that had been pushed by Congressman Richard A. Gephardt (D-Mo.). The Gephardt amendment would require the reduction of imports from countries that do not act decisively to reduce their large trade surpluses with the United States. Japan was one prime target, South Korea another. "We can amend the Gephardt language," Rostenkowski said, "but we cannot compromise the principle involved."[1]

In fact, the Ways and Means Trade subcommittee did compromise the principle somewhat in the trade package that it sent along to the full committee on March 12. Specifically, it eliminated the mandatory percentage cut in foreign countries' trade surpluses with the United States that was a prime feature of the Gephardt amendment. The subcommittee bill still was more protectionist than the Senate Finance Committee bill—and much more so than the administration found acceptable. In a March 18 letter to Ways and Means Committee members, U.S. trade representative Clayton Yeutter outlined administration objections to the emerging House bill. "If the [objectionable] provisions are not either eliminated or substantially improved," Yeutter wrote in his detailed nine-page letter, "I would find it exceedingly difficult to recommend that the president sign any trade bill including them. . . ."[2]

House Ways and Means Committee submits its own proposed legislation

Ways and Means Trade subcommittee revises House bill

[1] John Cranford, "Trade Bill: Options Aired, Markup Postponed," *Congressional Quarterly*, March 7, 1987, p. 433.
[2] John Cranford, "Conflicts Sharpen as House Trade Bill Advances," *Congressional Quarterly*, March 21, 1987, p. 519.

On the Senate side, the trade bill the Finance Committee approved on May 7, 1987 followed very closely the outlines of Senator Bentsen's February proposals. The committee vote was an overwhelming 19–1. The only dissenting vote was cast by Malcolm Wallop (R-Wy.), who attacked the bill's "definite protectionist slant."

Additional Senate and House committees contribute

Finance and Ways and Means were the key committees responsible for developing trade legislation. The package was so broad, however, that a number of other committees in both the House and Senate were involved in its content. The Senate Judiciary Committee worked on a measure that would for the first time protect U.S. firms from foreign manufacturers who use patented processes without paying royalties. The Senate Commerce Committee worked on an amendment that would allow the Secretary of Commerce to investigate the national security or "essential commerce" effects of a foreign firm's proposed merger, joint venture with, or acquisition of a U.S. company. In all, nine Senate committees contributed to the trade bill.[3] In the House, 11 committees were involved in the trade legislation package—including the Rules Committee that, with its legislative management responsibilities, combined separate bills coming out of a number of the other committees into a single comprehensive measure to be acted on by the full House.

House and Senate pass separate revised trade bills

The House passed its trade bill—known formally as the Trade and International Economic Policy Reform Act of 1987—on April 30, 1987. After four weeks of vigorous debate, the Senate passed its bill on July 21—known officially as the Omnibus Trade and Competitiveness Act of 1987. The margins of passage in both chambers were about two to one. As is almost always the case with complex legislation, the House and Senate trade bills differed; the next step was the convening of a *conference committee:* a joint committee of the House and Senate charged with reconciling the differences and reporting a single measure back to the two chambers for final action. The House-Senate conference first convened on August 7. The committee grew to an enormous size of nearly 200 members, 155 from the House and 44 from the Senate. The bills that were being reconciled were highly detailed packages, each covering about 1,000 pages.

Conference committee reconciles differences

Other political players were intimately involved in the continuing deliberations on the trade bill, even though they weren't formally represented on the conference committee. The Reagan administration actively negotiated with House and Senate members to try to obtain a final version more to its liking. If the administration was satisfied, Congress would avoid a presidential veto. In addition, a great variety of business and labor organizations continued to lobby actively for specific provisions dear to their hearts. The elaborate search for compromises went on for months, well into 1988.

---

[3] Drew Douglas and David Rapp, "Foreign Relations, Judiciary, Labor Add to Trade Measure," *Congressional Quarterly*, June 6, 1987, pp. 1181–83.

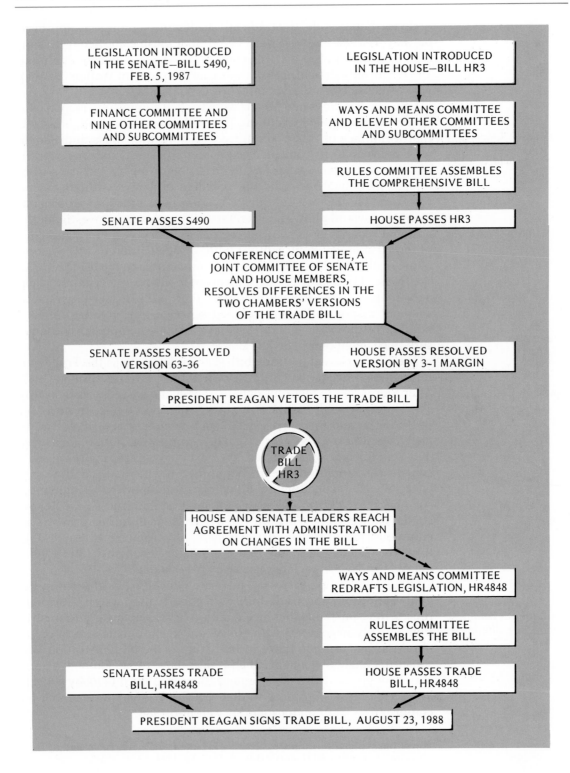

LEGISLATION INTRODUCED
IN THE SENATE—BILL S490,
FEB. 5, 1987

LEGISLATION INTRODUCED
IN THE HOUSE—BILL HR3

FINANCE COMMITTEE AND
NINE OTHER COMMITTEES
AND SUBCOMMITTEES

WAYS AND MEANS COMMITTEE
AND ELEVEN OTHER COMMITTEES
AND SUBCOMMITTEES

RULES COMMITTEE ASSEMBLES
THE COMPREHENSIVE BILL

SENATE PASSES S490

HOUSE PASSES HR3

CONFERENCE COMMITTEE, A
JOINT COMMITTEE OF SENATE
AND HOUSE MEMBERS,
RESOLVES DIFFERENCES IN THE
TWO CHAMBERS' VERSIONS
OF THE TRADE BILL

SENATE PASSES RESOLVED
VERSION 63–36

HOUSE PASSES RESOLVED
VERSION BY 3–1 MARGIN

PRESIDENT REAGAN VETOES THE TRADE BILL

TRADE
BILL
HR3

HOUSE AND SENATE LEADERS REACH
AGREEMENT WITH ADMINISTRATION
ON CHANGES IN THE BILL

WAYS AND MEANS COMMITTEE
REDRAFTS LEGISLATION, HR4848

RULES COMMITTEE
ASSEMBLES THE BILL

SENATE PASSES TRADE
BILL, HR4848

HOUSE PASSES TRADE
BILL, HR4848

PRESIDENT REAGAN SIGNS TRADE BILL, AUGUST 23, 1988

Figure 6.1
The 1988 Trade Bill
Here is the route that the 1988 trade bill took from its original introduction in the House and Senate, February 5, 1987, to final passage on August 23, 1988, after sustaining one presidential veto.

One item that deadlocked conference deliberations in early 1988 involved the issue of how to deal with foreigners who sold high-tech, military-related equipment to the Soviet Union. House conferees wanted retaliatory measures included, specifically to punish the Toshiba Corporation of Japan and Konsberg Vaapenfabrikk of Norway. Senate conferees wouldn't budge in their opposition to these provisions. Finally, in late March, the conferees accepted a compromise that would bar the two foreign firms only from selling to the U.S. *government* for the next three years. Even this relatively mild sanction was waived if essential parts were involved or existing contracts provided for sales.

By early April, House and Senate conferees had finally narrowed differences down to a few issues. The toughest of these was a requirement that U.S. corporations with 100 or more workers notify employees 60 days in advance if it were going to close a plant—to move it somewhere else, to consolidate factories to get greater efficiency, or any other reason. Business groups strongly opposed this measure; labor strongly backed it. The Reagan administration opposed the measure. Labor Secretary Anne Dore McLaughlin called it "inherently anti-competitive, anti-growth, and anti-trade." If it is kept in, she said, the president will veto the bill.[4]

Strong opposition to certain provisions

Congressional leaders wouldn't budge. Legislation worked out by the conferees—including the plant-closing provision—was reported back to the two chambers. It passed the House by a huge three-to-one margin on April 21, which meant that many Republicans (68 in fact) joined Democrats in supporting it. This tally meant that on the House side the bill was essentially veto-proof. A two-to-one margin is all that is required to override a presidential veto. The Senate was a different matter. Though the bill passed, the margin was 63 to 36, three votes short of the 66 that would be needed to override. (One member, Joseph Biden, D-Del., was recovering from serious surgery, so the total who in fact could vote on this measure was 99.) John Danforth (R-Mo.), who led GOP supporters of the bill, pronounced it virtually dead.

Conference committee bill passes House and Senate

The president vetoed the trade bill. The House overrode the veto by 308 to 113. Just one Democrat backed the president's position; 60 Republicans voted to override him. On June 7, however, the Senate sustained the president: 61 senators voted to overturn his veto. Only one Democrat, William Proxmire of Wisconsin, was opposed to the final bill.

President Reagan vetoes trade bill

This particular trade bill was dead—but not any trade bill. The president probably would have preferred having no bill at all, but many Republicans in Congress felt the folks back home expected them to pass some bill. They pushed the president and his aides to limit

[4]Elizabeth Wehr, "Dispute Over Final Trade Bill Narrows to a Few Tough Issues," *Congressional Quarterly*, April 9, 1988, pp. 936–37.

their objections to just a few provisions, so that these items could be stripped from the original bill and the measure then passed. Reagan agreed. Finally, on August 3, over eighteen months after Senator Bentsen offered his initial proposals, after intense lobbying, countless committee meetings, and endless compromises, an omnibus trade bill that the president could accept passed the Senate, having passed the House three weeks earlier. Reagan signed it into law on August 23. (See Figure 6.1.)

Objectional provisions stripped from vetoed measure

No one has gotten all or even most of what he or she wanted. Many, including the administration, had managed to block provisions they most opposed. The final law was less protectionist than labor had hoped, more protectionist than free traders wanted. Edmund T. Pratt, Jr., chairman of the Emergency Committee on American Trade and chairman of Pfizer, Inc., a big pharmaceutical company, said the legislation reflected "a broad national consensus on an appropriate trade policy for the United States."

Compromise trade bill is signed into law

ORGANIZATION OF CONGRESS

The American Congress is charged with representing the public in making laws. In this it resembles other national legislatures, such as the British Parliament, the French National Assembly, and the West German Federal Parliament. It differs from them, though, in its constitutional independence from the executive. As discussed in chapter 5, **separation of powers** distinguishes all of American government, including the relations of Congress and president. Separation of powers was certainly evident in work on the 1987–88 trade legislation.

A majority of the world's democratic governments are *parliamentary* in form, where executive authority is derived from the legislature. In such countries as Australia, Canada, Great Britain, Sweden, West Germany, Italy, India, and Japan, the chief executive official—variously called the prime minister, premier, or chancellor—holds a seat in the national legislature. So do the heads of the principal executive departments, called, together with the prime minister, the cabinet, council of ministers, or, simply, the government. They hold the reins of power in the government because they are the leaders of the legislative majority and are voted into office by the majority coalition. In the American scheme, the legislature and the executive are separately chosen and constitutionally distinct.

Parliamentary government and executive power

Bicameralism

Within Congress, the idea that power should be divided expresses itself through **bicameralism.** Legislative authority is assigned to two co-equal chambers, the Senate and the House of Representatives. Although two-house legislatures are not uncommon, the U.S.

Bicameralism

arrangement, where the two chambers share power equally, is rare. In parliamentary systems like Great Britain, West Germany, and Japan, one house has much more authority than the other. The British House of Commons, for example, elects the government and plays the major role in shaping legislation, while the House of Lords has come to have a distinctly inferior role.

In the United States, the framers provided for two chambers different in size, constituency, and term of office of their members. The House of Representatives, with a membership based on population, was (and is) the larger of the two bodies. In the first and second Congresses it had 65 members, compared to the Senate's 26. Since 1910 House membership has been fixed at 435. Composed of two senators from each state, the Senate had 96 members from 1910 until the late 1950s; when Hawaii and Alaska entered the Union, the total reached the present 100.

Congressional elections

The Constitution stipulates that the House of Representatives must be chosen through direct popular election; members are voted into office from districts of roughly equal population. In contrast, reflecting the federal character of the American union, the Constitution provides equal representation in the Senate for each state, regardless of state populations. Until ratification of the Seventeenth Amendment in 1913, the commitment to different constituencies for the Senate and House also included different election procedures: House members through direct popular ballot, senators by their state legislatures. The Seventeenth Amendment changed the latter provision by requiring direct popular election for the Senate. Regarding term of office, all House members are elected every two years. Senators serve six-year terms, with one-third of them up for election every biennium.

Contrasting legislative styles

The framers also believed that each chamber should possess its own distinctive legislative character. The House was to be what Madison called "the grand repository of the democratic principle of government."[5] With its short terms and popular election, it was expected to be sensitive to public opinion. At the same time, the House was thought likely to display certain weaknesses common to large, popularly elected legislatures: instability, impulsiveness, unpredictability, inclination to change decisions, and "a short-run view of good public policy." The Senate would be a counterbalance. It would be the source of "a more deliberate, more knowledgeable, longer-run view of good public policy."[6]

This sense of contrasting legislative styles is illustrated in a revealing anecdote about the two chambers. Thomas Jefferson had been in

[5] James Madison, *Notes of Debates in the Federal Convention of 1787* (Athens, Ohio: Ohio University Press, 1976), p. 39.
[6] Richard F. Fenno, Jr., *The United States Senate: A Bicameral Perspective* (Washington, D.C.: American Enterprise Institute for Public Policy Research, 1982), p. 3.

Television comes to the Senate.

France during the Constitutional Convention. Upon returning to the United States, he asked his fellow Virginian George Washington why the latter had agreed to a second chamber, rather than providing for a single-house legislature responsible to the people. "Why," asked Washington, "did you pour that coffee into your saucer?" "To cool it," Jefferson allegedly replied. "Even so," Washington responded, "we pour legislation into the senatorial saucer to cool it." Not all of the framers' expectations have been fulfilled. The Senate is quite capable of acting precipitately, and the House coolly and deliberately. All in all, though, the requirement that both chambers must consider and approve a piece of legislation before it becomes law has remained an important practical element of American legislative practice. As political scientist Richard Fenno observes, while "the framers did not . . . create one precipitate chamber and one stabilizing chamber . . . they did force decision-making to move across two separate chambers, however those chambers might be constituted."[7]

Effects of terms of office

Such characteristics of the Senate and House as the former's smaller size, larger constituencies, and less frequent elections have also led the two chambers to operate somewhat differently. For example, Fenno concludes that senators' six-year terms do insulate them a bit from the fluctuating currents of public opinion. Some senators acknowledge the "statesman" proposition: their longer terms make it easier for them to do what they think is right. One senator interviewed by Fenno in the first year of his term observed candidly that "I wouldn't have voted against [a piece of legislation] . . . as I did last Saturday if I had to run in a year. The six-year term gives you insurance. Well, not exactly—it gives you a cushion. It gives you some squirming room." Reflecting upon the Senate's 1978 passage of the controversial Panama Canal Treaty, which ceded sovereignty of the Canal back to Pan-

[7] Ibid., p. 5.

ama, another senator doubted that "you would have ever gotten [it] through the House. Not with the election coming up and the mail coming in so heavily against it. The [private] sentiment in the House might not have been any different from what it was in the Senate. But you could never have passed it."[8]

HOUSE AND SENATE RULES

Like other democratic legislatures, Congress has developed various rules and procedures governing the way it handles the flow of legislative business. While the impetus for them has typically been nothing more than the need to establish orderly and expeditious procedures, the rules have sometimes become highly consequential politically, as members have learned how to manipulate them for their own particular legislative objectives.

Before it becomes law, any bill must be passed in exactly the same form by both House and Senate.

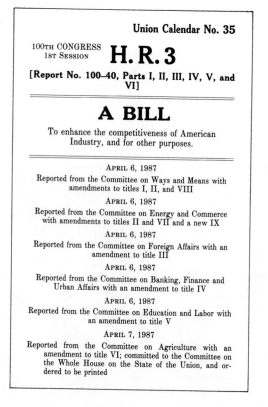

Union Calendar No. 35

100TH CONGRESS
1ST SESSION **H. R. 3**

[Report No. 100–40, Parts I, II, III, IV, V, and VI]

A BILL

To enhance the competitiveness of American Industry, and for other purposes.

APRIL 6, 1987
Reported from the Committee on Ways and Means with amendments to titles I, II, and VIII

APRIL 6, 1987
Reported from the Committee on Energy and Commerce with amendments to titles II and VII and a new IX

APRIL 6, 1987
Reported from the Committee on Foreign Affairs with an amendment to title III

APRIL 6, 1987
Reported from the Committee on Banking, Finance and Urban Affairs with an amendment to title IV

APRIL 6, 1987
Reported from the Committee on Education and Labor with an amendment to title V

APRIL 7, 1987
Reported from the Committee on Agriculture with an amendment to title VI; committed to the Committee on the Whole House on the State of the Union, and ordered to be printed

---

[8] Quoted in ibid., p. 37. For an insightful study of self-perceived constituency pressures on members of the House of Representatives, see idem, *Home Style: House Members in Their Districts* (Boston: Little, Brown, 1978).

Extended Debate and Filibuster

Filibuster

Because it is much smaller than the House, the Senate is able to operate much more informally. Senate rules afford members greater freedom in floor debate. Senators are permitted to speak as long as they see fit on bills and other legislative issues, whereas the time for House debate is strictly rationed. Frequently, however, senators in the minority on a bill use the extended-debate provision not to air their views fully but to block a vote they know they would lose. The **filibuster** is simply a legislative talkathon, an effort by a minority to hold the floor so long that the majority gives up its effort to secure passage of a bill—because of the press of other business—or at least makes concessions. Senate history is full of instances where determined senators have literally talked bills to death. Southern senators' use of the filibuster to block civil rights legislation in the 1940s and 1950s is the most notable instance, but many different Senate blocs have filibustered for many legislative ends.

Cloture and Unanimous Consent Agreements

Cloture

Senators are jealous of their individual prerogatives and unwilling to eliminate the extended-debate provision. They have recognized, however, the need to cut off debate in some instances where it was being abused to thwart the majority. The **cloture** rule was first adopted in 1917. In its present form, it permits stopping debate upon the vote of three-fifths of the entire Senate membership—60 votes. When cloture

Sometimes filibusters have gone on so long that cots have had to be set up in the Capitol for congressmen.

is invoked, the bill must be brought up for final action without more than 100 hours of additional debate.

In order to expedite work on legislation, the Senate often dispenses with its time-consuming formal rules and follows privately negotiated agreements submitted to the full chamber for its unanimous approval. These agreements specify the time and procedures of debate on a bill, what parts of it are open to amendment, and, sometimes, when the vote on final passage is to take place. **Unanimous consent** means just what it says; such agreements do not come into force if even one senator objects.

Unanimous consent

House Rules and the Rules Committee

With 435 members, the House of Representatives has to be more structured and less individualistic than the Senate. If, for example, it gave its members the right of extended debate, it would literally be paralyzed. One of the ways the House has responded to its need for more formal and restrictive rules of operation has been to empower a committee on procedure.

The Rules Committee

Before any bill reaches the House floor, it must receive a special order or rule governing the terms of amendment and debate. Issuing these special orders is the task of a committee of the House, the Rules Committee. The rules specify such matters as how long a bill may be debated and how the time for debate is to be apportioned, and what kinds of amendments can be offered. In recent years, rules have become especially complex, requiring in some cases prior notice in the *Congressional Record* (the official report of congressional proceedings) of any amendment to be introduced, the authorization of only certain members to introduce amendments, and so on.

Rules Committee's political clout

As might be expected, the Rules Committee has often used its procedural control over House business for policy ends—in particular, to block legislation that the committee opposes. For a long period, roughly from the end of World War I until 1970, its independence from House majority leadership made the Rules Committee a potent obstructive force. While in theory the House could always discharge the Committee and bring a bill directly to the floor, it was reluctant to do so, in part because members were not much inclined to cross so influential a body. Over the past decade, however, the obstructiveness of the Rules Committee has been greatly reduced. Still firmly in the role of traffic cop, it has been made to function in a manner much more responsive to the majority party leadership.

Suspension Procedures

For speedy handling of noncontroversial legislation, the House has adopted a procedure whereby every Monday and Tuesday members

Suspension of rules

may vote to suspend the rules and consider minor bills—provided that no amendments (provisions added to a bill after it has been introduced) are offered, debate is limited to 40 minutes, and two-thirds approval is required for passage (rather than the usual simple majority). Concerned that some important legislation might slip through even given these restrictions, the Democratic caucus—which is the assembly of all House Democrats—has directed the Speaker to remove from consideration any bills requiring the expenditure of more than $100 million in one year. The Speaker is the chief presiding officer of the House. He is also the leader of the majority party, and is elected by that majority to his post.

Discharge Petitions

Discharge petitions

To dislodge a bill stalled in a House committee for more than 30 days following referral, the discharge rule allows the House to remove the committee from jurisdiction upon the petition of at least 218 members—a House majority. The petition is then placed on the discharge calendar; if the discharge petition is supported by a majority when it is called for a vote, the bill being discharged is brought to the floor for immediate consideration.

THE COMMITTEE SYSTEM

An army, the old adage has it, moves on its stomach. Its food supply determines its capacity to advance. In much the same way, it may be said that Congress moves on its committees. The legislative process in Congress is very much a committee process. Congressional committees play such an important role in large part because of congressional workload. American government does much more today than it did in the nineteenth century. More complicated pieces of legislation must be conceived, drafted, debated, and enacted. The number of bills introduced and laws enacted tell part of the story. Just 207 bills were introduced in the eighth Congress, which sat between 1803 and 1805; 111 were passed. By contrast, 9,885 bills and joint resolutions were introduced in the ninety-ninth Congress (1985–1987), and approximately 483 measures were enacted into law. Total federal spending provided for by Congress in 1803 was less than $8 million; in 1988, federal spending stood at $1.06 trillion.

Larger workload, expanding committees

One congressional response to these increasing demands has been longer sessions. In the early nineteenth century, Congress met for only short periods each year: after fall harvesting and before spring planting. Many members were farmers, and their needs had to be accommodated. Even as late as World War I, Congress was in session only nine months out of every twenty-four. Today, however, the national legislature is in nearly continuous session, punctuated by fairly short recesses for vacation, campaigns, and district work. A more important response to the growth of legislative business has been to do most of the work in committees. A chamber of 435 representatives, or 100 senators, operating as a committee of the whole for the consideration of legislation, cannot begin to cope with the volume and variety of the contemporary legislative agenda.

Parliamentary government and committees

The dominant role of committees in the American legislative process cannot be explained solely by the amount of work to be done, however. The British Parliament also enacts a lot of complex legislation, but it has fewer committees than Congress, and more importantly, it relies on them much less for the conduct of its affairs. The reason for this is the tight party discipline that prevails in Parliament, leaving no room for strong autonomous committees. The government, consisting of the majority-party leadership, dominates the legislative process. It certainly does not want, and has not permitted, strong legislative committees to develop; the latter would only undermine the government's control.[9]

As a general rule, the stronger the political parties are in a legislature, and the tighter the control they maintain, the weaker committees are. In the U.S. Congress, party discipline and control are weak, and the committees are very strong.

Types of Committees

Standing committees

Congress has four principal types of committees: 1) *standing*, 2) *select* or *special*, 3) *joint*, and 4) *conference*. Together with their many subcommittees, the **standing committees** of Congress are where most of the work of legislating takes place. They are called "standing" because they are permanent units with continuing membership and staff. Among the 16 standing committees of the Senate are Agriculture, Nutrition, and Forestry; Appropriations; Armed Services; Energy and Natural Resources; Finance; Foreign Relations; and Judiciary. House standing committees (of which there are 22) include Appropriations; Armed Services; Banking, Finance, and Urban Affairs; Budget; Education and Labor; Public Works and Transportation; Rules; and Ways and Means. Every bill introduced into either house is referred to a standing committee responsible for the policy area in which it falls. The committee and its relevant subcommittee have the power to amend the measure as they see fit, and to delay action or speed it on its way. The committees sift through the immense volume of legislation introduced each session, work out compromises, and try to hammer out workable legislation.

[9] S. A. Walkland, "Committees in the British House of Commons," in John D. Lees and Malcome Shaw, eds., *Committees in Legislatures: A Comparative Analysis* (Durham, N.C.: Duke University Press, 1979), p. 256.

Select and special committees are of two main varieties: those established for the purpose of investigating problems and reporting on them to the parent chamber, as in the case of the House Select Committee on Aging and the Senate Select Committee on Intelligence; and those with membership from one party only, set up to perform party functions. Among the latter are the National Republican Senatorial Committee, which dispenses campaign funds to Republican Senate candidates, and the House Democratic Steering and Policy Committee, which acts as a kind of executive committee of the Democratic caucus and nominates Democrats for election by the caucus to the various standing committees when vacancies occur. In the one-hundredth Congress (1987–1989), there were twelve select and special committees in the House of Representatives, ten in the Senate.

Select and special committees

Joint committees serve as coordinating vehicles within the bicameral legislature, drawing their membership from both the House and Senate. In recent decades, they have been used largely for congressional oversight (discussed later in this chapter) and policy exploration. Joint committees have functioned in such areas as atomic energy, defense production, and the reduction of federal expenditures. There were five joint committees in the one-hundredth Congress, the most important of which were the Joint Committee on Taxation and the Joint Economic Committee.

Joint committees

Conference committees grow out of the requirement that every bill must pass the House and Senate in exactly the same form before it can become law. Conference committees adjust differences between the two chambers. They are set up to deal only with specific pieces of legislation; they have no life beyond the measures for which they were convened. When the House and Senate conferees agree upon a report, they submit it for approval to the full chambers, and it must be accepted or rejected without amendment. When both houses accept a conference report, the measure is passed and sent to the president for signing. If either chamber rejects a conference report, however, the bill is returned to the same or to a newly constituted conference committee. Conferees are supposed to consider only those portions of bills on which the two chambers disagree; and when the differences are modest, the conferees' discretion is in fact quite limited. But when the House and Senate versions differ more drastically, conference committees have much greater discretion and sometimes produce legislation at variance from what either chamber had envisioned. To curb runaway conference committees, the Legislative Reorganization Act of 1970 required them to supply the full chambers with statements on the reasoning behind their recommendations and the policy effects. This act also stipulated that conference committee reports could not be officially considered until at least three days after they were presented—when, hopefully, some members had found time to review the reports.

Conference committees

THE AGE OF SUBCOMMITTEES

House and Senate committees have long had subcommittees, for the same reason that the parent chambers themselves first established committees: to break the business of legislating into units of manageable size. Given the increasing volume and complexity of legislation, recourse to specialized subcommittees was unavoidable. For example, the House Appropriations Committee—charged with reporting spending bills for every area of federal activity—has thirteen subcommittees. Each subcommittee handles appropriations in one relatively manageable sector: agriculture, defense, transportation, and so on. (Figure 6.2 shows the place of subcommittees in the legislative process.)

Seniority and spreading the action

While the number of subcommittees has increased, especially in the House, where the count grew from 83 in the eighty-fourth Congress (1955–1957) to 143 during the one-hundredth (1987–1989), having gone as high as 151 in the ninety-fourth (1975–77), the big change has come in subcommittee autonomy. In the half-century or so from World War I until 1970, both the House and Senate permitted their affairs to be dominated by very strong and independent committee chairmen—congressional "barons" they were often called. These chairmen acquired and maintained their positions through **seniority:** a time-honored and rarely violated practice where the most senior member of the majority party on a committee was appointed chairman. Virtually impervious to removal no matter how arbitrary their conduct, the chairmen exercised broad control over committee business. They determined when committee meetings would take place, whether or when specific bills would be considered, what jurisdiction subcommittees would be assigned, what staff would be appointed, and so on. Subcommittees were then firmly under the thumb of any parent committee chairman who chose to exercise the powers available to him. In the early 1970s, however, a vast redistribution of power occurred in Congress, especially in the House of Representatives. Authority was taken away from the "barons" and redistributed among rank-and-file members. Known as **spreading the action,** this internal democratization has had wide ramifications; one major result is subcommittee autonomy.

A New Bill of Rights

Subcommittee autonomy

In January 1973 a committee of the House Democratic caucus, chaired by Julia Butler Hansen of Washington, recommended a plan which came to be known as the "Subcommittee Bill of Rights." It freed subcommittees from the control of the parent committee chairmen. Each subcommittee's jurisdiction is now determined by all the majority party members of the parent committee and is not easily altered. Bills

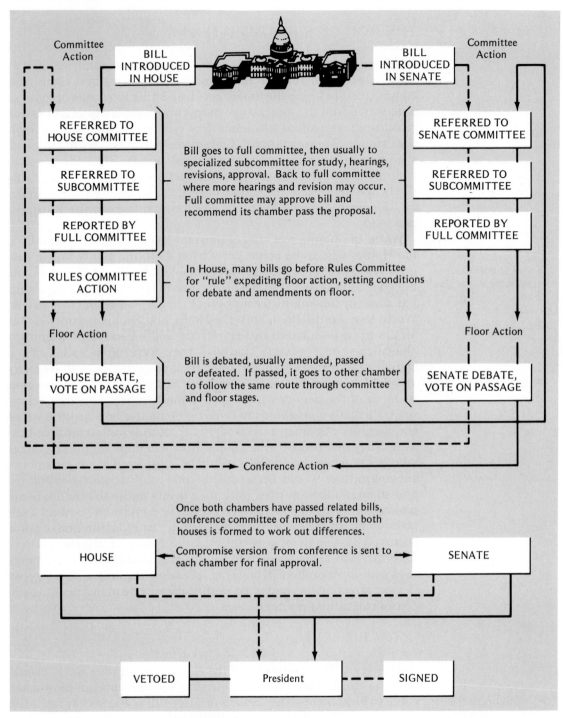

Committee Action

BILL INTRODUCED IN HOUSE

BILL INTRODUCED IN SENATE

Committee Action

REFERRED TO HOUSE COMMITTEE

REFERRED TO SUBCOMMITTEE

REPORTED BY FULL COMMITTEE

RULES COMMITTEE ACTION

Bill goes to full committee, then usually to specialized subcommittee for study, hearings, revisions, approval. Back to full committee where more hearings and revision may occur. Full committee may approve bill and recommend its chamber pass the proposal.

REFERRED TO SENATE COMMITTEE

REFERRED TO SUBCOMMITTEE

REPORTED BY FULL COMMITTEE

In House, many bills go before Rules Committee for "rule" expediting floor action, setting conditions for debate and amendments on floor.

Floor Action

HOUSE DEBATE, VOTE ON PASSAGE

Bill is debated, usually amended, passed or defeated. If passed, it goes to other chamber to follow the same route through committee and floor stages.

Floor Action

SENATE DEBATE, VOTE ON PASSAGE

Conference Action

Once both chambers have passed related bills, conference committee of members from both houses is formed to work out differences.

HOUSE

Compromise version from conference is sent to each chamber for final approval.

SENATE

VETOED

President

SIGNED

Source: Congressional Quarterly Guide to Current American Government, Spring 1986 (Washington, D.C.: CQ, Inc., 1986), p. 145.

◀

Figure 6.2
How a Bill Becomes Law
This graphic shows the most typical way in which proposed legislation is enacted into law. There are more complicated, as well as simpler, routes, and most bills never become law. Bills must be passed by both houses in identical form before they can be sent to the president. The path of a House bill is traced by a solid line, that of a Senate bill by a broken line. In practice most bills begin as similar proposals in both houses.

are automatically referred to the appropriate subcommittees in accord with the established jurisdiction. Subcommittees meet when they choose and subcommittee chairmen select subcommittee staff. Members of the majority party (in the House, this has been the Democrats continuously since 1955) bid in order of seniority for vacant subcommittee chairmanships, and are approved by a caucus of all parent committee Democrats. In short, committee chairmen can no longer appoint the subcommittee chairmen, "stack" subcommittee membership, or otherwise control members' work.

Spreading the action has been carried further. Under other provisions approved by the House Democratic caucus, no member can chair more than one subcommittee. No member can fill a second subcommittee vacancy before every other Democrat, submitting his claim in order of seniority, has gained one. In December 1976 the Democratic caucus ruled that no chairman of a full committee could chair a subcommittee on another committee; and in 1978 it decreed that upon reelection a Democratic representative could retain only one subcommittee membership—rather than two as was previously the case—before newly elected members could put in their bids.[10]

The House of Representatives had 22 standing committees and 143 subcommittees during the one-hundredth Congress; the Senate, 16 standing committees with 84 subcommittees. Counting special, select, and joint committees, with their subcommittees, Congress had a grand total of roughly 311 separate committees. The old back-bencher's dream of "every member a chairman" had come remarkably close to being realized. Over half of all House Democrats had a chairmanship in the one-hundredth Congress; in the smaller Senate, 49 of the 54 Democrats held one or more chairmanships.[11]

STAFFING CONGRESS

Over the past two decades, congressional staff has greatly expanded. Like the increase in subcommittees, the staff explosion has come in part as a response to greater demands of legislative business. The big staff expansion also reflects a successful search for independence. Congressional analyst Allen Schick notes that staff is the currency permitting congressmen to gain greater expertise and hence independence for the legislature from the executive branch, and for rank-and-

[10] James L. Sundquist, *The Decline and Resurgence of Congress* (Washington, D.C.: Brookings Institution, 1981), p. 382. The subcommittee movement received an initial boost from the Legislative Reform Act of 1946 which, among other things, reduced the number of standing committees from 43 to 19. As Roger Davidson and Walter Oleszek observed in *Congress Against Itself* (Bloomington, Ind.: Indiana University Press), many of the discarded committees became subcommittees of the now-larger remaining committees (p. 57).

[11] *1987–1988 Congressional Directory, 100th Congress*, pp. 445–570, passim.

file members from committee chairmen and other congressional leaders.[12]

Members' Staff

The greatest expansion has occurred among aides employed in the service of individual congressmen. Members' staffs more than tripled in size between the 1950s and the 1980s in both the House and Senate (Figure 6.3). Congressmen have put many of their new assistants to work back in their legislative districts. At present over 2,500 are so assigned—almost six per congressman. Members have found this useful in serving their constituents' needs for help in dealing with government, and useful as well as a little electoral machine made available to them year-round at public expense.

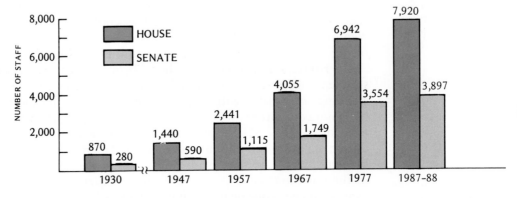

Figure 6.3
Personal Staffs of House and Senate Members since 1930

Source: Norman J. Ornstein et al., *Vital Statistics on Congress, 1987–88 Edition* (Washington, D.C.: American Enterprise Institute for Public Policy Research, 1987), p. 142; and for 1987–88, by officials of the House and Senate.

Committee Staff and Congressional Agency Staff

The number of assistants assigned to committees also grew over the 1960s and 1970s. Between 1979 and 1983, however, House committee staff growth leveled off, and Senate committee staffs were reduced by almost one-sixth. The cut on the Senate side occurred as the Republicans took control of the Senate in 1981 for the first time in a quarter-century and proceeded to fulfill their pledge to scale back committee staffing. But in the mid-1980s both House and Senate committee staffs again began to expand.

The four major research agencies of Congress—the General

[12]Allen Schick, "The Staff of Independence: Why Congress Employs More but Legislates Less," paper presented at the White Burkett Miller Center for Public Affairs, University of Virginia, October 1980, p. 13.

Accounting Office (GAO), the Library of Congress, the Congressional Budget Office (CBO), and the Office of Technology Assessment (OTA)— **Congressional research agencies** employ more than 10,000 additional staff members. Perhaps three-fourths of this total are not really congressional staff in anything more than a technical sense. The Library of Congress performs a general service in maintaining and making available to scholars the world's largest research library collection; only its Congressional Research Service works directly for Congress. And the GAO is a small army of auditors and accountants overseeing all federal spending. Figuring in cleaning and maintenance people, and the Capitol Police Force, congressional staff numbers more than 31,000. Of these, fewer than 20,000 actually work on legislative business.[13]

Legislatures Abroad

No other national legislature staffs itself so lavishly. The Canadian parliament comes closest, and it employs only about one-tenth as many assistants as Congress.[14] The contrast between Congress and Great Britain's Parliament is even more striking. House of Commons committees are very lightly staffed. In 1987, each member of Parliament (MP) received a personal allowance for secretarial and research assistance of (in dollar equivalents) about $36,500—about one-eleventh of what was provided at that time to a member of the U.S. House of Representatives.[15]

The Cost of Legislating

Each member of the U.S. House of Representatives in 1988 received a personal allowance of $406,560 for staff support and $105,500 to **Expense allowances** $306,500 for "official expenses," depending on certain contingencies such as the distance of his district from Washington. On the Senate side, each senator received between $716,000 and $1,440,000 for staff salaries, the precise amount determined by the size of the state he represented. In addition he was given extensive allowances for postage, travel, telephone, office furnishings, and the rental of office space in his home state. Whereas the total cost of operating Congress in 1955 was about $70 million, the price tag had climbed to $1.9 billion by 1988.[16]

[13] *Vital Statistics on Congress, 1987–1988 Edition,* pp. 137–40, passim.
[14] Michael Malbin, *Unelected Representatives: Congressional Staff and the Future of Representative Government* (New York: Basic Books, 1980), p. 10.
[15] *British Political Facts* (Strathclyde, Scotland: The Centre for the Study of Public Policy, University of Strathclyde, 1979); British Consulate General, New York, N.Y., unpublished 1988 data.
[16] These data are from Roger H. Davidson and Walter J. Oleszek, *Congress and Its Members* (Washington, D.C.: Congressional Quarterly Press, 1984), pp. 133, 245; and *Vital Statistics on Congress, 1987–1988 Edition* (Washington, D.C.: AEI, 1987), pp. 150–57, passim; Executive Office of the President, OMB, *Budget of the United States Government, FY 1989,* p. 6f–10.

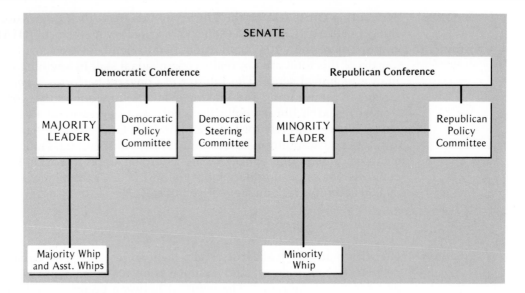

SENATE

Democratic Conference

Republican Conference

MAJORITY LEADER

Democratic Policy Committee

Democratic Steering Committee

MINORITY LEADER

Republican Policy Committee

Majority Whip and Asst. Whips

Minority Whip

Figure 6.4
Party Organization in the 100th Congress

The Speaker

Lack of party cohesion

PARTY ORGANIZATION

Those members of Congress who are Democrats, and those who are Republicans, vote as solid blocs against each other on all issues involving the partisan organization of the House and Senate. For example, majority-party members in the House always vote together and elect their leader to the office of **Speaker**—the chief presiding officer. Whichever party has a majority in each house names the chairmen of all the standing committees and subcommittees, and allocates to itself a majority of committee seats. Republicans and Democrats in both houses also establish their own party leadership bodies, shown in Figure 6.4.

Partisan discipline and coherence does not, however, extend beyond the divvying up of "the spoils of office." On the substance of policy, the Democratic and Republican parties in Congress cannot hold together. The observation of political scientist E. E. Schattschneider, made over 45 years ago, remains a valid description of the lack of party cohesion in Congress:

> The roll calls in the House and Senate show that party votes are relatively rare. On difficult questions, usually the most important questions, party lines are apt to break badly, and a straight party vote, aligning one party against the other, is the exception rather than the rule. . . . Often both parties split into approximately equal halves. . . . At other times one party votes as a unit but is joined by a substantial fraction of the other. Finally, a predominant portion of one party may be opposed by a predominant portion of the other party, while minorities, more or less numerous, on each side cross party lines to join their opponents . . .

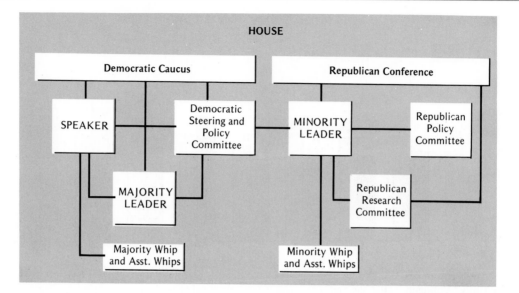

HOUSE

Democratic Caucus | Republican Conference

SPEAKER · Democratic Steering and Policy Committee · MINORITY LEADER · Republican Policy Committee

MAJORITY LEADER · Republican Research Committee

Majority Whip and Asst. Whips · Minority Whip and Asst. Whips

Figure 6.4 (continued)   [overall] the roll calls demonstrate that the *parties are unable to hold their lines in a controversial public issue when the pressure is on.*[17]

Recent congressional voting bears out Schattschneider's generalization. In the first session of the one-hundredth Congress (1987), only *Party unity voting* 53 percent of all recorded votes were what *Congressional Quarterly (CQ)* called "party unity" votes. And *CQ*'s usual standards for such votes reflect the general lack of cohesion in the congressional parties. A "party unity" vote is one where at least a bare majority of Democrats oppose a bare majority of Republicans.

Party unity voting, as it commonly is measured, has increased rather dramatically in the House of Representatives, but has not changed in the Senate. In 1978, just 33 percent of House votes saw a majority of Democrats opposing a majority of Republicans; in 1987, however, 64 percent of all votes were of the party unity variety (Figure 6.5). This latter figure is the highest recorded since *CQ* began computing party unity scores in 1955.

The increase in partisan voting in the House seems to have several different sources. Jim Wright (D-Tex.) became Speaker in 1987, upon *Sources of partisan* the retirement of Thomas P. O'Neill. Wright has made a concerted *voting* effort to tailor floor votes in such a way as to bring in all factions of his party. One tool that he has used involves getting the lopsided Democratic majority on the Rules Committee to craft highly restrictive rules for floor debate. When the Democrats get a House majority to vote for such a rule, they can prevent Republicans and conservative Democrats from collaborating on compromise amendments. In

[17] E. E. Schattschneider, *Party Government* (New York: Rinehart, 1942), pp. 130–32.

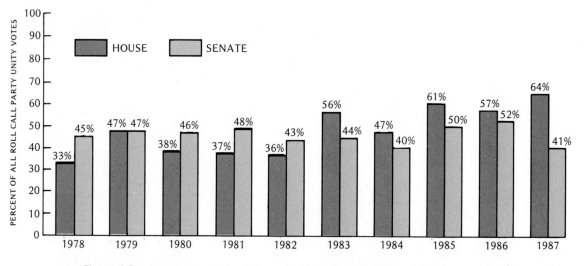

PERCENT OF ALL ROLL CALL PARTY UNITY VOTES

HOUSE SENATE

Year	House	Senate
1978	33%	45%
1979	47%	47%
1980	38%	46%
1981	37%	48%
1982	36%	43%
1983	56%	44%
1984	47%	40%
1985	61%	50%
1986	57%	52%
1987	64%	41%

Figure 6.5
"Party Unity" Voting in Congress since 1978 (in percent)

Source: Congressional Quarterly, November 15, 1986, p. 2902; January 16, 1988, pp. 101, 102, are "recorded votes in the Senate and House that split the parties, a majority of voting Democrats opposing a majority of voting Republicans."

addition, as Speaker, Wright has adopted a highly partisan style—matching and encouraging the more partisan and confrontational approach favored by many younger House Republicans.

The increase in party unity voting in the House of Representatives began to be evident before Wright became Speaker, though, and it clearly has other precipitants. The most important of these is the increased ideological coherence of the two parties in the House. There are fewer conservative Democrats, especially from the South—reflecting in part the increasing role of blacks in southern Democratic politics—and fewer moderate to liberal Republicans. As a more liberal House Democratic delegation faces a more conservative Republican membership, a growth of party unity voting has naturally followed.

Increase in party unity voting

Responding to the more ideologically coherent makeup of the two parties in the House, *CQ* began in 1987 computing new, more demanding measures of party unity voting. From this work we see that in 1987, 75 percent or more House Democrats opposed 75 percent or more Republicans on 32 percent of all roll calls. Just 20 percent for roll-call votes in the Senate met this "75 percent standard."

Still, party voting remains low in the American Congress as compared to most democratic legislatures. Even in the House where partisanship has been on the rise, the parties were cohesively aligned against each other—90 percent or more Democrats on one side, 90 percent or more Republicans on the other—on only 10 percent of roll call votes in 1987.[18]

Low party voting as compared to other democratic legislatures

[18]"Parties Close Ranks When Control Is at Stake," *Congressional Quarterly*, January 16, 1988, pp. 101–9.

American political parties are relatively *undisciplined*, a subject we discuss further in chapter 13. In most democracies the government—the prime minister and the cabinet—are members of the legislature and are voted into their executive posts by the legislative majority. Were Conservative MPs in the British House of Commons to cross party lines and vote with the opposition Labor party, they would, in the parliamentary tradition, be declaring "no confidence" in the Conservative government and would remove it from office. The very structure of legislative–executive relations in a parliamentary system strongly encourages party discipline and unity. But the opposite applies in the American system, given separation of powers. The president holds office for a fixed term, independent of Congress. His tenure is unaffected by how congressmen vote. Party leaders try to exert pressure, of course, and they can appeal to feelings of party loyalty. There are no compelling structural incentives for party unity voting.

THE COMPOSITION OF CONGRESS

Requirements for office

The Constitution sets only three requirements for congressional membership: 1) Before taking office, senators and representatives must have been citizens of the United States for at least nine and seven years, respectively; 2) a senator must be at least 30 years of age and a representative at least 25 years; and 3) each member must be an

"*I propose legislation. I do my best to aid in the process of government. And I try like hell to keep my name out of 'Doonesbury.'*"

Drawing by Ziegler; © 1985 The New Yorker Magazine, Inc.

inhabitant of that state in which he shall be chosen. Not surprisingly, though, the membership of Congress has a much more distinctive cast than these general and nonrestrictive standards dictate.

Party Membership

Partisan ties are surely the most important entrance requirements. Although political party organizations are relatively weak in the United States compared to other democracies, and many Americans now hold their party loyalties very lightly, one still does not, with rare exception, gain election to Congress without a strong party connection—and, specifically, without ties to either the Democratic or the Republican party. The largest group of senators and representatives to come to office in the past half-century unattached to either of the two major parties were the 17 elected in 1936. No Congress since World War II has had more than three members who were not Democrats or Republicans. Every congressman and senator elected in 1988 belonged to one of the two major parties.

Democratic party domination of Congress

Since the New Deal realignment made them the majority party more than a half-century ago, the Democrats have dominated Congress with a consistency unequaled by any other party in American history. Of the last 29 Congresses (from the seventy-third chosen in 1932 to the one-hundred and first elected in 1988) only two had Republican majorities in both House and Senate—the eightieth, elected just after World War II, and the eighty-third, which came in with Dwight Eisenhower's first-term victory in 1952. The Democrats have had majorities, usually very large ones, in the House of Representatives for all but four years since 1930. When the GOP ("Grand Old Party," as the Republicans came to be called in the late nineteenth century) gained control of the Senate in Ronald Reagan's big 1980 victory, and retained it in 1982 and 1984, these were only their third, fourth, and fifth upper-chamber successes since 1932. The box score for the last 29 Congresses shows a lopsided electoral game: 24 Congresses with the Democrats controlling both houses, two with the Republicans controlling both, and three with split-party control. The early 1980s are the closest the Republicans have come to a "congressional era" since the Great Depression. Their Senate majorities from 1981 through 1986 represent the only time in 50 years that they have controlled either house of the national legislature for three consecutive terms.

Social and Religious Background

Congressmen generally look like members of a national political elite. They are more highly educated than the public at large, come disproportionately from a few prestigious occupations, and are far above average in wealth. Virtually every senator and congressman has a college degree. A majority have done some form of graduate work, with law school training by far the most common. In 1987, 184 House members and 62 senators listed their previous occupation as lawyer.[19] In the same year, 142 in the House and 28 in the Senate had been businessmen or bankers. Public service / politics ranked third, with 94 representatives and 20 senators claiming this background. Education was fourth, with 38 representatives and 12 senators having been teachers, professors, or educational administrators. Journalism and agriculture now run fifth, with all other professions very thinly represented. Early in the twentieth century, the Senate acquired a reputation as a club for millionaires. Its present composition does little to dispute that status. About a third of all senators are now millionaires—a position they did not derive from their relatively modest senatorial salaries of $89,500 in 1987–88. House members are generally of upper-middle-class standing; only 30 or so are millionaires.

Educational and economic makeup of Congress

The religious makeup of congressmen differs significantly from that of the general public. But this is not unusual for a group of national leaders, for certain denominations are generally stronger among high-status groups. Of all senators and representatives in 1987, 27 percent were Catholics, roughly the proportion of Catholics in the general populace. But Episcopalians and Presbyterians—small denominations in the country, with members of notably high social status—had large numbers of congressional adherents; while the biggest Protestant denomination nationally, the Baptists, had relatively few adherents in Congress. Eleven percent of the members of both houses in 1987 listed themselves as Episcopalians, 11 percent as Presbyterians, and only 10 percent as Baptists. Seven percent were Jewish.[20]

Religious makeup of Congress

Women and blacks in Congress

Every Congress in American history has been composed disproportionately of white males. In recent years, though, the number of women and blacks has been edging upward. In the elections of 1986, 23 blacks won election to the House of Representatives—three more than in the preceding Congress. All of them are Democrats. The 23 women elected to House seats in 1986, together with the two senators who are women, surpasses by one the total of 24 elected in 1984. Women in the 100th Congress were evenly divided between the two parties: twelve were Democratic representatives, eleven Republican representatives, one a Democratic senator, and one a Republican senator (see Table 6.1).

---

[19] *Vital Statistics on Congress, 1984–1985 Edition*, pp. 21, 24.
[20] These data have been adapted from *Vital Statistics of Congress, 1984–1985 Edition*, pp. 28–29; and from an analysis performed by staff of *Congressional Quarterly* following the 1986 elections (*Congressional Quarterly*, November 8, 1986, pp. 2861–63).

Table 6.1
Women and Blacks in Congress since 1917

	Women		Blacks	
Congress	*D*	*R*	*D*	*R*
65th (1917)	–	1	–	–
70th (1927)	2	3	–	–
75th (1937)	6	1	1	–
80th (1947)	3	5	2	–
85th (1957)	9	7	3	–
90th (1967)	5	6	6	1
95th (1977)	13	5	16	1
99th (1985)	12	12	20	–
100th (1987)	13	12	23	–

Source: Congressional Quarterly Weekly Report, November 8, 1986, p. 2863; 1987–1988 *Congressional Directory,* 100th Congress, passim; U.S. Bureau of the Census, *Statistical Abstract of the United States,* 1986, p. 249; idem, "The Social and Economic Status of the Black Population in the United States: An Historical View, 1790–1978," *Current Population Reports,* series P-23, no. 80, 1979, p. 154; M. Christopher, *Black Americans in Congress* (New York: Crowell, 1976), pp. 309–11.

THE CHANGING CONGRESS

Today's Congress is the product of two centuries of evolution and change. While its formal position in the American constitutional scheme is essentially the same now as it was in 1789, its role in the dynamic process of policy making is very different. Congressional–presidential relations have seen important shifts, and Congress's internal distribution of power has changed as well.

Early Legislative Predominance

Through much of the first century after independence, Congress was the dominant branch of U.S. government. This status was in accord with the preferences of most Americans. Their experience with the British Crown and governors of the colonies had engendered among them a strong mistrust of executive authority. After independence, this mistrust expressed itself in state constitutions that "produced what was tantamount to legislative omnipotence."[21] The national government under the Articles of Confederation made no provision at all for executive authority.

The new constitution drafted in 1787 was a highly conscious effort to end government-by-the-legislature and provide for a coherent, active,

---

[21]Charles C. Thach, Jr., *The Creation of the Presidency, 1775–1789: A Study in Constitutional History* (Baltimore, Md.: Johns Hopkins University Press, 1969), p. 34.

countervailing executive authority. Yet even the Constitution's framers expected Congress to dominate the new governmental system. And following the first 15 years or so under the Constitution—when the great Federalist leaders in President George Washington's cabinet, and subsequently President Thomas Jefferson and his aides, provided relatively strong executive leadership—Congress did in fact become the governmental fulcrum.

Congress at the center

The Congressional Caucus

Henry Clay and the House caucus

At the beginning of the nineteenth century, the House of Representatives was the more prominent of the two legislative chambers. Most legislation in the early years originated there rather than in the Senate. House leadership was especially strong under Henry Clay, who served as Speaker for three separate terms: 1811–14, 1815–20, and 1823–25. Clay dominated the House caucus of the Democratic-Republican party—the assembly of all members of that party in the lower chamber—while the caucus was the most influential element of American government. Up until the 1820s, the caucus picked the ruling Democratic-Republican party's presidential candidates: Thomas Jefferson in 1804, James Madison in 1808 and 1812, and James Monroe in 1816. The president was in effect the nominee of a party system centered in the House of Representatives.

John Quincy Adams in Congress

Indicative of the standing of Congress in general, and of the House in particular, is the career of John Quincy Adams of Massachusetts, the son of the second president and himself the sixth president (1825–29). After losing his bid for a second presidential term, Adams ran for the House, won, and went on to play an active and distinctive part in House affairs. Today, we simply cannot imagine a president seeking election to the House of Representatives following his term as chief executive.

The Senate Giants

By the 1830s the balance of strong leadership had shifted from the House to the Senate. Henry Clay's decision in 1831 to run for a Senate seat is symbolic. The Senate's smaller membership and longer term of office proved attractive to nationally aspiring leaders. In addition, the election of senators by the state legislatures gradually led to the most important state party leaders becoming senators. With such political muscle, the Senate's stature grew. From the time of Andrew Jackson up to the Civil War, Senate giants like Clay of Kentucky, Daniel Webster of Massachusetts, and John Calhoun of South Carolina were the most prominent American politicians.

The Civil War changed the legislative–executive balance temporarily by putting a premium on presidential leadership. But with the end of the war and the assassination of President Lincoln in 1865, the

Henry Clay holding sway over the House.

Congressional ascendancy

era of congressional ascendancy resumed with a passion. Finally in control of both houses of Congress, the so-called "Radical Republicans" moved quickly to impose their own vision of Reconstruction on the defeated South. The house impeached President Andrew Johnson in 1867, and the Senate almost got the two-thirds majority needed to convict him and remove him from office. (Johnson's impeachment will be discussed in detail in chapter 7.)

Age of strong party leadership

While Johnson's successors managed to stabilize the powers of the presidency, the predominance of Congress was largely unchallenged for the rest of the century. A young political scientist, Woodrow Wilson, voiced this reality in the title of his classic work, *Congressional Government*, published in 1885. Wilson noted that "the business of the President, occasionally great, is usually not much above routine. Most of the time it is mere administration, mere obedience to directions from the masters of policy, the Standing Committees [of Congress]."[22] Over the 1880s and 1890s, however, power shifted within Congress as strong party leadership developed in both House and Senate. This gave the country its only era of legislature-based party government. There were two stages to this development.

The Ascendancy of the Speaker

In the first, the Speaker of the House of Representatives managed to accumulate an impressive array of prerogatives. By the time Thomas

[22] Woodrow Wilson, *Congressional Government* (New York: Houghton-Mifflin, 1913; first published, 1885), pp. 253–54.

The Speaker as "boss"

B. Reed held the post in 1889–91 and 1895–99, the office had assumed such governmental authority that the Speaker was likened to a prime minister. This ascendancy was short-lived. Even in their heyday, strong Speakers like Reed and his successor, Joseph Cannon, were burdened with such nicknames as "Boss" and "Czar." Reformers in both parties had a potent weapon with which to attack them: appeal to a populace inclined to view strong party leadership as undemocratic. In 1910, a House revolt against Cannon greatly weakened the Speaker's authority.

The Caucus and Its Power

The battle over the caucus

There was one final attempt at disciplined party government, this time with the caucus of House Democrats as the instrument of control. In 1911, the caucus directed Democrats on various committees not to report any legislation other than that submitted by the leadership "unless hereafter directed by this Caucus."[23] Two years before, the caucus had adopted a rule whereby a two-thirds vote in caucus would subsequently bind all party members. When a bill came up for a vote members were expected to vote as the party caucus instructed them. Violation resulted in the loss of such party entitlements as committee assignments. A similar rule applied in the Senate.

The outcry against government-by-caucus built up quickly. Republicans were outraged because the domination of the Democratic caucus left them with little influence. Reformers thought "King Caucus"

SPEAKER REED KNOWS HIS BUSINESS.
From the *World* (New York).

[23] Wilder H. Haines, "The Congressional Caucus of Today," *American Political Science Review* 9 (November, 1915), p. 697.

*Joseph Cannon,
Speaker of the House
early in this century.*

was as objectionable as the Speaker's control had been. The Secretary to the National Voters' League, established in 1913 by prominent proponents of congressional reform, charged that the Democrats had not abolished "Cannonism"—referring to the regime of Speaker Joseph Cannon—but only disguised it. A minority still ran Congress, now through the caucus rather than the office of Speaker.[24]

Defense of the caucus

Democrats fought back in defense of the caucus with some of the most coherent arguments for party government ever heard in the American legislature. Democratic Speaker Champ Clark of Missouri argued that

> responsibility rests upon the majority, and we shrink not from acknowledging our responsibility to the country and of acting accordingly. . . . We intend to place our ideas upon the statute books on the great questions now pressing for solution. . . . We must have organization in order to enact the will of the people into law, and we have got it. . . .[25]

But soon even Democrats joined in the attack on the caucus system. For a party member to be required by a binding caucus vote to back a bill that he disagreed with was unworthy of the Congress of the United States, Senator Gilbert Hitchcock of Nebraska argued in 1913. "Like all caucuses, I believe the fact to be that our Democratic caucus degenerated into a political machine."[26] Outside Congress the attack was even stronger. "King Caucus" was dethroned, never to be restored.

[24] Lynn Haines, *Your Congress* (National Voters' League, 1915), pp. 67, 76–77.
[25] *Congressional Record*, September 24, 1913, pp. 51, 57–59.
[26] *Congressional Record*, August 29, 1913, pp. 38, 58–59.

Leadership Shifts to the Presidency

By 1915 the brief American experiment with congressional party government had been abandoned. In the absence of central party leadership, power flowed back to the committees and to the chairmen, who dominated committee action. At the same time an equally momentous shift was propelling policy initiative away from the legislature altogether and to the presidency. Whereas government-by-the-legislature prevailed throughout most of the nineteenth century, government-by-the-president has been the rule in much of the twentieth century.

Why did initiative and leadership shift from Congress to the president? One factor was the growth of an industrial economy, which required an expansion of federal regulation and management. Theodore Roosevelt, a Republican who served as president from 1901 to 1909, was the first to recognize and articulate the growing public feeling that stronger presidential leadership was needed to handle the greater demands on government. He argued that "it was not only his [the president's] right but his duty to do anything that the needs of the nation demanded unless such action was forbidden by the Constitution or by the laws. . . ."[27]

Power shifts to the president

Although the Republican presidents of the 1920s were less assertive than either Theodore Roosevelt or Democrat Woodrow Wilson, they could not escape responsibility when things went sour. Herbert Hoover, rather than Congress, received most of the blame for the Great Depression and for the perceived inadequacy of the government's response to it. And the subsequent success of Franklin Roosevelt in providing vigorous leadership to combat problems of the Depression solidified the public's inclination to look to the presidency rather than to the legislature.

Presidential responsibility

After 1933, Congress found it increasingly necessary to confer responsibilities upon the executive branch. Given the commitment to greater governmental management of the economy and provision for public welfare, there was little alternative; a legislature is ill-suited to managing complex programs. But if it was inevitable that Congress would lose some ground to the presidency as big (executive) government developed in this century, it was by no means inevitable that executive growth would be uncritically endorsed and the presidency depicted in heroic terms. In the three decades or so after 1935, a mythology developed around the presidency. The president came to be seen as the great engine of democracy, "a kind of magnificent lion who can roam widely and do great deeds."[28]

The president as the "engine of democracy"

[27] Theodore Roosevelt, *An Autobiography* (New York: Scribners, 1925; first published, 1913), p. 357.
[28] Clinton Rossiter, *The American Presidency*, rev. ed. (New York: New American Library, 1960), p. 84.

The Great Depression produced widespread hardship—including the spread of shanty towns, nicknamed "Hoovervilles," outside many large cities.

A House of Misrepresentatives?

The other side of the coin was a growing inclination to disparage Congress. If the president was the engine that drove American government along its necessary course, Congress was the brakes, capriciously applied so as to make the journey fitful and incomplete. James McGregor Burns argued that Congress was so organized as to make coherent majority action exceedingly difficult.

> Even if majority support has been won for a program, organized minorities in either house can exploit the frailties of congressional organization and procedure to thwart the majority. Each chamber has an absolute veto on the other. In the Senate a band of dissidents can scuttle the program; even one determined senator can greatly dilute it.[29]

The great danger in all this was "legislative paralysis," the inability to mount needed governmental action except through sporadic bursts of successful presidential initiative. In Burns's critique, Congress was nothing short of the "House of Misrepresentatives."

Congress and the constitutional system

In the Congresses of 1935–65, with the absence of strong party leadership, power was fragmented, and the formulation of coherent policy often did depend upon executive initiatives. The dominant voice of the committee chairmen, who held their posts through seniority, not because they were loyal to the national party programs, detracted from Congress's representativeness. Still, the critique of Congress, like the accompanying cult of the presidency, lacked balance. If Congress

---

[29] James MacGregor Burns, *Congress on Trial* (New York: Harper & Brothers, 1954), p. 123.

was sometimes a roadblock to new policy initiatives, that was broadly in accord with explicit constitutional intent. In providing for separation of powers and checks and balances, the framers intentionally sided with barriers to precipitous governmental action. Supporters of the programs of activist presidents like Franklin Roosevelt and John Kennedy had reason to criticize congressional resistance, but those who opposed these presidential initiatives had equal reason to applaud the restraints Congress imposed. And Congress often did cooperate with presidents to produce an enormous amount of legislation during the New Deal and in succeeding decades. Congressional action was not nearly as slow, reactive, or conservative as its critics of the 1930s, '40s, and '50s suggested.

THE CONTEMPORARY CONGRESS

Congressional
resurgence

By 1965, Americans had for several decades been given a picture by the press and other commentary of the presidency as the repository of boldness and vision, and Congress of recalcitrance and conservatism. There was enough truth to these assertions to give them credibility, but there were also enough flaws in them to invite a powerful rebuttal in subsequent years. Four developments in 1965–75 changed presidential–congressional relations and the prevailing view of them. First, Congress was gripped by a new surge of political individualism. It has always been an institution where the individual member has been given much power and independence. But in the 1960s it experienced new demands by members that changed its internal operation and made it far more assertive vis-à-vis the president. Second, the idea that a strong president was good for the nation was shaken by a stream of events that came in rapid succession, especially the Vietnam War. Third, belief that presidential initiative was synonymous with liberal-progressive government was upset as the United States entered an era of aggressively conservative presidents. Suddenly, Congress became the progressive branch. And fourth, there was Watergate. The Watergate scandal gave the cult of the virtuous presidency a hard kick in its solar plexus, and for a time knocked most of the air out of it. The temporary weakening of the presidency—with Richard Nixon forced to resign from office, Gerald Ford left to pick up the pieces, and Jimmy Carter desperate to project a new model of presidential comportment—gave Congress an extraordinary opportunity to reassert itself.

Congressional Individualism

Political individualism—the antithesis of party regularity and cohesion—has been both a cause and an effect of the weakness of political

Political individualism

party organizations in the United States. The new wave of political individualism of the 1960s was heightened by the communications media. Television, a personality-emphasizing institution, became the dominant medium of mass communication in the 1950s and 1960s. From this and other structural changes a new type of congressman gradually emerged: more assertive and less inclined to defer to leadership, whether in Congress or the executive branch.[30]

Democrats and congressional reform

Three recent elections (1958, 1964, 1974) are especially important in the conversion of Congress because they brought in large numbers of Democratic newcomers. The Democrats have been the party in which changed outlooks and expectations have had the greatest actual impact—especially since, as the majority, they have had the power to implement new practices. Democrats gained 51 House seats in the elections of 1958, a year in which the country was gripped by the worst recession since World War II. In 1964, when Republican presidential nominee Barry Goldwater was buried electorally by Lyndon Johnson, Republicans lost 37 seats in the House. And in the election following the Watergate scandal (1974), House Democrats picked up a whopping 52 seats. These three big Democratic "freshman classes" generated a new assertiveness. They also pushed for shifts in the balance of power in Congress itself, especially in the House of Representatives, by spreading the action widely among all Democratic members. From roughly the end of World War I until the late 1960s, the majority party member who had served longest on a committee automatically became its chairman and was virtually assured of retaining that post as long as he remained in Congress. But in the late 1960s and early 1970s the seniority system was modified, with the provision that the Democratic caucus could displace chairmen who proved insufficiently responsive to the membership. As noted earlier, the power and autonomy of the subcommittees was greatly extended and the number of subcommittees increased. The staff available to individual members and to legislative committees was also greatly expanded. Through these and other means, power was distributed more widely among the rank-and-file of the majority party, and, to a much lesser degree, among the minority party as well.

Some Effects of Strong Presidents

America's involvement in Vietnam was a political watershed for the country. The loss of life which the war exacted, its staggering mate-

---

[30] In discussing "the forces fueling the individualistic tone of the present-day Congress," Thomas E. Mann puts the case bluntly: "As far as elections are concerned, senators and representatives are in business for themselves. . . . They are political entrepreneurs . . . seizing opportunities, generating resources, responding to pressures. . . ." Thomas E. Mann, "Elections and Change in Congress," in Thomas E. Mann and Norman J. Ornstein, eds., *The New Congress* (Washington, D.C.: American Enterprise Institute, 1981), p. 53.

President Lyndon B. Johnson working on a major address to the nation on his Vietnam strategy.

rial cost, the domestic protests it engendered, and the government's seeming inability to achieve a satisfactory resolution shook and divided the nation. For liberal Democrats, this was especially painful, since it was an activist liberal Democratic president, Lyndon Johnson, who led the country into heavy involvement in the Vietnam fighting. Many Democrats changed their thinking about the virtues of bold executive leadership.

A strong president and Vietnam

If Vietnam attested to the fact that strong presidents could serve ends that many deemed ill-advised, conservative activists like Richard Nixon and Ronald Reagan have taught many liberals that the "great engine of democracy" could be a strong force against their policy interests. In 1965 liberals could look back on 32 years of a presidency dominated by liberal Democrats, with Dwight Eisenhower's eight years merely a "breath-catching" interlude. In 1985, though, they looked back on the 32 years since Eisenhower's election as a period when Republicans dominated the presidency—a hold broken only by the eight years of the Kennedy and Johnson administrations and, somewhat dubiously from a liberal perspective, the four years of Jimmy Carter.

Strong presidents and conservatism

The Watergate Scandal

The errors of judgment and the betrayal of responsibility by a president and many of his closest aides—what Watergate has come to mean

Senators Howard Baker and the late Sam Ervin of the Senate Select Committee during the Watergate hearings of July 1973.

for many—capped off widespread disillusionment with presidential power, which had been growing since the mid-1960s. While most Americans still esteemed the office and looked to it for leadership, the presidency was stripped of the sometimes uncritical reverence that had enveloped it since the 1930s. In August 1974, few Americans would describe the president as "a kind of magnificent lion who can roam widely and do great deeds." The lion was caught lying and drummed out of office by a Congress responsive to public sentiment. Suddenly, separation of powers was looking a lot better than it had a decade earlier.

Watergate and the presidency

LEGISLATIVE RESURGENCE

Picture a legislature composed of ever more assertive and individualistic politicians, who concluded with increasing frustration that they had relinquished too much authority and initiative to the executive. Then picture them occupying a branch of government constitutionally independent of the executive and co-equal to it. Finally, picture them suddenly liberated from the myth that their executive-branch rivals had a corner on political wisdom and virtue. "I seen my opportunities and I took 'em," the eminent Democratic politician from New York, "Boss" George Washington Plunkett of Tammany Hall, offered

Three areas of congressional reassertion

as his political epitaph earlier in this century.[31] Watergate presented Congress with such an opportunity. The result was congressional resurgence. Three areas where Congress reasserted itself are especially important. One involves the **power of the purse,** especially the congressional efforts to develop a national budget more coherently. A second is the expansion of **legislative oversight** over the departments and agencies of the executive branch. The third, related to oversight, involves expanded congressional use of the **legislative veto** as part of an effort to ensure that executive-agency actions conform to legislative wishes. As we will see, the legislative veto ran into a constitutional challenge in the 1980s.

The Budget Process

One important aim of Congress in its resurgence of the 1970s was to recapture its **power of the purse.** The immediate target was the Nixon administration's sweeping use of **impoundment:** holding back funds that Congress had appropriated for various stated purposes in its regular budgetary actions.

The practice of impoundment developed early in the twentieth century for a specific purpose, and with Congress's blessings. After 1921, the Bureau of the Budget (now the Office of Management and Budget) established the practice of apportioning appropriated funds to the various federal departments in quarterly installments. In so doing it sometimes discovered that more dollars were available than were needed to meet the statutory purpose, and it placed these in reserve—a type of impoundment of excess funds. Congress welcomed this practice and gave it formal recognition in a 1950 law. When Richard Nixon took office in 1969 he found himself under another more specific congressional directive bearing on impoundment. Congress had instructed the president in a 1968 measure to trim some $6 billion from the spending it had approved so as to bring revenues and expenditures into greater balance. "We have appropriated more than we should have," Congress in effect said to the president. "You find places to cut $6 billion."

Building on this base, Nixon asserted a broad authority to impound funds. He believed that spending under the "Great Society" programs of the Johnson administration had surged out of control, and he saw impoundment as a means of achieving cuts beyond what he could persuade a profligate Congress to make. Speaking for the administration, then deputy director of the Office of Management and Budget (OMB) Caspar Weinberger argued that the president's consti-

Marginal notes:

Power of the purse

Impoundment

Nixon's use of impoundment

[31] See William Riordan, *Plunkett of Tammany Hall* (New York: E. P. Dutton, 1963), p. 3. The Society of Tammany, known as Tammany Hall, was a fraternal organization that controlled the New York Democratic party from roughly the middle of the nineteenth century until the middle of this century.

tutional responsibility to "take care that the laws be faithfully executed" sometimes necessitated impounding appropriated funds. The president, said Weinberger, must look beyond individual appropriations acts to all laws he is supposed to execute—including laws that place a ceiling on the national debt. When the intentions of different statutes conflict, as when appropriations' measures call for spending in excess of revenues, contrary to debt limitation statutes, the president may try to reconcile the conflicting requirements through impoundment.

Behind such rhetoric, a power-play of breathtaking proportions was being attempted. For the first time a president was asserting the general right to scuttle programs that had been duly enacted into law, by preventing funds appropriated for them from being expended. For example, in 1972 Nixon eliminated a whole series of Department of Agriculture programs and cut some $9 billion from funds appropriated for the Environmental Protection Agency. Had this sweeping use of impoundment been sustained, the nature of executive-legislative relations and separation of powers would have been significantly altered. The fact that the Nixon administration even entertained its expansive claims on impoundment showed how far presidential assertiveness and congressional retreat had proceeded.

Fiscal incoherence

As the battle over impoundment waged, many congressmen were occupied with another budget-linked problem, this one of long duration: How could greater coherence be brought to the whole budgetary process? As things stood, the taxing and spending halves of the program the president presented to Congress were assigned to different committees in both the House and Senate and acted on independently. On the spending side, a number of separate *appropriations bills* (bills allocating funding for programs and agencies) were enacted each session, each handled by a different appropriations subcommittee and considered by Congress independently of one another. Beyond this, a growing proportion of governmental expenditures were outside the control of the appropriations committees altogether, having been mandated by "backdoor spending" provisions included in legislation written by various standing committees.[32] How could priorities be determined and the overall impact of individual spending decisions on the total budget be properly assessed and controlled? The United States didn't have a fiscal policy, one commentator noted, only "a fiscal result."[33]

Financially, the left hand did not know what the right hand was doing. As a result, many in Congress concluded in the late 1960s and early 1970s that much more was wrong than the president's challeng-

[32]"Backdoor spending" as used in Congress refers to expenditures beyond the control of the appropriations committees, such as social security payments, farm price support payments, and pensions paid to retired government employees.
[33]Edwin L. Dale, Jr., *New York Times*, June 15, 1975.

ing them through impoundment. Representative Al Ullman of Oregon, the most senior Democrat on the House Ways and Means Committee, lamented that

Need for reform

> the only place where a budget is put together is the Office of Management and Budget downtown. When they send their recommendations to us we go through a few motions of raising or lowering the spending requests, but we have lost the capacity to decide our own priorities. Until we can devise a vehicle for putting those non-appropriated funds in the same basket and coming up with an overall limitation we have not faced up to the issue at all.[34]

Congressional Budget and Impoundment Act

Congress finally acted to remedy this situation and passed the Congressional Budget and Impoundment Control Act in June 1974. It was signed into law by Richard Nixon just four weeks before he left office. The administration had already given up on impoundment as a tactic in the face of adverse court decisions, and most of the impounded appropriations had been released.

The budget and impoundment act provided that the president may only propose to Congress that it cancel or defer spending previously authorized. In cases where the president simply proposed deferring expenditures to some future time, the act stipulated that his action would stand unless either house voted to overrule him. But if the president sought to terminate a program provided by statute or hold back funds for reasons of fiscal policy, his initiative would be cancelled unless a bill explicitly rescinding the original appropriation was enacted within 45 days. Impoundment has not been a matter of contention between the president and Congress in recent years. As we will see below, though, the specific provisions of the 1974 legislation dealing with this issue have been affected by a key 1983 Supreme Court decision.

Budget committees and the CBO

The other part of the 1974 legislation imposes a new organization on congressional budget making. A budget committee in each house, together with staff of the Congressional Budget Office (CBO)—all established by the 1974 act—arrive at recommendations on the basic outlines of fiscal policy. The budget committees and the CBO are supposed to consider such questions as how large a deficit is desirable or permissible given the state of the economy, and what taxing and spending measures are consistent with this target. Then, according to the plan, they specify spending levels for all major programs—national defense, agriculture, health, and welfare—taking into account recommendations from the standing committees that consider legislation in each of these areas. The budget committee recommendations are reviewed by House and Senate and, as modified, go into the first annual budget resolution in May. The resolution recommends

[34]*Congressional Record*, October 10, 1972, pp. 34600–2.

overall federal spending levels and sets financial guidelines. Each substantive committee, whether Agriculture, Education and Labor, or Foreign Affairs, is given an expenditures target that it is supposed to observe as it takes up the bills that come to it.

Budget reconciliation

In September, the House and Senate budget committees report a second resolution that reflects the May commitments along with new judgments on national economic needs. If the spending decisions Congress made during the spring and summer exceed the total provided by the September resolution, budgetary discipline can be imposed through a reconciliation process. Under reconciliation, Congress can direct the standing committees to report bills that either raise revenues or cut spending.[35] In effect, the budget committees have emerged in the role of fiscal watchdogs within Congress. They are an institutional voice for restraint against the continuing demands for new programs and increased spending coming from the substantive committees.

Presidential use of reconciliation

In 1981, the Reagan administration and its congressional allies made heavy use of the reconciliation provisions of the budget act in a novel way, as part of their efforts to get major cuts in government spending approved by Congress. The budget act envisioned reconciliation occurring at the end of the budget process to bring spending into accord with the targets set by the second budget resolution. In 1981 the administration succeeded in getting Congress to employ reconciliation at the beginning of the budget process, to make reductions in existing programs. In May and June, following dramatic battles, budget resolutions were passed that contained reconciliation instructions requiring House and Senate committees to make cuts of some $36 billion.

Effects of the budget act

After extensively reviewing the process provided by the Congressional Budget and Impoundment Control Act, political scientist Leroy N. Rieselback concluded that "the revised procedures have generated a variable record marked by both successes and failures."[36] Among the positive contributions are the enhancement of Congress's capacity to understand the huge and enormously complex national budget, through the work of the Congressional Budget Office; and the creation of an opportunity to impose budgetary discipline through the reconciliation process. On the negative side, the new budget committees set up by the 1974 legislation in effect simply add another layer of participants on top of the old key players, the appropriations and

[35] A detailed account of the new budget process in Congress can be found in Allen Schick, *Congress and Money* (Washington, D.C.: The Urban Institute, 1980). See also James P. Pfiffner, *The President, the Budget, and Congress: Impoundment and the 1974 Budget Act* (Boulder, Colo.: Westview Press, 1979); and Roger H. Davidson and Walter J. Oleszek, *Congress and Its Members* (Washington, D.C.: Congressional Quarterly Press, 1985), chap. 12.

[36] Leroy N. Rieselback, *Congressional Reform* (Washington, D.C.: CQ Press, 1986), p. 97.

taxation committees, which remain powerful. Now even more interests must be accommodated before a budget resolution can be passed.

The Congressional Budget Office (CBO) was envisioned as a staff agency that would function in a nonpartisan fashion, providing members of Congress with the data they need to develop a sound national budget. For a while, the CBO got good marks from both Democrats and Republicans. Alice Rivlin (who served from 1975 to 1983) and Rudolph Penner (1983 to 1987) were highly regarded for their work as CBO directors. But following Penner's resignation in March 1987, House and Senate leaders were unable to agree upon a permanent replacement. Lacking a strong director, the CBO found itself increasingly embroiled in partisan arguments and charged with compromising its essential independence. It remains to be seen whether the CBO will be weakened for the long term or will be able to regain its earlier reputation for competence and independence.

Legislative Oversight

Legislative oversight involves efforts by Congress to supervise the vast executive establishment set up to administer laws it has enacted. Prior to the 1930s, when the national government was small, oversight was a fairly easy matter. Today, government is so large and does so much that effective oversight is difficult to manage.

During the 1970s, Congress began placing much more emphasis on its oversight function. It broadened the spending oversight of the General Accounting Office (GAO). More importantly, it extended the number and independence of its subcommittees and greatly expanded their staffs. One result was more time for oversight hearings and related meetings. In addition, Congress began routinely adding onto legislation the requirement that executive agencies notify the appropriate committee(s) before promulgating program changes, so that the committees could call hearings if they chose and bring their influence to bear, perhaps taking steps to reverse the agency actions. Such legislative stipulations typically provide for a waiting period of 30 to 60 days between the time the agency notifies the committee(s) and the time its administrative action is due to take effect.

Congress also began asserting a near-absolute right to information as part of its oversight functions. An amendment to the 1974 foreign aid bill required that all covert actions of the Central Intelligence Agency be reported "in a timely fashion" to the "appropriate committees" of Congress. Cabinet members and other agency heads were required to furnish information Congress wanted, under threat of being cited for contempt if they refused. In December 1982, for example, a contempt citation was issued against Anne M. Burford, then administrator of the Environmental Protection Agency (EPA), for refusing to turn over documents concerning EPA enforcement of the 1980

Legislative oversight

Increased use of the oversight function

EPA and the right to know

"Superfund" hazardous waste cleanup law to the House Public Works Committee and the House Energy and Commerce Oversight Subcommittee, as requested. Acting on instructions from President Reagan and the Justice Department, Burford had claimed executive privilege, alleging that disclosure of contents would jeopardize the outcome of EPA lawsuits then in progress.[37] It was only after a year and a half of charges and countercharges by Congress and the Reagan administration that contempt charges against Mrs. Burford were dropped.

Overuse of congressional oversight?

Presidents and their executive department subordinates have come to feel, not surprisingly, that congressional oversight has expanded beyond reasonable limits. And more neutral observers agree that at times the new congressional demands are burdensome. An area of intense controversy involves congressional oversight of intelligence agencies. As the Iran-Contra affair unfolded in late 1986 and 1987, many in Congress were angered that they had not been kept informed of the missile sales to Iran. These sales had begun in August 1985, but they were not known to Congress until they were reported in a Beirut newspaper in November 1986. Congressional dissatisfaction prompted efforts to extend and make more specific the reporting requirements imposed on the executive in covert operations—to reduce the "wiggle room" it had left in the 1980 legislation.

These efforts have been opposed by the Reagan administration and by many in the intelligence community, in part on the grounds they would make it hard to maintain the level of secrecy essential in risky covert operations. Congress is "overreacting to its [the intelligence community's] role in the Iran-Contra affair," charged John K. Greaney, executive director of the 3,500 member Association of Former Intelligence Officers.[38]

The Legislative Veto

Congress and the legislative veto

The **legislative** or **congressional veto** provision was first employed in a 1932 law. President Herbert Hoover was authorized to reorganize agencies by executive order, but it was further required that each such order be transmitted to Congress, where it could be disapproved by either house within 60 days. This provision turned the usual legislative–executive relationship upside down: The president was allowed to write the equivalent of law, but Congress could subsequently veto (reject) what he had written.

In the 1960s and 1970s, Congress turned increasingly to the legislative veto, because it found the provision useful in meeting two somewhat contrary objectives: giving the president and executive

---

[37] *Congressional Quarterly,* December 18, 1982, p. 3077.
[38] Quoted in David C. Morrison, "An Eye on the CIA," *National Journal,* April 16, 1988, p. 1009.

agencies the authority to act, and keeping Congress very much in the picture, able to overturn executive actions. By 1980, 200 laws containing more than 250 legislative veto provisions were on the books. One-third of these were enacted after 1975.

Some examples:

(1) *War Powers Resolution* (1973). Absent a declaration of war, the president could be directed by concurrent resolution (passed by both houses, but not requiring the president's signature) to remove U.S. armed forces engaged in hostilities abroad.

(2) *Department of Defense Appropriation Authorization Act* (1974). National defense contracts obligating the United States for any amount over $25,000,000 could be disapproved by the resolution of either house.

(3) *Naval Petroleum Reserves Act* (1976). The president's extension of the production period for naval oil reserves could be vetoed by resolution of either house.

(4) *Omnibus Budget Reconciliation Act* (1981). The Secretary of Education's schedule of expected family contributions for Pell Grant recipients could be rejected by resolution of either house. Secretary of Transportation's plan for the sale of government's common stock in the rail system could be vetoed by concurrent resolution.

Types of legislative vetoes. Congressional veto provisions varied in the ease with which they permitted Congress to overrule agency actions. From the president's standpoint, the least objectionable type of veto was one where both houses had to concur before the executive action was disallowed. But one-house vetoes were more common, where, if either the House or Senate said no, the executive initiative was dead. In some cases, the one-house veto was delegated to one or more committees of one chamber, or to a subcommittee. In 1979, Congress even gave one of its agencies, the Office of Technology Assessment, power to veto the design of research for a study the Veterans' Administration was making—which is getting pretty far into the details of executive agency actions.

One- or two-house vetoes

It isn't surprising that presidents didn't like Congress's increasing recourse to the legislative veto, even though they recognized in many instances that Congress would not have given them authority to act at all unless it retained a ready means of blocking the action. President Jimmy Carter reflected general presidential sentiment when he argued in 1978 that legislative vetos were "intrusive devices that infringe on the Executive's constitutional duty to faithfully execute the laws."[39] Heavy use of the veto involved Congress in the day-to-

Presidential concern over the legislative veto

[39] Jimmy Carter, "Message to the Congress," June 1978, in *Public Papers of the Presidents of the United States–Jimmy Carter, 1978* (Washington, D.C.: Office of the Federal Register, National Archives and Records Service, 1979), book 1, p. 1147.

day practice of rule making, properly the domain of executive agencies.

With the argument between president and Congress over the legislative veto unresolved, the U.S. Supreme Court entered the dispute, through its ruling in the case of *Naturalization Service* v. *Chadha* (1983). This case began back in 1974 when Jagdish Rai Chadha, a Kenyan East Indian who had overstayed his student visa, won a verdict from the Immigration and Naturalization Service (INS) suspending his deportation. A year later, though, the House of Representatives exercised the one-house veto that had been written into an immigration act and overturned the INS action. Under the veto, Chadha had to be deported after all, even though INS had decided he could stay in the United States. Chadha appealed to INS and to the federal courts, in a complicated legal battle. A U.S. Court of Appeals agreed with Chadha's contention that the legislative veto provision of the immigration act was unconstitutional, in violation of separation of powers.

The Supreme Court upheld the Appeals Court ruling. Six of the nine justices felt that Congress had stepped unconstitutionally into the executive branch's domain and had skirted the requirements of bicameralism. Writing for the majority, Chief Justice Warren Burger concluded: "To accomplish what has been attempted by one House of Congress in this case requires action in conformity with the express procedures of the Constitution's prescription for legislative action: passage by a majority of both Houses and presentment to the President."[40]

In the wake of the *Chadha* decision, all of the legislative veto provisions on the books were undoubtedly unconstitutional and hence unenforceable. Political scientist Barbara Craig points out that Congress moved quickly to find replacements for the veto.[41] In many cases it is now required to pass a joint resolution either of *approval* or *disapproval*. All joint resolutions must be presented to the president for his signature or veto, but the difference between these two forms is substantial. The joint resolution of disapproval is now used most commonly. As an example, in July 1985 Congress passed a Federal Trade Commission (FTC) authorization that would allow it to reject proposed regulations issued by the FTC. The regulations would be overturned if a resolution disapproving them were passed by both houses of Congress and signed by the president. If Congress did not act, the FTC rules would take effect ninety days after being submitted to Congress. If Congress acted and the president vetoed the joint resolution, Congress would have to repass it by two-thirds majorities before its rejection of the FTC rules would take effect.

The Court's challenge
to the legislative veto

Joint resolutions

[40] *Immigration and Naturalization Service* v. *Jagdish Rai Chadha* et al., *United States Law Week*, June 21, 1983, p. 4918.
[41] Barbara Hinkson Craig, *Chadha: The Story of an Epic Constitutional Struggle* (New York: Oxford University Press, 1988), pp. 235–37.

In a few areas, including some arms sales, Congress has wanted to impose a tougher restriction on the president. In a resolution of approval, the specific arms sale (or other executive action) must be approved by both houses of Congress and signed by the president *before* it can be implemented.

What is the status of laws containing legislative veto provisions, where Congress has not modified them following the *Chadha* decision? A case presenting this issue was decided by the Supreme Court in March 1987. In it the Court upheld an employee protection plan set up by the Airline Deregulation Act of 1978 to help airline employees who lost their jobs as a result of deregulation. Alaska Airlines and other carriers argued that this plan was now void, because the provision of the statute creating it authorized the secretary of labor to issue implementing regulations subject to a veto by either house of Congress. The veto provision was clearly invalid after *Chadha*. Were the substantive provisions of the worker protection plan to be scrapped too?[42]

Writing for a unanimous Court, Justice Harry A. Blackmun held that "the legislative history of the [employee-protection plan] supports the conclusion that Congress would have enacted the . . . provisions even without a legislative-veto provision. . . ." Hence, the worker protection plan remains in force; only the veto component is invalid. The Court here was applying its familiar *severability* standard. "The unconstitutional provision," Blackmun wrote, "must be severed unless the statute created in its absence is legislation that Congress would not have enacted." He made clear, though, that some other laws could not survive the loss of their veto clauses: "Some delegations of power to the executive or to an independent agency may have been so controversial or so broad that Congress would have been unwilling to make the delegation without a strong oversight mechanism."

The Court rules on a legislative veto provision

THE TWO CONGRESSES

Congress performs two very different functions: that of *lawmaker* and that of *representative assembly*.[43] As lawmaker it is charged with passing the laws that the United States requires to address its various public problems. As a representative assembly it responds to very different needs. Composed of 535 senators and representatives, each with his own electoral interests, Congress must hear and respond to the claims of diverse constituencies. And the sum total of these claims may not always be consistent with the requirements of sound public policy for the nation.

[42] The case is *Alaska Airlines Inc.* v. *Brock* (1987).
[43] Davidson and Oleszek, "Introduction: The Two Congresses," in *Congress and Its Members*, pp. 7–12.

Two Roles, Two Records

Recognition of these different, sometimes opposing, legislative functions came a long time ago, in the early days of legislatures in Europe. On November 3, 1774, the great British politician and philosopher Edmund Burke described the constituent-oriented British Parliament as "a congress of ambassadors from different and hostile interests, which interests each must maintain, as an agent and advocate, against other agents and advocates." Then Burke set forth the idea of the same Parliament as lawmaker for the nation, "a deliberative assembly of one nation, with one interest, that of the whole—where not local purposes, not local prejudices, ought to guide, but the general good, resulting from the general reason of the whole."[44]

Congress as representative assembly

Any assessment of Congress should not lose sight of its different functions. In the opinion of many observers, Congress is doing very well as a representative assembly—as well as or better than at any point in its history. As a lawmaking institution the same Congress receives criticism and concern from inside its own ranks as well as from without. Its very success in one role contributes to its difficulties in the other.

Resources for Representation

Congress is exceptionally well tooled to function as a representative assembly. The 435 House districts are now of the same population size. The right to vote in congressional and other elections has been extended to all citizens. The extreme inequalities in the power of individual members in past Congresses has been greatly reduced. Staff resources now available to Congress permit individual members to respond to constituency interests more fully than ever.

Public opinion and Congress

Americans seem to appreciate the successful adaptation of Congress as a representative chamber. Public opinion polls have regularly asked respondents how good a job they think their congressional representatives are doing. Without exception in recent years, congressmen have received high marks. At the same time, however, the public gives low marks to Congress as a policy-making institution. In Harris surveys, for example, only 15 percent of the public say they have a "great deal of confidence" in the leadership provided by Congress.[45] The public thinks the Congress of individual representatives is performing well, while it sees the Congress as a policy institution doing poorly.

[44] Edmund Burke, "Speech to Electors at Bristol," in *Burke's Politics*, Ross J. S. Hoffman and Paul Levack, eds. (New York: Knopf, 1949), p. 116.

[45] In 1975, for example, 13 percent said they had a great deal of confidence in Congress; in 1978 the proportion was 10 percent; in 1980, 18 percent; in 1983, 20 percent; in 1985, 16 percent; and in 1988, 15 percent.

Opportunities for Interest Groups

Interest groups and subcommittees

Many of the steps that have added to the representative capacities of Congress have been highly disintegrative to Congress as a whole. Power is fragmented, and coherent national policy making hard to achieve. One result has been to strengthen the hand of interest groups. Groups are now able to take their cases directly to individual congressmen, without any party mediation, and establish close working ties with the subcommittee(s) in their areas of interest. Politically active interest groups are a necessary and proper part of a free society. Given the far-flung activities of modern government, it was unavoidable that there would be a proliferation of organized special interests. But in the current era, these special interests have been permitted to operate upon a highly individualistic, fractured Congress—giving them excessive influence.

The problem of the contemporary Congress is not that it is unresponsive. But what Edmund Burke two centuries ago called the "interest . . . of the whole—where not local purposes . . . ought to guide, but the general good . . ." has sometimes been poorly served.

Congressional Reform

Changes needed to correct this problem have been hard to achieve and almost certainly will continue to be so. While the fragmentation of power in Congress is widely deplored, even among many congressmen themselves, it generally serves the electoral and representation needs of individual congressmen. Why should a congressman who has his own subcommittee and a large staff, which can be employed to help his electoral fortunes and to advance legislation which he or his constituents favor, surrender these resources? To function better as a lawmaking body, Congress needs more discipline, a defined hierarchy, and leaders who can bargain with the executive branch and with interest groups, and then commit the Congress to the best overall mix of programmatic responses. But discipline, hierarchy, and leadership are not the best prerequisites for a representative assembly. And they do not coincide with the electoral needs and career expectations of today's legislator.

Congress as lawmaker

Some of the congressional reforms of the last two decades have responded effectively to the demands on Congress as a lawmaker for the nation. But most of the changes Congress embraced over the 1960s and 1970s reflected its needs as a representative assembly and the interests of its individual members. As Congress has changed, the imbalance between its representative and lawmaking functions has become more pronounced.

SUMMARY

Congress differs from other democratic legislatures in two important regards. One involves separation of powers. In the American scheme—though not in the more common parliamentary arrangement—the legislature and the executive are separate institutions. It is possible, and common, for the two to be controlled by different parties. The two branches must work together if American government is to function, but the Constitution makes them co-equal and independent.

Also setting Congress apart is the extent to which power is dispersed within it. Committees and subcommittees are strong; central party leadership is weak. Nowhere in the democratic world is the individual legislator so independent—and so powerful.

For a brief time in the late nineteenth and early twentieth centuries, Congress experienced strong party organization and discipline; this was gone by 1915. Over the last two decades, power has been even more widely dispersed among the membership, as the prerogatives of the once-dominant committee chairmen have been cut back, the number of subcommittees expanded and their independence buttressed, members' staff increased, and more.

In recent years Congress has experienced a resurgence, in part the product of external events and in part of its own making. The idea that strong presidential leadership is the "great engine of democracy," so widely held from the time of Franklin Roosevelt through the mid-1960s, was shaken by a stream of events, the most important of which were the Vietnam War and Watergate.

As this shift of assessment occurred, Congress began asserting itself more vigorously. It passed important new legislation dealing with national budget making. It applied its oversight powers so extensively that even some neutral observers thought it sometimes overreached its constitutional boundaries. It took a little-used provision, the legislative veto, and applied it routinely as a convenient means of blocking executive agency actions that it disagreed with—even matters like a ruling of the Immigration and Naturalization Service that suspended the deportation of Jagdish Rai Chadha. The Supreme Court ruled in Chadha's case that Congress was using the legislative veto unconstitutionally to get around the requirements of bicameralism and separation of powers. In many cases Congress is now required to resort to joint resolutions of disapproval, which must be passed by both houses and are subject to the president's veto.

Congress functions both as a representative assembly and as a national lawmaker. While each is vitally important, these roles do not necessarily get along very well together. Over the last two decades, a series of reforms have strengthened the legislature's capacity to perform its representative functions. But some of these reforms have also had a disintegrative effect, strengthening the position of the individual representative at the expense of the capacity for central leadership—and the capability of legislating effectively for the nation.

FOR FURTHER STUDY

Barbara Hinkson Craig, *Chadha: The Story of an Epic Constitutional Struggle* (New York: Oxford University Press, 1988), pp. 235–37.

Roger S. Davidson and Walter J Oleszek, *Congress and Its Members* (Washington, DC: Congressional Quarterly Press, 1984). A careful, balanced interpretation of the operations of the contemporary Congress and of the changes that have affected congressional operations.

Richard F. Fenno, *Home Style: House Members in Their Districts* (Boston: Little, Brown, 1978). A penetrating examination of the impact on the behavior of congressmen of their ties with their home district constituents.

Leroy N. Rieselback, *Congressional Reform* (Washington, DC: Congressional Quarterly Press, 1986). A comprehensive account of the congressional reforms of the last two decades and the impact they have made on Congress.

James L. Sundquist, *The Decline and Resurgence of Congress* (Washington, DC: Brookings Institution, 1981). Describes the efforts of Congress in the late 1960s and 1970s to regain powers that in the preceding decades had been surrendered to the president and the executive branch.

Michael Barone and Grant Ujifusa, *The Almanac of American Politics, 1988* (Washington, DC: National Journal, 1988). Published every two years, the almanac provides comprehensive descriptions of every congressional district, the voting records of members of Congress on major issues, interest group ratings of congressional voting on liberalism-conservatism continuums, and more.

Congressional Directory, 1987–1988 (Washington, DC: U.S. Government Printing Office, 1987). Published for each Congress, the Directory contains biographies of all members of Congress, provides listings of the members of all committees and subcommittees, gives addresses and telephone numbers for congressional offices, indicates principal staff assistants, and more.

Congressional Quarterly, Weekly Report and Annual Almanac (Washington, DC: Congressional Quarterly, Inc.) The most comprehensive regular reporting of developments on Capitol Hill, including reviews of all major bills introduced into Congress and complete records of all roll call votes.

Norman J. Ornstein et al., *Vital Statistics on Congress, 1987–88 Edition* (Washington, DC: American Enterprise Institute, 1987). An extremely valuable reference for statistics on Congress, including political, educational, religious background of senators and representatives; election and campaign finance data; congressional committees and staff size and operating expenses; workload; budget; voting alignments.

Chapter 7

The Presidency

A few days before his assassination in November 1963, President John F. Kennedy penned a personal note to political historian Clinton Rossiter, commenting on Rossiter's book on the presidency. Rossiter had introduced his study with a quotation from Shakespeare's *Macbeth*. The Scottish general, about to seize his country's throne, relates to his "first lady" a dream in which "Methought I heard a voice cry 'Sleep no more!' " Rossiter felt this a fitting commentary on a prime feature of the American presidency: the enormous demands placed on the office.[1]

Kennedy wrote that, while that quotation was apt, he believed there was an even better one in Shakespeare's *King Henry IV, Part 1*. Glendower boasts that "I can call spirits from the vasty deep." Hostpur replies: "Why, so can I, or so can any man; but will they come when you do call for them?" For Kennedy, it was the gap between the calling and the coming, between the large amount a president seeks to accomplish and the little he can accomplish, that best characterizes the position of this democratic chief executive.

The American presidency is a peculiar office. A president has great visibility and great practical importance in our scheme of government. But he also experiences, even at the height of his popularity and power, great limitations on his capacity to carry the country in the direction he intends. He is in one regard the symbol of America's sense of nationhood and the repository of political leadership and legitimacy. In another sense, though, he is a checked and balanced political executive, sharing the power of American national government not only with a constitutionally independent and politically

---

[1]Clinton Rossiter, *The American Presidency* (New York: New American Library; 2d rev. ed., 1960). The *Macbeth* quotation is from Act II, scene II.

Vice President George Bush was elected president on November 8, 1988. See the Appendix to this book (pp. A29ff.) for discussion of the transition and first hundred days of his administration.

independent-minded Congress, but with a potent federal judiciary, and with other units in the executive branch that are notably independent of his authority. This pervasive mix of power and limits, political majesty and modesty, led the distinguished British political scientist, Harold J. Laski, to describe the American president as "both more and less than a king, more and less than a prime minister."[2]

In the first part of this chapter, we examine the key structural features of the American presidency. We will see that the limitations on presidential power are impressive. The framers sought to avoid the possibility of presidential dictatorship, and in this worthy aim they have been proved successful. But in the process they created a presidency that is better able to "call spirits from the vasty deep" of American public policy than to ensure that these spirits will answer and be moved.

[2]Harold J. Laski, *The American Presidency: An Interpretation* (New York: Harper and Brothers, 1940), p. 11.

In the second section of the chapter we turn to a description of what a modern president does, of the many different roles and responsibilities we have thrust upon his office. The president wears many hats, from party leader to formulator of legislative programs, from commander-in-chief of the armed forces to administrator-in-chief of the executive branch. It is not easy to find someone who can do all of this well. A president cannot be expected to do all of it alone, of course.

In the third section we review the institutional presidency, the collection of aides and offices that now comprise the Executive Office of the President. We then turn to a subject always present in discussions of the American presidency: the nature of presidential power, how it is realized, and how adequate it is when set against what we expect presidents to accomplish. We conclude the chapter with a discussion of what Americans think about the presidency as an office, and how they assess the performance of recent presidents.

Then, in the Appendix to this book, we look at the spectacle, always momentous, of the transition from one presidency to the next—here the transition from the Reagan presidency to the Bush presidency. What changes did the Bush administration signal in its first 100 days?

WHAT KIND OF A CHIEF EXECUTIVE?

In their constitutional definition of the essential powers and character of the presidency, the framers were breaking new ground. Nowhere in 1787 was there a prototype for the national executive they had in mind. During the nearly two centuries since Article II of the Constitution was drafted, the American presidency has remained a unique office, one where executive authority has been organized and articulated differently from any of America's sister democracies.

A REPUBLICAN EXECUTIVE

The nature of the presidency

We saw in chapters 4 and 5 that the political ideals guiding the Constitution's framers, derived from European political thought of the seventeenth and eighteenth centuries, were called "republican"—emphasizing both popular sovereignty and individual liberty. This meant in part that political institutions would no longer have a class and hereditary base but would instead gain their legitimacy from their reliance on the popular will. The American presidency was set up to be consistent with the enlightened expectations of the times. The president would not resemble a king—not even a limited mon-

President John F. Kennedy.

Tames

arch favored by so many European thinkers of that time. He would be elected for a fixed term of four years, with re-election possible; any native-born citizen (or citizen at the time of the Constitution's adoption) of at least 35 years of age would be eligible to stand for office. These provisions represented a monumental break from the hereditary, aristocratic practice that still prevailed in Europe.

At the same time the framers were fearful of unrestrained majority rule and the possibility that the American chief executive might be too inclined to appeal to popular passions in ways harmful to minority rights. They sought to insulate the office by having the public participate in presidential selection only indirectly. Their chosen mechanism was the **electoral college.** As it turned out, the framers made two mistakes, one mechanical, the other philosophical—and both had to be corrected before the presidency as we know it emerged.

The electoral college

Article II provided that each state should appoint, "in such Manner as the Legislature thereof may direct, a Number of Electors, equal to the whole number of Senators and Representatives to which the state may be entitled in the Congress. . . ." These electors would meet in their respective states on a day designated by Congress and cast their votes for president. Any eligible person receiving an absolute majority of the votes cast would be declared president. If no one received a majority, the House of Representatives—with each state delegation having a single vote—would select the president from among the five contenders with the highest number of electoral votes.

A Mechanical Failure

Almost immediately, the electoral college arrangement malfunctioned. The procedures did not distinguish between electoral votes

cast for president and those cast for vice president. In the election of 1800, Thomas Jefferson of Virginia, the presidential choice of the new Democratic-Republican party, and Aaron Burr of New York, Jefferson's vice presidential running mate, each received the same number (73) of electoral votes. Everyone knew that Burr's 73 votes were for vice president, but they were not so designated. Something of a constitutional crisis resulted. The election was thrown into the House of Representatives, with an inevitable invitation for political chicanery given to the anti-Jefferson opposition. And the overly ambitious Burr sought to take advantage of this unforeseen opportunity to engineer his own election as president.

Jefferson did prevail, but it was evident there was a defect needing immediate remedy. The Twelfth Amendment was proposed by Congress on December 9, 1803, and was declared ratified on September 25, 1804, when the legislatures of 13 of the 17 states (the required 75 percent) had approved it. The amendment provided that the electors would cast separate and distinct ballots for president and vice president.

A Philosophical Failure

The framers had an incomplete appreciation of the powerful democratic forces stirring in the new nation. As a key public office, the

presidency had to reflect the democratic temper of American society. And it was in fact quickly democratized, without changing a word in the Constitution, through the agency of the developing party system. There were two steps through which the emerging political parties took over the electoral college procedures and converted them into a means for ratifying popular preferences for president. The first came as early as 1796, as selection of presidential electors in the state legislatures became a party contest between the Federalists and the Democratic-Republicans. The people voted one party or the other into majority status in the respective state assemblies, and these legislative majorities then picked electors pledged to vote for their parties' presidential nominees.

The second step was taken about three decades later, and involved picking presidential electors not by state legislatures but through direct

popular balloting. More and more states made this changeover in the 1820s and 1830s. The election of 1824—finally decided in the House of Representatives in favor of John Quincy Adams—saw the beginnings of popular presidential electoral contests in 18 of the 24 states.

Still, only 360,000 popular votes were cast nationally, and in so pivotal a state as New York the issue was wholly decided within the legislature. Four years later the popular vote jumped to 1,150,000, in a country where the voting-age male population was about 2,400,000. And by 1832, when Democrat Andrew Jackson won reelection over Henry Clay, candidate of the opposition National Republicans, presidential elections had been virtually transformed into the contest we know today: Eligible voters in each state went to the polls on election day and cast ballots for their choice for president by picking a slate of electors publicly pledged to him.

This democratization of the presidency strengthened the office. James Sterling Young has observed that

> nomination and election by popular acclaim [gave] the presidency the stature of popular spokesmanship and an independent electoral strength which was convertible, on occasion, to bargaining advantages over Congress. . . . In a nation pervasively mistrustful of government, democracy, and democracy alone, [converted] a figure of authority into a personage of national influence.[3]

AN INDEPENDENT EXECUTIVE

Powers of the president

The framers, influenced by their classical liberal preference for dispersed power, provided for an executive branch separate from the legislature and independent of it for its tenure in office. To ensure its independence, the executive had to have powers conferred directly by the Constitution, not by another branch of government. Section 2 of Article II made the president commander-in-chief of the armed forces, and established his power to make treaties and to appoint ambassadors, federal court judges, and "all other Officers of the United States." Other constitutional provisions gave the president an explicit legislative role through the veto power (Article I, section 7), and conferred upon him sweeping administrative responsibilities in that "he shall take Care that the Laws be faithfully executed" (Article II, section 3).

A CHECKED AND BALANCED EXECUTIVE

But if the president was to be constitutionally independent of the other branches, especially the legislature, he was to be subject to restraints by them lest he get too strong. We saw in chapter 5 that every basic constitutional grant of authority to the president is constitutionally limited. The president is commander-in-chief of the armed

[3] James Sterling Young, *The Washington Community, 1800–1828* (New York: Harcourt, Brace, 1966), p. 253.

forces, but it is within Congress's power to declare war and "to raise and support Armies." He has broad appointive powers, but his appointments require "the Advice and Consent" of the Senate. He has the power, in the conduct of foreign affairs, to make treaties, but the Senate's consent is required before the treaties come into force. The president stands at the helm of the ship of state and supervises the execution of all the laws of the United States—a formidable grant of authority, made even more formidable in the modern era by vast increases in the scope of legislation—but Congress determines what these laws shall provide and may repeal them at any time.

Impeachment

Impeachment

The ultimate congressional check on the chief executive is removing him from office. We have seen that the framers wanted the president to be independent of Congress for his election and tenure in office. But they envisioned the need, in an extreme case, for cashiering an executive who grossly violated his oath. They provided in Section 4 of Article II that the president (and other "civil Officers of the United States") shall be dismissed if impeached and convicted of "Treason, Bribery, and other High Crimes and Misdemeanors." Such removal has not been undertaken lightly. Impeachment proceedings have been advanced in Congress against only two presidents: Andrew Johnson in 1868 and Richard Nixon in 1974. The **impeachment** process has two stages. The House of Representatives formally brings charges—which is what impeachment means. If it votes to impeach, the president (or other officer) is then tried by the Senate. "When the President of the United States is tried," Article I, Section 3 stipulates, "the Chief Justice [of the U.S. Supreme Court] shall preside: And no person shall be convicted without the concurrence of two thirds of the Members present."

The impeachment of Andrew Johnson

The impeachment of Andrew Johnson. Only one president has ever been formally impeached by the House and tried by the Senate. Andrew Johnson of Tennessee succeeded Abraham Lincoln as president in 1865, upon the latter's assassination, and almost immediately got into deep political trouble. Johnson had been put on the ticket in 1864 as part of the effort to reach out in reconciliation to the South; Johnson was a southerner who opposed secession. But he was not a Republican—instead, he was a (pro-) "War Democrat"—so he began his presidency on the wrong foot with the highly partisan Republican majority in Congress. Passions were very high following the long and costly Civil War. Any president, even Lincoln, would have been hard pressed to control these passions as he charted policies for postwar Reconstruction. Johnson lacked the necessary skills, and his rupture with congressional Republicans deepened. Most historians do not believe

The impeachment trial of President Andrew Johnson.

that Johnson was in fact guilty of "High Crimes and Misdemeanors" —bad policy choices and inept political management would seem the harshest charges that could be sustained—but he was impeached by the House on February 24, 1868. The vote was unanimous.

With Chief Justice Salmon P. Chase presiding, Johnson's Senate trial opened in March 1868. After about two months of often bitter argument, votes were taken on May 16 and 26. A majority voted to convict, but not the two-thirds majority required by the Constitution. By the narrowest of margins (35 for conviction, 19 against) Andrew Johnson was left in office to serve out the remainder of his term.

Richard Nixon and Watergate. Richard Nixon, the only other president subjected to impeachment proceedings, was never actually

Richard Nixon's resignation

impeached—and hence never tried in the Senate. But he is the only president forced from office by these constitutional provisions. Richard Nixon resigned as president on August 9, 1974, when it was clear that he had lost the public backing needed to govern, and that the House would impeach him if he did not resign. Few Americans—and neither the president's friends nor his congressional opponents— wanted the agony of a Senate trial.

The events leading to Nixon's resignation are now referred to by the single word "Watergate." But the scandal that forced him from office grew from a complex of developments.[4] The actual Watergate

[4]*Congressional Quarterly's* two-volume account *Watergate: Chronology of a Crisis* (Washington, D.C.: Congressional Quarterly, 1973) is especially helpful because it brings together all of the basic events, testimony, etc.

Military personnel roll up the carpet as a helicopter readies to escort President Nixon from the White House lawn after his resignation speech on August 9, 1974.

incident was the June 17, 1972, break-in at the offices of the Democratic National Committee (DNC), located in a Washington commercial and residential complex known as the Watergate. Notwithstanding denial by the president himself, the burglary—undertaken for the purpose of political espionage—was subsequently linked to Nixon's campaign organization, the Committee to Re-elect the President, and to White House aides. Although the incident did not materially affect the outcome of the 1972 elections (Nixon won by a 23 percent margin), the subsequent disclosures of a conspiracy to cover up the crime implicated the president and many of his staff and campaign officials. Through the efforts of Federal District Court Judge John J. Sirica (who presided over the initial trial of the men who broke into the DNC offices), congressional investigators, enterprising journalists, and others, the president's complicity in the Watergate cover-up was brought out with increasing clarity over 1973 and early 1974. The final blow was the discovery of tape recordings, made on Nixon's initiative, of conversations in his office that showed his certain knowledge of the cover-up efforts. This revelation of presidential lying and obstruction led to a storm of public protest that culminated in Nixon's resignation on August 9.

Watergate was more than a break-in and cover-up. It was a product of the intense passions and protests of the Vietnam War period, and the feeling among administration officials that they were under siege politically. It reflected, too, a decade of presidential aggrandizement, where the traditional sense of presidential restraint was violated by increasingly assertive—one might say arrogant—behavior. The fram-

End of an era of presidential aggrandizement

ers had decided against any ceremonial titles for the president; the occupant would simply be addressed as "Mr. President." But in the 1960s and early 1970s that sense of democratic proportion had been lost. Painful though the process was, Watergate and congressional resurgence helped bring it back.

A VIGOROUS ONE-PERSON EXECUTIVE

Models of a strong executive

Popular feeling in the 1780s and 1790s that the presidency must not in any way resemble the British monarchy was strong and emotional. After all, a war had been fought and won to free the colonies from the absolute tyranny of a king. For most Americans, King George III was the model of a strong executive—and this model was not a comforting one when the new Constitution proposed to build up the executive power. The framers were acutely sensitive to this climate and did not want to advance anything that resembled monarchy.

George Washington's vision of the presidency

But the framers were convinced that the country needed more vigorous executive leadership than it had under the Articles of Confederation. The resolution of this tension in favor of a powerful but checked executive was a tribute to George Washington, who was almost universally expected to be the first occupant of the office. Washington favored a strong executive and worked hard to gain approval for it. The deep respect most Americans had for his character proved decisively important. Pierce Butler of South Carolina, a Convention delegate who was among those most skeptical about the wisdom of a strong executive, later argued that the president's authority would not have been drawn so expansively "had not many of the members cast their eyes toward General Washington as president; and shaped their ideas of the Powers to be given a president *by their opinions of his virtue.*"[5] Washington passionately rejected casting the president as a kind of monarch, and the delegates as well as their countrymen trusted him.

There was good reason for this trust. Washington's aversion to monarchy and his deep commitment to republican institutions was eloquently expressed in a passage from a letter he wrote on August 1, 1786, to John Jay of New York:

> What astounding changes a few years are capable of producing. I am told that even respectable characters speak of a monarchical form of government without horror. From thinking proceeds speaking; thence to acting is often but a single step. But how irrevocable and tremendous! What a triumph for the advocates of despotism to find that we are incapable of governing ourselves, and that systems founded on the basis of equal liberty are merely ideal and fallacious! Would to God that wise measures

[5] Farrand, ed., *Records of the Federal Convention of 1787*, 3:302. Emphasis added.

be taken in time to avert the consequences we have but too much reason to apprehend.[6]

Presidential check on Congress

There was a second critical factor that swung the Convention behind a strong presidency: the delegates' commitment to the liberal ideal of checked and balanced power. For the same reason that the Convention initially insisted that the legislature have powers to rein in the executive and the judiciary, it came to agree with the "presidentialists" who argued that the executive must have enough authority to check the legislature. James Madison of Virginia, the delegate who most reflected the Convention's mainstream, moved over the course of the debates in Philadelphia to back a strong president as a barrier to congressional autocracy.[7]

DUTIES OF THE PRESIDENT

Presidents and their aides sometimes unburden themselves on how demanding the job of president really is. (This always seems a bit curious, since they have worked so hard to get the chance to assume

Presidential authorization is needed for the launch of American bombers and missiles in the event of a national emergency. A military attaché always accompanies the president, carrying a black briefcase that contains the necessary authorization codes.

[6] Jared Sparks, ed., *The Writings of George Washington, Being His Correspondence, Addresses, Messages, and Other Papers, Official and Private* (Boston: Hillard, Odiorne, and Metcalf and Hillard Gray, 1835), vol. 9, pp. 187–89.
[7] Ibid., 3:35.

Box 7.1
Presidential Responsibilities

Chief of State: The president is the ceremonial head of the American government.

Chief Executive: To the president falls the constitutional charge to "take care that the laws be faithfully executed."

Commander-in-Chief: He controls and directs the American armed forces.

Chief Diplomat: He has prime responsibility for the conduct of U.S. foreign policy.

Chief Legislator: The president is expected to play a large role "guiding Congress in much of its law-making activity."

Chief of Party: He has a partisan role as the leader of his political party.

Voice of the People: He is "the leading formulator and expounder of public opinion in the United States."

Protector of Peace: In the face of challenges, domestic as much as foreign, the president is expected to promote national security and tranquility.

Manager of Prosperity: The president is now expected "to foster and promote free competitive enterprise, to avoid economic fluctuations . . . and to maintain employment, production, and purchasing power," in the words of the Employment Act of 1946.

World Leader: More than just chief diplomat of the U.S., he has broad responsibilities for the Western alliance and for international affairs globally.

Source: Rossiter, *American Presidency,* pp. 16–40, *passim.*

---

the burden.) Indeed, the responsibilities of a modern president are so numerous and diverse that it has become virtually certain that no occupant of the office will ever perform all of them well. Box 7.1 shows some of the principal dimensions of the president's job as it has evolved over two centuries of American political experience.

Responsibilities

All the president's roles continue to be very real and very demanding. As the only government official elected from a national constituency, the president commands media attention in articulating broad public wants and needs. Since the New Deal, Americans have believed that the president plays the largest part in the national government's prime responsibility to intervene in the economy to restore, maintain, or extend economic well-being. The president not only serves as

Chief of state

The guided missile cruiser USS Fox (right) keeps a protective eye on two Kuwaiti vessels near the Persian Gulf— 1988.

Commander-in-chief

the head of government, but also as chief of state: the ceremonial head of the nation. (While prime ministers are the head of government in parliamentary democracies, officials who do not bear significant governmental responsibilities, such as the British monarch, are chief of state.)

The president is head of the U.S. military establishment—a force currently consisting of 2.2 million men and women and a vast array of advanced weapons. Given the economic, technological, and military strength of the United States, the president's utterances and actions in foreign policy impact greatly on the world community. The president is responsible for the security of the country. When a serious crisis threatens American lives and interests—whether the disabling aftermath of a hurricane on the Gulf Coast or the prospect of war in the Middle East—he is expected to take calming or restorative action. Rather than sitting back in the Oval Office waiting for Congress to act, the president must formulate a comprehensive set of programs, present them to Congress, and lobby actively for their enactment. In many of his leadership roles he is expected to transcend narrow partisanship. Yet both his allies and his opponents expect him to uphold the philosophy and electoral interests of the political party on whose platform he was elected. (A platform is an agenda of party goals and programs as adopted every four years by the national nominating conventions of each party.)

Public Relations

Just as the president has an extraordinary array of responsibilities, so he needs an extraordinary array of skills. First and foremost, he must have the *external political skills* required to win the nomination of a major political party and ultimately a national election.

Campaigner. The candidate must be able to move among his fellow citizens and convince them to support him over other able and ambitious politicians. He must be able to speak effectively to small groups of businessmen to whom he turns for campaign contributions, to public rallies in city squares, and to national audiences linked by the crucial medium of television. He must have the stamina and the will to crisscross the country in the extended campaigns that have come to distinguish American presidential politics. The first big event in the 1988 campaign was the Iowa caucuses on February 28, but most of the serious contenders—including, certainly, George Bush and Jack Kemp on the Republican side, and Michael Dukakis, Jesse Jackson, and Richard Gephardt for the Democrats, were hard at work a year earlier. The pressures on presidents and would-be presidents as campaigners are enormous.

Communicator. Presidents need highly developed external political skills once in office as much as they did when campaigning. To maintain his popular standing and advance his programs, a president uses appearances at conventions of various interest groups, press conferences, and televised speeches. Friend and foe alike dubbed President Ronald Reagan the "Great Communicator" for his highly developed skills in televised speech making, though he never was comfortable with the televised news conference.

Working with Other Politicians

Internal political skills are no less vital to presidential success. The president is the most important—though only one—member of the political leadership community in the United States. On a daily basis, he must interact with fellow leaders—senators, governors, heads of labor unions and major business corporations—to try to persuade them to follow his lead. Political scientist Richard Neustadt has noted that any president's success in advancing his programs and interests depends in large measure upon "the residual impressions of tenacity and skill" that he conveys to the leadership community. Even a president whose popular standing is high will have trouble leading effectively if his professional reputation is low.[8]

Dwight Eisenhower, fresh from his decisive victory in 1956, backslid and equivocated, convincing a large proportion of political Washington that he lacked the skill and determination to set a coherent course for either his party or the country in domestic affairs. "Ike's" general popularity was high but his professional reputation was low.

Campaigner

Communicator

Internal political skills

Eisenhower's public reputation

[8] Richard E. Neustadt, *Presidential Power* (New York: Wiley, 1980), pp. 47–48.

Two years later, Neustadt argues, the situation was reversed. The Democrats had scored big gains in the recession-dominated congressional elections of 1958, and Eisenhower's popularity with the public had dropped. But through skillful and determined action on behalf of his programs, the president in 1959 greatly improved his professional reputation.

The internal political skills required to impress the political community are sometimes quite different from the external skills needed to move the public at large. Strength, determination, steadfastness, the capacity to fight hard for one's policies without personalizing the disagreements, and the sense of when and how to compromise to achieve the largest possible portion of one's program objectives are especially valued by politicians. They are critical to a president.

Administrative Skills

The president is a politician, but he is also an executive—and his leadership is likely to suffer seriously if he does not possess a high measure of administrative skill. The executive branch is a huge enterprise: 3.1 million civilian employees were involved in the expenditure of more than $1 trillion in 1988. The president need have, and can have, little to do with the day-to-day running of the executive branch, but he is ultimately accountable for overseeing and guiding a business so large that it dwarfs corporate giants like General Motors, Exxon, and IBM. (The sizes of various government departments are compared with those of the largest private U.S. businesses in the next chapter, Figure 8.1.)

Managing complex organizations has long been thought to involve special abilities and training. Schools of business administration each year turn out thousands of graduates with advanced training in corporate management. Yet little thought seems to be given to the skills needed to manage the most challenging of all executive positions, the American presidency. It is almost as if we are confident that the necessary skills will automatically materialize. Of course the president has no shortage of experts ready to advise him on the proper organization and operation of the executive branch. And his personal staff—the White House—includes hundreds of managers. But it is misleading to insist that a president does not need to be a skilled manager because he can hire outstanding managerial talent. Even choosing compatible, responsible, and able subordinates demands exceptional administrative skill.

President as manager

Policy Skills

In our chief executive we expect a composite leader: the president as CEO and the president as politician. Yet even this demanding mix is of no value without the crucial skill: *policy judgment*. The president

Box 7.2
One political scientist's tongue-in-cheek "job advertisement" for a modern-day president

Wanted—Chief Executive for Large, Troubled Public Enterprise

Must be dignified and capable of personifying the aspirations of all elements in a diverse and extremely heterogeneous organization. Must be a successful manager, capable of supervising several million employees, most of whom cannot be directly rewarded or punished. All employees except personal staff will also work for a rival employer. Must be skilled in diplomacy and have good knowledge of world affairs. Should be up on military matters as well. Must be capable of program development for entire enterprise. Job performance will be reviewed after four years, at which time applicant's record will be compared with the promises of numerous aspirants for his position. Applicant must be skilled in economics. A premium will be placed on ability to deal with complex fiscal, monetary, and regulatory matters. Should be good at maintaining alliances with other large public enterprises who do not always share common purposes. Applicant must have power drive but pleasant personality, a good sense of humor, and must be flexible and open to criticism. Must be trustworthy but shrewd. Must be a good speaker and skilled at press relations. Boundless energy is a must. . . . There is no certain deadline [for applicant], but early application is helpful, since the board will have to be convinced that the above qualifications are met.

Source: W. Wayne Shannon, "As If Politics Were About Government: Presidential Selection from a Governance Perspective," paper presented to the New England Political Science Association, March 1980.

must not only do "it" well but must determine what "it" is that needs to be done. He establishes the policies for which his political and managerial talents are employed, and is the final judge on policy direction. He does not need to be expert in every program area—he has a large staff to assist in his administration's programs—but he must choose wisely in the substance and politics of policy if his administration is to succeed.

Policy judgment

We remember Franklin D. Roosevelt as a great president in large part because his New Deal policies were an effective response to national needs in the 1930s. Although, of course, some of the individual programs were flawed, the overall policy direction that FDR imposed looks good through the eyes of history. This is what we hope for in the policy approach of every president—that when the immediate emotions, partisan and otherwise, are past, his approach will have addressed ably the country's most pressing needs.

FDR's success at policy making

Charles Wilson Peale's portrait of George Washington.

Leadership: The Whole Is Greater Than the Sum of Its Parts

In geometry the whole is always precisely equal to the sum of its parts; in social experience it is usually more or less. At its best, presidential leadership moves the nation as far as possible in the directions the public favors, by means that are acceptable given prevailing values and institutional requirements. While the product of a successful synthesis is easily perceived, how to achieve it through individual leadership skills is not readily understood or achieved.

Washington's political judgment

The record of the country's first president, George Washington, attests to the complex character of the leadership synthesis. Washington was not an outstanding public orator. Neither was he at ease in bargaining and compromising with his fellow politicians. He displayed no special administrative skills. By conventional standards he was not a brilliant man—although he was intelligent—and he possessed no unusual sophistication in addressing the policy issues of his day. Yet Washington was widely acclaimed by his contemporaries, and by later generations, as a great political leader.

One reason for Washington's success was simply that he was in the right place at the right time. He was a respected and experienced military man from Virginia, still young enough to lead at the time (1775) that the second Continental Congress was looking for a southern commander-in-chief to give national balance to its largely New

England army. At the end of the war with Great Britain, Washington, the victorious general, was considered a national hero. This strengthened his reputation as president. He was a man of personal force, magnetism, and unquestioned integrity. But, above all, Washington's political judgment on the big questions of his day proved right. He saw the necessity of giving the squabbling states a coherent national government, and he worked consistently for the nation against powerful state and regional pressures. He believed that national unity was the prime need of his time, and he devoted his presidency to its realization. Washington appreciated the importance of establishing the legitimacy of the infant republic's political institutions and he repeatedly acted in ways of great practical importance to the building of this legitimacy—as in his decision to withdraw from the presidency in 1796 while he was still in good health, letting the process of orderly democratic succession work.[9]

Overall, George Washington practiced politics with energy and intelligence for the lofty ends of national unity and democratic legitimacy. The mix of personality, reputation, formal leadership skills, and transcendent good judgment that enabled him to succeed (historian James Thomas Flexner described him as "the indispensable man" in early American nation building) is not easily captured by presidential job descriptions or analyses.

THE INSTITUTIONAL PRESIDENCY

"The president needs help." This was the conclusion of the Committee on Administrative Management, appointed by President Franklin Roosevelt in 1936. The scope of presidential responsibility had become such, the committee felt, that it was necessary to enlarge and formalize the president's staff support. Acting on the committee's recommendations, Roosevelt in 1939 established the Executive Office of the President (EOP). The key units in the EOP were the White House Office, comprising the president's immediate staff, and the Bureau of the Budget (now the Office of Management and Budget—OMB), the executive's agency for budget making and review created by Congress in 1921.

This was the beginning of the *institutional presidency,* built around an elaborate staff structure. The total of White House assistants to President Herbert Hoover had been just 26 in 1930, and annual expenditures for this staff were under $1 million. Even figuring in

---

[9] See Seymour Martin Lipset's insightful account of "Washington's role [in] the institutionalization of legal-rational authority in the early United States," *The First New Nation* (Garden City, N.Y.: Anchor Doubleday, 1967), p. 25. For a more general discussion of Washington's role in the political life of late eighteenth-century America, see James Thomas Flexner, *Washington: The Indispensable Man* (Boston: Little, Brown, 1969).

An elaborate staff
structure

other executive branch help, such as the Bureau of the Budget, Hoover's assistants numbered under 100. Of course, it wasn't until 1857 that public funds were appropriated by Congress at all to pay even the salary of a private secretary to the president. The size of Herbert Hoover's staff still seems extremely modest against the backdrop of the vast increases of the past half-century. EOP personnel in the years immediately after FDR's 1939 executive order totaled roughly 300; by the time of Dwight Eisenhower's presidency in the 1950s it had climbed to 600. In 1970, with Richard Nixon in the White House, EOP personnel had increased to some 2,000, when a leveling-out and then a modest reduction finally occurred. In Ronald Reagan's administration, the EOP had 1,600 to 1,700 employees.

The White House Office

It is as true today as it was in 1937 that the president needs help. It is not at all clear, however, just how that help is best provided or what changes would be most useful. In the 1930s, more help meant more people. But the corps of advisers and assistants has become so large that more people are no longer the answer to how to provide the president with the help he needs. In fact, some experts believe that the White House staff should be further reduced.[10]

Organizing the White House staff. How well any group of staff members actually serve their executive is determined, of course, by the intelligence, experience, personality characteristics, and energy they bring to their jobs. But when staff size increases beyond a handful, organization comes into play. How his White House Office is organized to perform the tasks placed upon it helps determine the success any president enjoys.

Organizational styles

Some presidents want to interact regularly with many different aides. They resist rigid hierarchy in their staff. Stephen Hess refers to this style of staff organization as "circular."[11] As practiced by Franklin Roosevelt, Lyndon Johnson, and Jimmy Carter, the circular mode has a number of senior assistants reporting directly to the president. Other presidents, such as Dwight Eisenhower and Richard Nixon, have been comfortable with a more hierarchical arrangement that places larger coordinating and integrating responsibilities upon a chief of staff. H. R. Haldeman, Nixon's chief of staff until the Watergate scandal forced his resignation, was often criticized for using an authoritarian approach in running the White House and barring the

---

[10] *A Presidency for the 1980s*, a report by a panel of the National Academy of Public Administration (Washington, D.C.: National Academy of Public Administration, 1980), p. 17.

[11] Stephen Hess, *Organizing the Presidency* (Washington, D.C.: Brookings Institution, 1976), p. 3.

door to the president. But two senior Nixon aides, speechwriter (now *New York Times* columnist) William Safire and National Security Adviser (later Secretary of State) Henry Kissinger, have reported that Haldeman was only performing ably the role Nixon set for him. The president wanted time for solitary contemplation and he wanted to be shielded from staff intrusions.[12]

Demands on staff. There are some enduring demands on staff organization. Because presidential time is a scarce commodity, staff arrangements must be such that items needing the president's attention get it—in the best form for his action—while other items are carefully kept away. Staff must permit the president to work most efficiently, leave him accessible to officials who need to see him (and whom he needs to see) but not let him be overwhelmed by intrusions, bring him the questions he *must* decide (but not every question he *could* decide). Then, when the president has chosen a course, an effective staff helps him sail it with as little expenditure of his time as possible.

Naturally, all this is easier said than done. For, while staff are supposed to serve the president's interests, they inevitably also have and serve their own. Every presidency suffers because key White House aides become absorbed in individual pursuits of power and recognition. "No conceivable staffing arrangements will meet all his needs," wrote presidential scholar Hugh Heclo, "and yet every arrangement carries the potential of submerging his interests into those of his helpers and their machinery."[13] The rarefied atmosphere of the White House poses problems for the proper functioning and, in a sense, mental health of the staff who dwell therein. The West Wing of the White House—where the Oval Office and facilities for senior presidential aides are located—is the physical center of the American political universe. Even an occasional visitor to the West Wing cannot fail to detect the air of restrained excitement. It is easy for staff to let this go to their heads, or to succumb to the pressure-cooker atmosphere.

Power, especially the ultimate singularity of power, gives the White House its distinctive atmosphere and style. In Congress, formal constitutional authority always rests in many hands; in the White House, it rests in one pair of hands. George Reedy, a long-time aide to President Lyndon Johnson, notes: "In the Senate no course stands the remotest chance of adoption unless a minimum of fifty-one egotistical men are persuaded of its wisdom. . . ." At the other end of Pennsylvania Avenue, a course carries the day when, and only when, it has the approval of one man. "The life of the White House," says Reedy,

Staff strains and pursuits

At the center of power

[12] William Safire, *Before the Fall* (Garden City, N.Y.: Doubleday, 1975); and Henry Kissinger, *The White House Years* (Boston: Little, Brown, 1979).
[13] Hugh Heclo, "The Changing Presidential Office," in Arnold J. Miltsner, ed., *Politics and the Oval Office* (San Francisco: Institute for Contemporary Studies, 1981), p. 163.

"is the life of a court."[14] There is, then, great pressure on staff members to behave like courtiers, to court the favor of the president as the source of whatever power staff members possess. Any aide known to have the president's support or approval is strong; any aide denied access or approbation is weak. In such a setting it takes unusual strength of character to tell a president he is wrong. Having staff mature enough and confident enough to do this is important for the well-being of the nation.

Staffing the Reagan White House. One of the key tests of any White House staff is how well they adapt to the president's style of work and, especially, how effective they are in compensating for the inevitable weaknesses in his approach. The performance of Reagan's staff at various points in his two terms illustrates the importance of this dimension.

Reagan's approach to White House staff responsibilities

Some presidents, such as Jimmy Carter, have had problems arising from their getting too involved in the details of their administrations' actions. So much is happening that a president can easily be overwhelmed by the details, making it hard for him to set direction boldly on the really key matters where his intervention is needed. Ronald Reagan's approach was at the opposite pole—and displayed a different set of weaknesses. Reagan believed that a president should make the big decisions and concentrate on mobilizing the support—whether in Congress or in the public—needed to sustain these decisions. When it comes to developing and managing the specifics of his policies, he should delegate great responsibility to his White House staff and cabinet executives. In many regards, Reagan's judgment here seems sound; it accords with the views of many who have studied the issue of how chief executive officers, in the private sector and in government alike, should budget that scarcest of all critical resources, their time. But Reagan's approach imposed heavy demands on his staff. If he was going to be inattentive to many of the big and important details of his administration's programs, they surely had to be both very attentive to and highly skilled in dealing with them.

Reagan's first-term staff

Reagan's staff in his first term got generally high marks, from opponents as well as friends. Robert Strauss, a seasoned Democratic politician who has served as his party's national chairman, called the original staff "simply spectacular. It's the best White House staff I have ever seen."[15] James Baker won the esteem of most observers as chief of staff of the Reagan White House from 1981 through 1984. According to Martin Anderson, who was Reagan's domestic policy advisor in 1981 and 1982, the senior staff of the first term adapted well to the president's "unique management style."

[14] George E. Reedy, *The Twilight of the Presidency* (New York: New American Library, 1970), pp. xi, 17–18.
[15] Quoted in the *Christian Science Monitor*, May 15, 1981.

Ronald Reagan . . . had one distinctive personality trait that was highly unusual, perhaps unique for someone who rose to the high levels of managerial responsibility he attained. He made no demands, and gave almost no instructions. Essentially, he just responded to whatever was brought to his attention and said yes or no, or I'll think about it. . . . His style of managing was totally different from the model of the classic executive who exercised leadership by planning and scheming, and barking out orders to his subordinates.[16]

All the key first term staffers understood Reagan's unusual approach and worked within it. "We just accepted Reagan as he was and adjusted ourselves to his manner. If that was the way he wanted to do things, fine. At the time it seemed like a small thing, an eccentricity that was dwarfed by his multiple, stunning qualities."[17] Other close advisers who came later, including Donald T. Regan, who was chief of staff from early 1985 through early 1987, offer a picture fundamentally consistent with Anderson's.[18]

What worked satisfactorily, even very well with a senior staff who accommodated themselves to it effectively, could become a disaster if another group of advisers were not up to the responsibilities the president's style imposed upon them. The Iran-Contra debacle in Reagan's second term dramatically illustrated the weakness always present in his high-risk approach.

The Iran-Contra affair   The Iran-Contra affair had its beginnings in 1985, in Reagan administration frustration over worsening conditions in the Middle East—especially the taking hostage of U.S. citizens in Lebanon by groups supporting the Ayatollah Khomeini's regime in Iran. The administration secretly approved two shipments of small arms by Israeli intelligence to leaders in Iran thought likely to be helpful in securing the hostages' release and, ultimately, in reestablishing satisfactory relations between western countries and Iran. At various stages in this process, three American hostages were actually released. In January 1986 President Reagan authorized additional arms shipments to Iran; implementation of the initiative was delegated to several staff members of the National Security Council—which is part of the Executive Office of the President (see below). The cover of the operation was blown in November 1986 when, after a deliberate leak by one of the Iranian middlemen, an article describing events was published in a Lebanese magazine. An investigation by the U.S. attorney general, prompted by the storm that followed the "arms for hostages" revelations, showed that some profits from the arms sales were diverted to the Contra rebels in Nicaragua. Robert C. McFarlane, national security adviser from October 17, 1983, to December 4, 1985,

---

[16] Martin Anderson, *Revolution* (New York: Harcourt Brace Jovanovich, 1988), p. 295.
[17] Anderson, *Revolution*, pp. 289–90.
[18] See, for example, Donald T. Regan, *For the Record* (New York: Harcourt Brace Jovanovich, 1988).

his successor as NSC staff chief, Admiral John Poindexter, and an NSC assistant, Lieutenant Colonel Oliver North, were the key figures in these transactions.

More than a little incredulity greeted the response of President Reagan that he had been kept entirely in the dark on important aspects of the Iran-Contra developments, including the diversion of arms sales profits. Subsequent investigations by a special review board, by House and Senate Select Committees, and by independent counsel Lawrence E. Walsh, who was named to investigate criminal charges, made it clear, though, that the president really was not informed. Problems of "runaway staff"—pursuing their own ideas of what is right or necessary—are hardly uncommon in large bureaucracies. The president's approach had left him especially vulnerable, however, based as it was on extensive delegation and inattention to detail.

"Runaway staff" and presidential vulnerability

The first investigative body to report was the president's Special Review Board, chaired by former U.S. Senator John Tower and including as well former NSC Adviser Brent Scowcroft and former Secretary of State Edmund Muskie. In retrospect, the board's report was in many ways the most impressive of all the commentary the affair elicited. It faulted both the president and his key advisers. "The NSC system will not work unless the president makes it work," the Tower Report notes, and in this "complex, high-risk operation and so much at stake, the president should have ensured that the NSC system did not fail him." Throughout the long course of the ill-fated Iran initiative, Reagan's key advisers had ample opportunities to compensate for weaknesses in the president's management approach. As General Scowcroft put it, "there should have been bells ringing, lights flashing, and so on." This did not happen. The Review Board strongly criticized failings of McFarlane, Poindexter, and North, but it didn't spare the actions, and especially the inactions, of more senior officials.[19]

THE EXECUTIVE OFFICE OF THE PRESIDENT

The personal staff of the White House are the most visible part of the institutional presidency. They are, however, only one unit out of ten in a presidential staff structure, called the Executive Office of the President (EOP), that employs over 1,600 people and costs just over $124 million to operate (in 1988). Figure 7.1 shows the various units of the EOP, when each was formally established, and the number of staff within it. All EOP agencies report directly to the president, and the top officers of each are appointed by him. But, unlike senior staff

[19] Report of the *President's Special Review Board*, February 26, 1987.

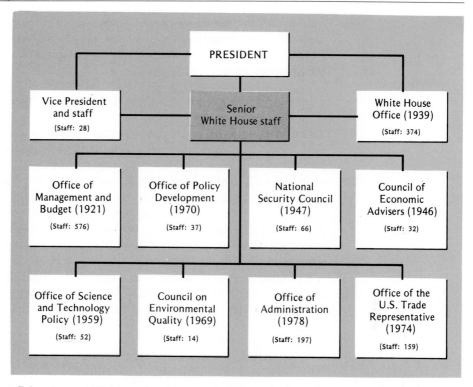

Figure 7.1
The Executive Office of the President
Year in parenthesis represents date when office received formal statutory recognition. Omitted from staff figures are approximately 100 employees performing household management and similar tasks. Staff size figures are for 1987–88.

Source: U.S. Senate Committee on Governmental Affairs, *Organization of Federal Executive Departments and Agencies,* January 1, 1988.

of the White House Office, the heads of a number of other EOP units must receive Senate confirmation—including the three members of the Council of Economic Advisers, the director of the Office of Management and Budget, and the special representative for trade negotiation. And, while the president has considerable discretion in reorganizing the EOP, many of its units outside the White House operate under the specifications of statutes enacted by Congress. The Council of Economic Advisers, for example, functions under the terms of the Employment Act of 1946; and the National Security Council (NSC), under the National Security Act of 1947.

National Security Council

The NSC has four statutory members: the president, the vice president, the secretary of state, and the secretary of defense. In addition, the director of the Central Intelligence Agency and the chairman of the Joint Chiefs of Staff are statutory advisers. NSC staff are under the direction of the Assistant to the President for National Security Affairs. The role of the council and its staff was intended to be purely advisory—the president calling upon them as he saw fit to get the balanced information he needed in making foreign policy. The Tower Commission strongly criticized the kind of involvement by NSC staff in the implementing of policy that was so dramatically evident in the Iran-Contra affair.

Office of Management and Budget

The OMB is the largest agency in the Executive Office of the President, successor to the Bureau of the Budget established in 1921. Its 600 or so staff members help the president accomplish his political objectives in formulating and administering the budget, reviewing the organizational structure and management procedures of the entire executive branch, developing regulatory reform proposals, and assessing program objectives. When a president is trying to achieve major governmental change, he is likely to lean even more upon the staff resources of the OMB.

The OMB and NSC, along with the White House Office, are the most important units of the Executive Office of the President. Their functions, as well as the functions of other units, are discussed further in chapter 8.

THE VICE PRESIDENT

It is doubtful that any political office in the United States has been the subject of as many jokes as the vice presidency. Benjamin Franklin did not like the idea of a vice presidency to begin with, and he suggested that the holder of the office should be addressed as "His Superfluous Majesty." In declining a vice presidential nomination by the Whig party in the middle of the nineteenth century, Senator Daniel Webster of Massachusetts said that "he did not propose to be buried until he was already dead." Thomas Marshall, who served for eight years as Woodrow Wilson's vice president, gave us the classic vice presidential joke: "Once there were two brothers. One ran away to sea; the other was elected vice president. And nothing was ever heard of either of them again." (Marshall was perhaps best known for his wit. He created another classic line when he whispered during a Senate debate over which he was presiding that "what the country *really* needs is a good five-cent cigar.")

Succession

It was the country's first vice president, John Adams, who provided the most perceptive summation of the office: "I am nothing, but I may be everything." A vice president's constitutional powers are feeble: he presides over the Senate (when he wants to) and casts the

Vice President Lyndon Johnson is sworn in as president immediately following the assassination of President Kennedy.

deciding vote if the Senate is deadlocked (which rarely happens); that is all. But he is, in the constitutional sense, "a heartbeat away from the presidency." Article II provides that "in Case of the Removal of the President from Office, or of his Death, Resignation, or Inability to discharge the Powers and Duties of the said Office, the Same shall devolve on the Vice President. . . ." Thirteen of the nation's forty presidents first served as vice presidents; nine of the presidents succeeded to the presidency upon the death or (in one instance) resignation of an incumbent.

"A heartbeat away from the presidency"

Assistant to the President

Since the vice president has no significant constitutional powers, except the constitutional role of standing first in the line of succession, he is wholly dependent upon the president for his assignments. Historically such assignments have been extremely modest. No vice president through Alben Barkley (who served under Harry Truman from 1949 to 1953) was given major governmental or political responsibilities. The reasons for this are clear. Vice presidential candidates have often been chosen for political and geographic balance on a ticket. As we saw, Lincoln picked Andrew Johnson of Tennessee as his running mate in 1864 because he wanted a pro-union southern Democrat to strengthen a broad unionist appeal. New York liberal Franklin Roosevelt wanted Texas conservative John Nance Garner for ticket balance in the 1932 presidential race. Thus chosen, vice presidents rarely became friends and confidants of their presidents, and they lost out to more trusted assistants in contests for the president's ear.

But over the last three decades the picture of vice presidential weakness has substantially altered. Without any single dramatic development, a new consensus has taken form. The enormity of presidential responsibilities, together with the substantial possibility that a vice president will succeed to them, requires that individuals not be chosen as vice presidential candidates unless they are presidential material. It follows that presidents should not toss their vice presidents into ceremonial oblivion, but should assign them real responsibilities so that they will be prepared to take on presidential duties if necessary. As presidents have begun to act on this strong, if informal, consensus, they have come to find that active, well-informed vice presidents are handy to have around.

The first notable departure occurred with Eisenhower and Nixon in the 1950s. The two men were not close, personally or politically; they were far apart in age and experience. Eisenhower had decidedly ambivalent feelings about his vice president and seriously considered dropping him from the ticket in both 1952 and 1956. Despite this, the president's strong inclination to delegate responsibility and his lack of interest in Republican party affairs led him to assign his vice president major political tasks. Nixon was also picked to represent the United States on highly visible and important foreign trips. Richard Nixon entered the vice presidency in 1953 as a quite junior Republican politician from California; he left in 1961 as the most prominent Republican (after the retiring Eisenhower), and a man who had come within a whisker of winning election in his own right against Democrat John F. Kennedy in November 1960. Kennedy's choice of Lyndon Johnson as his vice presidential running mate in 1960, and Gerald Ford's designation of Nelson Rockefeller as vice president in 1974, were also important steps in the rise of the office. Johnson and Rockefeller were powerful, strong-willed figures. Their willingness to accept the vice presidency was symbolically important. Kennedy never really trusted Johnson politically, and Ford could not make the use of Rockefeller that he wanted to because Republican conservatives so disliked the former New York governor. But no office that held political forces like Lyndon Johnson and Nelson Rockefeller could really be described as "His Superfluous Majesty."

Expanding vice presidential responsibility

Nixon, Johnson, Rockefeller

The Vice Presidency Today

Jimmy Carter and Ronald Reagan completed a seemingly permanent elevation of vice presidential responsibilities. Both made their vice presidents—Walter Mondale and George Bush, respectively—close associates and confidants, movers in the inner circles of administration affairs, even though neither president—vice president team had been close prior to their election. A new imperative is working. Presidents now need able and informed vice presidents. Vice presidents know that their role now requires them to function as loyal assistants to their presidents. Mondale won Carter's complete trust and confidence. Bush became a close political friend and associate of Reagan. This pattern is likely to continue in the Bush administration and the vice presidency of Dan Quayle.

PRESIDENTIAL POWER

Power of persuasion

Richard Neustadt, a former presidential assistant, argues that the power of the presidency gets depicted too much in terms of formal authority and not enough in terms of persuasion.[20] A president is strong or weak, succeeds or fails in his governing tasks, on the basis of whether he can convince the many political groups and offices with whom he must deal "that what the White House wants of them is what they ought to do for their sake and on their authority." In part Neustadt is describing political life under separation of powers. A president's entire legislative program lies beyond his formal powers of command. He has resources to persuade Congress to enact his policies, but he has few means to force legislators to enact them. Democracy limits cases of command and stresses the need for consent. In the extreme case where the consent of the governed is lost totally, a president's constitutional command powers become an empty shell. As we saw in the months just before the Watergate scandal forced his resignation, Richard Nixon retained the formal authority of the presidency but he was without the capacity to persuade. His most basic, practical power had slipped away.

Is Persuasion Enough?

The constitutional command powers of an American president are not very great when placed against his diverse responsibilities and the nation's high expectations of his performance. If a president cannot secure broad approval for his initiatives among the public at large and the political leadership community—especially in Congress—his position is weak. Whenever the country has had effective presidential "rulership," James Young observes, it has received it "within a constitutional framework [that was] deliberately *designed to make rulership difficult.*"[21] We saw in chapter 5 that critics of the separation of powers find the United States too dependent on having a president

[20] Neustadt, *Presidential Power*, pp. 26–43.
[21] Young, *Washington Community*, p. 252. Emphasis added.

able to move by persuasion. They grant that at those times when a politically adroit president enjoys high popularity, the system responds effectively. But too often the president's persuasive resources are insufficient to overcome the fragmentation inherent in the separation of powers.[22]

Contradictory Judgments

There is reason to be skeptical about such judgments. Any time political institutions manage to sustain strong popular support over a span of two hundred years, the presumption should be that they are doing something right, at least in the thinking of those governed by them. The American public has shown little dissatisfaction with the constitutional limits on the presidency. And there is no agreement among experts as to whether the United States has a problem with regard to presidential power and, if so, what it is. The presidency of John F. Kennedy in the beginning of the 1960s was hailed by many experts as "Camelot." The vigorous young executive had an office through which he could make good things happen. Arthur Schlesinger, Jr., noted in 1965 that Kennedy's presidency was based on the belief that

Kennedy and "Camelot"

> the Chief Executive . . . must be "the vital center of action in our whole scheme of government." The nature of the office demanded that the President place himself in the very thick of the fight . . . [that he] be prepared to exercise the fullest powers of his office—all that are specified and some that are not.[23]

The presidency was strong, and it was good that it was strong.

Following Kennedy's assassination, however, the activist president who was his successor used his office to lead the United States into a war that saw an American army of half a million men engaged in a small Asian country. The Vietnam War lasted twice as long as any previous military conflict in which the United States had been involved and claimed more American lives than any conflict other than the Civil War and World War II, and it prompted massive dissent at home. Vietnam dominated Lyndon Johnson's administration and that of his successor, Richard Nixon. Watergate followed almost immediately upon Vietnam. Now many of the same commentators who had proclaimed and endorsed a strong presidency denounced the presidency as bloated in its powers, imperial in its bearing and style, and dangerously open to personal abuses of power. The presidency was strong—but there was trouble in its strength.[24]

A strong presidency or a weak presidency?

Enter Jimmy Carter. He banished "Hail to the Chief" as the presi-

[22] James L. Sundquist, *Constitutional Reform and Effective Government* (Washington, D.C.: Brookings Institution, 1986). See, too, Donald L. Robinson, ed., *Reforming American Government* (Boulder, Co.: Westview Press, 1986).
[23] Arthur M. Schlesinger, Jr., *A Thousand Days* (Boston: Houghton Mifflin, 1965), p. 120.
[24] Idem., *The Imperial Presidency* (New York: Popular Library, 1973), p. 359.

President John F. Kennedy at his inaugural ball on January 20, 1961.

dent's song and donned his cardigan for low-key chats with the public. In matters of far greater substance, especially the conduct of U.S.

Carter: a weakened presidency?

foreign policy, he wanted a more restricted role for the president and for the nation. Quickly, though, events such as the seizure of the U.S. embassy in Iran and the holding of its staff as hostages for fourteen months came to be seen as dramatic signs of the Carter administration's weakness and the decline of American power. The presidency was now weak—and it was bad that it was weak.

These oscillations must have had an impact on the people who saw them, even on presidents. Having seen the glorifications of a strong

Changing lessons on presidential power

presidency, might not Lyndon Johnson and Richard Nixon have been encouraged to think that greater assertiveness on their part was really in the national interest? Having been warned repeatedly of the dangers of an "imperial" presidency, might not Jimmy Carter have drawn back more than he should and otherwise would have from the assertion of executive leadership? After Reagan succeeded Carter, however, the situation seemed almost immediately to change. The new administration won support, even in the Democratic-controlled House of Representatives, for substantial portions of its foreign, defense, and domestic programs. The new president seemed amply able to set the tone and direction for American national government. Indeed, discussion shifted to whether a Reagan revolution was altering basic governmental commitments developed over the preceding decades. In Reagan's second term there was talk of his becoming a "lame duck"—a president who could not again seek re-election and whose political clout was thus diminished. For the most part, though, the idea of a weak presidency found little currency in the Reagan years.

The presidency is an office of which much is expected in the American governmental system. It has fairly modest and much-checked formal powers, but great resources for political leadership by persuasion. Different presidents have employed the power of persuasion for contrasting ends, in constantly shifting political circumstances. There is as yet no consensus as to whether the president's powers and institutional position should be changed, much less as to a particular set of changes to be obtained.

ASSESSING PRESIDENTS

Presidents' reputations have undergone some startling changes. No president is all good or bad, of course; each reveals a mix of positive and negative attributes. At any given time, one facet of a president's performance is emphasized; later it may be a quite different facet. Assessments of Herbert Hoover, the country's thirtieth president, reflect this pattern of sharp interpretative shifts over time. Until the Great Depression, Hoover was widely considered a humanitarian, an outstanding organizer and doer, and a progressive Republican. His work

President Herbert Hoover.

in organizing relief help to avert starvation in Belgium after World War I earned him international acclaim on both organizational and humanitarian grounds. The election of 1928 was not, at the time, viewed as a contest between Republican conservative (Hoover) and a Democratic liberal (New York Governor Alfred E. Smith), but rather as one between two moderate progressives; many observers thought Hoover's credentials as a progressive were better than Smith's.

Then came the Great Depression and President Hoover's responses to it. A new picture of Hoover emerged: of a very conservative, insensitive man who was a failure at managing the great economic crisis. Over the last 15 to 20 years, however, the picture has again changed. Students of Hoover's presidency have adopted a far more complimentary view of his political commitments and performance. One study published in 1975 declares Hoover to be a "forgotten progressive." "There is a good deal of talk today about a 'new' Hoover. Disparate political groups ranging from the far right to the far left think they are rediscovering him, because his progressive philosophy contained ideas whose time has finally arrived."[25]

Both the positive and the negative judgments of Hoover were correct in part. He was a progressive man of great managerial talent. His administration's response to the Great Depression was by no means only short-sighted and conservative. But Hoover did find it hard to recognize the immense impact of the Depression on the thinking of his fellow citizens, and his response to criticism was to "hunker down" and to emphasize less humanitarian aspects of his political approach. Not surprisingly, as Joan Hoff Wilson points out, the prevailing judgment during the Depression and its immediate aftermath filtered out the positive dimensions of Hoover's work, while interpretations since the 1960s have seen it through a different, less critical filter.

Dwight Eisenhower's presidency has also prompted striking shifts of interpretation. General Eisenhower came to the presidency a hero of the American effort in World War II. As president, however, his lack of a bold domestic policy and his view that the presidency was to be used sparingly rather than vigorously invited criticism, especially from those who expected the president to be a doer of great deeds along the model of FDR. But, recently, Eisenhower's strengths are again being emphasized in something of an "Eisenhower revival." His refusal to be pushed into military action in Vietnam appears far more commendable after the sad experience of that war.[26] His modest judgments on the possibilities of governmental action appear sounder after a long spell of governmental activism than they did before. That Eisenhower had a coherent sense of leadership—which,

Herbert Hoover: a reassessment

An Eisenhower revival

---

[25] Joan Hoff Wilson, *Herbert Hoover: Forgotten Progressive* (Boston: Little, Brown, 1975), p. 269.
[26] See Louis W. Koenig, *The Chief Executive*, 4th ed. (New York: Harcourt Brace, 1981), p. 349.

President Dwight Eisenhower.

while very different from FDR's, is impressive in its own right—has come to be better appreciated by leading students of his presidency:

> On reexamination, Eisenhower's approach to presidential leadership emerges as distinctive and consciously thought-out, rather than an unfortunate example of airless drift. . . . When carefully explicated, this approach promises to add significantly to the repertoire of assumptions about how the expanded modern presidency can be conducted.[27]

Even Richard Nixon's presidency is already being reinterpreted. When he was forced to resign his office in disgrace, on August 9, 1974, following the Watergate scandals, it seemed unlikely that Nixon would soon see any substantial political rehabilitation. But by the mid-1980s just such was occurring. *Newsweek* exemplified the changing view of the press, when in a cover story on the former president in 1986, it observed that "the premise of his rehabilitation is that—Watergate aside—Nixon left a legacy of solid achievement, especially in foreign affairs."[28]

What will be the verdict on the Reagan presidency well in the future, when the emotions generated by immediate political battles have largely subsided? The sharp turns in the presidential ratings of the

Personality and the presidency

[27] Fred I. Greenstein, "Eisenhower as an Activist President: A Look at New Evidence," *Political Science Quarterly*, Winter 1979–80, p. 596; and idem., *The Hidden-Hand Presidency: Eisenhower as Leader* (New York: Basic Books, 1982).
[28] The Road Back," *Newsweek*, May 19, 1986, p. 27.

public and experts alike should make us a bit cautious in responding. We do know, though, that Reagan will ultimately be judged by much the same standards as the man for whom he cast his first presidential ballot, Franklin D. Roosevelt. FDR's administration changed permanently the role of American national government, expanding its economic management, regulatory, and welfare functions. Because the direction of these changes is seen as generally sound from the perspective of fifty years, Roosevelt's reputation remains firmly established. Whereas FDR expanded government, Reagan sought to curb its growth. The immense changes he encouraged in tax policy alone will have persisting effects. (We discuss these in chapter 16.) The large federal deficits of the Reagan years will be assessed for their long-term implications. From judgments about these and other matters involving the federal role and economic policy, history will reach more general conclusions about the strength, or the weakness, of the Ronald Reagan presidency.

Whatever the verdict on the substance of his administration's programs, Ronald Reagan the man is likely to be seen by history much as his contemporaries have seen him—as someone of unusual grace and strength of personality. Various scenes exemplify these characteristics—such as the president brought to surgery on March 30, 1981, with a bullet in his left lung following an assassination attempt, quipping to his doctors that "I hope you're Republicans." In a book that often reflects his anger over being fired as chief of staff during the Iran-Contra affair, Donald Regan paints a number of similar pictures. About to undergo cancer surgery on July 13, 1985, the president bantered with Regan and then engaged in a spirited discussion of the importance of cutting taxes and not raising federal spending.[29] If it all sounds like a movie, remember that movie actors have not really been shot in the chest or faced with colon cancer.

Many people who know Ronald Reagan have testified that the public man and the private person are one in the same. But both reveal contradictions. "Affable" was probably used more than any other adjective to describe Reagan, but aide Martin Anderson says he was as well "warmly ruthless."[30] He would cause discomfort to others "freely and easily," Anderson writes, if it were necessary in something he wanted to accomplish. Outgoing and an engaging conversationalist, Reagan was remarkably private and self-centered. Only one other person, his wife Nancy, ever entered his inner circle. Described as laid back and passive, Reagan displayed a fierce ambition that carried him from the small towns of central Illinois, to a career in Hollywood, to two terms as governor of the largest state government and two as president. Often called an ideologue, he built a political

A verdict on the Reagan presidency?

The strength of Reagan's personality

---

[29] Regan, *For the Record*, pp. 235–36.
[30] Anderson, *Revolution*, p. 288.

President Ronald Reagan.

career on compromise and pragmatism.[31] All in all, Ronald Reagan did not easily fit into the molds into which we try to place our presidents.

Presidential Character

Not only do conclusions about the merits of a particular presidency change over time; so do judgments about what we should look for in a prospective president. In the 1930s, 1940s, and 1950s little emphasis was placed on the requisite personality traits of a potential president. If pressed, one would have conceded that certain types of personalities were better suited to the office, more likely to give the country the performance it wanted. But personality did not seem a critical factor. Neither Roosevelt, Truman, nor Eisenhower—the three

[31] For an insightful account of some of these many contradictions, see Garry Wills, *Reagan's America* (New York: Doubleday, 1987).

men who occupied the presidency between 1933 and 1961—made us anxious by apparent deficiencies in their personalities.

Importance of presidential character

In succession during the 1960s and early 1970s, however, the United States had two presidents whose personalities raised concern among many people. Lyndon Johnson and Richard Nixon seemed too driven, too aggressive, too inclined to view as hostile the political world with which they had to deal. Personality emerged as a more important variable than it had been for assessing potential presidents. Political scientist James David Barber gave more systematic emphasis to these general concerns in his book *The Presidential Character*. Barber described Johnson and Nixon as "active-negative" personality types. The active-negative "seems ambitious, striving upward, power-seeking. His stance toward the environment is aggressive and he has a persistent problem in managing his aggressive feelings. . . . Life is a hard struggle to achieve and hold power, hampered by the condemnations of a perfectionist conscience."[32] Barber argued that "active-negatives" can be identified before they get to the presidency, and that it is important to do so because their presidencies are likely to be deeply troubling for the nation. Others are less confident that we know enough to practice political psychology successfully, except in extreme cases.

The Public's Ratings

Americans are not reluctant to criticize presidents for inadequate performance in office, but at the same time they recognize that the job has been extremely demanding. By large margins, the public thinks that Congress has become more difficult to deal with, that the communications media are more critical of presidents than they used to be, that the problems presidents are expected to solve have become increasingly complicated, and that the public itself may now be too demanding (see Figure 7.2). People want their presidents to set high standards, but they do not expect them to be persons without faults or immune to the problems that affect others.

Survey of recent presidential performance

Americans are sophisticated critics of their presidents. Louis Harris and Associates conducted a poll in 1987 in which people were queried: "I'd like to ask you about the last nine presidents of the United States. Please keep in mind Roosevelt, Truman, Eisenhower, Kennedy, Johnson, Nixon, Ford, Carter, and Reagan. If you had to choose one, which president do you think . . . was best on domestic affairs?" Respondents were then asked to rate presidents in this and other areas. They answered that Roosevelt and Kennedy were best on domestic matters, Kennedy and Nixon best on foreign affairs; that Kennedy most inspired confidence; that Nixon set the lowest moral standards;

[32] James David Barber, *The Presidential Character* (Englewood Cliffs, N.J.: Prentice-Hall, 1985), p. 9.

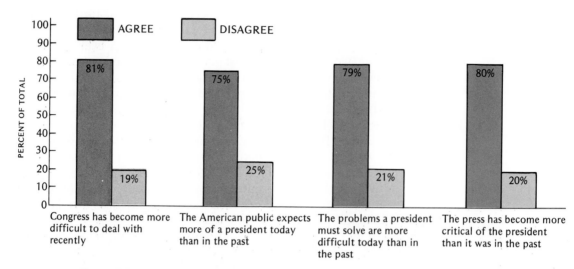

AGREE   DISAGREE

81%   19%   75%   25%   79%   21%   80%   20%

PERCENT OF TOTAL

Congress has become more difficult to deal with recently

The American public expects more of a president today than in the past

The problems a president must solve are more difficult today than in the past

The press has become more critical of the president than it was in the past

Figure 7.2
Public Answers to the Question: Please Tell Me Whether You Agree or Disagree with the Following Statements about the Presidency

Source: "Attitudes Toward the Presidency," a survey conducted in December 1979 by the Gallup Organization for the Corporation for Public Broadcasting.

and that Carter was least able to get things done (Table 7.1). The survey shows a public that makes more complex judgments about presidents, rather than assigning them to two bins labeled "good" and "bad."

Table 7.1
Americans Rate Their Presidents (in percent)

	FDR	HST	DDE	JFK	LBJ	RMN	GRF	JEC	RWR
Best on domestic affairs	20	7	7	25	4	3	2	5	10
Best in foreign affairs	8	6	9	23	1	22	2	6	10
Least able to get things done	1	2	3	3	7	10	14	43	7
Most inspired confidence	15	7	8	39	1	1	2	4	13
Set the lowest moral standards	2	2	1	8	7	41	3	12	9
Likely to be viewed by history as best over all	28	9	6	29	1	3	1	2	13

Question: "I'd like to ask you about the last nine presidents of the United States. Please keep in mind Roosevelt, Truman, Eisenhower, Kennedy, Johnson, Nixon, Ford, Carter, and Reagan. If you had to choose one, which president do you think [read each item] . . . was best on domestic affairs . . . was best in foreign affairs . . . was least able to get things done . . . most inspired confidence in the White House. . . ." Sample size was 1,252.

Source: Survey by Louis Harris and Associates, February 20–24, 1987.

SUMMARY

The framers had contrasting objectives in mind when they designed the presidency. They wanted to end the extreme executive weakness that distinguished government under the Articles of Confederation. But they also wanted the president so checked and balanced that he could not rule arbitrarily.

As the contemporary presidency attests, they succeeded to a large degree in these pursuits. The singularity of the office—the Constitution vests "the executive power of the United States" in one individual, the president—adds greatly to its visibility and persuasive force. But the president remains subject to great constitutional restraints, the most basic one being separation of powers: Every law the executive administers, every dollar it spends, requires the action of a separate and very independent branch of government, the Congress.

Many different types of responsibilities have been put on American presidents by the Constitution and modern political necessity. The president is at once party leader and ceremonial chief of state, manager of domestic prosperity and leader of the Western alliance, administrator-in-chief, commander-in-chief, and legislator-in-chief. Sometimes his plate seems to get a little too full. To accomplish all the different things expected of him, a president would have to possess a truly amazing collection of skills. He would have to be a great communicator and campaigner, an adroit politician among politicians, a consummate administrator, a great conceptualizer of policy—and comprising all these and more, a great democratic leader. Perhaps it isn't too surprising that we don't always quite get everything in one individual.

Of course, the president gets a lot of help. Formalized in 1939, the Executive Office of the President (EOP) is composed of a series of staff agencies. At the center is the White House Office, consisting of senior presidential assistants and other staff. The Office of Management and Budget and the National Security Council are two other pivotal units of the EOP.

No one argues that presidential staffs suffer from any lack of numbers. But getting them to function coherently and efficiently on behalf of presidential objectives is always hard. Often derided in the past as mere standby equipment, the vice presidency seems to have emerged as the source of high-level presidential assistance.

Some observers worry that the formal powers and institutional resources of the presidency are insufficient, when set against the demands placed on the office. Policy stalemate or incoherence, resulting from the executive–legislative separation, is the greatest concern. But over the last quarter-century, assessments of presidential power have undergone great fluctuations, under changing political circumstances and types of presidential leadership. There is now nothing approaching general agreement on any type of institutional change.

Assessments of presidents, by experts and the public, have undergone quite striking shifts over time. Performance that looks deficient by standards elevated by the experience of one generation, often looks better against the backdrop of another generation's problems. The things we worry about or look for most in potential presidents also change, although a president's personality or character is an enduring concern.

FOR FURTHER STUDY

Martin Anderson, *Revolution* (New York: Harcourt Brace Jovanovich, 1988). An insightful account of the workings of the Reagan presidency, by an economist who held a high staff position in it.

James David Barber, *The Presidential Character: Predicting Performance in the White House*, 3rd ed. (Englewood Cliffs, NJ: Prentice-Hall, 1985). An analysis of presidential behavior based on an effort to categorize key features of presidents' personalities.

Edward S. Corwin, *The President: Office and Powers, History and Analysis of Practice and Opinion* (New York: New York University Press, 1940). This work also appears in a revised 5th edition by Randall W. Bland, *et al*, eds, entitled *The President: Office and Powers, 1787–1984* (New York: New York University, 1984). A comprehensive description of the presidency by one of its leading students.

Thomas E. Cronin, *The State of the Presidency*, 2nd ed. (Boston: Little, Brown, 1980). A text that provides an especially comprehensive and balanced account of the office.

Richard E. Neustadt, *Presidential Power: The Politics of Leadership from FDR to Carter* (New York: John Wiley and Sons, 1980; first published, 1960). One of the most insightful accounts ever written of the nature of presidential power, the limitations on it, and the resources available for its exercise.

Bert A. Rockman, *The Leadership Question: The Presidency and the American System* (New York: Praeger, 1984). A thoughtful contemporary discussion of the position of the president in the American governing system.

Clinton Rossiter, *The American Presidency*, 2nd revised ed. (New York: New American Library, 1960; first published, 1956). A short, highly readable description of the American presidency, including a discussion of the many different roles the president is required to perform and the various skills needed for these.

Chapter 8

The Executive Branch

The executive branch of the federal government includes the president, his key aides and cabinet officials—and about *3 million* other civilian employees. The total is itself enough to remind us that the administration of modern government has become a huge undertaking, a far cry from what it was two centuries ago. In 1790 the entire federal executive establishment encompassed about 2,000 persons, and most of them operated post offices. The federal government is far and away the country's largest employer. Not only does it have to struggle to manage federal programs and policies; it confronts major problems in managing itself.

THE PRESIDENT AND THE EXECUTIVE BRANCH

Every four years Americans elect a president who is vested constitutionally with "the executive Power . . . of the United States of America." Yet if this grant seems unambiguous, the president's relationships with the many departments and agencies that comprise the executive branch—and in particular the extent of his authority over them—are in fact varied and complex. Later in this chapter we look specifically at the different units that make up the federal executive and how they are organized. At the outset, though, we need to get a sense of the diversity in the arrangements that have evolved for expressing "the executive power."

Many of the key administrative units of the executive branch are supposed to respond to presidential direction. This is true of departments such as State and Defense. Carrying out American foreign policy and seeing to the national defense are major undertakings. The

departments established to attend to these matters have grown to be able to meet their diverse responsibilities. With about 1.1 million civilian employees and more than 2 million men and women on active duty, Defense is the largest department in the executive branch. Even State, a very small executive department, employs over 26,000. To suggest that departments such as these, with their layers of policy-making units and staffs, simply respond to what the president wants done would be silly indeed. Still, a determined president has the means of seeing that in the broad outlines of policy State and Defense do his bidding.

President selects chief executive officials

The president alone decides who will be the chief executive of each department. His choices for secretary of state and secretary of defense require Senate approval, but in the American constitutional tradition the Senate grants the president very wide latitude to pick the people he wants in such posts. If the president is dissatisfied with any aspect of a secretary's performance he can remove him. Individuals appointed to these high-ranking positions are often strong willed, with ideas of their own about what policies are required. And they often have their own bases of support such that a president must expend some scarce political capital if he chooses to dismiss them before they want to go. Nonetheless, they recognize the president's constitutional and political primacy in the fields of foreign and defense policy. They are his agents.

Other agencies in the executive branch were established with different notions of their proper responsiveness to presidential direc-

From the Department of Defense to the National Park Service, the size and diversity of the executive branch is enormous.

A. Weiner

tion. Sometimes it has been deemed desirable for an executive agency to be insulated from political pressures; so it is constituted in such a way as to remove it from a president's control. An example here is the Federal Reserve, the central bank of the United States, an executive branch organization that has enormous responsibilities in the area of U.S. monetary policy. (The Federal Reserve is described in detail in chapter 16.)

Insulation of certain executive agencies

At the apex of the Federal Reserve system is its Board of Governors. The seven governors are appointed by the president and must be confirmed by the Senate, but to insulate them from political pressure they are appointed for unusually long terms of 14 years. Terms of board members are also so arranged that one expires every two years, making it harder for a president to appoint a majority. The idea is that management of the country's money supply shouldn't reside with an official who might be tempted to manipulate it to help his party in the next election to the country's detriment in the long run. As we will see in chapter 16, the Federal Reserve needs the president's support for its monetary policies to be successful; the president in turn needs the Fed's cooperation if his economic programs are to be properly advanced. The two have strong incentives to work together. But the president does not control the Fed and its policies in the way he determines U.S. foreign policy. The Fed's chairman and the other six governors know that they have been appointed to an agency designed to operate independently of the president and regular political pressures—and often, though not always, they act accordingly.

The Federal Reserve

EVOLUTION OF THE EXECUTIVE BRANCH

For all the present scale of the executive branch of the national government, the constitutional foundations for it are modest. Article II states that the president "shall nominate, and by and with the Advice and Consent of the Senate, shall appoint Ambassadors, other public Ministers and Consuls, Judges of the Supreme Court, and all other officers of the United States, whose Appointments . . . shall be established by Law. . . ." It further stipulates that Congress may "vest the Appointment of such inferior Officers, as they think proper, in the President alone . . . or in the Heads of Departments." Every federal department and agency has come into existence through simple legislation enacted by Congress, and each may be reorganized or eliminated at any time in the same way.

Birth of executive departments

When the first Congress convened in 1789, its members agreed that several executive departments should be established and that each should be headed by a single official—appointed, as the Constitution required, by the president with the Senate's advice and consent. The departments of State, Treasury, and War (the latter renamed and reorganized in 1947 as the Department of Defense) were set up in 1789, as was the office of Attorney General (now the Justice Department). The Post Office Department was also created in 1789, but its present-day successor, the U.S. Postal Service, is no longer a department of cabinet rank.

Only four of the present thirteen executive-branch departments—State, Treasury, Defense, and Justice—trace their lineage all the way back to Washington's presidency. Four others—Interior, Agriculture, Labor, and Commerce—were established in the late nineteenth and early twentieth centuries. The remaining five have been established since 1950: Health, Education, and Welfare (HEW) in 1953; Housing and Urban Development (HUD) in 1965; Transportation in 1966; Energy in 1977; and Education in 1979. The last of these came into being when the old Office of Education was separated from HEW and given independent departmental status. HEW was renamed and recast as the Department of Health and Human Services (HHS).

Early Executive-Branch Activity

The first federal employees

The earliest executive offices were restricted to the minimum number of areas—finance, foreign policy, defense, postal service, and law. They also had very limited duties and needed few employees. For example, the State Department at the outset had only 9 staff members besides the Secretary! A quarter-century after the Constitution was ratified, federal employees numbered just over 4,800. Of these, only 500 or so worked in Washington; most were scattered in towns around the

Table 8.1
Civilian Employees of the Federal Government,
1816–1987

Year	Total number of employees	Number employed in the Washington, D.C. area
1816	4,837	535
1821	6,914	603
1831	11,491	666
1841	18,038	1,014
1851	26,274	1,533
1861	36,672	2,199
1871	51,020	6,222
1881	100,020	13,124
1891	157,442	20,834
1901	239,476	28,044
1911	395,905	39,782
1921	561,142	82,416
1931	609,746	76,303
1941	1,437,682	190,588
1951	2,482,666	265,980
1961	2,435,804	246,266
1971	2,874,166	322,969
1981	2,858,742	350,516
1987	3,100,379	349,313

Source: United States Bureau of the Census, Historical Statistics of the United States, Colonial Times to 1970, Part 2; pp. 1102–03; U.S. Office of Personnel Management, Federal Civilian Workforce Statistics: Employment and Trends as of January 1988, p. 10.

country providing the one service that required many workers—delivering the mail. By 1816 there were over 3,200 U.S. post offices; as the country grew, so did the number of post offices, reaching about 30,000 in 1871. Total federal employment climbed gradually from about 4,800 in 1816 to 51,000 in 1871, and most of this growth was accounted for by the postal service (Table 8.1).

In our own time the largest executive department—indeed, the largest single employer in the country—is the Department of Defense (DOD). DOD employed just over three million Americans in 1986, including more than 2 million active-duty military personnel, and 1 million directly hired civilian workers. Compared to this, the American armed services were tiny throughout most of the country's history. Total military personnel numbered just 7,000 in 1801, 21,000 in 1840, 28,000 on the eve of the Civil War, and 42,000 in 1871 (when postwar demobilization had been completed).[1]

Department of Defense

[1]Students interested in more detailed information on the size of the national government in general, and of the military branches in particular, over the country's history are referred to two publications of the U.S. Bureau of the Census: Historical Statistics

During the drought of 1988, the Department of Agriculture offered assistance to farmers.

Government as a Promoter of Interests

After the Civil War new federal agencies and programs were established with the intent of promoting the special interests of various segments of the population. Lawrence Dodd and Richard Schott have noted that

> whereas the original departments had been built around specific federal functions—the War Department for national defense, State for the conduct of foreign relations, and so on—the latter half of the nineteenth century witnessed the creation of certain offices, bureaus, and departments of the federal government around group interests. Farming, the largest occupation in its day, secured recognition with the establishment of a Department of Agriculture that gained full cabinet status in 1889. Education interests got a foothold with the creation of a Bureau of Education (1869) in the Interior Department, forerunner of the Office of Education. The emergence of organized labor, whose ranks were swelled by the industrial revolution, led to the creation of the Department of Labor in 1888. Not far behind were small business and commercial interests that helped secure the establishment of a Department of Commerce in 1903 (actually a joint Department of Commerce and Labor until 1913).[2]

of the United States: Colonial Times to 1970, bicentennial ed., 2 vols. (Washington, D.C.: U.S. Government Printing Office, 1975); and *Statistical Abstract of the United States*, published annually by the Government Printing Office. The growth of the American armed services each year from 1789 to 1970 is shown on pages 1141–43, part 2, of *Historical Statistics*.

[2]Lawrence C. Dodd and Richard L. Schott, *Congress and the Administrative State* (New York: Wiley, 1979), p. 27.

These clientele-oriented departments for the most part were originally intended not to subsidize or regulate but to promote—for example, by collecting and disseminating relevant statistical information and supporting research.

One of the new agencies was, however, a major provider of cash benefits. After the Civil War, the leading veterans' organization, the Grand Army of the Republic (GAR), was fabulously successful in persuading Congress to establish and then liberalize veterans' pensions; the Pension Office (within the Department of the Interior) administered these benefits. In 1891 the Commissioner of Pensions could claim that his was "the largest executive bureau in the world." It had over 6,000 staff members, supplemented by thousands of local physicians paid on a fee basis. Over 40 percent of the entire national government budget in the early 1890s was devoted to veterans' pensions and other benefits. Political scientist James Q. Wilson notes that in the Pension Office

Federal agencies and group interests

> the pattern of bureaucratic clientelism was set in a way later to become a familiar feature of the governmental landscape—a subsidy was initially provided . . . to a group that was powerfully benefited and had few or disorganized opponents; the beneficiaries were organized to supervise the administration and ensure the funding of the program; the law authorizing the program, first passed because it seemed the right thing to do, was left intact or even expanded because politically it became the only thing to do.[3]

Governmental Regulation

Another important group of federal agencies and commissions involved in economic regulation began to evolve in the late nineteenth century, many of them outside the major cabinet-level departments. While the United States has had less governmental ownership of economic enterprises than most other democratic countries, and has attempted less central economic planning, it has extended governmental regulation of the economy further than most democracies. The government tries to realize various public objectives in the economic arena by regulating what private businesses do.

The first major federal regulatory commission was the Interstate Commerce Commission (ICC), set up under the Interstate Commerce Act of 1887. The ICC was given responsibility for regulating carriers—initially railroads and shipping lines—that transported products cross-country. Not surprisingly, the need for such sustained national regulation was first felt after the Civil War as the industrial economy developed and its parts became vastly more interdependent.

Interstate Commerce Commission

[3]James Q. Wilson, "The Rise of the Bureaucratic State," in Francis E. Rourke, ed., *Bureaucratic Power in National Politics*, 3rd ed. (Boston: Little, Brown, 1978), p. 64.

R. Burroughs

The Federal Aviation Administration (FAA) is the regulatory agency responsible for airline safety.

The Interstate Commerce Act and the Sherman Anti-Trust Act (1890) were the most important pieces of legislation in the first round of federal regulatory expansion. In a second round, between 1906 and 1915, key legislation included the Food and Drug Act (1906), the Federal Trade Commission Act (1914), and the Clayton Act (1914) which, like the Sherman Act before it, was an antitrust law. In a third wave during the 1930s, a host of new regulatory statutes were passed, including the Communications Act (1934), the Securities Exchange Act (1934), the National Labor Relations Act (1935), and the Civil Aeronautics Act (1938). The latest round came in the late 1960s and early 1970s with passage of consumer protection and environmental legislation, including the Truth-in-Lending Act (1968), the Clean Air Act (1970), and the Clean Water Act (1972). A great variety of agencies and commissions have been created to administer these laws, such as the Federal Trade Commission (1914), the Federal Communications Commission (1934), the National Labor Relations Board (1935), and the Environmental Protection Agency (1970).

Growth of the Executive Branch

The departments and agencies of the federal executive have expanded in every era of U.S. history as the business of government has in some way been enlarged. By any measure, however, the greatest growth has occurred over the last half-century. If the measure is the *number* of government employees, the time of maximum growth was the 1930s and 1940s. During these decades, total federal personnel increased by more than 400 percent—from about 600,000 when Franklin Roosevelt took office in 1933 to roughly 2.5 million in 1953 when Republican Dwight Eisenhower ended the Democrats' 20-year control of the executive (Table 8.1). On the other hand, if the measure of federal growth is *expenditures*, the time of greatest increase has been the last 20 years. Federal expenditures climbed from $118 billion in 1965 to $1.06 trillion in 1988.

Size of federal agencies

Today, we see as one end product of this expansion the prominent presence of governmental agencies, especially federal agencies, among the largest organizations in the country. Ranked by their expenditures (in the case of government) or by their sales (for business corporations), the three largest organizations in the United States are all executive branch agencies: the Departments of Health and Human Services, Defense, and Treasury. General Motors surpassed all other private corporations, but its total sales in 1987 were only about 29 percent as great as the expenditures of HHS. Expenditures by the largest state government, California, were comparable to the sales of

Many complain about governmental regulation.

A "camel" truck designed by government committee

Figure 8.1

The Largest Governmental and Private Business Organizations (by dollars of corporate sales or governmental outlays, or by number of employees, for the year 1987)

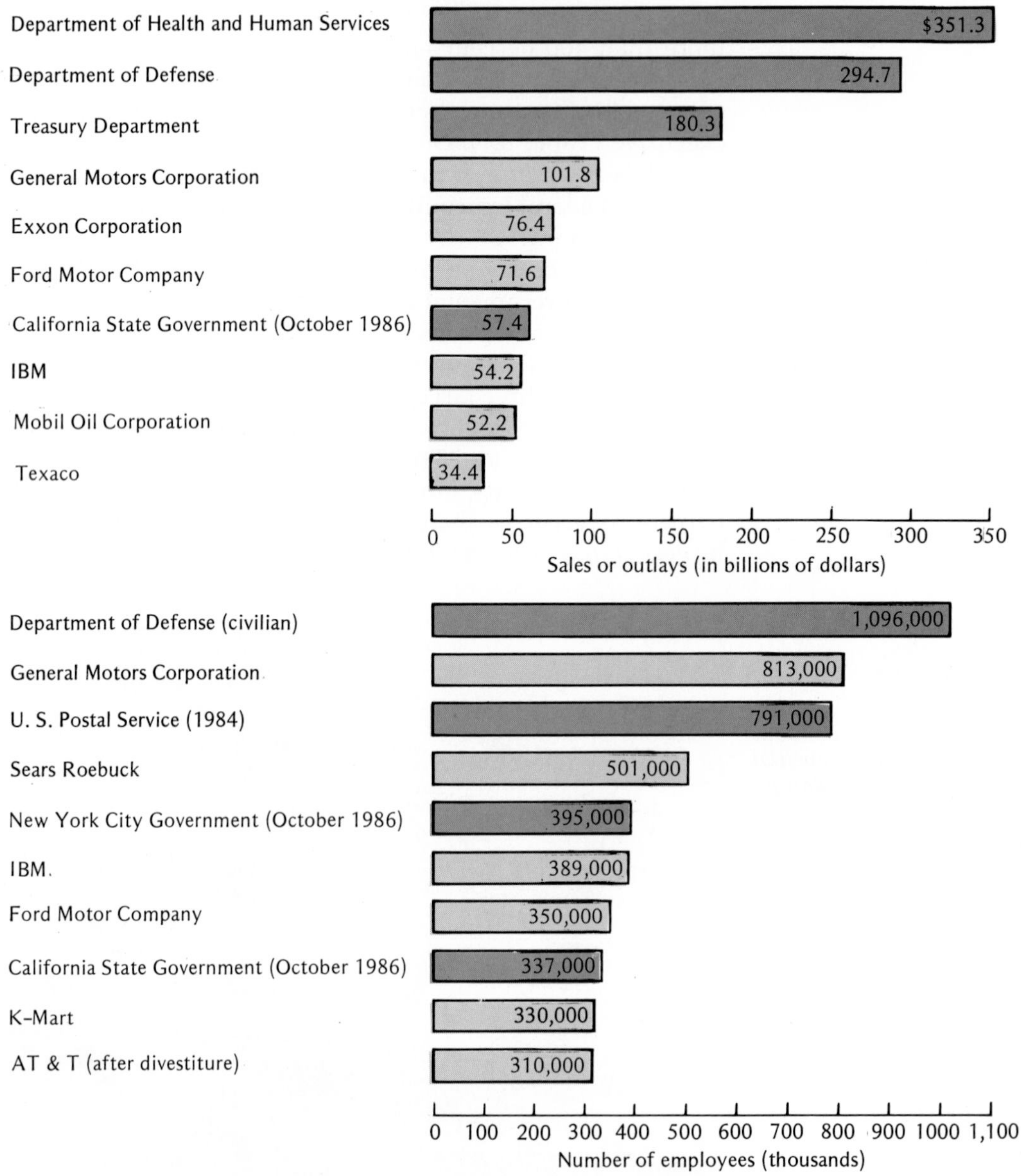

Organization	Sales or outlays (in billions of dollars)
Department of Health and Human Services	$351.3
Department of Defense	294.7
Treasury Department	180.3
General Motors Corporation	101.8
Exxon Corporation	76.4
Ford Motor Company	71.6
California State Government (October 1986)	57.4
IBM	54.2
Mobil Oil Corporation	52.2
Texaco	34.4

Sales or outlays (in billions of dollars)

Organization	Number of employees (thousands)
Department of Defense (civilian)	1,096,000
General Motors Corporation	813,000
U. S. Postal Service (1984)	791,000
Sears Roebuck	501,000
New York City Government (October 1986)	395,000
IBM	389,000
Ford Motor Company	350,000
California State Government (October 1986)	337,000
K-Mart	330,000
AT & T (after divestiture)	310,000

Number of employees (thousands)

Source: Executive Office of the President, Office of Management and Budget; *Budget of the United States Government*, FY 1989, p. 6g–8; *Fortune*, April 25, 1988, pp. D11, D37; U.S. Bureau of the Census, *State Government Finance in 1986*, p. 19, *Public Employment in 1986*, p. 9, *City Employment in 1986*, p. 20; idem, *Statistical Abstract of the United States*, 1988, p. 310; U.S. Senate, Committee on Governmental Affairs, *Organization of Federal Executive Departments and Agencies*, 1988.

the largest companies (Figure 8.1). Comparing the number of employees, one comes to the same conclusion. The Defense Department employs about 260,000 more civilian workers than does General Motors, the largest private employer.

THE FEDERAL EXECUTIVE TODAY

The principal departments and agencies of the federal executive branch are shown in Figure 8.2. Thirteen of them—the executive departments—are shown to outrank all other agencies. This position reflects an interesting mix of status considerations, historical experience, and practical political reality.

Cabinet Rank

The meaning of cabinet rank

The heads of these thirteen departments, each of whom holds the title of secretary, collectively form the president's cabinet, and their departments are described as "of *cabinet* rank."[4] In the American system, the cabinet lacks any constitutional or even statutory base. In contrast to parliamentary systems, where the cabinet collectively exercises governmental authority, in the United States it has no clear governing role. Presidents often work closely with individual cabinet officers, of course, but rarely with the cabinet collectively. Cabinet rank is simply a symbolic affirmation of importance within the executive hierarchy.

From where does this importance stem? As the director of the then Bureau of the Budget stated in 1961 when he testified on a bill that would establish a new executive department,

> Departmental status is reserved for those agencies which (1) administer a wide range of programs directed toward a common purpose of national importance; and (2) are concerned with policies and programs requiring frequent and positive presidential direction and representation at the highest levels of Government.[5]

Departmental status

Departmental status and cabinet rank symbolize basic national commitments and a breadth of policy responsibilities beyond what obtains in the case of other agencies. The breadth of their policy responsibilities and their elevated status do not mean, though, that the cabinet departments are in all cases the largest executive-branch units, in either overall budget or number of employees. The U.S. Postal Service, which does not have department status, has more employees than any cabinet department other than Defense. Effective March

---

[4] A few other officials, such as the U.S. ambassador to the United Nations, also hold cabinet rank.
[5] Statement of David E. Bell, June 21, 1961.

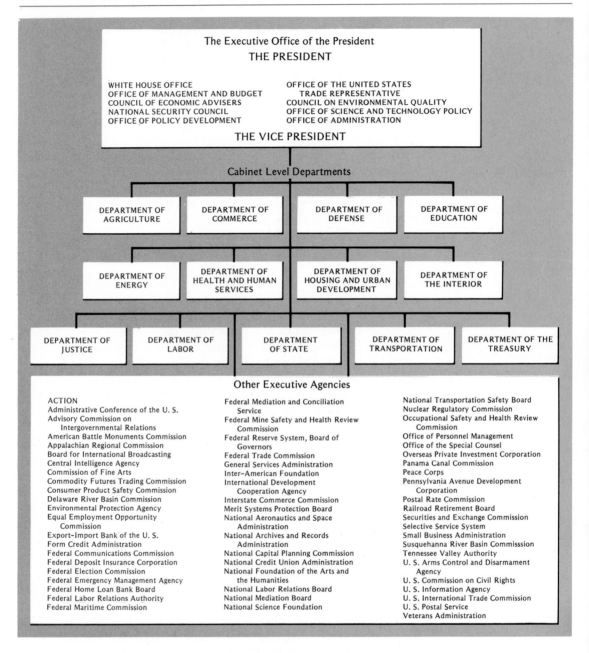

The Executive Office of the President
THE PRESIDENT

WHITE HOUSE OFFICE
OFFICE OF MANAGEMENT AND BUDGET
COUNCIL OF ECONOMIC ADVISERS
NATIONAL SECURITY COUNCIL
OFFICE OF POLICY DEVELOPMENT

OFFICE OF THE UNITED STATES
 TRADE REPRESENTATIVE
COUNCIL ON ENVIRONMENTAL QUALITY
OFFICE OF SCIENCE AND TECHNOLOGY POLICY
OFFICE OF ADMINISTRATION

THE VICE PRESIDENT

Cabinet Level Departments

| DEPARTMENT OF AGRICULTURE | DEPARTMENT OF COMMERCE | DEPARTMENT OF DEFENSE | DEPARTMENT OF EDUCATION |

| DEPARTMENT OF ENERGY | DEPARTMENT OF HEALTH AND HUMAN SERVICES | DEPARTMENT OF HOUSING AND URBAN DEVELOPMENT | DEPARTMENT OF THE INTERIOR |

| DEPARTMENT OF JUSTICE | DEPARTMENT OF LABOR | DEPARTMENT OF STATE | DEPARTMENT OF TRANSPORTATION | DEPARTMENT OF THE TREASURY |

Other Executive Agencies

ACTION
Administrative Conference of the U. S.
Advisory Commission on
  Intergovernmental Relations
American Battle Monuments Commission
Appalachian Regional Commission
Board for International Broadcasting
Central Intelligence Agency
Commission of Fine Arts
Commodity Futures Trading Commission
Consumer Product Safety Commission
Delaware River Basin Commission
Environmental Protection Agency
Equal Employment Opportunity
  Commission
Export–Import Bank of the U. S.
Form Credit Administration
Federal Communications Commission
Federal Deposit Insurance Corporation
Federal Election Commission
Federal Emergency Management Agency
Federal Home Loan Bank Board
Federal Labor Relations Authority
Federal Maritime Commission

Federal Mediation and Conciliation
  Service
Federal Mine Safety and Health Review
  Commission
Federal Reserve System, Board of
  Governors
Federal Trade Commission
General Services Administration
Inter-American Foundation
International Development
  Cooperation Agency
Interstate Commerce Commission
Merit Systems Protection Board
National Aeronautics and Space
  Administration
National Archives and Records
  Administration
National Capital Planning Commission
National Credit Union Administration
National Foundation of the Arts and
  the Humanities
National Labor Relations Board
National Mediation Board
National Science Foundation

National Transportation Safety Board
Nuclear Regulatory Commission
Occupational Safety and Health Review
  Commission
Office of Personnel Management
Office of the Special Counsel
Overseas Private Investment Corporation
Panama Canal Commission
Peace Corps
Pennsylvania Avenue Development
  Corporation
Postal Rate Commission
Railroad Retirement Board
Securities and Exchange Commission
Selective Service System
Small Business Administration
Susquehanna River Basin Commisssion
Tennessee Valley Authority
U. S. Arms Control and Disarmament
  Agency
U. S. Commission on Civil Rights
U. S. Information Agency
U. S. International Trade Commission
U. S. Postal Service
Veterans Administration

Figure 8.2
The Executive Branch

Source: U.S. Senate, Organization of Federal Executive Departments and Agencies, January 1, 1988.

15, 1989, the numbers of cabinet departments grew from 13 to 14: the Veterans Administration became the Department of Veterans Affairs.

Table 8.2
Federal Expenditures by Agency

Departments and agencies (cabinet departments are capitalized)	1987 outlays (billions of dollars)
DEFENSE	394.7
HEALTH AND HUMAN SERVICES	351.3
TREASURY	180.3
AGRICULTURE	50.4
Postal Service (1986)	30.7
Veterans Administration	27.0
Office of Personnel Management	27.0
TRANSPORTATION	25.4
LABOR	23.5
EDUCATION	16.8
HOUSING AND URBAN DEVELOPMENT	15.5
ENERGY	10.7
National Aeronautics & Space Administration	7.6
INTERIOR	5.0
Environmental Protection Agency	4.9
JUSTICE	4.3
STATE	2.8
Railroad Retirement Board	2.4
COMMERCE	2.1
President: Executive office and directly appropriated funds	10.5
Legislative and judicial branches	3.0
Other agencies	14.3

The above figures represent actual 1987 outlays, with the exception of the Postal Service, for which 1986 data are provided. In this last case, the total includes expenditures of nongovernmental as well as governmental revenues. The Postal Service is largely self-financing.

Source: Executive Office of the President, OMB, Budget of the U.S. Government, FY 1989, pp. 6f-171, 6g-8; U.S. Bureau of the Census, Statistical Abstract of the United States, 1988, p. 520.

Independent Agencies

When agencies such as the Central Intelligence Agency (CIA), the Veterans Administration, the Environmental Protection Agency (EPA), and the General Services Administration are referred to as "independent," it means simply "outside the executive departments." Many of them are in no sense independent of presidential direction. The director of the CIA and the administrator of the EPA are subordinate to the president in the same way as the secretaries of State and Transportation.

Some of the **independent agencies,** however, really have been removed from presidential direction. The U.S. Postal Service (USPS) is a case in point. In urging that the Post Office Department be reorganized as an independent, noncabinet Postal Service, President Richard Nixon argued that efficiency would be served by freeing the agency "from direct control by the president, the Bureau of the Budget, and the Congress," and relatedly from partisan political pressure. Under the Postal Reorganization Act of 1970, the Postal Service got much of the independence Nixon recommended. It is headed by an eleven-person board of governors, appointed by the president with Senate confirmation. The governors serve nine-year overlapping terms. The administrative head of the Postal Service, the postmaster general, is appointed by and responsible to this board of governors—*not the president.* The Postal Service is largely self-financing, and it can borrow money and sell bonds as it sees fit, as long as its total indebtedness does not exceed $10 billion. Only about 1.5 percent of its current operating budget comes from congressional appropriations—principally subsidies for mailings by some nonprofit groups and pension payments for postal workers who were employed prior to 1970.

Still, the USPS remains a federal agency, and it sometimes is required by Congress and the Office of Management and Budget to do things that it doesn't want to do. For example, in a budget agreement between the administration and Congress reached in December 1987, the Postal Service was required to help the federal government save $1.2 billion over fiscal years 1988 and 1989. The legislation mandated that money had to come from savings in the USPS operating budget and not from increased borrowing or higher postal rates. In response, the agency cut retail window hours, curbed weekend mail sorting, and suspended about 700 capital improvement projects. Predictably, the reductions in service brought howls of protest from postal patrons.

Arguments over the Postal Service's status are continuing. Some conservatives favor "privatization," turning mail delivery over to private enterprise and ending the federal monopoly on first-class mail. Others, including Representative Mickey Leland (D-Tex.), who chairs the House Post Office and Civil Service Subcommittee on Postal Operations, think the 1970 reorganization went too far in removing Congress's oversight of the USPS.[6]

Foundations and Institutes

A number of **foundations** and **institutes** have been established in the executive branch to promote science and scholarship. The first to be established, the Smithsonian Institution, is now a century and a half old. James Smithson of England bequeathed his entire estate to the United States, to establish in Washington an institution "for the increase and diffusion of knowledge. . . ." Federal subsidies followed. But only after World War II did the federal government's investment

[6]Richard Cowan, "Postal Service Faces Era of 'Power Sharing,' " *Congressional Quarterly*, February 27, 1988, pp. 507–11.

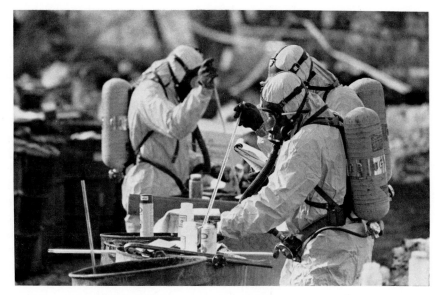

EPA workers inspecting chemical waste dumps.

in science and the arts become massive, with the establishment of the National Science Foundation, the National Institutes of Health (and its many components such as the National Cancer Institute and the National Heart Institute), and most recently, the National Endowment for the Arts and the National Endowment for the Humanities.

In all of these cases it was felt that a degree of agency insulation from regular political direction was in order. The oldest of the federal scientific establishments, the Smithsonian has the greatest autonomy. Its business is conducted by a board of regents that consists of the vice president, the chief justice of the Supreme Court, three members of the Senate, three members of the House of Representatives, and six others appointed by joint resolution of the Congress. The chief executive officer of the institution is chosen by this highly independent board. When the National Science Foundation was established in 1947 to provide federal funding for scientific research, especially at the nation's colleges and universities, the scientific community worked hard to achieve for the new facility a high measure of independence from political interference. The aim was to create a kind of university structure within the executive branch, and this was substantially realized. Policy-making authority resides in a 24-person National Science Board, appointed for six-year terms by the president, with the advice and consent of the Senate.

The Smithsonian and the National Science Foundation

Independent Regulatory Commissions

Another large group of federal agencies, the **independent regulatory commissions,** were set up with the idea that they should be insulated

Independent
regulatory
commissions

from regular presidential leadership and political direction. One of these organizations, the Board of Governors of the Federal Reserve System, was described earlier in the chapter. The first of the independent commissions was the Interstate Commerce Commission, established in 1887 to regulate such carriers as railroads and shipping lines engaged in interstate commerce. Eleven others were subsequently created.[7] Economic regulation is not the exclusive province of the independent commissions—various bureaus in the regular departments, such as the Food and Drug Administration (FDA) within Health and Human Services, and the Occupational Safety and Health Administration (OSHA) in the Labor Department, play prominent regulatory roles—but the commissions are key regulatory bodies.

Regulatory
commission structure

In contrast to most of the important executive departments and agencies, the regulatory commissions are headed by boards rather than single executives. By law these boards must be bipartisan. The commissioners' terms are long (five years or more) and overlapping, and commissioners may be dismissed by the president only for "inefficiency, neglect of duty, or malfeasance in office." Commissioners cannot be fired simply because the president doesn't like their views. The president still has influence over regulatory commission policies. He appoints commissioners. Even with their long overlapping terms, he usually gets to see his appointees established as a majority on each regulatory body; he is certain to do so if he serves a second term. The requirement of bipartisanship in commission membership is of little consequence; a Republican president can always pick conservative Democrats, and a Democratic president liberal Republicans.

THE BUREAU

The bureau
The **bureau** is the basic unit of federal administration. The word "bureaucracy" was coined in eighteenth-century France, a neologism formed from the French word for a place where officials worked (the bureau) and a suffix derived from the Greek word for "rule." The root meaning of bureaucracy connotes "rule by officialdom." The *Dictionary of the French Academy* defined "bureaucratie" in 1798 as "power, influence of the heads and staff of governmental bureaux."[8] In subsequent usage, "bureaucracy" has lost some of its original stress on "rule," but the idea of appointed officials organized around an

---

[7]Ten of these were still functioning in 1985: the Commodity Futures Trading Commission, the Consumer Product Safety Commission, the Federal Communications Commission, the Federal Energy Regulatory Commission, the Board of Governors of the Federal Reserve System, the Federal Maritime Commission, the Federal Trade Commission, the National Labor Relations Board, the Nuclear Regulatory Commission, and the Securities and Exchange Commission.

[8]Martin Albrow, *Bureaucracy* (New York: Praeger, 1970), p. 17.

*Government bureau-
crats come in for a lot
of ribbing—some good
natured, some reveal-
ing frustration.*

administrative office is still central to most modern conceptions of bureaucracy.

Nature of bureaus

Today, bureaus are the administrative organization set up to actually operate the various programs of the executive departments—as in the Bureau of the Census of the Department of Commerce. The same type of administrative structure is sometimes called an "office" (the Office of Surface Mining Reclamation and Enforcement of the Department of Interior), an "administration" (the Food and Drug Administration of the Department of Health and Human Services), or a "service" (the Internal Revenue Service of the Department of the Treasury). James Fesler notes that "these operating units are so important in federal administration that one could regard the executive branch as literally a 'bureaucracy'—that is, a government by bureaus—and could treat the departmental and presidential levels merely as superstructure."[9] Most of the executive departments are really collections of bureaus. Some bureaus are older than the departments in which they are now located. The Bureau of Land Management was established in 1812, thirteen years before the Interior Department, of which it is now a part, was formed. And five bureaus are actually larger (in number of employees) than the Department of State, Labor, Energy, Housing and Urban Development, and Education. (These are the Social Security Administration, the Internal Revenue Service, the Public

[9]James W. Fesler, *Public Administration, Theory and Practice* (Englewood Cliffs, N.J.: Prentice-Hall, 1980), p. 45.

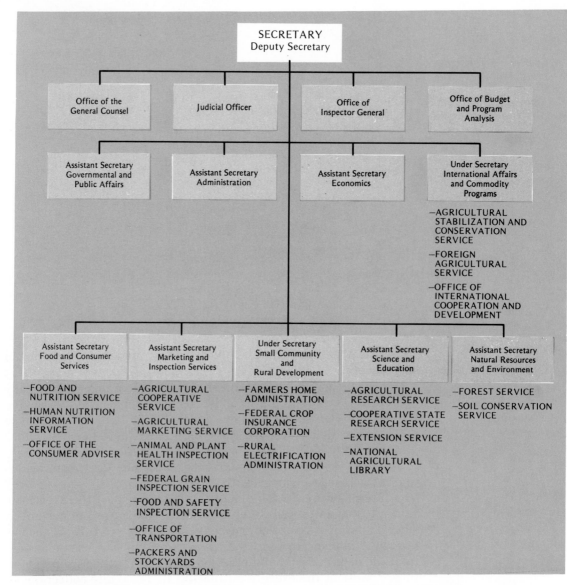

Figure 8.3
United States Department of Agriculture (the bureaus are shown in capital letters)

Source: *The United States Government Manual*, 1987–88, p. 104.

Health Service, the Forest Service, and the Army Corps of Engineers—for civil functions.)

To understand the scope of federal government activities and the kinds of programs and services the government provides, we must look beneath the "umbrella" departments to the constituent bureaus, offices, administrations, and services. Figure 8.3 shows the operating structure of the Department of Agriculture—a middle-sized executive department. More than twenty services (bureaus) run the department's wide-ranging programs. A number of these services are huge governmental agencies. For example, the Farmers Home Administration, established to provide credit for people in rural areas unable to obtain credit at reasonable rates elsewhere, makes loans to low-income persons to buy houses in the open country, to farm owners and operators for land conservation purposes, to those wanting to repair farm homes and service buildings, to young people (ages 10–21) who want "to establish and operate income-producing enterprises of modest size," and many others. In 1988 the Farmers Home Administration employed 19,000 people and expended roughly $6.8 billion.

Department of Agriculture's organization

The main federal bureaus, with their large, ongoing program activities, have naturally become focal points for interest groups and, in turn, look to interest groups to help protect and maintain themselves. And congressmen serving on the committees and subcommittees with jurisdiction over the programs that bureaus manage have come to take a close interest in bureau affairs. A complex and important set of policy systems has gradually emerged in the federal executive, with the bureau typically at the center. As we look more closely at these systems, we will draw our examples primarily from the Department of Agriculture (USDA) and agricultural programs, although much the same relationships apply to many other client-oriented departments, such as Labor, Commerce, Energy, and Transportation.

Bureaus and the federal government

The Bureau: Hub of Federal Policy

A president is elected, and upon taking office he appoints a group of political executives to give direction to his administration's programs. The formal authority of these executives, and their political influence deriving from the mandate the voters give the president, are substantial. But many observers stress the limits rather than the extent of their power. For the president and his cabinet secretaries often have less enduring roles in federal programs than do the heads of governmental bureaus. The former come and go; the latter seem to go on forever.

A president may serve one term, two at most. The people he appoints to administer the executive departments on average have even shorter terms. For example, from 1960 through 1972, about 40 percent of all cabinet secretaries served under 24 months; over 50 percent of all undersecretaries and assistant secretaries held their posts two years or less.[10] "The single most obvious characteristic of Washington's political appointees," political scientist Hugh Heclo observes, "is their transience."[11] Among the political executives of the federal govern-

Transience of political appointees

[10] Arch Patton, "Government's Revolving Door," *Business Week*, September 22, 1973, p. 12.
[11] Hugh Helco, *A Government of Strangers* (Washington, D.C.: Brookings Institution, 1977). p. 103.

ment, everything seems to be constantly in flux. They have come to government from all corners of national life. Many of them have had little or no contact with one another prior to receiving their presidential appointments. They must try to master exceedingly complex jobs in short periods of time and in the context of almost entirely new executive teams.

Durability of bureau roles

The political direction coming to the bureau from the president, and the cabinet secretary or assistant secretary, is short-term and episodic. In contrast, the relationship between the bureau and the political interests that have a stake in its programs endures. This contrast between the transience of political executives and the durability of the policy environments in which they must work tells us much about why practical control over programs resides to such a large degree in the bureaus and with the political interests organized around them. The strength and durability of bureaus' role in federal policy results, too, from the mutually supporting nature of their ties to interest groups. When two different organisms are associated in a manner of mutual benefit, biologists call their relationship "symbiosis." In this sense, the association of bureaus and interest groups is a symbiotic one.

Interest Groups and Bureaus

Consider the Rural Electrification Administration (REA) within the USDA. It delivers important services to rural dwellers—organized through the National Rural Electric Cooperative Association—such as helping rural electric and telephone utilities obtain financing through loans and loan guarantees. In turn, the Rural Electric Cooperative Association has served as a personal lobby for the REA, lobbying congressmen on behalf of the REA's programs and budget. Political scientist Theodore Lowi notes that a principal agricultural interest group, the American Farm Bureau Federation, has had a similar connection with the Extension Service of the Agriculture Department throughout its entire history.[12] And Harold Seidman, who served as assistant director of the Bureau of the Budget from 1964 to 1968, observes, "Each of the agencies dispensing federal largess has its personal lobby: the Corps of Engineers has the Rivers and Harbors Congress; the Bureau of Reclamation, the National Reclamation Association; the Soil Conservation Service, the National Association of Soil and Water Conservation Districts."[13]

Some depict these ties as grubby and self-serving. But the matter is considerably more complicated. A federal program like rural electrification began with a clear and respectable need: it cost much more to extend electric and telephone service to remote rural areas than to

[12] Theodore J. Lowi, *The End of Liberalism* (New York: Norton, 1979), p. 72.
[13] Seidman, *Politics, Position and Power*, p. 164.

cities and towns, because wires had to be strung across miles of isolated and sparsely settled territory to reach a few paying customers. The REA stepped into the breach by providing the funding. It is neither surprising nor troubling that the bureau and the interests it served established a firm and mutually supporting association. Once enough of these ties have been established, however, the position of the cabinet secretary and assistant secretaries becomes very weak, because they find it hard to control the bureau's policy commitments. Furthermore, the line between legitimate interest in extending needed services and the narrow interest of group/agency self-advancement is both blurred and easily crossed.

The interest group/ bureau connection

The symbiotic nature of the ties between bureaus and interest groups has led some to question conventional descriptions of group power. In many of the cases we have been describing, it would be misleading to suggest that a powerful interest group has muscled its way in and forced government to do its bidding. Rather, the agency and the interest group have compatible objectives and need each other.

Congress and Bureaus

Just as the associations of interest groups and bureaus are often enduring, so are those of congressional leadership and bureaus. As we saw in chapter 6, power in the U.S. Congress is highly fragmented, distributed across an elaborate system of over 300 committees and subcommittees. Each executive agency bureau falls within the jurisdiction of one or several subcommittees that develop legislation defining bureau programs and provide funding for them. A subcommittee chairman usually pays close attention to the work of "his bureau" because he may care deeply about it, because it matters to his constituents, and/or because he thereby gains power. Here again the symbiosis. Congressmen and bureau administrators need and use each other. And the permanence of their ties and interaction, coupled with the transience of cabinet secretaries and other senior political executives, further encourages the remarkable fragmentation of executive authority.

Congressional ties to bureaus

Congressmen do not have formal grants of administrative responsibility, but they often play large roles in guiding agency programs. In fact, a congressman's reach over executive-branch programs sometimes far exceeds that of cabinet secretaries. For example, Representative Jami Whitten of Mississippi, chairman of the House Appropriations Committee and, as well, chairman of the Appropriations Subcommittee on Rural Development, Agriculture, and Related Agencies, has been called the "permanent secretary of Agriculture." Over the last quarter-century, a time when the Democrats have continuously controlled the House of Representatives, Whitten's say in agricultural programs has been immense.

The Life of the Bureau Chief

Bureaucratic autonomy

The administrators who head federal bureaus are responsible not just to their executive superiors—the cabinet secretaries and the president. In a very real sense they are also responsible unofficially to congressional committee leaders and to influential interest groups. This means that bureau chiefs have a confusing mix of "masters"—but also that they can attain a striking degree of political autonomy. If astute and inclined to play one master against another, a bureau chief can achieve a measure of longevity and program control that does not exist in the administration of other democratic governments. Within our pluralistic government, bureaus are not merely administrative units, but also the focal points of a system of dispersed power. Bureau chiefs are typically policy makers, not merely administrators of policies others make.

"Iron triangles"

Once in place, the bureau-subcommittee-interest group triangle becomes a familiar and comfortable policy environment for its participants. And they will resist attempts at reorganization. Committee leaders often don't like change because it might disrupt their established channels of oversight and influence. Interest groups fear that new arrangements might weaken their claims. And bureau chiefs find their own autonomy and influence enhanced by established and enduring congressional and group ties. Many efforts at change initiated by presidents and cabinet secretaries have crashed against these "iron triangles." Figure 8.4 shows a current triangle.

Change is made especially difficult by the fact that the triangular interactions often involve intensely held inside interests and weak or diffuse outside concerns. For example, a program of agricultural price supports—maintaining farm prices at levels deemed fair to farmers—

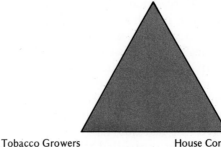

Agricultural Stabilization and Conservation Service,
Price Support and Loan Division,
Peanuts and Tobacco Section, U.S. Department of Agriculture
(executive bureau)

Tobacco Growers
(interest group)

House Committee on Agriculture,
House Subcommittee on Tobacco
and Peanuts
(Congress)

Figure 8.4
A Modern Iron Triangle

Agency programs and
the public interest

may benefit only a small group of farmers at the expense of a large group of consumers. But the interests of the former are intense while those of the latter are by comparison weak and disjointed. It isn't always this way, though. Sometimes outside interests can become strong enough to overturn established policy systems. One recent example has to do with the public's concern over the environment. By 1970 environmental interests had gained enough political muscle to get Congress to establish the Environmental Protection Agency (EPA). The EPA assumed authority in a variety of areas that had been under the jurisdiction of old-line departments. For instance, it took over the regulation of pesticides that had formerly been lodged with a bureau in the Department of Agriculture. Firms manufacturing pesticides felt more comfortable with their ties to the USDA and resisted the shift. But the environmental lobby succeeded in severing the old interest group–bureau bond.[14] Today environmental groups look upon the various offices or bureaus of the EPA as their own, much as agricultural interest groups have for a long time viewed the USDA as their own.

The Public Interest

This description of interest-group ties to bureaus does not give us much help in determining whether the resultant programs are legitimate ones, as judged by the standard of the public interest. Interest groups invariably claim that the programs they favor serve larger national ends, not just their own interests, and often they sincerely believe they do. Different groups will inevitably construe the public interest in different ways. The fact that an interest group strongly backs a program does not mean that the program is bad. What is clear is that American public-policy formation, built as it is around a multiplicity of interest-group, bureau, and congressional committee interrelations, is remarkably fragmented.

As Figure 8.5 suggests, the federal bureau is frequently the hub of a set of interactions involving 1) *administration leadership*, 2) *congressional leadership* (usually defined at the committee or subcommittee levels, 3) *inside group interests*, and 4) *outside interests*. The strength of any one part will vary from one program area to another and may shift over time. For example, a politically popular president and an effective cabinet secretary may well be able to build upon public support for change to override the preferences of inside interests and established congressional committee preferences. Conversely, a strong subcommittee chairman, especially if he is operating in conjunction with well-organized inside interests and in the absence of sustained opposing efforts by the president, may be able to push bureau activities decisively in a direction that he favors. Inside interests—such as

The bureau: the hub
of policy making

[14] Peter Woll, *American Bureaucracy*, 2nd ed. (New York: Norton, 1977), p. 104.

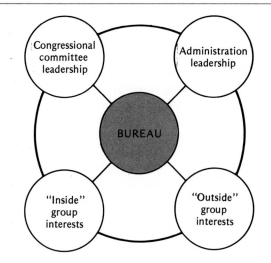

Figure 8.5
The Policy Wheel in Executive Organization

those of farm groups in USDA programs—are often highly influential, but they may be overridden by the growth of outside interests. While their relative strength varies from case to case, the component parts of the policy wheel seem to be constants. And viewed from the perspective of executive branch organization and operation, the bureau is typically the focal point of the policy wheel.

THE PRESIDENT AND THE BUREAUCRACY

Neither the president nor his chief appointees—such as cabinet secretaries—are involved in matters of hiring or dismissing most of the 3 million executive branch employees. The bulk of these workers are covered by provisions of one or another civil service system, the largest of which is administered by the government's central personnel agency, the Office of Personnel Management (OPM), discussed later in the chapter. When President George Bush took office on January 20, 1989, he already was responsible for appointing about 8,000 political executives and other assistants.

Executive recruitment

Even filling these 8,000 posts is an enormous chore. No president or small group of presidential assistants knows 8,000 people prepared to leave their present jobs and serve ably in diverse posts throughout the executive branch. Recent presidents have set up quite elaborate recruitment efforts, but the results have still often been disappointing. For certain positions the problem is not choosing among a number of worthy candidates but rather encouraging able people to leave jobs in the private sector—where they receive higher salaries and much greater security and privacy—and come to Washington.

Of the 8,000 executives whom the president can appoint, perhaps

The Executive
Schedule

700 are key managers. They include cabinet secretaries and other agency heads, and such second-tier political executives as deputy secretaries and assistant secretaries. They are appointed by the president to positions within a job classification scheme known as the **Executive Schedule.** It has five levels, each with established compensation (the Executive Schedule pay rates). Box 8.1 shows which jobs fit into which levels of the schedule.

Box 8.1
The Executive Schedule

Level 1: The heads of executive departments, like the Secretary of State, the Secretary of Defense, and the Secretary of Transportation. 1988 salary for executives at this level: $99,500.

Level 2: The heads of major agencies, of the Executive Office of the President, such as the Office of Management and Budget; the heads of large independent agencies including the National Aeronautics and Space Administration, the Central Intelligence Agency, the Veterans Administration, and the Federal Reserve. 1988 salary: $89,500.

Level 3: The heads of other independent agencies, such as the General Services Administration and the Small Business Administration; commissioners of the major regulatory agencies, including the Interstate Commerce Commission and the Federal Trade Commission; the heads of government corporations, such as the Federal Deposit Insurance Corporation and the Tennessee Valley Authority; the directors of scientific foundations, such as the National Science Foundation; the heads of important administrations or bureaus within executive departments, such as the director of the Federal Bureau of Investigation and the Comptroller of the Currency. 1988 salary: $82,500.

Level 4: The heads of smaller independent agencies like the Selective Service System, the Equal Employment Opportunity Commission, the St. Lawrence Seaway Development Corporation; the chiefs of important bureaus within the executive departments. 1988 salary: $77,500.

Level 5: The heads of minor agencies like the Renegotiation Board and the Foreign Claims Settlement Commission; the directors and deputy directors of other constituent units within executive departments and agencies. 1988 salary: $72,500.

Source: Adapted from Seidman, *Politics, Position, and Power,* pp. 243–44; Salary figures, courtesy OPM, executive administration.

Presidential Control

Presidents and their cabinet secretaries often complain that they lack sufficient control over the executive-branch bureaucracy. But here they in fact are referring to only a very small segment of all federal workers. As we have seen, the president appoints the top political administrators and can fire them if they fail to do his bidding. The bulk of federal workers, of course, do not play policy roles at all. They issue Social Security checks, deliver the mail, process tax returns, and more. These jobs are vital to government, but they involve routine operations that presidents have no interest in "controlling." Most of these positions are handled through civil service systems.

Career officials

Presidents' concern over bureaucratic unresponsiveness revolves around a relatively small group of career officials—numbering not more than 50,000—who are involved in policy but who are not subject to presidential appointment or dismissal authority. At the bureau level, virtually all key staff, the bureau chief included, are career officials. Presidents and cabinet secretaries come and go; senior career personnel usually stay much longer. Their relative longevity and dominant place in the bureaus—which have large policy-making responsibilities—give them great influence.

Any administration, anxious to implement its programs, and encountering all kinds of obstacles in the American system of divided power, is bound to feel some frustration when it encounters bureaucratic resistance. Presidents and their political appointees often express the concern that career officials don't fully support administration policies and indeed resist them. On occasion, amid mutual complaints and recriminations, pitched battles actually break out between the two sides.

Nixon and the Bureaucracy: A Case Study

Perhaps the most dramatic instance of tension between political executives and career officials came during Richard Nixon's tenure in office. The tension stemmed from the suspicion, even animosity, that some in the political leadership of the Nixon administration felt toward the career bureaucracy—feelings that seem to have been reciprocated. In a manual prepared by White House staff, Nixon appointees were warned that the career service was stacked against the administration: "Because of the rape of the career service by the Kennedy and Johnson Administrations . . . this Administration has been left a legacy of finding disloyalty and obstruction at high levels while those incumbents rest comfortably on career civil service status."[15] The anger extended to the president himself, as is evident from

[15] This document has been included in the Report of the Select Senate Committee on Presidential Campaign Activities, *Executive Session Hearings*, "Watergate and Related Activities," 93rd Cong., 2nd sess., Washington, D.C., 1973, 19:9,006.

these comments of his captured by his White House taping system and released following the Watergate investigation:

> "You've got to get us some discipline George [George Shultz, then OMB director, now secretary of state]. You've got to get it, and the only way you get it, is when a bureaucrat thumbs his nose, we're going to get him. . . . They've got to know, that if they do it, something's going to happen to them, where anything can happen. I know the Civil Service pressure. But you can do a lot there. There are many unpleasant places where Civil Service people can be sent. We just don't have any discipline in government. That's our trouble. . . . So whatever you—well, maybe he is in the regional office. Fine. Demote him or send him to the Guam regional office. There's a way. Get him the hell out.[16]

Nixon and the bureaucracy

In a February 1971 news conference, the president publicly described his opponents in the federal bureaucracy as "dug-in establishmentarians fighting for the status quo."[17] And in an interview later that year, he told reporter Howard K. Smith that "I think it is repugnant to the American system that only the bureaucratic elite at the top of the heap in Washington [believes it] knows what is best for the people. . . ."[18]

The plan to reorganize executive departments

Nixon's distrust of career federal administrators seems excessive, but it was not entirely misplaced. When Nixon entered the White House, Democrats far outnumbered Republicans among top career executives of the federal government. Many of the administrators brought in under Democratic presidents Kennedy and Johnson had real disagreements with Nixon's programs.[19] To secure greater White House control over the executive branch, the Nixon administration tried a number of things. In his 1971 State of the Union message, Nixon proposed merging eight existing domestic departments into four new super agencies: the Departments of National Resources, Human Resources, Economic Affairs, and Community Development. Congress would not go along. But immediately after his November 1972 victory, the president moved ahead anyway. He named four cabinet members—the secretaries of Treasury, Agriculture, HEW, and HUD—as *presidential counselors*. By making them White House office staff as well as cabinet officers, he gave them functional responsibilities over economic affairs, natural resources, human resources, and community development, respectively. At the same time, he appointed trusted political staff to positions throughout the executive branch "in direct charge of the major program bureaucracies of domestic

[16] Tape of meeting held April 19, 1971. A transcript was published in the *New York Times*, July 20, 1974, p. 14.
[17] Richard M. Nixon, news conference, February 17, 1971, printed in *Public Papers of the Presidents, 1971* (Washington, D.C.: Government Printing Office, 1972), p. 167.
[18] Howard K. Smith interview of Richard M. Nixon; the text may be found in *Public Papers of the Presidents, 1971*, p. 463.
[19] Joel D. Aberbach and Burt A. Rockman, "Clashing Beliefs Within the Executive Branch," *American Political Science Review* 70 (June 1976): 456–68.

government."[20] By manipulating the civil service personnel system, his administration also sought to change the partisan makeup and policy commitments of the most senior levels of the career service.

Nixon's attempts to achieve central political direction over the sprawling federal administration soon got sidetracked as his administration was engulfed by Watergate. Fighting for survival, it lacked both the energy and the political clout required to follow through on its struggle with the bureaucracy. But were Nixon's ideas for change well conceived? On the one hand, the idea of an independent civil service pursuing its managerial tasks according to politically neutral standards of professional competence remains an attractive one. Nixon's efforts to "take over" the bureaucracy were a frontal challenge to that ideal. At the same time, as Richard Cole and David Caputo have observed, the Nixon administration held office at a time when the ideal of a neutral bureaucracy was further than usual from realization.[21] A host of new federal programs and activities were established in the 1960s. As this happened, some newly hired career-service officials behaved more as partisans of the programs they were brought in to manage then as neutral administrators.

The ideal of a neutral bureaucracy

The Reagan Administration and Federal Workers

Many experienced government officials think that the problem of bureaucratic unresponsiveness is often overstated. They maintain that most career officials will respond to effective leadership from political appointees and that, most of the time, it is only the inept political executives who encounter disabling resistence. Even when an administration takes office determined to change policy substantially, it can usually gain the sufficient *assistance*—rather than the determined *resistance*—of career civil servants. The Reagan administration's record offers much support for this view. An occasional political official in a sensitive post—such as Reagan's first appointee as administrator of the Environmental Protection Agency, Anne Burford—got embroiled in bitter battles, but most skilled appointees seemed to have had little difficulty directing their career staffs, even when major program changes were the order of the day.

The big battles in the Reagan administration didn't involve managing the upper bureaucracy, but rather stemmed from clashes with federal employee unions. The most heated of these revolved around the efforts of Reagan's first appointee as director of the Office of Personnel Management (OPM), Donald J. Devine. From early 1981 until his departure in the spring of 1985, Devine, a former political science professor, attempted to implement a sweeping series of changes bear-

The battle of OPM

[20] Richard P. Nathan, *The Plot That Failed* (New York: Wiley, 1975), pp. 61–62.
[21] Richard L. Cole and David A. Caputo, "Presidential Control of the Senior Civil Service," *American Political Science Review*, June 1979, p. 394.

ing on federal employment, centering on compensation, that reflected administration ideas on needed improvements. Devine won some battles, but lost many others—and ultimately he lost his job.

"Federal employee likes and dislikes are important to me," Devine remarked in testimony before the Senate Civil Service Subcommittee in March 1982, "but so is getting the public's work done." He was by no means the first federal personnel official to believe that "getting the public's work done" required some changes not to the liking of employee unions. But he was certainly the most inclined to do battle for changes he believed necessary. To his opponents, Donald Devine was too ideological and political, and fundamentally unsympathetic to employee interests. To his defenders, he was someone willing to take on entrenched federal unions on behalf of management reforms needed to improve executive agency performance and cut excess costs. Not many observers were neutral. "Federal workers vilify him, while conservative supporters of the Reagan administration idolize him," was the *Washington Post*'s apt summary.[22]

Retirement benefits were one area where Donald Devine sought changes in the rules governing federal employment. He thought that civil service retirement programs were far too costly. In fact, many members of Congress in both parties thought that something should be done to curb the growth of costs in the Civil Service Retirement System (CSRS), but Devine was the one pushing cuts and he became the prime target of employee union protests.

One reason for the high total costs of federal retirement was the provision that employees could retire as early as age 55 with full benefits, after 30 years of service; their pension checks would then be raised automatically each year by cost-of-living adjustments (COLAs) pegged to the rate of inflation. All in all, the federal government's total pension costs in 1982 were roughly 25 percent of its payroll costs. With OPM's leadership the Reagan administration pushed measures to cut the rate of the annual cost-of-living increases, and to raise both employee retirement contributions and the retirement age.

The administration wanted all federal workers to contribute more to their retirement system. Congress wouldn't go along, but in 1983 it did pass legislation that brought *new federal employees* (hired after December 30, 1983) under Social Security, a step that had been recommended by the bipartisan National Commission on Social Security Reform (appointed by President Reagan in 1982). This meant that they would have to pay Social Security taxes. Working through the Fund for Assuring an Independent Retirement (FAIR), some 25 groups representing several million active and retired employees waged a furious lobbying campaign against being brought under Social Secu-

Donald Devine and the OPM controversy

Curbing CSRS cost growth

Attempts to reform the federal retirement program

[22] Keith B. Richburg, "Devine: Workers' Bane, Conservatives' Idol," *Washington Post*, June 7, 1985, p. A25.

rity. Throngs of federal employees and postal workers ascended Capitol Hill, bused in by FAIR.

Another area where Donald Devine led an administration attempt to change federal employee compensation involved "merit pay" or **Merit pay reform** "pay for performance." In March 1983 OPM proposed regulations that would extend the pay-for-performance system that was already in effect for roughly 7,000 "senior executive service" (SES) managers and supervisors. (See pp. 279–80 for a discussion of the SES.) The new OPM regulations would have eliminated the automatic pay increases for 1.4 million low- and middle-level federal workers, basing raises instead on job performance.

Again, employee unions strongly resisted Devine's efforts. Unions have traditionally seen merit pay as a cover for management attempts at gaining more control over workers—"bribing" the compliant and (by withholding pay increases) punishing the noncompliant. "We are convinced that OPM, with the blessings of the Reagan administration, is attempting to replace the civil service system with one of political patronage," argued Kenneth T. Blaylock, who was then president of the American Federation of Government Employees (AFGE), the largest federal employee union.[23] A bitter, protracted battle ensued between Devine and OPM and the employee unions. It was fought out in Congress and the federal courts. For the most part, the unions managed to block implementation of the changes OPM proposed.

After Devine left OPM, Congress and the Reagan administration still had to grapple with the same difficult issues involving the compensation and status of federal workers. In May 1986, following three **Devine leaves OPM** years of argument, agreement was finally reached on one of these issues—a new retirement system for employees hired after January 1, 1984. The new Federal Employees' Retirement System (FERS) provides a three-part pension package: basic Social Security benefits, supplemented by a government employee pension and by a tax-deferred savings plan into which the government must contribute and workers may. FERS cuts total costs by gradually raising the minimum retirement age from 55 to 57, by eliminating automatic cost-of-living increases for retirees under age 62, and by reducing by 1 percent the annual increases for retirees 62 and older. The changes are expected to eventually reduce government's pension costs from 25 percent of payroll to 23 percent. This cut is far less than what the administration wanted, but the administration finally accepted the package as the best it could get. The cut is more than the employee unions wanted, but they could fairly claim that "it could have been much worse."

---

[23] Devine and Blaylock, quoted in "Federal Workers Battle OPM Proposals. . . . ," *Congressional Quarterly*, April 30, 1983, p. 836.

ORGANIZATION OF THE FEDERAL CIVIL SERVICE

The merit system

Over 90 percent of all federal civilian workers are now covered under some kind of **merit system.** What is meant by a merit system? Basically, the term has been closely linked in the United States with civil service, referring to procedures for the appointment of civil servants on the basis of competitive examinations rather than political sponsorship. Civil service merit systems came into being in the late nineteenth century to replace the so-called spoils system, under which each administration had a free hand to hire and fire virtually all federal workers: "To the victor, the spoils." The initial idea of a merit-system alternative was largely negative, focusing on the importance of keeping political influence out of appointments and promotions.

Reforming the civil service

The Pendleton Civil Service Act of 1883 was the first important piece of reform legislation at the federal level in the United States. Borrowing heavily from the practices of the British civil service of the time, the Pendleton Act required competitive examinations for federal appointments, guaranteed tenure of office (assuming competent performance), and required civil service workers to be politically neutral (not to use their posts to advance party goals or to discriminate on a partisan basis). Initially only about 10 percent of the federal work force was covered by Pendleton Act provisions, but the proportion grew steadily. Today, more than nine out of ten federal workers are covered by a merit system.

Sample questions for the examination administered by the Office of Personnel Management for the job of Junior Federal Assistant, GS-4.

Later legislation, especially the Hatch Acts of 1939 and 1940, extended protection of the civil service by barring on-the-job political pressure. The Hatch Act of 1939 placed severe restrictions on practi-

---

Sample Questions 23 through 32 — Verbal Skills

The sample questions in this part will include questions on both meaning of words and reading comprehension. Read each question carefully and mark your answers on the Sample Answer Sheet.

23. *Previous* means most nearly
   A) abandoned   C) timely
   B) former   D) younger

24. *Unanimity* means most nearly
   A) emphasis   C) harmony
   B) namelessness   D) impartiality

25. To *acquiesce* means most nearly to
   A) assent   C) complete
   B) acquire   D) participate

26. *Innate* means most nearly
   A) eternal   C) native
   B) well-developed   D) prospective

27. *Feasible* means most nearly
   A) capable   C) practicable
   B) justifiable   D) beneficial

28. Probably few people realize, as they drive on a concrete road, that steel is used to keep the surface flat and even, in spite of the weight of buses and trucks. Steel bars, deeply imbedded in the concrete, provide sinews to take the stresses so that they cannot crack the slab or make it wavy.

   The paragraph best supports the statement that a concrete road
   A) is expensive to build
   B) usually cracks under heavy weights
   C) is used exclusively for heavy traffic
   D) is reinforced with other material

cally all political activities of federal employees except voting; the Hatch Act of 1940 extended coverage to state and local government workers whose jobs were funded in whole or in part by the federal government. The specific intent of this legislation was to prevent political executives from putting the squeeze on their subordinates within the bureaucracy. Since it would be difficult to differentiate "friendly persuasion" from subtle forms of coercion, even voluntary political work by government employees was banned.

The largest merit system today, encompassing 1.7 million workers, is administered by the Office of Personnel Management (OPM). The OPM was established in 1978 as one of two successor agencies to the old Civil Service Commission. By law, a number of agencies are outside the OPM-run civil service, including the U.S. Postal Service and its 640,000 full-time employees. Other "excepted" agencies are the Federal Bureau of Investigation, the intelligence agencies, the Foreign Service of the State Department, and the Tennessee Valley Authority. All of these operate their own independent merit systems.

Getting a Civil Service Job

Staffing the federal bureaucracy first involves calculating the personnel requirements of the departments and agencies. With passage of the Civil Service Reform Act of 1978, such planning became the responsibility of the OPM. The OPM announces examinations designed to measure applicants' qualifications for various openings, processes applications, and administers the tests. The tremendous range of the jobs being filled is suggested by Table 8.3. Some exams are narrowly fitted to specific positions; others are of the "broad-band" variety—that is, designed to certify applicants for a range of different posts in government.

Actually, many candidates for civil service jobs never take a written test. Middle-level and upper-level positions in the civil service (GS grade levels 9–18) require the "unassembled" examination, which isn't an examination at all. Each candidate submits a statement that describes his or her relevant educational background and other pertinent training or experience, and lists persons, such as previous employers and teachers, who could be contacted for informed evaluations. What the candidate submits for these senior professional and managerial jobs in the government is exactly what he or she would for a comparable position in a university or a private business corporation.

Civil service examinations

Why call it an "examination"? The elusive goal is a type of objective certification that removes any opportunity for bias on the part of those doing the hiring. But no one has been able to devise satisfactory written examinations for many complex professional and managerial positions. Those who know what such posts require must assess can-

Table 8.3

Full-Time Civilian White-Collar Employees of the Federal Government
(by selected occupational categories)

Employment categories	Number of employees
General Administrative, Clerical & Office Services	450,267
Engineering & Architecture	166,976
Medical, Dental & Public Health	141,698
Accounting and Budget	132,747
Business & Industry	95,273
Legal & Kindred	74,680
Supply	60,546
Social Sciences, Psychology & Welfare	56,972
Investigation	56,423
Biological Sciences	54,824
Personnel Management & Industrial Relations	50,431
Physical Sciences	44,378
Transportation	41,325
Education	30,287
Information and the Arts	21,708
Quality Assurance	19,458
Equipment, Facilities & Service	17,738
Mathematics & Statistics	15,363
Library & Archives	10,083
Veterinary Medical Science	2,728
Copyright, Patent, Trademark	2,042

Source: U.S. Office of Personnel Management, *Federal Civilian Workforce Statistics Monthly Release, Employment Trends as of March 1986,* pp. 70–75.

didates in terms of training and experience and arrive at the best judgment as to who are most qualified. Yet the greater the need for judgment, the greater the opportunity for bias or favoritism. One interesting indication of the quest for objectivity is that the *curriculum vitae* submitted by candidates for upper-level civil service positions are actually "graded" with numeric scores.

Veterans in the Civil Service

Veterans' preferences

Probably the most substantial denial of the merit principle in the federal civil service system is extraneous to the examination process. All veterans of the armed services who sustained a service-related disability get 10-point bonuses added to their examination scores; all other veterans get 5 points (except for those who entered the military after 1976 and served only in peacetime). In addition to their 10-point bonuses, disabled veterans are placed at the head of the eligible register for all openings except scientific and professional positions at GS-9 and above. This means that they must be put on the list for hiring ahead of nonveterans, even those with much higher examination scores.

Veterans' preferences don't end there. Normal civil service procedure requires the OPM to send an agency a list of three certified candidates for an opening, leaving the agency free to pick from the list the individual it considers most qualified. But when a veteran appears on a list ahead of a nonveteran, the agency *must* pick him unless it gets the OPM's approval not to do so. Not surprisingly, veterans' organizations pay close attention, keeping the pressure on. At the other end of the employment process, when an agency is required to cut back on its work force ("reduction in force" or rif), the law states that veterans cannot be riffed before nonveterans in the same type and grade of work. Often veterans are retained while nonveterans with greater seniority are laid off.

The preferences accorded veterans in the civil service seriously challenge the merit system. Of course, veterans' preference provisions were put in not with merit in mind, but rather as an additional recognition of those who served in their country's defense. But another big problem arises: few women are veterans. Thus women are rather systematically excluded from the preferential treatment the veterans' bonus confers. How should this problem be addressed?

The Carter Proposals

The 1978 Civil Service
Reform Act

In 1978 President Jimmy Carter attempted to find a solution. In his proposals for the Civil Service Reform Act, Carter endorsed a number of reductions in veterans' preferences. Among them, veterans would receive preference in governmental appointments only for a limited time after their discharge, rather than for life. Women's groups strongly backed these changes, but in the end the veterans' groups won out. The act was passed without most of the proposed reductions in preferential treatment for veterans.

Dismissing Civil Service Workers

Another dilemma presents itself when questions of dismissing workers arise. Civil service arrangements were implemented in large part to preclude the political favoritism of the spoils system. One way to make it hard to fire people by requiring that a "preponderance of evidence" establish an employee's unacceptable performance before he or she could be dismissed. Anything less than that, it was felt, would make it too easy for supervisors to continue political favoritism by simply claiming that work was deficient. Strong federal employees' unions now add their weight as well to the side of protecting employees' rights.

But the same civil service regulations and union pressure that make

Reprinted by permission of UFS, Inc.

Difficulty of firing incompetent workers

it hard to dismiss employees for such illegitimate reasons as political preference also make it hard to fire lazy, unreliable, or insufficiently competent workers. Leonard Reed argues that "for many fine and capable civil servants, the acceptance of the incompetent and the slacker affects their own attitudes and performance. For federal executives the invulnerability of the unproductive worker makes a mockery of the whole concept of efficient management."[24]

Anecdotes about this problem abound. A classic example of the perils a supervisor may encounter if he tries to dismiss an employee is recounted by the former head of the Office of Personnel Management, Alan Campbell. The supervisor in question was trying to justify the dismissal of an employee

> whose repeated absences from her duty station placed undue pressures on her co-workers. The supervisor spent 21 months preparing documentation and conferring with personnel officers, and finally succeeded in building his case. However, at the end of that time, the supervisor received a poor performance rating from his superiors for the neglect of his other duties. Had the employee appealed the case might yet be unresolved.[25]

Commenting on this case, James Fesler notes that it is even more difficult to bring about the dismissal of a worker who tries but who

---

[24] Leonard Reed, "Firing a Federal Employee: The Impossible Dream," in Charles Peters and Michael Nelson, eds., *The Culture of Bureaucracy* (New York: Holt, Rinehart and Winston, 1979), p. 208.

[25] Alan K. Campbell, "Civil Service Reform as a Remedy for Bureaucratic Ills," in Carol H. Weiss and Alan H. Barton, eds., *Making Bureaucracies Work* (Beverly Hills: Sage Publications, 1980), pp. 161–62.

is simply incapable of performing his job competently.[26] The American public concurs that incentives and sanctions for government workers are inadequate, and that federal workers' output often lags behind that in the private sector.[27] But in all this, we should be on the watch for exaggeration. Many politicians, journalists, and other commentators have long enjoyed getting in their criticisms of "over-protected, inefficient bureaucrats." Over the last decade, 5,000 to 6,000 workers who had been on their jobs beyond the probationary period have been dismissed for cause each year, and many others have been induced by their superiors to retire from government service. Still, undoubtedly, the federal civil service has erred on the side of job protection.

Dismissals and the 1978 Civil Service Reform Act

To try to correct the imbalance, the 1978 Civil Service Reform Act gave greater authority to agency heads in matters of dismissals, and streamlined discharged and demotion procedures. Now when an employee is dismissed for unacceptable performance and appeals to the Merit Systems Protection Board, the dismissal will be upheld if supported by "substantial evidence" rather than "a preponderance of evidence."

Apart from these changes, large (and increasing) numbers of federal workers are in positions where some of the regular civil service job protections have not been applied. Involved here are the roughly 500,000 persons in the so-called "expected service." These workers were not hired through *competitive* civil service tests but rather through the "unassembled" exam procedure described above. Their ranks include attorneys, chaplains, scientists, interpreters, and the like. Hiring for GS ranks 9 and higher has in recent years been almost exclusively through the excepted service. Responding to the fact that these workers do not have as extensive appeal rights as other civil service employees subject to adverse personnel action, the House passed legislation in February 1988 bringing them under the same basic provisions that have applied to the others. Considering these regular provisions excessively protective, the Reagan administration naturally opposed extending them to the excepted service. Action on the House-passed bill was pending in the Senate in mid-1988.

---

[26] Fesler, *Public Administration*, p. 107.

[27] For example, a national survey conducted by the Roper Organization in November 1981 found 60 percent of the opinion that government employees work "less hard . . . [than] people in comparable jobs in private industry." Only 5 percent thought they generally work harder, and 31 percent saw little difference between the two. The distributions were about the same on the question of whether government workers are more or less likely to come up with new ideas, or to be recognized for good ideas when they have them.

THE SENIOR EXECUTIVE SERVICE

Executive Schedule and General Schedule

The highest-ranking career administrators have been brought into the Senior Executive Service (SES). Established by the 1978 Civil Service Reform Act, the SES now includes roughly 7,000 managers in the three highest General Schedule (GS) grades of federal employment and in Levels IV and V of the Executive Schedule. (There are 18 grades in all in the General Schedule; the Executive Schedule covers top government executives not under the General Schedule.)

Mobility and Neutral Competence

The idea of neutral competence

The civil service reformers who pushed for the SES wanted a corps of senior career administrators not locked into particular bureaus and programs. Rather than being tied to specific positions, members of the SES are supposed to constitute a mobile pool of top managerial talent, available for assignment where needed in the executive branch.

A second, related goal was to provide the executive branch with a staff of skilled career managers who see themselves and, in turn, are seen by presidents and political appointees as sources of neutral competence rather than program advocacy. It should be possible, civil service reformers have long thought, to create in the United States a cadre of skilled, experienced career officials able and willing to serve any properly constituted administration, and in turn trusted and relied upon by administrations with contrasting political goals. The SES should not be merely skilled administrative "hired guns." "Just tell us what to do, boss" is not the desired end. Civil servants take an oath to uphold the Constitution, and out of this commitment grows a defensible basis for making judgments independent from those of the political executives of the day. Beyond this, senior administrators have a responsibility to argue back to their political superiors (even if they ultimately acquiesce), for their experience and understanding must be brought into play: "S.E.S personnel should embody the 'institutional memory' that has so often rescued political leadership from disastrous adventures."[28]

Early in his career as a political scientist, Woodrow Wilson gave expression to the idea of larger ends and interests to be served by public administrators:

Woodrow Wilson on bureaucracy

The question for us is, how shall our series of governments within governments be so administered that it shall always be to the interest of the public officer to serve, not his superior alone, but the community also with the best efforts of his talents and the soberest service of his conscience? How shall such service be made to his commonest interest by

[28] John A. Rohr, "Ethics for the Senior Executive Service," *Administration and Society* 12 (August 1980):211.

contributing abundantly to his sustenance, to his dearest interest by furthering his ambition, and to his highest interest by advancing his honor and establishing his character? And how shall all this be done alike for the local part and the national whole?[29]

The ideal senior bureaucracy

The ideal SES, then, would be prepared to serve ably different groups of political executives, accepting their claims to political leadership. In this way, the Constitution's grant of executive power to the president and his appointees would be honored, and with it the democratic requirement that the people should be the ultimate arbiters of policy through those whom they elect. At the same time a higher ethic of administration would be interposed, predicated on enduring standards for sound constitutional government.

The British Experience

Britain: a history of bureaucratic neutrality

Students of American public administration have long felt that some nations—among them, Great Britain—have done a better job than the United States in producing cadres of senior career officials with a high *esprit de corps* and a reputation for neutral competence in the service of shifting political executives. In Britain, the civil service's "administrative class" of about 7,500 officials assists cabinet ministers in all facets of governing: providing them with information about what is happening within their departments, identifying alternate courses of action, and translating the policy goals of the party in power into concrete programs and legislation. The ideal of neutral competence figures prominently in the work of the senior British civil service, for once a policy is determined by a minister or by the cabinet, career administrators are supposed to execute it loyally even when they personally disagree with it. As one British administrator put it: "The soul of the service is the loyalty with which we execute ordained error."[30]

Some observers maintain that the British model has been over-idealized.[31] Even if this is so, the American sense of how the British civil service operates contributed a great deal to the development of the SES and the conception of how it should operate.

SUMMARY

Over the last two centuries, a vast governmental system has evolved to administer the American federal government. The executive branch now

[29] Woodrow Wilson, "The Study of Administration," *Political Science Quarterly*, June 1887; reprinted in Political Science Quarterly, 56 (December 1941):505.
[30] As quoted in Ian Gilmour, *The Body Politic* (London: Hutchinson, 1969), p. 198.
[31] Norton Long's brief discussion of this is perceptive. "The S.E.S. and the Public Interest," *Public Administration Review*, 41 (May/June 1981):306–7.

includes over one hundred cabinet departments, independent agencies, regulatory commissions, foundations, boards, and related organizations, and employs about three million men and women in civilian service.

The executive agencies with the broadest policy mandates and the greatest prestige are the thirteen departments with cabinet rank. Four of them trace their lineage back to the beginning of George Washington's first administration: State, Treasury, Defense (originally the War Department), and Justice (originally the office of the Attorney General.) The other nine departments are, in the order in which they were established: Interior, Agriculture, Commerce, Labor, Health and Human Services, Housing and Urban Development, Transportation, Energy, and Education.

The Constitution vests executive authority in the president, but effective presidential direction of the sprawling executive branch is not easily achieved. While the president appoints the heads of the various executive agencies and their principal deputies (with the Senate's advice and consent), and may remove most of these officials without congressional action, Congress plays an active role in executive-branch management. One reason why congressional influence is so great involves the strength and independence of the bureaus, the main units of program responsibility and administration. Headed typically by senior career civil servants, bureaus are tied not just to the departments and agencies of which they are a part, but also to the congressional committees that legislate the substance of their programs and appropriate their budgets.

Sometimes bitter battles have broken out between presidents and their political appointees on one hand, and senior career administrators in the various executive agency bureaus on the other hand, as presidents and their political appointees have sought to exercise greater policy control and direction over the bureaucracy. In an effort to break the cycle of conflict and recrimination, the Carter administration proposed, and Congress enacted, the 1978 Civil Service Reform Act. One portion of this Act establishes the Senior Executive Service, compromised of about 7,000 high career administrators. These officials of the permanent government would be less tied to specific bureaus and programs and more a source of much-needed neutral competence in executive branch administration.

Apart from the issue of political direction and responsiveness, personnel management for the civil service involves classic public administration problems. How can one preclude civil servants being fired because of political favoritism, while permitting them to be dismissed for such proper reasons as incompetent performance? Federal employment has acquired the reputation for erring excessively on the side of job security—a reputation it seems to have earned.

Other problems confronting the federal civil service stem from contrasting objectives in its staffing practices: providing preferential treatment for veterans on the one hand while trying to ensure that government jobs will be open to all on the basis of merit rather than favoritism on the other.

FOR FURTHER STUDY

Lawrence C. Dodd and Richard L. Schott, *Congress and the Administrative State* (New York: Wiley, 1979). A most useful account of the complex relationships of Congress with the agencies of the executive branch.

James W. Fesler, *Public Administration, Theory and Practice* (Englewood Cliffs, NJ: Prentice-Hall, Inc., 1980). A penetrating description of public bureaucracies, their organization, and their operations.

Hugh Heclo, *A Government of Strangers* (Washington, DC: Brookings Institution, 1977). A major treatment of the relationship between political appointees to the executive branch and career civil servants.

Frederick C. Mosher, *Democracy and the Public Service*, 2nd ed. (New York: Oxford University Press, 1982). Provides a useful description and analysis of recent developments affecting career civil service—including the unionization of governmental employees, the operation of merit systems, professionalization, etc.

Charles Peters and Michael Nelson, eds., *The Culture of Bureaucracy* (New York: Holt, Rinehart and Winston, 1979). A thoughtful, sometimes satiric account of the values and culture of bureaucratic Washington.

Harold Seidman and Robert Gilmour, *Politics, Position, and Power: From the Positive to the Regulatory State* (New York: Oxford University Press, 1986). A brilliant description of how government agencies operate and an important critique of proposals for bureaucratic reform, by Seidman, a former deputy director of the Bureau of the Budget (now Office of Management and Budget).

Aaron Wildavsky, *The New Politics of the Budgetary Process*, revised ed. (Glenn View, Illinois: Scott Foresman, 1988). The best account of the nature of the federal budgetary process and its implications for American public policy.

Office of the Federal Register, National Archives and Records Administration, *The United States Government Manual 1987–1988* (Washington, DC: U.S. Government Printing Office, 1988). Published annually as the official handbook of the federal government, the *Manual* is a comprehensive source of information on all agencies, including all units of the executive branch.

Chapter 9

The Judiciary

On July 1, 1987, Ronald Reagan announced his nomination of Judge Robert H. Bork to the Supreme Court seat recently vacated by Justice Lewis F. Powell, Jr. That announcement launched what was to become an epic confirmation battle, a battle that formally ended four months later, on October 23, when the U.S. Senate refused its consent to the Bork nomination, 42 senators voting in favor and 58 against.[1] Dramatic as a political confrontation between president and Congress and important in its implications for the future direction of Supreme Court decisions, the Bork battle was the latest engagement in a continuing struggle over the politics and policies of the federal courts.

Four elements loom large in the background of the Bork dispute: (1) the heightened policy role of the federal courts today; (2) the record of court appointments of the Reagan and Carter administrations, which have involved the application of more explicitly political and ideological standards; (3) the growing recognition by both parties in the late 1980s that a critical tipping point has been reached in the courts' political balance; and (4) a new partisan balance in Congress resulting from the Democrats' 1986 success in regaining a Senate majority after six years of GOP control. Prior to the nomination of Judge Bork, an observer probably could not have known whether the nomination would succeed or fail—but he could have predicted that an explosion was waiting to happen. (See Table 9.1.)

---

[1] Article 2, Section 2, of the U.S. Constitution establishes the institutional framework for Supreme Court appointments. It provides that the president "shall nominate, and by and with the Advice and Consent of the Senate, shall appoint . . . Judges of the Supreme Court. . . ." Senate "consent" requires approval of the nomination by a simple majority—at least one more than half of the senators voting.

Table 9.1
Table 9.1
Members of the U.S. Supreme Court, June 1988

Name	Place of birth	Age as of 12/1/88	Law school from which graduated	President who appointed
Brennan, William Joseph, Jr.	Rumson, NJ	82	Harvard	Eisenhower (1956)
White, Byron Raymond	Fort Collins, CO	71	Yale	Kennedy (1962)
Marshall, Thurgood	Baltimore, MD	80	Howard	Johnson (1967)
Blackmun, Harry A.	Nashville, IL	80	Harvard	Nixon (1970)
Rehnquist, William Hubbs*	Milwaukee, WI	64	Stanford	Nixon (1971) Reagan (1986)
Stevens, John Paul	Chicago, IL	68	Chicago	Ford (1975)
O'Connor, Sandra Day	El Paso, TX	58	Stanford	Reagan (1981)
Scalia, Antonin	Trenton, NJ	52	Harvard	Reagan (1986)
Kennedy, Anthony McLeod	Sacramento, CA	52	Harvard	Reagan (1988)

*Rehnquist was nominated to the U.S. Supreme Court in 1971 by Richard Nixon; he was nominated as chief justice by Ronald Reagan in 1986.

Courts as Policy Makers

The framers of the Constitution intended that the federal courts—especially the Supreme Court—would be a major political institution, one of the three branches of national government that would check and balance the other two in determining public policy. Yet if federal court judges were to be politicians, they would be politicians of a special sort, bound by norms and practices rooted in the law and distinct from those applying to the executive and legislature.

Presidents have routinely nominated for the federal bench mostly those of their own party, and in their selection have often concerned themselves with how their nominees would settle some major unresolved judicial question of the day—for example, Franklin Roosevelt's determined (and successful) effort to get a Supreme Court that would uphold key New Deal legislation. Other than in this regard, until recently the political standards for judicial selection were typically quite casual. We often read about how "unpredictable" a nominee's subsequent decisions on the bench are, and how presidents have been "surprised" by their nominees' subsequent judicial records. In fact, the limited nature of the political scrutiny ensured that a president's court nominees would be a highly heterogeneous group on most issues of judicial policy.

Political Shift in Selecting Judges

Over the last quarter-century a shift has occurred in the selection of federal judges. A surge of new legislation in the 1960s and 1970s established expansive performance standards and entitlements in

Lopez

Chief Justice William H. Rehnquist, center, with the associate justices of the Supreme Court. From the left, Thurgood Marshall, Antonin Scalia, William J. Brennan, Jr., John Paul Stevens, Sandra Day O'Connor, Byron R. White, Anthony M. Kennedy, and Harry A. Blackmun.

many areas, from education to the environment. As court cases arose under these new laws, federal judges were pushed more extensively into the policy-making process. What is more, as a result of court decisions they often found themselves involved in much the same fashion as political executives and legislators—for example, overseeing the operations of public school systems and prisons and settling the detailed requirements of environmental legislation.

From this experience a new view of the courts took shape—a view of their role as more explicitly political and as necessarily involved in the regular policy process. Inevitably, a wide array of interests began examining prospective court appointees, lobbying and even campaigning for and against them much as has been done traditionally for executive and legislative seats. Jimmy Carter was not notably partisan or ideological, but studies show his appointees to the federal courts of general jurisdiction to be a distinctively liberal group. In turn, Reagan's appointees have proven distinctively conservative.[2]

Sheldon Goldman, a leading student of appointments to the federal judiciary, finds

> on balance and with few exceptions, the Reagan administration during the second term appears . . . to have been successful in recruiting quali-

[2] The results of a number of empirical studies of the voting and opinions of district and appeals judges have been summarized by Sheldon Goldman in "Reagan's Second Term Judicial Appointments: The Battle at Midway," *Judicature*, April-May 1987, pp. 335–38.

fied individuals who share the administration's judicial philosophy. . . . [They] have been men and women of accomplishment and . . . they generally compare favorably with the appointments of previous administrations.[3]

Reagan's concern over judicial philosophy Nonetheless, the Reagan administration in its second term added to the impression amply conveyed in its first, that it was being, as one participant described it, notably "meticulous in its concern about [the] judicial philosophy" of its nominees.[4] Goldman argues that the appointment of Edwin Meese III as attorney general helped draw the lines of ideological conflict a little sharper. Meese was more outspoken in articulating a conservative judicial philosophy than was his immediate predecessor, William French Smith, attorney general during Reagan's first term.

The Shifting Balance of Power

The fact that the last two presidents were in a position to make an unusually large number of federal court appointments has further heightened political sensitivity. Jimmy Carter did not have a chance to appoint anyone to the Supreme Court, but in his one term he appointed more district and appeals judges than any previous president—including Franklin Roosevelt, who was in office over twelve years. In 1978, faced with a sharp rise in federal court litigation, Congress passed the Omnibus Judgeship Act, creating 177 new federal district judgeships and 35 new appeals court posts. Carter was in office at the time, so it fell to him to fill these new positions. (See Table 9.2.)

Table 9.2
Numbers of Federal Judges Appointed by
Presidents Roosevelt through Reagan

President	Number of judges	In approximate number of years
Franklin Roosevelt	194	12
Harry Truman	136	8
Dwight Eisenhower	170	8
John Kennedy	129	3
Lyndon Johnson	156	5
Richard Nixon	226	5.5
Gerald Ford	60	2.5
Jimmy Carter	258	4
Ronald Reagan	358	7.5 through June 1988

[3] Ibid., p. 338.
[4] This assessment was offered by Bruce Fein, who played a leading role in the Justice Department screening prospective judges in Reagan's first term. Quoted in "Conservatives Pressing to Reshape Judiciary," *Congressional Quarterly*, September 7, 1985, p. 1760.

By the end of his second term, Ronald Reagan had been able to make even greater changes proportionately than Jimmy Carter in the makeup of the federal judiciary. As of June 30, 1988, the president had nominated and seen confirmed 358 lifetime judges—about half of the entire federal bench.[5] Both supporters and opponents of Mr. Reagan's views have come to see his political legacy in court appointments as especially large and consequential.

Carter's and Reagan's judicial appointments

Partisan Conflict

Developments in the partisan arena helped set the stage for the political explosion that followed the Bork nomination. In the Reagan landslide of November 1980, the Republicans won a Senate majority—the first time they controlled either house of the national legislature since 1954. They retained their Senate majority in the 1982 and 1984 elections. This base contributed greatly to the Reagan administration's legislative successes in many areas. It was especially important in the area of judicial appointments, where the Senate has a large constitutional role while the House of Representatives is not involved.

The Democrats regained control of the Senate in 1986 by a 55–45 margin. That they made a net gain of 8 seats was important in the obvious sense that it meant the Republicans now had to win over members of the opposition in order to carry any issue in the Senate. Even more important than the actual number of seats, though, on the matter of confirmation of Court appointees was the fact that control of the machinery of the Senate shifted from the Republicans to the Democrats. Beginning in January 1987, the Judiciary Committee had a Democratic chairman (Senator Joseph Biden of Delaware). Scheduling of confirmation hearings was now something the Democrats, not the Republicans, could determine. The majority staff of the Judiciary Committee would be chosen by the Democrats and its examination of prospective judges would proceed in the direction the Democrats determined. All in all, whenever the Democrats decided to oppose a nominee for a judgeship they had greater resources to do so effectively than they had during the preceding six years.

Democrats gain control of the Senate

The Bork Controversy: A Battle of Ideas

The confirmation hearings on Robert Bork were dominated by a major argument over judicial philosophy. Bork felt, as did his backers, that in deciding constitutional issues judges should stick closely to the intentions of those who framed and ratified the Constitution. Once he

[5] In addition to the more than 700 federal judges with full-time status, about 290 others have "senior" status—meaning they are semi-retired with reduced case loads. The vast majority of these senior judges were appointed by Reagan's predecessors.

"abandons the lawyer's task of interpretation" of these stated or clearly implied intentions underlying the various constitutional provisions, the judge finds himself with no guidelines other than his own preferences and values.[6] If he chooses to assert these, Bork maintains, the courts lose legitimacy.[7]

Bork believed that in a constitutional democracy like the United States,

Bork's judicial philosophy

> the moral content of law [in the sense of the larger ends it is to serve] must be given by the morality of the framer or the legislator, never by the morality of the judge. The sole task of the latter—and it is a task quite large enough for anyone's wisdom, skill, and virtue—is to translate the framer's or the legislator's morality into a rule to govern unforeseen circumstances.[8]

"The original Constitution," Bork observed, "was devoted primarily to the mechanisms of democratic choice."[9] It did not prescribe a set of answers to the many substantive questions coming before the polity, but rather a governmental structure and practice for arriving at those answers. At its core is the principle of majority rule, with its stipulations that popular majorities, through the legislators, governors, presidents, and other officials they elect, should decide policy on most issues, both large and small.

Judicial interpretation of the Constitution

The U.S. Constitution is not completely majoritarian. It modified majoritarianism with the principle that some rights are so important that they must not be infringed by any group, however large. The Supreme Court draws its legitimacy from the need—in a democratic system predicated not just on majority rule but also on minority rights—for a nonelective branch, insulated from majoritarianism, to patrol the boundaries and determine the areas in which majority preferences may not determine policy. But, in Bork's view, for this to work the Court must limit itself to implementing the minority rights guarantees that those who framed the original Constitution and its later amendments intended.[10] Judges must not simply substitute their own values.[11]

---

[6] Robert Bork, "The Struggle Over the Role of the Court," *National Review*, September 17, 1982, pp. 1137–38.

[7] Ibid., p. 1138.

[8] Robert Bork, "Tradition and Morality in Constitutional Law," in Mark W. Cannon and David M. O'Brien, eds., *Views from the Bench* (Chatham, N.J.: Chatham House Publishers, 1958), pp. 171–72.

[9] Ibid., p. 170.

[10] Robert Bork, "Neutral Principles and Some First Amendment Problems," *Indiana Law Journal*, Fall 1971, pp. 1–35.

[11] Ibid., p. 6.

An Alternate View

One area in which the practical implications of "strict construction" generated heated criticism during the Senate hearings encompasses issues of personal rights and liberties, many involving family privacy, that are not specifically referred to in the Constitution. These are sometimes called "unenumerated rights." The case of *Griswold* v. *Connecticut*, 381 U.S. 479 (1965), is an important one in the contemporary argument over these rights. By seeing where the Court came down in this case, and where Bork faulted it, we gain insights into an ongoing policy dispute.

Griswold v. *Connecticut*

In *Griswold* the Supreme Court decided the constitutionality of Connecticut's birth control law which banned the sale and use of contraceptives and barred physicians and clinics from counseling on birth control. Over the years this statute had been largely ignored. Indeed, in an earlier case, *Poe* v. *Ullman*, which reached the Supreme Court in 1961, a challenge to the law was dismissed for lack of justiciable controversy: The Court found that despite the common sale of contraceptives, no one had ever been tried for violating the law. (For a definition of justiciability, see pp. 320–21.) The Catholic Church's position against the use of contraceptives goes far toward explaining why the statute was enacted: Roman Catholics were a majority of the Connecticut population and the Church's influence on relevant policy questions was strong. The fact that many Catholics, as well as members of other faiths, disagreed strongly with the Church on birth control explains why the law was in practice substantially ignored. It remained on the books nonetheless. Following the *Poe* v. *Ullman* ruling, the Planned Parenthood League of Connecticut was able to initiate a new test case challenge that met the Court's earlier objections by actually getting someone arrested for violating the statute.

Poe v. *Ullman*

The issue before the Court in *Griswold* was not, of course, whether Connecticut's birth control measure was wise legislation. Rather, the issue was whether, by enacting it and keeping it on the books, the popularly elected legislature of the state had strayed into an area where it constitutionally was obliged not to go, infringing on individual rights.

The Court held in *Griswold* that fundamental rights exist that are not expressly enumerated in the Bill of Rights or elsewhere in the Constitution. In the majority opinion, Justice William O. Douglas argued that "specific guarantees in the Bill of Rights have penumbras, formed by emanations from those guarantees that give them life and substance." Some of these guarantees create "zones of privacy." The present case, Douglas maintained, "concerns a relationship lying within the zone of privacy created by several fundamental constitutional guarantees. . . . We deal with a right of privacy older than the

Fundamental rights not enumerated in the Constitution

Bill of Rights—older than our political parties, older than our school system. Marriage is a coming together for better or for worse, hopefully enduring, and intimate to the degree of being sacred." Government simply can't encroach upon this right of being sacred." Government simply can't encroach upon this right to privacy as Connecticut was doing through its birth control ban. The Connecticut law was declared unconstitutional.

Two justices, Hugo Black and Potter Stewart, dissented. Black argued that

> the Court talks about a constitutional "right of privacy" as though there is some constitutional provision or provisions forbidding any law ever to be passed which might abridge the "privacy" of individuals. But there is not. There are, of course, guarantees in certain specific constitutional provisions which are designed in part to protect privacy at certain times and places with respect to certain activities. . . . I realize that many good and able men have eloquently spoken and written, sometimes in rhapsodical strains, about the duty of this Court to keep the Constitution in tune with the times. . . . For myself, I must with all deference reject that philosophy. The Constitution makers knew the need for change and provided for it. Amendments suggested by the people's elected representatives can be submitted to the people or their selected agents for ratification. That method of change was good for our fathers, and being somewhat old-fashioned I must add it is good enough for me.

Black would not have overturned the Connecticut law.

Bork's view of Griswold

In his Senate confirmation testimony, Bork suggested that there might be some acceptable alternate basis for reaching the same result that the Court's majority reached in *Griswold*, but he continued to insist, as he had on many previous occasions, that the Court's reasoning had been fundamentally flawed. His position is basically the same as Black's.[12]

By itself *Griswold* was not the most momentous case, but it led to other, more far-reaching decisions. In its controversial decision on abortion, *Roe* v. *Wade* (1973), the Supreme Court applied the basic right of privacy construction that it had announced in *Griswold* in striking down a Texas statute that had made abortion a state crime if performed for reasons other than saving the life of the mother. Justice Harry Blackmun held in the majority opinion in *Roe* that "this right to privacy . . . is broad enough to encompass a woman's decision whether or not to terminate her pregnancy." (We discuss *Roe* in more detail later in this chapter.)

Roe v. Wade and the abortion controversy

A bitter national debate has gone on since 1973 over abortion and the Court's *Roe* decision. The appointments of Justices Sandra Day O'Connor and Antonin Scalia—both of whom have been critical of *Roe*—had already shifted the balance on the Court on abortion from what it was in 1973. The prospect of Robert Bork's appointment troubled those on the "pro-choice" side of the abortion debate, especially

---

[12] Bork, "Neutral Principles and Some First Amendment Problems," p. 9.

given the strength of his attack on the reasoning that underlay the Court's ruling. Would Bork be the key fifth vote in a new Court majority to reverse or substantially weaken *Roe?* And more generally, would he tip the Court's balance in other cases to a narrower construction of the rights of privacy?

Bork: A Radical Departure?

In testifying against Judge Bork's confirmation, Laurence Tribe, a prominent constitutional scholar, argued that the judge's position is

> a uniquely narrow and constricted view of "liberty" and of the Supreme Court's place in protecting it. It sets Judge Bork apart from the entire 200-year-old tradition of thought about rights that underlies the American Constitution. And it suggests an incapacity to address in any meaningful way a whole spectrum of cases that we can expect will be vital in our national life during the next quarter-century.[13]

Critics of Bork's view of the Constitution

The core of the problem, as Tribe and other critics saw it, was Bork's radical view of the U.S. Constitution: that the people of the United States in ratifying the Constitution surrendered to government all the natural rights they had believed themselves to have possessed except for those specifically enumerated in the Bill of Rights. "Despite Judge Bork's espousal of a theory of 'original intent,' " Tribe argued,

> no understanding of the Constitution could be further from the clear purpose of those who wrote and ratified the Constitution and its first ten amendments. The principal aim of the original Constitution—and the impetus for the insistence as a condition of ratification, upon a Bill of Rights to preserve natural rights that had been recognized for centuries—was to create a national government that, although sufficiently powerful to bind together states of great diversity, would not threaten the individual liberty that the people retained and did not cede to any level of government.[14]

Bork's challenge to unenumerated rights

The U.S. Supreme Court from the beginning of the Republic, Tribe maintained, has recognized that the people of the United States retained various "unenumerated rights." The American nation is bound together by a broad and vital conception of individual liberty. This conception has evolved and enlarged with the passage of time. "Judge Bork's rejection of the Supreme Court's historic role in articulating *an evolving concept of 'liberty'* protected by the Constitution—not simply protecting a *fixed* set of 'liberties' from an evolving set of threats," Tribe insisted, challenges deeply held American expectations and values.[15] The Judiciary Committee majority took this same stand.

[13] Testimony of Laurence H. Tribe before the Senate Judiciary Committee, September 22, 1987, p. 9 of the typescript of Tribe's prepared remarks.
[14] Ibid., pp. 10–11.
[15] Ibid., p. 16.

The Vote

In late September and early October, after an unusually spirited battle, the Senate tide flowed strongly against Bork's nomination. He lost the support of virtually all the senators who had been cross-pressured and undecided. In the Senate Judiciary Committee vote of October 6, all eight committee Democrats opposed confirmation; one Republican, Arlen Specter of Pennsylvania, joined the Democratic majority; the remaining five committee Republicans voted for confirmation. The nomination went to the Senate floor with the committee recommending, nine to five, that the Senate not grant its consent to the appointment. On October 23, 1987, the full Senate rejected the nomination of Robert H. Bork to be an associate justice of the Supreme Court by a margin of 42 in favor, 58 against. Only two Democrats, Boren of Oklahoma and Hollings of South Carolina, voted to confirm. Six Republicans—Chaffee of Rhode Island, Packwood of Oregon, Specter of Pennsylvania, Stafford of Vermont, Warner of Virginia, and Weicker of Connecticut—voted no.

The Nomination of Ginsburg

After Bork's defeat, the president named a second nominee, Douglas H. Ginsburg, age 41, since 1986 a judge on the U.S. Court of Appeals for the District of Columbia. Almost immediately, Ginsburg's nomination ran into trouble. White House and Justice Department staff who had done the screening had presented Judge Ginsburg to the president as someone whose nomination could be presented to the Senate without fear of embarrassment. Here the president was ill-advised. A number of embarrassing revelations came to light, the most publicized of which was that Ginsburg had smoked marijuana both as a student at Cornell and as a young law school professor at Harvard. Some made a distinction between the two situations, being far more troubled by his use of marijuana as a law school faculty member than as an undergraduate. On another front, Ginsburg was faulted for a possible conflict of interest in his 1986 handling of a case bearing on the cable television industry, when he was head of the antitrust division of the Justice Department. At the time, Ginsburg owned stock in a cable TV company.

More damaging than these revelations, however, was the growing sense of uncertainty among senators and others who examined his nomination about what Judge Douglas Ginsburg was really like. Bork's views had been highly developed and aired publicly often—at times, it seemed to his supporters, almost too often—as opponents seized on earlier statements to fault him. But at least everyone knew where Bork stood. Where Judge Ginsburg stood on the substance of what a Supreme Court justice does—broad constitutional interpretation—

was simply not known. In the end, it was the picture of Ginsburg as insufficiently experienced and the uncertainties about his qualities of mind and the kind of Supreme Court justice he would be that ultimately brought him down. Against the backdrop of much public hoopla about his marijuana use, some conservatives in the administration such as Education Secretary William Bennett called upon him to have his name withdrawn. And on November 7, 1987, just nine days after the president had picked him, Douglas Ginsburg capitulated.

Kennedy to the High Court

Judge Anthony Kennedy of the Ninth Circuit Court had been a finalist in the previous round of nominee selection, and the possibility of his nomination had been favorably received by many senators. He quickly emerged as the favorite in round three. On November 11, President Reagan named him to the vacant seat on the Supreme Court. In the White House ceremony announcing his nomination, Kennedy set at least one record. He became the first Supreme Court nominee in American history to be quizzed by the press at such a ceremony on his use of marijuana. Reporters wanted to know if investigators had asked if he'd ever smoked marijuana. Judge Kennedy replied: "They asked me that question and the answer was no, firmly no."

From the outset, senators on both sides of the aisle indicated that Judge Kennedy would be easily confirmed. This was partly due to both sides being exhausted by the tumultuous battle of the preceding four months. As one participant put it, "there's institutional battle fatigue around here." Senator Edward Kennedy, who had been so critical of Judges Bork and Ginsburg, limited himself to saying that he was interested in examining the new nominee's lengthy judicial record. "I look forward to the hearings and to meeting Judge Kennedy."

Whereas Judge Bork had been controversial and outspoken, Judge Kennedy was noncontroversial and soft-spoken. In his twelve years on the Court of Appeals for the Ninth Circuit, Kennedy had written over 400 opinions and had given a great many speeches. Through these he had conveyed a sense of personal moderation and balance. "His opinions are more sensitive than strident," was the conclusion of Tribe, a leading critic of Judge Bork.

Personal affability and moderation are important characteristics, but they are not elements of a political philosophy. An individual may hold quite conservative views, or quite liberal ones, and display a moderate and relaxed personal style. What is Anthony Kennedy's judicial outlook? It appears similar to Robert Bork's. Judge Kennedy had clearly subscribed to "interpretivism." Before coming to the High Court, for example, in a 1986 speech Kennedy argued that "the Constitution was written with care and deliberation, not by accident. . . . The Constitutional text and its immediate implications, traceable by

Kennedy: moderate, noncontroversial

Kennedy's judicial philosophy

some historical link to the ideas of the framers, must govern the judges." If these principles don't govern judges' interpretation of constitutional questions, they and the courts find their claims to impartiality and even legitimacy in jeopardy.

"It is great irony of contemporary history," Judge Kennedy remarked,

> that those who argue most passionately for creative judicial intervention in effect advocate abolition of an independent, nonelected judiciary. The unrestrained exercise of judicial authority ought to be recognized for what it is: the raw exercise of political power. If in fact that is the basis of our decisions, then there is no principled justification for our insulation from the political process.[16]

Hearings on the Kennedy nomination began on December 14, 1987. While the president of the National Organization for Women had strongly attacked the Kennedy nomination, most of the interest groups that had jumped so actively into the fray against Bork stayed on the sidelines this time. On February 3, 1988, Kennedy was unanimously confirmed by the Senate, 97–0.

Kennedy is confirmed by the Senate

A Political Balance Sheet

Who were the winners and losers in this protracted political battle? Apart from Judges Bork and Ginsburg, who obviously lost in the sense that neither attained the Court seat he wanted, that question is not as easy to answer as it might at first appear. As is so often the case in the American system built on separation of powers and divided governmental authority, each of the principal participants won and lost.

President Reagan was deeply committed to putting Judge Bork on the Supreme Court. Administration officials have stated that when Lewis Powell announced his retirement, the president made it clear that he really had only one candidate in mind for the post. Reagan failed in his efforts to convince the country that Bork was the man for the job, and he saw the Senate turn down his nomination by a heavy margin of 58 votes to 42. On the other hand, while disappointed by Bork and embarrassed by Ginsburg, Mr. Reagan realized his goal of seeing appointed a conservative justice whose "interpretivist" judicial philosophy was very close to what the president had repeatedly said he wanted.

Reagan succeeds in appointing a conservative justice

For their part, the liberal groups and the Democratic leadership committed themselves to an all-out fight against the Bork nomination, and they carried the day decisively. They not only gained the necessary votes to block confirmation, but they convinced the coun-

---

[16] Judge Anthony M. Kennedy, "Unenumerated Rights and the Dictates of Judicial Restraint," speech made at Stanford University, July 1986.

A cartoonist's depiction of President Reagan's appointment of Justice Kennedy after attempts to get Judge Bork (right), then Judge Ginsburg (left), on the Supreme Court.

try that Bork would have been unsettling as a Supreme Court justice. At the same time, however, in the end they saw another conservative justice, nine years Bork's junior, take a seat on the highest court.

Reagan's conservative judicial legacy

Ronald Reagan's appointees to the federal bench are often described as his lasting legacy in the sense that many of these judges will be deciding cases into the 1990s and beyond. This legacy is certain to be a conservative one. For example, studies of the decisions of Reagan appointees show them less likely than Carter appointees to support criminal litigants.[17] On the Supreme Court itself, the three justices nominated by Reagan—Sandra Day O'Connor, Antonin Scalia, and Anthony Kennedy—together with Richard Nixon appointee William H. Rehnquist, whom Reagan elevated to chief justice in 1986, and John Kennedy appointee Byron R. White, appeared to emerge as a new if precarious conservative majority as the Court's 1987–88 term ended. Anthony Kennedy cemented a majority for the conservatives in seven of the eight 5–4 decisions in which the Court's other eight members split along liberal–conservative lines. Kennedy supplied the fifth vote for the more conservative block, for example, in the decision to consider in the 1988–89 term overruling *Runyon* v. *McCrary* (1976), a civil rights decision that interpreted an 1866 statute expansively, making it the basis for a broad range of discrimination suits involving private parties. And he joined the majority in two 5–4 decisions upholding death sentences for convicted murderers.

A "conservative revolution" not likely

Still, the courts are unlikely to effect a "conservative revolution" in American law. The big changes in areas such as civil liberties and the rights of persons accused of crimes that were brought about by the courts in the 1960s will for the most part stand as settled law. In his confirmation hearings, Anthony Kennedy made this point forcefully. There was great argument over these changes at the time they were made, he said, but the legal system has generally adapted to them. Just as Americans expect more in governmental services today than they did a half-century ago, so they expect a more expansive set of guarantees of individual rights than they did earlier. Federal judges will reflect these widely shared judgments.

Difficulty in predicting partisan labels for the judiciary

But reference to liberal and conservative blocs on the Court is always a tricky business. In interpreting the Constitution justices frequently confront the need to make distinctions that don't fit neatly under standard ideological or partisan labels. In June 1988, for instance, the Court handed down an important decision upholding the constitutionality of the 1978 law that provides for judicial appointment of "independent counsels" to investigate alleged crimes by high executive branch officials and that insulates them from presidential con-

---

[17]C. K. Rowland, Robert A. Carp, and Donald Songer, "The Effect of Presidential Appointment, Group Interaction, and Fact-Law Ambiguity on Lower Federal Judges' Policy Judgments: The Case of Reagan and Carter Appointees," paper presented at the 1985 annual meeting of the American Political Science Association.

trol by barring their removal except for good cause, subject to judicial review. The Reagan administration had challenged the constitutionality of the statute, arguing that it violated separation of powers by intruding upon the executive branch's powers and responsibilities for criminal prosecution. Writing for a 7–1 majority, Chief Justice Rehnquist rejected the administration's arguments: "We do not think that the act works any Judicial usurpation of properly executive functions. . . . The act does give a Federal court the power to review the Attorney General's decision to remove an independent counsel, but in our view this is a function that is well within the traditional power of the Judiciary."[18]

Only Justice Scalia voted to support the administration's position in this case. The Supreme Court is a political institution, sitting right in the middle of important parts of the policy making process in the United States, but it plays its political role according to a special set of constitutional requirements. Predicting justices' votes by where they stand on a liberal–conservative dimension is an undertaking fraught with peril.

COURTS AS POLITICAL INSTITUTIONS

Judicial review

The courts follow procedures and are governed by standards vastly different from the other branches. The practice of **judicial review**— whereby an independent judicial branch reviews and gives final construction to legislative and executive acts and determines their constitutionality—is key to the courts' political role. As it has developed in the United States, judicial review is exercised by state as well as federal courts, although the Supreme Court makes final binding determination of whether legislation is consistent with the Constitution.

Judicial Review

Supreme Court: federal system umpire

A distinction must be made between judicial review of laws enacted by Congress and those enacted by state legislatures. The framers saw the Supreme Court playing umpire in the federal system, striking down state legislation that clashed with the requirements of national law. Alexander Hamilton argued in *Federalist Paper* 22 that true national government would be impossible if each state court system could separately decide what the Constitution and federal legislation require. It is essential "to establish one court paramount to the rest, possessing a general superintendence and authorized to settle and declare in the last resort a uniform rule of civil justice." Section 25 of the Judi-

[18] *Morrison* v. *Olson* (1988).

ciary Act of 1789 (enacted by a Congress of which many of the framers were members) explicitly conferred upon the Court authority to review state court decisions involving state actions in which a federal claim was raised.

On the issue of the Court's striking down acts of Congress, however, the historical record is more ambiguous. Some framers argued strongly for this power, as Hamilton did forcefully in *Federalist Paper* 78: "There is no position which depends on clearer principles than that every act of a delegated authority, contrary to the tenor of the commission under which it is exercised, is void. No legislative act, therefore, contrary to the Constitution, can be valid." But who is to decide if an act contradicts the Constitution? Shouldn't Congress itself be the judge? Hamilton was adamant that this was not intended.

Judging constitutionality

> It is far more rational to suppose that the courts were designed to be an intermediate body between the people and the legislature in order, among other things, to keep the latter within the limits assigned to their authority. The interpretation of the laws is the proper and peculiar province of the courts. A constitution is, in fact, and must be regarded by the judges as a fundamental law. It therefore belongs to them to ascertain its meaning as well as the meaning of any particular act proceeding from the legislative body.

Marbury v. *Madison.* A decade and a half after the Constitution was ratified, Supreme Court Chief Justice John Marshall echoed Hamilton's argument:

> The Constitution is either a superior paramount law, unchangeable by ordinary means, or it is on a level with ordinary legislative acts. . . . If the former part of the alternative be true, then a legislative act contrary to the Constitution is not law. . . . It is, emphatically, the province and duty of the judicial department, to say what the law is.

Marshall concluded that "a law repugnant to the Constitution is void; and that courts, as well as other departments, are bound by that instrument."

Marbury v. Madison

The case in which Marshall delivered this momentous ruling was *Marbury* v. *Madison*, decided in 1803. William Marbury had been an official in the administration of President John Adams. Along with more than fifty of his fellow Federalists, he was nominated and confirmed for a federal judgeship just before Adams left office in March 1801. Final work on Marbury's commission was completed so late, however, that it did not get delivered before Thomas Jefferson and his new administration took office. Angered by the attempt to stack the federal judiciary with so many Federalists, Jefferson ordered that Marbury's commission (and others similarly not delivered) be held back. Marbury took his case to the Supreme Court, seeking an order requiring the Jefferson administration to give him his appointment.

John Marshall had been secretary of state in Adams's administration, and it was actually his oversight that had led to Marbury's commission not being delivered. By the time the Supreme Court heard Marbury's appeal, Marshall was chief justice. The case seemed to present him with a no-win dilemma. If the Court issued the order Marbury wanted, Jefferson and his secretary of state, James Madison, would certainly ignore it. The Court had no means to enforce compliance. And, as a new institution trying to establish itself, the Court might suffer permanent damage from such a precedent. But if it did not issue the order, the Court would be seen to be caving in to Jefferson's point of view.

An historic ruling on constitutionality

In the ruling for a unanimous Court, Marshall found a way to escape this dilemma and expand upon the Court's authority. Since the president had signed the commissions and the secretary of state had recorded them, the appointments were in order. The Jefferson administration was wrong in not releasing them to Marbury and his colleagues. Having thus rebuked Jefferson and Madison, Marshall turned to the question of whether the Supreme Court had the authority to issue the order Marbury wanted—and he concluded that it did not. He held that a minor provision of the Judiciary Act of 1789 under which Marbury *had sought remedy had added unconstitutionally* to the Court's original jurisdiction and had to be struck down. Thus was the Court's power to declare an act of Congress unconstitutional first formally enunciated.

In subsequent years, the Hamilton-Marshall position on judicial review triumphed completely. But it was by no means generally accepted at the time. Sheldon Goldman found that, insofar as judicial review of congressional acts was considered at all by most framers, it was endorsed only in a narrow form: as a means whereby flagrant violations of the Constitution by Congress or the president could be declared void.[19] It would be a weapon in reserve, to be used rarely as a check in extreme cases, not the expansive power it has in fact become.

Extending judicial review. Since its beginnings, the U.S. Supreme Court has held over 900 state acts to be unconstitutional, and has voided more than 120 federal statutes in whole or in part.[20] Up until the Civil War, only two congressional acts had been held unconstitutional; the rate of such findings increased substantially in the late nineteenth century and has increased even more in the twentieth century. Four-fifths of all federal statutes (or portions thereof) struck down by the Court have been voided since 1900.

[19] Sheldon Goldman, *Constitutional Law and Supreme Court Decision-Making* (New York: Harper and Row, 1982), p. 12.
[20] Congressional Research Service, *Constitution of the United States of America, Analysis and Interpretation* (1980 supplement), Senate Document 96-64, 1982; and Henry J. Abraham, *The Judicial Process* (New York: Oxford University Press, 1980), pp. 304–10.

Judicial review and
civil liberties

Since the late 1930s, national legislation found unconstitutional has been especially heavy in one area—*civil liberties and civil rights.* Of the 40 provisions of federal law struck down between 1943 and 1979, "all but two [were voided] because they infringed certain personal rights and liberties safeguarded under the Constitution."[21] For example, in *Afroyim* v. *Rusk* (1967), the Court declared unconstitutional a section of the Nationality Act of 1940 which stripped American citizens of their citizenship if they voted in a foreign election; the Court held that under Section 1 of the Fourteenth Amendment Congress lacked the constitutional authority to enact any legislation denying Americans their citizenship without their express consent. And in two companion cases (cases at the same time and similarly decided), *Blount* v. *Rizzi* and *United States* v. *The Book Bin* (1971), statutes authorizing the Post Office Department to cut off service to mail-order houses dealing in pornography were struck down as unconstitutional violations of First Amendment guarantees of freedom of expression.

Judicial review abroad. Comparable powers of judicial review are by no means commonly held by courts in other democracies. In Great Britain the constitutional doctrine of the supremacy of Parliament means that the courts may not strike down any law that the legislature has enacted. In France, only a circumscribed power resembling judicial review exists, and it resides not in the courts but in the Constitutional Council (which includes a number of ranking political officials, among them all living past presidents of France). Private individuals cannot challenge a law's constitutionality; only the president, the premier, the heads of the two houses of the legislature, or a group of at least 60 members of the legislature by petition may do so.

Judicial review and
courts abroad

Other countries have developed certain aspects of judicial review, but not the full-blown form one sees in the United States. In West Germany no ordinary court is permitted to decide constitutional questions in the course of litigation. A Federal Constitutional Court has wide-reaching powers to decide all controversies involving the meaning of the German Basic Law (the country's constitution). In Canada and a handful of other countries, most of which have federal systems of government, the ordinary courts exercise judicial review much as the United States. For example, in Canada authority to declare acts of Parliament void clearly does not flow from English common law—Canada's legal heritage—which recognizes the principle of parliamentary supremacy, and the Canadian Constitution says nothing at all about judicial review power. Nonetheless, through continuing use judicial review has developed into an unwritten rule, "a

[21] Abraham, *Judicial Process*, p. 297.

binding convention of our [Canadian] Constitution."[22] The roots of judicial review in Canada can be "traced to pragmatic considerations flowing implicitly from the principle of federalism. . . ." With their separate state or provincial governments, federal systems need some central body able to decide when state actions contradict national legislation. The regular courts have assumed this role in a number of former British colonies, including Canada and Australia.

Judicial Policy Making

The American courts' power of judicial review is one resource in a more general capacity to make policy. When the Supreme Court holds that an act that Congress has passed and the president has signed violates the Constitution and hence cannot be enforced, it obviously is setting national policy. But rulings on constitutionality are not the only or even the most important instrument for judicial policy making. Most of the work of the courts does not involve constitutional adjudication, but rather the interpretation of ordinary legislation.

Due to the age of some justices, President Bush will probably have, as President Reagan had, a unique opportunity to shape the Supreme Court.

GREAT RETIREMENT PARTY! WE'LL HAVE TO DO THIS AGAIN REAL SOON!...

[22] Richard J. Van Loon and Michael S. Whittington, *The Canadian Political System* (Toronto: McGraw-Hill Ryerson, 1981), p. 179.

Whenever a legislature enacts a law, it makes policy; but the scope of these policy initiatives varies widely. There is a vast difference between the public policy implications of a new parking ordinance and sweeping Social Security legislation. Similarly, a court's policy role is much more limited when it applies a specific drunk-driving law than when it interprets an act setting complex new environmental goals and requirements. As a general rule, the narrower the scope of a law and the more precisely and unambiguously its terms are prescribed, the less policy discretion courts have. The wider the substantive reach of a law, and the more expansive the goals it proclaims, the greater are the court's policy powers stemming from interpretation.

Interpreting legislation

Making Policy by Deciding Cases

The courts are a special type of political institution, bound by a set of norms and practices distinct from those of all other governmental units. They make policy within a structure and tradition that exerts great influence over the results. The best way to get a sense of the special properties of judicial policy making is to examine decisions rendered by the U.S. Supreme Court. A court makes policy by deciding *cases in law*. An **opinion of the court** entails the resolution of a particular policy dispute presented in a case brought before it. As the highest court in the land, the Supreme Court usually hears cases of only substantial national policy importance.

Decisions of the Supreme Court are an unusual blend of practical political action and political philosophy. The latter comes into play so prominently because the Court's influence depends in significant part upon its success in convincing other actors—the president, members of Congress, lower-court judges, lawyers, and, to some extent, the public at large—of the intellectual soundness of its legal interpretations. When the law in question is the Constitution itself, the Court expounds on the most fundamental values of the American polity. Through Court decisions, concrete disputes get resolved but, at the same time, large philosophic questions are consciously explored. Because the Court is often divided, and one or more judges in the minority issue dissenting opinions, the argument gets joined directly and, on occasion, with great force.

The Supreme Court and political philosophy

Brown v. *Board of Education of Topeka* (1954)

Three key Supreme Court decisions of the last several decades illustrate concretely aspects of the reach of judicial decision making in important areas of contemporary public policy. Together these rulings provide a good sense of how much the Court can accomplish, and how it is sometimes uniquely situated to act decisively when the other branches cannot act.

Linda Brown speaks at the University of Kansas on civil rights nearly thirty years after the famous Brown school desegregation decision.

Segregation and the
Fourteenth
Amendment

The first of these three cases is probably the single most important Supreme Court decision of recent years. In **Brown v. Board of Education of Topeka** (1954), the Court signaled a vast shift of national policy in race relations. *Brown* and its companion cases came to the Supreme Court as specific challenges to what was then the general southern and border state practice of maintaining two separate public school systems: one for whites and one for blacks. At issue was the requirement of section 1 of the Fourteenth Amendment: "No state shall . . . deny to any person within its jurisdiction the equal protection of the laws." Did the prevailing segregation of black students deny them equal protection mandated by the Fourteenth Amendment? Box 9.1 gives excerpts from the Court's decision.[23]

When Congress passes a statute treating a central question of national policy, the objective set forth in the statute is not always promptly and harmoniously achieved. So it is with Supreme Court

[23] References to Court decisions are written in a distinctive format. For example, the citation for the *Brown* decision often appears as follows: 347 U.S. 483; 98 L. Ed. 873 (1954). "U.S." stands for *United States Supreme Court Reports;* "L. Ed." refers to *Lawyers' Edition.* These are two separate publications—the first by the U.S. Government Printing Office, the second by a private publishing company—that print the complete text of every Court decision. The first number is always the volume in which the opinion is located; the second number is the page on which the opinion begins.

Box 9.1

Brown v. Board of Education of Topeka (1954)

Facts. Five cases originating in the states of Kansas, South Carolina, Virginia, and Delaware, and in the District of Columbia, came to the Supreme Court for reargument on June 8, 1953. All involved challenges to the constitutionality of racial segregation in public schools. In each, black schoolchildren through counsel sought admission to community schools to which they had been denied access. The lead case involved a suit by Oliver Brown to require the Board of Education of Topeka, Kansas, to admit his eight-year-old daughter Linda to a then all-white public school only five blocks from her home.

Decision. In a unanimous opinion the Court held that the segregation that the plaintiffs complained of violated the guarantee of equal protection of the laws under the Fourteenth Amendment to the U.S. Constitution. Mr. Chief Justice Warren, delivering the opinion of the Court, said in part:

> . . . Today, education is perhaps the most important function of state and local governments. In these days, it is doubtful that any child may reasonably be expected to succeed in life if he is denied the opportunity of an education. Such an opportunity, where the state has undertaken to provide it, is a right which must be made available to all on equal terms.
>
> We come then to the question presented: Does segregation of children in public schools solely on the basis of race, even though

decisions. *Brown* was immediately engulfed in intense controversy. At once hailed by some for signaling the demise of the "separate but equal" doctrine instituted in 1896, it was vigorously denounced by others as a usurpation of state prerogatives. In March 1956, 101 of the 128 members of Congress from 11 southern and border states issued a tract that labeled the *Brown* decision "a clear abuse of judicial power" and applauded states intending to "resist enforced integration by any means."[24] Massive resistance in many southern states followed for years after.

Intense controversy over Brown

Nonetheless, when Chief Justice Earl Warren, speaking for a unanimous Court, concluded, "We have now announced that such segregation is a denial of equal protection of the laws," the nation was launched on a new policy course that would entail major changes in educational programs by local, state, and national government. Nar-

[24] U.S. Congress, Senate, "Declaration of Constitutional Principles," *Congressional Record* #102 (March 12, 1956):4460.

the physical facilities and other "tangible" factors may be equal, deprive the children of the minority group of equal educational opportunities? We believe that it does. . . . To separate them [children in grade and high schools] from others of similar age and qualifications solely because of their race generates a feeling of inferiority as to their status in the community that may affect their hearts and minds in a way unlikely ever to be undone. The effect of this separation on their educational opportunities was well stated by a finding in the Kansas case by a court which nevertheless felt compelled to rule against the Negro plaintiffs: "Segregation of white and colored children in public schools has a detrimental effect upon the colored children. The impact is greater when it has the sanction of the law; for the policy of separating the races is usually interpreted as denoting the inferiority of the Negro group. A sense of inferiority affects the motivation of a child to learn. Segregation with the sanction of law, therefore, has a tendency to [retard] the educational and mental development of Negro children and to deprive them of some of the benefits they would receive in a racial[ly] integrated school system. We conclude that in the field of public education the doctrine of "separate but equal" has no place. Separate educational facilities are inherently unequal. Therefore, we hold that the plaintiffs and others similarly situated for whom the actions have been brought are, by reason of the segregation complained of, deprived of the equal protection of the laws guaranteed by the Fourteenth Amendment. . . .

Brown: the success of checks and balances

rowly construed, separation of powers and checks and balances envision a situation where the excesses of one branch are curbed by another. In a more general sense, this constitutional doctrine allows for the failure of one part of government in discharging its constitutional duties to be corrected by another part of government not subject to the same political constraints. The work of the Supreme Court in *Brown* shows this process at its best. By the 1950s, many Americans believed that the presence of segregated schools throughout the South grossly denied the constitutional claim to equal rights for all citizens. But opinion among the white majority in southern states was such that local government would not act to end segregation. Congress had ample legislative authority to act, but the near-unanimous opposition of southern congressmen, many of whom held positions of great authority in the congressional committee system, was sufficient to block legislation. Of all the units of government in a position to act, only the Supreme Court was sufficiently insulated from such political pressures to take corrective steps.

Baker v. Carr (1962)

Legislative
apportionment

The school desegregation decisions are by no means the only occasion when the Court has moved to correct an abuse that other units of government had authority to handle but for various political reasons did not. **Legislative apportionment** provides another important recent instance. The right to vote is one of the most basic elements of democratic citizenship. But achieving a system that guarantees the ideal of "one person, one vote" can be difficult. A great variety of political devices have been used to curtail the full exercise of this right, one of the most common involving juggling the size and boundaries of legislative districts so that some people's votes carry more weight than others'.

The idea that legislative districts should be of approximately equal population size—except in the U.S. Senate, which provides equal representation for each state—has been widely endorsed as general electoral policy. In practice, however, legislative districts in states around the country were often wildly disproportionate in size prior to 1962. As cities grew, residents of small towns and rural areas, fearful of the rising political power of their urban brethren, defended provisions that gave their areas overrepresentation.

Apportionment in
Connecticut

Apportionment in Connecticut is an instructive example (see Figure 9.1). The Connecticut Constitution of 1818 stipulated that all towns already incorporated were entitled to two representatives in the lower house of the state legislature, but that towns established after that date would be entitled to only one.[25] This was changed slightly in 1955, when all towns with populations of at least 5,000 were given two representatives. Yet in 1960 an extraordinary situation existed: Hartford, with over 160,000 inhabitants, had only two representatives, while the old colonial town of Union, with just 383 residents, also had two.[26] Under this apportionment scheme, the small towns controlled the legislature and their representatives blocked any effort to reapportion. The large urban and suburban areas favored reapportionment, but they were too underrepresented to achieve it.

Colgrove v. Green

Court challenges. Inevitably, voters victimized by legislative malapportionment in U.S. House of Representatives districts and state legislative districts looked to the courts for redress. For a long time the judiciary preferred not to meddle in legislative apportionment on the grounds that it was the exclusive province of a coequal branch of government. For example, the Supreme Court ruled in *Colgrove* v. *Green* (1946) that the "times, places and manner of holding elections" provision of Article I, Section 4, of the U.S. Constitution gave Con-

[25] David M. Roth, *Connecticut: A History* (New York: Norton, 1979), p. 113.
[26] *State of Connecticut, Register and Manual, 1960*, pp. 198, 272.

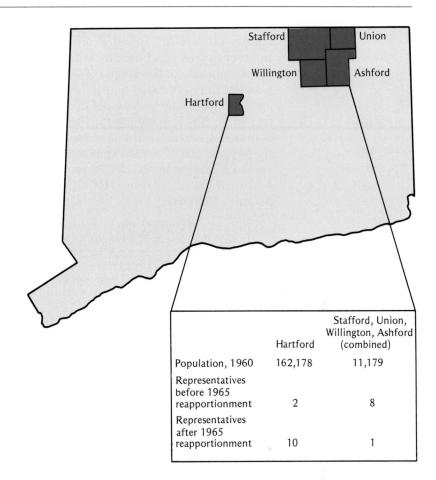

Figure 9.1
Apportionment in Connecticut Before and After Reapportionment of 1965

	Hartford	Stafford, Union, Willington, Ashford (combined)
Population, 1960	162,178	11,179
Representatives before 1965 reapportionment	2	8
Representatives after 1965 reapportionment	10	1

gress the authority to ensure equitable representation in U.S. House districts; hence, it was up to Congress, or the state legislatures, to take care of any imbalances. "Whether Congress faithfully discharges its duty or not, the subject has been committed to the exclusive control of Congress."

Baker v. Carr

In the landmark case of ***Baker v. Carr*** (1962), however, the Court abandoned its long-standing reservations and jumped into the political thicket. Speaking for a 6–2 Court majority, Justice William Brennan rejected the earlier view that apportionment presents a political question for which there were no appropriate judicial responses. The inequitability of legislative districts, Brennan held, can properly be subjected to judicial standards under the equal protection clause of the Fourteenth Amendment. Justice Tom Clark wrote a concurring opinion which probably reflected the underlying motivation of the Court's majority most faithfully. (Justices write concurring opinions when they agree with the basic decision of the court but want to further explain their own reasons for reaching the judgment.) Justice

Clark conceded that "although I find the Tennessee apportionment statute offends the Equal Protection Clause, I would not consider intervention by this Court in so delicate a field if there were any other relief available to the people of Tennessee."

In the flurry of cases that followed *Baker,* the court enlarged upon and implemented its new policy. In *Wesberry* v. *Sanders* (1963), Justice Hugo Black, speaking for the majority, held that "the command of Article I, section 2, that representatives be chosen 'by the people of the several states' means that as nearly as is practicable, one man's vote in a congressional election is to be worth as much as another's." And in *Reynolds* v. *Sims* (1964), Chief Justice Earl Warren for the majority held that

Wesberry v. *Sanders*

Reynolds v. *Sims*

> the right of suffrage can be denied by a debasement of suffrage or dilution of the weight of a citizen's vote just as effectively as by wholly prohibiting the free exercise of the franchise. . . . Legislators represent people, not trees or acres. Legislators are elected by voters, not farms or cities or economic interests. . . . The Equal Protection clause requires that the seats in both houses of a bicameral state legislature must be apportioned on a population basis.

Implementing the *Baker* decision

While *Baker* and other apportionment decisions produced more than a little grumbling among legislators and other politicians, compliance followed swiftly. In contrast to *Brown,* where powerful interests continued for many years to try to subvert or at least restrict the decision, *Baker* and the rulings subsequent to it were immediately fulfilled. This occurred in part because legislative apportionment simply did not generate the passions of race relations. In part, too, it occurred because the means of enforcement or execution were more straightforward. The courts could simply block elections under legislative apportionment schemes that did not meet the standards of population equality. In a few years, the Supreme Court brought about a fundamental shift in national policy on legislative apportionment at the local, state, and national levels.

Roe v. *Wade* (1973)

Sometimes when it makes public policy, the Court enjoys the good fortune of being on the side of the angels. *Brown* and *Baker* are cases in point. Whatever judgments prevailed in the past, few people would now argue that a state's maintenance of a rigidly segregated school system is other than a clear denial of equal protection under the law. The Court articulated an emerging national consensus on a matter of basic democratic practice. But in many other instances, the Court finds itself in the middle of an argument on which thoughtful men and women entertain sharply divergent views—and continue to long after the Court's judgment has been rendered. In such cases, the Court gets enmeshed in unresolved—sometimes unresolvable—political argument. Its decisions affect policy but fail to convince substantial segments of the populace on what policy should be.

A good illustration is **Roe v. Wade** (1973), the Court's much-discussed and much-criticized decision on abortion. Justice Harry Blackmun delivered the opinion for a 7–2 Court majority in *Roe*, striking down a Texas statute that had made abortion a state crime if performed for reasons other than saving the life of the mother. Similar statutes long on the books in a majority of other states were invalidated through the application of this decision.

Blackmun's majority opinion emphasized the core right of privacy:

> This right of privacy, whether it be founded in the Fourteenth Amendment's concept of personal liberty and restrictions upon state action, as we feel it is, or, as the district court determined in the Ninth Amendment's reservation of rights to the people, is broad enough to encompass a women's decision whether or not to terminate her pregnancy.

At the same time, Blackmun's opinion explicitly recognized the constitutional basis for *some* substantial state regulation of abortion. It rejected "Jane Roe's" (not the real name of the Texas woman bringing the suit) argument "that the woman's right is absolute and that she is entitled to terminate her pregnancy at whatever time, in whatever way, and for whatever reason she alone chooses." It held that "a state may properly assert some important interests in safeguarding health, in maintaining medical standards, and in protecting potential life."

In its effort to reconcile the right of a woman to have an abortion if she wants with "important state interests in regulation," the Court introduced the much-debated "trimester" standard, which broke pregnancy into three distinct terms and outlined the permissible restrictions that a state may impose in each one. In the first three months of pregnancy, the Court held, the decision to have an abortion must be left entirely to a woman and her physician, although the state can forbid abortions by non-physicians. During the second trimester, the state may regulate abortion but only in ways reasonably related to maternal health. And during the final three months of pregnancy, the state can if it chooses forbid all abortions except those necessary to save the mother's life.

The Court's decision in *Roe*, which has set national policy on abortion, illustrates the difficulty in locating clear *constitutional* guidelines for many contemporary disputes. The Constitution simply does not say anything that applies unambiguously to state regulation of abortion, and judges are of necessity thrown back on their own values and their sense of what is good public policy. In such cases, those on the losing side of the issue usually charge the Court majority with improper "judicial legislation": finding a controlling constitutional standard where one does not exist. The dissenting opinions in *Roe* by Justices William Rehnquist and Byron White echoed this criticism.

Court ruling on abortion

Arguing the right of privacy

"Trimester" standard

No clear constitutional guidelines

The decision, Justice Rehnquist wrote, "partakes more of judicial legislation than it does of the determination of intent of the drafters of the Fourteenth Amendment." In his notably truculent dissent, Justice White found

> nothing in the language or history of the Constitution to support the Court's judgment. The Court simply fashions and announces a new constitutional right for pregnant mothers and, with scarcely any reason or authority for its action, invests that right with sufficient substance to override most existing state abortion statutes.

In the years since the *Roe* ruling, Americans have remained deeply divided over abortion—and so has the Supreme Court itself. The basic decision handed down in *Roe* has not been altered, but the Court minority inclined to some modification of the decision has grown, standing at *four justices* in 1986, just one short of a majority. The nomination and subsequent confirmation of Sandra Day O'Connor in 1981, in the seat that had been held by Justice Potter Stewart, contributed to the shift in the balance. Before his retirement in 1986, Chief Justice Burger had shown himself increasingly dissatisfied with the aftermath of *Roe*. William Rehnquist, Burger's successor as chief justice, and Antonin Scalia, Rehnquist's successor as associate justice, have been critics of *Roe* v. *Wade*. Anthony Kennedy, who replaced Lewis Powell on the Supreme Court, will play a key role in future decisions.

Continuing dissatisfaction with Roe decision

Public opinion and the
Roe v. Wade (1974)
decision.

Thornburgh v.
American College of
Obstetricians and
Gynecologists

The closeness and depth of the split on abortion issues in the present Court were evident in *Thornburgh* v. *American College of Obstetricians and Gynecologists*, a ruling handed down in June 1986. The Court divided 5–4, with the majority voting to strike down as unconstitutional provisions of the 1982 Pennsylvania Abortion Control Act that required that doctors provide women seeking abortion with detailed information about the risks and alternatives and keep detailed records. The Act specified that women must be given materials describing the "probable anatomical and physiological characteristics of the unborn child at two-week gestational increments from fertilization to full-term, including any relevant information on the possibility of the unborn child's survival." "The printed materials . . . seem to us to be nothing less than an outright attempt to wedge the Commonwealth's [Pennsylvania's] message discouraging abortion into the privacy of the informed-consent dialogue between the woman and her physician," wrote Justice Blackmun for the majority. "Perceiving, in a state implementing the state's legitimate policy of preferring childbirth to abortion, a threat to or criticism of the decision in *Roe* v. *Wade*, the majority," argued Justice White in his dissent, "strikes down statutory provisions that in no way contravene the right recognized in *Roe*. I do not share the warped point of view of the majority. . . ." The position of Anthony Kennedy will be a key factor in future abortion decisions.

Recent Developments in Judicial Intervention

Expansion of judicial intervention

In their constitutional role of saying what the law is, American courts have been heavily involved in policy formation throughout the country's history. But over the last two decades there has been a significant broadening of judicial intervention—and this has generated intense controversy. "Today no action of government seems complete without litigation," judicial scholar Martin Shapiro writes.

> Our newspapers tell us of judges who forbid the transfer of air-force squadrons from one base to another, delay multi-million construction projects, intervene in complex negotiations between public employers and their employees, oversee the operation of railroads, and decide the location of schools. . . . Judges now joyously try their hand at everything from the engineering of atomic reactors to the validation of I.Q. tests. They run school districts, do regional land use planning, redesign welfare programs, and calculate energy needs. . . . Today there seems to be no public policy issue, no matter how massive, complex, or technical that some judge somewhere has not felt fully capable of deciding, aided only by the standard processes of litigation.[27]

Judicial intervention in agency management

Departing from past practice, many federal district courts and some state courts are now inclined to become directly involved in the daily management of major public agencies: prisons, mental hospitals, facilities for the elderly, local school systems. In *Wyatt* v. *Stickney* (1972), federal district judge Frank M. Johnson found "intolerable and deplorable" conditions prevailing in Alabama's largest state mental health facility. The court held that, as a matter of due process under the Fourteenth Amendment, hospital inmates "unquestionably have a constitutional right to receive such individual treatment as will give each of them a realistic opportunity to be cured or to improve his or her mental condition. . . ." In support of this finding, the court set forth detailed constitutional standards of care and treatment. Similarly, in *Hamilton* v. *Schiro* (1970), Federal District Judge Herbert W. Christenberry ordered the mayor of New Orleans to "immediately implement" directives for the reform of New Orleans prisons: providing specified medical and dental services, constructing a new hospital, guaranteeing "adequate security for medical personnel to facilitate the needs of the medical program," maintaining a year-round recreational program, building an indoor recreation area, and limiting the number of prisoners in the main facility.

To achieve such sweeping changes in the programs and administrative practices of executive agencies, courts frequently appoint special administrators. In *Hamilton* v. *Schiro*, Judge Christenberry

[27] Martin Shapiro, "Judicial Activism," in Seymour Martin Lipset, ed., *The Third Century: America as a Post-Industrial Society* (Chicago: University of Chicago Press, 1979), p. 125.

appointed a "master" to investigate New Orleans prison conditions; he subsequently transformed the master's findings into a decree and then continued to hold jurisdiction until the reforms were implemented. In *Gates* v. *Collier* (1972), Federal District Judge Elbert P. Tuttle placed the Mississippi state penitentiary under the direct supervision of a "monitor," who was instructed to examine the prison's records, review the way management was operating the prison, and report his findings to the court.

Judicial administrators

Court-directed reforms of state and municipal institutions to meet "conditions-of-confinement" and "right-to-treatment" standards often require major public expenditures. "More often than not, this has been accomplished by leveraged judicial threat. . . ."[28] For example, in *Hamilton* v. *Love* (1971), the federal judge warned that

The cost of implementing court decisions

> if the state cannot obtain the resources to detain persons awaiting trial in accordance with minimum constitutional standards, then the state will not be permitted to detain such persons. . . . This court, of course, cannot require the voters to make available the resources needed by public officials to meet constitutional standards, but it can and must direct the release of persons held under conditions which violate their constitutional rights. . . .

If the state did not appropriate the money that the judge considered necessary, he would order it to turn loose persons accused of serious crimes. In a 1978 ruling, another federal judge ordered Rhode Island's maximum security prison closed within the space of one year, the period of time he thought adequate to build a satisfactory replacement.

One important source of the courts' activism is a general expansion of the perceived responsibilities of government. In discussing Congress and the presidency, we have seen how these institutions have grown in the modern period as they have taken on a host of new tasks pursuant to public well-being. Americans expect a broader range of governmental services and protections than they did in the past. Like other political leaders, judges have responded—sometimes wisely, sometimes foolishly—to these increased expectations and demands. As the courts have become involved in a wider range of policy questions, groups have organized to participate more effectively in this judicial setting. There has been a major expansion of public advocacy law centers. At the beginning of the 1960s only one such center existed in the United States: the National Association for the Advancement of Colored People's Legal Defense Fund. During the 1960s and 1970s, however, law centers for public advocacy, receiving government or foundation aid, "were established in almost every field of social policy—welfare, education, housing, health, environment—and for almost

Courts in an age of bigger government

[28] Robert S. Gilmour, "Agency Administration by Judiciary," *Southern Review of Public Administration*, 6 (Spring 1982):26.

every group of potential clients. . . ."[29] The growth of such centers and staff with the resources to litigate on behalf of policy interests has naturally heightened demands on the courts.

Problems with Increased Judicial Intervention

The development of a more activist judicial branch is a natural response to changes in American society and politics. But it is not problem-free. One problem is that the courts are not responsible, as legislators or executives are, for the costs of their actions. A court ordering school busing does not have to find the money to pay for it; one that blocks the construction of a new power-generating facility does not have to find the electricity to meet future needs.

Rights versus interests

A related problem involves the increased difficulty in adjusting priorities and finding compromises when interests get expressed as basic legal rights. Martin Shapiro cites the issue of handicapped persons obtaining public transportation. When such a question is brought before the executive and legislative branches, decision makers can argue about whether expending millions of dollars on bus lifts and subway elevators is merited, considering the benefits that would accrue from alternate uses of the same funds. However, "once a court declares that the handicapped have a right to equal access to public transportation, then the money must be spent even if the cost-benefit ratio is insane." Shapiro maintains that courts too often use the language of *rights* rather than *interests;* and the more court intervention expands, the harder political compromise and adjustment becomes, "for they [the courts] are always demanding that the particular interest that they choose to prefer at the moment be given absolute priority over all of the other interests at play."[30]

THE COURT SYSTEM OF THE UNITED STATES

Jurisdiction

American federalism posits two distinct levels of government: national and state (with local government a subdivision of state). This federal structure extends into the judiciary. Two distinct sets of courts operate in the United States: federal courts exist side by side with courts established by the fifty states. In the pages that follow, we will examine the important question of **jurisdiction:** which cases originate in the federal courts and which in the state courts. The country's highest judicial authority, the Supreme Court of the United States, is at the apex of the dual court system; by deciding appeals from both the highest state courts and lower federal courts, it establishes necessary uniformity in national law and legal practices.

[29] Nathan Glazer, "Towards an Imperial Judiciary?" *Public Interest,* 41 (1975):116.
[30] Shapiro, "Judicial Activism," p. 130.

Federal Courts

National court structure

The basic national court structure includes the **U.S. district courts,** which function as trial courts or courts of original jurisdiction (where a case is first tried); the **U.S. courts of appeals,** which are the lower federal appellate courts (hearing appeals of decisions rendered in lower courts); and, of course, the **U.S. Supreme Court.** In 1988, there were 94 district courts and 12 U.S. courts of appeals.

Circuit courts of appeals

Evolution of the federal court system. The Judiciary Act of 1789 created 13 federal district courts, with a district judge assigned to each. The act also provided for three federal **circuit courts,** with one district judge and two Supreme Court justices riding each circuit to hear appeals. While bills were introduced from time to time over the next 90 years to create separate circuit courts of appeals with resident judges and substantial jurisdictions, none were enacted until 1891. Lawrence Friedman describes the long political argument over creating federal courts of appeals as "one of the most enduring political struggles in American political history."[31] The Circuit Court of Appeals Act of 1891 at last established a new tier of courts to hear most of the appeals growing out of district court actions.

District courts

In 1903, Congress created **special three-judge U.S. district courts** to consider suits filed by the attorney general under the Sherman Anti-Trust Act or the Inter-State Commerce Act. These special district courts were made up of two judges from the court of appeals and one judge from the district court in the area. Appeals from these three-judge courts would go directly to the U.S. Supreme Court. In 1910 the Mann-Elkins Act additionally empowered these special courts to hear cases brought by private individuals involving the constitutionality of state or federal statutes, and to issue injunctions to block enforcement of the challenged statutes. The heavy volume of civil rights litigation after 1960 included a large increase in petitions brought to the three-judge district courts, as civil rights groups challenged the constitutionality of various state laws governing race relations.

Reorganization of federal courts

Other changes during the 1920s brought the federal court system to the basic form we know today. Following extensive lobbying by the American Bar Association and the urgings of Chief Justice William Howard Taft, Congress further expanded the jurisdiction of the federal courts, and strengthened their administration by authorizing the chief justice to assign federal judges to temporary duty anywhere in the system, and creating the Conference of Senior Circuit Judges (later named the Judicial Conference), which would meet annually to discuss common judicial administrative problems.

[31] Lawrence M. Friedman, *A History of American Law* (New York: Touchstone Books, 1973), p. 120.

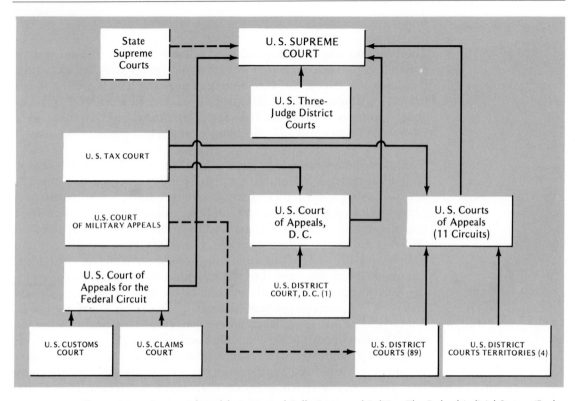

Figure 9.2
Federal Judicial Organization

Source: Adapted from Howard Ball, *Courts and Politics: The Federal Judicial System* (Englewood Cliffs, N.J.: Prentice-Hall, 1980), p. 74. The arrows show the direction of appeals through the system.

Present organization. Figure 9.2 shows the present organization of the federal courts. Along with the district courts, courts of appeals, special three-judge district courts, and the Supreme Court, there are a number of other specialized courts. The Federal Court Improvement Act of 1982 established a twelve-judge ***U.S. Court of Appeals for the Federal Circuit,*** merging two special courts of long standing. The new court has exclusive jurisdiction over appeals from district courts of decisions involving patent rights, as well as appeals from the Merit System Protection Board and Boards of Contract Appeals. It also has exclusive jurisdiction in international trade, and acts as an appeals court in cases involving claims against the U.S. government.

U.S. Court of Appeals

Another special federal court is the ***U.S. Claims Court:*** a trial court handling claims against federal agencies arising out of governmental contracts. The ***U.S. Customs Court*** consists of a chief judge and eight associate judges. Congress created it to hear cases involving rulings by U.S. customs collectors. It serves as the trial court for disputes between private citizens (and business corporations) and the govern-

Special federal courts

ment over the amount of customs duties, the value of imported goods, and decisions to exclude certain merchandise from the country. The **U.S. Tax Court,** made up of a chief judge and fifteen associate judges, was originally part of the executive branch under the Internal Revenue Service. Congress transformed it into a specialized court in 1969 under its taxing powers granted by Article I, Section 8, of the Constitution. The Tax Court is still a quasi-administrative agency, independent of the Internal Revenue Service, rather than a court in the traditional sense. Its jurisdiction includes taxpayers' challenges to IRS rulings. The last specialized federal court is the **U.S. Court of Military Appeals.** Composed of three civilian judges, it reviews all appeals from military court-martials.

Jurisdiction

What determines which cases are heard in this federal court system or by state courts? Part of the answer may be found in Article IV, Section 2, of the U.S. Constitution, which permits federal court jurisdiction in "all cases, in law and equity" that meet one of two sets of standards—involving either the subject matter of the case or the character of the parties to the suit. Under the first standard, federal courts have jurisdiction in

First standard of jurisdiction

1) cases arising under the U.S. Constitution, a federal law, or a treaty;
2) cases involving admiralty and maritime laws.

Second standard of jurisdiction

Under the second standard, federal jurisdiction is granted when

3) the U.S. government is a party to the suit;
4) one or more state governments is a party;
5) the controversy is between citizens of different states;
6) a case involves an ambassador or some other official representative of a foreign country;
7) a case arises between citizens of the same state because of a dispute involving land grants claimed under titles of two or more states.

When the federal courts have jurisdiction, cases typically originate in the U.S. district courts. Congress has given the district courts only original jurisdiction; they are the "workhorse" trial courts where the cases and controversies are first heard. The U.S. courts of appeals and the Supreme Court have only limited original jurisdiction; most of the cases reaching them do so on appeal.

Article III, Section 2, sets the outer limits of federal court jurisdiction, but nothing in the Constitution prevents Congress from assigning certain portions of this jurisdiction to state courts, on a concurrent or even on an exclusive basis. **Concurrent jurisdiction** means that a case may originate in either a state or a federal court; **exclusive jurisdiction** means it is assigned exclusively to one or the other. For example, Congress has provided that if the dollar amount in civil suits involving citizens of different states exceeds $10,000, the case may be tried in either a federal district court or a state court. Otherwise, exclusive jurisdiction is granted to the state courts. This provision was enacted to reduce the federal court workload. U.S. district courts have the sole power to hear all proceedings in bankruptcy. This exclusive federal jurisdiction accounts for a substantial portion of the district courts' workload: there were 561,278 bankruptcy filings in 1987 alone. In addition, Congress has granted exclusive original jurisdiction to the federal courts in all prosecutions for violation of federal criminal laws.

In most instances where a case arises under a state law, exclusive original jurisdiction is held by the trial courts of that state. Appeals may be brought, though, from the highest state courts to the U.S. Supreme Court when a substantial federal question is raised. And challenges to state laws on the grounds they violate the U.S. Constitution or federal statutes may in some instances be initiated in the special three-judge federal district courts.

How Cases Reach the U.S. Supreme Court

Congress determines the jurisdiction of the U.S. courts of appeals. Essentially two kinds of cases have been given to these appellate courts to review and decide: appeals from federal district court rulings and reviews of decisions of federal administrative boards and commissions. In the latter, the appeals courts exercise a form of original jurisdiction, in the sense that appeals of many administrative agency rulings first enter the judicial system at this level.

The original jurisdiction of the U.S. Supreme Court—where it is the first court to hear a case—is very limited. Cases taken up by the Court under its original jurisdiction have averaged less than one a year. The vast majority of cases reaching the Supreme Court come on appeal from other courts, specifically from the highest state courts, the three-judge federal district courts, and the U.S. courts of appeals. The Constitution gives Congress broad power to determine the Supreme Court's appellate jurisdiction; Congress has in turn given the Supreme Court great discretion to decide which cases it will devote its scarcest resource—time—to hearing.

Certiorari. Most cases that the Court reviews come to it through one of two procedures. The first involves the **writ of certiorari:** an order

Concurrent and exclusive jurisdiction

Limited original jurisdiction of the Supreme Court

Writ of certiorari

to a court whose decision is under challenge to send the records of the case to a higher court so that the latter may review the decision. One of the parties to a lower-court decision petitions the higher court to issue the writ. Legislation enacted by Congress in 1925 gave the Supreme Court power to grant or deny writs of certiorari at its own discretion. As Howard Ball notes, through this authority "the justices of the Supreme Court carefully select a very small percentage of petitions to the Court for review on the merits. In order for the Court to take the case, it must—in the estimation of the sitting justices—be a controversy of major proportions."[32] At least four of the nine justices must agree in order for a writ of certiorari to be issued.

Right of appeal

Appeal. The second main avenue to Supreme Court review is by the legal right of **appeal.** The Supreme Court must accept cases on *appeal* when 1) the highest court of a state declares a federal law or a portion of it to be unconstitutional, 2) the highest court of a state upholds state law when it is challenged on the grounds that it violates the U.S. Constitution or an act of Congress, 3) a U.S. court of appeals holds a section of a state constitution or a state statute unconstitutional, and 4) a lower federal court declares an act of Congress unconstitutional and the U.S. government is a party to the suit. Appeals may also be brought directly to the Supreme Court from the three-judge district courts—but the Court in practice rejects many of these cases "for lack of a substantial federal question."

Special Procedures in Supreme Court Action

The Supreme Court has evolved a number of rules and procedures bearing on what sorts of cases it will hear. One of the most important is the insistence that the Court will intervene only when there is a definite case or controversy involving bona fide adversaries. The Court will not issue advisory opinions. It will not hear contrived cases developed merely to test a law. This limits, of course, the Court's control over the timing and the form of various issues brought to it.

Standing to sue

Standing. For a party to bring a suit he must have **standing.** This means he must show that he has sustained or is threatened with real injury.[33] A famous finding of lack of standing involved Dr. Wilder Tileston, a Connecticut physician who wanted to challenge his state's legislation preventing "the use of drugs or instruments to prevent conception, and the giving of assistance or counsel in their use." The U.S. Supreme Court held that

[32] Howard Ball, *Courts and Politics: The Federal Judicial System* (Englewood Cliffs, N.J.: Prentice-Hall, 1980), p. 108.
[33] See Caren Orren, "Standing to Sue: Interest Group Influence in the Federal Courts," *American Political Science Review*, 70 (1976):723.

no question is raised in the record with respect to the definition of [Dr. Tileston's] liberty or property in contravention of the Fourteenth Amendment. . . . [Hence] the appeal must be dismissed on the ground that appellant has no standing to litigate the constitutional question which the record presents.[34]

In a subsequent case (discussed earlier in this chapter), Estelle Griswold, executive director of the Planned Parenthood League of Connecticut, and Dr. C. Lee Buxton, medical director of a center that the league operated, were convicted of violating the same Connecticut statute and fined $100 each. Personally affected or injured, they had standing. The Court granted their appeal, made on the grounds that the law violated their Fourteenth Amendment rights. In *Griswold* v. *Connecticut* (1965) the Court declared Connecticut's birth control statute unconstitutional.

Class-action suits. A ***class-action suit*** is one filed by an individual on behalf of himself and perhaps many hundreds or thousands of others allegedly wronged in the same fashion. The petitioner in a class-action suit must show unequivocally that he is a member of the affected class and not simply someone sympathetic to it. Among the well-known instances of successful class-action suits are the school desegregation cases of 1954, which were initiated on behalf of all pupils affected by the prevailing educational segregation in the school districts under challenge. In a number of cases in the 1970s, the Supreme Court narrowed the availability of the class-action challenge by stipulating that a person bringing such a suit must notify all the members of the "class" potentially benefiting and must bear the costs of notification.[35] Personal injury and more than nominal involvement with others for whom a legal challenge is mounted have been significant facets of the rule of standing.

Class-action suits

Justiciability. Another important limitation that the courts have imposed on their intervention in policy disputes involves ***justiciability.*** At issue here is not whether an individual has standing to sue, but whether courts are institutionally suited to provide remedies in the particular type of case. Political scientist Sheldon Goldman identified several central questions that bear upon justiciability:

Justiciability

> Is there something that a court can do for a plaintiff assuming that the plaintiff is in the legal right? Is the dispute moot (no longer a dispute)? Is the subject matter of the dispute one that is essentially a political question best resolved by the political branches of government? Is the subject amenable to judicial resolution?[36]

[34] *Tileston* v. *Ullman*, 318 U.S. 44 (1943).
[35] See, for example, *Eisan* v. *Karlyle and Jacqueline*, 416 U.S. 979 (1974).
[36] Goldman, *Constitutional Law*, p. 8.

At first glance, arguing whether a litigant has standing to sue, or whether a particular controversy is justiciable, may seem simply an abstract preoccupation of the legal profession. In fact, these judicial standards are important factors defining the special kind of political role American courts play. If every significant political issue were considered justiciable, and if every interested person could bring suit, the federal courts would be handling the entire range of political controversies dealt with by the executive and legislative branches. Judicial rules such as those involving standing and judiciability are an expression of judicial respect for separation of powers.

Rules to maintain separation of powers

Administration of the Federal Courts

We have come to expect that those who direct government agencies will favor developments that increase their agencies' workload and responsibilities. More work can mean more staff and bigger budgets, and the opportunity for greater influence. Interestingly enough, leading officials of the judicial branch take the opposite position. During his tenure as chief justice Warren Burger argued forcefully in recent years that courts in general—but especially federal courts—now perform tasks they need not. The answer, he maintained, is not primarily more staff—although he thought additional judges are needed—but going outside traditional judge-directed proceedings altogether (more informal conciliation efforts now being tried in many states), and delegating functions to lower courts.

Do courts perform too many tasks?

Looking to state courts, Justice Burger questioned whether judges are needed initially to preside over probate matters (involving wills and estates), to resolve child custody cases, or to handle divorces. Regarding federal courts, he expressed doubts that judges are required at the outset to administer bankrupt estates "when only a small proportion of these cases involve contested issues requiring judicial decision, and when these cases can readily be referred to a federal judge." He strongly urged getting the federal courts out of "diversity of citizenship" cases, which, according to former Solicitor General Erwin N. Griswold, have become anachronisms.[37] Asked Chief Justice Burger, "How long must we wait to keep out of federal courts an automobile intersection collision which reaches federal courts simply because one driver lives in Newark and the other in New York? Or one in Virginia and one across the Potomac in Washington?"[38]

Jurisdiction charges

A litigation explosion. These efforts to trim the courts' workload must be seen against the vast increase in recent years in the number of disputes brought to courts for resolution. Justice Burger noted that

[37] Erwin N. Griswold, "Helping the Supreme Court by Reducing the Flow of Cases into the Courts of Appeals," *Judicature* 67, 2 (August 1983):60.
[38] Warren E. Burger, *1982 Year-End Report on the Judiciary*, p. 3.

in the first year his predecessor, Earl Warren, was chief justice (1953), the Supreme Court had 1,312 case filings and issued 65 signed opinions. During the 1987–88 term, the Court had 5,021 cases on its docket and as of June 1988 had issued 105 signed opinions.

Overload of court cases

The entire legal system has been challenged by extraordinary increases in cases. In 1987, 282,274 new cases were filed in federal district courts. Of these, 238,982 were civil cases, nearly double the number filed in 1975. And 35,176 appeals were brought to the U.S. courts of appeals, up from less than 17,000 in 1975 and just 7,000 in 1965.

Legislative assistance for judges

Federal court organization has changed slowly in response to these heightened demands. District court judges are now provided with a variety of assistants; along with stenographers, court reporters, bailiffs, and law clerks, they are assigned administrators and United States magistrates. The professional court administrators take from the judges much of the burden of overseeing the courts' increasingly complex administrative machinery. Under the Federal Magistrates Act of 1968, judges are permitted to appoint magistrates (for eight- and four-year terms of office) to assist in processing court caseloads. In 1987 magistrates handled over 466,000 court proceedings—including trial jurisdiction in 96,000 misdemeanor cases and over 134,000 preliminary proceedings in arrest warrants, search warrants, bail reviews, detention hearings, arraignments, etc. Even with these improvements, the workload of federal judges spirals upward. Richard Posner projects a possible caseload for the year 2000 of almost 845,000.[39]

SELECTION OF FEDERAL JUDGES

Just as the courts are a special type of political institution, so judges are a special type of politician. The political side of judgeships extends throughout the process by which they are selected for the bench. As Joseph C. Goulden observed, "judges are of political, not divine, origin. . . ."[40] What is the political process through which judges reach the bench?

Article III of the U.S. Constitution says little about judicial selection. It provides only that judges of the Supreme Court and of the lower courts "shall hold their offices during good behavior"—that is, for life terms. Article II, Section 2, stipulates that the president shall have the power to nominate, and with the "advice and consent of the Senate" to appoint "ambassadors, other public ministers and consuls, judges of the Supreme Court, and all other officers of the United States. . . ."

[39] Richard A. Posner, *The Federal Courts: Crisis and Reform* (Cambridge, Mass.: Harvard University Press, 1985), p. 93.
[40] Joseph C. Goulden, *The Bench Warmers* (New York: Weybright and Talley, 1974), p. 23.

The formal process for selecting federal judges seems straightforward. The president proposes a candidate and submits his name to the Senate; if the Senate concurs by majority vote, the president's nominee is confirmed and takes office. But as it has evolved over two centuries, the process is considerably more complicated than the constitutional form might suggest. Different practices apply in selecting federal district judges, judges of the courts of appeals, and justices of the Supreme Court.

Formal selection of judges

District court appointments. The constitutional requirement that the Senate approve judicial nominees, coupled with the fact that district judges serve jurisdictions within individual states, has led to the informal but powerful practice of **senatorial courtesy** in district court appointments. Once a nomination has been sent to the Senate, it is given to the Senate Judiciary Committee. The Judiciary chairman routinely sends out what are known as "blue slips." These are forms that alert the senators from the nominee's home state and ask for their opinions and information concerning the nomination.

Senatorial courtesy

In effect, through the blue slip the Judiciary Committee asks the senators whether the president's nominee is acceptable. If a senator receiving the blue slip is of the same party as the president, his failure to return it with a statement of endorsement is taken under senatorial courtesy as a veto of the nominee. The willingness of the Senate to grant de facto veto power to senators of the president's party from the nominee's state is a form of mutual back scratching. By following the practice, a senator knows that when a nominee from his own state is submitted, his brethren will grant him this same courtesy—more precisely, this same power. When the senators from the nominee's state are not of the president's party, this right of veto does not apply. This reflects political realism, for to require a president to consult senators of the other party with the same care and diligence with which he consults senators of his own party would upset the normal sense of political fairness.

De facto veto power over district court nominees

The Senate's willingness to veto a nominee who does not receive proper home-state clearance is rarely tested, because a system of prior consultation has developed. Before the nomination is ever submitted, negotiations take place between the senators from a prospective nominee's state and the attorney general or deputy attorney general representing the administration. The extent to which Justice Department officials will defer to the home-state senators' wishes depends upon instructions from the president. Presidents Eisenhower and Kennedy made it clear that their Justice Department subordinates were authorized to negotiate for the best possible nominees. Lyndon Johnson was willing to defer to the preferences of the home-state senators as long as the individuals they recommended were not clearly unacceptable to him. The only absolute in this process is that a nomination will surely fail if the home-state senator or senators of the president's party strongly oppose it.

Prior consultation

ABA evaluations

Independently of the above process, candidates for district court appointments are informally investigated by the Justice Department; their names are then given to the Standing Committee on Federal Judiciary of the American Bar Association. The committee ranks these nominees on a scale: "exceptionally well qualified" "well qualified," "qualified," or "not qualified." At early stages in the review process, the ABA committee provides the Justice Department with information on what is likely to be the rating of the leading contenders; poor preliminary ratings may be the basis for eliminating candidates from further consideration.[41] Nominees are sometimes approved, however, even when they receive "not qualified" ABA ratings. This may reflect the clout of the nominee's home-state senators. Or it may reflect doubts about the ABA's standards in particular cases. For example, the ABA committee will not approve anyone who has reached the age of sixty-four—a standard many senators do not generally accept.

Courts of appeals appointments. President Jimmy Carter changed the procedures for choosing nominees to the U.S. courts of appeals.

Courts of appeal appointments

Through an executive order he established the United States Circuit Judge Nominating Commission to make recommendations for nominations based on merit. Working through panels that it set up for each of the eleven circuits, the commission forwarded to the president the names of persons deemed most qualified on the basis of "character, experience, ability, and commitment to equal justice under law." Since the president first determined the composition of the panels and then chose the court nominees from the lists presented to him, his role remained decisive. President Ronald Reagan disbanded the Circuit Judge Nomination Commission, returning to the pre-Carter selection procedures, with senators and others recommending candidates to the Justice Department.

Supreme Court appointments. Since the Supreme Court has national jurisdiction, the tradition of senatorial courtesy has never applied to

Supreme Court appointments

nominations to it. The president makes nominations with broad national policy considerations in mind, and traditionally the Senate has granted him considerable leeway. This does not mean that the president's nominations always have smooth sailing in the Senate. In the nineteenth century, about one out of every three nominations failed; in the twentieth, about one in nine.[42] The last four presidential nominees to be rejected were Clement Haynsworth and Harrold Carswell, Nixon nominees in 1969 and 1970; and Robert Bork and Douglas Ginsburg, Reagan nominees in 1987.

[41] See Sheldon Goldman and Thomas P. Jahnige, *The Federal Courts as a Political System,* 2d ed. (New York: Harper and Row, 1976), pp. 49–50. For a review of Reagan administration practices in selecting federal judges, see Goldman, "Reagan's Judicial Appointments at Midterm," *Judicature* 66 (March 1983):342.

[42] Goulden, *Constitutional Law,* p. 19.

Routes to the Judiciary: Backgrounds of Federal Court Appointees

Federal court appointments throughout U.S. history, including those to the Supreme Court, have typically gone to members of the president's party. Even when presidents reach across party lines for nominations—as Richard Nixon did when he chose Lewis F. Powell, Jr., of Virginia for a Supreme Court opening in 1971—they usually pick individuals of a philosophic bent similar to their own. While nominally a Democrat, Powell's conservatism was compatible with the views of the president who picked him. In this century, only three presidents have given more than 10 percent of their judicial appointments to individuals outside their own parties, none more than 20 percent.

Partisan and policy considerations in court appointments

Presidents appoint to the bench fellow partisans and people who, as best they can determine, hold compatible policy perspectives. They also frequently send other political signals in making their appointments. Jimmy Carter appointed women and ethnic minorities to the federal judiciary in greater numbers than any other president. (Carter had unusual opportunities to reconfigure the federal bench because Congress created 152 new federal judgeships in 1978.) He had pledged to make the federal judiciary more diverse and pluralistic with regard to ethnicity and sex. As Table 9.3 shows, he succeeded. About 14 per-

Table 9.3

Judicial Appointments of Recent Presidents by Sex and Ethnicity (in percent)

	Women	Blacks	Hispanics
U.S. Courts of Appeals			
Johnson	3	5	*
Nixon	0	0	*
Ford	0	0	*
Carter	20	16	4
Reagan	8	1	5
U.S. District Courts			
Johnson	2	4	3
Nixon	1	3	1
Ford	2	6	2
Carter	14	14	7
Reagan	7	1	1

*Data not available.

Source: Johnson, Nixon, and Ford: Sheldon Goldman, "Carter's Judicial Appointments: A Lasting Legacy," *Judicature* 64, 8 (March 1981): 344–55. Carter appointments: *Congressional Quarterly*, December 8, 1984, p. 3075. Reagan appointments as of June 1988: CQ Research Department, based on data from Department of Justice.

cent of Carter's appointees to U.S. district courts were women, compared to just 1.6 percent of Johnson's, .6 percent of Nixon's, 1.9 percent of Ford's, and 7 percent of Reagan's (towards the end of his second term in office). In all, Carter appointed 40 women, 38 blacks, and 16 Hispanics to the federal bench; and Reagan, close to the end of his presidency, 25 women, 4 blacks and 3 Hispanics.

Political considerations

Informal political criteria also guide presidents in their Supreme Court appointments. For example, nominations have at times served to recognize social groups that had been excluded from full participation in American social and political life. President Lyndon Johnson finally broke the color bar when he appointed Thurgood Marshall to the Supreme Court in 1967; President Ronald Reagan broke a similar barrier in 1981 when he appointed Sandra Day O'Connor the first female Supreme Court justice. The current Supreme Court is composed of six justices whose party background prior to appointment was at least nominally Republican, and three who were Democrats. Among the current sitting justices, one was appointed by Dwight Eisenhower, one by John Kennedy, one by Lyndon Johnson, two by Richard Nixon, one by Gerald Ford, and three by Ronald Reagan.

PUBLIC OPINION AND THE COURTS

Public criticism of judicial leniency toward criminals

In many regards, Americans give their courts high marks. Yet, for all of this general approval, the last twenty years have seen growing public unease directed at the courts. The unease has one clear, overriding source or cause: anger over the rising incidence of crime. Studies have shown that public fears and concerns about crime have risen significantly and that they include the sense that the courts have failed to do their part in seeing to it that the guilty are properly punished. A January 1986 national survey by ABC News and the *Washington Post* found 62 percent of the view that "judges should be handing out longer . . . sentences to criminals than they generally do. . . ." Only 5 percent wanted shorter sentences, while 19 percent said sentences now were generally of the right length and 14 percent had no opinion. The concern does not distinguish between state and federal courts. Nor is the Supreme Court especially criticized; no one decision arouses massive resentment. Americans simply think judges have been too lenient with criminals. Two-thirds of the public disapprove of the way the criminal courts are doing their job.[43] In 1972, 66 percent of the public said the courts have not "dealt harshly enough with criminals"; the proportion rose to 79 percent in 1975 and 88 percent in 1986 (Figure 9.3). Another survey showed that 84 percent of the public favored harsher prison sentences for persons convicted of crimes.[44] In chapter 15 we

[43] Poll taken by the *Los Angeles Times*, January 1981.
[44] Poll taken by the *Roper Organization*, January 7–21, 1984.

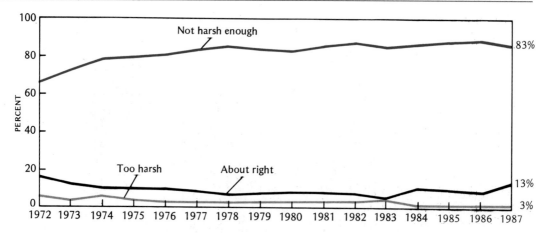

Figure 9.3
**What the problem is:
Public wants tougher
penalties for criminals**

Question: In general, do you think the courts in this area deal too harshly or not harshly enough with criminals?
Source: Surveys by the NORC, University of Chicago, taken in the spring of the years shown.

will look more closely at some court rulings bearing on the rights of persons accused of crimes that have helped spur these reactions. Concern about crime and judicial handling of it detracts from what is otherwise strong public backing for the courts and their performance in the American system of divided governmental powers.

SUMMARY

The framers of the U.S. Constitution provided for a system of federal courts as a third separate branch of the national government. Together with a set of lower federal courts, the Supreme Court was made the repository of "the judicial power of the United States."

The courts are in many ways weak institutions, compared to legislatures and executives. In Alexander Hamilton's words, they are without the powers of the purse and the sword. But the authority to say what the law is has proved a formidable one. One facet of it is *judicial review,* the power to review acts of legislatures and actions of executive officials to determine whether they are in conformity with the Constitution, and to declare them void if they are held not to be.

The framers believed that American federalism required federal courts to exercise judicial review over state legislative actions; otherwise there could be no uniform and respected national law. The Supreme Court would be the umpire of the federal system.

Whether the framers believed that judicial review should extend to declaring unconstitutional acts of a co-equal branch of national government is less clear. Hamilton asserted strongly that judicial review of acts of Congress was essential. Most of those who drafted the Constitution apparently gave little thought to this question, and expected that if the courts were to invalidate congressional acts they would do so only when there was the clearest violation of constitutional requirements.

In interpreting constitutional provisions or statutes, courts make law as surely as legislatures do. Furthermore, federal courts are now often heavily involved in administrative matters. This growing intervention has prompted criticism, including the charge of "judicial legislation"—that judges are too inclined to discover constitutional or statutory provisions mandating what are in fact their own political views and values. But every branch of government is now activist compared to times past, partly in response to increased public demands for governmental efforts to redress all manner of problems.

The fact that courts are political institutions that make policy does not mean that there is nothing special about how they enter the policy process. Courts operate within a context defined by a limiting set of judicial rules and standards. Real cases or controversies in law, involving appellants who have suffered injury that is appropriately redressed through judicial action, are the prime vehicle for judicial action. Separation of powers requires that the courts follow procedures distinct from those governing political executives and legislatures.

The United States has a dual court system, with federal and state courts existing side by side and sometimes sharing jurisdiction. *Concurrent jurisdiction* means that a case may originate in either a state or a federal court; *exclusive jurisdiction* means it is assigned exclusively to one or the other. When a case arises under a state law, exclusive original jurisdiction usually belongs to the trial courts of that state. However, appeals may be brought from the highest state courts to the U.S. Supreme Court when a substantial federal question is raised.

The process for selecting judges varies greatly from one court to another. The majority of state-court judges are elected, commonly on nonpartisan ballots. All federal justices are appointed by the president, with the Senate's advice and consent.

For appointments to the federal district courts, the practice of *senatorial courtesy* is followed: The Senate will not confirm the president's choice unless that individual is acceptable to the senators of the president's party from the state in which the judge would sit. Presidential appointments to the Supreme Court are scrutinized, instead, in terms of broad national policy considerations and whether the requisite level of judicial competence has been met.

FOR FURTHER STUDY

Henry J. Abraham, *The Judicial Process*, 5th ed. (New York: Oxford University Press, 1986). A comprehensive introduction that explains the operations of the state and federal courts and locates the American judicial system in a comparative context.

Sheldon Goldman, *Constitutional Law and Supreme Court Decision-Making* (New York: Harper and Row, 1982). A careful, systematic description of the principal Supreme Court rulings and developments in American constitutional interpretation. Idem., *Constitutional Law: Cases and Essays* (New York: Harper and Row, 1987).

Sheldon Goldman and Thomas P. Jahnige, *The Federal Courts as a Political System*, 3rd ed. (New York: Harper and Row, 1985). Interprets the federal courts as a set of political institutions, bound by their own unique versions of political interests and dynamics.

J. Woodford Howard, Jr., *Court of Appeals in the Federal Judicial System* (Princeton, N.J.: Princeton University Press, 1981). An important examination of judicial decision making in three U.S. Circuit Courts of Appeals.

David M. O'Brien, *Storm Center: The Supreme Court in American Politics* (New York: W. W. Norton, 1986). A major recent interpretation of the nation's highest court, including such elements of the court's internal operations as the role of law clerks and of administrative staff.

Richard A. Posner, *The Federal Courts: Crisis and Reform* (Cambridge, MA: Harvard University Press, 1985). A valuable description of problems confronting the federal court system, including the explosive growth in the number of court cases, written by a former law school professor now on the U.S. Circuit Court of Appeals.

Martin Shapiro, *Courts: A Comparative and Political Analysis* (Chicago, IL: University of Chicago Press, 1981; paperback, 1986). A major interpretation that examines court systems cross-nationally.

Part 4

Participation

Chapter 10

Public Opinion

Democracy endows public opinion with a moral or ethical status: democratic government simply does not exist if citizens' preferences on the many questions of public policy are not respected—even if the majority's wishes must sometimes be subordinated to basic minority rights. As we will see in this chapter, however, the task of understanding what the public wants policy to be is not easy or straightforward. This is especially true because the public often wants a number of different things, each worthy, that come into conflict in complex policy decisions. This *ambivalence* is a dominant characteristic of public opinion.

Questions of government's performance and proper role are a good case in point. In remarks that he made after becoming chairman of the National Commission on Public Service in 1987, Paul Volcker observed that

> We Americans have always been ambivalent about government. For that matter, we started out that way. Instinctively, we still have a lot of feeling that that government is best that governs least; nonetheless we are quick and caustic with our complaints and our rhetoric when government doesn't produce what we expect of it. And as we've grown in size and in the complexity of our society, for better or worse we've asked and expected more of government.[1]

The tension Volcker was describing was displayed sharply in a survey taken by the Roper Organization in the fall of 1986. Eighty percent of those polled said that cuts in government's social programs threat-

---

[1] Volcker is best known for his work as chairman of the board of governors of the Federal Reserve system, a position he held from 1979 through 1987.

ened the future of the American dream. But at the same time, 88 percent said that government's interference in people's lives posed that same threat.

The fact is that large numbers of Americans see government at once as problem and solution. Solid majorities told Gallup interviewers in the spring of 1987 that they thought the federal government controlled too much of our lives. In the same survey, three-quarters said that the federal government should run only those things that cannot be run at the local level. Sixty-three percent agreed that "when something is run by government, it is usually inefficient and wasteful." (See Figure 10.1). In another survey, this one commissioned by the Advisory Committee on Intergovernmental Relations (ACIR) in June 1987, two-thirds maintained that the national government wastes the most tax money, while only 14 percent cited state, and 8 percent local, government. This harsh view of the federal government was strongest among professionals, those with some college or a college degree, and those earning over $40,000—groups that are the most knowledgeable about government and the most likely to vote.

At the same time, though, two-thirds of those polled by Yankelovich Clancey Shulman said they wanted the federal government to be very involved in helping people receive an affordable education (67

Agree ▮   Disagree ▯

The federal government should run only those things that cannot by run at the local level

75%
19%

When something is run by the government, it is usually inefficient and wasteful

63%
31%

The federal government controls too much of our daily lives

58%
37%

The federal government should by *very* involved or only *somewhat* involved in . . .

Very involved ▮   Somewhat ▯

Helping people meet their health needs

74%
24%

Helping people who are poor

69%
29%

Helping people receive an affordable education

67%
30%

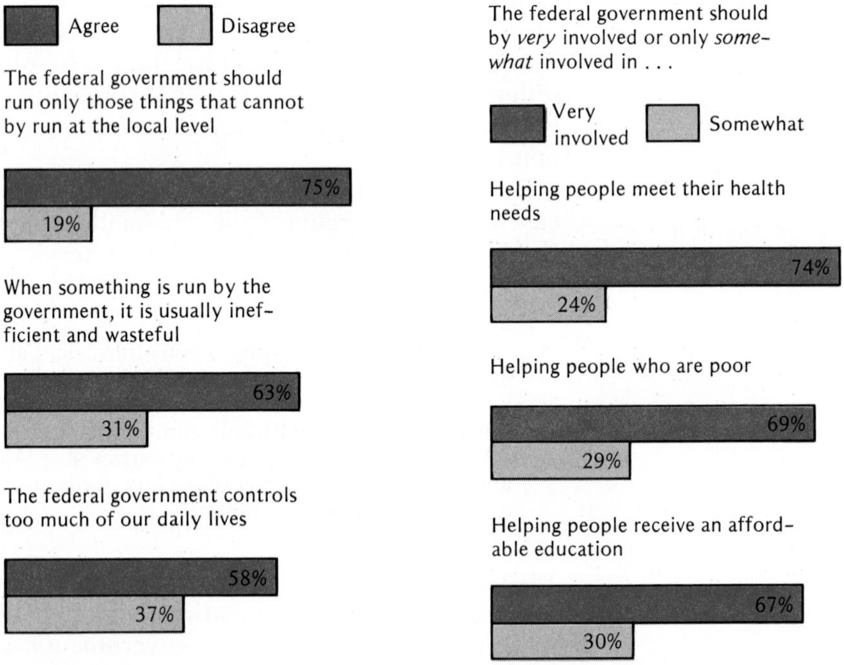

Figure 10.1
Government Is Too Big . . . But Should Be Bigger

Source: Survey by the Gallup Organization for Times Mirror Co., April 25–May 10, 1987; Survey by *Time*/Yankelovich Clancey Shulman, February 17–18, 1987.

percent). Seventy-four percent said the federal government should be very involved in helping people meet their health needs, and 69 percent felt that way about helping the poor. The public appetite for government services and assistance remains robust.

In early 1987, the Roper Organization asked Americans to assess Reagan's proposed budget. Only one in ten thought overall spending was too low—no real change from the 11 percent who gave that response in 1983. A near majority (47 percent) said the budget called for too much spending; only about 25 percent saw it as pretty much on target. The share of the population believing that spending was too high had actually increased over the preceding several years. When the public was asked to assess a list of individual spending programs, however, responses were quite different. Solid majorities felt that we should be spending more on the homeless, education, social security benefits, health aid to the poor, and job creation. Large majorities felt that the United States should either be spending more or that we were spending about the right amount on the environment, agriculture, price supports or subsidies, science and basic research, improving mass transit, aid to the cities, and space exploration.

The same tensions are evident surrounding the question of government regulation. In an NBC News/*Wall Street Journal* survey taken in October 1987, 37 percent said there is too much government regulation of the economy. Only 21 percent said government was not doing enough, while 31 percent put regulation at about the right level. The April 1987 survey conducted by Gallup for the Times Mirror Company showed considerable skepticism about governmental regulation, with 55 percent agreeing that "government regulation of business usually does more harm than good." And yet another NBC News/*Wall Street Journal* poll in March 1987 found majorities favoring more regulation with regard to job health and safety (50 percent) and the environment (61 percent). (See Figure 10.2.) Government should be involved in these areas, the public says, because it is needed to check the activities of another big institution, business. Americans simply don't believe that business will do the job by itself.

The mix of answers like those cited above become a lot less confusing if one keeps in mind that most Americans approach questions of the government's role and performance on a case-by-case basis, without any overall organizing notion of the state as inherently helpful or harmful. A good sense of this emerges from a survey done in the spring of 1987 by the University of Chicago's National Opinion Research Center. Respondents were asked to locate themselves on a scale: Choosing one end affirmed that the national government should do everything possible to improve the living standards of all poor Americans; selecting the other end was to insist that this is not the government's responsibility and that each individual should take care of himself. Twenty-nine percent put themselves in the first camp, 24

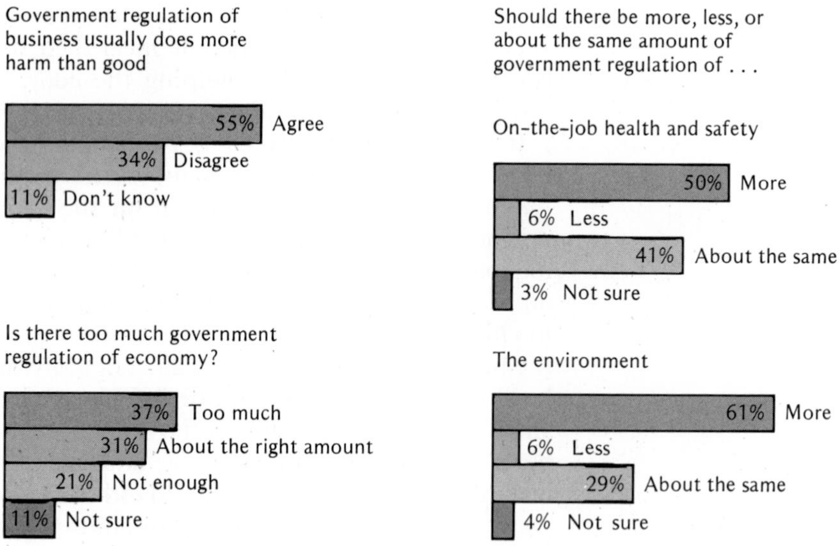

Government regulation of
business usually does more
harm than good

55%	Agree
34%	Disagree
11%	Don't know

Should there be more, less, or
about the same amount of
government regulation of . . .

On-the-job health and safety

50%	More
6%	Less
41%	About the same
3%	Not sure

Figure 10.2
**Regulation Is Often
Harmful . . . And We
Need More of It**

Is there too much government
regulation of economy?

37%	Too much
31%	About the right amount
21%	Not enough
11%	Not sure

The environment

61%	More
6%	Less
29%	About the same
4%	Not sure

Source: First question: survey of the Gallup Organization for Times Mirror Company, April 25–
May 10, 1987. Other questions: Surveys by NBC News/*Wall Street Journal,* March 15–17;
October 25–27, 1987.

percent in the latter. Forty-four percent, however, put themselves at
a mid-point on this scale which was labeled "agree with both positions."

Other surveys show the same thing. Pollsters—and politicians—keep
trying to get the public to declare itself as pro- or anti-government.
Americans keep responding that they are neither, or both—or, more
precisely, that they just don't see why the issue must be cast in such
terms.

The lesson isn't that people are so fickle as to make public opinion
a joke. As we will see, public opinion displays both form and coherence. The lesson is that public opinion is not a unidimensional thing,
like the temperature of a sample of water. It isn't, "47 percent believe
that. . . ." It is rich and variegated, full of shades and gradations. *Measuring* public opinion is a challenge, *responding* to it an even greater
one.

PUBLIC OPINION AND DEMOCRATIC GOVERNMENT

Political scientist V. O. Key defined public opinion as "those opinions
held by private persons which governments find it prudent to heed."[2]
Government acts on an issue when it is understood to be of public

[2]V. O. Key, Jr., *Public Opinion and American Democracy* (New York: Knopf, 1961),
p. 14.

rather than purely private consequence—and public opinion involves preferences and perspectives on public issues. We amend Key's definition slightly: **Public opinion** is the aggregate of citizens' personal opinions on questions considered part of public as opposed to private life. All of the preferences, hopes, fears, aspirations that people hold do not necessarily comprise public opinion, because many of them involve strictly private choice. The color a person prefers in a house, the type of music one likes best, the college one wants his or her children to attend are not public issues; there isn't public opinion on Beethoven and Billy Joel, although there are certainly musical tastes that can be measured.

Distinctions are often made among *opinions, attitudes,* and *values.* **Opinions** connote less deeply rooted judgments on current policies, leaders, and events. "What is your opinion on the president's trip to China?" Political **attitudes** suggest more fundamental perspectives on enduring social and political questions, such as attitudes toward race relations. **Values** are people's ideals and the commitments they make, involving religious beliefs, standards for interpersonal relations, moral and ethical judgments. All three comprise public opinion in the term's broadest sense.

Opinions, attitudes, and values

The Debate over Role

In *The American Commonwealth,* English theorist James Bryce saw the role of public opinion gradually advancing through a series of stages, "from its unconscious and passive into its conscious and active condition." He foresaw the possibility of a new stage, not then realized,

Rule by public opinion

> if the will of the majority of the citizens were to become ascertainable at all times, and without the need of its passing through a body of representatives, possibly even without the need of voting machinery at all. . . . [When this happens] popular government would have been pushed so far as almost to dispense with, or at any rate to anticipate, the legal modes in which the majority speaks its will at the polling booths. . . . To such a condition of things the phrase, "Rule of public opinion," might be most properly applied, for public opinion would not only reign but govern.[3]

The advent of scientific public opinion polling in the 1930s was seen by some observers to make possible the ultimate evolution of public opinion's role envisioned by Bryce. Did not the polls permit "the will of the majority of citizens . . . to become ascertainable at all times"? The most important figure in the founding and early development of public opinion polling, George H. Gallup, clearly thought

Birth of scientific public opinion polling

---

[3] James Bryce, *The American Commonwealth* (New York: Macmillan, 1916), vol. II, pp. 261–62.

so. The polls, he argued, "can make this a truer democracy."[4] Anything that enlarges the sway of public opinion over governmental decision making is desirable.

Others rejected the direct democrats' expectations for public opinion as simplistic and unattainable. The distinguished journalist Walter Lippmann, in *The Phantom Public*, offered one of the strongest rebuttals over a half-century ago. The populace is poorly equipped in its level of information and interest for what "rule by public opinion" suggests. Mass publics just don't involve themselves in the details of policies and legislation, only in broad questions of ends and means. They are perfectly capable of passing judgment on the general objectives and approach of a governmental program, and they are competent to decide which party or candidate is best able to carry out the program. But this is where their role stops. As Lippmann saw it, democratic theory had created much confusion through its overstated definition of the proper role of the public and public opinion. Thus democracy

A critique of public opinion

> has never developed an education for the public. . . . It has, in fact, aimed not at making good citizens but at making a mass of amateur executives. It has not taught the child how to act as a member of the public. It has merely given him a hasty, incomplete taste of what he might have to know if he meddled in everything. The result is a bewildered public and a mass of insufficiently trained officials.[5]

Can Public Opinion Be Manipulated?

Other issues enter the debate over the proper role of public opinion: Are people's political opinions basically their own, reflective of their true inner values and interests, or are they in some sense manufactured for them by powerful interests?

The helpless public. Many theorists have insisted that mass publics are all too easily manipulated, and the image of an ill-informed and emotional populace, preyed upon by demagogues, has often been invoked. The success that dictators Benito Mussolini and Adolf Hitler had in the 1920s and 1930s in rallying many of their countrymen behind anti-democratic, expansionist, and racist appeals added to such fears. European theorists of that time, such as Gustave Le Bon and Robert Michels, argued that the "common man" was just too susceptible to demagoguery for democracy to work well, if at all.[6] In Europe

Fear of manufactured public opinion

[4]George H. Gallup, "Polls and the Political Process—Past, Present, and Future," *Public Opinion Quarterly*, Winter 1965, p. 549. See, too, George Gallup and Saul Forbes Rae, *The Pulse of Democracy: The Public Opinion Poll and How it Works* (Westport, Conn.: Greenwood Press, 1968; first published 1940).
[5]Walter Lippmann, *The Phantom Public* (New York: Harcourt, Brace, 1925), pp. 61–108 *passim*, pp. 144–45, 147–49.
[6]See Gustave LeBon, *The Crowd* (New York: Penguin, 1977; first published 1919); and Robert Michels, *Political Parties* (New York: Dover, 1959; first published in English, 1915).

in the early days of democratic experience, conservative theorists were the most likely to express foreboding about the ease with which the masses could be persuaded to support bad leaders and bad policies—not surprising since traditional conservatism had been uncomfortable with the idea of democracy in all of its forms. But in our own day, the left as well as the right expresses fears about manufactured public opinion.

False consciousness. Some theorists invoke the idea of "false consciousness," in which the public is seen as manipulated into views that are not really its own. Marxist theorist Herbert Marcuse argued, for example, that the great wealth of the contemporary United States has enabled it to smother discontent in a blanket of affluence and in effect buy consent to policies that elites favor. The "establishment" has succeeded in imposing on the public an outlook that serves its own needs.

Is public opinion a farce?

> We are again confronted with one of the most vexing aspects of advanced industrial civilization: the rational character of its irrationality. Its productivity and efficiency, its capacity to increase and spread comforts, to turn waste into need, and destruction into construction, the extent to which this civilization transforms the object world into an extension of man's mind and body makes the very notion of alienation questionable. The people recognize themselves in their commodities; they find their soul in their automobile, hi-fi set, split-level home, kitchen equipment. The very mechanism which ties the individual to his society has changed, and social control is anchored in the new needs which it has produced.[7]

Of course, if one wants to belittle a democratic society, it is convenient to argue that the public opinion to which it professes such respect and obedience is basically a farce, the product of elitist manipulations. But many commentators in many different settings have raised questions about how authentic public opinion really is. In present-day America it isn't just critics of democracy who portray the public as easily manipulated. This assessment underlies the perspectives of many in the advertising and public relations professions (although they profess no unease about it). Advertising theorists insist that improvements in their techniques, together with new communications technology and vast commitments of financial resources, permit the engineering of public acceptance of products, institutions, and ideas.

Selling the candidate. From the claim that consumer tastes and product preferences can be induced, it was not a very great step to the conclusion that political tastes can also be shaped by advertising. Over the last two decades, a small army of advertising people, media

[7] Herbert Marcuse, *One Dimensional Man* (Boston: Beacon Press, 1964), pp. xii–xiii, 7–9 *passim.*

The film, The Candidate, *portrayed the "selling" of a candidate who, after his election, says to his campaign manager, "What do I do now?"*

Advertising candidates

specialists, and other campaign consultants have assumed a dramatically enlarged role in American electioneering, around the basic premise that techniques that sell soap can sell candidates and causes. V. O. Key observed:

> Propagandists and advertising men encouraged the acceptance of the most exaggerated estimates of their powers. Given enough money, they could sell soap, cigarettes, policies, presidential candidates. . . . Eventually the image of public opinion as an irresistible giant yielded to the image of the all-powerful opinion manipulators, engineers of consent and molders of mass opinion.[8]

Debate over marketing candidates

The idea that "selling is selling" is now commonly expressed. A veteran political consultant, who had been "selling" candidates for many years, decided he would like a change of pace and secured a senior post in a large advertising agency specializing in consumer products.

> When I first spoke to them, they were a little concerned that perhaps my background in marketing candidates was not just right for the new post

[8] Key, *Public Opinion,* p. 6.

selling . . . [a well-known consumer product]. But as we talked, they saw that I was right, that there really isn't any difference. If you are good at selling, what difference does it make if you are promoting a candidate or a soft drink?[9]

Many consultants insist that public consent to candidates can quite easily be engineered, assuming that the "product" (i.e., the candidate) cooperates. When his candidate loses a race, the consultant often complains that "he just wouldn't do what we told him to do." Political consultants also argue that manipulating political opinion is no less reputable than manipulating consumer tastes. Media consultant Michael Kaye makes the latter claim unashamedly: "If I sell a car, I am not a bad guy. The minute you add one ingredient, the politician, all of a sudden it becomes distasteful or wrong. I am still waiting for someone to say why it is wrong. Why is it wrong to sell politicians?"[10]

This increasingly manipulative tone, so evident in the 1988 campaign, troubles many observers. Of course a candidate should be presented in his best light. But democracy assumes—more, requires—the presence of public opinion that reflects the people's needs and interests, not those of advertising hucksters. Does public opinion live up to its democratic billing?

The needs of the public

We do not ask whether public opinion can ever be fooled or manipulated; of course it can be. Over a century ago Abraham Lincoln told a visitor to the White House that "you may fool all the people some of the time; you can even fool some of the people all the time. [But] you can't fool all the people all the time." Lincoln's whimsically put but serious point is the same one that occupies us here. In the pages that follow, we explore what is known about American public opinion to learn whether it still meets Lincoln's expectation. We will see how general properties and overall patterns bear on the argument whether public opinion is authentic and autonomous or the plaything of those who would manipulate it for their own ends.

PROPERTIES OF PUBLIC OPINION

Public opinion undoubtedly has certain common characteristics in all or most countries, but its patterns are also shaped by the specific social, economic, and political experience of individual nations. What we see in the United States reflects the country's two hundred years under one set of democratic institutions, the absence of sharp class polarization, the levels of public education and communication, and other formative elements.

---

[9] Personal communication to the author, July 1, 1983.
[10] Michael Kaye, quoted in Larry J. Sabato, *The Rise of Political Consultants* (New York: Basic Books, 1981), p. 321.

An Informed Public?

On first review, survey research seems to raise serious doubts about whether Americans know enough about the various questions of public affairs to play the part democratic theory assigns them. A cursory examination of poll data reveals extraordinary lack of interest and unawareness, even on basic facts of political life. This finding lends support to those who argue that mass publics can readily be manipulated because they know so little about issues they are supposed to decide.

Lack of knowledge about leaders

A national poll taken by the Roper Organization in 1975 showed that only 36 percent of adult citizens could identify their two home-state U.S. senators.[11] This small poll presented respondents with a list of prominent politicians and asked whether "you feel you know a lot about, or feel you know a fair amount about, or very little about, or have never heard of" each of them. A quarter of those surveyed said they had never heard of, or knew little about, Gerald Ford—the incumbent president! In a 1981 NBC News/Associated Press poll, 44 percent claimed never to have heard of Speaker of the House Thomas P. O'Neill, and 72 percent not to have heard of Defense Secretary Caspar Weinberger. A Roper Organization poll taken in May 1984 found that only 22 percent could put Mario Cuomo in the correct general category of "a governor or mayor," even though this incumbent Democratic governor of New York was the focus of considerable media attention. Five percent described Cuomo as a foreign head of state, and three percent as a sports star. Sixty-four percent said they didn't know who he was. Early in 1986 over half the U.S. adult public couldn't name Mikhail Gorbachev as the head of the U.S.S.R., although the press had been giving extensive coverage to the new Soviet leader.[12]

Inattention to policy specifics

Looking at levels of factual information about important political events and programs, we see even more unawareness. In November 1982, only a third of adults polled had even a slight sense of the size of the current federal deficit—that is, could give an estimate within a hundred billion dollars. Yet the size of the deficit was a hot issue. When asked in fall 1981 which country, the United States or the Soviet Union, is a member of the NATO alliance, only 47 percent correctly identified the United States.[13] Since America had taken the lead in forming the North Atlantic Treaty Organization with its European allies after World War II, and the NATO pact remained the most

---

[11] Poll taken by the Roper Organization, December 6–13, 1975.
[12] Poll taken by ABC News and the *Washington Post*, February 6–12, 1986.
[13] These data are from a poll taken by ABC News/*Washington Post*, October 14–18, 1981. The question asked was: "One of these two nations, the United States or the Soviet Union, is a member of what is known as the NATO alliance. Do you happen to know which country that is, or are you not sure?" Forty-seven percent said the United States, 2 percent the Soviet Union, while 50 percent were not sure.

important of all U.S. alliances, the fact that less than half felt confident enough to pick the U.S. over the U.S.S.R. as a NATO member is fairly startling. In the spring of 1986, after years of debate about the Reagan administration's policies toward the Sandinista government in Nicaragua, only 38 percent interviewed nationally correctly identified the United States as supporting "the people fighting against the [Nicaraguan] government."[14]

A cautionary note on direct democracy

As we will see, rushing from findings like these to the conclusion that meaningful public opinion does not exist is unjustified. But there is doubt about the wisdom of submitting every important policy issue to a referendum vote. Many Americans lack basic factual information, even with high levels of education and plentiful political communication. We should also be cautious about claims like "82 percent of Americans favor" this or that program. Often the public just does not have enough information and awareness to justify them.

How Stable and Structured Is Public Opinion?

Consider two hypothetical individuals. The first eats, sleeps, and breathes politics. He devours the *New York Times* and other leading newspapers, and closely follows virtually every major issue. When asked his views on a particular program, he answers confidently, because he has reached his conclusions through a painstaking accumulation of pertinent facts. His opinions have a bedrock firmness. The second individual, in contrast, pays little attention to the intricacies of governmental programs and political arguments. He gives the daily newspapers only a cursory glance, except on the sports pages. When asked his views on a program, his answers are more a spur-of-the moment reaction than a considered judgment. If individuals of the latter type predominate, public opinion on many governmental questions may be highly unstable.

Fluctuations of opinion responses

An influential study by political scientist Philip E. Converse addressed this subject. Converse concluded that the amount of political information people have goes far toward determining the structure, constraint, and stability of their beliefs. Without much factual information, the beliefs of large segments of the populace bounce around wildly over time. Between 1956 and 1960, the Institute for Social Research at the University of Michigan posed the same questions to the same people on three separate occasions, asking their views on issues such as school desegregation, federal aid to education, foreign aid, and federal housing. Many respondents moved from one side to the other on these questions in successive interviews. After closely examining this pattern, Converse concluded that most of the movement was not true opinion change but rather the result of

[14] Poll conducted by CBS News and the *New York Times*, April 6–10, 1986.

"Glad you brought that up, Jim. The latest research on polls has turned up some interesting variables. It turns out, for example, that people will tell you any old thing that pops into their heads."

Drawing by Saxon; © 1984 The New Yorker Magazine, Inc.

respondents answering in essentially a random fashion. Only a distinct minority had something close to hard-core opinions. "For the remainder of the population, response sequences over time are statistically random."[15]

If this is true, it carries substantial implications for the role of public opinion in democratic government. Giving great weight to the clear, considered preferences of the people is supported by everyone sympathetic to democracy. But should views that are virtually "statistically random" be accorded such weight? If the public really knows little about most policy disputes—even those that have been extensively discussed—and if the opinions it expresses are very lightly held, why should politicians or anyone else pay attention to them?

Philip Converse's work stimulated further research on the subject. Several investigations concluded that Converse's findings held up only for a particular period in time: the 1950s. During the mid- to late 1960s, these studies concluded, the relatively issue-less politics of the Eisenhower years gave way to heated divisions over civil rights, Vietnam, and social issues. When the political parties and their nominees began taking distinct positions on such divisive issues, they imparted

Sharper divisions in the 1960s

[15] Philip E. Converse, "The Nature of Belief Systems in Mass Publics," in David Apter, ed., *Ideology and Discontent* (New York: Free Press, 1964), p. 242.

to voters ideological cues that had been lacking in the previous decade. This led to more constrained public responses.[16]

General Values versus Programs Specifics

Another type of public opinion research yields conclusions very different from Converse's or even those of his critics. It focuses on the overall patterns of responses Americans give. These turn out to be remarkably stable and predictable. The Gallup Organization has polled American opinion continuously since the mid-1930s, rarely missing so much as a month. Gallup asks questions on foreign policy, the role of government, many different domestic programs, a wide range of social issues from abortion to race relations, and more. The findings in each of these areas at all times show a clear, persisting structure in what people are saying. Through all the changes in political events and circumstances, Americans make basic distinctions and express general preferences that in the aggregate don't look random or uninformed.

The basic source of this contradiction in assessments of public opinion can be traced to a central distinction that democratic theory has long made: Mass publics can hold underlying values and express broad preferences coherently, even while they are inattentive to much of the detail of governmental programs and policies. As we have seen, Walter Lippmann took it as evident that the public is unlikely to initiate specific programs or immerse itself in their detailed specifications. But it can choose perfectly well between contrasting approaches presented to it by political leaders. Political scientist Harwood Childs argued that

> the general public is especially competent, probably more competent than any other group—elitist, expert, or otherwise—to determine the basic ends of public policy. . . . On the other hand, the general public is not competent to determine the best means for attaining specific goals, to answer technical questions, to prescribe remedies for political, social, and economic ills, and to deal with specialized issues far removed from the everyday experience and understanding of the people. . . .[17]

Elmo Roper was one of the founders of modern public opinion research. In 1942 he reviewed what he had learned from his first decade

Strong underlying public values (margin note)

[16] For studies concluding that Converse's findings were time-bound and not reflective of the pattern that appeared in the 1960s, see Norman Nie and Kristi Andersen, "Mass Belief Systems Revisited: Political Change and Attitude Structure," *Journal of Politics*, August 1974, pp. 541–91; John C. Pierce and Douglas D. Rose, "Non-Attitudes and American Public Opinion: The Examination of a Thesis," *American Political Science Review*, June 1974, pp. 626–49; and Norman H. Nie, Sidney Verba, and John R. Petrocik, *The Changing American Voter* (Cambridge, Mass.: Harvard University Press, 1976), especially chap. 7.

[17] Harwood Childs, *Public Opinion: Nature, Formation and Role* (Princeton, N.J.: Van Nostrand, 1965), p. 350.

of survey investigations:

Elmo Roper on the public's judgment

> I believe that a great many of us make two mistakes in our judgment of the common man. *We overestimate the amount of information he has; we underestimate his intelligence.* I know that during my eight years of asking the common man questions about what he thinks and what he wants I have often been surprised and disappointed to discover that he has less information than we think he should have about some question we consider vital. But I have more often been surprised and elated to discover that, despite his lack of information, the common man's native intelligence generally brings him to a sound conclusion.[18]

Public inattention to program specifics

Roper's commentary may seem to wax a bit sentimental: in effect, "underneath all that ignorance, there beats a heart of pure gold." But it states the wisdom of the distinction orthodox democratic theory has made between the public's role, and that of leaders and activists, in the process of democratic government. Most people do not have responsibility for writing laws or otherwise determining the specific shape of programs, and they clearly do not pay much attention to programs at such a level. While we might wish that schools would do a better job of giving students information on government or that more people would spend more time deepening their knowledge, this is a different matter than whether the public can play the role specified by democratic theory: determining what Harwood Childs called "the basic ends of public policy." A populace may be quite attentive to those ends, and notably clear and consistent in its specifications on them, without having much factual knowledge of program details. One cannot account for the findings of a half-century of public opinion research in the United States without granting that great coherence in underlying attitudes and values coexists with great inattentiveness and confusion on the details of policy.

Public Opinion and National Defense: A Case Study

Public ambivalence on foreign policy

By looking closely at public opinion in selected policy areas, we can get a clearer understanding of its stability and underlying structure. In foreign affairs and defense, for example, it is not hard to find proof that many people do not pay much attention to policy details. But it also becomes apparent that Americans have coherent values and expectations that guide their assessments of leaders and events, and that these views have been remarkably consistent for a very long period of time. Since World War II, Americans have accepted the need for their country to exert sustained international leadership. The "we can go it alone" isolationism that shaped U.S. defense and foreign policy for much of the country's history collapsed after 1941. Dis-

[18] Elmo Roper, "So the Blind Shall Not Lead," *Fortune*, February 1942, p. 102. Emphasis added.

trustful of the Soviet Union, Americans have insisted over the past four decades that their country's defenses be at least the equal of the U.S.S.R.'s, and they have backed up this view by supporting high defense expenditures. At the same time, the public has rejected a strident or bellicose foreign policy, and it has always been reluctant to see American troops committed to foreign wars. It has wanted policy to walk the line between strength and stridency. All steps that can reasonably be taken to relax tensions between the United States and the Soviet Union (and other countries) should be taken, but not those that would weaken the U.S. military position and leave it vulnerable to external threats.

Public opinion on defense spending

Each component of the above outline of public opinion is deeply rooted, and the public has shown that it is prepared to make sacrifices or accept consequences in seeing it carried out. For example, since World War II the United States has maintained a large and expensive military establishment. (See chapter 19 for a detailed description of the national defense commitment.) In fiscal year 1988 alone, defense outlays stood at nearly $300 billion, while veterans' benefits claimed another $28 billion. Against this backdrop, pollsters have asked national samples of Americans whether they think the country is spending too much, the right amount, or too little on defense. With only a few exceptions—at the height of the Vietnam War—every time this question has been asked, a majority of the populace has maintained that U.S. military expenditures were either at about the right level or lower than they should be (see Figure 10.3).

Figure 10.3 is based on surveys taken by the National Opinion Research Center (NORC) of the University of Chicago and on surveys by the Roper Organization. The year-to-year change shown by both sets of polls indicates a clear response to external events. During the Carter administration, for instance, both surveys found growing unease about the adequacy of U.S. military preparedness and growing support for increased military spending. The proportion of the public wanting defense cuts fell steadily, reaching a low of just 12 percent in 1980, Carter's last year in office. Then, as the Reagan administration pushed for and gained bigger military budgets, the proportion of the public concluding that the proper level of spending had been surpassed climbed significantly. The percentages reported vary a bit from one survey organization to the other, but notice the overriding coherence and structure—belying any suggestion of "statistical randomness."

Public Opinion and Inherent Personal Values

The further one probes, the more one sees a public that holds firmly to core values and assessments in each area of public policy. One may agree or disagree with the wisdom of the public's positions, of course.

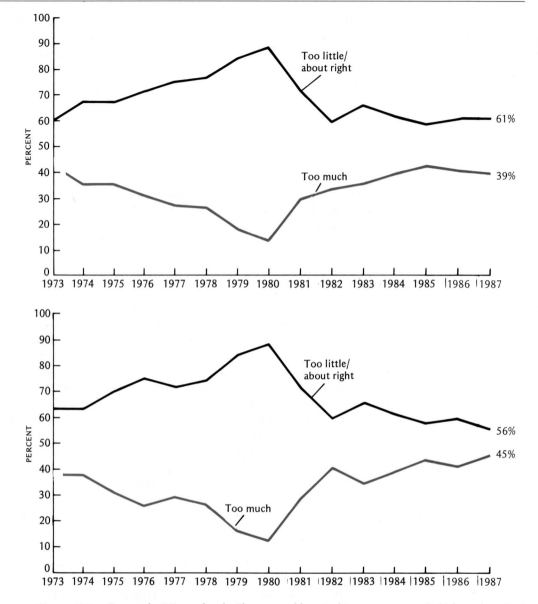

Figure 10.3
Is the U.S. Spending Too Much on Defense?: Two Polls, Two Results

Top graph: "We are faced with many problems in this country, none of which can be solved easily or inexpensively. I'm going to name some of these problems, and for each one I'd like you to tell me whether you think we're spending too much money on it, too little money, or about the right amount—the military, armaments, and defense?"
Source: Survey by the National Opinion Research Center, General Social Surveys, conducted in the spring of each year shown.
Bottom graph: "Turning now to the business of the country—we are faced with many problems in this country, none of which can be solved easily or inexpensively. I'm going to name some of these problems, and for each one I'd like you to tell me whether you think we're spending too much money on it, too little money, or about the right amount—the military, armaments, and defense?"
Source: Survey by the Roper Organization, conducted in December of each year shown.

But one cannot dismiss them as flighty, erratic, or greatly susceptible to manipulation. A century and a half ago, the great French social theorist Alexis de Tocqueville commented on the great stability, even obdurateness, of American public opinion in holding to a basic course defined by some enduring values:

Tocqueville on the stability of public opinion

> I hear it said that it is in the nature and habit of democracies to be constantly changing their opinions and feelings. This may be true of small democratic nations, like those of the ancient world, in which the whole community can be assembled in a public place and then excited at will by an orator. But I saw nothing of the kind among the great democratic people that dwells upon the opposite shores of the Atlantic Ocean. *What struck me in the United States was the difficulty of shaking the majority in an opinion once conceived of.* ... [The public] is engaged in infinitely varying the consequences of known principles ... rather than in seeking for new principles.[19]

Public Opinion on Social Issues: A Case Study

Recent empirical research bears out Tocqueville's shrewd assessment: The public stays with and elaborates a few basic commitments, and resists being moved in new directions. Changes occur through "infinitely varying the consequences of known principles ... rather than in seeking for new principles." Core values are not replaced or rejected; they are applied in a different way to new claims.

Individualism extended: the changing view of women in politics

One of the most powerful sets of American values, we noted in chapter 3, involves individualism. A high moral claim is granted to arguments on behalf of extending individual rights and opportunities. In recent decades, this value has been applied to groups and interests somewhat different from those of the past. Women's views of their position in American society, for example, have been undergoing important changes. "What about our rights and interests as individuals?" many women are now asking. The value of individualism is not new, but this application of it is. The American public has had to adjust to a new status for women, and hence men, in the home, the workplace, and other social settings. One can chart this adaptation through public opinion as roles more in accord with current expectations of individualism gradually receive wider acceptance. Elect a woman president? In 1937, when Gallup first asked a sample of the public nationally whether they would vote for a qualified woman for president if their party nominated one, only 32 percent said they would. Since then, the proportion has steadily increased: to 50 percent in 1949, 59 percent in 1967, and 87 percent in 1987. There is a clear and predictable structure to the change, shown in Figure 10.4, as the old emphasis on individual rights and opportunities gets redefined and reapplied.

[19] Alexis de Tocqueville, *Democracy in America* (New York: Vintage Books, 1958), vol. 2, pp. 271–72. Emphasis added.

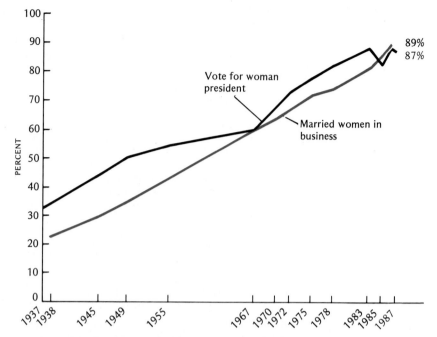

Figure 10.4
A Changing Role for Women

Question: Would you vote for a woman for president if she qualified in every other respect? (1937). If the party whose candidate you most often supported nominated a woman for president of the United States, would you vote for her if she seemed qualified for the job? (1949, 1955). If your party nominated a woman for president, would you vote for her if she were qualified for the job? (1967–86).

Question: Do you approve of a married woman earning money in business or industry if she has a husband capable of supporting her? (1938, 1970). Do you think married women whose husbands make enough to support them should or should not be allowed to hold jobs if they want to? (1945). Do you approve or disapprove of a married woman earning money in business or industry if she has a husband capable of supporting her? (1972–86); Gallup, 1987.

Source: Woman president: Surveys by American Institute of Public Opinion (Gallup) 1937–71; National Opinion Research Center, General Social Surveys, 1972–86.

Married women in business: Surveys by American Institute of Public Opinion (Gallup) 1938, 1970; Roper Organization for Fortune, 1945; National Opinion Research Center, General Social Surveys, 1972–86.

Ambivalence of Opinions

Public ambivalence on the role of government

We noted at the outset of this chapter that on a great many policy questions the public is highly ambivalent—pulled this way and that by conflicting values. "What are we expected to do?" politicians sometimes ask incredulously. Voters are fickle and erratic. Public opinion is a poor guide to policy action because it is so often on both sides of the fence. Americans *do* have mixed minds about many things— including the proper role and scope of contemporary government. Those who are flatly pro-government or anti-government are rare; most people make conflicting assessments. These responses, though, do not seem to be an immature desire to have one's cake and eat it too.

Instead, this ambivalence follows naturally from the joining of legacies from America's ideological past with some contemporary developments. It is often assumed that the American tradition is anti-state, but this isn't so. The founders of the American republic were an unusual breed philosophically: strongly committed to the state and architects of a new national union under the Constitution, but also certain that a government unchecked would usurp and tyrannize. This mix of pro- and anti-government perspectives taught the public to revere coherent and active national government, and at the same time to be vigilant against governmental abuse. Americans began their modern political experience without an ideological tradition wholeheartedly for or against the state.

Historical mix of pro- and anti-government perspectives

Recent experience has enlarged the scope and meaning of this legacy. During the New Deal, the national government assumed new responsibilities and won general approbation for its performance in meeting them. When the society grew markedly richer in the post–World War II years, popular expectations of what should be achieved in both the private and the governmental sectors rose. Americans came to expect more leisure time, more consumer goods, higher standards of living, and, as well, more governmental service in protecting the environment, extending educational opportunities, helping those in need, ensuring adequate income in old age and retirement, and more. Without any profound bias either for or against the state, large majorities of the public saw the government's role in achieving a fuller life inextricably scrambled with the various private roles. For them, the proper questions were "Is it practicable?" and "Does it work?"

Heightened expectations after the New Deal

The other side of this nonideological posture toward the state has involved a readiness to criticize government whenever its actions seemed not to work or advance a better life. Over the 1960s and 1970s, as it began doing so much more, American government presented a much bigger target for criticism. None of this suggests a lack of coherence in public thinking on the role of government. The dualism mirrors the position in which American society finds itself. The idea of a division of labor that is at the core of representative government seems to be reinforced by these findings of ambivalence in public attitudes: It is the task of those who head the institutions of government to strike an appropriate balance between the contending public impulses.

Increased readiness to criticize government

Competing Goals and Values: The Case of Foreign Affairs

The ambivalence in attitudes toward government is evident in other policy areas, such as the debate over whether a nuclear freeze should be enacted—involving a halt to the testing, production, and installation of more nuclear weapons. Whenever pollsters have asked whether the United States should agree to a nuclear freeze with the Soviet Union, the answer has been an overwhelming yes. A CBS News/*New York Times* poll of May 1982 found 72 percent favoring a freeze, compared to only 21 percent opposed and 7 percent of no opinion. But when this poll posed additional questions on the freeze, it revealed a complex mix of colliding values. What if a freeze resulted in the Soviet Union's having somewhat greater nuclear strength than the United States? Would you still favor it? Only 30 percent said they would. What if the United States had to freeze its weapons development first in order to get the Soviet Union to enter into an agreement? Would you then be in favor? Only 26 percent would. There was no *single* opinion on the freeze issue; the public has more than one value it wants served.

What we have seen of the complex, often conflicting tugs of public opinion on a specific issue like a nuclear freeze is broadly evident on other foreign policy questions. We want peace—and we want to see the spread of Communism resisted. We want to see checks put on the arms race—and we want a strong defense, second to none. We want to sit down and talk with the leadership of the Soviet Union and we endorse the holding of summits—and we are deeply suspicious of the Soviet Union, doubting, for instance, that they will abide by their agreements. We don't want a bellicose foreign policy—but we do want a strong, determined foreign policy. We don't favor an "old West" style of vigilantism in dealing with terrorism—but we do want to see terrorism resolutely resisted and punished, even if such punishment does not quickly expunge the cancer. We see threats to U.S. interests in Central America arising from the alliance of the Sandinista government in Nicaragua with the Soviet Union—and yet we are loathe to see the United States drawn further into a military conflict in Nicaragua (as the data in Figure 10.5 indicate).

STUDYING PUBLIC OPINION: POLLING AND ITS INFLUENCE

Public opinion, we have said, is the sum of citizens' personal views—opinions, attitudes, and values—on public issues. It gets expressed in many ways. People write letters to newspapers, hold rallies, cast votes on election day. But increasingly over the last half-century, public opinion has been expressed through polls conducted among representative samples of the populace. The idea that public opinion is what polls say it is represents quite a leap from earlier conceptions. Public opinion used to be seen as an almost mysterious force, a swelling up of popular feelings on this issue or that. Now it is practically a statistical exercise: "67 percent of Americans believe . . . while 24 percent think that . . . and 9 percent are undecided."

Threats to U.S. Interests

Question: Do you think the government of Nicaragua threatens the security of other Central American countries, or not?

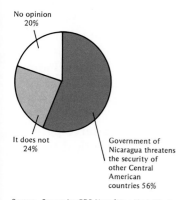

No opinion 20%

It does not 24%

Government of Nicaragua threatens the security of other Central American countries 56%

Source: Survey by CBS News/*New York Times,* April 6-10, 1986.

Question: Do you think Nicaragua will provide military bases for the Soviet Union?

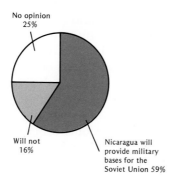

No opinion 25%

Will not 16%

Nicaragua will provide military bases for the Soviet Union 59%

Source: Survey by CBS News/*New York Times,* April 6-10, 1986.

Question: Do you think it's important to the security of the United States to eliminate Communism from Latin America, or can Communist governments exist in Latin America without threatening U.S. security?

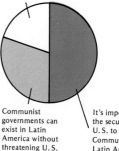

No opinion 20%

Communist governments can exist in Latin America without threatening U.S. security 30%

It's important to the security of the U.S. to eliminate Communism from Latin America 50%

Source: Survey by CBS News/*New York Times,* April 6-10, 1986.

But Don't Get Involved Militarily

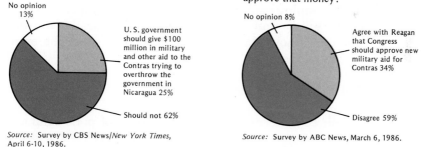

Question: Do you think the U.S. government should give $100 million in military and other aid to the Contras trying to overthrow the government in Nicaragua?

No opinion 13%

U.S. government should give $100 million in military and other aid to the Contras trying to overthrow the government in Nicaragua 25%

Should not 62%

Source: Survey by CBS News/*New York Times,* April 6-10, 1986.

Question: President Reagan is asking Congress for new military aid for the Nicaraguan rebels known as the "Contras." Do you agree or disagree with Reagan that Congress should approve that money?

No opinion 8%

Agree with Reagan that Congress should approve new military aid for Contras 34%

Disagree 59%

Source: Survey by ABC News, March 6, 1986.

Figure 10.5
American Opinion on Nicaragua

Polls can be wrong. They can yield misleading pictures of what the public's thinking is—for reasons we will discuss in the pages that follow. But they came to be relied upon, once their techniques were perfected, because all other outlets or expressions of public opinion were so open to the possibility that they have left out large numbers of people. Letters to the editor and rallies are notorious in this regard; they reflect some people's opinions, of course, but whose? How faithful a slice are they of the total body of public thinking? Even if expressions of opinion that require active effort, like attending a march to protest some governmental action, should receive more weight because the effort suggests greater commitment, the fact is that such expressions are partial rather than complete. The views of more activist segments of the population may not accord with majority sentiment.

Opinion polling can claim to be truly democratic. Samples are drawn so as to represent all groups and classes in proportion to their actual size in the entire population. Questions can be framed more or less neutrally and precisely, and everyone's answers fairly recorded. Polling offers a more objective means of gauging public opinion. As a result, systematic polling has become the dominant tool for opinion measurement. An assortment of groups and institutions, including the communications media, politicians, business corporations, and other interest groups have concluded that opinion polling is useful enough to them to justify spending large sums of money on it. The polling industry has become a big one, and it plays a large part in contemporary politics. Polls have become a staple of political assessment and commentary in every advanced industrial democracy.

Systematic polling: the dominant tool of opinion measurement

Polling and the Social Sciences

Public opinion surveys are an instrument of social science research. Political scientists and sociologists, in particular, have found surveys a means of measuring more efficiently and reliably many topics central to their disciplines. For example, political scientists utilize opinion surveys to study voting decisions. They use them to examine the makeup of political party coalitions: which groups back which party, with what strength and what regularity, for what objectives. Sociologists employ carefully designed surveys to measure such phenomena as ethnic and religious prejudice. The academic study of public opinion is now almost wholly dependent upon the opinion survey method.

Polling and the Media

Measured in terms of the total number of polls conducted and the financial support for them, scholarly research is a small part of polling, however. It is dwarfed by other uses. Increasingly over the last two decades, communications media have found polls extremely useful in news reporting. They employ surveys to forecast election outcomes and to explain why people voted as they did. They track public sentiment on a broad assortment of current issues, as part of their regular news coverage. The surveys taken by CBS in conjunction with the *New York Times*, ABC News together with the *Washington Post*, NBC News in association with the *Wall Street Journal*, and the *Los Angeles Times* are not only media-sponsored but media-managed efforts conducted in-house by their own staffs. Many local newspapers and television stations also sponsor polls.

Polling and Campaigns

The requirements of news reporting and social science research differ; both of these in turn are different from the directly political use of polls. Today it is rare when a candidate for major office does not commission polls to assess what voters want and how well his campaign is registering. Presidential candidates routinely set up large polling operations that conduct surveys almost daily during the campaign. Pollsters have become important campaign strategists, working hand in hand with media experts and other consultants in planning all aspects of campaigns. Candidates are not the only political actors using polls. Interest groups sponsor surveys on subjects of political importance to them and then introduce results into political debate, often to demonstrate that the people really endorse what the group is urging. The American Medical Association (AMA) is one interest group that makes heavy use of polls in its lobbying efforts. Polls have become widely used political weapons. In recent lobbying on environmental issues, for example, both sides have emphasized poll findings in their efforts to set the terms of the debate favorable to what they want done.

How Polling Developed

"Must I drink the whole bottle," Belgian mathematician Adolphe Quetelet once asked, "in order to judge the quality of the wine?" If the answer were yes, wine tasting would be a quite different art. A small sample is sufficient to judge, providing it has all of the important characteristics of the larger unit. This principle of sampling is today employed by researchers in many fields. When marine biologists chart the chemical properties of a bay, they cannot submit all of it to laboratory analysis, nor do they collect samples wherever they feel like it. They draw portions of the water from different spots throughout the area, at different depths, using procedures so that their samples reflect the range of properties of the entire bay. Sampling in public opinion research follows this same general idea. (See Box 10.1 on "How Polls Are Taken.")

The *Literary Digest* and the Birth of Systematic Polling

One event a half-century ago dramatized the basic premises of sampling applied to the study of public opinion, and helped change the course of opinion research: the famous "*Literary Digest* fiasco" of 1936. The *Literary Digest* was a large circulation magazine with articles on topics of general interest: economic, cultural, political, and so on. As early as 1895, it began collecting the names of prospective subscrib-

Box 10.1
How Polls Are Taken

Of a number of books and manuals available on public opinion polling, among the best is Charles W. Roll and Albert H. Cantril, *Polls: Their Use and Misuse* (Cabin John, Md.: Seven Locks Press, 1980). Here, very briefly, are some of the "nuts and bolts."

Polling by mail, telephone, and in person. The least expensive type of polling is the mail questionnaire. And in some instances, especially where one needs to pose a lengthy and complex set of questions to a very interested group within the population, data gathering by mail can be very effective. But most of the time this approach yields unacceptably low returns of completed questionnaires, and it is very slow.

The pioneering survey research organizations in the United States began their work almost exclusively with in-person interviewing; Gallup and Roper still do much of their interviewing in respondents' homes. The advantage of this form is the opportunity it presents a skillful interviewer to establish rapport with respondents. Many people seem to be more willing to explore controversial subjects in a thoughtfully conducted in-person interview than over the telephone.

But telephone interviewing is taking over the industry. It is faster and cheaper than in-person interviewing. Over 97 percent of all households in America now have telephones, so the old argument that telephone interviewing leaves out large numbers of less affluent people no longer applies. Survey organizations are finding that, especially in the high-crime sections of cities, refusal rates are lower when interviewing is done by telephone rather than in person. The ABC News/*Washington Post*, CBS News/*New York Times*, NBC News, and *Los Angeles Times* polls are all conducted by telephone.

Drawing a sample. In the early years of U.S. polling, samples of the population were drawn largely through the *quota* method. (Quota sampling is still common outside the United States.) In this type of sampling, census information is utilized to find the distribution of the population by such relevant attributes as age, education, income, and region. A frame is then designed so that the makeup of the interviews conducted matches the overall population distributions. Interviewers are instructed as to how many respondents they are to

ers as part of its general efforts to increase circulation, and its mailing list rapidly grew to include millions of names. In 1920 the magazine's editors first hit upon the idea of using these lists as a base from which to test political sentiment. By 1928 the *Digest* was conducting a presidential poll in which 18 million ballots were distributed through their mailing lists. Those receiving ballots were asked to check off their choice for president and return their "vote" to the magazine. The *Digest* tabulated them and printed the results at inter-get in the various specified categories: so many men and women, so many people 18 to 29 years of age, etc. This approach is quite efficient, but it has major drawbacks and has largely been abandoned in the United States. Chief among the drawbacks is the fact that the interviewer makes the decision as to which individuals are to be interviewed. The element of randomness is lost. And various forms of bias creep in. Anyone who has ever been out with interviewers working on quota samples has heard such statements as "Oh, I'm not going to interview *him*, he looks so grouchy."

Probability sampling. U.S. survey firms now rely on sampling procedures that make use of probability principles. The idea behind them is to give every individual an equal or known chance of falling into the sample. One common approach is to divide the population into categories on the basis of the size and location of the places people live. Particular areas (such as city blocks) are then chosen on a systematic or random basis. So many interviews are assigned for each block, selecting every *n*th household. People are interviewed solely because the place they live is within an area included in the sample.

Random-digit dialing (RDD). This approach applies the theory of probability sampling to telephone interviewing. A survey firm obtains from the telephone company a tape of information on the working three-digit prefixes (called COCs, for central office codes) in telephone numbers and the assigned banks of the latter four digits. COCs are then selected at random, and a number of interviews to be completed is assigned to each COC—depending on how many working residential numbers there are within it. Random-digit numbers are then generated for each COC or prefix. Calls are continued until the desired number of interview completions is achieved.

Sampling error. Statisticians know how to calculate what the chances are that a sample will be representative of the population. "Sampling error" refers to the extent to which the results in a sample can be expected to differ from the results that would have been obtained if everyone in a population had been interviewed. *Sampling error* encompasses only a small fraction of possible *survey error*. Inaccurate poll results can stem from bad question wording, poor interviewing, sloppy sampling, and many other sources. Sampling error per se is exclusively statistical. The laws of probability can result in samples that are unrepresentative of the total population.

vals during the campaign. It showed the grand total in its last issue before the election.

Over several elections, the *Literary Digest* poll results corresponded remarkably closely to actual election results—and its prestige naturally rose. In 1928, for example, the poll predicted a victory for Republican Herbert Hoover with 63 percent of the popular vote; Hoover won the election with 59 percent. Four years later, the *Digest* poll indicated that the Democratic candidate, Franklin Roosevelt, would

The cover of the Literary Digest *announcing the "final returns of the mammoth nation-wide presidential poll."*

win handily, and he did. The final poll results in 1932 were within 1.5 percent of the actual vote distribution. In 1936, however, the poll fell on its face—and in such a dramatic fashion that the magazine itself was discredited. All during the 1936 campaign, the *Digest* issued reports on the return of its mailed ballots showing Republican Alfred Landon well ahead of incumbent Franklin Roosevelt. The *Digest's* final report, based on nearly 2.4 million ballots, pointed to a resounding Landon victory. Republicans were shown carrying 32 states with a total of 370 electoral votes, and winning 54 percent of the popular vote. In the actual balloting on November 5, however, Roosevelt won 61 percent of the popular vote and 523 of the 531 electoral votes. Landon was buried under the biggest landslide in American political history. Why the *Digest* poll failed became a topic of intense discussion.

In fact, the *Literary Digest's* failure was predicted well in advance of the election, and its source was explained by George Gallup and a number of others who were founding public opinion research in the United States on the basis of new sampling procedures. As Gallup pointed out, while the 2.4 million returned ballots seemed an impressive number, they could be no more reliable than the sampling frame from which they were drawn: the magazine's mailing list. And that list was skewed toward the middle and upper middle class. In the 1936 election, where class lines were relatively sharp, and lower- and working-class voters much more supportive of Roosevelt than those in the middle class, the bias of the *Digest's* sample was immense. Another problem was that the magazine mailed out over 20 million ballots but received back just over 10 percent of them; it had no way of determining whether those taking the trouble to "vote" were even a cross-section of those receiving the ballots, much less of the entire American electorate. And the *Digest's* method of polling was insensitive to opinion shifts occurring at later stages of the race, because it provided for only one mailing during the campaign.

For many who followed the *Literary Digest* fiasco, perhaps the most striking thing was the contrast between the immense, cumbersome efforts of the magazine and the lean, efficient new scientific surveys pioneered by Gallup, Elmo Roper, and Archibald Crossley. Whereas the *Digest* "surveyed" millions, the new polling methods sampled only a few thousand. But because the latter could achieve samples that corresponded at least roughly to the makeup of the entire population, they were dramatically more successful. The "little" Gallup poll was largely right, while the huge *Literary Digest* effort was embarrassingly wrong—a juxtaposition that brought the new age of polling in with a bang. As George Gallup and Saul Forbes Rae were to observe later, "One fundamental lesson became clear in the 1936 election: the heart of the problem of obtaining an accurate measure of public opinion lay in the cross-section, and no mere accumulation of ballots could hope to eliminate the error that sprang from a biased sample."[20]

Problems in Opinion Polling

The major breakthrough in sampling made by Gallup and Roper in 1936 forever changed the way public opinion is measured. Later work by statisticians improved upon the sampling techniques, but the underlying principles had been sound. Today, the problem with polls generally has little to do with the way samples of respondents are drawn from the total population. But the polls' performance is not problem-free.

Polling experts are often asked whether opinion research is really scientific. Modern-day polling certainly draws upon scientific knowledge, especially on how to draw samples that reliably reflect attributes of the entire population. Scientists do use survey findings in their research, just as they use many other types of data. But polling as such is not a science; it is a set of techniques, informed by science,

Sampling bias and imbalance

Advent of scientific surveys

Is opinion research scientific?

[20] George Gallup and Saul Forbes Rae, *The Pulse of Democracy* (Westport, Conn.: Greenwood Press, 1968; first published 1940), pp. 54–55.

that are utilized for a great variety of purposes. Some of these uses are problem causing. Yet even when opinion surveys are used in the most dispassionate and carefully designed types of research, they may still yield invalid results. The methods of science do not always yield reliable knowledge. For many different reasons, ranging from weaknesses of theory to problems in the data collection, inaccurate pictures sometimes emerge from polling. Poll findings should not be accepted uncritically.

Swift Results from a Slow Machine

One set of problems arises from the incompatibility of survey research methods with some of the needs of journalism. The *press,* meaning all mass communications media, must work quickly in order to do its mandated job, to bring the story promptly to the audience. From this basic requirement, speed and timeliness have become highly regarded values. But to do its job, polling must typically move slowly; time is required to frame questions properly, pretest and refine them, do the field work, transform the resulting data to computer-readable form, and perform careful analysis of them. The results of opinion polling on issues of consequence also typically require extensive, time-consuming explanation and exposition.

Tendency toward oversimplification

News media must often move quickly in their canvass of political events, and a great variety of developments vie for press attention. Given this competition for media time and space, public opinion on, for example, a new strategic arms limitation treaty with the Soviet Union or the fighting in Central America can rarely expect to receive as much as 90 seconds of television newscast or 500 words in a newspaper article. An obvious problem arises when such accounts cannot begin to properly explicate the subject. In such cases—which are common, not exceptional—"tight editing" equals "gross oversimplification."

Focused conclusions

Good news reporting has focus and arrives at relatively clear and unambiguous conclusions. In contrast, good opinion research typically reveals such characteristics of public thinking as tentativeness, ambivalence, and lack of information or awareness. The journalist wants crisp answers to such questions as: Is the United States public becoming more conservative? Do Americans want to see a tougher line taken against the Soviet Union? Do they support U.S. policy in Nicaragua? Frequently, though, results of the best survey research aren't consistent with journalists' needs. Conclusions emerging from polling on the various issues often fail to sustain the focused conclusion that is the staple of good news reporting. Today, with the press so heavily involved in the financial sponsorship and even the actual management of polls, there are powerful incentives to act as though poll findings are typically newsworthy. Law professor Michael Wheeler maintains that "the most flagrant error of the press is the common practice of reporting polls as if each American holds a firm opinion on every topic."[21]

Political Distortions

The political use of polls

Problems resulting from polling appear even greater when one looks at its uses in the rough-and-tumble world of American politics. Politicians and interest-group officials have learned that polls can be impressive weapons. In a democracy, it is always comforting to be able to demonstrate that "the people agree with the position I am taking." To this end, poll findings are employed, often highly selectively, on behalf of various interests. Many consumers of politically biased poll reports probably have a hard time distinguishing between them and valid information on public opinion.

One striking illustration of politically motivated distortions of survey findings came in testimony that pollster Louis Harris gave on October 15, 1981, to the Subcommittee on Health and Environment of the U.S. House of Representatives. The message that Harris delivered, drawing on surveys that his organization had conducted, was that any effort by Congress to modify the Clean Air Act—which was up for review—would meet the strongest possible public condemnation. The Clean Air Act is one of the most important pieces of national environmental legislation, and some of its provisions have been the subject of heated debate. We discuss the act in chapter 11.

In his response to Democrat John Dingell of Michigan concerning the Clean air Act, Harris stated;

> I am saying to you just as clear as can be that clean air happens to be one of the sacred cows of the American people, and the suspicion is afoot, however you slice it, that there are interests in the business community and among Republicans and some Democrats who want to keelhaul that legislation. And the people are saying: "Watch out. We will have your hide if you do it."[22]

Inaccurate interpretations of polls

Harris's surveys and those of other organizations did indeed show widespread public backing for the goal of a clean environment. But these data did not suggest that there was any clear public opinion on the specifics of the Clean Air Act. Indeed, survey research had established that most people knew almost nothing about specific provisions of the act—as is the case with most such legislation. Mr. Harris's suggestion that Americans were insisting passionately that Congress

[21] Michael Wheeler, "Reining in Horse-Race Journalism," *Public Opinion*, February / March 1980, p. 42.

[22] For further discussion of the Harris testimony and public opinion data on environmental issues, see Everett Ladd, "Clearing the Air: Public Opinion and Public Policy on the Environment," *Public Opinion*, February / March 1982, pp. 16–20.

make no changes in the act was inaccurate. A perfectly valid expression of political values or preference was being offered in the guise of scientific poll results.

In many cases, political interests assert themselves in polling by framing questions in such a way as to strongly encourage the desired political answer. Consider the following survey question on public reactions to the much-publicized pollution of the Love Canal in upstate New York:

Bias in survey questions

> As you know, residents near the Love Canal, in the Niagara Falls, New York area, were reported to have stillbirths, cancer, deformed children, and chromosome damage as a result of the dumping of hazardous chemical wastes. The people who live near the Love Canal want to move out and are suing the chemical company there and the federal government for $3 billion for damages done to them. How serious a problem do you think the dumping of toxic chemicals is in the country today—very serious, only somewhat serious, or hardly serious at all?[23]

The only remarkable finding was that, after so obviously biased and leading an introduction, there were still some people (7 percent of the total) who answered "hardly serious at all." The question set out to make the case, and it determined what the answers would be.

Such biased approaches are all too common. In October 1982, in a poll ostensibly taken to determine American attitudes toward Israel and the Palestinian question following Israel's invasion of Lebanon, the question was asked of those who said they thought Israel was justified in its actions:

> If you knew that during the ceasefire between Israel and the PLO from July 1981 to June 1982, the PLO observed the ceasefire and launched no rocket attacks while Israeli bombing caused the deaths of almost 100 people, would you still feel that Israel was justified in invading Lebanon?[24]

Aided by so obviously prejudicial a lead, this question found what its sponsors wanted, that about half of those who had indicated support for Israel's action shifted their stand.

The Difficult Task of Question Wording

All survey research, to the extent it tries to understand the public's thinking rather than provide ammunition to advance a cause, confronts a perplexing set of challenges in the area of question wording. When misleading results accrue from surveys, deficiencies in question form and language are now the principal source of the problem.

[23] Survey by Louis Harris and Associates, June 1980.
[24] Survey by Decision-Making Information for the Institute for Arab Studies, October 1982.

WE'RE TAKING A POLL TO SEE IF POLLS ARE ACCURATE POLLS... AS POLLS CLAIM THEY ARE—

1984 CHICAGO TRIBUNE

Double-barreled questions

Technical problems. Some survey items inadvertently pose two separate questions within one, making it impossible to know what respondents are actually answering: "Please tell me whether you agree or disagree with the following statement: It is important that the federal deficit be substantially reduced and that spending for national defense be cut below the president's proposal." This is called a "double-barreled" question. Even if the first part of this statement were separated to stand by itself, there would still be an easily recognizable problem: "It is important that the federal deficit be substantially reduced" poses a variation of the old "motherhood and apple pie" factor. Who is going to declare himself against it? Everyone wants to reduce the federal deficit; the problem comes in finding a way to accomplish the objective with the least harm to other values. A great many different types of problems in question design have been detected. The polling literature has given helpful guidance in avoiding these pitfalls.

Ambivalence and low levels of information. Other problems are trickier to handle. It is especially difficult to frame questions on subjects where the level of relevant information among the general public is low. "One very real difficulty with interpreting opinion data from surveys is that since many people are responding to questions to which they have not given much previous thought, their replies can vary with even subtle differences in the way the questions are worded."[25]

[25] Robert S. Erikson, Norman R. Luttbeg, and Kent L. Tedin, *American Public Opinion* (New York: Wiley, 1980), p. 29.

On abstract policy issues, as we have seen, the public's opinions often haven't taken clear form. How questions are worded helps determine the apparent majority position. That problem is compounded when the public has mixed feelings on an issue being investigated.

Question wording presents only minimal problems for the experienced survey research specialist when:

When polling is easy

1) the level of relevant information among respondents is high;
2) the public has focused on the issue in the context of an actual decision;
3) the choice presented is not complex;
4) the issue is not distinguished by major public ambivalence.

A common instance where the above conditions apply is asking respondents how they plan to vote late in a campaign, when the candidates of both parties are well known and the decision is a real one for most respondents because they will actually be making it shortly in the polling booth.

When polling is hard

When the opposite of all of these elements apply, however—when the information level is low, opinions have not crystallized, the question is highly complex, and many people are ambivalent—even the most sensitive approach to question wording can yield unreliable results. Any version of the question is likely to produce findings significantly different from other equally valid and informed questions. The latter conditions can be found in varying degrees in polling on virtually every complicated policy issue. The deeper one probes, the tougher the problem appears.

> The prevailing model underlying the discipline of survey research is that of the single opinion. A person holds an opinion, which he communicates to an interviewer. When he is influenced to change his mind, he replaces his former opinion with another one. This model has the virtue of great simplicity, but it makes no sense, because conflicting and contradictory opinions may be held simultaneously and because they constantly jostle one another for dominance.[26]

The very design of the structured public opinion survey may be incapable of dealing with the complexity of opinion, given the mix of contrasting values and expectations that vie one with another for priority in our thinking on issues.

Bogart's conclusion is not that opinion research is incapable of yielding useful knowledge. Instead, he gives greater force to the caution that "the mechanics of survey research, like any other human enterprise, are subject to a substantial range of error. . . ." Survey

---

[26] Leo Bogart, *Silent Politics: Polls and the Awareness of Public Opinion* (New York: Wiley-Interscience, 1972), p. 17.

questions are like the blind men before the elephant—each reaches out trying to grasp and comprehend something it really cannot see.

Solutions to Polling Problems

As polls become more widely used, those of us who "consume" them need to become "smarter shoppers." Governmental legislation restricting polling doesn't seem to offer a satisfactory solution, because polling appears to fall well within the bounds of free inquiry, which the U.S. Constitution mandates, and because much useful information is gathered from polls. The answers, then, must involve more knowledge about polls and wiser use of them.

More information needed about polls

Journalists need to learn more about polls. Courses on public opinion research that are specially tailored to the needs of the press are already being developed. Journalists also need ready access to larger bodies of polling information. Is a particular question biased or otherwise defective? It is becoming possible for journalists to plug into data banks that contain large numbers of related questions, and this should stimulate more informed press coverage.

Higher standards needed in polling

Citizens who read poll results need to be more sensitive to the distortions that can arise from polling. The cautions contained in this chapter are a starting point. Groups of responsible polling organizations try to set higher standards for their profession, and these efforts need to be supplemented. The National Council on Public Polls (NCPP) and the American Association for Public Opinion Research (AAPOR) already do important "self-policing" with regard to professional standards. They need to do more, especially to publicize problems inherent in question form and wording, the area of greatest deficiency in opinion research.

HOW AMERICANS VIEW THEIR SOCIETY

Some of the most important aspects of a country's public opinion involve views not of issues and events but of the country itself. How confident are a people in their social and political institutions, and in their values? How satisfied or dissatisfied are they with the way their leaders have managed governmental affairs?

A Crisis of Confidence?

This dimension of public thinking has loomed large in the United States over the last 15 to 20 years because of the abundant evidence of national self-dissatisfaction. This dissatisfaction has been noted by many different observers, including our recent presidents. On July 15, 1979, President Jimmy Carter addressed the public on the theme that many citizens had lost confidence in themselves and their country's future. The result was a severe challenge to the very fabric of American democracy. The threat, the president argued,

> is nearly invisible in ordinary ways. It is a crisis of confidence. It is a crisis that strikes at the very heart and soul and spirit of our national will. We can see this crisis in the growing doubt about the meaning of our own lives and in the loss of a unity of purpose for our nation. The erosion of our confidence in the future is threatening to destroy the social and political fabric of America.

After the bitter experiences of the long Vietnam War, after soaring energy prices and double-digit inflation, after the Watergate scandal and a heightened sense of the frailties of government, many other Americans worried that the public had become less certain about the country and the ideas and institutions on which it was founded. Some noted academic observers concluded, in effect, that history had at last caught up with the United States. In 1975 Daniel Bell saw a long-term loss of faith by Americans in their country's future.[27]

Many opinion polls taken between 1965 and 1980 did indicate a big drop in national self-confidence. During the Vietnam years, according to Harris polls, Americans began expressing markedly diminished confidence in the "people in charge of running" the various central institutions of the society. Over the 1960s and 1970s, according to surveys conducted by the Institute for Social Research of the University of Michigan, large majorities of Americans came to see their political leadership as insufficiently competent and sensitive to the public interest. In 1958 only 18 percent of respondents agreed that "the government is run by a few big interests looking out for themselves," but by 1980 the proportion had soared to 77 percent. The proportion of Michigan survey respondents who said they believed that "quite a few [of the people running the government] don't seem to know what they are doing" stood at 28 percent in 1964, jumped to 45 percent in 1970, climbed further to 52 percent in 1976, and crested at 63 percent in 1980.

Drop in national self-confidence

Dissatisfaction with government performance

What the Public Was Saying

Underlying faith in the American system

If the populace intended literally all of the criticisms that these various poll findings suggest, then a severe blow was struck to American confidence and self-esteem over the 1960s and 1970s. All along, though, other measures advised against a literal reading. For example, polling data suggested that the people had not changed their basic conception of the nation or their commitment to it, but rather that they

[27] Daniel Bell, "The End of American Exceptionalism," *The Public Interest*, Fall 1975, pp. 197–98.

were simply angry about aspects of leadership performance and were looking for ways to let this be known. A May 1975 Yankelovich survey that found nearly three-fifths of Americans claiming their country was in "deep and serious trouble," also discovered that 82 percent professed confidence that in the future "our country will be strong and prosperous."

Such discrepant results show the importance of distinguishing among different levels—and hence different results—of public criticism:

	Level	Result
Mood:	Dissatisfaction with leaders and their performance ⟶	Public wants its leaders to "do a lot better."
Confidence:	Loss of confidence in basic institutions and processes ⟶	Public is receptive to significant institutional change.
Legitimacy:	A crisis of legitimacy ⟶	Public looks for a new structure to the social and political order.

After the buffeting the country took in the 1960s and 1970s, it would have been surprising if the public mood were not testy. This need not mean, however, that the public had lost confidence in the country's central institutions and certainly not that the system had lost its basic claim to loyalty and legitimacy. And in fact, surveys have consistently shown strong popular support for all aspects of the basic design of American social, economic, and political institutions.

Slumps and Winning Streaks

Political scientist Jack Citrin has noted the strength of the American system's ideological underpinnings. What happened in the late 1960s and 1970s was simply that the United States experienced a long "slump."

> Political systems, like baseball teams, have slumps and winning streaks. Having recently endured a succession of losing seasons, Americans boo the home team when it takes the field. But fans are often fickle; victories quickly elicit cheers. And to most fans what matters is whether the home team wins or loses, not how it plays the game. According to this analysis, a modest "winning streak" and, perhaps, some new names in the lineup may be sufficient to raise the level of trust in government.[28]

[28] Jack Citrin, "Comment: The Political Relevance of Trust in Government," *American Political Science Review*, September 1984, p. 987.

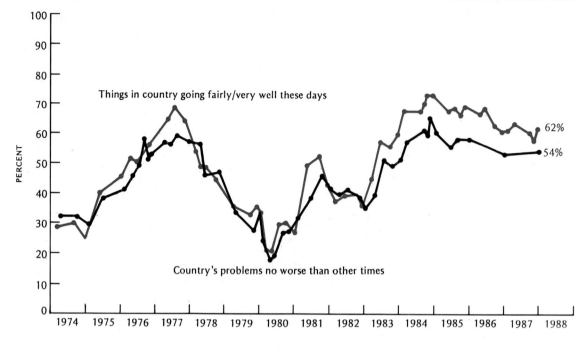

Figure 10.6
How Are Things Going in the Country Today?

Question: How do you feel that things are going in the country these days—very well, fairly well, pretty badly, or very badly?
Question: In commenting on how things are going in the country, some people tell us that the problems we face are no worse than at any other time in recent years. Others say the country is really in deep and serious trouble today. Which comes closest to your own feelings—the fact that: Problems are no worse than at other times. . . . The country is in deep and serious trouble. . . ?
Source: Surveys by Yankelovich, Skelly and White (1974 through February 1986); and Yankelovich Clancy Shulman (March 1986 to present).

Ups and downs in public confidence

Recent experience bears out Citrin's only partly whimsical analogy. As divisive and dispiriting events like the Watergate scandal and the Vietnam War have faded, confidence in the nation's direction and performance has climbed. As Figure 10.6 shows, in May 1980 only 21 percent of Americans interviewed by Yankelovich, Skelly, and White said that things in the U.S. were going very well or fairly well. By July 1986, however, the proportion had risen sharply to 69 percent. Other poll questions show the same sharp rise in national confidence and optimism from the lows experienced in 1979 and 1980, the closing years of Jimmy Carter's presidency, when the prolonged holding of American hostages in Iran seemed to encapsulate the nation's frustrations. In August 1979 just 12 percent of those interviewed by Gallup said they were "satisfied . . . with the way things are going in the U.S. at this time"; 84 percent were dissatisfied. By 1986 these proportions had been dramatically reversed: 69 percent in the Gallup poll of March 4–10, 1986, said they were satisfied, only 31 percent dissatisfied.

Americans are, in Citrin's metaphor, very demanding fans. They expect their home team to have a strong winning record. When things are not going so well they are quick to enter their complaints. Following the Iran-Contra revelations that began in November 1986, public satisfaction again declined somewhat. And following the stock market crash in October 1987, the proportion saying things were generally going well in the country fell to 58 percent, down 11 points from the high in July 1986 (Figure 10.6). Still the public's overall verdict in the 1980s has been quite favorable.[29]

SUMMARY

Public opinion is assigned a critical role in a democracy. Government by the people, democracy, must mean government responsive to the public's preferences for leaders and policies, or it is a sham.

Questions have been raised from a variety of perspectives as to whether public opinion can meet democracy's requirements. Many observers have argued that the mass public is insufficiently informed about and attentive to the issues on which its judgment is supposed to be controlling. Critics have portrayed the public as too easily manipulated by demagogic leaders. In the United States, some charge, the "establishment" has succeeded in imposing on the people outlooks that serve its, not their, needs. Arguments made by advertising and public relations theorists in a way back up the critics, through their stress on how easily consent to candidates and causes can be engineered.

Opinion research in the United States does reveal a public strikingly inattentive to the details of even the most consequential and controversial policies. This suggests a potential for manipulation. But the research also indicates great stability and coherence in the public's underlying attitudes and values. Americans show themselves perfectly capable of making the distinctions needed to determine what Harwood Childs called "the basic ends of public policy," and of pursuing these logically and clearly. There is a persisting structure to American opinion that belies the picture of a populace helpless before the "engineers of consent."

To observe that the public holds strongly to basic values is not to assert that its preferences are always clear or readily followed. People are frequently ambivalent—committed at one and the same time to opposing or competing goals. They think that contemporary government is too big, too powerful, and too costly, and they would like to see it reined in. But they also look to government for help in solving a great variety of problems, and don't think there is any alternative to an expansive role for the state. Such pushes and pulls of contending values dominate American public opinion.

The public's ambivalent responses pose some tricky measurement problems for opinion research. It is no easy task to frame questions so as to give

[29] See Jack Citrin, Donald Green, and Beth Reingold, "Confidence in the Reagan Years," *Public Opinion*, November-December 1987, pp. 18–19 ff.

proper weight to the contending objectives people so often bring to complex policy issues. In general, problems related to question design contribute more to deficiencies in opinion research than any other factor.

Pioneered a half-century ago by George Gallup and Elmo Roper, systematic polling has become the dominant tool for opinion measurement. A wide assortment of groups and institutions—including academic social scientists, the press, politicians, business and other interest groups—all find polling valuable in their work. But each makes its own special use of poll information, very different from those of the others. Journalists look to polls as sources of news, whereas political interest groups want poll findings that buttress their positions or help them chart strategies. Given the varied uses, the maxim *caveat emptor* is very much in order: the buyer or consumer of poll reports should be wary.

Some of the key aspects of American public opinion involve views of the country itself. In the late 1960s and 1970s, a great many indicators, including opinion polls, suggested that there had been an alarming drop in national self-confidence. But close examination showed that the populace had not changed their basic sense of the nation or commitment to it. Instead, they were troubled about leadership performance and were anxious to let that be known. "Political systems," Jack Citrin observed, "like baseball teams, have slumps and winning streaks," and the United States had been in a slump. In the 1980s, the fans seem less restless but no less demanding.

FOR FURTHER STUDY

Leo Bogart, *Silent Politics: Polls and the Awareness of Public Opinion* (New York: Wiley-Interscience, 1972). A brilliant analysis of what public opinion is and isn't, and how polls can be used in the study of public opinion.

Robert S. Erikson et al., *American Public Opinion*, 3rd ed. (New York: Macmillan, 1988). A good review of polling information on American public opinion in various policy areas.

George Gallup and Saul Forbes Rae, *The Pulse of Democracy* (Westport, CT: Greenwood Press, 1968; first published, 1940). One of the founders of modern public opinion polling, George Gallup, defends the enterprise as one that can enlarge and strengthen democracy itself.

Eytau Gilboa, *American Public Opinion Toward Israel and the Arab-Israeli Conflict* (Boston: D.C. Heath, 1987). A careful, systematic review of American opinion in an area of great importance in U.S. foreign policy.

Benjamin Ginsberg, *The Captive Public: How Mass Opinion Promotes State Power* (New York: Basic Books, 1986). A forceful argument that increased instantaneous access to mass public opinion has enabled governments to manage it for their own purposes.

V. O. Key, Jr., *Public Opinion and American Democracy* (New York: Knopf, 1961). A systematic examination by a leading political scientist of the properties of public opinion and its role in American government and politics.

Robert E. Lane, *Political Ideology* (New York: Free Press, 1962). A classic examination of how people think about political life, based on lengthy interviews with fifteen citizens in one American city (New Haven, CT).

Walter Lippmann, *Public Opinion* (New York: Macmillan, 1960; first published, 1922). A classic account of public opinion—how it is formed and how it helps shape politics.

Chapter 11

Interest Groups

James Madison's assessment of interest groups—which he called "factions"—in *Federalist Paper* 10 is an American classic. (See Appendix, pp. A21–A25 for *Federalist Paper* 10.) Any society will inevitably have a great many contending interests, he argued, because "the latent causes of faction are . . . sown in the nature of man. . . ." People will hold different opinions and interests on such matters as power, religion and, especially, economics. If by chance we couldn't think of a good reason to divide up into contending interests we would invent one. Madison observed: "So strong is this propensity of mankind to fall into mutual animosities that where no substantial occasion presents itself the most frivolous and fanciful distinctions have been sufficient to kindle their unfriendly passions and excite their most violent conflicts."

In Madison's view, interest groups are in many regards undesirable. They are invariably narrow and self-serving. Indeed, he defined a faction as "a number of citizens . . . who are united and actuated by some common impulse or passion, or of interest, *adverse to the rights of other citizens, or to the permanent and aggregate interests of the community*" (emphasis added).

This should not mean, though, that Madison thought the new American nation should strive to throttle interest groups. It could never eliminate the diversity of interests. And if it ever sought to prevent the organized expression of those interests it would lose the most precious thing it was striving to obtain—freedom. "Liberty," he insisted,

> is to faction what air is to fire, an aliment without which it instantly expires. But it could not be a less folly to abolish liberty, which is essential to political life, because it nourishes faction than it would be to wish the annihilation of air, which is essential to animal life, because it imparts to fire its destructive agency.

The only way to proceed, then, is try to organize society and especially government so as to force groups into situations where they must compete and none can get too strong. We explored this approach in general terms in chapters 3 and 4. Arguments have gone on throughout U.S. history as to whether certain groups—large business corporations, for example—have not in fact gotten too strong. Various proposals have been made to regulate interest group behavior. In recent years, for example, a lively argument has proceeded on whether some groups have undue electoral influence because they contribute so much money to political campaigns, and we discuss the growth of *political action committees* (PACs) later in this chapter. In chapter 12 we review legislation that has been enacted to regulate private interest money in campaigns and proposals to curb these contributions further. Whatever one thinks about the need for more regulation of groups, though, the core of Madison's arguments is impressive. Organized interests are necessary elements of a free society.

A Nation of Joiners

After visiting the United States in the 1830s, Alexis de Tocqueville wrote that "in no country in the world has the principle of association been more successfully used or applied to a greater multitude of objects than in America." Americans were a nation of joiners. Tocqueville explained this propensity, interestingly, in terms of individualism: "The citizen of the United States is taught from infancy to rely upon his own exertions in order to resist the evils and the difficulties of life; he looks upon the social authority with an eye of mistrust and anxiety, and he claims its assistance only when he is unable to do without it. . . ."

Joining together with other like-minded persons to attack common problems expresses a sense of individual responsibility and self-confidence:

High levels of participation

> If a stoppage occurs in a thoroughfare and the circulation of vehicles is hindered, the neighbors immediately form themselves into a deliberative body; and this extemporaneous assembly gives rise to an executive power which remedies the inconvenience before anybody has thought of recurring to a pre-existing authority superior to that of the persons immediately concerned. . . . In the United States associations are established to promote the public safety, commerce, industry, morality, and religion. There is no end which the human will despairs of attaining through the combined power of individuals united into a society.[1]

[1] Tocqueville, *Democracy in America*, vol. 1, p. 198.

A Nation of Interest Groups

Tocqueville's observation still applies. This general proclivity for forming private associations to meet public needs extends to the pursuit of political interests. The variety of interest groups in the United States ranges from strictly local associations, such as small-town chambers of commerce (which try among other things to influence town councils on off-street parking or zoning regulations) to massive national associations like the American Federation of Labor and Congress of Industrial Organizations (AFL-CIO), the principal U.S. labor union federation, and the National Association of Manufacturers (NAM), a huge industry association comprising over 13,000 companies. Every conceivable issue before the American polity at the national, state, and local levels has a distinct set of interest groups and associations trying to shape policy on it.

Number and diversity of interest groups

How many interest groups are there in the United States? No one can say precisely. While some groups are exclusively political and required by law to register as lobbyists (see below) and hence can be counted, many other groups intervene only sporadically in political affairs and never register. They often don't even think of themselves as interest groups, even though they sometimes work actively for political goals. For example, the 346,000 individual churches and parishes in the United States, with a total membership of about 143,000,000, exist primarily for religious and social purposes. But on occasion, these churches and their national denominational organizations try to influence public policy, often on social questions such

Trade unionists protesting the rising tide of foreign imports.

as abortion, school prayer, and the death penalty. Churches are also at times outspoken on questions of national defense and foreign policy, such as the development of nuclear weapons.

Business interests   Virtually every large business corporation in the United States and many small businesses have strong legislative interests. General Motors and Boeing Aircraft are affected by governmental actions in many ways: Each gets government contracts, is subjected to a welter of federal and state regulations, pays taxes, has a big stake in international trade policy. Are most businesses interest groups? Sometimes, and to some extent. Business firms exist for many purposes and objectives other than those political, but at times they function as interest groups as they try to influence what government does.

THE INTEREST GROUP ARENA

As the federal government has come to play an ever-larger role in national life over the last fifty years, more and more groups have come to be actively concerned with influencing federal action. Lobbying has burgeoned.[2] The most comprehensive accounting of Washington lobbyists is the volume *Washington Representatives*, a privately published listing of "persons working to influence government policies and actions to advance their own interests." In 1977, 4,000 names were listed; just a decade later, in 1987, *Washington Representatives* listed about 11,000 who fitted its definition of national lobbyists.

Inevitably, people with good connections to Congress and the executive branch—and this includes, in particular, former members of those branches—have come to be in high demand as interest-group representatives. Ethical issues abound. Sometimes the law is broken. The case of Michael K. Deaver is instructive.

Michael Deaver and   After he left his post as White House deputy chief of staff in 1985,
lobbying   Deaver set up a public relations firm, Michael K. Deaver and Associates. There is no doubt that the firm's primary assets were the many contacts and ties Deaver himself had established over his twenty years as an aide to Ronald Reagan—and especially during his four-plus years as a White House official. Many of the interests Deaver began to represent were foreign governments concerned with and affected by various U.S. actions. His clients (and their annual fees) included the embassy of the government of Canada ($100,000); the government of Singapore ($250,000); the Ministry of Commerce and Industrial Development of the government of Mexico ($250,000); the government of Korea and the International Cultural Society of Korea ($475,000); and the Royal Embassy of Saudi Arabia ($500,000). In

[2]The term "lobby" came into use in seventeenth-century England, when a large anteroom near the House of Commons was referred to as the "lobby." Those who approached members of Parliament, trying to persuade them to vote a certain way, were lobbying.

reports that he filed with the Justice Department (as required by the Foreign Agents Act), Deaver reported contacts with U.S. cabinet officers and other administration officials on behalf of his foreign government clients—including meetings with Treasury Secretary James Baker III, Secretary of State George Shultz, and Commerce Secretary Malcolm Baldrige.

The principal charge that was brought against Michael Deaver was that he violated conflict-of-interest laws by representing Canada on acid rain (see p. 397) shortly after helping to determine administration policy on the issue as a White House official. Deputy Counsel of the General Accounting Office James Hinchman stated in May 1986 that there was "enough basis" for believing that the law governing permissible lobbying activity following federal service had been violated to warrant referring the case to the Justice Department. The end results were the appointment of an independent counsel to determine whether Deaver had broken the Ethics in Government Act or any other federal statute, and Deaver's subsequent indictment and conviction on perjury charges.

A long line of former presidential assistants have gone on to successful careers as Washington lobbyists, in part trading off old ties to public officials. Most have not run afoul of the law. Still, ethical problems are always present in situations where former high officials lobby past colleagues. And the problem hardly stops with White House aides. Retired congressmen often stay in Washington as lobbyists. Retired generals become representatives for defense contractors. Reporter Neal Peirce found that, as of June 1986, 16 former officials of the government of Austin, Texas, were occupying posts that involved lobbying city hall.[3]

Types of Interest Groups

The Federal Regulation of Lobbying Act, passed in 1946, requires that groups attempting to influence legislation before Congress register and report the amount they expend in lobbying efforts. This legislation is full of loopholes and it contains almost no enforcement provisions. Any organization that really prefers not to register finds it easy to avoid doing so. As a result, the number of formally registered groups is certainly smaller at any given time than the number of organizations actively engaged in lobbying. But the law states an obligation that many groups heed. More than 5,000 groups were registered in 1987.

The roster of those registered gives a sense of the extent and diversity of interest groups nationally. Among them are major business

---

[3] Neal R. Peirce, "Locals, Too, Exit Through the Revolving Door," *National Journal,* June 21, 1986, p. 1556.

Conflict of interest

The only major recent growth in American trade unions has come among government employees.

associations, such as the Business Roundtable and National Association of Manufacturers; individual corporations, from American Express to Phillips Petroleum to the Kellogg Company; trade and professional associations, including the American Petroleum Institute, the American Meat Institute, the Electronic Industries Association, the National Education Association, and the American Medical Association; trade unions such as the American Federation of State, County, and Municipal Employees AFL-CIO, and the Amalgamated Clothing and Textile Workers' Union AFL-CIO; and a wide variety of organizations known as citizens' groups, among them the National Rifle Association, the National Clean Air Coalition, the Sierra Club, and the Religious Coalition for Abortion Rights.

Registration of lobbyists

These registered interest groups are only the tip of the iceberg. There are, for example, some 6,200 national trade and professional associations alone, and virtually every one of them has policy interests. The asbestos industry has five trade associations. Nine associations represent brewers. There are four trade associations for china tableware and four for chocolate. The trucking industry has approximately sixty trade associations. About fifteen associations promote the interests of businesses that produce and sell wine. More than 4,000 individual business corporations retain representatives in Washington, D.C. By the beginning of the 1980s, Washington had also become the leading headquarters city, with about 30 percent of all national non-profit associations headquartered there.[4]

[4]Robert H. Salisbury, with John P. Heinz, Edward O. Laumann, and Robert L. Nelson, "Soaking and Poking Among the Movers and Shakers: Quantitative Ethnography Along

State and local groups

Interest groups operate at the state and local levels as well. In Connecticut, for example, where groups and their representatives are required to report to a State Ethics Commission, some 450 individuals were registered as lobbyists in 1986, representing about 375 groups and associations. Many organizations that try to influence policy nationally have state affiliates which, quite independently, pursue state policy objectives. The AFL-CIO is a national interest group, but there are fifty state AFL-CIO units that have their own staffs and their own state-related legislative agendas. All in all, the interest-group world in the United States is massive. Tens of thousands of individuals and groups expend hundreds of millions of dollars each year in efforts to shape public policy. Little wonder that Thomas P. O'Neill, House of Representatives speaker from 1977 through 1986, remarked with exasperation that "everybody in America has a lobby."

The Most Common and Durable Source of Faction

The economic basis of interest-group activity

The sheer volume of interest groups does not mean, however, that all the different kinds of interests in the country are more or less equally engaged in interest-group activity. Some interests are disproportionately represented. Madison saw the pattern two centuries ago. He wrote in *Federalist Paper* 10 that while every type of political interest gets mobilized in a democracy,

> the most common and durable source of factions has been the various and unequal distribution of property. Those who hold and those who are without property have ever formed distinct interests in society. Those who are creditors, and those who are debtors, fall under a like discrimination. A landed interest, a manufacturing interest, a mercantile interest, a monied interest, with many lesser interests, grow up of necessity in civilized nations, and divide them into different classes, actuated by different sentiments and views.

The prime source of organized interests, then, is economic status. Interest groups spring up to represent claims of different sectors in the economy (Madison listed farming, manufacturing, trade, and banking as the most important) and the interests of economic "haves" and "have nots." The consuming conflict of America in the 1780s was not between rich and poor. It was among farm interests in different parts of the country, and between farm interests and the mercantile and monied interests concentrated along the northeastern seaboard. When he wrote *Federalist Paper* 10, Madison had just spent a decade absorbed in the struggle of these various regionally organized eco-

---

the K Street Corridor," paper presented at the annual meeting of the American Political Science Association, Washington, D.C., August 30–September 2, 1984. See also *National Trade and Professional Associations of the United States*, 23rd ed. (Washington, D.C.: Columbia Books, 1988).

nomic interests. The Constitutional Convention of 1787 itself had to mediate the contending claims of representatives of the different economic sectors.

Is this interpretation of interest-group organization and conflict valid today? The answer must be a qualified yes. The United States has seen an extraordinary array of contending groups and interests throughout its history. Groups defined by ethnic and cultural interests (blacks and whites, old-stock immigrants and newer arrivals, Protestants and Catholics, Christians and Jews) have often been centrally involved in the struggle. Still, the lion's share of interest-group activity has involved economic interests, with the horizontal or sector split far more prominent than the vertical or haves-versus-have-nots split. We see this today when we look at interest-group activity in Washington. In 1987 more than 2,500 separate interest groups were involved in new registrations with the clerk of the U.S. House of Representatives and the secretary of the Senate, under the terms of the Federal Regulation of Lobbying Act. Their overwhelmingly economic bias is evident. As Table 11.1 indicates, 58 percent of all new registrants were business corporations and another 20 percent trade associations. About four-fifths of all groups registering or reregistering as lobbyists in 1987 had predominantly economic objectives. They cover the widest range of economic pursuits. The many different sectors of economic life, represented by the variety of business corporations and trade associations, distinguish this interest-group world.

The continuing prominence of economic interests

Table 11.1
Lobby Registrations Filed with U.S. House of
Representatives by Type of Group,
April 1, 1987–March 31, 1988 (in percent)

Business corporations	58
Trade associations	20
Labor unions	1
State and local governments	3
Citizens' groups (misc.)	15
Other	1
Total	2,588 registrations

Source: Data compiled from *Congressional Quarterly,* weekly reports of September 12, September 19, September 26, October 17, October 24, November 7, December 12, 1987; and January 23, March 5, April 8, April 23, May 14, 1988.

Governments Lobbying Government

These economic interests in what government does extend beyond business and labor to government itself. We described in chapter 5 the expansion during the 1960s and 1970s in federal programs providing aid for states and municipalities. Responding to these new programs and the billions of dollars distributed through them each year, state and local governments dramatically extended their Washington lobbying. In this period, for instance, the state of Louisiana, the Kansas Corporation Commission, the city of New Orleans, Los Angeles county, and the state of Maryland all registered as congressional lobbyists. Thirty states and more than 100 cities and counties have established offices or hired agents in Washington. The National Governors' Association has been especially active. Its marble building, called the Hall of the States, is just a stone's throw from the U.S. Capitol. This association maintains a staff of over 100. Near the Hall of the States is the new headquarters of the National Association of Counties (NACO). A mile away, the National League of Cities has a new office complex, housing lobbyists for many individual municipalities. The headquarters of the U.S. Conference of Mayors is also nearby. These state and local government lobbies are now a major part of Washington interest representation.

Governments lobbying government is not confined to the states and municipalities; the federal government lobbies itself. Various agencies that have a great stake in congressional appropriations and other legislative provisions actively lobby Congress. Every cabinet department has a top congressional liaison person of assistant-secretary rank and several subordinates to assist in these efforts.

Public-Interest Groups

Serving the public interest

One of the most widely discussed developments in interest group activity in recent years is the prominent role of public-interest groups. A **public-interest group** is "one that seeks a collective good, the achievement of which will not selectively or materially benefit the membership or activists of the organization."[5] The roster of public-interest groups includes environmentalists, such as Friends of the Earth, the National Wildlife Federation, and the Sierra Club. Others seek to reform the organization and conduct of American political life, the most prominent being Common Cause. Consumers Union tries to mobilize the diffuse interests of purchasers rather than producers. Foreign-policy goals such as arms control have been the focus of the Arms Control Association and the World Federalists.

Do these groups really speak for the public interest? While the concept of public interest is not simple or unambiguous, it calls attention to the general claims and needs of the whole population as opposed to those of special and private interests. Groups are rarely organized around the broadest and most unselfish aspirations of a society. Rather

[5] Jeffrey M. Berry, *Lobbying for the People* (Princeton, N.J.: Princeton University Press, 1977), p. 7.

The American Cancer Society at times lobbies as a public-interest group.

SMOKING POLLUTES YOU AND EVERYTHING ELSE

they grow to advance narrower objectives. Indeed, it is typically the special nature of their claims that spurs their organization. Many public-interest groups, including those that take stands on environmental questions, consumer affairs, and governmental reform, argue that there are general public interests in their respective areas that are sometimes denied by the actions of special interests like private business corporations. Yet when public-interest groups make their own proposals, they very often articulate another set of special interests and perspectives. Nonetheless, they encourage a competition of ideas and claims; and the values they pursue do not lead to the narrow economic benefit of their members.

Growth of public-interest groups

The growth of public-interest groups is a product of larger changes in the composition of American society. As noted in chapter 2, there has been a recent and huge increase in the number of college-educated men and women employed in professional occupations. With this expansion has come the vast growth of a relatively new stratum of political actors: people who are well-educated, highly skilled, and attentive to issues rather than political patronage.[6] One of the ways the expanding stratum of middle-class activists has expressed itself

[6] For an account of the expansion of one part of this new group of political activists, see James Q. Wilson, *The Amateur Democrat* (Chicago: University of Chicago Press, 1962).

is through public-interest groups. There are now several thousand public-interest organizations operating at the local, state, and national level in the United States.[7] And this development has not been confined to the United States. Groups protesting the use of nuclear power for the generation of electricity have been active throughout Western Europe and Japan. The "green movement," expressing environmental concerns, is similarly influential in other industrialized nations. The largest environmental group in France, for example, Les Amis de la Terre (Friends of the Earth) advances environmental programs and policies similar to those of Friends of the Earth and the Sierra Club in the United States.

Expanding Sector Coverage by Interest Groups

In numerical terms business-related interest groups still predominate. But extensive group organization now exists in many sectors outside the traditional ones of business and labor. For example, the social, economic, and political interests of women are represented by scores of organizations nationally and by thousands of group affiliates at the state and local levels. Education is a major activity in the United States and almost every conceivable dimension of it has formal representation.

Some groups, it should be noted, are not as heavily represented by organized interest groups; the poor and minorities are the most prominent of these. For example, while the National Association for the Advancement of Colored People (NAACP) and the National Urban League are well-established and have long been active in advancing the goals of black Americans, interest-group involvement in this area is less substantial than in other sectors such as environmental and educational concerns, to say nothing of business.

Women's groups. This expression of interests is not limited to widely publicized organizations associated with the women's movement, such as the National Organization for Women (NOW). Women who work for the national government are represented by Federally Employed Women (FEW). The widows of Army, Navy, Air Force, and Marine veterans have interests in survivor benefit programs, represented by the National Association of Military Widows. For women in education there are such groups as the National Council of Administrative Women in Education and the American Association of University Women. To advance athletic programs, there is the National Association for Girls and Women in Sports. Few areas where women's inter-

Women's groups

---

[7] Roger M. Williams, "The Rise of Middle Class Activism: Fighting 'City Hall,'" *Saturday Review*, March 8, 1975, pp. 12–16; Jeffrey M. Berry, *The Interest Group Society* (Boston: Little, Brown, 1984).

Table 11.2
Selected National Women's Organizations

American Association of University Women: women graduates of regionally accredited colleges, universities, and recognized foreign institutions.

Federally Employed Women (FEW): women and men who work for the federal and District of Columbia governments.

Federation of Organizations for Professional Women: women's caucuses and committees in professional associations and organizations, and people interested in equal educational and employment opportunities for women.

General Federation of Women's Clubs: nonpartisan organization of volunteer women, interested in conservation, education, home life, public affairs, and the arts.

League of Women Voters of the United States: women and men interested in nonpartisan political action and study.

National Association of Military Widows: provides referral information to military widows on survivor benefit programs.

National Association of Women Business Owners: individuals, primarily women, who own their own businesses.

National Council of Negro Women: coalition of international organizations and individuals.

National Federation of Republican Women: volunteers for support of Republican candidates for national, state, and local offices.

National Organization for Women (NOW): individuals interested in all rights for women.

National Women's Political Caucus: persons interested in greater involvement of women in politics.

Women's Equity Action League: nonpartisan organization that works for economic advances and equality for women.

ests are found in the contemporary United States now lack formal organization (see Table 11.2).

Educational groups

Educational groups. School teachers work through the American Federation of Teachers, AFL-CIO, and the National Education Association. Private schools are represented by such groups as the Lutheran Educational Conference of North America, the National Association of Independent Schools, the National Catholic Education Association, and the Christian College Coalition. College and university interests get expressed through varied groups, among them the Association of American Colleges, the Association of American Universities, the American Council on Education, the American Association of University Professors, the Council of Graduate Schools in the United States, the Council for the Advancement of Small Colleges, the Women's College Coalition, and the National Association for Equal Opportunity in Higher Education (see Table 11.3).

INTEREST-GROUP RESOURCES

The thousands of interest groups in the American political scene vary greatly in the impact they are able to have on public policy. Some

Table 11.3
Selected National Educational Organizations

American Association of School Administrators: chief school executives and other administrators at district or higher level, and teachers of school administration.

American Association of University Professors: college and university faculty and graduate students.

American Council on Education: colleges, universities, and education associations.

American Federation of Teachers, AFL-CIO: preschool through postsecondary level teachers.

Association of American Universities: public and private universities with emphasis on graduate and professional education and research.

Association of Catholic Colleges and Universities: colleges, universities, and individuals interested in Catholic education.

Council for American Private Education (CAPE): national organizations serving private elementary and secondary schools.

Council for Exceptional Children: teachers, researchers, administrators, students, social workers, psychologists, and physicians who work with handicapped or gifted children.

Council for Graduate Schools in the United States: degree-granting graduate schools and graduate programs at private and public colleges and universities.

National Association for Equal Opportunity in Higher Education: predominantly black colleges and universities.

National Coalition of Public Education and Religious Liberty: coalition of groups that oppose federal aid to nonpublic schools.

National Congress of Parents and Teachers: parent-teacher associations.

National Education Association: teachers, from elementary through postsecondary level, and other educational professionals.

National Retired Teachers' Association: retired teachers.

United States Student Association: college and university student government associations.

have far greater resources than others. While it is not possible to specify exactly how much influence a group will have, given its particular mix of resources, it is possible to identify the principal types of resources that groups call upon as they try to influence policy.

Size of Membership

In a democratic political system, the size of an interest group's following is and should be an important factor. Numbers matter. About 13.1 million men and women belong to the labor unions that make up the AFL-CIO, which unquestionably adds weight to the representation AFL-CIO leaders make on behalf of various programs. Through the staff and organization of their unions, labor officials have formal ties and channels of communication to many people. But a number of factors restrict the weight of numbers. For one thing, every large group is certain to have a membership with very heterogeneous interests. AFL-CIO lobbyists claim to speak for millions of trade unionists, but in fact few pieces of legislation come before Congress where this is truly persuasive. Politicians know that unionists are divided on most political matters—much like any comparably large body of Americans. One almost never encounters the situation on a controversial question where 90 percent of the union membership is on one side and just 10 percent on the other. In the 1988 presidential election, for example, when the AFL-CIO and most member unions endorsed Democrat Michael Dukakis and made a concerted effort on his behalf in the general election battle against George Bush, their efforts clearly produced results. Dukakis did much better, for instance, among workers who belonged to unions than he did among non-unionized workers in the same general economic position; part of the leadership message got across to the members. Still, Dukakis won the support of just 58 percent of trade unionists and their families, according to the CBS News/*New York Times* election-day survey. The situation had been much the same in the 1984 election (Table 11.4).

Table 11.4
Presidential Vote by Union Membership, 1980, 1984, and 1988 (in percent)

	1980			1984		1988	
	Carter	Reagan	Anderson	Mondale	Reagan	Dukakis	Bush
Members of labor households	47	44	7	54	46	58	42
Members of households where no one belongs to a union	35	55	8	37	63	42	58

Source: Election-day surveys by CBS News and the New York Times, November 4, 1980, November 6, 1984, and November 8, 1988.

Policy splits within groups

It is not surprising that splits develop between union leadership and the rank-and-file membership on various policy questions. Any large group attracts its members for limited objectives—in the case of the labor unions, to improve wages and working conditions. Sustained by this base, labor leaders then proceed to take stands on a broad range of important policy questions, such as race relations, taxing and spending, and foreign affairs. These positions are by-products of an institutional arrangement organized for another purpose. There is no reason to expect leaders to represent the rank and file's view directly outside of the objectives for which the group membership was developed. This does not mean that the 13 million member AFL-CIO is a feeble giant. More than any other organization it is listened to when it speaks for American labor. Its membership supports an organizational structure that is often skillfully committed in election contests and policy debates. But the impact of these numbers is diluted by the great heterogeneity of interests they entail.

Financial Resources

Numbers are only one element determining a group's influence. Money is another critical political resource. Some groups have a lot of it, others very little. Lobbying by business corporations and trade associations—groups that are relatively weak in number of members—is often very well financed. Groups use money in a variety of ways to advance their interests, most of which are straightforward and legal. Well-financed associations of business or professional people, like the National Association of Manufacturers and the American Medical Association, employ large and politically astute staffs. They mount effective public-relations campaigns, utilizing the mass media to present their positions. In general, they use their financial resources to get their messages before legislators, other political decision makers, and the public, to an extent quite beyond the reach of groups that lack such substantial funding.

Buying access to officials

Interests that can draw on large financial resources can also increase their access to officials, something that is troubling even when it is completely legal. One common means of increasing or protecting access is by making campaign contributions to candidates. Electioneering is very expensive, and it is becoming steadily more so, especially as the use of television expands. Candidates turn to well-financed groups for campaign contributions, and the groups often oblige. These groups do not think they are buying votes and typically they are not, but they do think their contributions entitle them to get in the door and make their case the next time an issue of importance to them comes along. Or they are afraid that if they refuse an influential incumbent's request for a contribution, he or she may be unreceptive to their future appeals.

Expansion of PACs

New federal campaign-finance legislation in the 1970s encouraged expansion in the number of political action committees (PACs), discussed in greater detail in chapter 12. PACs are the political campaign arms of business, labor, professional, and other interest groups, legally entitled to raise funds on a voluntary basis and to make contributions to favored candidates and parties. The number of these special-interest-group organizations grew from just 600 in 1974 to over 4,000 at the end of 1987, according to a report issued by the Federal Elections Commission. PACs are now a major vehicle for bringing private money into electoral campaigns (Figure 11.1).

Organization

There has been increasing attention in recent years to the importance of sophisticated formal organization as a group resource—such as using computers in extensive direct-mail campaigns, and building coalitions of groups to better integrate lobbying efforts. Interest groups

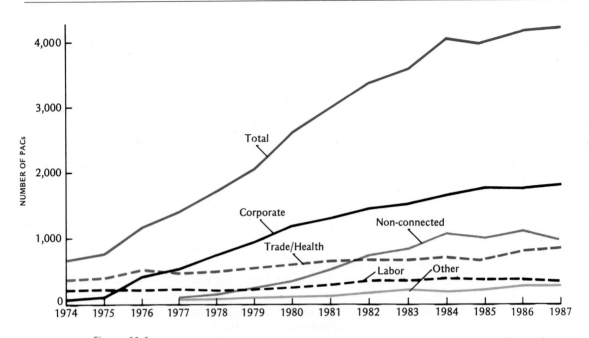

Figure 11.1
Growth of Political
Action Committees

Source: Federal Elections Commission Annual Report of January, 1982; FEC releases of January 20, 1986, and January 18, 1988.

are better organized today then ever before, and thus the disadvantages of ineffectively organized groups are greater than ever before.

Organization is an even more critical resource because American government is so fragmented and awash with contending claims and interests. Getting one's case across in this noisy, cluttered, diverse, and pluralistic setting requires planning and systematic effort. The old stereotype of the effective lobbyist as one who knows the right people and meets with them periodically to cut deals is increasingly out of touch with a political environment that puts a premium on careful organization in group dealings with a big and complex government.

Intensity of Interest

When a legislator casts a vote that a group of his constituents favors, he often hears nothing about it from them. But when he goes against some deeply felt interest, even if it is one held by only a distinct minority, the complaints are loud and persisting. Constantly bombarded, even the most principled legislator takes pains to limit criticism wherever he can without doing violence to his basic policy commitments. If an interest group has the capacity to hurt him politically, the legislator has a vested interest in placating it, especially if he can do so relatively easily. This helps explain why groups with

The National Rifle Association has been an active opponent of gun-control legislation.

JAMESON PARKER: Husband, Father, Actor, Hunter, Member of the National Rifle Association.

"Until a few years ago, I had hardly touched a gun. And I certainly didn't know much about the NRA. But when I began hunting and target shooting, a gun store owner told me, 'The first thing you ought to do is join the NRA.' Frankly, I was hesitant. But he gave me some NRA literature and I began to see the NRA isn't what I perceived it to be.

"I realized the NRA is a bunch of intelligent people that stand for the positive aspects of gun ownership. They teach gun safety. They represent the millions of law-abiding hunters, gun collectors and competitive shooters in this country. Thank God they do. I love guns. I love hunting. I believe in my right to defend my home and my family. But I also accept the responsibilities that accompany these freedoms.

"You can tell my image of the NRA has really changed. With my membership, I hope I can change a few minds, too, about who the NRA really is. It's people like me." **I'm the NRA.**

The NRA's Hunter Services Division offers programs and publications for hunter safety and education, including the comprehensive "Basic Hunter's Guide." If you would like more information about our publications, or would like to join the NRA, write Harlon Carter, Executive Vice President, P.O. Box 37484, Dept. JP-20, Washington, D.C. 20013.

intensely held interests often get their way on questions where a majority of the public and a majority of the legislators themselves, in their own private judgments, hold to the other side. For example, public opinion surveys have shown that large majorities of the American public favor stronger gun-control legislation.[8] Yet congressional efforts to get stronger laws, opposed by groups like the National Rifle Association (NRA), have failed. This is not because the legislators doubt

[8] Gallup, for example, asked in April 1986: "In general, do you feel the laws covering the sale of handguns should be made more strict, less strict, or kept as they are now?" Sixty-one percent said they wanted the laws to be stricter, only 8 percent less strict; 31 percent favored keeping legislation about as it is now. Gallup poll, April 11–14, 1986.

the polls or have been personally convinced by NRA lobbyists of the inherent wisdom of the latter's views; nor is it a result of bribery or other illicit means of persuasion. In a system where central party organization is weak and individual legislators operate largely on their own, there are strong incentives to placate interest groups. The NRA's intensity of concern, compared to the less focused involvement of most of the public, gives it a capacity to cause trouble. Congressmen are sorely tempted to appease the group unless they are strongly committed to gun control.

Interest groups sometimes "target" senators and representatives whose stands on issues they find especially unsatisfactory; that is, they commit resources to defeating them in the next election. These efforts may at times contribute to their desired end, but at least as often, it seems, they backfire. Many voters resent it when an interest group wages electoral warfare on their congressman. Groups with intensively held interests gain their major successes in a different way, by convincing wavering legislators who do not have strong feelings on an issue that it just is not worth antagonizing the group on the matter.

"Targeting" political opponents

Striking Alliances

Some groups pursue objectives that fit with prevailing views of the populace, while others cannot count on such public support. Some interests are able to call upon strong allies, while others find themselves quite isolated when they try to advance their policy goals. Even if other major resources, such as money and organization, could be equalized, a group committed to promoting more rapid economic growth would have an advantage over one that wants to extend the rights of homosexuals; the former rides the tide of favorable public opinion and has many allies, while the latter bucks public opinion and can count on little help from most other groups. The literature on interest-group activity probably places too much emphasis on the mechanical features of interest representation. The type of interest pursued is by itself very important, and groups fortunate enough to favor policies that strike a responsive chord elsewhere in the society thereby enjoy a major advantage.

TACTICS AND STRATEGIES OF INTEREST GROUPS

On every major question of American public policy, and on a great many relatively minor ones, interest groups work to persuade governmental officials to take actions consistent with what the groups think should be done. This may mean passing a law, imposing or removing a regulation, funding a program, changing the tax code, committing the country to some new objective, or countless other actions within the scope of modern government. Interest-group tactics and strategies are as diverse as the objectives for which groups intervene in public life.

Legislating for the Environment: A Continuing Interest-Group Struggle

The Clean Air Act

Some of the hottest and most interesting interest-group battles of recent years have occurred on environmental issues. In the latter part of the 1960s American public opinion began to swing rather sharply in favor of greater national efforts at making the country's environment safer and cleaner than it had been. Environmental groups such as the Sierra Club, the National Audubon Society, and the National Wildlife Federation became active proponents of new legislation. On the other side, business corporations and related associations often took issue with the environmentalists' proposals—claiming, for example, that the legislation would impose economic hardships on them and would harm the U.S. economy generally. One major piece of legislation, the Clean Air Act, prompted a continuing, almost classic interest-group campaign. The contending groups utilized many of the tactics that have become staples in contemporary lobbying. Looming in the background have been large questions of policy direction and compelling public interests.

The legislation. In 1970, Congress passed the Clean Air Act, which required the Environmental Protection Agency (EPA) to determine what concentrations could be safely permitted for seven major air pollutants, and then to see to it that these levels were not exceeded. The act was intended to gain major reductions in air pollution in order to promote the health of the general public, meet the special needs of such groups as the elderly and those with health problems affected by pollution, and prevent pollution damage to crops, livestock, buildings, and so on.[9]

These general objectives seem straightforward, but in fact the act is highly complex, and the detailed regulations issued by the EPA pursuant to its responsibilities under the law are even more complicated. Citizens who want to understand fully the controversies that

---

[9]It should be noted that air pollution control legislation goes back as far as 1955, when technical assistance was first offered to the states by the federal government in their efforts to improve air quality. The original Clean Air Act (CAA), passed in 1963 and amended in 1965 and 1966, was for the most part ineffective, since it depended solely on the voluntary cooperation of the states. The Clean Air Act (Amendments) of 1970 was the first comprehensive legislation dealing with the problem of air pollution nationally. Standards were set, and the newly constituted Environmental Protection Agency was charged with administration of the program. Amendments in 1977 established penalties for noncompliance and gave statutory force to EPA policies.

have ensued around this statute must master such terms and acronyms as NAAQS (National Ambient Air Quality Standards), PSD (Prevention of Significant Deterioration) provisions, RACT (Reasonably Available Controlled Technology), BACT (Best Available Controlled Technology), LAER (Lowest Achievable Emission Rate), and SIP (State Implementation Plans), among others.

The argument. The debate over the act has not involved its general goals but rather has centered around various standards enforced to achieve the goals, such as standards for the acceptable level of auto emissions. It has also involved tradeoff questions: How do you ensure environmental cleanliness without excessively obtrusive regulation? How do you protect the environment without setting back other important policy goals such as economic growth, creation of new jobs, and greater use of coal and other domestic energy resources? Many groups, including virtually all affected industries—auto, chemical, and oil companies, some trade unions, state agencies involved in implementation of the EPA standards, and others—had concluded by 1981 that the act unreasonably hampered some legitimate economic objectives and produced regulatory confusion. But many other groups—including virtually all environmentalist associations, some trade unions, government-reform groups like the League of Women Voters, and others—feared that business-led efforts to amend the act would go too far and set back the cause of a clean and healthful environment.

Debate over standards to achieve environmental goals

Business groups said they wanted "to reform the Act in certain limited ways, with a view toward boosting GNP and employment and restoring the nation's competitive position in world markets."[10] They favored such specific changes as modification of the emissions standards and deadlines affecting the auto industry, and an end to the "off-set" rule affecting the building of new plants. Under the "off-set" rule, any company wanting to build in an area where the air did not meet pollution standards not only had to install the best possible pollution control equipment, but also had to buy "emission off-sets" from companies already operating in the area. That is, the incoming business had to get other companies to reduce their emissions by at least as much as the new plant would add to the overall volume of pollutants being released in the area.

Business perspectives

Environmental groups wanted to avoid any weakening of the clean air legislation. They wanted to retain the "off-set" policy. They wanted to keep strict deadlines for compliance. They feared that, in the words of Democratic Congressman Henry A. Waxman of California, chairman of the House subcommittees charged with environmental legis-

Environmental group perspectives

[10] Statement of the National Environmental Development Association, as printed in *Environment*, July/August 1981, p. 20.

lation, the industry-backed amendments were, cumulatively, "a blueprint for the destruction of our clean air laws."[11]

Tactics: Building coalitions. A key feature of group tactics in the clean air fight was the formation of formal coalitions. Many corporations, trade associations, labor unions, and environmental groups lobbied actively on an individual basis. But, in addition, they worked together in organized alliances for and against amending the act. On one side, various business and trade associations—including the Chamber of Commerce of the United States, the American Petroleum Institute, the National Coal Association, the Iron and Steel Institute, the Chemical Manufacturers' Association, the National Association of Manufacturers, the Business Roundtable, the Paper Institute, and the Edison Electric Institute—channeled much of their activity through the Clean Air Working Group. Another influential coalition was the National Environmental Development Association/Clean Air Act Project (NEDA/CAAP). Many of the major businesses that banded together in this alliance had obvious and direct stakes in applications of the legislation—oil companies like Exxon, chemical companies like du Pont, and automobile manufacturers like General Motors. But special effort was made to enlist other organizations that didn't have such immediate interests. International Business Machines (IBM) was brought into NEDA/CAAP, a nice addition because it was so little affected by the act: Computers are a "clean" industry. The Building and Construction Trade Unions, AFL-CIO, were also included, attesting to labor-business agreement on the need for changes in the legislation.

On the other side, many environmental groups joined together to form the National Clean Air Coalition (NCAC). Represented here was the core of the environmental movement—Friends of the Earth, the Sierra Club, the National Wildlife Federation, the Wilderness Society, and others. NCAC was also at pains to diversify its coalition, and it brought in such "disinterested" groups as the League of Women Voters and a number of trade unions, including the United Steel Workers of America and the Amalgamated Clothing and Textile Workers' Union. (See Table 11.5).

The establishment of coalitions of interest groups on behalf of broad policy positions is by no means unique to the battle over amending the Clean Air Act. It has become a generally important part of lobbying. Just as trade associations appeared to pool the resources of individual companies, so group coalitions have developed to integrate lobbying on behalf of broad policy goals. One prominent coalition or "working group" which has operated in Washington in recent years is the Trucking Alliance. It brought together in favor of dereg-

Marginal notes:
Two contending coalitions

Coalition-building: essential to lobbying

[11]Remarks by Representative Henry A. Waxman, as quoted in the *New York Times*, June 20, 1981, p. 10.

Table 11.5
Contending Groups in the Battle over the Clean Air Act

Don't amend the Act *The National Clean Air Coalition*	*Amend the Act* *The National Environmental Development* *Association/Clean Air Act Project*
Amalgamated Clothing & Textile Workers	Allied Chemical Corporation
Americans for Democratic Action	Ashland Oil, Inc.
American Lung Association	Atlantic Richfield Company
Center for Auto Safety	Building and Construction Trades Department, AFL-CIO
Citizens for a Better Environment	Campbell Soup Company
Environmental Action	Celanese Corporation
Environmental Defense Fund	Chevron U.S.A., Inc.
Environmental Policy Center	Consolidation Coal Company
Friends of the Earth	Crown Zellerbach Corporation
International Association of Machinists & Aerospace Workers	Dow Chemical Company
Izaak Walton League of America	Dravo Corporation
League of American Bicyclists	E. I. du Pont de Nemours & Company
League of Women Voters of the United States	Exxon Company, U.S.A.
Sierra Club	Fluor Corporation
National Audubon Society	General Electric Company
National Consumer League	General Motors Corporation
National Farmers Union	Getty Oil Corporation
National Parks & Conservation Association	International Business Corporation
National Wildlife Federation	International Paper Company
Natural Resources Defense Council	Kaiser Aluminum & Chemical Corporation
Oil, Chemical & Atomic Association	Mobil Oil Corporation
United Steelworkers of America	Occidental Petroleum Corporation
Wilderness Society	Pennzoil Company
Western Organization of Resource Councils	Phillips Petroleum Company
	PPG Industries, Inc.
	Procter & Gamble Company
	Shell Oil Company
	Standard Oil Company (Indiana)
	Standard Oil Company (Ohio)
	Stauffer Chemical Company
	Sun Company, Inc.
	Tenneco Chemicals, Inc.
	Texaco Inc.
	Texas Oil & Gas Corporation
	Union Oil Company of California
	Westvaco
	Weyerhaeuser Company

ulation of the trucking industry such normally contending groups as Common Cause and Ralph Nader's Congress Watch on the one hand, and the National Association of Manufacturers and the American Conservative Union on the other. Another coalition is the Longshore Action Committee, which united 74 different groups, from the National Association of Manufacturers to the American Farm Bureau Federation, on behalf of legislation curtailing a federal program that compensates longshoremen, and workers in such related industries as shipbuilding and harbor construction, for on-the-job injuries. The Consumer Issues Working Group lobbied for eight years (successfully) against establishment of a federal Consumer Protection Agency. The Alaska Coalition, an alliance of environmental groups, secured passage of legislation to preserve from development large segments of the state of Alaska.

Various factors have contributed to the increasing recourse to carefully organized coalitions, in place of the more independent and loosely coordinated lobbying in the past. For example, power in Congress, once concentrated in the leadership and committee chairmen, was dispersed much more widely among the membership by the reforms of the late 1960s and 1970s. At the same time, congressional staff grew tremendously. Lobbyists found that they had to influence many more people to accomplish their goals. This suggested that they pool resources.[12] The use of coalitions as in lobbying over Clean Air Act revisions was also a step by interest groups to avoid speaking with a babble of conflicting voices. The coalition approach required groups to get their houses in order before going to Congress. Extensive interaction and compromise are necessary to hammer out reasonably united coalition positions. In the process, a whole new layer gets added to lobbying. Interest groups must spend much more time lobbying each other to build plausible coalitions and formulate common legislative approaches.

Tactics: Finding allies where you can. We tend to think of business and labor as opposing interest groups, and they often are. But as it turned out, many businesses and labor unions shared an interest in amending the Clean Air Act. Automobile manufacturers felt that the legislation created unfair burdens for their industry; so, too, did the United Auto Workers' Union. The UAW is a liberal union and usually aligns itself against the business community. But the financial troubles of auto manufacturing have meant financial troubles for auto workers, and the UAW committed itself to working with business to modify the act.

Most important legislative battles involve bipartisan support for proposed changes and bipartisan opposition to them. This was the case with the Clean Air Act amendments. For example, the bill containing amendments strongly backed by industry (H.R. 5252) was introduced by six members of the House of Representatives: three Democrats and three Republicans. Among them were John Dingell, a liberal Democrat from the sixteenth congressional district of Michigan, covering parts of Detroit as well as the city of Dearborn; and James T. Broyhill, a conservative Republican from the tenth congres-

Bipartisan alliances

---

[12] Bill Keller, "Coalitions and Associations Transformed Strategy, Methods of Lobbying in Washington," *Congressional Quarterly*, January 23, 1982, p. 119.

sional district of North Carolina, a largely rural district including the western Piedmont section of the state. Dingell served as chairman of the Committee on Energy and Commerce—the parent committee for environmental legislation—and Broyhill was the ranking minority member of that committee. Such bipartisan alliances on controversial measures are rare in the legislatures of most democratic countries, but they are the rule in the U.S. Congress, where party ranks are broken with abandon. Interest groups understand the importance of ad hoc legislative alliances, and they seek out "friends" on particular measures where they can find them. A liberal Democrat like Dingell would not usually be found working in tandem with a conservative Republican like Broyhill. But in this case the UAW, whose members are a big part of John Dingell's constituency, favored the same changes that industry wanted.

Tactics: Providing information. Congressmen, required to move from one issue to another, need information and technical guidance on complex issues like the Clean Air Act revisions. Interest groups are more than happy to provide them. The Business Roundtable, for example, financed a $400,000 study of various proposed changes in the clean air legislation. The Chamber of Commerce of the United States issued detailed "suggestions for improving the Act." On the other side, the National Clean Air Coalition set forth its positions and recommendations.

The need for policy guidance

Congress wanted more than technical information; it wanted policy guidance. Many congressmen, not just those notably friendly to industry, wanted to know what aspects of the act most troubled business. In the same way congressmen wanted to know which of the proposed changes especially bothered environmental groups. "You can't have everything you want. What are your priorities?" This was an important part of the information exchange between the contending groups and Congress.

Tactics: Grassroots lobbying. During the debate on amending the Clean Air Act, interest groups made countless representations to congressmen. But they also sought to mobilize individuals and groups back home to communicate with their representatives. Environmental groups worked actively through their state and local networks. One very active business group, the U.S. Chamber of Commerce, devoted extensive resources to rallying municipal chambers of commerce around the country, to get them involved in trying to persuade their local congressmen to support amending the act.

Tactics: Public opinion. Polling is an increasingly important part of lobbying efforts. Groups vie with one another in telling legislators that they should do what the group wants because it is also what the

Polls as "weapons"

people want. We saw in chapter 10 that the way questions are worded can affect the opinions people voice on complicated policy issues. Recognizing this, interest groups sometimes sponsor or otherwise encourage polls where questions are worded so as to prompt the desired answers. Or they emphasize only part of the answers people give— the part favorable to the group's position. The object is to get a message to legislators: "Polls are showing that big majorities of Americans want this action taken. If you don't go along, you or your party are going to pay the price for defying the will of the people."

Public opinion on the Clean Air Act

Sometimes an interest group does not have an incentive to bend information from opinion surveys. Sometimes the people really do want what the group wants. And sometimes the issue is not one where politicians are likely to believe there is firm public opinion on either side, as when the questions are too narrow and technical. But more and more in big policy controversies, poll findings are being manipulated to fit in with a larger lobbying effort. This was the case in the debate over amending the Clean Air Act. Both industry and environmental groups commissioned new surveys and stressed results that seemed favorable to their respective sides. The U.S. Chamber of Commerce hired the Opinion Research Corporation (ORC) to conduct a national survey on the act in late 1981. "Most Americans support changing the nation's Clean Air Act," the Chamber argued in interpreting the ORC poll findings.[13] House Democrats opposed to amending the act brought in pollster Louis Harris to assure legislators that his surveys showed Americans saying, "Keep your cotton picking hands off that environmental law."[14]

Who won? The argument over the clean air legislation had all of the ingredients of a classic _High Noon_ interest-group confrontation. The stakes were large: the requirements of a growing economy on one hand and vital health and aesthetic needs on the other. Two big coalitions of interest groups went into battle—industry versus environmentalists—each claiming to be on the side of the angels. Each used its full complement of lobbying tactics. The public was both interested and confused.

Party split on the Act

Each of the two political parties was internally divided on the question of amending the Clean Air Act. The bill that industry favored, H.R. 5252, had the strong backing of the Reagan administration. President Reagan urged amendments that "while protecting the environment, will make it possible for industry to rebuild its productive base and create more jobs." But H.R. 5252 also had the support of some key House Democrats, including John Dingell, chairman of the Energy and Commerce Committee. On the other side, opposed to

[13] News release of the Chamber of Commerce of the United States, December 8, 1981.
[14] Testimony by Louis Harris before the Subcommittee on Health and Environment, U.S. House of Representatives, October 15, 1981.

Some groups organize to confront problems in their local communities. Here, residents express their opposition to a proposed dumpsite for radon-contaminated soil.

the bill, was Dingell's Democratic colleague, Henry Waxman, the chair of the Subcommittee on Health and the Environment. Many Senate Republicans were also opposed to the Reagan administration and industry position. The bill reported out by the Senate Environment and Public Works Committee made only modest changes in the Clean Air Act and was generally supported by environmentalists.

What was the final outcome of this long interest-group battle? The environmental groups won hands down. The House Energy and Commerce Committee was deadlocked, and H.R. 5252 was never reported out. No amendments of any kind passed either the House or the Senate. While environmental groups would have liked to enact changes of their own to further strengthen clean air standards, their main goal was to resist industry-backed changes that they thought weak-

Environmentalists win

ened the legislation; in this they had complete success. The effort to amend the Clean Air Act in the ninety-seventh Congress (1981–83) ended with Congress sharply divided over what to do, and thus making no changes at all.

The Next Stage: Acid Rain

After beating back industry and Reagan administration efforts to overhaul the Clean Air Act, the environmental lobby went on the offensive, its efforts centering on proposals to control acid rain. A by-product of coal-fired plants concentrated in the midwest, acid rain is blamed for damage to fishlife and forests, particularly in the northeastern United States and Canada. Emissions of sulfur dioxide and nitrogen oxides are the culprits. These gases react chemically in the atmosphere, raising the acidity of rain water.

The proposed legislation to curb acid rain itself got stalemated in Congress. As Henry Waxman, chair of the Energy and Commerce Subcommittee on Health and the Environment, noted, "as a general proposition, it's easier to stop legislation than pass legislation." Utilities and coal, steel, and automobile producers in the midwest opposed the suggested remedies. Reflecting this, the most active congressional opponents of the proposed legislation were John Dingell (D-Michigan), chairman of the House Energy and Commerce Committee, whose home state is the leading auto producer; Edward Madigan (R-Illinois), whose state produces high-sulfur coal; and Thomas Luken (D-Ohio), whose Ohio Valley district contains many coal-fired power plants. "This is a sectional bill," Lukens charged, "and it is people from Ohio and Pennsylvania and places like that who are going to bear the brunt." On the Senate side, the proposed legislation had a powerful opponent in Majority Leader Robert Byrd (D-West Virginia), whose state is a lead producer of coal that has a high sulfur content.

In 1988, a new push was made to break the six-year deadlock on acid rain legislation. The proposed statute would require states to submit to the Environmental Protection Agency plans for cutting sulfur dioxide and nitrogen oxide emissions by specified amounts. If a state failed to submit an acceptable plan within 27 months of the legislation's enactment, the law would automatically impose control standards on each plant in the state.

Once again, though, no agreement was reached on acid rain legislation. "I tried my best, but we didn't quite make it this year," remarked George J. Mitchell (D-Maine), the author of the Senate bill. Mitchell had negotiated compromises with Senate Democratic leader Robert C. Byrd (W.Va.) who for years had opposed tough acid rain legislation because he feared the consequences for his state's coal

Stalemate over acid rain legislation

industry and miners. But the compromises wound up satisfying no one. Environmentalists were especially unhappy with what they described as a substantially weakened bill.

Contrasting Types of Interest Group Efforts

The big interest-group battles over environmental legislation reveal many facets of interest-group activities. But no case study can illustrate the whole range; in other policy areas, group objectives, competition, and tactics are different.

Narrower objectives. The clean air debate involved broad and highly visible issues. The public may not have understood the technical points being debated, but the basic controversies around the competing claims of environmental and economic objectives were of general public concern. In contrast, many instances of interest-group intervention involve narrower issues which, though important to specific groups, do not pose questions central to the entire polity. Independent service station operators try to get Congress to pass legislation prohibiting the major oil companies from operating service stations. Dairy farmers seek to maintain a federal price support-program for milk products they cannot sell at a set price. The domestic shipbuilding industry wants to continue to receive federal subsidies initiated to make U.S. shipbuilding more competitive with foreign yards.

The "10-5-3" plan   Sometimes the financial stake in seemingly narrow group objectives is very large. In 1978 a number of business groups came together to set priorities for changes in tax provisions affecting corporations. Meeting around a breakfast table at the Sheraton-Carlton Hotel in Washington, representatives of the major business federations settled upon an accelerated depreciation plan as their prime objective. The "10-5-3" plan, as it came to be known, referred to the length (in years) of new depreciation schedules for buildings, equipment, and vehicles, respectively. Basically, the new schedules allowed for faster tax write-offs. In 1981, having convinced the Reagan administration and congressional Democrats and Republicans to back "10-5-3," the business coalition saw its prized provision written into the new tax legislation. Billions of tax dollars were at issue and "10-5-3" was virtually a password in the business community. But the public, and many informed observers, never saw broad questions of policy direction in the accelerated depreciation proposals. Press coverage was minimal outside of business periodicals. Few Americans knew anything at all about the "10-5-3" depreciation plan. There simply was not any public opinion on it. Only a small proportion of the efforts interest groups make to influence policy receive significant press coverage and are the subjects of relatively focused popular opinion.

No battle of the groups. On occasion, as with some environmental legislation, elaborate armies of contending groups organize on each side of an issue. Working with friendly congressmen, each of these coalitions tries to bring undecided legislators to its side. But in many other cases, most of the organization and activity takes place on one side only. For example, the business interests favoring "10-5-3" did not confront an opposing army of groups wanting to block their proposed changes. Much of the conflict leading up to enactment of "10-5-3" was within the business community itself, as different associations had different tax priorities that had to be adjusted before business could speak with a reasonably united voice. Interest-group conflict isn't uncommon, of course, but the elaborate mobilization of contending groups that happened with the Clean Air Act revisions occurs on a limited number of issues.

Lobbying the executive branch and the judiciary. In many instances, lobbying efforts center not on Congress (or a state legislature) but on executive branch departments and agencies. Earlier in American history, when the enterprise of government was less developed, the scope of policy initiatives by administrative agencies was tightly circumscribed. Today, however, government does so much and programs are of such complexity that program administration is often a central part of policy formation. Executive bureaucracies have become a main arena of interest-group activity.

Lobbying reaches the judiciary as well. As we saw in chapter 9, a primary means of group intervention in the judicial arena comes

Judicial test cases

through *test cases.* The National Association for the Advancement of Colored People (NAACP) Legal Defense Fund has provided skilled attorneys and directed a long series of court challenges to racial discrimination. Similarly, the American Civil Liberties Union (ACLU) has concentrated its efforts in the courts rather than in the executive and legislative branches. In recent years, many of the newer public-interest groups, including those concerned with environmental issues, have also relied heavily on litigation: for example, by seeking court rulings to restrict the construction of nuclear power plants or to extend the scope of governmental regulation under environmental statutes.

The importance of "standing"

The highly technical issue of *standing* (as we saw in chapter 9) has a bearing on the extent to which public-interest groups can advance policy goals through litigation. In order to have standing to sue, a party must show that he has sustained or is threatened with real injury. The more stringent the requirements the courts set, the harder it is for groups to mount judicial challenges to statutes they oppose. On the whole, federal courts have over the last decade shifted a bit toward stiffer requirements of demonstrated injury in order for standing to be granted in challenges brought by public-interest groups, a development that reflects the impact of Reagan appointees to the courts.[15]

Amicus curiae briefs

Interest groups pursue their objectives in the judicial arena in other ways, apart from initiating and supporting litigation: They "speak" to the judges and try to persuade them to adopt philosophies that the groups find attractive. Courts are a special part of the political process, and the etiquette for group attempts at persuasion is different for them than for other governmental institutions. When a group wants to convey its policy views to Congress, it sends its representatives directly to the legislators, or it may take out full-page ads in leading newspapers. Judges are not supposed to be lobbied in such ways, and for the most part they are not. To get the message through, a prime vehicle is the filing of *amicus curiae* (friend of the court) briefs. In a major case, it is not uncommon to find scores of interest groups filing *amicus* briefs on behalf of one or the other of the primary litigants. These briefs contain legal argument, but they are also a formal mechanism through which groups make known to judges their policy interpretations and preferences. The use of *amicus* briefs in important civil rights cases is discussed further in chapter 15.

GROUPS AND AMERICAN DEMOCRACY

As noted earlier, Tocqueville argued in the 1830s that Americans were unusually active in interest groups and voluntary associations. Con-

---

[15] See Rochelle L. Stanfield, "Out-Standing in Court," *National Journal*, February 13, 1988, pp. 388–91.

temporary studies come to this same conclusion. Gabriel Almond and Sidney Verba found a quarter-century ago that a higher proportion of citizens belonged to voluntary associations in the United States than in Britain, West Germany, Italy, or Mexico.[16] Americans were much more likely, moreover, to have multiple group memberships. A later study by Sidney Verba and Norman Nye showed 32 percent of Americans as active members in community organizations, compared to 15 percent in the Netherlands, 11 percent in Japan, and 9 percent in Austria.[17] The sheer numbers of groups and the vigorous roles they play are a distinctive feature of U.S. experience. Why is this so?

Conditions for Active Group Participation

One would expect relatively free and open societies to have more extensive group participation than those with authoritarian regimes. But, as we have seen, even in established democracies like Britain, the Netherlands, West Germany, and Italy, activity lags behind that exhibited in the United States. A highly educated and affluent populace has the time, training, confidence, and other resources necessary for group organization, much more than the public of a poor country, where educational and communications resources are restricted. But, again, the United States is not alone in having the requisite education, sources of information, and economic position. Explanation for the unusually extensive group organization in America, compared to other industrial democracies, lies elsewhere.

Diversity

Diversity. One factor seems to be the heterogeneity of American society. James Madison felt in 1787 that one of the virtues of a large republic like the one provided for by the Constitution was the capacity to sustain a more diverse set of groups or factions to compete against each other. American experience has borne out Madison's expectations. The United States comprises a great variety of groups— ethnic, religious, cultural, regional, and more.

Individualism

Individualism. We noted at the beginning of this chapter that Tocqueville thought the strength of American individualism contributed importantly to the country's vigorous group life. One might think the opposite: that practitioners of rugged individualism would be social and political loners. Tocqueville saw that, in the United States, a nation of self-confident and assertive individuals would produce a welter of

[16] Gabriel A. Almond and Sidney Verba, *The Civic Culture: Political Attitudes and Democracy in Five Nations* (Princeton, N.J.: Princeton Univ. Press, 1963), pp. 301–2.
[17] Norman H. Nye and Sidney Verba, "Political Participation," in Fred I. Greenstein and Nelson W. Polsby, eds., *Handbook of Political Science* (Reading, Mass.: Addison-Wesley, 1975), vol. 4, pp. 24–25.

group action, as people banded together to accomplish various objectives. Passivity, or the absence of a sense of individual efficacy, are the true deterrents to a vigorous associational life. "I'm important—and I can do something" spurs the formation of voluntary associations.

Decentralization. Groups organize around units where decisions get made, and governmental arrangements are a key factor determining what these units are. Centralized governmental systems, like those of Britain and France, produce interest-group centralization. Britain has, for instance, just one national organization of farmers and one major business association. There is no counterpart in France to the fifty state AFL-CIO units, for the simple reason that there is no counterpart in France to the fifty states.

Autonomy. In many democracies, major groups are closely tied to the political parties. For example, the largest French labor organization, the Confédération Génerale du Travail (CGT), has been controlled by the French Communist party. Another French labor federation—Force Ouvrière—is directed by the Socialist party. In Great Britain, the umbrella trade union federation, the Trades Union Congress (TUC), is closely tied to the Labour party. The British and French cases are quite different in one regard: In France the parties dominate the labor unions, while in Britain the reverse is true, the unions are a major force guiding the Labour party. Neither case, however, is comparable to the American situation where autonomous labor unions pursue their own interests. Many AFL-CIO officials feel closer to the Democratic party, of course, and often back its candidates, but the party and the unions are truly independent. This fits the general U.S. pattern of interest-group autonomy.

Groups and Group Power

We have seen the propensity of the populace for vigorous group participation and the central role that well-organized and well-financed interest groups play in governmental decision making. What remains is to examine the central issue of group power as it relates to democratic governance. Specifically, are groups too strong? Do the maneuverings of special interests threaten the public interest? The research on these questions support a complex conclusion: Interest groups and their active involvement in political life are 1) inevitable, 2) desirable, and 3) a continuing source of problems.

Inevitable. Interest groups are inevitable for the basic reasons Madison noted in *Federalist Paper* 10. The presence of liberty, essential and desirable, ensures an abundance of self-serving groups. And it would be utopian to think that this country could have dynamic groups and associations without some of them acquiring resources that give them a competitive advantage over others. While the United States need not adopt an "anything goes" posture before the claims of organized interests, both the active presence of interest groups and the disproportionate resources of some of them are inevitable features of American democracy.

Desirable. Many proponents of democracy find interest groups not only inevitable but also desirable. Committed to popular sovereignty, democrats must applaud conditions whereby bodies of people who share political interests seek their expression and realization. Advocates of democracy may condemn certain forms of group activity, but they can hardly dispute that interest groups are the primary means through which popular sovereignty is realized. We might contrast this with totalitarian societies, where there is a continuing aversion to interest-group activity. Essential to the definition of totalitarianism, as that concept is applied to national socialism in Hitler's Germany or to Soviet communism, is the sustained effort to stamp out all forms of intermediate group life that might challenge the regime and organize people for independent political activity. On December 13, 1981, army and police in Poland began applying massive force to suppress Solidarity as an independent trade union. The mere existence of this strong interest group, independent of the regime, was a denial of the regime's exclusive claim to represent the interests of the Polish people. The presence of strong independent interest groups imposes important limits on the power of government.

Democratic theory has long emphasized the essential place of a vigorous system of interest groups and other mediating structures through which the varied interests making up a society are organized and expressed.[18] Through groups people are given meaningful identities, and the alienation of mass society is reduced.[19] Organized groups also play important roles in articulating the demands and needs of the many diverse interests within a population.[20]

Problem causing. From James Madison on, the operation of organized interests has prompted concern among Americans attentive to the health of their country's democracy. In the early twentieth century, a political movement known as Progressivism grew up with a prime objective of purging excessive interest group influence from political

Interest groups and democracy *(margin note)*

Progressivism *(margin note)*

[18] For a thoughtful general statement of the essential place of interest groups in a democratic society, see Ernest Barker, *Reflections on Government* (New York: Oxford University Press, 1958).
[19] See, for example, William Kornhauser, *The Politics of Mass Society* (Glencoe, Ill.: Free Press, 1959); and Seymour Martin Lipset, *Political Man* (Garden City, N.Y.: Anchor Books, 1963), especially chaps. 1 and 2.
[20] David B. Truman, *The Governmental Process* (New York: Knopf, 1951).

parties, legislatures, and governmental administration locally and nationally. The Progressives saw American democracy dominated by a struggle between "the interests" and "the people," and they sought political reforms that would shift the balance of power from the former to the latter. The Progressives were especially troubled by what they considered the excessive power of big business interests—"the trusts"—as they had developed in such industries as oil, steel, and banking. In 1913, Woodrow Wilson, just elected president and with ties to the Progressive movement, issued a statement denouncing the role of special interests in current legislation.

Woodrow Wilson on special interests

> I think that the public ought to know the extraordinary exertions being made by the lobby in Washington to gain recognition for certain alterations of the tariff bill. Washington has seldom seen so numerous, so industrious, or so insidious a lobby. . . . It is of serious interest to the country that the people at large should have no lobby and be voiceless in these matters, while great bodies of astute men seek to create an artificial opinion and to overcome the interests of the public for their private profit. . . . The Government in all its branches ought to be relieved from this tolerable burden and this constant interruption to the calm progress of debate.[21]

Concern over special interests today

Americans still lament the role of pressure groups and pressure politics. Citizens have complained as much in recent years about the power of "Big Oil" as their counterparts seven and eight decades ago did about "the trusts." Lobbying is considered an often unsavory activity that carries the onus of excessive influence by big private money. There is a vivid perception of too-cozy relationships between interest groups and politicians, of wheeling and dealing behind closed doors for ends antithetical to the public interest. Three different concerns are often tangled in the general indictment of excessive group influence. One is the fear that some interests may actually come to dominate American government as a coherent power elite. A second is that groups are able to take over not the entire government but rather a great number of specific policy areas where they have special interests and get their way with little general public scrutiny or control. The third concern is about the fact that some interests are much better organized and represented than others.

Group tyranny. Madison addressed the problem of group tyranny directly, and he and the other framers of the Constitution thought they had found a satisfactory, long-term answer. We saw in chapter 4 that their answer was to so divide power, and check and balance it, that group tyranny would be impossible. A government of dispersed authority operating in a diverse and pluralistic society would be sufficient to maintain popular sovereignty and individual liberty.

[21] *State Papers and Addresses by Woodrow Wilson, President of the United States* (New York: George H. Doran, 1918), pp. 9–10.

Boom Town

—from THE HERBLOCK BOOK (Beacon Press, 1952)

Policy making in the iron triangle. Political scientist Grant McConnell dismissed the idea of power-elite domination, observing that the American interest-group world is highly fragmented and decentralized. Political organization in the United States, he noted, has been based persistently on "small constituencies."[22] The fragmented groups of small constituencies have

> on the whole had limited ends; their tactics have been limited and often more economic than political. Where they have been openly political, they have relied upon group self-help through the exercise of well-isolated segments of public authority rather than upon action through political parties and elections.[23]

Madison wanted political organization based on small constituencies to serve as a check on group power, and today the United States has that arrangement to a degree that might surprise even its brilliant proponent.

The present problem grows out of the very success of the Madisonian solution. As Americans have come in recent decades to accept an enlarged mission for government, thousands of new lobbies have developed around the expansive governmental system. As the Advi-

[22] Grant McConnell, *Private Power and American Democracy* (New York: Knopf, 1966), p. 342.
[23] Ibid., p. 345.

sory Commission on Intergovernmental Relations has noted, "Every program, every protective regulation, every tax loophole appears to have acquired its coterie of organized beneficiaries." The proliferating interest groups found the traditional dispersion of authority much to their liking. For, while the whole of government was impervious to control by any group, the many separate parts proved to be uniquely susceptible to special-interest pressures.

Fragmenting power and proliferating special interests

We saw in chapter 8 how interest groups, congressional subcommittees, and executive-agency bureaus have operated relatively closed policy systems in many discrete program areas. "Molecular government," Joseph Califano called it when he was secretary of Health, Education, and Welfare and thus unusually well placed to observe the problem. "Washington has become a city of political molecules," he observed, "with fragmentation of power, and often authority and responsibility, among increasingly narrow, what's-in-it-for-me interest groups and their responsive counterparts in the executive and legislative branches."[24] National policy is too often made not for the nation but for narrow, autonomous sectors defined by special interests. The total of programs determined in each sector makes up national policy—but it is a national policy no one planned or intended.

Do special interests balance each other?

Grant McConnell was among the first to identify this contemporary problem with interest groups. "There is a comfortable assumption," he wrote in 1966, "that interest groups will balance each other in their struggles and produce policies of moderation."[25] Unfortunately, he noted, recent American experience shows the incompleteness of this interpretation. "Repeatedly during the past half-century, relatively homogeneous groups have been effectively organized and have assumed a strong degree of power over particular areas of public policy through close collaboration with segments of government. . . ."[26]

In solving the problem that Madison considered the primary one of democratic governance—preventing groups from dominating the totality of government—institutional arrangements were established that have led to a different problem: Special interests do not control the nation, but their influence over discrete policy sectors makes coherent national policy that is properly responsive to the public interest difficult to achieve.

Over- and under-representation. Criticizing the argument of some analysts that the great variety of organized groups contending with each other preserves a pluralistic balance, political scientist E. E. Schattschneider observed that "the flaw in the pluralist heaven is that the heavenly chorus sings with a strong upper-class accent."[27]

[24] Remarks by Joseph A. Califano, Jr., before the Economic Club of Chicago, April 20, 1978.
[25] McConnell, *Private Power*, p. 362.
[26] Ibid., p. 338.
[27] E. E. Schattschneider, *The Semi-Sovereign People* (New York: Holt, 1960), p. 35.

The economically privileged enjoy greater group representation than do the poor.

Disproportion between interest groups

There are a number of reasons why businessmen and other high-status groups have a disproportionately large place in the interest-group process. They have the financial means to sustain organized group action. This is notably the case with corporate executives, who are able to command the resources of major corporations. Also, people with large amounts of formal education have skills and training that equip them better to engage in complex political action. Economist Mancur Olson explained another facet: In certain types of small groups, an individual may find that his personal gain from achieving some collective good—a benefit for the entire group—is so substantial that it is in his interest to support an organization set up to advance it even if he has to pay all the cost of the organization effort himself. The high degree to which business interests are organized in the United States results, then, from the fact that the business community "is divided into a series of . . . 'industries,' each of which contains only a fairly small number of firms."[28] Each firm, operating through relatively compact units such as the trade associations, has a big stake in voluntarily contributing to the organized group activity because of the large individual gain it may expect.

The role of political parties in representing the disadvantaged

One can probably never attain a condition where all segments of the population are equally represented by interest group efforts. Some segments simply have greater resources and incentives for group action. This does not mean that the economically disadvantaged cannot have their needs represented. What it does mean, as Schatt-schneider and McConnell have argued, is that adequate representation of the poor and the disadvantaged is unlikely to be achieved through the interest-group structure.

> Such protection as they have had has come from the centralized features of the political order—parties, the national government, and the presidency. . . . Many of the values Americans hold in highest esteem can only be realized through large constituencies, some indeed only by a genuinely national constituency.[29]

A free society must permit the free organization of groups and must confer on them considerable latitude in making their claims. But adequate attention to broad national interests, including the claims of people insufficiently spoken for by interest groups, requires the interventions of such primary representative institutions as political parties and the presidency. Only a *vox populi* expressed by elected representatives bound to do the people's business can counterbalance the "upper-class accents" coming from interest groups.

[28] Mancur Olson, *The Logic of Collective Action* (Cambridge, Mass.: Harvard University Press, 1965), p. 34.
[29] McConnell, *Private Power*, pp. 349, 366–67.

SUMMARY

The United States displays a great variety of interest groups and, in general, a high level of group participation. While organized interests can be found in every sector touched by public policy, economic policy has prompted the greatest profusion of groups. In recent years, though, other sectors such as women's affairs, education, and environmental issues have seen a proliferation of interest groups. Public-interest groups, those that pursue collective goals that are not of immediate material benefit to their members, have also expanded greatly.

Various resources determine the extent of group influence. *Numbers* are important, as groups speaking for large constituencies can make a special claim upon political attention. But having a large constituency often means that the group also encompasses a great heterogeneity of interests, and on many issues it cannot really speak for the bulk of its members.

Money is always a critical resource. Well-financed groups can hire skilled staff, make campaign contributions, advertise, and do other things needed to gain favorable attention for their proposals. Groups speaking for *intensely held interests* have an advantage over those whose memberships, though perhaps larger, are not strongly engaged. Some interests are able to find support broadly across the society, while others must largely go it alone.

The tactics used by interest groups have been evolving. The organization of formal coalitions of groups around key policy interests is now common. It has been prompted in part by the greater dispersion of power in Congress. Groups have always been concerned with public opinion, but they now devote greater resources than previously to the measurement of opinion through polls and to efforts to demonstrate through poll data that the people are on their side.

American interest groups operate in a political environment where the parties are organizationally weak and often split internally. The groups have learned, then, to find their allies where they can across party lines. They also operate in a governmental system of divided powers; and they must concentrate on executive agencies and the judiciary as well as Congress, and on the state capitals as well as Washington.

It is always tempting to reach for a simple, focused conclusion on the role of interest groups in American democracy, like "They are too strong and threaten the public interest." But political life is too complicated for that. Groups are an *inevitable* part of democratic experience, reflecting the free choice of interests to express themselves. Groups are a *desirable* part of democratic experience, barring excessive power by government, providing people with greater representation and identification. And interest groups are a *problem-causing* side of democracy as they dominate specific policy sectors and give greater voice to some interests than others. Group power, speaking for small constituencies, must be balanced by recognition of the claims of the entire public through national institutions and electoral mandates.

FOR FURTHER STUDY

Jeffrey M. Berry, *The Interest Group Society* (Boston: Little, Brown, 1984). A thoughtful account of the relationship of interest group politics to broader aspects of the American political system, including especially the relationship of interest groups to political parties.

————, *Lobbying for the People* (Princeton, NJ: Princeton University Press, 1977). Still the best available account of "public interest groups" like Common Cause and the Sierra Club, and the role they play in contemporary American politics.

Theodore J. Lowi, *The End of Liberalism: Ideology, Policy, and the Crisis of Public Authority*, 2nd ed. (New York: Norton, 1979). A brilliant analysis and a trenchant criticism of interest-group politics as it has evolved in the United States over the last half-century.

Grant McConnell, *Private Power and American Democracy* (New York: Knopf, 1966). A penetrating examination of the role and power of interest groups, which argues that specific clusters of interests dominate the various narrow areas of public policy.

Mancur Olsen, Jr., *The Logic of Collective Action: Public Goods and the Theory of Groups*, 2nd ed. (Cambridge, MA: Harvard University Press, 1971). Applies economic analysis to the relationships between individuals, their self-interest, and their commitments to interest groups.

E. E. Schattschneider, *The Semi-Sovereign People* (New York: Holt, 1960). An elegant study which argues that interest groups represent disproportionately a set of established, upper-class interests.

David B. Truman, *The Governmental Process*, 2nd ed. (New York: Knopf, 1971). Advances a theory of interest groups and applies it in explaining how decisions get made in the American governmental process.

Chapter 12

Voting and Elections

This chapter examines the machinery through which Americans choose their leaders, and the nature and extent of electoral participation. We begin by looking at the legal requirements for voting in the United States and at the expansion of the franchise over the nineteenth and twentieth centuries. We next turn to voter turnout and how electoral participation in this country compares to that in other democracies. After briefly reviewing the basic structure of U.S. elections, which involves a single-member district, simple-majority system, we discuss modern-day campaigning. Chapter 13 follows up this chapter with an analysis of the American party system.

A striking feature of the 1988 presidential campaign was the contrast between the two levels at which it was waged. The first level was painfully superficial; it involved the elections industry—television, polls, the press, and campaign technicians. Here, all politics was image. Though the industry paid lip service to the issues, it was preoccupied with style. It valued an adroit one-liner more than a thousand carefully chosen words. The apparatus for presenting candidates to the electorate—the centerpiece of which was the celebrated 30-second sound bite—would not allow an Aristotle to escape banality. But the second level had structure and meaning. It involved a more fundamental competition—featuring party philosophies against the backdrop of economic conditions and social change. For all the emphasis in the first level on campaign imagery, there is no evidence that any presidential election has been so decided. Sorting out the fluff and the substance is necessary to make sense of American elections and their results.

EXPANDING THE FRANCHISE

Until the Civil War, the Constitution left decisions on who could vote to the states. Article I, Section 2, required that "the House of Representatives shall be composed of Members chosen every second Year by the People of the several States. . . ." But the manner in which the people would exercise this basic right was determined by the state governments. The Constitution stipulated only that the right to vote for House members must be conferred on all those who have the right to vote for "the most numerous Branch of the State Legislature." If you could vote for a state representative, you had to be permitted to vote for your national congressman.

The other principal offices of the national government were not to be chosen directly by the people at all. Members of the U.S. Senate, two from each state, were to be selected by the state legislatures (Article I, Section 3); direct popular election of senators did not come until 1913, with the ratification of the Seventeenth Amendment. On the election of the president, the Constitution provided for an electoral college: "Each State shall appoint, in such Manner as the Legislature thereof may direct, a Number of Electors, equal to the whole Number of Senators and Representatives to which the State may be entitled in the Congress . . ." (Article II, Section 1). The president would then be chosen by a majority in the electoral college. This basic provision remains in force, but in the 1820s and 1830s the primary role in choosing the president shifted to the entire electorate: Most states provided for quadrennial elections in which electors pledged to one

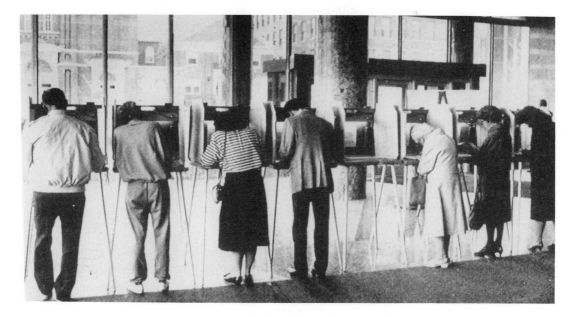

presidential candidate or another were picked by popular ballot. Today people still vote for president indirectly, determining by the majority vote in each state which slate of pledged electors is chosen, and hence which presidential candidate wins the state's electoral vote. If no candidate wins a majority of electoral votes nationally, the House of Representatives chooses the president, with each state casting a single vote.

This latter situation has occurred only twice, the first time in 1800, because of a flaw in the initial constitutional language (since corrected by the Twelfth Amendment). Thomas Jefferson and his vice presidential running mate, Aaron Burr, got the same number of electoral votes in 1800 because no distinction had been made between votes cast for president and those for vice president.

The other time an election was decided in the House of Representatives was 1824, when Andrew Jackson won a plurality of electoral votes, but not an absolute majority in a four-candidate contest: The Twelfth Amendment provides that the House must choose among the three top electoral vote-getters—in this case Jackson, who got 99 electoral votes, John Quincy Adams (84), and William H. Crawford (41). The fourth major candidate, Henry Clay, threw his support to Adams, who was then chosen as president.

Early Economic Restrictions on Voting

Property ownership

At the state level, the early arguments over who should be entitled to vote centered around property ownership. When the Constitution was ratified, the idea that all adult citizens should vote, without regard to their economic position, was considered radical and was espoused by only the most extreme democrats. As a result, states commonly established property-holding and tax-paying qualifications for voting. These qualifications were fairly modest: "between one-half and three-quarters of white adult males living in the United States in 1789 were qualified to vote."[1]

Even these limitations quickly fell before the charge that they were undemocratic. By the administration of Andrew Jackson (1829–37), the franchise had been broadened in much of the United States to include virtually all white male adults. Property qualifications for voting survived into the 1840s in only several southern states and Rhode Island. Virginia did not abolish them until 1852.

Extending the Vote to Blacks

After property restrictions were removed, two large groups remained without the right to vote: all women and most black Americans. Until

[1] Bruce A. Campbell, *The American Electorate: Attitudes and Action* (New York: Holt, Rinehart and Winston, 1979), pp. 12–13.

the Civil War, the overwhelming majority of blacks lived in the South and were slaves. President Lincoln's Emancipation Proclamation in 1863, the victory of the Union armies in 1865, and the ratification of the Thirteenth Amendment abolishing slavery in that same year were important acts in extending citizenship to blacks. But the practical achievement of many basic rights, including the right to vote, came very slowly.

Voting and the Fifteenth Amendment

The first major legal step for voting by blacks was taken in 1870 with the ratification of the Fifteenth Amendment. For the first time, the Constitution contained a formal stipulation on who could vote: "The right of citizens of the United States to vote shall not be denied or abridged by the United States or by any State on account of race, color, or previous condition of servitude." Important though this provision was, it was effectively nullified throughout the South after the end of Reconstruction in 1876 through a variety of mechanisms. Many southern states required the payment of *poll taxes* to discourage voting by blacks (and by some poor whites as well), and *literacy tests* further diminished black voting.

The white primary

The most formidable legal barrier was the so-called **white primary.** The Fifteenth Amendment required that *states* not deny the vote. Southern states responded by arguing that the Democratic party—which after Reconstruction was predominant throughout the region—was a private association to which this constitutional stipulation did not apply. The "private" Democratic parties of the southern states proceeded to exclude blacks from participation in their primaries, where the most important election contests occurred. Unable to vote

The drive after 1960 to encourage blacks to vote.

in Democratic primaries in the one-party South, blacks were thus effectively disenfranchised by law. Not until 1944 did the United States Supreme Court strike down the white primary. In *Smith* v. *Allwright*, the Court ruled that the party primaries were part of a continuous process for choosing public officials. Since the primaries were enforced by the states, by certifying nominees chosen in them for inclusion on the ballot in the general elections, preventing blacks from voting in Democratic primaries was in fact state action in violation of the Fifteenth Amendment.[2] In 1940, only 250,000 blacks had been registered in the South; by 1946, just two years after *Smith* v. *Allwright*, the number had doubled, and by 1960 it had reached 1.4 million.

Only in the last quarter-century, however, has the right to vote been wholly guaranteed and extended to black Americans in the South. The Civil Rights Acts of 1957, 1960, 1964, and 1965, which we discuss further in chapter 15, had as their primary goal the final removal of racial discrimination in voting. Widely regarded as the most important civil rights legislation ever enacted in the United States, the 1965 law suspended literacy tests and other such devices in all states and counties where less than fifty percent of the voting-age population had been registered in 1964. It also provided for the appointment of federal examiners to register voters in these areas and to supervise the entire election process. And it required that officials in these states submit to the U.S. attorney general any election law changes that they proposed to make; the attorney general could veto the changes if he found them discriminatory. Dramatic increases in black registration and voting immediately followed the enactment of this legislation.

Voting rights legislation in the 1950s and 1960s

In 1975, the Voting Rights Act of 1965 was extended to 1982 with several additional provisions: making permanent the previously temporary ban on literacy tests, and extending coverage to "language minorities" in areas where over five percent of the voting-age population were of a single-language minority and less than fifty percent were registered or had voted in the 1972 presidential election. Hispanics were affected more than any other group. In 1982, the Voting Rights Act was again extended for another seven years. Through these actions, racial barriers to voting were at last effectively removed.

Extending the Vote to Women

The debate over women's suffrage developed at about the same time as that over black voting, but was resolved much faster. Until 1869, women were denied the vote everywhere in the United States—everywhere in the world, for that matter. The territory of Wyoming

[2] *Smith* v. *Allwright*, 321 U.S. 649 (1944). Three years earlier, in *U.S.* v. *Classic*, 313 U.S. 299 (1941), the Supreme Court had reached the general determination that "where the primary is by law made an integral part of the election machinery," Congress has the power to regulate primary as well as general-election voter participation.

The efforts of the women's suffrage movement in the late nineteenth and early twentieth centuries culminated in the ratification of the Nineteenth Amendment to the Constitution in 1920.

(reflecting frontier individualism) became in 1869 the first part of the country to grant women the vote. It was followed by Colorado in 1893, Utah in 1896, and eleven other states between 1897 and 1918, until extension of the vote to women was guaranteed nationwide, with the ratification in 1920 of the Nineteenth Amendment: "The right of citizens of the United States to vote shall not be denied or abridged by the United States or by any State on account of sex."[3]

Achieving the Vote

With the formal guarantee of voting rights to women and to blacks, the long battle to achieve universal suffrage was largely concluded. Minor debate over the age requirements for voting remained. Until 1971, the voting age in most states was set at 21. The Twenty-sixth Amendment lowered the age requirement to 18 throughout the country. No one has proposed reducing the voting age further.

[3] Data on the extension of the franchise to women by various states prior to passage of the Nineteenth Amendment are from *Historical Statistics of the United States: Colonial Times to 1970* (Washington, D.C.: Government Printing Office, 1971), part 2, p. 1068.

Universal suffrage came slowly. It was not fully achieved in the eighteenth century, when American democracy was born, but rather in our own century, indeed, in the last 25 years. In assessing this slowness, we need to temper our judgment of the past by recognizing that the United States was a leader, not a follower, in extending the vote. America was the first nation in which a mass electorate gained firm control of the processes of picking political leaders. In 1880, when fourteen percent of adult males in the United States could not vote, the proportion was far higher elsewhere. In England at that time, about forty percent of adult males could not vote.[4] Women's suffrage did not become national in the United States until 1920—but it was not provided for at all until 1945 in France, 1946 in Italy, 1952 in Greece, and 1971 in Switzerland.

Universal suffrage

PARTICIPATION IN AMERICAN ELECTIONS

As the franchise has been guaranteed to all citizens, there has been a heightening of concern over the relatively low proportion of eligible voters who actually cast ballots. According to official statistics, only fifty-three percent of voting-age residents voted in the 1984 presidential election, ten percent below the turnout in the 1960 Kennedy-Nixon contest (Figure 12.1). An even smaller proportion—roughly 51 percent of the voting-age population—participated in the 1988 presidential contest.

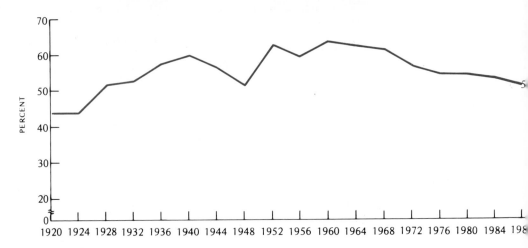

Figure 12.1
Percent of Voting-Age Population Voting for President since 1920

Source: 1932–84: U.S. Bureau of the Census, *Statistical Abstract of the United States, 1979,* p. 513; 1986, p. 255. 1920–28: Idem, *Historical Statistics of the United States: Colonial Times to 1970,* 2:1073.

[4] Morton Keller, *Affairs of State* (Cambridge, Mass.: Harvard Univ. Press, 1977), p. 523.

Low off-year voting

Turnout is even lower in voting for the U.S. House of Representatives. In 1976 it dropped below the 50 percent mark for the first time in a presidential election year since the 1940s, and it was only 48 percent in 1984. In "off-year" voting for the House, without the added spur and visibility of the more publicized presidential contest, participation is lower still. Only 38 percent of the voting-age public participated in the 1982 House contests, and just 38 percent voted in 1986.

A Confounding Decline

Declining voter participation

The country's low and somewhat declining voter participation is made more striking by its occurrence in the face of developments designed to spur voting. The drop-off in turnout of the last decade and a half has taken place at the very time the poll tax was outlawed, discrimination at polling places on the basis of race or language was prohibited, residency requirements were greatly eased, unreasonable registration dates were discarded, and many states initiated procedures to enhance participation such as mobile registrars, postcard registration, and even election-day registration.[5] Other developments associated with higher participation have also been occurring, the most notable of which is the steady increase in the amount of formal education. As data presented later in this chapter show, the strongest observed link between social characteristics of the population and inclination to vote involves education: The more of it citizens have, the higher their participation levels in elections of all types.[6] And yet as the formal education of the populace has been growing so impressively, voter turnout has been falling.

Voter turnout in the U.S. and other democracies

Concern has been spurred further by comparisons of voter turnout in the United States to that in other democracies. Although, as we will see, comparisons are more difficult to make than is sometimes supposed, the mean (or average) turnout in national elections 1945–80 was 95 percent in Australia and the Netherlands, 87 percent in West Germany, 81 percent in Norway, 79 percent in France, 77 percent in Great Britain, 76 percent in Canada, and 73 percent in Japan—while in American presidential elections during this period turnout was just 59 percent.

Is Voter Turnout a Problem?

The United States is the world's oldest democracy and a pioneer in the extension of the vote to the entire population, but it appears to have one of the lowest voter-participation rates among the world's

[5] Curtis Gans, "The Cause: The Empty Voting Booths," *Washington Monthly*, October 1978, p. 28.
[6] See Raymond E. Wolfinger and Steven J. Rosenstone, *Who Votes?* (New Haven, Conn.: Yale University Press, 1980).

democracies. America has taken a number of measures to spur registration and the population now seems better equipped to vote, given
its high formal education, but still turnout is falling off. A debate is
going on over the source and nature of the problem and its consequences.

Some argue that low turnout diminishes the capacity of those not
participating to represent their interests and shape policy. For example,
after reviewing data suggesting that the decline in turnout between
1960 and 1976 did not take place evenly across the population but
was sharpest among whites of low income and education, Howard
Reiter expressed concern that this "may make federal policymakers
less responsive to their [lower-status whites'] desires than they used
to be. This may be especially significant for the Democratic party,
which has claimed to speak for lower and working-class interests."[7]
Frances Fox Piven and Richard Cloward maintain that U.S. voter registration statutes requiring that individuals themselves come forward to get registered—rather than being registered automatically
by a government agency—are in fact a greater barrier to the poor
than to the affluent. As a result these statutes serve to underrepresent
the poor and shift the electorate more to the right than it otherwise
would be.[8]

Other experts disagree. Ruy A. Teixeira argues that "quite simply,
for many Americans voting just doesn't seem worth the bother. . . .
Nonvoting [is hardly] an indicator of suppressed radicalism or any
other political viewpoint." While nonvoters differ from voters in some
regards, such as educational background, they don't differ much in
political outlook. From a partisan point of view, "the question of
mobilizing nonvoters is logically inseparable from the question of
mobilizing voters. A party unable to sway the existing pool of voters
with its message would be unlikely to change its fortunes by mobilizing more nonvoters to vote."[9]

Voter participation is central to the democratic process, and the
debate over the consequences of nonvoting is an important one. As
we will see, however, the whole subject of who votes and who doesn't
and what this means is quite complicated. We need to try to assemble
some pertinent information. One source of confusion on American
voter turnout as opposed to other democracies is the lack of fully
comparable statistics. The conclusion our data so obviously suggest,
that voter turnout is lower here than abroad, is valid. But important

Effects of low voter turnout

The facts on voter turnout

---

[7] Howard L. Reiter, "Why Is Turnout Down?" *Public Opinion Quarterly*, Fall 1979, p.
310. See, too, Reiter, *Parties and Elections in Corporate America* (New York: St. Martin's
Press, 1987), pp. 134–57.
[8] Frances Fox Piven and Richard Cloward, *Why Americans Don't Vote* (New York: Pan-
theon, 1988).
[9] Ruy A. Teixeira, "Will the Real Nonvoter Please Stand Up?" *Public Opinion*, July/
August 1988, pp. 42, 44. See, too, Teixeira, *Why Americans Don't Vote: Turnout Decline
in the United States, 1960–84* (Westport, CT: Greenwood Press, 1987).

qualifications on this conclusion are often overlooked. Voter turnout for the United States is regularly computed on the basis of votes as a percentage of the *voting age population;* in all other countries, turnout is calculated on votes cast as a percentage of *registered voters.* Additionally, in the United States only valid votes are counted in the total turnout, while in the other countries invalid and blank ballots are also in the total figure. These statistical dissimilarities make turnout in the United States seem lower than it actually is.

Registration and voting

Part of the reason why data are published with one statistical convention for the United States and another elsewhere is that American registration laws result in a substantial proportion of the voting-age population not being registered in any given election. Were turnout in the United States represented as a proportion of only those actually registered, it would convey a sense of very robust participation that would be misleading. (Table 12.1 shows that in recent elections the

Table 12.1
Turnout of Registered Voters

	Vote as a percentage of registered voters	Compulsion penalties	Automatic registration
1. Belgium	94.6	Yes	Yes
2. Australia	94.5	Yes	No
3. Austria	91.6	No (some)	Yes
4. Sweden	90.7	No	Yes
5. Italy	90.4	Yes	Yes
6. Iceland	89.3	n.a.	n.a.
7. New Zealand	89.0	No (some)	No
8. Luxembourg	88.9	n.a.	n.a.
9. W. Germany	88.6	No	Yes
10. Netherlands	87.0	No	Yes
11. United States	86.8	No	No
12. France	85.9	No (some)	No
13. Portugal	84.2	n.a.	n.a.
14. Denmark	83.2	No	Yes
15. Norway	82.0	No	Yes
16. Greece	78.6	Yes	Yes
17. Israel	78.5	No	Yes
18. United Kingdom	76.3	No	Yes
19. Japan	74.5	No	Yes
20. Canada	69.3	No	Yes
21. Spain	68.1	Yes	Yes
22. Finland	64.3	No	Yes
23. Ireland	62.2	No	Yes
24. Switzerland	48.3	No (some)	Yes

"Compulsion penalties" refers to whether or not law in each country provides for penalties (fines, etc.) for not voting.

Source: David Glass, Peverill Squire, and Raymond Wolfinger, "Voter Turnout: An International Comparison," *Public Opinion,* December/January 1984, p. 52. The authors based this table on the most recent national election held in each country as of 1981.

percentage of *registered voters* turning out in presidential elections is in line with turnout in national elections in other democracies.)

Most democracies have registration procedures *intended* to register automatically virtually the entire adult citizenry; for these nations measuring turnout as a proportion of registered voters is appropriate. But as British political scientist Ivor Crewe has pointed out, "The accuracy of the turnout figures [for all countries except the United States] depends on the efficiency of the electoral registers on which they are all based. . . ."[10] In those instances where "the registers omit those unlikely to exercise their right to vote (the homeless, tenants of single rooms, immigrants), *turnout figures will be artificially inflated.*" Any situation where significant numbers of people are not counted among registered voters makes turnout appear higher than it really is; computing turnout on the basis of those registered always inflates participation rates since no registration system ever records all voting-age residents.

At the time of the 1984 U.S. presidential election, the noninstitutionalized voting-age population of the United States was about 172 million. The number of valid ballots cast for president was 92.7 million—hence the turnout figure of just over 53 percent. But just 115 million Americans were registered to vote in 1984. Among those who were registered, the turnout was 80 percent.

Why were 57 million voting-age residents of the United States not registered? Certainly many of them did not register because they did

Reasons for nonregistration

not intend to vote. Registration and voting in the United States are part of one continuous act of electoral participation. The government does not assume the responsibility of registering people but rather requires that citizens initiate the step; millions of people who for whatever reason do not plan to vote just do not register. But among the unregistered residents are millions who are off the rolls not because of lack of interest but because by law they cannot register or vote. Perhaps as many as 9 million resident aliens of voting age in the United States don't have the citizenship required for voting. The Census figures on voting-age residents also regularly include "institutional" populations. Those jailed for felonies are barred by law from registering and voting. Many other people who are institutionalized, like inmates of mental facilities, cannot vote. All of this means that millions of people in the United States who are of voting age are barred from registration by reasonable, consciously developed legal standards. By continuing to compute turnout on the basis of all those of voting age, we substantially overstate the magnitude of American nonvoting.

[10] Ivor Crewe, "Electoral Participation," in David Butler, Howard R. Penniman, and Austin Ranney, eds., *Democracy at the Polls: A Comparative Study of Competitive National Elections* (Washington, D.C.: American Enterprise Institute for Public Policy Research, 1981), p. 232.

Voter Participation across History

If turnout is low in America, it has long been that way. As we saw in Figure 12.1, participation in 1924 (as a percentage of the voting-age population) was just 43 percent, 10 percentage points lower than in 1984. And electoral participation in 1936 was only slightly higher than at present. Yet a very different cast has been given to participation in Roosevelt's big victory of 1936 than to such recent contests as Ford–Carter in 1976, Reagan–Mondale in 1984, and Bush–Dukakis in 1988. With the country in the midst of a great depression, which had sapped national confidence, Roosevelt came to office, told the people that they had "nothing to fear except fear itself," and proceeded to chart a bold course that rallied much of the populace to his banner. Opposition to the new initiatives was also vigorous, and the 1936 election was a spirited referendum on the New Deal. This historical account seems valid. But then why was voter participation in this buoyant referendum about the same as in recent elections in which, according to many accounts, the public has often been unenthusiastic about the candidates of both parties, dissatisfied with the quality of leadership, and uneasy about the programmatic approaches the parties were offering?

Voter turnout in nonthreatening elections

There is a dimension of nonvoting in the United States unrelated to dissatisfaction with democratic performance or with the parties and their leaders. As S. M. Lipset, among others, has noted, American nonvoting is "a reflection of the stability of the system" and confidence that the next election will not produce threatening or dangerous results.[11] Elections in many countries involve contenders far more dissimilar in their programs and outlooks than are the Democrats and Republicans in the United States. The two major American political parties are middle-class alliances that share many basic ideological commitments. For a Democrat, the prospect of a Republican being elected is not usually wildly threatening, and vice versa. In Britain, the division between the leadership of the Labour and Conservative parties is much greater; in France, the gap between the Communist party and the Center-Right is greater still. Less interested or involved people are more likely to participate electorally in contests where they see the stakes to be high. As a stable democracy that has operated under the same constitutional structure for two centuries, the United States has a political system that is not so stress-filled, and many people feel they can afford the luxury of not voting.

One rebuttal to this argument is that voter turnout was much higher in the United States in the late nineteenth century than at present. According to data collected by Walter Dean Burnham, voter turnout was 75 percent in the presidential election of 1892, 79 percent in 1896,

[11] Seymour Martin Lipset, *Political Man* (Garden City, N.Y.: Doubleday, 1960), p. 181.

Voter turnout
historically

and 73 percent in 1900.[12] Turnout undoubtedly was higher in the last century than in our own, but not as much higher as these statistics would suggest. Voting fraud occurred more frequently in the nineteenth century because it could be committed so easily. Stipulations on eligibility requirements were few and easily avoided. The paper ballots were printed by the political parties, not by the government. The counting of votes was often controlled by the parties and, in areas of one-party dominance, padding of the totals was commonplace. As a result, the number of votes reported in nineteenth-century elections was probably, as a routine matter, considerably larger than the number of voting-age citizens actually casting ballots. One often-cited instance of exaggeration of turnout is that of West Virginia, where the reported turnout in 1888 was actually 12,000 votes higher than the total eligible to vote!

Sources of Diminished Voter Turnout

The diminished role of
political parties

When all these factors are considered, it is still clear that current voter turnout in the United States has dropped off over the last quarter-century. One reason involves the status of political parties, as we will see in chapter 13. Parties have undergone in recent decades a great variety of changes. While it is certainly not true that all of these shifts have left them weaker than they were in earlier eras, *local party organizations* have on the whole been weakened. In times past, strong, local party organizations had the institutional resources needed to

Drawing by D. Fradon; © 1973 The New Yorker Magazine, Inc.

[12] These data have been published in *Historical Statistics of the United States: Colonial Times to 1970*, part 2, pp. 1071–72.

increase turnout. They canvassed potential voters and urged participation on behalf of party nominees. They conducted "get out the vote"
drives, took people whom they expected to vote for the party's candidates to and from the polls, and in general helped maintain a sense
of partisan awareness and interest in the electorate. Today, in many
areas of the United States, parties do such things less vigorously than
they used to.

A second factor in low voter turnout involves the scale and remote-
ness of the governmental process. Survey data, for example, show

Frustration with big government

that large and growing segments of the population now feel that the
complexity of politics and decision making have become beyond their
control. Seventy-two percent of those interviewed in a recent survey
agreed that government "seems so complicated that a person like me
can't really understand what's going on." Modern government is big
and distant. It seems set apart from the average citizen's world,
something which encourages frustration and resentment. Fifty-nine
percent held that "the government is pretty much run by a few big
interests looking out for themselves. . . ."[13]

The general sense of distance between the individual citizen and
"big government" is likely to persist. In nineteenth-century America,
most of government's work began and ended at the local level. It was
easier, in such a context, for the individual voter to believe that the
decision he made on election day shaped governmental action. A citizen in Bucksport, Maine, in 1840 saw a shorter and more direct link
between his vote and actual governmental response than any American can today. While one may conclude that voting remains a basic
check on government and recognize that collectively the millions of
votes cast determine who the nation's leaders will be, the scope of
modern government must detract from a sense of voter efficacy and
confidence, especially among those who have little training to understand such complexity.

Who Votes?

The importance of education

People of high socioeconomic status generally vote at a much higher
rate than those of low status, data analysis from massive surveys conducted by the Bureau of the Census shows. Education is especially
important: it "has a very substantial effect on the probability that
one will vote."[14] In 1984, people with college degrees voted at a rate
of 36 percentage points higher than those with eight years of schooling or less (Table 12.2). Income and occupation were independently
much less important: Once education is held constant, income differences have little effect on rates of voter participation. Yet, the varia-

[13] Center for Political Studies, University of Michigan, 1984 election surveys.
[14] Wolfinger and Rosenstone, *Who Votes?*.

Table 12.2
Reported Voting Rates in 1984 of Selected Groups

Characteristic	Persons of voting age	Percentage reporting they voted
Total	170,000	59.9
Male	80,300	59.0
Female	89,600	60.8
White	146,800	61.4
Black	18,400	55.8
18–20 years old	11,200	36.7
21–24 years old	16,700	43.5
25–34 years old	40,300	54.5
35–44 years old	30,700	63.5
45–64 years old	44,300	69.8
65 years old and over	26,700	67.7
North and West residence	112,400	61.6
South residence	57,600	56.8
Years of school completed:		
8 years or less	20,600	42.9
9–11 years	22,100	44.4
12 years	67,800	58.7
More than 12 years	59,500	67.5*
		79.1**
Employed	104,200	61.6
Unemployed	7,400	44.0
Not in labor force	58,400	58.9

*One to three years of college.
**Four years or more of college.

Source: Nelson W. Polsby and Aaron Wildavsky, *Presidential Elections: Contemporary Strategies of American Electoral Politics,* 7th ed. (New York: Macmillan, 1988), based on data from U.S. Bureau of the Census, *Current Population Reports,* Series p-20. Nos. 192, 253, 359, and 405. From *Statistical Abstract,* 1974, p. 437; 1977, p. 491; 1981, p. 499; 1986, p. 256.

tions in rates of voting by education level are very large within all income groups.[15] Education

> imparts information about politics . . . and about a variety of skills, some of which facilitate political learning. . . . Schooling increases one's capacity for understanding and working with complex, abstract, and intangible subjects, that is, subjects like politics. . . . Learning about politics doubtless heightens interests; the more sense one can make of the political world, the more likely that one is to pay attention to it.[16]

[15] Ibid., pp. 23–28.
[16] Ibid., p. 18.

Presumably, the increasingly complex and abstract character of politics makes education a bigger factor in determining the likelihood of voting.

An immediate stake. Another factor that comes into play is whether individuals have highly concrete interests in election outcomes. Those who do are more likely to vote. For example, farm owners, who are highly dependent on governmental decisions for their livelihood, are notably active participants. So, too, are governmental employees, who are affected by what government does just as other citizens are, but who in addition have their wages and other conditions of employment determined by elected officials.[17]

Age. Voter turnout is lowest at the beginning of adult life, increases to reach a plateau in middle age, and then declines in old age.[18] Beyond this, the lower levels of voting by young adults are much more pronounced outside the ranks of the college-educated than for those with college training.

> In other words, the start-up costs of voting [developing a level of understanding and interest in politics] are not borne equally by all young people. The cost of entering the political system is relatively small for the educated, but for those without such skills the costs are [as a statistical expression] nearly three times as great.[19]

Partisan implications. How much do voters differ from nonvoters in political terms? Voters are generally of higher socioeconomic standing and have more formal education than nonvoters, but are their political interests and values different? If voters and nonvoters are very different politically, then the widespread nonvoting in contemporary American politics means that our electorates can be highly unrepresentative.

As a group, voters used to be slightly higher in Republican identification than the entire adult population by a few percentage points.[20] This may be changing, however. In 1986, voters were a bit more Democratic than the voting-age populace as a whole. The main story is that political differences between voters and nonvoters are small. "On some issues voters are a shade more liberal than the entire population; and on others they are a trifle more conservative. . . . In short, on these issues voters are virtually a carbon copy of the citizen population. Those most likely to be underrepresented are people who lack opinions."[21] The tiny differences between voters and the entire citi-

Having a stake in the outcome

Voter turnout by age

Political nature of voters and nonvoters

---

[17] Ibid., pp. 30–35.
[18] Lipset, *Political Man*, p. 189.
[19] Wolfinger and Rosenstone, *Who Votes?*, p. 60.
[20] Ibid., pp. 109–10.
[21] Ibid., p. 109.

zenry on various policy issues "suggest that on these political questions people who vote are representative of the population as a whole."[22]

Other Forms of Political Participation

Americans may turn out at the polls at a lower rate than their counterparts in other democracies, but they exercise their control over the political process through a much more extensive array of elections than any other citizenry. Over 500,000 offices are filled by election in the United States within every four-year election cycle. "No country can approach the United States in the frequency and variety of elections and thus in the amount of electoral participation in which its citizens have a right."[23] No other country chooses the lower house of its national legislature as often as every two years, as the United States does. No other country has such a broad array of offices—including judges, sheriffs, city treasurers, attorneys general—subject to election. No other country (with the exception of Switzerland) approaches the United States in the number or variety of local referenda on policy issues. The United States is almost alone in using primary elections as the vehicle for choosing party nominees; in most democratic nations party organizations pick the nominees. Ivor Crewe concludes that "the average American is entitled to do far more electing—probably by a factor of three or four—than the citizenry of any other democracy."

This suggests a critical modification of the common observation that voter participation is low in the United States. *Turnout* in national elections is indeed low, but in other regards voter *participation* is very high. The American electorate expresses itself in more political decisions through casting ballots than the electorate of any other country. In fact, some observers suggest that the very frequency of elections in America serves to reduce the proportion turning out in any given contest: "Ho-hum—another election."

Elections are not the only way in which people participate politically.[24] And, outside the electoral arena, Americans appear highly participatory compared to their counterparts in other countries. We noted in chapter 11 the high level of involvement in interest groups and voluntary associations in the United States. As in voting, participation in these other political activities is strongly related to socioeconomic status (Table 12.3). Only 26 percent of those with less than a high school education said in 1984 that they were "very interested"

Frequency of American elections

Political involvement

[22] Ibid., p. 111.
[23] Crewe, "Electoral Participation," in *Democracy at the Polls*, p. 232.
[24] Ronald Mason argues that political science has placed too much stress on the narrowly electoral forms of political participation. See Ronald M. Mason, "Toward A Non-Liberal Perspective on Participation," paper presented at the Midwest Political Science Association Meeting, April 1980.

Table 12.3
Political Interest and Participation by Socioeconomic Position (in percent)

	Very interested in political campaigns	Contributed money to a candidate during the 1984 campaign	Attended political meetings, rallies, or other political activity
Education			
College graduate plus advanced training	49	16	13
College graduate	42	9	12
Some college	35	6	11
High school graduate	27	2	6
Less than four years of high school	26	1	3
Family income			
$50,000 or more	37	11	8
35,000–49,999	36	6	7
25,000–34,999	32	7	9
20,000–24,999	34	4	10
15,000–19,999	27	3	8
10,000–14,999	29	2	7
Under $10,000	29	1	7

Source: Center for Political Studies, University of Michigan, 1984 election surveys.

in political campaigns, compared to 27 percent of high school graduates, 35 percent of those with some college, 42 percent of college graduates, and 49 percent of those with advanced degrees. Only 1 percent of those with little education indicated that they had made a financial contribution to a candidate, compared to 16 percent of those with the highest levels of formal training.

THE STRUCTURE OF ELECTIONS

The arrangements under which votes are cast and tallied often exert considerable influence on election outcomes. And no set of electoral mechanics is politically neutral. For example, the *single-member district, simple-majority* electoral system used by the United States leads to results different in important regards from those encouraged by systems built around *plural-member districts* and *proportional representation.*

Translating Votes into Seats

Perhaps the most important single feature of an electoral system is the way it translates the votes people cast into the election of legislators and other officeholders. Consider a hypothetical example. *Vot-*

The impact of electoral systems

ersland is a small country with 1,000,000 registered voters and three political parties. The Liberty party is backed by 40 percent of the people, the Equality party by 30 percent, and the Brotherhood party by 30 percent. Votersland held its 1984 national election under an arrangement where the country was divided into 100 districts, each with 10,000 electors. The party winning the most votes in each had its candidate chosen as the district's congressman. Since the Equality party's 40 percent was evenly distributed across the country (as were the votes of its rivals), it had a plurality in every district. Thus the results were:

Liberty	100 seats
Equality	0 seats
Brotherhood	0 seats

As would be expected, there was a storm of protest. A party with just 40 percent of the popular vote had, in a free and open election, gained all the seats. Bowing to demands for electoral change, the legislature proceeded to rewrite the law. The new statute provided that no candidate would be declared the winner unless he received an absolute majority (50 percent or more) of the vote. If no one did, there would be a runoff election between the two candidates with the highest totals in the first round.

The 1986 elections were conducted under these new rules. The total popular vote was exactly the same as in 1984, but this time that meant no one was elected in the first round. The Liberty party had 40 percent in each district, more than its rivals but not a majority. Before the second round, the Equality and Brotherhood parties reached an arrangement whereby the one coming in third (and thus disqualified for the second round) in a district would throw its support to the party that came in second. In half the districts this was Equality, in half Brotherhood. Voters followed their leaders' wishes, and when the second-round votes were tallied, the results in half the districts were Liberty, 0 seats, Equality, 50 seats. In the other half, the final tally read Liberty 0, Brotherhood 50.

With no shift in the popular vote, representation of the Liberty backers fell from 100 to 0. Naturally, protests again erupted, and once more the rules were changed. This time the districts were abolished, and congressmen were elected on the basis of the distribution of the partisan vote nationally. Each party submitted a list of 100 candidates, with the understanding that a percentage of them would be declared elected exactly in proportion to its share of the popular vote. These new rules were tried in the 1988 elections. The popular vote was distributed as in the two previous contests. This meant that the first 40 candidates on Liberty's list were elected, the first 30 on Equality's, and the first 30 on Brotherhood's.

The Votersland example is obviously contrived, assuming such things as the popular vote being evenly distributed across an entire country, and not changing from one election to the next. But the example is fair and revealing. It shows how in perfectly free elections very different results can be obtained just by changing electoral mechanics. Variants of the three sets of rules used in the example are actually found in democratic countries around the world.

The American Electoral System

Single-member district system

The United States conducts most of its elections under a single-member district, simple-majority, single-ballot system. Elections for seats in the U.S. House of Representatives, the Senate, state legislatures, for governorships, and for many other offices fit within this general order. It is a **single-member district** system because the area covered by the election—the entire United States in the case of House of Representatives elections, a given state for state legislative contests—is carved into a series of districts, each of which elects a single representative. In contrast, many countries employ systems with **plural-member districts**—where a single constituency chooses more than one representative. The United States has some plural-member district elections—for example, in cities where the entire council or board of alderman is chosen by voters at large rather than in single-member council or aldermanic districts. But single-member districts are the rule.

The simple-majority, single-ballot system

The American arrangement is a **simple-majority** and **single-ballot** system: The candidate who gets the most votes in his district is awarded the seat on the basis of a single casting of ballots. The alternative is an absolute-majority requirement, where the winner must not only get more votes than any rival but must get more than 50 percent of all ballots cast. This requires, in some instances, recourse to a second ballot or runoff election between the two highest contenders. Some *primaries*, especially in southern states, include provision for runoffs. Jesse Jackson made an issue of this provision during the 1984 Democratic presidential contest. Like other black leaders, he saw the runoff primary as discriminatory, allowing white voters to pool their strength for the surviving white candidate against the black candidate in the second-round election. Many Democratic officials defended the runoff as essential when the first-round election has so many candidates that no one can get a majority. Primaries aside, one finds in a typical United States election (as for the House of Representatives) an arrangement where all candidates run in districts from which only one person is elected, and the candidate with the most votes in the single general-election ballot is declared the winner, whether or not he or she has an absolute majority of the votes cast.

Some other countries operate with this single-member district, simple-majority arrangement, but they are confined largely to the English-speaking world. Britain is the political progenitor of this system. A majority of the world's democracies—including Italy, West Germany, Sweden, Israel, and Japan—count votes and award seats through some form of plural-member districts with **proportional representation** (PR). In such systems representatives are chosen from districts in which more than one candidate is elected. In Norway, for example, in 1980, 155 seats in the national legislature were spread over 20 voting constituencies; in Japan, 511 seats were allocated among 130 constituencies; and in the Netherlands, all 150 seats in the lower house of the national legislature were elected from a single constituency: the entire nation. The idea of PR is to divide seats among the contending parties in proportion to the percentage of the vote won by each of the parties. In theory, if a party receives 27 percent of the vote in a given legislative election, under PR it should get about 27 percent of the seats. The particular electoral mechanics employed under PR vary; some come closer than others to an exact link of vote and seat proportion. But the underlying idea is always the same. For PR to work, you must have plural-member districts, and you must then divide the seats among the contending parties in proportion to their percentages of the votes cast.

Which System Is Best?

What are the relative advantages and disadvantages and the partisan implications of the single-member and PR systems? The Votersland example makes evident one of the chief biases of single-member, simple-majority arrangements: They can produce big imbalances between the proportion of votes and seats won by a party. Congressional elections in the United States have often reflected this. In 1978, for example, U.S. congressional elections, the Democrats won 54 percent of the popular vote nationally but gained 64 percent of the seats; in 1984, 50 and 58 percent.

The reason why the votes–seats ratio is not even more uneven than it is in U.S. congressional elections involves the distribution of Republican and Democratic votes around the country. Both parties have their "safe" seats: those where they enjoy a fairly comfortable majority and manage to win almost every time. In recent years the Democrats have regularly done better in House seats than in popular vote, but not so much better that the Republicans have had to cry "foul." Neither party wants to change the prevailing electoral machinery.

Is the simple-majority system, as it operates in U.S. elections, basically unfair because it typically gives the winning party more seats than its share of the popular vote would suggest? Not necessarily. If an exact ratio of votes to seats is the goal, the U.S. arrangements are obviously flawed. But by another standard for assessing systems of representation, elections are vehicles for choosing a government by the principle of majority rule. Absolute proportionality in votes won and seats gained is not universally held essential to that end. In fact, sometimes proportionality makes it hard to form a coherent government. A common criticism of PR is that it fractures legislatures by producing such a mix of parties that governing is difficult. The purer the form of PR, the more likely fracturing will occur. The price of the fairness of a pure system of PR may be prolonged governmental instability.[25] The Dutch PR arrangements, for example, have led to a proliferation of parties: in 1971, 14 parties secured seats in the national legislature.

What should an electoral system accomplish?

Which system is best cannot be answered, then, without attention to differing electoral goals. If elections are seen as means for gaining "an ideological census, a declaration of the voters' fundamental position on the left-right spectrum," as British political scientist David Butler puts it, there is much to be said for a pure PR arrangement, since the legislature should be a direct reflection of the proportional party preferences of the electorate. But if the goal is seen as one of choosing "viable governments" and giving such governments legitimacy, Butler suggests, the single-member system may be better. He argues that

> a clear answer may be better for the country than a mathematically exact one . . . a legislature that is a perfect mirror of what the electorate felt on one particular polling day may not be as satisfactory a basis for effective government as one that offers a cruder but more decisive reflection of majority trends.[26]

Third Parties

The single-member district, simple-majority system the United States uses for most of its electoral contests helps maintain a two-party system and penalizes third parties. In order to secure representation, a minor party must not only find considerable support in the populace but achieve more support in some districts than the established major parties. If it becomes the choice of 10 percent of voters in many different districts, it wins no seats. Thus third parties are constantly vulnerable to the charge that a vote for one of them is essentially a wasted vote, since it is unlikely to join enough others to constitute a plurality of all votes cast. If the American Congress were elected on the basis of PR (without any other aspect of American society or politics being changed), the United States would almost certainly move immediately from a two-party system to a multi-party one—and the purer the form of PR employed, the greater the proliferation of parties that would result.

[25] David Butler, "Electoral Systems," in *Democracy at the Polls*, p. 19.
[26] Ibid., pp. 22–23.

Third parties in the
U.S. and Britain

In Great Britain, where there have been three or four important parties, the penalty that the single-member, simple-majority system imposes on those not among the top two is vividly shown. In the 1983 elections, for example, the new Alliance of the Liberal and Social Democratic parties garnered an impressive 26 percent of the popular vote, just 2 percentage points behind the second-place Labour party; the Alliance gained only 3 percent of the House seats, however, compared to 31 percent for Labour.

Primary Elections

Primary elections

Another important key feature of American electoral arrangements is the *primary election* for choosing party nominees. In no other democracy are party candidates chosen largely by rank-and-file adherents through primaries. The direct primary in the United States developed early in the twentieth century and was effectively promoted by the Progressives. They argued that leaving the choice of candidates to the party "bosses" was undemocratic, and that the fullest participation of the rank-and-file in candidate choice was desirable. American individualism provided fertile soil for this appeal. Use of primaries is now so extensive that party organizations typically have little control over candidate selection. The choice is made by party voters in election contests that are as regular and routine a part of the electoral process as are the general elections. State governments supervise all facets of the primaries, including the printing of ballots.

Closed primaries and
open primaries

Open and closed primaries. Today most states use **closed primaries**, where only voters registered as party members may participate. Seven states, however, use **open primaries**, where any voter may cast a ballot, regardless of his or her party registration. The open primary has the troublesome feature of allowing supporters of the opposition to help decide who the party's nominees will be. Sometimes, these opponents understandably cast their ballots for the candidate they think will be easiest to beat in the general election. The most open of all the primaries is used in the state of Washington. A voter may cast his ballot in the Democratic primary for governor, the Republican primary for U.S. Senate, and so on, alternating as he sees fit through all of the offices.

Presidential primaries. Primaries are now widely used to pick delegates to the national parties' presidential nominating conventions. In 1988, 40 states employed primaries, although in several of these states, they applied to only one party. Historically, presidential primaries have come in a number of varieties: primaries that actually elect delegates to the national conventions, and those that merely give voters an opportunity to express their preferences (so-called "beauty contests"), advisory to some party committee or convention that chooses the delegates; primaries that bind the delegates to support, for at least one ballot, the nominee for whom they were pledged at the time of the primary, and those that pick delegates who are then free to exercise their own preferences at the national convention. Today, most presidential primaries bind delegates for the first convention ballot.

Within this general arrangement, primaries vary greatly in how they allocate delegates. New Hampshire law provides that all candidates receiving 10 percent or more of the vote will receive delegates in proportion to their shares of the primary vote. New Hampshire Democrats will allocate their delegates in exactly the same way. California is a different story. Republicans in the nation's largest state pick their delegates through a winner-take-all primary: The Republican candidate who wins the most primary votes wins all delegates to the national nominating convention. Democrats in California, however, employed in 1988 a proportional allocation formula: Delegates were elected from each of the state's 45 congressional districts; each candidate who gained at least 15 percent of a district's popular vote—the proportion specified in national party rules—won delegates in proportion to his or her vote share. Since only 7 or 8 delegates were chosen from each district, the system is far less perfectly proportional than if all California delegates were elected at large—it is hard to divide 7 with perfect proportionality, but it stands in sharp contrast to the GOP's winner-take-all arrangement.

Since the 1960s, Democrats have debated the question of what kind of allocation formula is best. Some in the party argue that a strict proportional system is fairest—because it gives candidates the same

Choosing candidates in presidential primaries

"ARE YOU SURE THIS IS THE WAY IT WAS SUPPOSED TO WORK?"

Reprinted with special permission of King Features Syndicate, Inc.

Proportional allocation

share of the delegates as of the popular vote. Other groups argue that winner-take-all is most effective—since it tends to produce a clear winner rather than fragmenting the delegates. At the end of the 1988 primary season, the Democrats moved further toward proportional allocation. The National Convention's Rules Committee voted to prohibit states from electing delegates on a winner-take-all basis by congressional district—the system they used in 1988 in Illinois, Maryland, New Jersey, Pennsylvania, and West Virginia.

Winner-take-all

Republicans have been more comfortable with winner-take-all arrangements, which are acceptable in national party rules. Individual states have their own ideas, however, as we have seen in the case of New Hampshire, and a great variety of allocation arrangements are found around the country. The most common Republican arrangement provides for winner-take-all election of delegates on both a congressional district and statewide basis: A portion of the delegates are assigned to each congressional district in the state, and the Republican candidate who gets the most votes in each district wins all of its delegates. The remainder of the state's delegates go to the candidate who wins the most votes statewide.

Caucuses

Presidential caucuses. The other general system of delegate selection in presidential nominations is the **caucus.** In a typical caucus arrangement like Iowa's, rank-and-file party adherents gather in precinct meeting houses. In some caucus arrangements, those favoring a candidate who does not have enough local support to win a delegate are allowed to go (after the first division) with the group supporting their second choice. The idea of the caucus is that it provides more substantial involvement than just casting a ballot: it involves spending an evening with one's neighbors and publicly declaring for a candidate. At the same time, it is like a primary in that any voter registered with the party may attend its caucuses and participate in delegate selection. Caucuses take more of a voter's time than primaries do, and turnout in them is much lower.

Two systems yield different results

The sharply differing levels of turnout in primaries and caucuses means that the two systems readily yield different results. In 1988, for example, Jesse Jackson was unable to win a primary in any state except those where the Democratic electorate was heavily black—Alabama, Georgia, Louisiana, Mississippi, Virginia, and the District of Columbia. He won caucuses all over the country, however—Alaska, Delaware, Michigan, and Vermont, as well as Texas and South Carolina. On the Republican side, Pat Robertson did not win a single primary. But he was able to bring his supporters out in sufficient numbers to win low-turnout caucuses in Alaska, Hawaii, and Washington, and he finished ahead of George Bush in the Iowa caucuses (won by Robert Dole).

Box 12.1
How the Iowa Caucuses Work

All precinct caucuses are open by law to all persons of voting age living in the precinct. On the Republican side, any qualifying individual need only profess his "Republican affiliation"; he need not be a registered Republican. If he is challenged—if someone asserts that he is really a Democrat intruding into a Republican gathering—the GOP committee for the precinct has final word on whether to admit him.

At 7 p.m. on caucus day on the Republican side, those attending each caucus are invited to make nominations for president in what is only a "straw poll." All those nominated have their names placed on a chalk board, paper is passed out, and each attendee indicates his preference. The results are forwarded to GOP state organizations and are advisory only. Then the actual work of delegate selection begins. Each precinct gathering elects delegates to county conventions. While the delegates thus chosen need not be pledged to any presidential contender, most are, and the delegates chosen in each precinct meeting usually divide in candidate preference very much along the proportions of the straw poll. The county conventions (attended by all delegates chosen by every precinct caucus in the county), in turn select delegates to a state convention; the state convention picks the delegates who represent the state in the presidential nomination convention itself. Seems complicated? It is. It was designed to encourage active participation, not to be easy and straightforward.

Iowa Democrats follow much the same procedure as the Republicans, with these differences: To participate in the Democratic caucuses, one must be a registered Democrat, not simply profess an affiliation. Instead of participating in a straw vote, caucus attendees divide into groups according to their presidential preference, and correspondingly elect delegates to the county convention. If 20 percent in a caucus favor a given candidate, 20 percent of its county convention delegates will go to him. The county conventions follow the same procedures in electing its delegates to the congressional district convention: At the latter, the major portion of the national convention delegates—the "district-level delegates"—are elected by preferential ballot. A 15 percent threshold operates, eliminating any presidential candidate who does not receive 15 percent of the vote. The remainder of the national delegates—the "at large" delegates—are formally selected at the party's state convention.

CAMPAIGNS

For those who love to campaign for elective office, or enjoy watching campaigns, the United States is a veritable horn of plenty. Nationally, the great presidential sweepstakes comes every four years; 435 House of Representatives seats are contested every biennium, as are a third of the Senate seats. At the state level, campaigns for governor, executive offices such as attorney general, and seats in state legislatures proceed on two- and four-year cycles. County, city, and town elections—for such offices as mayor, seats on town councils, county boards of supervisors, boards of education, and judgeships—are interspersed around the federal and state election calendars. Add to all this the primary elections that are held to choose nominees and you have the American saga: "The Endless Campaign."

Length of Campaigns

By the spring of 1986, campaigning for the 1988 Republican presidential nomination was already well underway in Michigan, as part of an unusually elongated new delegate selection process established by Republicans in that state. Some 10,000 local activists filed on May 27, 1986, to run for precinct delegate, the first rung on a ladder leading to a state party convention early in 1988 that picked delegates to the 1988 GOP National Convention. A number of Republican presidential hopefuls, including Vice President George Bush, New York Congressman Jack F. Kemp, and television evangelist Marion G. (Pat)

The 1988 campaign started well before New Hampshire voters welcomed the candidates to their February 16, 1988, primary.

Robertson, and their local supporters, competed to see who could field the most precinct delegate candidates. On August 5, 1986, Michigan Republicans trooped to the polls to cast ballots for the rival delegate candidates; those selected then went to county conventions that elected state convention delegates. The very idea of a formal step leading ultimately to the selection of a presidential candidate being taken 27 to 30 months before the election strikingly illustrates what we mean by "the endless campaign."

Running for Congress: A case study. The contest for the 1980 Democratic nomination for the House seat in Connecticut's 2nd congressional district is a concrete illustration of why many people are concerned about the heavy demands today's lengthy campaigns impose. In 1979, the incumbent congressman from the 2nd district, Christopher Dodd, decided he would seek the Senate seat being vacated through the retirement of Senator Abraham Ribicoff. A number of Democrats expressed interest in succeeding Dodd in the House. One of them was Samuel Gejdenson, 31 years old, the owner of a small farm in the sparsely settled eastern Connecticut town of Bozrah. Although he had served two terms in the state legislature, Gejdenson was little known in Democratic circles and started the race with virtually no party backing. But he was willing to campaign unceasingly. With almost no money and a modest volunteer staff (his campaign manager was still in his teens) Gejdenson traveled for months around his sprawling district, attending every party function and social affair he could. The effort paid off. Gejdenson won a closely contested primary, in which one of his rivals had the party endorsement, and then went on to nip his Republican opponent in the November election.

In many ways Gejdenson's unexpected triumph is a heartening success story, showing how even in an age when campaign costs have skyrocketed, a political unknown can, through diligent pursuit and a gift for personal campaigning, win election to the U.S. Congress. But it raised a troubling question: What about other worthy individuals who have the skills and interests needed to serve in Congress, but who are unable because of the demands of their jobs or unwilling to submit to endless campaigning? "Who would drop everything else and campaign for months on end, attending every little party and social function in the district?" Gejdenson's campaign manager was asked. "Why, someone like Sam," he replied, "who didn't have much of a job and who would see getting elected to Congress as the opportunity of a lifetime." (In 1988, Gejdenson easily won re-election to a fifth term in the House.) Some defend the campaign trial as appropriate: a test of political zest and aptitude. Others wonder whether the campaigning side of elective office may not now loom proportionally too large.

Gejdenson's campaign

Assessing the
campaign process

Money and Campaigns

The number and length of campaigns in the United States, and the extent to which they now require large amounts of expensive resources such as television time for speeches and advertisements, means that American electioneering is a very expensive business. Money has become a central problem in contemporary campaigning. Without substantial funding, parties and candidates cannot reasonably make their appeals to the electorate. Money can also become too important and be used in ways that abuse and bias popular choice. In the United States, as in other democracies, there is a continuing argument over what arrangements need be made so that the important task of communicating with voters can proceed without certain special interests that have disproportionate access to funding gaining an improper advantage.

Until the 1970s, the law governing federal campaign financing in the United States was the Corrupt Practices Act of 1925. It set a statutory maximum of $25,000 for total expenditures in a U.S. Senate

Signs like this one prohibit any electioneering within 300 feet of a polling place.

POLLING PLACE

ELECTIONEERING PROHIBITED

On the day of any primary, general or special election, no person may, within a polling place, or in any public area within three hundred feet of such polling place do any electioneering, circulate cards or handbills of any kind, solicit signatures to any kind of petition, engage in any practice which interferes with the freedom of voters to exercise their franchise or disrupts the administration of the polling place, or conduct any exit poll or public opinion poll with voters.

No person may obstruct the doors or entries to a building in which a polling place is located or prevent free access to and from any polling place. Any sheriff, deputy sheriff, or municipal law enforcement officer shall prevent such obstruction, and may arrest any person creating such obstruction.

No person may except as provided in RCW 29.34.157, remove any ballot from the polling place before the closing of the polls or solicit any voter to show his or her ballot.

No person other than an inspector or judge of election may receive from any voter a voted ballot or deliver a blank ballot to such elector.

Any violation of this section is a misdemeanor under RCW 9A.20.010 and shall be punished under RCW 9A.20.020(3), and the person convicted may be ordered to pay the costs of prosecution.

$100.00 FINE (and cost of Prosecution) MAY BE IMPOSED FOR VIOLATION OF THE ABOVE CONDITIONS. No one but Election Officers, (R C W 29.51.020) Persons voting, and One Challenger for Each Political Party allowed.

RETURN TO COUNTY AUDITOR

C 84

FORM E 305 TRICK & MURRAY SEATTLE 61500

Under the terms of the Federal Election Campaign Act, candidates for federal office are required to file very detailed reports of their campaign expenditures. Shown here is a page from a report filed by U.S. Senator Pete Wilson of California. (Courtesy the Federal Elections Commission)

SCHEDULE B	ITEMIZED DISBURSEMENTS		Use separate schedule(s) for each category of the Detailed Summary Page	PAGE OF 3
				FOR LINE NUMBER

Any information copied from such Reports and Statements may not be sold or used by any person for the purpose of soliciting contributions or for commercial purposes, other than using the name and address of any political committee to solicit contributions from such committee.

NAME OF COMMITTEE (in Full)

Californian's for Senator Pete Wilson

Full Name, Mailing Address and ZIP Code	Purpose of Disbursement	Date (month, day, year)	Amount of Each Disbursement This Period
A. Joanne Kozberg 721 No. Linden Drive Beverly Hills, CA 90210	Reimb. for: Telephone service, Pacific Bell Disbursement for: Primary | General Other (specify)	11/20/85	38.75
B. Texaco P. O. Box 2000 Bellaire, TX 77401-2000	Business travel Disbursement for: Primary | General Other (specify)	11/20/85	112.09
C. The Paper Store 613 Massachusetts Ave., N. W. Washington, D. C. 20002	Supplies Disbursement for: Primary | General Other (specify)	11/21/85	115.67
D. U. S. Postmaster San Francisco, CA	Postage Disbursement for: Primary | General Other (specify)	11/22/85	4.32
E. State Compensation Insurance Fund P. O. Box 85488 San Diego, CA 92138	Workman's Comp Insurance Disbursement for: Primary | General Other (specify)	11/25/85	140.00
F. Mary A. Micai 3803 Marquette Place, #44 San Diego, CA 92106	Temporary help Disbursement for: Primary | General Other (specify)	11/26/85	108.00
G. Sheridan Plaza LaReina 6101 West Century Boulevard Los Angeles, CA 90088	Banquet facilities Disbursement for: Primary | General Other (specify)	07/25/85	339.97
H. Julie Miller 5725 Eldergardens San Diego, CA 92020	Temporary help Disbursement for: Primary | General Other (specify)	07/26/85	16.00
I. Toyo Griffith Park Florists 5900 Hollywood, CA 90028	Flowers (ie: Condolence, get well) Disbursement for: Primary | General Other (specify)	07/25/85	102.35

Corrupt Practices Act of 1925

race and $10,000 for a House campaign. These spending limits were wholly unrealistic, and they were ignored. Finance reports were supposed to be filed with the clerk of the House or the secretary of the Senate, but enforcement of this requirement, too, was lax. In a message dealing with the campaign finance legislation, President Lyndon Johnson described it as "more loophole than law."

Campaign finance reform. In the early 1970s, Congress finally enacted legislation that provided for more meaningful regulation of federal elections. In 1971, Congress adopted the Federal Election Campaign Act (FECA). This law required candidates and committees to file detailed, timely reports on who was financing their campaigns and how much they were spending. It also imposed limits on how much a candidate for federal office could spend on communications media. Also enacted in 1971 was a checkoff provision allowing taxpayers to contribute $1 each from their annual federal income tax payments to a general campaign fund to be divided among eligible presidential candidates.

Two and a half years later, Congress passed sweeping amendments to the FECA. These amendments set the first spending limits for presidential candidates, covering both the pre-nomination and general election phases of the campaign. They established new expenditure limits for congressional campaigns. And they provided public funding for presidential elections: Federal matching grants would cover half the cost of the pre-nomination part of the contests and all of the cost of the general election phase, within tight spending limits. Candidates could decide not to accept federal funds, in which case they would be exempt from the spending limits. A new independent body, the Federal Election Commission (FEC), was set up to oversee this program. The six FEC commissioners are now appointed by the president to serve staggered six-year terms; no more than three can be from any one political party.

The campaign contribution limits provided by the 1974 legislation (as subsequently amended) are shown in Table 12.4. Under these limits, an individual may contribute no more than $1,000 to any candidate or candidate's committee in a given election, $20,000 to a party's national committee in a calendar year, $5,000 to any other political committee, and no more than $25,000 in all per year. This was to prevent the wealthy from making huge contributions that might "buy" special treatment or give them undue influence.

FECA and the FEC

Campaign contribution limits

Table 12.4
Federal Campaign Contribution Limits

	To each candidate or candidate committee per election	To national party committees per calendar year	To any other political committee per calendar year	Total contributions to federal candidates per calendar year
Contributor:				
Individual	$1,000	$20,000	$5,000	$25,000
Multicandidate committee*	$5,000	$15,000	$5,000	No limit
Other political committee	$1,000	$20,000	$5,000	No limit
Republican or Democratic senatorial campaign committee, or the national party committee, or a combination of both	$17,500 to U.S. Senate candidate† during the year in which candidate seeks election	Not applicable	Not applicable	Not applicable

*A multicandidate committee is any political committee with more than 50 contributors which has been registered for at least six months and, with the exception of state party committees, has made contributions to five or more federal candidates.

†Limitation applies to either candidate for nomination or candidate for election to post of U.S. senator.

Source: Federal Election Commission, *Contributions*, March 1984; idem, *Federal Election Campaign Laws*, Jan. 1984, p. 49.

Funding presidential contests. American presidential elections are now conducted with public funding. In the pre-convention stage, before the parties have picked their nominees, candidates are entitled to receive federal matching funds. To qualify, they must receive contributions of at least $5,000 from people in 20 or more states, with no single contribution exceeding $250. Once these provisions are met, federal funds are made available covering 50 percent of a candidate's total expenditures up to the prescribed limits. In 1988, this meant that a candidate could receive as much as $27 million in federal funds prior to the party conventions if he stayed in the race all the way. During the general election campaign in 1988, both Bush and Dukakis were permitted to spend about $45 million. Millions more were spent indirectly on behalf of both candidacies.

Funding for presidential elections

Candidates not of a major party who get at least 5 percent of the vote in the current presidential election are entitled, following the election, to receive federal funding in proportion to their share of the total vote cast. Their parties also qualify for federal support in the next election. In 1980, when Carter and Reagan each received $29.4 million in federal funds for the general election campaign, independent John Anderson was granted $4.2 million. He qualified because he gained 6.6 percent of the popular vote. Anderson's independent movement would have received federal finds in 1984 if it had chosen to enter a candidate.

Funding for congressional elections

In campaign financing outside the presidency, private sources remain predominant, although about 20 states provide some public subsidies for state-level contests. There has been lively debate over the desirability of making federal funds available to congressional candidates. Bills have been introduced providing for public finance in races for the House and Senate, but they have foundered on partisan wrangling. The Republican party has developed a very effective, broadly based fund-raising effort on behalf of its congressional candidates, and it sees Democratic support of public funding and tight expenditure limits as an attempt to eliminate its advantage.

Are campaigns too expensive? One persisting set of issues involves the sheer cost of present-day campaigning. State campaign spending data are now available in better form than ever before; from these various sources Herbert E. Alexander, director of the Citizen's Research Foundation, estimated that $525 million was expended on state and local politics in the 1983–84 election cycle, and $850 million in 1987–88. Using FEC data, Alexander further estimated that total money expenditures for federal elections were just under $1.3 billion in 1983–84 and just over $2.1 billion in 1987–88.

Is this just too much money? In one sense, this issue is a hard one to deal with because any observer can decide for himself how much is "too much." But do we have any *objective standards* that can help us reach a judgment?

Evaluating the level of
campaign spending

Those inclined to argue that present campaign spending is not too high often compare current expenditures for this "vital act of democratic participation" with what we spend for fairly frivolous things—like snowmobiles, lipstick, and chewing gum. Those who think present spending levels are too high find this response unsatisfactory, and there is much to commend this position. Spending for electioneering has nothing to do with spending for chewing gum, and the comparison can have only a certain sophomoric appeal. But there is a meaningful comparison. Campaign spending all comes back in one way or another to efforts to persuade voters—and, disproportionately, to efforts at persuasion that involve sending messages over television, radio, in newspaper advertising, in mailed flyers, and the like. The proper comparison, then, asks: How do the communications resources made available to candidates and parties compare to those available to other organizations and interests that vie for the attention of the American citizenry in communicating on politics and public issues?

Campaign spending as
part of public
communications

Specifically, is there any evidence that campaign spending for political communication by candidates and parties has grown disproportionately, compared to total public affairs communications? Candidates and parties try to bring their views on issues and events to voters' attention, to influence voters' electoral choices. If this party/candidate role in the larger process of political communications has grown inordinately, compared to other parts, that fact would at least suggest that limits *might* be desirable. But if instead the party/candidate share of total spending relating to communications on public issues has steadily shrunk, it is hard to see precisely why we should want to shrink it further. Surely party/candidate communications to voters is a legitimate part of political communications in this and any other democracy.

Early on in American history, the parties exercised the decisive role in political communications. Today, however, the United States is very far from the party-dominated communications of its early years. Americans receive the bulk of their information on political issues not from the parties but from national communications media that maintain a steadfast independence of all party influence, much less direction, as the cornerstone of their professional self-definition. Network news programs command many millions of viewers. The resources committed to the public affairs communications by the television networks alone dwarf those available to parties and candidates. CBS News takes in for its evening news program far more than both the Democratic and Republican parties at all levels take in for every act of political communication within their domains. It is hard, then, to see a sound basis for the argument that party spending for campaigning is in some absolute sense too high. Is it desirable for the party/candidate role to be even more subordinate to that of the national communications media and the journalistic profession? The case has not been made. In contrast, political scientists going back to

Woodrow Wilson have made the case that parties are important instruments of the democratic process, and that their institutional roles need to be expanded, not weakened.

Is one party advantaged? Substantial balance or parity between the two major parties has been achieved in several major areas of campaign finance, although some imbalances still exist. With regard to the much-discussed PAC contributions, FEC data show that in the 1985–86 election cycle all forms of PACs together contributed $79 million to Democratic congressional candidates and $61 million to Republicans—continuing the clear though fairly modest Democratic edge evident in preceding elections. All Democratic House and Senate candidates received about $119 million in 1985–86 in contributions from individuals; the Republicans did somewhat better, taking in $148 million. The net receipts of Democratic House and Senate candidates were about $231 million, those of Republicans $240 million. Direct spending by the Democratic and Republican presidential nominees has been roughly equalized through the public finance provisions of the FECA, first employed in 1976.

"Institutional" fundraising

The biggest imbalance in campaign resources involves "institutional" fundraising. The Republicans enjoy a large advantage over the Democrats in funds raised by the National Committee and the House and Senate campaign committees (Table 12.5). FEC data for 1985–86 show the Republicans raising roughly $255 million to the

Table 12.5
Political Party Fundraising, 1985–86

	Adjusted receipts
Democratic	
National committee	17,235,406
Senatorial	13,397,809
Congressional	12,322,969
Assoc. State Chair.	7,618,834
Conventions, other national	259,674
State/local	14,008,888
Total Democratic	64,843,580
Republican	
National committee	83,780,156
Senatorial	84,438,546
Congressional	39,796,974
Other national committees	86,813
Conventions, other national	110,366
State/local	47,031,995
Total Republicans	255,244,850

Total funds raised during 1985–86 election cycle.

Source: Federal Election Commission, press release of May 5, 1988.

Democrats' $65 million. The GOP's fundraising achievements have
made it a formidable electoral force—one admired by its friends and
envied by its opponents.[27] The Democrats have had some recent success, though, in reducing the GOP's advantage.

Political action committees. As a result of the campaign finance legislation enacted in the 1970s, the role of **political action committees**
(PACs) has expanded greatly. PACs are organizations formed by business corporations, trade associations, labor unions, and the like, to
raise and disburse funds to advance political objectives. The emergence of corporate and labor PACs followed a long period in which
such activity was restricted by law. In 1907, the Tillman Act banned
corporate gifts of money to candidates for federal elective office or to
any committees that supported such candidates—which does not mean,
of course, that the contributions actually stopped. The ban was incorporated into the Federal Corrupt Practices Act of 1925, which extended
the prohibition to cover contributions of "anything of value." The
Smith-Connally Act of 1943 and the Taft-Hartley Act of 1947 banned
contributions to federal-office candidates by unions from their members' dues.

The Federal Election Campaign Act of 1971 introduced an important change in this area. It permitted the use of corporate funds and
union treasury money for "the establishment, administration, and
solicitation of contributions to a separate, segregated fund to be used
for a political purpose." These funds have become known as PACs.

**Political action
committees**

[27]Herbert E. Alexander, "Political Parties and the Dollar," *Society*, January/February
1985, p. 56.

Table 12.6
PAC Contributions (1985–86) to Federal Candidates (in millions of dollars)

	Candidate status			Party affiliation of recipient	
Type of PAC	Incumbent	Challenger	Open seat	Democrat	Republican
Corporation	37.7	3.9	7.8	19.2	30.2
Trade/member/health	26.5	3.0	4.9	16.8	17.6
Labor organization	17.9	7.6	5.5	28.7	2.3
Non-connected	9.8	4.9	4.7	11.2	8.2
Other	4.2	.5	.6	2.8	2.4
Total	96.1	19.9	23.5	78.7	60.7

Source: Federal Election Commission, release of May 21, 1987, p. 2.

Under the law, an individual can give up to $5,000 to a PAC. By July 1987, 1,779 corporate PACs were registered with the Federal Election Commission, along with 797 trade association PACs, 382 representing labor unions, and about 1,250 more in assorted other categories. PACs contributed in 1985–86 about $116 million to candidates in federal election campaigns. Seeking to keep on good terms with influential lawmakers, PACs supported incumbents over challengers by a wide margin (Table 12.6). Table 12.7 shows the 20 biggest PACs in 1985–

Table 12.7
Top 20 PAC Contributors to Federal Candidates, 1985–86

Realtors Political Action Committee	$2,782,338
American Medical Association PAC (AMPAC)	$2,107,492
National Education Association PAC (NEA)	$2,055,133
UAW-V-CAP (United Auto Workers)	$1,621,055
Nat'l Assn of Retired Federal Employees PAC (NARFE-PAC)	$1,491,895
Committee on Letter Carriers Political Education	$1,490,875
Democratic Republican Independent Voter Education Committee (DRIVE) (Teamsters)	$1,457,196
Build PAC of the National Association of Home Builders	$1,424,240
Association of Trial Lawyers PAC (ATLA)	$1,404,000
Machinists Non-Partisan Political League	$1,364,550
Seafarers Political Activity Donation (SPAD)	$1,187,106
American Federation of State, County, and Municipal Employees P.E.O.P.L.E. (AFSCME)	$1,122,075
Active Ballot Club, A Dept. of United Food & Commercial Workers Int'l Union	$1,116,879
National Association of Life Underwriters PAC	$1,087,859
Dealers Election Action Committee of the National Automobile Dealers Association (NADA)	$1,059,650
Auto Dealers for Free Trade PAC	$1,016,699
Int'l Brotherhood of Electrical Workers Committee on Political Education	$969,840
National PAC	$952,000
Carpenters' Legislative Improvement Committee	$947,836
American Bankers Association BANKPAC	$934,440

Source: Federal Election Commission Release of May 21, 1987.

86, measured in terms of the total amount of their contributions to federal candidates.

Campaign Techniques and Technicians

Over the last quarter-century, changes in the technology of mass communications have transformed American electioneering. The biggest single factor, of course, is the increasing use of television: Candidates can reach far more people through television news coverage, political advertisements, and televised debates than through the most vigorous traditional campaigning. Still, most candidates are unfamiliar with television at the technical level; they don't know how to buy air time, how to schedule it most advantageously, or how to develop the most effective television appeals. The more they use television, and the more dimensions the medium offers (the spread of cable networks, for instance, has opened new possibilities) the more candidates must turn to media consultants. Technological change intrudes in other areas: The application of computers to direct-mail efforts has greatly enlarged the reach of political fundraising. Polling has become a large part of the apparatus of modern campaigns. In 1976, Patrick Caddell served as pollster to Democratic candidate Jimmy Carter, and by all accounts had a major influence on the Carter campaign. Caddell continued to be part of Carter's inner circle of advisers after Carter moved into the White House. Pollster Richard Wirthlin had a similar place in the 1980 and 1984 Reagan campaigns, and again the polling expert became an important presidential adviser. Peter Hart has continued to be active not only in polling for, but in advising Democratic candidates, as has Lance Tarrance for Republicans. In the 1988 presidential election, Robert Teeter served as pollster and a leading adviser to George Bush; Irwin ("Tubby") Harrison did the polling for Michael Dukakis.

Media advisers are also key actors in the new corps of political technicians. Roger Ailes was George Bush's chief of media in 1988. Leslie Dach played this role for Michael Dukakis. David Garth, Gerald Rafshoon, Charles Guggenheim, Douglas Bailey, and Robert Goodman are other media consultants who have attained national prominence.

Selling Soap and Electing Presidents

A student once wrote to the great nineteenth-century British prime minister, Benjamin Disraeli, asking how he should prepare for a career in public life. Disraeli replied that there were only two things he needed to know to succeed in politics. "You must know yourself, and you must know the times." Political scientists William Schneider observes:

"That is still true. Only these days, candidates have to hire political consultants to find out who they are and what's going on."[28]

Many others, we suspect, share Schneider's concern. The army of technicians surrounding candidates seems too engrossed in the manipulative side of things, and the candidates themselves often appear too inclined to listen to the new salesmen. "It's not like selling soap," we sometimes feel like shouting. "Electing a president is really serious and important. Don't worry so much about running really clever political ads, or coming up with a catchy slogan. Just give us the facts as best you can on where you hope to lead the country, and why you think you have the ability to get it there."

In the end, though, our frustration with long, overly manipulative presidential campaigns may be a little overdrawn. Voters are hardly helpless pawns. They have their own ideas about what the country needs and assess candidates against demanding standards. As *New York Times* columnist Tom Wicker notes,

Are voters being manipulated?

> this is a far more complex—even mysterious—process than the "selling soap" comparison so often invoked. Not even Ronald Reagan was elected for his smile or his hairdo, and no one will be in 1988 either. . . . Voters look ultimately for someone to believe in. What causes them to place their confidence in a candidate is not always clear, but it's seldom because he or she acts and talks like everyone else in the race, and even less often because of an artifice or posturing on television.[29]

Beyond the selling is the searching—and the searching should command our respect.

THE 1988 RACE FOR PRESIDENT

Both parties had long lists of presidential hopefuls in Campaign '88. On the Democratic side: former Senator Gary Hart of Colorado (forced by scandal to withdraw from the race in April 1987); Senator Joseph Biden of Delaware; Congresswoman Patricia Schroeder of Colorado; Senator Paul Simon of Illinois; former Governor Bruce Babbitt of Arizona; Congressman Richard Gephardt of Missouri; Senator Albert Gore of Tennessee; the Reverend Jesse Jackson; and the man who was to win his party's nomination decisively, Governor Michael Dukakis of Massachusetts. On the Republican side: former Senator Paul Laxalt of Nevada; former Secretary of State Alexander Haig; former Governor Pete DuPont of Delaware; Television evangelist Pat Robertson; New York Congressman Jack Kemp; Senate Republican Leader Robert Dole of Kansas; and Vice President George

[28] William Schneider, "What's Going to Sell in Next Year's Race?" *National Journal*, April 25, 1987, p. 1016.
[29] Tom Wicker, "The Seven Dwarfs," *New York Times*, July 4, 1987, p. 27.

Bush, who surprised a lot of people first by winning the GOP nomination handily and then by beating Michael Dukakis solidly in the November balloting.

George Bush was the Rodney Dangerfield of much of the campaign: He found it hard to get any respect. His voice was too high, pundits said, his syntax too garbled, his style too patrician, his personality too soft, and the man he chose as his running mate in his first "presidential decision"—Senator Dan Quayle of Indiana—was too inexperienced. Each time he triumphed, analysts managed to find an explanation that assigned responsibility for it elsewhere. When he beat Bob Dole decisively in the "Super Tuesday" primaries across the South in March, it was because southern Republicans wanted to affirm their admiration for Ronald Reagan—by voting for his designated heir. When Bush, whom polls had shown trailing, caught up with Dukakis at the time of the Republican convention, it was because the structure of the election—peace, prosperity, a popular president, an electorate satisfied with how things were going—was finally asserting itself. And when he pulled into the lead in the homestretch of the campaign, it was because Dukakis and his advisers had messed things up.

Elements of all these explanations are true. Michael Dukakis had obvious weaknesses as a candidate. He and his key advisers had never before run a national campaign and this inexperience showed. Clearly in the mainstream of post-1960s liberalism, Dukakis was not the man to help his party overcome the problems it has been having with its public philosophy. And no one should have expected him to bring to the campaign the Kennedy-like charisma that might have overcome the Republicans' structural advantage.

Nonetheless, Bush was a surprisingly strong candidate. On basic strategy, he took the heat as Ronald Reagan's unswervingly loyal vice president in the expectation, which was rewarded, of long-term gain. He was the caring moderate—who strongly defended all of the core elements of the conservative agenda. He was unremitting, and successful, in his efforts to place Dukakis securely in the line of post-1960s Democratic liberals. Coming after Reagan, Bush faced a daunting task in establishing his own political identity. Recognizing that the structure of the election favored the incumbent Republicans, Democratic leaders made a concerted effort to depict Bush as a weak leader, not up to the man he served as vice president. The drumbeat of this attack—lap dog, yes man, wimp, "born with a silver foot in his mouth"—met with considerable success over the spring and early summer. Bush went into the Republican convention in August facing a high measure of public doubt.

His acceptance speech at the convention was his first big opportunity to address these doubts in three key communities: the press, Republican activists, and the general public. He succeeded. Polls taken immediately after the GOP convention showed him viewed far more

Bush's public image

Dukakis's weaknesses

President-elect George Bush confers with President Ronald Reagan.

favorably than he had been in the preceding months. The two presidential debates had figured prominently in Dukakis's plans to win

Bush's rise in the polls

his personal competition with Bush. Prior to the first, most analysts thought Dukakis would extract some advantage from these confrontations. If nothing else, the lesson of past debates seemed to be that the candidate of the out-of-power party—Kennedy in 1960, Carter in 1976, Reagan in 1980, and Mondale in 1984—started with an initial advantage by having a bigger target to attack. But Bush held his own in his first meeting with Dukakis and, in the jury of public opinion, carried the second decisively.

Polls taken after presidential debates have shown two typically different stages of public reaction: the first, when viewers give their verdicts before being coached by news accounts, and the second, in the days after, when the "spin" put on by news analysts has had its impact. Polls taken right after the debate on October 13 gave Bush a larger composite margin over Dukakis than any previous set of debate-night polls had shown for any other candidate.

To win the 1988 election, George Bush probably didn't need to convince a majority of voters that in personal terms he was better suited than Michael Dukakis to be president of the United States. Gaining a tie with his opponent on those matters of strength, character, likeableness, and competence was all he needed, given the underlying advantage with which the Republicans entered the campaign. But he in fact won his personal competition with Dukakis. Pre-election polls consistently showed him farther ahead in personal ratings than in the trial heats. The one pair of campaign decisions where Dukakis gained a clear advantage over Bush was their vice-presidential choices.

Democratic vice-presidential nominee Lloyd Bentsen of Texas got generally high marks; Republican Dan Quayle, in the opinion of most observers, cost his ticket votes.

The Congressional Elections

While the Republicans again won the presidency in 1988—for the fifth time in the last six contests—the Democrats did well in other elections. They made net gains of one seat in the Senate, two seats in the House, and one governorship; and they maintained their commanding position in the state legislatures (Table 12.8).

The most striking feature of congressional voting is its burgeoning uncompetitiveness. The apparent manifestation of this problem is that virtually all incumbents of both parties who seek to do so now win re-election to the U.S. House of Representatives, typically by overwhelming margins. The underlying core of the problem is the virtually complete separation of House voting from judgments about the proper course of public policy. Much the same thing seems to be happening in state legislatures, for the same reasons.

Uncompetitive congressional elections

Political scientist David Mayhew was one of the first to call attention to the "vanishing marginals"—House seats where the winner's margin was small enough that the contest could be seen as competitive.[30] In 1960, while both parties had plenty of safe seats, 203 of the 435 contests were at least marginally competitive, with the winner

Table 12.8
Election Box Score

	1980		1982		1984		1986		1988	
	D	R	D	R	D	R	D	R	D	R
House of Representatives	243	192	269	166	253	182	258	177	260	175
Senate	46	53	46	54	47	53	55	45	55	45
Governors	27	23	34	16	34	16	26	24	28	22
Members of state legislatures	4,483	2,918	4,643	2,734	4,338	3,035	4,474	2,924	4,477	2,925
Control of state legislative chambers by party	63	35	71	26	65	31	66	29	69	29
States with both legislative houses and governor of same party	17	7	23	4	18	4	14	6	14	4
Proportions of all state legislative seats (in percent)	60	39	63	37	59	41	60	40	60	40

[30] David R. Mayhew, "Congressional Elections: The Case of the Vanishing Marginals," *Polity*, Spring 1974, pp. 295–317.

Table 12.9
Competitiveness of the U.S. House of Representatives' Districts, 1960–88

	Number of districts in which winner's margin in 1960 was:	Number of districts in which winner's margin in 1980 was:	Number of districts in which winner's margin in 1988 was:
Winner is unopposed	54	27	57
75–99%	43	94	91
70–74%	27	64	94
65–69%	49	60	62
60–64%	59	50	66
55–59%	112	61	36
52–54%	56	39	17
51% or less	35	40	12

being held to less than 60 percent of the vote. By 1980, though, only 140 House races saw the winner under 60 percent.

The process hasn't stopped. The 1988 House voting was the most uncompetitive in U.S. history. The winner was either unopposed or beat his opponent by 70 to 30 percent or more in 242 districts. A respectable showing for a challenger has become holding the victor to "just" 60 to 69 percent of the vote, a result obtained in 128 districts in 1988. The losing candidate got as much as 40 percent of the vote in just 65 contests, and he came within 10 percentage points of the winner—that is, losing by 55–45 or less—in only 29 of the 435 House races (Table 12.9). Open seats—those where no incumbent is running—are often quite competitive, but in 1988 there were just 26 of them. Only 6 incumbents seeking re-election lost, and 5 of them had been tinged by some form of scandal.

What accounts for the virtual disappearance of competitiveness in U.S. House elections? One big part of the story is the enormous advantage incumbents typically enjoy in resources for promoting their candidacies. Staff provided to House members tripled in the 1960s and 1970s (see p. 172), and congressmen have put many of their new assistants to work back home in their districts. They have found this useful in serving constituents' needs—and, not incidentally, useful as a little electoral machine made available to them year-round at public expense. Few challengers can match this resource for self-publicization.

Advantages of incumbency

Incumbents generally enjoy a large advantage as well in campaign contributions. Knowing that incumbents are likely to be re-elected and that they will have to deal with them in advancing their legislative objectives, the political action committees (PACs) of the various interest groups heavily back incumbents, regardless of party. In the last election cycle (1985–86), PAC dollars went to congressional incumbents over their challengers by about $96 to $20 million; and incomplete returns for 1987–88 suggest that the margin will be greater still. Even challengers in races targeted by their political parties for special effort usually have less financial support than the congressmen they seek to unseat.

Candidate visibility

In races for governor and U.S. senator—as well, of course, as that for president—many voters know something substantial about the candidates' policy stands or records. In these contests, even well-funded incumbents who are better known than their opponents may readily be defeated, when the electorate is in a mood for policy change. But congressmen simply don't have the "policy visibility" governors and senators do. Most voters know next to nothing about their representative's voting record. They are, though, more likely to have some vaguely favorable image of him than they are of his opponent.

Weakening party influence

Political party ties are the one thing that could upset this dynamic. That is, a voter might not know anything about a congressman's voting record but still vote against him in favor of a less-well-known challenger because he preferred the challenger's party. But over the last quarter-century, as incumbents have accumulated election resources greater than ever before in U.S. history, the proportion of the electorate bound by strong party ties has declined precipitously. Better educated and drawing their political information largely from the communications media, today's voters feel they need parties less than did their counterparts of times past.

In highly visible races like those for president, senate, and governor, voters typically acquire enough information to make up for the decline of the guidance party ties long provided. At the other end of the spectrum, in elections of school board members, aldermen, etc., voters often have enough close-up, personal knowledge of the candidates to reach informed judgments. In between, such as in House races, there is a problem. Party voting is no longer decisive, but substantive knowledge of the candidates' records is usually insufficient to furnish a substitute base for substantive choice. Enjoying huge advantages in resources for self-promotion, incumbents in such contests are now winning re-election routinely, by escalating margins. Literally no one but the incumbents themselves benefits from this profoundly unrepresentative system.

SUMMARY

Universal suffrage was not achieved in the eighteenth or nineteenth centuries in the United States or any other country. Most American states dropped property qualifications for voting in the early 1800s, but many of them did not permit women to vote until ratification of the Nineteenth Amendment in 1920. Full voting participation by blacks was not realized until the civil rights legislation of the 1960s.

Today there is concern over the low and somewhat diminished level of voter turnout in the United States. Just over 53 percent of voting-age residents cast ballots in the 1984 presidential election; this represented a slight rise over the 1980 voting rate, but it was still well below the turnout in 1960, the modern high in the United States.

The curious way the United States expresses its rate of voter participation—as a percentage of the resident adult population, even though millions of these residents by law cannot vote—makes turnout seem lower than it really is. But it *is* lower than in most other democracies. This is partly because the United States has so many elections that it is hard for any one to seem a special event. The low turnout is also partly a response to a system where political stresses have been relatively manageable. The perceived cost of not voting, in short, has not been nearly as high in the United States as in most other democracies.

Voter turnout has been lower in the twentieth century than in the nineteenth, although not as much lower as statistics suggest. The weakening of local party organization and the increasing distance and complexity of government have probably been major factors accounting for the drop-off in voting.

Two features of American electoral arrangements are especially distinguishing. One is the heavy use of primary elections to pick party nominees. The other is the reliance on the single-member district, single-ballot, simple-majority system for translating votes into seats. This system has done much to bolster the ascendancy of the two major parties. If the United States instituted plural-member districts with proportional representation, it is likely that third parties would proliferate.

The number of elections held in the United States and the duration of campaigns have put a premium on political fundraising. Over the last two decades campaign costs have climbed much faster than inflation alone would have required. Television has become an increasingly important campaign resource or facility. Total election expenditures, at all levels, exceeded $2 billion in 1988.

Important federal legislation covering campaign spending was enacted in 1971 and 1974. Limits were imposed on how much individuals and groups could contribute to federal candidates. Effective disclosure provisions were instituted, to be administered by the Federal Election Commission (FEC). Public funding was established for presidential elections, along with tight spending limits for candidates who accept governmental assistance.

The legislation also encouraged the formation of political action committees (PACs) by business corporations, trade associations, labor unions, and other groups, to collect and disseminate funds for political purposes. Though tightly supervised by the FEC, PACs have become the hub of current contention over money in politics. PACs give much more support to incumbents of both parties than to challengers.

FOR FURTHER STUDY

David Butler, et al, eds., *Democracy at the Polls: A Comparative Study of Competitive National Elections* (Washington, DC: American Enterprise Institute for Public Policy Research, 1981). A superb collection of articles comparing electoral experience in democracies around the world.

Congressional Quarterly, *Guide to U.S. Elections* (Washington, DC: CQ Press, 1985). A compendium of information on U.S. presidential elections from 1789 through 1984.

Michael J. Malbin, ed., *Money and Politics in the United States: Financing Elections in the 1980s* (Washington, DC: American Enterprise Institute, 1984). A set of essays that examine various aspects of how election campaigns are financed in the United States and the implications this financing has for American democracy.

Nelson W. Polsby and Aaron Wildavsky, *Presidential Elections: Strategies of American Electoral Politics*, 7th ed. (New York: Scribners, 1988). The best analysis of recent presidential elections in the United States.

Larry J. Sabato, *The Rise of Political Consultants* (New York: Basic Books / Harper and Row, 1981). A study of the changing dynamics of campaigning in the United States, centering on the increased role of professional campaign consultants.

Raymond E. Wolfinger and Steven J. Rosenstone, *Who Votes?* (New Haven, CT: Yale University Press, 1980). The best available study of who votes and who doesn't vote in the United States, based on analysis of surveys conducted by the U.S. Bureau of the Census.

Federal Election Commission, miscellaneous reports: campaign guides, federal election campaign laws, FEC reports on financial activity (of candidates, parties and PACs) and numerous other documents—many provided free—by the FEC, 999 E Street and 1325 K Street, NW, Washington, DC.

Chapter 13

Political Parties

During Franklin D. Roosevelt's presidency in the 1930s, the Democrats emerged as the country's majority party. Their ascendency was evident at all levels, from the cities and statehouses to Congress and the presidency. More Americans identified themselves as Democrats than as Republicans—even though the Republicans had been the majority party for more than three decades up to the Great Depression. This massive shift in party fortunes is known as the New Deal *realignment*.

Since the 1930s, politicians, journalists, and political scientists have often debated what conditions might produce another such major change in the makeup and relative strength of the party coalitions— and whether such a new realignment is underway. Republican successes in recent presidential elections have given fresh currency to this long-playing interest.

When George Bush defeated Michael Dukakis on November 8, 1988, it was the fifth time in the last six elections that the Republicans had won the presidency. Their successes are a clear indication of change in the parties' electoral fortunes since the New Deal years, and they would seem to point to the emergence of a new Republican majority. But other election results tell a different story. Throughout the span of Republican dominance of the presidency, the Democrats have been the clear majority party in Congress. In the state houses, too, the Democrats have had the upper hand. What has been happening to the strength and makeup of the two major parties? Does it spell realignment?

We will be examining various data that shed light on this question. At the outset we should note, though, that much of the disagreement on whether realignment has occurred (or is proceeding) seems to involve semantics. *Realignment* is commonly used in three different though related meanings: (1) major social groups changing their partisan loyalties and voting differently than they did in times past; (2) a significant net change in the partisan balance of power; and (3) the emergence of a new majority party. Has the American polity in recent years experienced realignment? Yes, if either the first or the second meaning is employed; no, if the third construction is the one intended.

Let's imagine a political Rip Van Winkle who falls into a deep sleep just after Franklin Roosevelt's presidency, and wakes up in the mid-1980s. He finds that white southerners, who had stood so solidly behind FDR (and all preceding Democrats back to the Civil War), have moved substantially into the Republican camp—such that when an attractive Democratic moderate won about half the white vote in the 1985 Virginia gubernatorial race his party hailed the result as a major comeback! He finds black voters now overwhelmingly Democratic and a major component of that party's national coalition. When Rip fell asleep New England was, as it had long been, the most Republican region. Now it is the least; Republicans do better in the South and much better in the Mountain states. Young voters were the Democrats' best group in the New Deal years. Now the young are the Republicans' best age group.

Republican Gains

By the standard of shifting group alignments, realignment has certainly occurred. But what about by the second standard—a shift in party balance? The GOP has strengthened itself in its share of party loyalties. The last half-century shows the Republicans at first severely weakened by the experiences of the Depression decade. They reasserted themselves in the latter half of the 1940s and 1950s but, even in the Eisenhower years, they did not reverse the pattern that saw the Democrats beating them in the contest for support among new voters. The GOP fell further back in the 1960s and early 1970s, hammered by their disastrous defeat in the 1964 election, by the Vietnam War turmoil of the early 1970s, and by the Watergate scandals. From this post-Watergate nadir, the party climbed back up to achieve basic parity with the Democrats. The GOP has been stronger in the mid- to late 1980s than at any time since the Great Depression, and vastly stronger than it was in the mid-1970s.

A shifting partisan balance of power

This chronicle of Republican ups and downs should remind us forcefully of two things: First, the partisan balance of power has been far from stable over the last half-century. It has changed significantly on several occasions. Second, while the underlying patterns of group attachments to the parties evolve slowly, the mix of current events, policies, and candidates is capable of moving each party's backing well above or below its base-line support. Political tides raise (or lower) all boats: Republican and Democratic strength in most social groups rises and falls, as the case may be, depending on how attractive their presidential candidates are, how things seem to be going in the country, and how basic party policies are viewed.

Party identification is the standard U.S. measure of underlying partisan strength. As they developed the profession during the 1930s, George Gallup, Elmo Roper, and other founders of polling recognized that they couldn't ask most people which party they "belonged to," because most Americans don't belong to political parties in the sense of holding formal membership and paying dues. Rather, we become Republicans and Democrats *by thinking of ourselves* as adherents of one party or the other. In the late 1930s Gallup began asking: "Do you *regard yourself* as a Republican, a Democrat, a Socialist, or an independent in politics?" Variations of this basic approach, emphasizing identification rather than membership, have been widely used over the last half-century.

Party identification

The exact proportions of Americans identifying as Democrats and Republicans vary from one survey to another, but a general pattern is evident. In 1988, most national surveys showed Democrats outnumbering Republicans by a clear but modest margin. A poll done by Gallup May 13–22, 1988, showed 38 percent Democratic, 28 percent Republican, and 26 percent independent, with 8 percent saying they had no preference. A series of four surveys taken during February, March, and May 1988 for the Americans Talk Security (ATS) project found 36 percent of its respondents (all of them registered voters) Democrats, 30 percent Republicans, and 32 percent independents.[1] Figure 13.1, based on surveys by CBS News and the *New York Times*, shows Democrats outnumbering Republicans by margins of between 5 and 9 percentage points in the winter, spring, and summer of 1988—margins much narrower than the Democrats enjoyed in the mid- to late 1970s and the early 1980s.

Democrats still outnumber Republicans

Whatever their precise mix, party loyalties have weakened for much of the U.S. electorate—a subject we will discuss later in this chapter. More and more voters are prepared to cast their presidential ballots for the candidate and party they see most likely to advance various policies and objectives. American elections increasingly hinge on perceptions of current performance capabilities rather than traditional loyalties rooted in such matters as regional and ethnic experience. On the question of which party does the better job managing the economy and keeping the country prosperous, the Democrats gained a huge advantage during the New Deal years. This advantage per-

Weakening party loyalties

---

[1] The Americans Talk Security Project involved a series of surveys focusing on foreign policy and defense issues in the 1988 campaign. Each survey used the same wording for all questions identifying respondents in terms of party identification and political ideology, and each used the same demographic categories. The four surveys combined here were conducted for ATS by the Daniel Yankelovich Group, Martilla and Kiley, and Market Opinion Research.

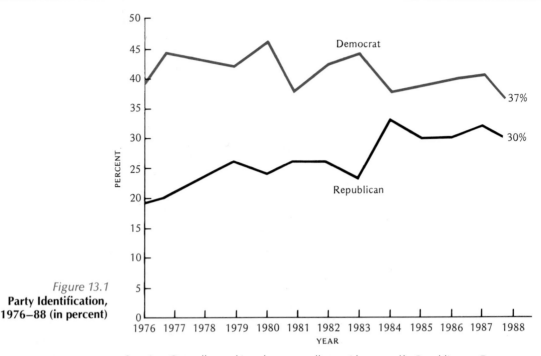

Figure 13.1
Party Identification, 1976–88 (in percent)

Question: Generally speaking, do you usually consider yourself a Republican, a Democrat, or what?

sisted beyond Franklin D. Roosevelt's presidency. Asked in March 1947 which party they preferred to have in office "if hard times come again," 51 percent of those interviewed by the Gallup Organization named the Democrats, just 30 percent the Republicans. Fifty-four percent in this survey credited the Democrats with being better able to keep wages high, only 22 percent the Republicans.

Near the end of Dwight Eisenhower's first term, the GOP had drawn even with the Democrats in terms of the proportion seeing it likely to "do better keeping the country prosperous." It couldn't hold this position, though, and by the end of Eisenhower's presidency a substantial plurality of Americans again credited the Democrats with being the party of prosperity. Figure 13.2 shows that the Democrats maintained this status through virtually all of the ensuing two decades, often by overwhelming margins.

In the 1980s, however, the Republicans caught up with the Democrats on this key performance measure. Recent surveys asking which party is better at keeping the U.S. economy healthy differ somewhat in their findings, both for technical reasons relating to the nature of sampling and because economic developments are constantly changing. Overall, though, these surveys found in the mid- to late 1980s a slight overall GOP edge in the numbers naming it as the party best for prosperity.

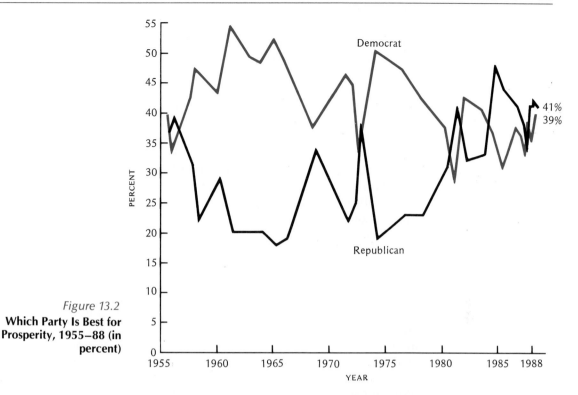

Figure 13.2

Which Party Is Best for Prosperity, 1955–88 (in percent)

Question: Looking ahead to the next few years, which political party—the Republicans, or the Democrats—do you think will do the better job of keeping the country prosperous?
Source: Gallup polls of dates shown. I have shown one asking in each year the question was asked—except in 1972 when I showed two askings, because the question got a very different response early in the year than it did at election time. I have shown *every* asking since January of 1987. The difference between the Democratic and Republican percentages shown and 100 percent are accounted for by respondents who said "no difference" or "no opinion."

Today's public makes a complex set of distinctions about partisan capabilities or performance, giving the Republicans an edge in some important areas and the Democrats in others. In general, pluralities credit the GOP with doing a better job handling the U.S.S.R., maintaining a strong defense, and curbing inflation. The Democrats are seen stronger on controlling defense spending, addressing unemployment, extending social services, and attending to those in need. On issues of war and peace, and, interestingly, on the federal deficit, the public splits evenly on which party does the better job.

Public assessment of party performance

Up for Grabs

A shift in the partisan balance need not involve the creation of a new majority. We see this historically with the emergence of the Republican party. The GOP became a major party at the time of the Civil War, but for the next thirty years—up until the mid-1890s—it operated in rough parity with the Democrats.

Republicans' edge in
presidential balloting

Today each of the two major parties has its strongholds. The Republicans have done especially well in presidential balloting. As noted, they have been victorious in five of the last six presidential elections, gaining 55 percent of the total two-party vote over this span. Since winning narrowly in 1968, the GOP's victory margins have been 23 percentage points in 1972, 10 points in 1980, 18 points in 1984, and 8 points in 1988. The one election the Democrats won, 1976, is in a sense the most graphic confirmation of the GOP's ascendancy: Jimmy Carter and the Democrats managed only the narrowest win in 1976, even though the Republican party had been decimated by the massive Watergate scandals that culminated in the forced resignation of a Republican president, Richard Nixon. The Republican presidential margins of the last quarter-century are large by any historic comparison. They are comparable to those the Democrats achieved during the New Deal elections (1932–48) and to the Republicans' own presidential ascendancy from 1896 through 1928.

Democrats' edge in
the House

Outside the presidency, though, the Democrats' position remains strong. They have enjoyed a majority in the House of Representatives continuously since 1955. In the 1988 voting, they renewed their decisive legislative majorities at both the national and state levels, winning 260 of the 435 House seats, 55 of 100 in the Senate, and 60 percent of all seats in the state legislatures.

Some observers explain these split results in terms of Americans' liking for separation of powers and checks and balances. If the direction the Republicans propose for national policy is to be encouraged by the election of Republican presidents, isn't some check on it useful in Congress and the state houses? Besides, many people are ambivalent about the role of government and other central policy issues. What better way to express their mixed feelings than by ordaining divided party control?

Political advantage of
incumbency

Such factors are undoubtedly at work. They are almost certainly not the main reason why congressional vote results have diverged so sharply from those of presidential voting. As we saw in chapter 12, voting for the House of Representatives hinges much more on the advantages of incumbency than on decisions to back one party's programs over the other's. Members of Congress now have large staffs and other resources of incumbency useful in advancing their re-election. Gaining high levels of name recognition and emphasizing their nonpartisan service to constituents, they can often divorce their own electoral fortunes from those of their parties' presidential nominees. In addition, incumbents frequently are able to outspend their challengers by substantial margins. Congressional incumbents of both parties enjoy a big edge over their challengers in campaign finance partly because many interest groups have a proclivity for backing incumbents—with whom they deal in pressing their various policy objectives. The Democrats entered the modern period with a big edge in congressional seats, and the advantages of incumbency have been theirs more than the Republicans'.

The current split-level voting system

The United States simply does not have a dominant party at present, and this condition may persist. Probably never as stable as it was once thought to be, party identification has shown a great deal of movement lately. In the television age, changes in the mix of issues, events, and leadership seem to have the potential for causing more rapid shifts in party fortunes than ever before.

Even more importantly, party voting has greatly declined. That is, the proportion of the electorate prepared to support one party or the other across the board, in all offices, has dropped off sharply from what it was in times past. Voting for the man (or woman) who is running for the office, rather than for the party, has become the rule. Ticket-splitting has reached massive proportions. In this context, the traditional conception of a "majority party" has been put in doubt.

THE NATURE OF PARTY IDENTIFICATION

To say "I am a Democrat" is to express a commitment deeper and more lasting than merely saying "I am going to vote for a Democratic nominee this election." Angus Campbell and his colleagues at the

"My God! I went to sleep a Democrat and I've awakened a Republican."

Drawing by Dana Fradon; © 1984 The New Yorker Magazine, Inc.

University of Michigan observed that "often a change of candidates and a broad alteration in the nature of the issues disturb very little the relative partisanship of a set of electoral units, which suggests that great numbers of voters have party attachments that persist through time."[2] But, granting that party identification taps some deeper form of party loyalty, just how stable is it, how are party ties formed, and how do they change?

Party identification since the 1950s

Work done by political scientists in the 1950s and 1960s suggested that for most voters party identification was bedrock stable, remarkably resistant to change even in the face of substantial shifts in political stimuli accruing from different mixes of candidates and issues in succeeding electoral campaigns. Over the last decade, however, analysts have revised this view. They now think that party identification is considerably more fluid than it had been portrayed.[3]

Greater fluidity in party identification

Behind the findings of greater fluidity is a more complex model of how party preferences are shaped and then continually acted upon by perceptions of candidates and issues in succeeding elections. For example, Benjamin Paige and Calvin Jones argue that "voters' party loyalties may both affect and be affected by comparative candidate evaluations or intended votes during a particular election campaign." A person's party loyalties may influence his perception of the candidates, of course, but it works the other way, too. How he feels about the candidates the parties nominate in an important election, like one for president, may affect how he feels about the parties themselves.[4]

Party loyalty and issue preference

Paige and Jones make a parallel argument with regard to how party identification relates to political issues. The party loyalties of voters influence how they see certain issues: Some voters in effect misperceive their party's stand on a program that matters to them, interpreting it as basically consistent with what they want; and some shift their own stance on less critical issues to make it consistent with what their party is saying. But the flow runs the other way, too. People form their party loyalties in part because of the issue preferences they have: For example, someone who in the 1930s believed that government needed to do more than it had been doing in social welfare was apt to be pushed toward a preference for the Democratic party, since the Democrats were developing a multitude of programs for a more ambitious federal role. Similarly, as the mix of salient issues changes

[2] Angus Campbell et al., *The American Voter* (New York: Wiley, 1960), p. 121.

[3] See, for example, Edward Dryer, "Change and Stability in Party Identification," *Journal of Politics*, 35 (1973):712–22; John E. Jackson, "Issue, Party Choice, and Presidential Votes," *American Journal of Political Science*, 1975, 161–85; Benjamin I. Paige and Calvin C. Jones, "Reciprocal Effects of Policy Preferences, Party Loyalties and the Vote," *American Political Science Review*, 73 (1979):1071–89; and Herbert F. Weisberg, "The Electoral Kaleidoscope: Political Change in the Polarizing Election of 1984," paper presented to the 1985 annual meeting of the American Political Science Association, New Orleans, LA.

[4] Paige and Jones, "Reciprocal Effects," p. 1079.

in succeeding elections, and as the interests and perspectives of individual voters shift, voters are often encouraged to change their feelings about the parties. The party to which they were initially committed perhaps becomes increasingly removed from their current program preferences, while the party they previously opposed comes closer to representing what they now want.

In short, a continuing interaction goes on among underlying party identification, candidate preferences, and policy choices. This is not to say that a voter is likely to be constantly changing his party loyalty—because, among other things, his political interests and perspectives are often relatively stable and the two parties do not wildly and capriciously change their general approach to policy and governance. Yet if their party identification shows persistence over time, voters are sometimes pushed to change their views of the parties as new issues and new candidates come along that give these voters new views of the parties.

Forming, and Changing, Party Loyalties

This important process—involving the underlying stability of party identification but also the mechanisms through which party loyalties can change—is better understood as we consider just how an individual voter may come to the party loyalties he or she holds. Seven different sets of factors seem to be involved.

1) *Home Team.* This hypothetical voter sees his party as the "home team." He "roots" for it in part for reasons having nothing to do with its policies. Most of us experience attachments that have no base in objective interests. I have been a lifelong fan of the Boston Red Sox, probably because I grew up in southern Maine, where the Red Sox are the home team. But my commitment to the Sox persisted when I was living in New York and California. Such attachments are not limited to baseball; similar ties bind people to political parties.

2) *Yesterday's Hero.* For our hypothetical voter, his party is also the one which, in years past, presented a candidate to whom he felt especially close. Perhaps it was Franklin D. Roosevelt or John F. Kennedy who left a strong, positive, lasting impression, or on the Republican side, Dwight D. Eisenhower. In years after, the Democrats are always FDR's party, or Jack Kennedy's party, or the Republicans are always seen favorably as Ike's party.

3) *Today's Choice.* Not only does he remember one or more of the leading politicians of his party in times past with special fondness; our voter is also comfortable with the current crop of party nominees. At the very least, he usually doesn't have any difficulty supporting the people his party is presenting for major offices. For example, initially attracted to the Democratic party by his admiration for Harry Truman, he is now equally enthusiastic about Michael Dukakis.

Party workers during a campaign.

4) *Past Cultural Ties.* Our voter grew up with a strong sense of cultural ties to his party. He might, for example, have been raised in a Boston Irish-Catholic family where Democratic attachments seemed natural, almost unquestionable. Or, on the other side, our voter may have been reared a Protestant in a small Indiana town, a cultural environment as securely Republican as Boston Irish-Catholicism has been Democratic. This is not simply the party as the home team but also as "the party where my people fit," the party whose social composition and cultural style seem far more supportive and attractive than those of the alternative. In wide sections of the North throughout much of American history, it was not much of an exaggeration to describe the Republicans as the Protestant party, the Democrats as the Catholic party. While these connections reflected religious and ethnic prejudice, they should not be dismissed as merely that. Important differences of style and culture separated Protestants and Catholics in the United States for much of the country's history and the two major parties were distinguished by them.

5) *Present Cultural Ties.* Our voter belongs today to a setting where matters of style and culture push him as strongly toward his party as those of times past made him comfortable there. It isn't simply that when he was growing up the Democrats or the Republicans were the party of "his people"; today the area where he lives and the social groups to which he belongs sustain the same partisan loyalty. The initial cultural predispositions to the party are constantly reinforced by present-day contact and experience.

6) *Past Policies.* Our voter found himself strongly in agreement with the principal programs and policies of his party at the time he made his formative political commitments. On the Democratic side he might have been deeply attracted to the programs advanced by the Roosevelt administration in the 1930s, or if he were from a younger generation, by the civil rights and social welfare policies of Lyndon Johnson's Great Society. On the Republican side, he might have had precisely the opposite policy responses: believing that the Democrats' programs involved an overreliance on government and that the Republicans' course of less government was sounder. In either case his party was not just the home team, not just the home of leaders he revered, more than a place where he was culturally comfortable: In broad terms it governed more or less along the lines he favored.

7) *Present Policies.* Today our voter still agrees with the basic commitments of his party. Of course he takes issue with its programs or promises in some instances, but overall he thinks it is pointing the country in the right direction. Its view of how America should be governed, and his own view, still fit together comfortably.

In this hypothetical case, where all seven sets of factors push the individual in the same partisan direction, his party identification is strong and unambiguous. He is securely Democratic or securely Republican. We need not worry about the precise weight of these seven factors or just how they interact: When they are all aligned in the same direction a strong party tie results and all seven contribute to that preference.

Factors in strong party identification

	Party A	Party B
1. Home Team	x	
2. Yesterday's Hero	x	
3. Today's Choice	x	
4. Past Cultural Ties	x	
5. Present Cultural Ties	x	
6. Past Policies	x	
7. Present Policies	x	

For some voters at least some of the time, the political world is in fact this consistent in its political stimuli. But for many voters in at least some instances, the various factors related to choice of party do not point in the same direction: Some push the voter toward one party, while others incline him away from it and toward the opposition.

Cross Pressures

Consider the case of a white southerner in his sixties at the time of the 1972 election. He had grown up with a picture of the Democrats as the home team. He remembered how much Franklin Roosevelt meant to him in the 1930s. He had strongly supported FDR's social welfare policies. When he was coming of age politically around 1925, the Democrats were the party in which his people, white southerners, had coalesced during the Civil War and Reconstruction, the party of white supremacy in southern politics, and the party that opposed Republican rule in Washington sustained by majority support in the Yankee North.

By 1972, however, much had changed. As the civil rights revolution swept the South and the national Democratic party committed itself firmly to racial change, it seemed less clear to him that the Democrats were the party of his people. FDR was his patron saint, but George McGovern certainly wasn't: He preferred Republican Richard Nixon, whom he considered a stronger leader. The programs of the New Deal had his backing but many of the newer Democratic policies, and not just those dealing with race, went contrary to his preferences. The fact that the rural South of his boyhood, an economically poor region that felt estranged from the industrial North, had become more urban and industrial made Republican policies now look much different to him, more palatable. Our voter was severely cross pressured. In the presidential election his choice was fairly easy: McGovern was not, as he saw it, the proper Democratic leader; Nixon was better and got his vote. But was he a Democrat or a Republican?

Cross pressures in party identification

	Democrats	Republican
1. Home Team	x	
2. Yesterday's Hero	x	
3. Today's Choice		x
4. Past Cultural Ties	x	
5. Present Cultural Ties		x
6. Past Policies	x	
7. Present Policies		x

Some southern whites even in 1972 had swung over and called themselves Republicans, but the great majority of those in older age groups born and raised in the region still saw themselves as Democrats. The Democratic party remained the home team, and the pull of past cultural, candidate, and policy loyalties was strong enough to maintain Democratic partisanship, especially since many state and local Democratic leaders were reinforcing the old ties even as developments involving the national parties were rupturing them.[5]

[5] For data supporting the generalization that in the late 1960s and early 1970s the majority of older native white southerners continued to think of themselves as Democrats even though they were being pushed away from their once secure Democratic loyalties, see Raymond E. Wolfinger and Michael G. Hagen, "Republican Prospects: Southern Comfort," *Public Opinion*, October / November 1985, pp. 8–13.

Partisan conversion of white southerners

While this doesn't tell us when a given percentage of native white southerners would be expected to jump ship and swim over to the Republicans, it does indicate the magnitude of the cross pressures. From it one could easily conclude that, unless the current mix of stimuli which were inclining many away from the Democrats changed, a major shift in party identification was inevitable. The longer the new pro-Republican influences persisted, the more *they became past as well as present*. The Democrats' lead over the Republicans in party identification among white southerners declined in the late 1970s and early 1980s; as late as the spring of 1984, however, the Democrats still had a substantial edge. Since 1985, though, the two parties have been basically even in the white south.

Partisan balance shifting to the Republicans

The percentage of white southerners identifying as Republicans in February through June 1985 was 10 points higher than it had been in the spring of 1983, an unusually large and rapid shift in underlying party loyalties across a large and diverse social group. Other polls confirm this picture (see Table 13.1). The partisan balance was tipped significantly in favor of the Republicans in the mid 1980s. We don't know precisely why this shift occurred when it did. We can hypothesize, however, that Ronald Reagan's popularity had much to do with it, coming after various events over the past quarter-century had already eroded Democratic loyalties.

Table 13.1
Party Identification of White Southerners (in percent)

1979			1983			1985			1988		
D	*R*	*I*	*D*	*R*	*I*	*D*	*R*	*I*	*D*	*R*	*I*
46	21	33	42	23	35	36	39	25	33	33	34
	D: +25			D: +19			R: +3			R: 0	

Source: Gallup polls in the years shown, except for 1988 when data are from combined February–June surveys conducted for the Americans Talk Security project.

Persistence of old identifications

The partisan conversion of the white southerners is a dramatic story—but also an exceptional one. A group rarely moves from a position where it has been strongly pushed toward one party to another where, just a quarter of a century or so later, it is decisively inclined to the opposition. More often, when developments involving cultural ties, candidates, and policy preferences move members of a group away from their old party loyalties they do so much more tentatively and incompletely. The more inconsistent or contradictory the new stimuli are, the greater the persistence of party identification based on old loyalties and preferences will be.

Party identification is the end product of a swirl of stimuli, involving past and present experiences and expectations for the future, that may or may not come together behind the choice of one party over the other, and that may or may not shift so markedly over a period of time as to produce a general partisan conversion. This perspective helps us avoid a blind determinism—as though party loyalties once set are immutable, or as though once set they can be changed only under the impact of a massive system-shaking crisis like the Great Depression. More modest changes in American society and politics can gradually shift the mix of stimuli for a group away from one party and toward another. This is why the dichotomy often suggested by questions about partisan change—is realignment occurring—is a bit simplistic. Realignment is a continuous process involving many groups, each with its own mix of partisan influences changing according to differing timetables.

Gradual shifts over time

Too many things are at work for there ever to be a single structure to realignment, a fundamental pattern repeated periodically. Only the process is constant: Past influences pushing various groups toward one party are sometimes eroded, in varying degrees of completeness over differing lengths of time, culminating eventually in major differences in the way the social groups align themselves.

CHANGING GROUP ALIGNMENTS

In forming party attachments individuals gain a frame of reference from the decisive events of the period when they first come to political consciousness—usually in their late teens or early twenties—which then shape their subsequent values and actions.[6] Of course, rich and poor youth, factory workers and college students, blacks and whites, may experience their generational scene in different ways. Still, whatever the specific generational unit, the early political values are likely to continue to influence the group's outlook even many years in the future.

Generational Experiences

Our discussion of the formation of partisan attachments permits us to refine the idea of political generations and apply it specifically to changes in party strength in the United States. A group comes of age politically at a time when certain political leaders are on the stage. These leaders are not viewed in the same way by everyone, of course, but some are decidedly more respected and popular than others. Sometimes these ascendent politicians are Republicans and sometimes they are Democrats. For new voters without a lot of past polit-

Experiences upon coming of age politically

[6] See Karl Mannheim, *Ideology and Utopia* (New York: Harcourt, Brace, 1936); idem, "The Sociological Problem of Generations," in *Essays on the Sociology of Knowledge* (New York: Oxford University Press, 1952), pp. 276–322; Sigmund Neumann, *Permanent Revolution* (New York: Harper and Brothers, 1942); Rudolf Herbele, *Social Movements* (New York: Appleton-Century-Crofts, 1951).

ical experience, the impressions gained from this powerful first personal exposure to political leaders may be very important. Similarly, a distinctive mix of issues dominates political argument as these new voters come of age politically; if the mix generally favors one party over the other—as was the case in the 1930s when the Democrats were developing new programs and initiatives—the impact on persons without much previous personal political experience is apt to be substantial.

Returning to the table on page 465 showing the factors that shape party identification, we can see how, for a large component of an age group, the ascendent political leaders and issues at the time they begin to be involved personally in politics can push disproportionately toward one party or the other—in the absence of past experience leading them in another direction.

As the group ages, it begins to have new and sometimes conflicting political experiences—but these are filtered through an established pattern of party loyalties that are likely to persist, unless and until the mix of new experiences produces a sustained break.

Do available data support this interpretation? Let's begin by looking at the party preferences of different age groups in the United States as shown by Gallup surveys taken in 1952 and in 1985 (Table 13.2).

Table 13.2
Party Identification by Age, 1952 and 1985 (in percent)

Age	1952			1985			Democratic (−) Republican	
	D	R	I	D	R	I	1952	1985
18–21	40	25	35	30	40	30	+15	−10
22–25	42	27	31	31	35	34	+15	− 4
26–29	43	26	31	31	35	33	+17	− 4
30–33	45	26	29	34	31	35	+19	+ 3
34–37	43	29	28	37	30	33	+14	+ 7
38–41	45	30	26	38	32	30	+15	+ 6
42–45	38	36	25	37	32	31	+ 2	+ 5
46–49	39	36	25	37	33	30	+ 3	+ 4
50–53	42	32	25	35	36	28	+10	− 1
54–57	39	38	24	41	32	27	+ 1	+ 9
58–61	41	37	21	42	35	23	+ 4	+ 7
62–65	39	39	22	48	32	21	0	+16
66–69	37	45	18	46	35	19	− 8	+11
70–73	40	43	17	47	35	17	− 3	+12
74–77	36	49	14	41	41	18	−13	0
78–81	34	50	16	40	41	19	−16	− 1
82 and over	31	57	12	40	42	18	−26	− 2
All ages	41	33	26	37	34	29	+ 8	+ 3

Source: Gallup polls conducted April through July 1952 (seven) and January through July 1985 (eight).

Survey data on
generational voting

The first thing we see is a striking difference in the party preferences of the age groups now as compared to 33 years ago. In 1952 the Democrats' best groups were the young and middle-aged; while the Republicans had large leads among the more elderly voters. In 1985, however, the Republicans were strongest among the young and the very old, while the Democrats had their greatest strength among people in their fifties, sixties, and early seventies.

Let's translate these data more directly into the frame of generational experience, showing groups by the time when they came of age politically rather than by current age. "Coming of age politically" will be expressed here as reaching 18 years, which seems adequate as a rough standard. Looking at Table 13.3, we see a broad array of groups,

Table 13.3
Republican and Democratic Party Identifiers by Years of Coming of Voting Age, 1952 and 1985 (in percent)

Year	Republican	Democratic (−) Republican	Democratic (−) Republican	Republican
1890–93	63	−26		
1894–97	54	− 8		
1898–1901	51	− 2		
1902–05	54	− 8		
1906–09	49	+ 2		
1910–13	48	+ 4		
1914–17	47	+ 6		
1918–21	46	+ 8		
1922–25	48	+ 4	0	50
1926–29	46	+ 8	0	50
1930–33	41	+18	+14	43
1934–37	39	+22	+14	43
1938–41	37	+26	+20	40
1942–45	39	+22	+10	45
1946–49	39	+22	+12	44
1950–53			0	50
1954–57			+ 6	47
1958–61			+ 6	47
1962–65			+10	45
1966–69			+10	45
1970–73			+ 6	47
1974–77			− 6	53
1978–81			− 6	53
1982–85			−14	57

Since the object of this table is to focus on the relative Republican versus Democratic strength in each generation, independents have been excluded from the calculations. To take an example of how the data should be read, among those who reached 18 years of age in the 1982–85 span, who identify with one or the other major party, 57 percent are Republican (and 43 percent Democratic).

Source: 1952 and 1985 Gallup polls.

from those who reached 18 years of age way back in the early 1890s—who were still part of the electorate in 1952—to people who reached voting age in the last few years. Using both the 1952 and the 1985 surveys extends the range of our generational examination. Some groups are represented in both the 1952 and the 1985 polls. Those who were just coming of political age in 1952 are now in their fifties.

The relative standing of the major parties varies substantially across generational groups in a fashion that corresponds in rough terms to what we know of decisive political experiences. For example, both the 1952 and 1985 Gallup polls show the Democrats' margin over the Republicans highest among those who came of age politically at the height of the Democrats' New Deal ascendancy. Since static enters into polling and poll responses, it is especially impressive that the picture provided by the two batches of surveys separated by thirty-three years is so consistent.

People who reached political maturity in the late 1930s and early 1940s were in 1952 unusually pro-Democratic—and they are so today.

Republicans had a big edge in the 1890s, but they began to lose this among new voters coming of age in the early twentieth century—reflecting in part the impact immigration had on the makeup of the population. In the 1930s the Democrats began to achieve an over-whelming generational advantage over the Republicans, which was not interrupted until the 1950s when various developments, among them Dwight Eisenhower's personal popularity, cut significantly into the Democrats' edge among new voters. The heyday of Kennedy's New Frontier and Johnson's Great Society saw the Democrats recover among new entrants, but over the last decade the GOP has, for the first time in a long while, begun to take the lead among those just coming into the electorate. More modest at first, the new Republican margin has widened substantially during the Reagan presidency, which has been a popular one.

These data help us understand why in recent years no dramatic overall swing to the Republicans has occurred in party identification, though the Democrats' position has diminished. The Democrats put together a long string where they bested the Republicans among new voters, and they continue to reap the benefits: People who came of age politically from the 1930s through the 1960s remain a large part of the electorate, and the impressive Democratic base built among these age groups has by no means been obliterated. In recent years, the Republicans have reversed the trend among new entrants; should they continue to have this success, they will in time shift the under-lying partisan base in their favor. Generational replacement contin-ues to occur, with older groups dying and new ones entering the electorate. But it is too soon for this process to have had a major impact overall. The Democrats are down from their once clear ascendance, but they still have a lot of generational capital.

Long-standing Democratic edge in party identification

Group Conversions

Their attachments thus set, these groups move slowly through the generational pipeline. The total of the different generational experiences among groups in the electorate at a given point is a major component of overall party strength, because party identification once formed persists. A party does best in its current share of party loyalties when it has its largest number of favorable generational groups still in the electorate. The Democrats were especially far ahead of the Republicans in the mid- to late 1970s, even though at that time they were not doing nearly so well as they had at earlier points in attracting new voters. They were living off their generational capital. Conversely, in the late 1930s and 1940s the Democrats had done very well in attracting new voters, but their lead over the Republicans among all voters was relatively modest because pre-New Deal (and more Republican) age groups were still a major part of the electorate.

Base-line party strength is determined in part by the mix of generational groups in the pipeline at any point in time. Current political and economic experience then moves each party above or below its base line. For example, if the Republicans control the presidency and the economy is booming, their share of party loyalties across most groups will rise; conversely, it will fall when the party is in power during a recession. But a party enlarges its base only slowly, by attracting disproportionate numbers of new voters entering the electorate.

Base-line party strength

There are exceptions to this process. On rare occasions, a party manages to convert quickly large numbers of people of all ages in a social group—when the policies it supports are especially and unambiguously attractive to the group or, conversely, when the other party's policies are exceptionally repulsive.

Black Americans and the Democratic Party

The shift of blacks to the Democratic party, first in the 1930s and then in the 1960s, is a case in point. This was no gradual shift in support through generational replacement. The New Deal experience had brought blacks into the Democratic party in large numbers. Through 1960, however, a substantial proportion, especially of older blacks, retained their attachments to the GOP—because of old memories of the Republicans as the party of Lincoln and because much of the Democratic party in the South was so strongly associated with policies of white supremacy.

The presidential election of 1964 was a critical one in the black community. The Johnson administration had committed itself to carrying forward the civil rights revolution while the Republicans, through the 1964 presidential candidacy of Barry Goldwater, were seen aligning with resistance to racial change. A massive, immediate partisan swing occurred. Since 1964 Republican support in the black community has been weak indeed.

Moreover, party differences among blacks by age, sex, education, income, region, and so on, are small. For example, the Democrats' margin over the Republicans among those with less than high school educations in 1988 was almost exactly the same as among black college graduates. Black Americans differ substantially in many important interests, outlooks, and values; this ethnic group is far from homogeneous. But when it comes to party choice, most blacks see the Democrats as preferable to the Republicans. Individual Republican candidates have managed to attract large numbers of black votes—as New Jersey's Republican governor Thomas Kean did in the 1985 gubernatorial election, when he apparently won over half the black vote. But overall, the pattern of overwhelming Democratic support, set in the mid-1960s, has persisted.

Democratic preference among blacks

Hispanic Americans' Party Preferences

The story is quite different for Hispanic Americans—showing the danger in referring sweepingly to the preferences of "minority groups." Hispanics and blacks are both ethnic groups that have experienced discrimination and that are composed disproportionately of people less well-off than the national average. But the black and Hispanic populations have had different historical and cultural experiences, and their party loyalties are different.

Moreover, the Hispanic communities in the United States are several rather than one. Those living in the South Atlantic states, especially Florida, have a heavy Cuban representation—people who left Cuba after Fidel Castro came to power. This group is as firmly Republican as the Mexican-American populations of the Southwest and Pacific Coast states are Democratic. Party differences by socioeconomic status are also substantial, with the Democrats strongest among those with the lowest incomes. The Democrats have a clear overall margin among Hispanics but the Republicans are still in the running.

Mixed voting among Hispanics

White Southerners and the Republican Party

In the last half-century there have been only two cases of "critical group conversion"—where an entire social group swings decisively from one party to the other. As we have seen, the shift of blacks to the Democrats is one; the move of white southerners to the Republicans is the other. As late as 1965 the Democrats had a lead of about 36 percentage points in party identification among white southerners, according to Gallup data. This margin eroded gradually from the late 1960s through the early 1980s; during the 1984 campaign it disappeared altogether. The shift has been especially great among young voters, who came of age politically at a time when the mix of race, economic policy, and candidates pushed so strongly in a Republican direction. During the Eisenhower years, young (18–24) whites throughout the South were overwhelmingly Democratic. Not even the slightest erosion of the historic group attachments could be seen. By 1985, however, the youngest white southerners had become solidly Republican. They remained Republican during the 1988 election.

Gradual shifts in regional voting

As the big shift in the South has occurred, more modest changes have taken place in other parts of the country. Voters in the Mountain states have moved toward the Republicans, while those in New England have swung toward the Democrats. The net effect of all of these shifts is a substantial change over the last three decades in the parties' regional bases. In 1952, New England was still the Republicans' best region in party identification—although not significantly better than the Midwestern and Pacific Coast states. The South was overwhelmingly Democratic, of course, and the Mountain states gave the Democrats a slight edge. In 1985 this New Deal regional alignment was nowhere to be seen. The Mountain states were the most Republican section of the country, followed by Midwestern, Southern, Pacific, and Middle Atlantic states. And New England, so securely Republican from the Civil War through the middle of the twentieth century, had become the most heavily Democratic part of the country.

Religious and Ethnic Groups and the Parties .

Dramatic when they occur, sweeping conversions of the kind we have seen for blacks and southern whites are rare. Much more common are group shifts that involve the gradual erosion of once-strong party ties and the establishment of new ones, as succeeding generations of group members come of age in a social and political environment different from what group members had experienced historically. The case of Catholics and Protestants is a fairly typical one.

Immigration and ethnic diversity

The ethnic diversity of the United States was extended throughout the late nineteenth and early twentieth centuries by heavy immigration from eastern, central, and southern Europe. This inevitably made for continuing ethnic conflict, much of it organized around Protestant and Catholic lines. Whereas the earlier British, Irish, and other Northern European immigrants had been heavily Protestant, later immigrants were much more heavily Roman Catholic and Jewish. Tensions generated by this ethnic change got sorted out along partisan lines. Outside the South where a different source for party loyalties pertained, Republicans became the party of older stock Protestants, the Democrats of newer stock Catholics. Differences in style and culture, and in policy interests, often left the partisan split between Protestants and Catholics wide and deep.

Protestant/Catholic
differences in partisan
loyalties

In the twentieth century social, economic, and political differences between Protestants and Catholics have declined greatly. For one thing, the older / newer immigrant distinction has grown more and more irrelevant as the United States has gotten further away from the period of its heavy immigration from Catholic Europe—the four decades or so from the mid-1880s to the mid-1920s. But Protestant / Catholic differences in partisan loyalties have lessened only gradually. As late as 1979, according to Gallup data, the Democratic edge over Republicans in party identification among white, northern Catholics was 31 percentage points, while the Republicans' margin over the Democrats among white, northern Protestants was 7 points—a net gap of 38 percentage points. In 1988, the GOP was stronger than it had been among both these groups. But Protestant / Catholic differences remain present in party identification. According to the ATS surveys, in 1988 northern white Protestants were 12 points more Republican than Democratic, while northern white Catholics were 8 points more Democratic than Republican—a net gap of 20 percentage points (Table 13.4).

Table 13.4
Party Identification by Religious and Ethnocultural Background (percent Republicans—left column each year—and percent Democrat minus Republican—right column each year)

	1947		1952		1955		1960		1965	
Protestants	Religion		36	+ 5	35	+ 7	36	+ 8	29	+19
Catholics	not		22	+28	26	+22	20	+36	13	+54
Jews	asked		13	+39	10	+48	9	+58	8	+54
Northern white	in 1947									
Protestants			44	−14	44	−12	46	−13	41	− 5
Northern white										
Catholics			23	+25	28	+19	21	+33	14	+52
Southern white										
Protestants			17	+49	22	+37	20	+44	20	+32
Blacks	34	+ 9	20	+35	18	+44	25	+28	9	+70
All respondents	35	+ 7	33	+ 8	32	+12	31	+16	24	+28
	1970		1975		1979		1984		1988	
Protestants	34	+ 5	25	+18	28	+15	31	+10	34	−1
Catholics	21	+31	13	+39	16	+33	24	+21	27	+13
Jews	5	+57	8	+50	10	+45	13	+47	18	+33
Northern white										
Protestants	44	−13	33	− 1	37	− 7	39	−11	39	−12
Northern white										
Catholics	22	+28	15	+37	16	+31	24	+19	28	+ 8
Southern white										
Protestants	27	+16	22	+24	25	+20	29	+15	34	− 2
Blacks	9	+67	5	+68	8	+66	5	+74	7	+61
All respondents	29	+14	21	+24	23	+21	28	+14	30	+ 6

Source: Gallup polls in the years shown, except for 1988 when data are from combined February–June surveys conducted for the Americans Talk Security project.

Socioeconomic Groups and the Parties

Throughout the New Deal years the Democrats were stronger among the "have nots" in the United States—whether measured by education, occupation, income, or some other component of socioeconomic status (SES)—than they were among the "haves."[7] These relationships persist at the present time in large measure, no doubt, as a straightforward response to the two parties' policies. Democrats continue to give more backing to programs designed specifically to assist low-income people; Republicans put more emphasis on restraining the growth of federal spending on domestic programs and on cutting taxes. Leaders of both parties believe, of course, that what they are proposing is really best for lower and upper SES groups alike: Republicans think that promoting vigorous economic growth with low inflation is the best way to advance the economic position of the less affluent; Democrats insist that low-income people require higher levels of governmental assistance than Republicans want to provide.

"Tell me, sir, is there any such thing as just a plain Republican, or are they all staunch?"

Drawing by Stan Hunt; © 1984 The New Yorker Magazine, Inc.

[7] For more detailed discussion of socioeconomic position and party ties in the New Deal years, see Everett Ladd, with Charles D. Hadley, *Transformations of the American Party System*, 2nd ed. (New York: Norton, 1978), pp. 64–74, 93–111.

Today as during the New Deal, however, the Democrats are more inclined to tax and spend for social welfare programs, and this has gained them support among lower SES groups and cost them backing among higher SES groups.

Are the differences in party support by socioeconomic position a case of the glass being half-full or half-empty? Is the *extent* of the differences what is remarkable, or is it rather how *limited* they are? Consider the differences by education. In 1988 according to the ATS data, the Democrats had a 30 percentage point edge among those with less than a high school education, while the Republicans led by 5 points among the college educated (Table 13.5). The GOP share of party loyalties among the college-trained population is 15 points higher than what it is among the grade school educated. A case can be made that these are fairly small differences, considering the gap between the groups in socioeconomic status. Differences among income groups are similar. According to the ATS surveys, Democrats outnumbered Republicans by roughly two to one among those with the lowest incomes (under $15,000 a year), while the Republican margin was almost as large among those with the highest incomes ($75,000 and up). People with family incomes in the $35,000–$75,000 range divided evenly in party loyalties (Table 13.5).

Party support by economic position

Table 13.5
Party Identification in 1988, by Socioeconomic Position (in percent)

	Democrat	Republican	Independent
Education			
Less than high school	50	20	30
High school graduate	37	29	34
Some college	35	32	33
College graduate	30	35	34
Income			
Less than $15,000	48	22	31
$15,000–24,999	37	33	31
$25,000–34,999	35	30	35
$35,000–49,999	35	29	36
$50,000–74,999	31	36	33
$75,000 and up	24	43	34

Source: Combined surveys taken for the Americans Talk Security project, February–June 1988.

Weakening Voter Loyalties

Though not the majority party, the Republicans have enlarged their coalition. In one basic regard, though, this realignment differs greatly from its predecessors. It is accompanied, indeed distinguished, by the continued weakening of voter loyalties to political parties in general. The larger change in voter alignments we are experiencing includes

Dealignment

Split-ticket voting

dealignment: a greater inclination on the part of many voters not to express any firm underlying party preference, and in general to make party identification a more causal matter than it ever before has been. The contemporary electorate is less anchored today than throughout most of American history. Whatever their future assessment of the Reagan administration and of Republican performance, or of the Democrats, voters are not going to re-create the extent and degree of stability in party ties that they displayed in the New Deal era. It takes less to move this electorate from one party to the other, from one election to the next.

One manifestation of the diminished strength of party ties is the high frequency of split-ticket voting. In this regard, 1984 fitted neatly into the experience of modern U.S. elections. Gallup regularly asks: "For the various political offices, did you vote for all the candidates of one party, that is, a straight ticket, or did you vote for the candidates of different parties?" For the last five presidential elections the proportions saying they voted a straight ticket have been a fairly *consistent minority:* 37 percent in 1968, 44 percent in 1972, 41 percent in 1976, 37 percent in 1980, and 43 percent in 1984. In a poll taken in September 1986 by Yankelovich Clancy Shulman, just 19 percent said they voted "mostly for Democratic candidates," and only 13 percent "mostly for Republicans." A full two-thirds of the electorate described themselves as "switching between the two parties."

Electoral volatility. A dealigned electorate is like an unanchored boat—it can be easily moved. American voters are highly volatile, moving this way and that over the course of a campaign and from one campaign to another. This does not mean that large numbers of voters will be in a state of flux every campaign. But the weak party loyalties characteristic of the contemporary electorate leave it inherently more volatile or changeable than electorates used to be.

Sources of dealignment. Discussions of the progress of electoral dealignment typically emphasize two broad sources: the *sociological* and the *political-institutional.* The sociological explanation notes that an affluent, leisured, highly educated public no longer perceives the need for political parties as intermediary institutions to the degree that less-educated and less-secure publics did in the past. The political-institutional explanation stresses the deterioration of political party organizations, producing a situation where increasingly ineffective party bodies give voters scant reason to back them strongly. It also notes that other institutions, especially the national communications media and the welfare state, have assumed functions that parties once performed.

While these factors are important, another key precipitant of dealignment has received little attention: Large segments of the

Ambivalence and dealignment

American public have become so ambivalent about the proper course of public policy that they are unable to give a clear endorsement to the competing positions of the parties. Today, Democrats and Republicans offer contrasting approaches that arguably are as distinct as at any time in the past, but most voters do not feel confident about either set of partisan answers. We discussed this ambivalence in chapter 12. With regard to the role of government, many voters are of mixed minds. They do not see any alternative to government's doing a lot, but they are clearly dissatisfied with its recent performance. Not certain just what course they actually favor, many Americans have been reluctant to give strong and unequivocal support to either party.

A Changing Political Climate

Discussions of change in the policy views and political philosophical outlook of Americans often revolve around two conflicting positions: (1) in recent years the public has swung clearly and unambiguously toward conservatism; and (2) nothing much has changed. Neither position in fact seems defensible. The persisting problems that the Democrats have been having in contests, like those for the presidency, that pose issues of national policy direction hardly can be accounted for if things are basically unchanged from the New Deal era. At the same time, the Democrats' overall competitive balance with the Republicans is hard to explain if the electorate has really opted for a coherently conservative posture. A third, intermediate position suggests itself. The policy preferences of the public have evolved—though not to some narrowly coherent conservatism. Americans want something new in the country's public policy, something different from a simple extension of the approach to political economy that the Democratic party pioneered in the 1930s and elaborated in the ensuing decades. Without expressing certainty about the Republicans' capacity to define a successful new approach, the public has shown its substantial displeasure with the Democrats' "old-time religion."

The 1980 presidential voting. Many Democratic leaders understood this in 1980. What gave them such concern following Carter's defeat was their sense that their party was floundering intellectually and that the country had turned against its approach to governing. In July 1980, New York Democratic Senator Daniel Patrick Moynihan argued that his party had become a stale force stubbornly defending the big establishment of modern government. "There is a movement to turn Republicans into Populists, a party of the People arrayed against a Democratic Party of the State." Moynihan went on to call this role reversal "terrifying" for the Democrats and one that might signal "the onset of the transformation of American politics." He conceded, further, that "of a sudden, the GOP has become a party of ideas."[8]

For some time, intellectuals like Moynihan had been highly critical of aspects of government performance and of the Democrats' response to these inadequacies. But concern over deficiencies in Democratic "ideas" became widespread across the party after the 1980 election. Senator Gary Hart of Colorado, who managed George McGovern's presidential campaign in 1972, and who in 1984 tried to channel the newer currents of Democratic liberalism in his own presidential bid, agreed with Moynihan that "the liberal wing of the Democratic party has run out of ideas. It has been operating on the Roosevelt momentum of programmatic, bureaucratic solutions to the domestic agenda," even though such currents as "increased taxpayer resistance to the growth of the costs of governmental programs, inflation, the realities of international economics, and a lot of other factors . . . have been catching up with that momentum."[9]

Above all, many Democrats agreed, a sense of inadequacy in their economic ideas or approach was their greatest problem. The onset of high inflation served as the focal point. Frustration with inflation could be seen across the social spectrum, but it was especially acute among the Democrats' traditional working-class and lower-middle-class constituents. And working-class voters had come by 1980 to believe, as fervently as upper-middle-class voters, that contemporary government, more than business and labor, had caused the inflationary surge. The electoral impact of this shift in class perceptions of government and the Democrats' handling of it was felt in 1980 when the party suffered its greatest losses among Americans who thought they were in trouble economically.

Professor David Vogel argues that a resolute pragmatism distinguishes the American approach to questions of political economy. "The American public has supported whichever 'side' has offered the most effective program for promoting real economic growth." From the 1870s through the 1920s, the ascendancy of private business and its success in limiting governmental intervention ultimately rested on business's capacity "to manage successfully the transformation of America from an agrarian to a modern industrial society." The Great Depression changed that.

> Americans supported the reforms of the New Deal because they represented an effective alternative for restoring the viability of the American private sector. . . . What gave political credibility to liberal forces in America during the quarter-century following the Second World War was their ability to argue effectively that the expansion of the welfare

Sidenotes:
Dissatisfaction with the Democrats' ideas

Public concern over inflation

Pragmatism and political economy

---

[8] Daniel Patrick Moynihan, "Of 'Sons' and their 'Grandsons,' " *New York Times*, July 7, 1980, p. 15.
[9] Interview conducted by the author with Senator Gary Hart, December 2, 1980.

state and the adoption of the principles of Keynesian economics were not only compatible with economic prosperity, but essential to it.[10]

In the 1970s, another shift occurred. The Democrats' approach was no longer associated with growing prosperity, and the American public became receptive to new ideas. This was the setting in 1980.

The 1982 congressional voting. In the 1982 vote for Congress, the public had its first opportunity to reaffirm or recast the tentative, somewhat ambiguous mandate it had extended two years earlier. The results of the 1982 balloting were viewed by some as indecisive. The Democratic party made gains in governorships and in the House of Representatives, but it did not gain massively. The Reagan administration was told by the public to change course, but it was not repudiated: "The Center, Rediscovered" was the way the *New York Times* put it.[11] Actually, the 1982 vote was a reaffirmation of the message the electorate conveyed in 1980: The Democrats' approach to political economy was flawed, and a new Republican departure should be given a try—even though that party's capacity to govern successfully was viewed skeptically.

Especially striking as an indicator of persisting voter dissatisfaction with the Democrats' approach were the answers to the question "Which of the two political parties do you think is better able to handle the nation's economic problems?" This was asked nationally in the NBC News election-day poll, and of samples of voters in 13 states. Historically, the Democrats' margin over the Republicans had been large and persistent on this type of question. Add to that the troubled state of the economy in 1982, with the GOP in power, and one might have expected a substantial majority to prefer the Democrats. In fact, only 36 percent nationally said the Democrats were best equipped, compared to 35 percent for the Republicans, 18 percent not seeing any difference, and 10 percent not sure or not answering. Even in a Democratic state like Michigan, especially hard hit by the recession, only 38 percent said the Democrats' approach to economic problems was better—just 5 percent more than preferred the GOP's approach.

Throughout the 1982 campaign, Americans were unhappy about the state of the economy and critical of many Reagan administration policies. On the question of whether the administration's general approach deserved endorsement or rejection, however, the 1982 verdict was to continue the Reagan experiment. A CBS News / *New York Times* poll asked, "Have you personally been helped or hurt?" Those saying "hurt" outnumbered those "helped" by better than two to one.

Backing for the Reagan experiment

---

[10] David Vogel, "The Inadequacy of Contemporary Opposition to Business," *Daedalus*, 109, 3 (Summer 1980):47–57.
[11] *New York Times*, editorial of November 7, 1982.

"Apart from the impact on you personally, has the national economy been helped or hurt so far?" Again, those saying "hurt" outnumbered "helped" by a large margin, nearly two to one. On the third question, however—"Do you think the economic program eventually will help or hurt the country's economy?"—the answers revealed the intent to continue. Sixty percent said the economy would be helped, compared to just 27 percent who thought it would be hurt in the long run. While the proportions varied from one survey to another over the course of Campaign '82, in every instance where this or a comparable question was asked, a plurality said they thought the economy would be helped in the long run.

The 1984 presidential voting. If the electorate were inclined during the pain of the recession of 1982 to continue its limited mandate for a new approach to political economy, it was unlikely to vote to shift direction in 1984, once the economy had turned up and it was at least arguable that the Reagan administration's approach was working.

All during the long 1984 presidential campaign, economic news was about as good as an incumbent administration seeking re-election could hope for. Even interest rates, which were high by historical standards, fell during September and October. *Valence issues* (how things are going) reinforced and strengthened the public's sense that the Reagan approach to economic management was generally sound and should be continued.

Valence issues and presidential voting

Thus the big act in the realignment drama of the late 1970s and early 1980s involved a movement of voters away from the Democrats on questions of political economy—under the dual challenge of high inflation (seen as government's fault) and frustration over the extent of government's growth. This movement provides part of the backdrop for the answers a national sample gave to CBS News / *New York Times* interviewers in a poll taken from September 30 to October 4, 1984. "Which party is better able to insure a strong economy?" Fifty-four percent said the Republicans; only 27 percent said the Democrats.

THE 1988 ELECTIONS

Perhaps the most striking thing about the 1988 election was how predictable it was. Just about everything happened as it should have, based on what we knew when the election year began. A major reason for this predictability is that the balloting took place well into the latest of our country's great partisan realignments, which we have been describing. When a realignment is new, its central features—changes in group ties to the political parties, issues cutting in novel directions, etc.—often startle us. But after we have seen them over a series of elections, we take them as givens. That's what happened in

1988. The election told us little we didn't already know; instead, it was confirming, or reaffirming. The New Deal era now seems as remote as the McKinley era.

Our present-day electoral alignment has five principal components, and the 1988 elections were a textbook illustration of them. First, as we have seen, a variety of groups vote differently now than they did in the New Deal years. The most notable are white southerners, long the strongest of Democratic supporters, who have become the strongest of presidential Republicans. The oldest voters, long the Republicans' best age cohorts, are now their worst. Men and women, who until a decade ago voted almost identically, today differ significantly: women are relatively more Democratic, men more Republican. Second, the present mix of issues differs from that of the New Deal period, and the Democrats' public philosophy has lost favor. Third, the Republicans are the majority party in presidential elections—precisely because their public philosophy is ascendant. Fourth, *dealignment*—the weakening of voters' ties to the parties—is a key factor distinguishing the current partisan competition from all previous ones. Finally, for well over a decade now the new alignment has displayed a split personality: one face evident in presidential voting, another in state and local contests.

Components of alignment

Group Voting

Michael Dukakis won the black vote in 1988 by the kind of margin that has been familiar since the civil rights revolution of the 1960s— 86 percent to 12 percent, according to the CBS News/*New York Times* election-day survey of 11,645 voters. Whites, in contrast, strongly backed George Bush.

The most striking feature of this vote on November 8 was the extent to which the Republicans' share among whites in the South exceeded that in the rest of the country. According to the election-day polls of NBC News and the *Wall Street Journal,* for example, Bush received 57 percent of the white vote nationally—but his margins in the South ranged from a low of 63 percent in Florida to a high of 80 percent in Mississippi. In the New Deal era white southerners' overwhelming support for the national Democratic party had two main sources: racial tensions and memories, reaching back to the Civil War. In fact they were the most liberal—i.e., New Deal policy supporting—regional group in the country. In the contemporary alignment, things have been almost exactly reversed. White southerners have become the most Republican regional group in presidential voting, because of the racial division that finds blacks overwhelmingly Democratic, and because they are now the most conservative regional group.

Southern voting

For a decade now the Republicans have been beating the Democrats in their competition for the support of new voters. This is highly important because, studies show, realignments involve not so much shifts in the loyalties of older voters, who have long political memories and experience, as the movement of those just beginning to form partisan attachments in a new political era. Today, voters in their late teens and twenties identify with the GOP in greater proportions than do any other age group.

Pre-election polls in 1988 showed Bush getting his biggest margins over Dukakis among the young, but the election-day surveys did not find this. Age-related differences in voting were not significant. The reason for this discrepancy between pre-election poll findings and actual results was made clear by a survey that CBS News and the *New York Times* conducted November 10–16. It found that young people, always the group least likely to vote, had an especially low turnout this year. Indeed, two-fifths of all nonvoters in the country were under 30 years of age. The CBS News/*New York Times* study showed that the young nonvoters would have picked Bush by a much bigger margin than the rest of the populace and that they were more pro-Bush than the young who voted.

The gender gap is of interest here as an example of group divisions not evident in previous eras. Realignments occur, of course, when old divisions fade while new ones appear, reflecting changing social needs and circumstances. In the wake of big gender-related shifts, which included a surge of women into the labor force, polls in the 1970s began showing differences of opinion between men and women on a range of policy questions. A gender gap first appeared in presidential voting in 1980. In 1988, according to the CBS News/*New York Times* exit poll, it was 15 percentage points: men favored Bush over Dukakis by a 16 percentage point margin, women by just one percentage point. The NBC News/*Wall Street Journal* poll put the gap at 14 points.

Public Philosophy

Campaign '88 got more than a little silly at times, with heated exchanges about "the L word" and endless speculation about how Dukakis should have responded to the charge that (shudder) he was a *liberal*. Underlying these fun and games, however, was a serious message: New Deal liberalism was a majoritarian public philosophy; post-1960s liberalism is a minoritarian public philosophy. This says nothing about who's right and who's wrong; it's a matter of votes. The Democrats' call for more government simply found higher support in the 1930s and 1940s than it does in the 1980s. And what we call the "social issues," scarcely a factor in New Deal balloting, are an important part of the liberal–conservative divide today. The configuration of American opinion on questions like crime, school prayer, abortion, permissiveness, problems in family life, and the like, is enormously complex. Overall, though, the Democrats' association with

Gaining the support of new voters

The gender gap

the liberal side of these questions has for two decades been costing them votes. It did again on November 8.

The Republican Presidential Majority

Democrats are again debating the lessons of the presidential balloting. "Did we just run a bad campaign, or is our problem deeper?" One lesson should by now be clear: Democrats are the minority party in contemporary presidential politics.

Does this mean Michael Dukakis could not have won? Of course not—no more than one could say that Democrat Woodrow Wilson could not win in 1912 and 1916, when the Republicans were the majority party. Minority parties win presidential elections as a result of any one of a number of circumstances: when they nominate more attractive candidates, when the majority party fractures, or when people think it's time for a change. Minority status simply means that the party begins each contest with an underlying disadvantage: The *regular* alignment of groups and cut of issues favors its opponents.

Could the minority party win?

When an out-of-power minority must contend for the presidency in a period of peace and relative prosperity, it is likely to lose. That was the Democrats' problem in 1988. The election results were not inevitable, but they were both likely and predictable. Bush's final margin of roughly 8 percentage points seems to be at the low end of the likely range, given the setting in which the contest was waged. Polls suggest that a higher turnout would have in fact resulted in a bigger Republican margin.

Dealignment

The New Deal realignment was accompanied by an unambiguous strengthening of Democratic party loyalties across the electorate. In contrast, the present realignment finds more and more people splitting their tickets and deciding their votes on grounds related to the candidates and issues in specific elections, rather than going down the line for their party. Party ties count for less today than at any point since a mature party system took shape in the United States in the 1830s.

Lessening party voting

In the case of less visible offices, such as members of Congress, where most voters know little about the candidates' records and officeholders enjoy prodigious advantages over their challengers in resources for painting their image in a vaguely rosy glow, the precipitous decline of party voting has resulted in an extraordinarily uncompetitive set of results. Incumbents now routinely win these contests by overwhelming margins. In the November 8 balloting, only 6 House incumbents who sought re-election were defeated. Only 29 victorious House candidates were held to margins of 10 percentage points or less (see Table 12.9). Incumbency, not party, is the decisive element.

When candidates take policy stands that to some degree encourage the desertion of their partisans, the extent of ticket-splitting can be quite extraordinary. In this year's Connecticut senatorial contest, for example, Republican Lowell Weicker ran with a liberal voting record, while his challenger, Democrat Joseph Lieberman, took more conservative stands on a number of social issues. The CBS News/*New York Times* election-day poll in Connecticut showed 38 percent of Republicans crossing over to vote for Lieberman, and 34 percent of Democrats backing Weicker.

Split-Level Results

The New Deal realignment was as complete and decisive as it was rapid. By 1936 the Democrats were unquestionably the majority party at all levels: They "owned" the presidency, dominated Congress, held sway in the state houses, and had a substantial lead in party identification. Today's realignment is anything but complete, as data from the November 8 balloting reminded us. Bush won strongly, carrying 40 states and 426 electoral votes; but the Democrats retained their ample majorities in Congress and the state houses.

Divided results are a fact. They mean that the Republicans have a power base in the presidency, the Democrats a base in Congress. But they do not have much to say about one of the silliest of our election-related debates—Who has the mandate?

After the 1988 balloting, some analysts argued that Bush's victory was nothing like the clear policy endorsement Ronald Reagan's victories represented. But the fact is that the Republicans have won the presidency five of the last six times, by a cumulative margin of 11 percentage points over their Democratic opposition. That may not be a mandate but it is certainly not the chance product of various short-term forces, such as how individual campaigns are run. It represents an expression of opinion on the parties' stands comparable in its decisiveness to that of the New Deal years.

PARTIES AS REPRESENTATIVE INSTITUTIONS

Discussion thus far has focused on the political parties as coalitions of voters and on how and why these electoral alignments have shifted from the 1930s into the 1980s. Parties are, however, more than voter coalitions; they are political institutions that play critically important institutional roles.

The American party system is the oldest in the world, fast approaching its second centennial. In the late 1790s, when parties took shape in the United States and began a struggle for control of government in popular election contests, their architects had no blueprints to follow. A new political institution was being established. Less than two hundred years later, political parties are found throughout the world.

The Birth of Political Parties

In the sweep of governmental experience, parties are very young institutions. They became necessary only after the revolutionary changes that gripped Western societies in the seventeenth and eighteenth centuries, and that dominated American origins: the collapse of aristocratic society; the extension of social and political egalitarianism; and the development of political ideologies, especially classical liberalism, that assigned the individual a far more elevated position than he had ever enjoyed.

Political parties are the children of egalitarianism. They appeared as a necessary institutional response to the idea of popular sovereignty, to the belief that the rank-and-file citizen should have final authority in the business of governing. In pre-egalitarian societies small groups of citizens organized to influence the affairs of state through cabals, cliques, and factions. The egalitarian revolution of the seventeenth and eighteenth centuries gave legitimacy to the idea that the entire public should be considered and consulted.

The legacy of popular sovereignty

Once the notion of popular sovereignty took hold, political parties evolved rapidly. They set up organizations among the populace and linked up local units with national leadership—for example, with party officials in the legislature. They provided common political identities for elites and the rank-and-file, promoting popular cohesion for and against contrasting philosophies of government. They put flesh on the skeletal idea of representation.

Edmund Burke and the Early Argument over Parties

Parties did not emerge without a struggle. For some time after the first stirrings of egalitarianism in the seventeenth century, philosophers and politicians had trouble conceiving a permanent and legitimate role for political parties. To those like the English leader and political theorist Henry St. John, Viscount Bolingbroke, parties were "a political evil,"[12] institutions of a dangerous and untried democracy. They would represent special interests against the national

[12] Henry Saint-John Bolingbroke, *A Dissertation Upon Parties*, in *The Works of Lord Bolingbroke*, vol. 2 (Philadelphia: Carey and Hart, 1841). The *Dissertation* was first published in England in 1733.

interest. They would break a nation into parts, involving it in endless squabbles, blocking the pursuit of the common good.

Prior to the nineteenth century, only one theorist raised and defended the idea of political parties as essential instruments of emerging representative government: the great British politician and philosopher Edmund Burke (1729–97). It is testimony to Burke's genius that he developed the case for a mature party system long before one came to exist. The proper question, as Burke saw it, was how the various interests in the country could be organized so as to determine policy. His answer was through political parties. "Party is a body of men united, for promoting by their joint endeavors the national interest, upon some particular principle in which they are all agreed."[13] He recognized that there would be different and competing ideas of how best to serve the national interest; all would inevitably prove futile unless their proponents organized for effective action. Once organized, political parties would become the necessary great connection between groups of citizens and governmental institutions.

National interests and the need for strong parties

Although parties as we know them did not yet exist, Burke was already what we would call a "strong party man." He believed that political figures should assess the various issues, decided which political group they would side with in order to advance a shared view of the public interest, and then give their party sustained support. Burke was not sympathetic to the argument that continuing support for a party requires a politician to subordinate the claims of his own conscience. What is incumbent upon a politician in a representative government, he insisted, is the thoughtful choice of a party whose "leading general principles in government" he can support. When an issue arises which is not of great moment, he should go along with his party, even if he happens to disagree with it. Only rarely, Burke thought, will a politician be required by deep conviction to separate himself from a party whose general goals he shares.

The case for party allegiance

Development of Parties in the United States

Burke's insights into the necessary place of parties in representative governments were not readily accepted. Here in the United States, where parties first matured, James Madison did not contemplate a place for them in the constitutional order. Madison did recognize the place of interest groups or factions, but he did not foresee an essential representative role for parties. George Washington's vision also was limited to an idea of special-interest-serving factions, which he considered a necessary evil as the by-product of liberty. In his farewell

[13] Edmund Burke, *Thoughts on the Cause of the Present Discontents,* in *The Works of Edmund Burke,* vol. 2 (London: Rivington, 1815), p. 335. *Thoughts* was written in 1770.

address in 1796 Washington warned "in the most solemn manner against the harmful effects of the spirit of party."

Thomas Jefferson and political parties

Thomas Jefferson had similar views, even though he was the architect of one of the world's first full-fledged parties: the Republicans, later called Democratic-Republicans, and eventually called the Democrats. The alliance Jefferson put together is the direct ancestor of the present-day Democratic party. But he considered parties troublesome enterprises, not great instruments for extending democracy. While president in 1804, Jefferson wrote William Short that "the party division in this country is certainly not among its pleasant features. To a certain degree it will always exist: and chiefly in mercantile places. In the country and those states where the Republicans have a decided superiority, party hostility has ceased to infest society."

Jefferson lamented that, while he had been quite prepared to offer his partisan opponents a few minor places in his government if they would cease to be an opposition force, they had spurned this! Even among the most prescient of Americans of the day, there was no real picture of parties as regular, necessary instruments through which the divergent views of the public are organized and expressed in an egalitarian polity.

The birth of American parties

Still, if Americans were uncertain as to the purpose of political parties, they nonetheless went ahead rapidly building them. The first stirrings of party were in the policy conflict between Hamilton and Jefferson in Washington's administration, a division which was part of a much broader argument over public policy in the new regime. As the dispute deepened, Hamilton turned to his friends in Congress, Jefferson to his—one result being that factional ties between executive and legislative leaders became much tighter. Hamilton's group took a name that raised memories of the successful fight for the Constitution: the Federalists. At this time the Jeffersonians called themselves the Republicans.

The incipient parties arose from divisions in national, rather than state, politics.[14] Thus party lines became clear in national politics before they did in state contests. The Republican party of Jefferson made its first organized efforts by endorsing candidates for Congress and for presidential electors; party tickets for state legislatures and other state offices came later.

A Core Democratic Function

Political parties sprang up so quickly because they were needed to link the people to government in the first egalitarian society. They

---

[14]For an excellent description, see Noble E. Cunningham, Jr., *The Jeffersonian Republicans* (Chapel Hill, N.C.: University of North Carolina Press, 1957).

aggregated the preferences of the public for political leadership and policy choice, and converted what was incoherent and diffuse to specific, responsive public decisions. There are three distinct but closely interrelated parts to this basic function.

Representation

Representation. The potential electorate in the United States (citizens of voting age) now numbers over 150 million. It is no small task to get candidates and programs that reflect the preferences of so large and diverse a public. Effective representation is achieved when government translates popular preferences into programs, and the public concludes that government is generally responsive to its wishes. Representation, then, requires a number of things that only parties can do: building coalitions and articulating policies that meet coalitions' needs, finding popular and effective candidates to win office and implement the policies, and offering alternative candidates to those in power, so that when popular majorities are dissatisfied with governmental performance, they have somewhere to turn.

Popular control

Popular control. Political parties are also necessary to enable citizens to control their government and ensure the responsiveness of public institutions. There are so many different elective offices in a country like the United States that citizens cannot consider their votes meaningful in controlling policy unless the many separate election contests are linked in some understandable fashion: For instance, balloting for the national legislature can be seen as a competition of one party against another, rather than as the unrelated competition of individuals.

Beyond this, only parties are in a position to so organize policy choices that mass publics can make judgments on them. Parties provide the "conduit or sluice by which the waters of social thought and discussion are brought to the wheels of political machinery and set to turn those wheels," as Ernest Barker once put it.[15] When they make elected officials in some sense collectively, rather than individually, responsible to the electorate, parties expand the level of meaningful popular control.

Integration. Today's government, with all of its far-flung activities, is incredibly complex. It has so many different parts responsive to so many different interests that the natural centrifugal pressures are

---

[15] Ernest Barker, *Reflections on Government* (New York: Oxford University Press, 1958; first published 1942), p. 39.

Integration

sometimes almost irresistible. Party is the one acceptable counter-acting, centripetal force. Governmental integration is especially demanding in the United States, because of the extreme dispersion of authority resulting from federalism and the separation of powers. In such a system, coherence in policy simply cannot be obtained unless parties are available for bridging governmental divisions, for example, by bringing together officials in the executive and legislative branches through common partisan ties and commitments.

CHARACTERISTICS OF THE AMERICAN PARTY SYSTEM

Even among democracies there is considerable variety in party arrangements. A distinctively American party system evolved early in the nineteenth century; to a striking degree, it has persisted.

A Two-Party System

By the time Democrats and Whigs grappled for power in the 1830s, a two-party system was securely in place. In most of the major election contests, and above all in those for president, only Whigs or Democrats won. Today, Democrats and Republicans similarly dominate the contests for elective office.

Most democracies operate with some type of multi-party system, in which at least three and often many more parties regularly draw substantial support. Even in Canada, where two parties—the Liberals and the Progressive Conservatives—have dominated federal governments, other parties have contested vigorously and often successfully for control of the provincial governments.

Why a two-party system?

As we saw in chapter 12, one reason for America's continuing attachment to this rare type of party competition is that our electoral arrangements impose severe handicaps on third-party challengers. Especially influential is the election of most candidates by the single-member district, simple-majority system. In each district one party's candidate wins the seat. The party that comes in second can argue plausibly that it is the realistic alternative for all those dissatisfied with the winner. Other parties are vulnerable to the charge that a vote for them is simply wasted. Another important reason why two parties have dominated contests for elective office throughout U.S. history is the fact of a highly consensual society distinguished by minimal ideological disagreements. As we noted in chapter 3, classical liberalism has enjoyed preeminence in American thought from the country's inception. The absence of competing ideological traditions has prevented parties representing different perspectives, such as the socialists, from finding a firm base on which to build. There

Obstacles to third-party formation

has been insufficient ideological room in which to establish third and fourth parties, especially since electoral mechanics have made it hard for such challengers to operate.

The unusual success American society has enjoyed has also held back third-party challenges. The national wealth of the United States, unsurpassed by any other country for at least a century and a half, together with a high degree of social mobility and a sense that opportunity for advancement is present, have strengthened American political and economic institutions and blunted the protests that almost certainly would have been stronger otherwise. The United States has not lacked political parties bred of protest, but protest parties have found it hard to generate a broad appeal. As socialist thinker Werner Sombart remarked of the socialists' experience in America, it has "come to grief on roast beef and apple pie."[16]

Protests over racial and other ethnocultural changes have sometimes nourished third-party protests. In the 1850s the American party, popularly called the "Know-Nothings," built a politically strong appeal on anti-Catholic and anti-immigrant sentiment. In 1968, George Wallace's American Independent candidacy won 13 percent of the presidential vote on white dissatisfaction with the civil rights movement and the course of racial change. But these parties of ethnic protest have not been able to sustain themselves.

Parties of Accommodation

The extraordinary continuity evident in the persistence of a two-party system is also seen in the pragmatic cast of American party competition and the weakness of exclusive ideological appeals. The major parties of a century and a half ago were not doctrinal or even strongly programmatic, and neither are their counterparts today. "Tweedledum and Tweedledee," some have called the two big U.S. parties. In one sense this depiction is inaccurate, for there have always been important policy differences between the parties. But the differences have not had the magnitude of doctrinal fissures. Though today we talk about a more "liberal" Democratic party aligned against a more "conservative" Republican party, Democrats and Republicans share much of the American ideological inheritance. In their pursuit of majority support in a nation not sharply polarized ideologically, the two parties have had to make broad appeals, and they have attracted adherents across the political spectrum.

This heterogeneous character of party coalitions has encouraged the parties to practice a politics of accommodation. American parties have been "creatures of compromise . . . vast, gaudy, friendly umbrel-

[16]Werner Sombart, "American Capitalism's Economic Rewards," in J. H. M. Laslett and S. M. Lipset, eds., *Failure of a Dream? Essays in the History of American Socialism* (Garden City, N.Y.: Anchor Books, 1974), p. 599.

"ACTUALLY, THEY REMIND ME OF THE CHOICE BETWEEN THE REPUBLICANS AND DEMOCRATS THIS YEAR."

las under which all Americans, whoever and wherever and however minded they may be, are invited to stand for the sake of being counted in the next election."[17] This contrasts sharply with the experience in many European countries where parties have often considered it unnatural, and in a sense even undesirable, for certain social groups to find them attractive. The British Labour party, for example, really doesn't expect or want backing from the country's business establishment.

Heterogeneous party coalitions

There are few places in the United States where the Democrats and Republicans do not work actively to secure the votes of virtually all identifiable interests and groups. On occasion, one party will be weak within a particular group—as the Republicans are among black Americans today. Ninety percent of black voters have regularly backed the Democrats in elections over the last twenty years, and Democrats outnumber Republicans among blacks in party identification by roughly 9 to 1. Because this condition challenges the tradition of broad-appeal accommodation politics, it is seen as a distinct liability both by the GOP and by most neutral observers, for it suggests that the GOP is not fully open to all ethnic groups in the society.

Broadening the appeal

Although the major American parties have not always successfully appealed to every group, our accommodationist two-party system has unquestionably encouraged a broadening of appeals and punished failures to do so. The typical range of both Democratic and Republican support within various social groups has been between the 40 and 60 percent marks; a party's support from a given group is considered seriously weak when it falls below 40 percent.

[17] Rossiter, *Parties and Politics in America*, p. 11.

Loose and Undemanding Alliances

Throughout U.S. history the two major parties have not required very much of either their rank-and-file supporters or the elected officials who bear their names. In this regard, American parties are the opposite of the intensely organized and disciplined Communist parties where the latter control the government, as in the Soviet Union, or where they are in seemingly permanent opposition, as in France and Italy.

Party membership. A citizen's ties to an American party are rarely formal. The Democrats and the Republicans don't have regularly enrolled, card-carrying and dues-paying members. There are no "official formalities" for admission, "no precise criteria of membership."[18] A voter becomes a Republican or a Democrat by a simple declaration, and he assumes no responsibilities when he makes that declaration. To participate in primary elections for selecting a party's candidates, a voter has at most to declare his affiliation at some specified time prior to the primary, and he may change his affiliation as he wishes. In primary elections in some states, he may even cast his vote in the selection of Republican or Democratic candidates without ever disclosing which party he prefers. These are the *open primaries*. Associating with a party is strictly and exclusively a matter of individual self-expression. "An American party," Clinton Rossiter wrote, "is not an army, not a church, not a way of life, not even a lodge. It asks nothing of one of its adherents but his vote, a few dollars, and, if he seems willing, a few hours of his time for manning the polls, licking stamps, and ringing doorbells; and it would settle willingly for a sure vote."[19]

Undisciplined elites. American parties are also undemanding of the leaders who operate under their standards. The Democratic and Republican parties at both the national and state levels are undisciplined and lacking in internal cohesion by comparison to governmental parties in most other democracies. In the U.S. Congress, Democrats vote together against all Republicans only rarely: just on organizing the House and Senate, as in the election of the Speaker of the House. Otherwise, as we saw in chapter 6, in the passage of legislation on issues large and small the parties split, with some Democrats and some Republicans voting together to form a majority, and others, the minority.

One reason for this lack of discipline and cohesion is the unusual separation of the executive and legislature in the United States. In

Open primaries

[18] Maurice Duverger, *Political Parties*, 2nd English ed. (London: Methuen, 1959), pp. 63–65.
[19] Rossiter, *Parties and Politics in America*, p. 25.

Separation of powers and the lack of party cohesion

most democracies, as we have seen, the executive—the prime minister and the cabinet—are members of the legislature and hold office because the assembly majority supports them. In Great Britain, Prime Minister Margaret Thatcher and her cabinet are in power because the Conservative party has a majority in the House of Commons and that majority backs the Thatcher government. Were Conservative Members of Parliament (MPs) to cross party lines and vote with the opposition Labourites, they would be declaring "no confidence" in the Thatcher government and would remove it from office. This structure requires that party members vote together. In the American system of separation of powers, the president holds office for a fixed term independent of Congress, and Congress is elected and holds office independent of the president. A Republican member of the House of Representatives can vote against programs proposed by a Republican president as frequently as he likes without jeopardizing the government's continuation in office.

Decentralization of power

The pronounced decentralization of power in the American parties is another source of their incohesion. Congressional Republicans and Democrats hold office not because of the blessings and assistance of national party leaders, but because of the work they and their supporters have done in the districts they represent. Successful congressional candidates of both parties "did not rise through disciplined organizations," and thus "they are individualists from the beginning of their political careers. As candidates they were self-selected, self-organized, self-propelled, self-reliant. . . ."[20]

Tradition of independence

A final important source of the lack of discipline and cohesion within the Democratic and Republican governmental parties is *tradition*. In most party systems, for a member of the legislature to go against his party is to betray it. The American tradition is very different. From the earliest party experience in this country, voting independently, and not being "beholden to party bosses," have been considered virtues. Few American congressmen have ever lost their seats because they developed reputations for "flinty independence."

With power so fractured and dispersed among state and local parties and candidates, it is inevitable that officeholders will frequently cross party lines. This is true whether the spur is principle or expediency: whether the officeholder thinks good judgment requires him to vote against his party or whether good politics ordains it.

Weak Party Organizations

In American political folklore, the activities of strong party organizations or "machines" are both celebrated and condemned. Such

[20] James Sundquist, "The Crisis of Competence in Our National Government," *Political Science Quarterly*, Summer 1980, p. 198.

political figures as E. H. "Boss" Crump, who headed the Democratic machine in Memphis from 1932 to 1948, and Richard Daley, who led the strong Democratic organization in Chicago for a quarter-century until his death in 1976, are among the legendary party "bosses." They dominated the machinery of their political parties and maintained strangleholds on almost all aspects of the political life of their cities.

Strong party organizations have indeed existed at various times in different parts of the United States, especially in big cities when large numbers of immigrants were arriving. These party machines provided services to the newcomers, helping them find jobs and assisting them in bringing their problems to government agencies. In turn, the parties could count on followings that would loyally back their candidates. But muscular party organizations have been the exception in the United States, not the rule. The strong current of political individualism throughout American culture generates resentment of strong party leadership. Our very vocabulary attests to this: disciplined organizations are referred to as "machines" and their leaders depicted as undemocratic "bosses."

Mechanisms have been established to strengthen the hand of individual citizens vis-à-vis party bodies. The most dramatic case is *nominee selection*. In most democracies party leaders determine the party candidates. In the United States rank-and-file voters select the nominees through primary elections. As we saw in chapter 12, no other country approaches the United States in the degree to which rank-and-file party adherents control the nominee selection process. Primaries were established during the Progressive era early in this century. In their insistence that nominations be controlled by the voters rather than by party officials, the Progressives had great success, because they appealed to the culture's distinctive individualism. Americans insist on their individual right to determine electoral outcomes, on *their* right, not that of party machines, to control the nomination process.

Primaries and nominee selection

"Let the people, not the bosses, pick the candidates" seems to most Americans a natural position. But in other democracies no comparable perspective obtains. In Japan party candidates are chosen by the party hierarchy. Choosing candidates through primary elections has no appeal to most Japanese voters. In Great Britain, France, and West Germany as well, control of nominations is thought by most voters to be properly a party organization affair. That the leadership of American party organizations does not determine nominees has meant that American parties are organizationally weaker than their counterparts in other democracies. Prospective nominees take their case directly to the voters; party officials have few sanctions over them. The Democrats and Republicans reflect durable loyalties; they have managed to hold their dominant place in electoral competition since the 1860s. Yet as organizations they are weak and undisciplined compared to most other major democratic parties.

Party organization in other democracies

It gets harder and harder for political parties to keep the American voter interested.

"*At this point in the campaign, you have to expect a certain amount of erosion.*"

Drawing by Stevenson; © 1984 The New Yorker Magazine, Inc.

PARTY REFORM

Selecting presidential nominees

From time to time, campaigns are mounted to reform various American political institutions. We saw in chapter 6, for example, the major changes that were made in congressional organization and procedures from 1965 to 1975, with the intent of correcting perceived problems. Political parties have also been affected by these recurring efforts at reform.

Party reform has often been intended to make the institution more democratic. Early in this century direct primaries were introduced to weaken party bosses and to give the rank-and-file a bigger role in what is perhaps the most important of all party functions: picking candidates for offices. Beginning in the late 1960s, the latest of the party reform attempts concentrated on changing the way presidential nominees are selected. These efforts have originated largely within the Democratic party.

The Democrats were deeply divided in 1968 between the wing that backed President Lyndon Johnson in his conduct of the Vietnam War and the large bloc in the party that bitterly opposed him on this issue.

The latter felt that nominating procedures unfairly benefited the party "establishment" under Johnson, who wanted Vice President Hubert Humphrey to succeed him. (Humphrey did win the 1968 Democratic nomination but was defeated by Republican Richard Nixon in the general election.)

Following their tumultuous 1968 presidential convention in Chicago, the Democrats established a commission to examine possible changes in the party's presidential nomination procedures and to make recommendations for changes to be implemented prior to the next nomination contest in 1972. This Democratic commission was chaired first by Senator George McGovern of South Dakota and later by Congressman Donald Fraser of Minnesota. Officially the Commission on Party Structure and Delegate Selection, the body was better known as the McGovern-Fraser Commission. Its report to the Democratic National Committee, *Mandate for Reform*, was presented in 1971.

The McGovern-Fraser Commission

The McGovern-Fraser Commission maintained that internal party democracy was the value to be promoted through reform, and that its achievement would make the party more representative of the populace and thereby stronger, more competitive, and generally better able to perform its role in the governing process. It recommended either that presidential delegates be chosen by caucuses and conventions open to all party adherents, with delegates apportioned among the contending candidates through proportional representation, or that they be selected through primaries. If a state Democratic party insisted on permitting its central committee to play a role in choosing delegates to the national convention, it had to limit the number thus selected to 10 percent of the total. Forbidden was the practice whereby "certain public or party officeholders are delegates to county, state, and national conventions by virtue of their official position." Being a major party official would no longer entitle anyone to a formal role in the party's presidential nominee selection.

Increased use of presidential primaries

These new rules led to the proliferation of presidential primaries. A later party report noted in 1978 that "while the McGovern-Fraser Commission was neutral on the question of primaries, many state parties felt that a primary offered the most protection against a challenge at the next convention."[21] There were 17 Democratic presidential primaries in 1968; the number rose to 23 by 1972 and to 30 in 1976. Less than half of all delegates to the 1968 Democratic convention had been chosen by primaries; nearly three-fourths of the 1976 Democratic delegates were thus selected. The new rules also weakened Democratic party organizations, as "state party organizations [took] *on more of an administrative role rather than a decision-making role in recent presidential nominations.*"[22]

[21] *Openness, Participation and Party Building: Reforms for a Strong Democratic Party*, Report of the Commission on Presidential Nomination and Party Structure, 1978, Morley Winograd, chairman, p. 24.
[22] Ibid. Emphasis added.

The Republicans showed little enthusiasm for the kinds of changes the Democrats were imposing. But the GOP nonetheless felt the impact of some of them, like the greater reliance on primaries, which were written into state law and were applied to both parties.

By the late 1970s, the McGovern-Fraser reform efforts were under strong criticism as actually weakening the party. Another reform commission was formed: the Commission on Presidential Nomination, chaired by Governor James B. Hunt of North Carolina. The Hunt Commission made its report to the Democratic National Committee (DNC) in early 1982, and the DNC gave final approval to its new rules for the 1984 presidential nomination process in March 1982. One important change was intended to bring party officials back again more substantially into the nomination process. The 1984 rules allocated 550 seats for *party and elected officials* as unpledged delegates. Some of these would be named by the House and Senate Democratic caucuses—with seats given to three-fifths of all congressional Democrats—and the balance would be named by state parties, giving priority to governors and big-city mayors. Unpledged delegate slots would also be reserved for each state's Democratic chair and vice-chair. Under the McGovern-Fraser rules, party leaders had been required to run for delegate seats like anyone else. Most of them would not run: It would be humiliating to lose, and winning might not be much better for they might anger an important group of constituents whose support they would need in their next election.

Other changes were designed to increase the chances of a decisive outcome in the search for delegates. We noted in chapter 12 that winner-take-all electoral systems encourage unambiguous electoral outcomes (clear winners and losers) while proportional representation aims at allotting seats in exact proportion to votes and thus may prevent anyone getting a majority. Hunt Commission rules led the Democrats further away from the type of proportional representation in delegate selection introduced first by the McGovern-Fraser Commission.

In establishing the guidelines for their 1988 convention, the party followed the recommendations of its rules review panel, the Fairness Commission—and made relatively few changes from what applied in 1984. It did further increase the number of "superdelegates"—party officials who receive convention seats automatically without having to run in primaries and caucuses. But it also lowered—from 20 percent to 15 percent—the percentage of votes a candidate must receive in each primary and caucus state to win convention delegates. This was a bow to Jesse Jackson, who argued that the higher cutoff in 1984 had unfairly deprived him of delegates.

The continuing Democratic struggle over rules for delegate selection took another turn during convention preparations in 1988. Jackson and his supporters sought major changes in the rules, cutting back the superdelegates—who had given him little support in 1988—

The Hunt Commission

The 1988 convention guidelines

and relying on a strictly proportional scheme for delegate selection—so that, for instance, 10 percent of the primary vote would yield 10 percent of the delegates. Michael Dukakis had the votes on the convention's Rules Committee to block Jackson's initiatives, but he decided to place harmony in 1988 over preservation of the rules that many party leaders had thought worked well. The number of superdelegates was cut by 250, and winner-take-all delegate selection arrangements were banned completely. The party was edging back to the philosophy that had underlain the McGovern-Fraser changes two decades earlier—emphasizing the importance of having convention delegates reflect exactly the balance of primary and caucus voting. Political scientist David E. Price, now a congressman from North Carolina, was especially critical of these changes, which will apply in 1992. "It's a familiar path that we see," he said. "Candidates meet their short-term needs but sell out the long-term interests of the party."[23]

SUMMARY

By two key criteria, partisan *realignment* has occurred in the United States in recent years. This means, first, that a number of social groups manifest new party loyalties and voting behavior. The shift in the partisan attachments of white southerners has been especially dramatic.

The partisan balance of power has changed. A weak second to the Democrats through much of the New Deal era and into the late 1970s, the Republicans have found their electoral position significantly strengthened.

If one insists, however, that realignment must include the emergence of a new majority party—not just new patterns of social group attachments to the parties and a shift in the partisan balance—then realignment still has not occurred. In the mid-1980s the two main parties stand in positions of rough parity.

Even as the party coalitions have shifted, voter ties to both parties have weakened. *Dealignment*, the moving of voters away from strong partisan loyalties, has accelerated over the past fifteen years. The electorate is now less anchored by party identifications than it used to be, and it can be shifted more easily by the issues of the time.

Political parties as we now know them first took form in the infant United States at the end of the eighteenth century. An institutional response to the new reality of political egalitarianism, they have become central institutions in all democracies and in many other countries as well. Parties are linkage institutions between the public and government. Properly organized in a democratic system, they can greatly increase voters' control over their governmental officials and public decision making.

[23] David Price quoted in Rhodes Cook, "Pressed by Jackson Demands, Dukakis Yields On Party Rules," *Congressional Quarterly*, July 2, 1988, p. 1799.

The American party system has a number of distinctive attributes. Almost alone in the world, it is a two-party system. For over a century, the Republicans and Democrats have won the overwhelming majority of votes and offices. American parties are inclusive and heterogeneous, practitioners of political compromise and accommodation. They do not have members, only adherents; they exercise remarkably little discipline over their elites. Party organization is weak in the face of strong currents of political individualism. Rank-and-file voters typically select nominees through primary elections. No other democracy gives party leaders so little control over candidate selection.

Efforts to reform the political parties have focused on making them more democratic in their internal operations. Over the last two decades, reform attempts have been concentrated within the Democratic party and have dealt with presidential nominating procedures. The 1984 Democratic rules sought to reverse a pattern begun by the party's McGovern-Fraser Commission in 1969, by modestly increasing the role of party and elected officials, and by opting for decisiveness at the expense of proportionality in the allocation of delegates. In 1988, though, the party adopted new rules for 1992 that edged back toward the McGovern-Fraser philosophy.

FOR FURTHER STUDY

Angus Campbell, et al., *The American Voter* (New York: Wiley, 1960). A major study that advances a theory of party identification and its role in American electoral decision making.

Xandra Kayden and Eddie Mahe, Jr., *The Party Goes On* (New York: Basic Books, 1985). Argues that political parties are adapting successfully to a changed political environment in the United States and that any notice of their death is decidedly premature.

Norman H. Nie, Sidney Verba, John R. Petrocik, *The Changing American Voter*, rev. ed. (Cambridge, MA: Harvard University Press, 1979). Argues that since the 1960s voters have become more inclined to evaluate candidates and parties on the basis of their issue positions.

Nelson W. Polsby, *Consequences of Party Reform* (New York: Oxford University Press, 1983). Advances a strong criticism of changes made in the presidential nominating system, especially by the Democrats, in the 1960s and 1970s.

Austin Ranney, *Curing the Mischiefs of Faction: Party Reform in America* (Berkeley, CA: University of California Press, 1975). The best available analysis of the theory and practice of party reform historically in the United States.

Clinton Rossiter, *Parties and Politics in America* (Ithaca, NY: Cornell University Press, 1960). A highly readable yet thoughtful account of what is distinctive about American political parties.

Giovanni Sartori, *Parties and Party Systems: A Framework for Analysis* (Cambridge: Cambridge University Press, 1976). A comparison of party systems in countries around the world.

Richard C. Scammon, Alive V. McGillivray, eds., *America Votes: A Handbook of Contemporary American Election Statistics* (Washington, DC: Congressional Quarterly, Inc., latest volume, 1987). A compendium of electoral data on each biennial election, by state, since 1948.

Chapter 14

The Media

Early in American history, much of the work of government was done locally, in the nation's then-predominant small towns and rural areas. It was "up close and personal": People could see it firsthand, talk with the decision makers, ask them to explain or defend their actions. Today things are greatly changed. The work of government is far more complex and remote. Most citizens literally never see in person the state and national government officials whose decisions have such large consequences for their lives. In today's conditions, if we are to gain the information we need about politicians, policies, and events, we will do so for the most part through *mass media of communication*—large-circulation national and metropolitan newspapers like the *New York Times*, the *Wall Street Journal*, and *USA Today;* popular news magazines such as *Time*, *Newsweek*, and *U.S. News & World Report;* and, especially, through radio and television.

From this basic development the media or "the press" has emerged as an ever more central social and political institution. It is relied upon—and complained about. The extent of its power, and how that power is employed, are much discussed. These and other matters bearing on the role of the media in modern American democracy will be discussed in this chapter.

THE POWER OF THE PRESS

There is no consensus on the proper place of the press in a political system. The "founding father" of the Soviet Union, V. I. Lenin, thought that the press should be subordinate to the state. Why, he asked in a famous speech made in 1920, should freedom of the press be allowed? "Why should a government which is doing what it believes to be right allow itself to be criticized? It would not allow opposition by lethal

DeLucia

Trucks mounted with satellite dishes line up outside the 1988 Democratic National Convention to transmit the news to stations across the country.

weapons. Ideas are more fatal than guns."[1] In contrast, democrats insist that government should sustain the full freedom of the press. Even the firmest advocates of this democratic ideal differ, however, on other issues surrounding this vital institution—such as how much power the press has—and should have.

It is not hard to detect the consequences of the use of power in certain instances, as when an authoritarian government uses its control of the police and armed forces to stifle opposition. But in many cases the effects are hard to measure: How much power does big business have in the United States? Organized labor? There is not even agreement on how to understand the concept of power in such instances, much less any precise measure of that power or what it achieves. We are on firmer ground when we talk not about power but about resources relevant to the exercise of power. The economic resources available to those who head certain major corporations in the United States can be described, and we can see where there is discretion in employing them and where there is not. This does not give us a definitive picture of the power or influence of American business leaders, but it does provide us with a better sense of their power potential vis-à-vis other groups. Similarly, by examining the resources available to the communications media, we gain a clearer understanding of what the debate over the power of the press involves.

Let us begin with a hypothetical question. What would be the consequences for democracy if these two conditions obtained: (1) Gov-

---

[1] V. I. Lenin, *Collected Works*, vol. 31 (Moscow: Progress Publishers, 1966), p. 207.

ernment scrupulously maintained a "hands off" position with regard to the press, not using its authority to limit who communicates what to whom, but (2) certain private interests held huge and disproportionate communications resources and used these to advance their own perspectives on politics? (By communications resources we mean facilities for collecting political information and presenting it to mass audiences.) What if certain private interests owned all the television stations and used them to reach mass audiences to push their own political preferences, ignoring or misrepresenting other points of view? Could democratic government function satisfactorily in this situation? Few think that it could. Press resources matter, and even scrupulous enforcement of the First Amendment cannot solve all problems regarding these resources.

Mass Audiences

Early in American history, concerns about press resources seemed remote. The economics and technology of communications allowed new communications media, typically newspapers, to be established easily, and no one could reach very large audiences. Resources were widely dispersed. As long as government did not intervene to throttle freedom of communication, there was little to worry about. For example, in New York, the nation's largest city, the *Morning Herald* was started in 1835 with just $500 and the *Tribune* in 1841 with $3,000.[2] Anyone with a little money and writing ability could set up a newspaper and compete effectively in the dissemination of political ideas. Newspapers reached at most a few thousand people, and it did not cost much to establish them.

Subsequent developments in transportation and communications changed this—making possible huge audiences and requiring great

Expanding communications and politics

financial outlays. On an average weekday evening, about 50 million Americans tune in to the national news broadcasts of CBS, NBC, ABC, and public television. Whereas most citizens can express their views to at most a few score of their fellows, anchorman Tom Brokaw of NBC News reaches 15 million or more nightly. The question of how much Brokaw and his counterparts influence American political life has been endlessly debated with few certain conclusions. But the mere act of creating audiences of the size generated by contemporary American television news programming has encouraged the perception that vast communications power is thus imparted.

Network television audiences are unusually large, but a number of print media have also acquired huge circulations. Table 14.1 shows the ten individual newspapers with the largest circulations. At the top of the list, with a paid circulation of nearly 2 million (and hence

[2] For a general discussion of press resources prior to the Civil War, see Frank Luther Mott, *American Journalism: A History of Newspapers in the United States through 250 years, 1690 to 1940* (New York: Macmillan, 1947), pp. 215–323.

Table 14.1
Paid Circulation of the Ten Largest U.S.
Daily Newspapers

Wall Street Journal	1,961,846
USA Today	1,324,223
New York Daily News	1,285,869
Los Angeles Times	1,113,459
New York Times	1,002,899
Chicago Tribune	765,371
Washington Post	761,142
New York Post	692,915
Detroit News	686,787
Detroit Free Press	649,312

Source: 1988 Editor and Publisher International Yearbook (New York: Editor and Publisher Co., 1988). The reporting date for circulation of above newspapers is September 30, 1987.

Major newspapers and magazines

perhaps 4 million readers daily) is the *Wall Street Journal*. *USA Today* had a national circulation of about 1,325,000 in 1987. With daily paid circulations of about 1,000,000 and 760,000, respectively, the *New York Times* and the *Washington Post* are read by very large proportions of the country's political, economic, and intellectual leaders, especially in the key New York and Washington areas.

A number of magazines have even larger circulations. (See Table 14.2.) At the top of the list among those that print primarily political

Table 14.2
Paid Circulation of Selected U.S. Magazines

News reporting and commentary	
Time	4,720,000
Newsweek	3,181,000
U.S. News & World Report	2,287,000
Harper's	176,000
Business	
Business Week	879,000
Fortune	744,000
Forbes	727,000
Political opinion	
National Review	116,000
The New Republic	94,000
The Nation	82,000
Commentary	47,800
The American Spectator	40,000
The Public Interest	12,000
Other	
TV Guide	16,800,000
Readers Digest	16,250,000
National Geographic	12,000,000

Source: The 1988 Gale *Directory of Publications,* 120th ed. (Detroit, Mich.: Book Tower, 1988).

news is *Time*, which sells 4.7 million copies each week and has a readership of more than 10 million. Among all monthly magazines, *Reader's Digest* leads, with a circulation of well over 16 million copies and some 40 million readers. In print and electronic journalism massive audiences have become the rule.

Financial Resources

The attainment of such huge audiences permits the great print and electronic media to generate enormous revenues, especially through the sale of advertising. In 1950 the television networks and the 107 local television stations had broadcast revenues of just $106 million. Thirty-six years later, in 1986, the big three commercial networks and the over 900 VHF and UHF stations enjoyed broadcasting revenues (largely from advertising) of over $22 billion. The three networks alone had revenues of $8.6 billion in 1986.[3]

The financial resources generated by the largest communications media are used for many things, including news coverage far beyond that of any previous period. For example, CBS News now has about two hundred full-time staff members in its Washington bureau, including 18 on-the-air reporters. The Associated Press's DC bureau has 100 reporters. In all, about 1,700 reporters are assigned to the White House alone. Big special news events attract throngs of report-

Staff resources of major media

The evening news—in the U.S. and in the Soviet Union.

[3] *Television and Cable Fact Book*, Services Volume, 1987 ed. (Washington D.C.: Television Digest, 1987), pp. 6, 10, 13.

ers. The 1988 Democratic Convention in Atlanta drew some 15,000 journalists—who far outnumbered the Convention's official participants. Such numbers make it possible for political actions to be probed and dissected to a detail unimaginable in the past.

The great financial resources of the major communications media permit them to support their staffs far more generously than in the past. Historically, journalists were a poorly paid professional group. At the *New York Times* in 1987, however, a reporter earned a minimum of $47,000 a year, and leading columnists and top editors received salaries several times as great. The most dramatic salary gains have been recorded in television news. In 1984, CBS News anchorman Dan Rather signed a contract that would bring him $36 million in salary over the next 10 years.[4] Anchors for big-city television stations were paid salaries of $500,000 and more. Not surprisingly, the enhanced pay of journalists and the huge audiences now open to those reporting for the leading media have increased the prestige and glamour of the journalism profession. Occupational prestige scores, which had shown journalism near the bottom compared to other professions, have over the last quarter-century recorded a sharp rise in reporters' status. And journalism school enrollments have swelled.[5]

There is no chance that the United States will return to the institutional arrangements that prevailed earlier in the country's history, when the communications resources available to any one individual

Changing status of journalism

---

[4] Ed Joyce, *Prime Times, Bad Times* (New York: Doubleday, 1988), pp. 350–52.
[5] See James Boylan, "News People," *Wilson Quarterly*, Special Issue, 1982, pp. 76–77; see, too, *1988 Editor and Publisher International Yearbook.*

or press outlet were so meager that they conferred little opportunity for undue political influence. In nineteenth-century America, the only way power over political communications could have become concentrated would have been for government to control the press. Given the technology of that time, freedom of the press was enough to ensure a highly dispersed, fragmented, pluralistic press. No longer.

ORGANIZATION OF THE PRESS

Though it is not a part of the government in any democracy, the press plays an essential public-sector role, performing functions central to political life. Even when it is wholly privately owned and operated, the press has broad public responsibilities, chief of which is seeing to it that citizens have access to the information they need to decide the issues before them.

In most democracies, a distinction is made in practice between those segments of the press that articulate particular group interests and perspectives, partisan or ideological, and those that are general-circulation vehicles of news dissemination. There is little debate over what public policy should be with regard to the former: Government should simply stay out of the way, allowing the journals of opinion to speak their mind freely. But with regard to general-circulation news media, there is argument in every democratic nation. How should the mass-audience press be organized to perform its broad public-sector responsibility of assuring the citizenry access to needed information?

Ownership

In the United States, there has been general agreement on one part of the answer: The press should be *privately owned and operated*, with the fewest possible governmental regulations and restraints. Democracy requires a free press, and freedom is most securely attained when government is kept at arm's length. The natural interplay of market forces will ensure a variety of general-circulation communications media that, in competition with one another, will see to it that the news is as fully and fairly reported as is practically possible. Note that this emphasis on free markets is akin to the more general American rationale for a private business system, which emphasizes the importance of free competition in meeting consumers' needs.

American newspapers and news magazines are private corporations, owned and operated much like other private businesses. Those wishing to establish a new paper capitalize it like those wishing to set up any other business; if they cannot maintain their news business profitably they cease to operate. Every year a number of newspapers and magazines are established while others close their doors.

The American press: a private enterprise

Newspaper births and deaths have largely balanced out in recent decades; there were 1,763 daily newspapers in the United States at the end of World War II and 1,645 in 1987.[6]

Radio and television ownership in the U.S.

The ownership status of the general-circulation *print media* in America is essentially what one finds in other democratic countries, where the print media are privately owned. The organization of radio and television in the United States differs substantially, however, from that in other democracies. The three major television networks—the Columbia Broadcasting System (CBS), the American Broadcasting Company (ABC), and the National Broadcasting Company (NBC)— together with a preponderance of local television stations, are privately owned businesses.

Radio and television ownership in Europe

In contrast, throughout Europe telecommunications was seen from the beginning as a public utility to be run as a national monopoly. Government's role in managing radio and television is still greater all across the European democracies than in the United States, although in recent years privately-owned media have been given increasing scope.

Public radio and television

The American telecommunications industry has not always been privately controlled, and is not exclusively private today. In 1918 the American Telephone and Telegraph Company was taken over by the federal government, and remained under public control until the middle of 1919. And today, the United States has public radio and public television stations which, while small compared to the size and number of commercial networks and their affiliates, play a significant role in broadcasting. The Public Broadcasting Act of 1967 established the Corporation for Public Broadcasting (CPB). With some of the features of the British Broadcasting Company, CPB is a public corporation responsible for developing noncommercial television and radio services. It provides financial support to public radio and television station operations. Most of the funds for the Corporation for Public Broadcasting come from government—state and local as well as federal—although public radio and television stations also depend on private contributions and grants from business corporations.

Financing the press in the U.S. and Europe

The contrast between the United States and much of Europe evident in the area of radio and television ownership is even sharper in the area of finances. Newspapers and news magazines in the United States do receive favorable postal rates. But all units of the press, print and electronic alike, depend on private resources, especially advertising, for their sustenance. They sell their product on the private market. Throughout Europe, however, there are extensive governmental subsidies. State-directed radio and television receive much of their revenue from annual license fees that owners of radio and

---

[6] Leo Bogart, "Newspapers in Transition," *Wilson Quarterly*, Special Issue, 1982, p. 69; See, too, *1988 Gale Directory of Publications*.

television sets must pay—much as motor-vehicle operators in the United States pay license fees. These fees are a type of user-directed tax. The print media also receive large and important subsidies. In Great Britain newspapers are exempted from the country's principal taxation, the value-added tax (VAT). Revenue from the sale of newspapers or from the sale of advertising is not subject to any VAT, and this confers what one observer calls "a colossal fiscal advantage, worth between five and ten percent of total [newspaper] revenue." In France the private press gets subsidized newsprint, low postal rates, and special tax privileges.[7]

Regulation

The one area where the U.S. government is significantly involved in the mass communications media is radio and television regulation. The Federal Communications Commission (FCC) licenses radio and television stations. A corporation wishing to establish a VHF or UHF television station cannot simply purchase the necessary equipment, hire staff, and begin broadcasting. The FCC must license it to operate on a particular frequency. The now rather detailed provisions of FCC licensing developed from the straightforward premise that some basic regulation of who could broadcast at what frequency was needed to prevent a hopeless scrambling of signals. There are no technical lim-

Barred from the island of Grenada during the American military intervention on the island in 1983, at least 500 journalists flocked to the neighboring island of Barbados and tried to file their stories from there.

[7] Anthony Smith, *The Politics of Information: Problems of Policy in Modern Media* (London: Macmillan, 1978), p. 175.

its on the number of newspapers or news magazines that can be disseminated in a particular market; but the airwaves are a finite common property, defined by the laws of physics, rather than simply by laws of supply and demand.

FCC regulation

If the basic rationale for governmental regulation of the broadcast media is unexceptionable, the result has been to establish a governmental agency—the FCC, which is an independent regulatory commission—with substantial authority. Television stations now must go before the commission every five years to renew their licenses. AM and FM radio stations must seek renewal every seven years. In practice they are rarely turned down, but there have been a few dramatic cases of denial. On what grounds can the FCC deny renewal? From the beginning of the broadcast industry, U.S. policy has stipulated that a license to broadcast, once conferred, is not permanent. Subsequent performance must be taken into account in determining whether renewal is to be granted. Stations are given access to a vital public resource, the airwaves. Do they use it responsibly? Are they attuned to the needs and interests of their broadcast areas? Few would argue that the FCC should automatically extend licenses regardless of what stations do on the air. But on the issue of what constitutes insufficient performance, confusion reigns. The sword rarely falls—but it is left hanging.

Fairness doctrine

Federal regulation of *news* broadcasting has occurred in three related areas: (1) the fairness doctrine, (2) the equal-time provision, and (3) the right of rebuttal. Involved are so-called "access rights" established initially through Section 315 of the Federal Communications Act of 1934 and its various amendments and interpretations. The ***fairness doctrine*** required broadcasters who aired material on controversial issues to provide reasonable time for the expression of opposing views. Critics of this provision long argued that it had the effect of discouraging the media from covering certain controversial issues, to avoid having to air opposing views in place of programs that generate revenue.[8] The broadcast industry opposed the regulation, and had challenged it in the courts on the grounds that it infringed First Amendment rights. In August 1987, the FCC voted 4–0 to repeal the fairness doctrine—partly responding to the legal challenge and partly reflecting the general commitment of Reagan appointees to deregulating the broadcast industry. These appointees believe that the dramatic expansion of television-viewing options—cable systems, videotape cassettes, etc.—has increased market competition and thus obviated the need for some of the traditional forms of regulation. Congressional Democrats sought to enact legislation requiring reinstatement of the doctrine, but their efforts were blocked in 1987 and 1988 by a threatened presidential veto.

[8] For a discussion of the effects see Doris A. Graber, *Mass Media and American Politics* (Washington: Congressional Quarterly Press, 1980), p. 93.

Equal-time provision

The ***equal-time*** provision, still in force, stipulates that broadcasters who permit one candidate for public office to campaign on their stations must give equal opportunities to every other candidate for that office. For example, they cannot sell air time to a Republican candidate for a U.S. Senate seat and deny the same type of time, at the same rates, to a Democratic, Libertarian, or other party candidate. Like the fairness doctrine, the equal-time provision has been under legal challenge as violating broadcasters' First Amendment rights. In 1988, however, the Supreme Court refused to hear an appeal of a lower court decision on the constitutional issue, in effect stating that it considered the equal-time rule to be constitutionally-permitted regulation.

Right of rebuttal

The ***right-of-rebuttal*** provisions are ancillaries of the fairness doctrine that have remained in force. They involve the right of individuals to respond to personal attacks made over radio or television that might be held to damage their reputations. In the case of *Red Lion Broadcasting* v. *Federal Communications Commission* (1969), a liberal newsman who had written a book critical of conservative Senator Barry Goldwater brought suit because he was denied free air time to rebut an aired attack on his book by a conservative clergyman. The clergyman headed a religious organization that bought and paid for the program on which the book was attacked. In the *Red Lion* case, the Supreme Court granted the newsman the air time he had demanded, free of charge, holding that maligned individuals deserve an opportunity to reply and that the public deserves the opportunity to hear opposing views.[9] Outside of radio and television broadcasting, the press in the United States has not felt the regulatory hand of government very heavily.

Libel Law

The application of libel laws in Great Britain and the United States provides an illustration of the comparative freedom of the American press from regulatory controls. What if a newspaper story about a political leader states things harmful to his reputation that can be demonstrated to be untrue? If he can prove in a court of law that the accounts are false, can he collect damages from the newspaper? In Britain, the answer is generally yes. Not surprisingly, the British press is reluctant to print critical materials when it is not certain that it can establish their accuracy. "British newspapers are often forced to delay publication until their evidence is watertight or until foreign newspapers and the underground press have made an item common knowledge."[10] The author of a story, the publisher, and those selling the paper or book can all be sued in Britain for defamatory libel.

[9]Graber, *Mass Media*, pp. 94–95.
[10]Max Belloff and Gillian Peole, *The Government of the United Kingdom: Political Authority in a Changing Society* (New York: Norton, 1980), pp. 336–37.

In the United States, more than defamatory inaccuracy must be proved before a conviction for libel may be sustained. In the 1964 case of *New York Times Company* v. *Sullivan*, the Supreme Court ruled that a "public official" seeking libel damages for a matter relating to his official conduct must prove that the false statement about him had been made with "actual malice"—that is, with conscious knowledge that the statement was false or with "reckless disregard" for whether it was or not. The Court held that, otherwise, the press or other critics would be restrained from speaking or writing for fear they could not readily demonstrate that what they had said was true. As a practical matter, it is very hard to prove that defamatory falsehoods about a public official were made with "actual malice," and the American communications media are largely free from the threat of libel action in their reporting on public officials.[11]

New York Times v.
Sullivan

Similar distinctions between the legal position of the American and British press can be seen in other areas. For example, the British Official Secrets Act, passed in 1911, makes the *unauthorized receipt* of official government documents, as well as their *unauthorized publication*, an offense. While the government has not used this legislation in an oppressive manner, the act is still a source of governmental restraint on the press. In contrast, in the United States, the Freedom of Information Act (1974) gives the press a strong legal base from which to force the government to release documents that they might choose to withhold. The burden is on the government to prove that some harm, as to national security, might come from release of the documents.

British Official Secrets
Act and the Freedom
of Information Act

Contradictory Trends

Communications media in the United States have been experiencing contradictory developments in terms of centralization and decentralization. Historically America did not have a national press. Its newspapers—unlike Great Britain's, for example—were predominantly local, circulating only in one urban area or state. In recent years, though, this has been changing. New communications technology has made it possible for a newspaper whose editorial staff is located in one city to transmit information via satellite to printing plants located throughout the country. The paper is then distributed from the local plants to newsstands and subscribers just like any other local paper. The *Wall Street Journal* was the first American newspaper to take full advantage of this new technology. The *New York Times*, perhaps the most prestigious paper in the country, began following suit in the

The growth of a
national press

[11] A. E. Dick Howard, "The Press in Court," *Wilson Quarterly*, Special Issue, 1982, pp. 87–90; see also *New York Times Company* v. *Sullivan*, 376 U.S. 254 (1964). In recent years, the Supreme Court has shown no sign of backing away from the strong protection it gave the press in *New York Times Company* v. *Sullivan*. For example, in June 1986, in *Anderson* v. *Liberty Lobby*, the Court made it easier for press defendants in libel cases to win pretrial dismissal of suits against them.

Television crews travel far and wide to report the news: here, a TV crew filming Palestinian demonstrations in the Israeli-occupied West Bank.

early 1980s, although the New York City base of many of its advertising clients presented serious obstacles. New York department stores usually do not want to pay for advertising in other geographic areas. In September 1982, the Gannett chain of newspapers established *USA Today*, the first daily in American history established as a nationwide, general-circulation, general-news publication. Fifteen months after its birth, "America's newspaper," as Gannett calls it, was selling about 1.2 million copies a day all across the country. No longer could it be said that the United States lacked a national press.

These recent centralizing developments have been in addition to the long-established role of the national wire services in news reporting. Local papers draw much of their coverage from the Associated Press (AP), United Press International (UPI), the *New York Times*, *Washington Post*, or *Los Angeles Times* wire services.[12] The masthead may say Bangor, Maine; Tucson, Arizona; Spokane, Washington; or Savannah, Georgia; but when it comes to news of national and international politics, a few centralized reportorial organizations, with great resources, dominate the scene.[13]

The first few decades of television were characterized by a very different condition than the one that prevailed historically with newspapers. Television-station ownership was dispersed, but both

National wire services

---

[12] The roots of the AP and UPI go back to 1848, when six New York newspapers banded together to share the costs of gathering foreign news. The major wire services now maintain huge staffs of reporters throughout the world.

[13] See Bogart, "Newspapers in Transition," p. 58.

Expanding television news networks

entertainment and national news reporting were highly central-ized—dominated by the three big commercial networks. Now, how-ever, the television industry is experiencing an extraordinary fracturing, as many new players challenge the stranglehold on audi-ence that ABC, CBS, and NBC long enjoyed. One major source of change has been the extension of cable television to more and more house-holds and with it, the emergence of new cable networks. Turner Broadcasting launched the Cable News Network (CNN) in 1980, and it is now committed to establishing yet another cable network, Turner Network Television (TNT). The USA Network is also in operation, along with other cable-based facilities including the Financial News Network (FNN) and the Christian Broadcasting Network (CBN). The Fox network is seeking to join CBS, ABC, NBC, and Public Broadcast-ing as a fifth broadcast network—operating through local stations rather than over a cable hookup. A number of new national news programs have been established in recent years, eroding the domi-nant position that the "Big Three" long enjoyed.

EVOLUTION OF THE PRESS

The communications media in the United States today differ greatly in size, resources, organization, and modes of operation from their counterparts in earlier periods. The press evolved in the years follow-ing ratification of the Constitution with very close ties to the infant political parties. Indeed, historians often refer to newspapers in the early years as "the party press."

Newspapers and Political Parties

As the new parties took shape, politicians began starting or enlisting newspapers to help them communicate their partisan interpretations of political events to their constituents. A leading historian of Amer-ican journalism, Frank Luther Mott, notes that

> as party feelings grew, a new reason for the existence of newspapers came to be recognized. Whereas nearly all newspapers heretofore had been set up as auxiliaries to printing establishments and had been looked upon merely as means which enterprising printers used to make a living, now they were more and more often founded as spokesmen of political par-ties. This gave a new dignity and a new color to American journalism.[14]

The *Gazette of the United States* was established in 1789 as a semi-weekly newspaper, with the avowed intent of telling the Federalist side of things. It was to be an organ of the new government. Its foun-der was a Boston school teacher, John Fenno. Fenno intended "to

---

[14] Mott, *American Journalism*, pp. 113–14.

hold up the people's own government, in a favorable point of light— and . . . by every exertion, to endear the GENERAL GOVERNMENT TO THE PEOPLE."[15] As the Republican opposition to the Federalists took shape, its leaders, especially Thomas Jefferson and James Madison, felt the need for a new paper in the capital to reflect their political point of view. Madison and Jefferson enlisted the services of Philip Freneau to edit and publish their paper, and the *National Gazette* appeared in October 1791. Other party-press ties were established around the country. The political tone of the press became so harsh, so reflective of partisan emotion, that Mott calls "the whole period of 1801–1833 . . . a kind of 'Dark Ages' of American journalism."

Another important feature of the press in the early years was its rapid assumption of a key role in American democratic life. For all their faults, early American papers succeeded in supplying common people with access to political information. The resultant growth of the press was phenomenal. At the beginning of the nineteenth century, the United States had about 200 little newspapers, few of which were published on a daily basis. By 1835, however, the country had more than 1,200 newspapers, about 65 of which were dailies. This gave the United States more papers and a larger total circulation than any other country.[16]

Development of an Independent Popular Press

In the years after the Civil War, new printing technology greatly reduced publishing costs. New communications technology, appearing first in the telegraph, permitted news to be transmitted electronically from one part of the country to another, or from Europe to the United States, almost instantaneously. As major cities developed, they provided the population and financial base for great mass circulation dailies. The number of newspapers increased phenomenally, from about 3,500 in 1870, to roughly 7,000 in 1880, to over 12,000 in 1890. As this occurred, the controlling audience for the American press shifted from partisan groups to a mass audience. Papers gradually emerged from domination by political parties. The press came increasingly to deal with a wide variety of subjects of popular interest in addition to politics.

A key figure in the development of the mass-circulation popular press in late-nineteenth-century America was Joseph Pulitzer (after whom the well-known journalism award, the Pulitzer Prize, has been named). Pulitzer got his start as a newspaper owner in 1878, when he bought the bankrupt *St. Louis Dispatch*. Successful with that paper

---

[15] *Gazette of the United States*, April 27, 1791, as quoted in Frank L. Mott, *Jefferson and the Press* (Baton Rouge: Louisiana State University Press, 1943), p. 15.
[16] Mott, *American Journalism*, pp. 167–68.

(which after a merger became the *Post-Dispatch*), Pulitzer moved into New York publishing in the 1880s. In 1883 he bought the *New York World* and announced what he intended to do with it:

> There is room in this great and growing city for a journal that is not only cheap but bright, not only bright but large, not only large but truly democratic—dedicated to the cause of the people rather than to that of the purse potentates—devoted more to the news of the New than of the Old World—that will expose all fraud and sham, fight all public evils and abuses—that will battle for the people with earnest sincerity.[17]

The energy and flare of the *World*, and its catering to popular tastes, quickly made it enormously successful. From a circulation of 20,000 in 1883, the *World* reached 100,000 in September 1884, 250,000 in 1886, and 374,000 in 1892. It had become the largest and, carrying vast amounts of advertising, the most profitable newspaper ever published.

Yellow journalism

In the late nineteenth century and the early years of the twentieth, the search for ever larger audiences produced a flourishing of what has been called "yellow journalism." Be sensational; and don't let facts slow you down—such might have been the motto of this new journalism. The battle for circulation between press lords Joseph Pulitzer and William Randolph Hearst in New York City in the 1890s displayed yellow journalism in its most rambunctious form. Perhaps

William Randolph Hearst wielded enormous power through his publishing empire.

The Yellow Peril

[17] Ibid., p. 434.

the most famous story of this press battle came in 1897, when Hearst sent a leading fiction writer, Richard Harding Davis, and a distinguished illustrator, Frederic Remington, to Cuba to investigate conditions in that Spanish colony and to send back features. James Creelman, who was also a reporter for Hearst, claims that the following telegraphic exchange took place:

> HEARST, JOURNAL, NEW YORK:
> EVERYTHING IS QUIET. THERE IS NO TROUBLE HERE.
> THERE WILL BE NO WAR. WISH TO RETURN. REMINGTON.
>
> REMINGTON, HAVANA:
> PLEASE REMAIN. YOU FURNISH THE PICTURES AND I'LL FURNISH THE WAR.
> HEARST.[18]

The Rise of Professionalism

Gradually a new ethos made its way through the American press; its watchword was "professionalism." Reacting against the political distortions arising from partisan domination of the press and those resulting from the insistent sensationalism of yellow journalism, some reporters concluded that their field needed to become a profession, with its own norms and ethical standards, like law and medicine. Intellectual independence—to describe things as they are—was a key objective in this pursuit of professionalism; care, objectivity, attention to factual detail were emphasized.

Establishment of journalism schools

Special programs were developed to teach journalists the technical tools of their profession and to instill in them professional standards. The first journalism curriculum was offered by the Wharton School of Business at the University of Pennsylvania. The first four-year program for journalism was set up in 1904 at the University of Illinois. And the first independent school of journalism was established in 1908 at the University of Missouri. In 1903 Joseph Pulitzer endowed a college of journalism at Columbia University, contributing $2 million. When the Columbia School of Journalism finally opened its doors in 1912, there were more than 30 colleges and universities offering formal training in the field. Books on the practice of journalism began to appear. And in 1910, newspaper editors in the state of Kansas adopted the first formal code of ethics for the profession.[19]

Journalistic independence

Perhaps the most important change brought about by this new professionalism was the growth of journalistic independence. The press should be independent of politicians, reporting on them and their actions as fully and fairly as possible. Journalists should be independent of the control of publishers who should run the business side;

[18] James Creelman, *On the Great Highway: The Wanderings and Adventures of a Special Correspondent* (Boston: Lothrop, 1901), pp. 177–78.
[19] Mott, *American Journalism*, pp. 604–5.

the pressroom should operate according to journalistic cannons. Newsmen should write without fear or favor, subject only to their own standards of ethics and professional competency.

The idea of journalism as an autonomous profession dramatically altered the way the mass media reported the news. This commitment is now a key part of the idea of "freedom of the press." The national media organizations, such as the *New York Times* and CBS News, draw their resources largely from American business; but the norm of journalistic independence has greatly minimized business influence in reporting and editorial coverage.

Radio and Television

The first commercial radio station in the United States began operating in 1922. Over the next quarter-century this new communications medium spread like wildfire. In late 1925 more than 575 stations were on the air, in 1940 about 850, and in 1950 about 2,150. With his famous "fireside chats," broadcast throughout the country in the 1930s, Franklin Roosevelt demonstrated that radio could do more than entertain: it could be a potent political instrument.

Emergence of radio and television news

Radio journalism remained much less influential than its print counterpart. So did television in the late 1940s and 1950s when it was establishing itself as a dominant entertainment medium. It was not until the 1960s that television news came into its own. The extension of evening television news programs from 15 minutes to 30 minutes in 1963 (for CBS News and NBC News, with ABC News following suit

With the widespread cable television hook-up, TV news is even more available to the public.

three years later) was a major step in the emergence of the electronic news media into the national limelight. As the networks learned that news could be more than a public service, that in an age of mass higher education there was an immense market for it, permitting the highly profitable sale of advertising, they began to devote much greater resources to news coverage.

Television's share of the total news audience has greatly risen over the last quarter-century. In one series of surveys, respondents were asked: "Where do you usually get your news about what's going on in the world today—from the newspapers, or radio, or television, or magazines, or talking to people, or where?" Figure 14.1 shows the changing mix. In 1959, just 29 percent listed television, not newspapers, as their prime news source; by the end of 1986, the proportion had risen to 50 percent. The proportion mentioning newspapers but not television dropped from 31 to 22 percent. In all, 63 percent of respondents to the December 1986 survey cited television as a principal source of the information they receive on public affairs, while only 35 percent listed newspapers as a major news source. Evans Witt, a public-opinion polling expert for the Associated Press, cautions that these data may exaggerate the public's shift to television as a source of public affairs information. People get their news from a variety of

Public reliance on television news

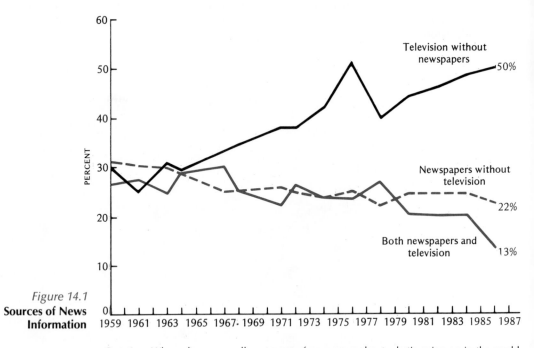

Figure 14.1
Sources of News Information

Question: Where do you usually get most of your news about what's going on in the world today—from the newspapers or radio or television or magazines?
Source: Surveys by the Roper Organization, for the Television Information Office, latest that of December 1986.

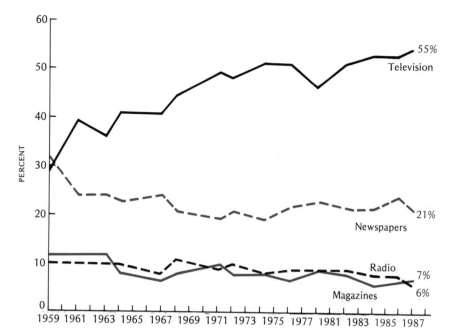

Figure 14.2
**Trustworthiness of
News Sources**

Question: If you got conflicting or different reports of the same news story from radio, television, the magazines, and the newspapers, which of the four versions would you be most inclined to believe—the one on radio or television or in magazines or newspapers?
Source: Surveys by the Roper Organization for the Television Information Office, latest that of December 1986.

sources and are not particularly aware of the process. They overemphasize the role of the more entertaining medium: television. This may be; still, there can be little doubt that television has become a vastly more important news source over the past quarter-century.

Americans also now indicate that they are more inclined to accept the television news version of a story than that of newspapers, radio, or magazines, in cases where these media present conflicting versions. In December 1986, 55 percent said they would tend to believe television, compared to 21 percent saying newspapers, 6 percent radio, and 7 percent magazines (Figure 14.2). Is the public asserting that "the camera cannot lie"?

THE PRESS AND GOVERNMENTAL INSTITUTIONS

The press envelops the government in the United States. Independent of those who wield governmental authority, but tied to them in a complex relationship both cooperative and adversarial, journalists form a critical part of government's primary audience. The president, his key aides, cabinet members, United States congressmen, and other officials interact more with the national press corps than they do with almost any other group—far more on a day-to-day basis than, say, with business and labor leaders.

The amount of contact American news reporters have with officials has long been a distinguishing feature of U.S. politics. In its openness to the press,

Interaction of press
and government
officials

> American government differs markedly from European (even British) governments. All European journalists are immediately struck by this difference. The American reporter not only has access to official announcements and press releases; he also has the opportunity of becoming the confidante of the official and of enjoying limited but regular access to his personal thoughts, official secrets, internal departmental gossip, and the like.[20]

Not only does the U.S. press play the primary role of disseminating information on what government does, but its members are a numerically imposing segment of the *political community*, interacting closely with governmental officials as the latter do their official work.

The Press and the Political Parties

The press's involvement in the political process applies with special force to party politics and electoral campaigns. The retinue of a presidential candidate typically includes a relatively small number of aides who travel with him and, if he is thought to have any likelihood of succeeding, a very large press contingent. The press's role is not confined to simply reporting what the candidate says and does. Members of the press have come to act as "talent scouts," screening the candidates, conveying the judgment that some are promising while others are without talent. Journalists act as race-callers or handicappers telling the public how the contest is going and why one candidate is ahead of another. They function at times as self-perceived public defenders, bent on exposing what they consider to be the frailties, duplicities, and sundry inadequacies of a candidate. They even sometimes slip into the role of "assistant campaign managers," informally advising a candidate and publicly, if indirectly, promoting his cause.[21]

The press in American
elections

The expanded campaign role of the national communications media is both a cause and an effect of the weakening of political parties. The extent to which the parties have introduced mechanisms for candidate selection that make voters-at-large the final judges has obviously made the press more important. The national nominating contests now center not in party committees or conventions but in mass-public-participation primaries across the country. The press has unpar-

[20] Paul H. Weaver, "The New Journalism and the Old—Thoughts after Watergate," *The Public Interest*, Spring 1974, p. 72.

[21] David S. Broder, "Political Reporters in Presidential Politics," in Charles Peters and Timothy J. Adams, eds., *Inside the System: A Washington Monthly Reader* (New York: Praeger, 1970), pp. 3–22 *passim*.

alleled resources for covering these contemporary campaigns; indeed, it is the only institution that can do it.

Press versus party as information source

But even if the political parties had not given up so much of their historic institutional responsibility for selecting candidates, the vast communications resources of the mass media would have severely challenged the parties. Political parties can no longer compete with the press as sources of information on candidates and the progress of electoral campaigns. Earlier in U.S. history, handbills printed by the parties and house-to-house canvassing by local party officials were the primary sources of electoral information, but today they cannot compete with the pervasiveness, visual force, immediacy, and general audience reach of television. It is the press that brings the campaign's personalities and issues into the homes and consciousness of American voters. Political parties are now ancillary structures in the whole process of communication between candidates and elected officials on one side and voters on the other.

The Press and the President

The relationship between the press and the president is a particularly consequential one. Washington is, of course, the center of U.S. government and the hometown of the national political elite; it is consequently the center for the national press. The Washington press corps dwarfs that of any other American city, and Washington is the hub for national news reporting. Though the Washington press hardly confines itself to reporting on the president and his administration, it does give the White House vast attention, partly because the presidency is a very important office in the country and partly because presidential actions lend themselves to highly visible and focused news stories.

The contrast between press treatment of the president and Congress demonstrates this point. The executive and legislative branches are coequal in the American constitutional scheme and in practical political power as well. The presidency is one person, however, while Congress is five hundred and thirty-five. From a news standpoint, reporting what happens in Congress is vastly more difficult, because of the numbers and because the story is usually less focused. As a result the press gives disproportionate attention to the president.

The extensive coverage given presidential actions and utterances, from the crucial to the trivial, has helped further elevate the presidency in contemporary American government. As television news became a more important part of the overall journalistic mix, the time-sensitive and visual properties of television made the distinctive singularity of the presidential office especially attractive, compared to the disjointed multiplicity of Congress. This bright spotlight the press has put on the presidency shows off strengths and makes the president seem larger than life; but it also illumines every weakness and alleged shortcoming. The inordinate press attention the president gets is a two-edged sword. We have seen presidents both rapidly elevated and diminished by this scrutiny. Political scientist Austin Ranney reminds us that

> no television correspondent or anchorman has ever won an Emmy or Peabody or even a promotion for a series of broadcasts focusing on what a marvelous job a president . . . is doing. Those rewards go to newspeople who expose the moral lapses, lies, and policy failures of public officials, and the president is the biggest game of all in the perennial hunt.[22]

Presidents and their aides thus have concluded that they must try to "manage" press treatment. The relationship is too important, and the consequences of negative scrutiny too great. Every modern presidency has devoted great attention—reaching well beyond the work of press secretaries—to turning the enormous powers of media coverage to the president's advantage. And still, for all the effort, no modern administration has emerged from its intricate dance with the national communications media without a sense of frustration.

Tension between president and press is inevitable because the two institutions have contrasting responsibilities. Arthur Krock, for many years head of the *New York Times* Washington bureau, notes that the job of the press is to uncover the news and then get the stories to the

Marginal notes:

Press spotlight on the presidency

Presidential "management" of the press

[22] J. Austin Ranney, *Channels of Power: The Impact of Television on American Politics* (New York: Basic Books, 1983), p. 141.

public. The more that is reported, the better. "But the statesman has other considerations. Is it [publication of a particular account of events or intended actions] premature? Will publication make the going more difficult? Will publication tend to confuse, rather than to clarify, the popular mind?"[23] A press is supposed to bring out "all the news that's fit to print," while a president is supposed to govern effectively. These contrasting objectives can never rest in perfect harmony. The amount of contemporary press coverage simply exaggerates the inherent tension.

President / press tension

The Press and Governmental Pluralism

In 1959, journalist and commentator Douglass Cater sought to describe the imposing role that the press had assumed in American government with an instructive title: *The Fourth Branch of Government*. News reporting is such a large and central undertaking in present-day democracy that it must be seen a formal, if extra-constitutional, "branch" of government itself.

The fourth branch of government?

From the standpoint of politicians, the press is both an opportunity and problem: an opportunity, because it provides them with coverage and publicity that they need to advance their candidacies and programs; a problem because press coverage may not reflect what they want brought to the public's attention. For the press, politicians are sources of exciting stories but also authors of attempts to manipulate them. From another perspective, the key element in press-politician ties is not the tensions that result but the important complementarity of their roles in American liberal democracy. James Madison and other founding fathers believed in a government of dispersed power, where no unit was too strong. The Constitution, as we have seen, has established an elaborate institutional framework to ensure the dispersion of governmental power. If this constitutional model is still sound, as many Americans believe it to be, the press, as the fourth branch of government, enlarges pluralism by further dispersing power.

Of course, the vast communications resources in the hands of an independent press are often employed in ways that governmental officials find troubling. And many neutral observers fear that in the last fifteen years or so segments of the press have become too inclined to probe for weaknesses and imperfections, thus helping to erode popular confidence in the governing process.[24] "The White House will

[23] Arthur Krock, as quoted by Douglass Cater, *The Fourth Branch of Government* (New York: Vantage, 1965), p. 19.

[24] For two important survey research studies by political scientists pointing to this conclusion, see Michael J. Robinson, "Public Affairs Television and the Growth of Political Malaise," *American Political Science Review*, June 1976, pp. 409–32; and Arthur Miller et al., "Type-Set Politics: Impact of Newspapers on Public Confidence," *American Political Science Review*, March 1979, pp. 67–84.

Dwayne Powell
Raleigh News and Observer
Los Angeles Times Syndicate

remain in a state of siege, as the normal transactions of the political system are unearthed, magnified, and then distorted by the media."[25]

Still, the net effect of the extensive, autonomous, quasi-governmental powers of the American communications media seems to be to further disperse governmental power. Those inclined to believe that Madison was basically right have reason to look with some satisfaction on the part the American communications media plays in contemporary governance. Those who have always felt that Madison erred by overemphasizing the advantages of fragmenting authority, to the point where coherence in policy making and other governmental actions is hard to achieve, have reason to be concerned about the increasingly prominent political role of the press as a kind of fourth branch. For the fourth branch does make it harder for the other three to act coherently. And the more effectively it exposes their failings, the more it diminishes them in general political terms. The autonomy and centrality of the press mean that political authority, in the broadest sense, is even more dispersed and fragmented than the Madisonian constitution itself requires.

Media's effect on governmental power

THE MEDIA, POLITICS, AND RESPONSIBILITY

Because the press plays a substantial part in political life, many are concerned with its *political outlook*—partisan and ideological. If the

[25] Richard Pious concludes his book *The American Presidency* with this lament. (New York: Basic Books, 1979), p. 417.

press is virtually a fourth branch of government, the political preferences of those who inhabit it merit attention. Those who believe that their own political preferences are underrepresented among journalists are naturally the most likely to protest against alleged press bias. For the last twenty-five years or so, conservatives and Republicans have more often accused the national press of bias than liberals and Democrats have. Liberal politicians who assert that the press is a hotbed of conservatism are rare, while conservative politicians who find the press a hotbed of liberalism are about as common as mosquitoes in the Everglades.

The liberal-conservative debate over the press has been a hot one at times. And it has made many members of the press defensive. We need to broaden the query into possible press biases, and answer three sets of questions.

Possible press biases

1) Do national journalists in the United States as a group reflect some distinctive political viewpoint? Are they, for example, more liberal or conservative in their own personal political preferences than Americans generally?

2) If the press has a distinctive political viewpoint, does this intrude in news reporting? Journalists might have some clear political preferences personally but do they keep these on the sidelines in professional work?

3) Is the issue of press liberalism/conservatism the key one? Are other aspects of the outlook of journalists more important in shaping their political role and performance than the side of the ideological or partisan spectrum on which a majority of them stand? Are there professional norms and outlooks in American journalism that impose certain biases in news reporting?

Press Liberalism

How liberal is the press?

Surveys leave little doubt that the tilt among national journalists in the United States is toward values and policies generally thought of as *liberal* (in the current meaning of that word). National journalists give more backing to liberal candidates than the American public does. Surveys show, for example, that in 1972, when Republican Richard Nixon won 61 percent of the vote in the country, only 19 percent of the journalists supported him while 81 percent backed Democrat George McGovern. In 1984, Ronald Reagan was backed by about 59 percent of the entire electorate but by just 26 percent of reporters and editors—the latter according to a national survey taken by the *Los Angeles Times*.[26] The *Times* poll also found that 55 percent of the journalists called themselves liberal and just 17 percent conservative. The pollsters reported that newspaper journalists were also

[26]The survey findings are summarized by S. Robert Lichter, Stanley Rothman, and Linda S. Lichter, *The Media Elite* (Bethesda, MD: Adler and Adler, 1986), pp. 38–41.

"*This is the nightly news, with Jim Watson in New York sitting in for Walt Bolling, who is on vacation, and Herb Henry in Washington sitting in for Stu Farnell, who is too liberal.*"

Drawing by Dana Fradon; © 1985 The New Yorker Magazine, Inc.

"markedly more liberal than others of similar educational and professional standing." On a wide variety of social and cultural issues—such as affirmative-action programs for blacks and other minorities, abortion, sexual norms and conduct—journalists are notably more liberal than the general public.

Many other groups, of course, give disproportionate backing to one side or the other of the political spectrum. Thus labor union leaders are heavily liberal and Democratic, while top officials of *Fortune 500* business corporations are generally conservative and Republican. The special interest—and, in some circles, concern—that is now expressed with regard to the political outlook of the national press reflects the press's unique role at the center of the dissemination of political information to the general public.

Press Liberalism and Bias in Reporting

It does not follow that if newspeople are disproportionately liberal, their reporting of the news must reflect a liberal bias. As Michael Robinson points out, "press behavior—not opinion—is the key. Bias that counts must be in the copy, not just in the minds of those who write it."[27] Robinson conducted a research project to find out if there were signs of liberal news bias in the press during the 1980 presidential campaign. After analyzing about 6,000 news stories, in print and electronic media alike, he did not find liberal bias. Not only did the

[27]Michael J. Robinson, "Just How Liberal Is the News? 1980 Revisited," *Public Opinion*, February/March 1983, p. 56; see, too, Robinson and Margaret A. Sheehan, *Over the Wire and on TV* (New York: Russell Sage Foundation, 1983).

content of stories not reflect any distinctive political leaning, but even more tellingly, the selection of stories to be covered did not betray bias.

This latter point is important and often overlooked. A story may be treated in an objective fashion, but if only a certain type of story is selected for coverage, bias could still result. As Robinson points out,

> if the press covered all business scandals objectively, but *only* covered business scandals, that agenda alone would support a theory of partisan bias. If the media always covered cost-overruns at the Pentagon but failed to cover any cheating in AFDC programs, that too would be political bias, regardless of how fair the reports themselves may seem.[28]

Are reporters biased?

Even on this level, he found few signs of liberal bias during the 1980 campaign. Of course, the fact that political bias was not evident in press coverage of that campaign does not mean bias is always absent. Campaign '80 might have minimized liberal-conservative bias because the Democratic incumbent was widely seen by liberals as well as conservatives to be ineffective. Not many liberals anywhere rallied strongly to Jimmy Carter in 1980. Four years later, in 1984, Robinson found that network coverage *was* more inclined to include criticism of Republicans Reagan and Bush than of Democrats Mondale and Ferraro. Nonetheless, he concluded that overall the networks "did not do nearly enough to overcome real events, real conditions, and real style. In short, the network coverage was so 'responsible' that it carried almost no weight in the campaign."[29]

Studies done during the 1988 campaign by the Center for Media and Public Affairs found that the distinguishing feature of media coverage was the amount of *bad* press *both* presidential candidates received. Both George Bush and Michael Dukakis attracted over twice as much unfavorable as favorable coverage on the networks' evening news broadcasts, the Center reported.[30] The networks did vary, however, with the CBS Evening News giving Dukakis relatively more favorable coverage while ABC's World News Tonight was a bit more favorable to Bush.[31]

Others have found clearer signs of press bias on certain issues. Stanley Rothman and Robert Lichter report that the press has greatly exaggerated the amount of opposition of informed scientists to the use of nuclear power to generate electricity. Their data indicate that a large number of scientists with knowledge about nuclear energy favor its use and do not reject it on safety grounds, but that press

[28] Robinson, "Just How Liberal Is the News?" pp. 59–60; see, too, Robinson and Sheehan, *Over the Wire.*
[29] Michael J. Robinson, "The Media in Campaign '84: Wingless, Toothless, and Hopeless," *Public Opinion*, February/March 1985, pp. 43–44.
[30] *Media Monitor*, Vol. 2, number 8, October 1988.
[31] *Media Monitor*, Vol. 2, number 9, November 1988.

reporting portrays the scientific community as deeply split on the issue.[32]

Some observers have concluded that the national press is especially receptive to certain kinds of issues linked to a liberal political outlook. For example, Michael Pertschuk—chairman of the Federal Trade Commission under President Carter, an ally of Ralph Nader, and a Democrat with strongly held liberal views—argues that one of the factors critical to the development of support for consumer-rights initiatives in the late 1960s and 1970s was "a newly aggressive corps of investigative and advocacy journalists, who shared the advocates' view of consumer initiatives as moral imperatives. . . ."[33] While he welcomed this development, Pertschuk himself saw the press as an ally rather than as an opponent or as what it claims to be—simply a fair-minded reporter of the news.

The press is composed of many different men and women who cover many different issues under often difficult reportorial conditions. It is not surprising that examinations of bias in press coverage have not yielded definitive conclusions as to the general rule. Few question that journalists are a liberal group in their personal political perspectives. But there is no comparable agreement that these personal views are often reflected in news coverage.

Are reporters more receptive to liberal issues?

Political Cynicism

What is clear is that most students of the press do not consider liberal-conservative bias the big issue. Recent studies emphasize the issue of *political negativism or cynicism,* suggesting that the distinguishing bias of the press results not from its political ideology but from its professional outlook. This may encourage holding up politicians and politics as more seamy and less worthy of public support than they in fact are. Paul Weaver argues, for example, that journalists generally, and television newspeople in particular, tend to see politics as in essence "a game played by individual politicians for personal advancement, gain, or power." From this perspective, politicians are naturally inclined "to exaggerate their good qualities and to minimize their bad ones, to be deceitful, to engage in hypocrisies, to manipulate appearances." The task of the press is to expose these bad tendencies of the political world.[34] Austin Ranney makes the same argument. There is not so much "a political bias in favor of liberalism or conservatism, as a structural bias." The latter encourages a cynical and excessively manipulative view of politics.[35]

[32] Stanley Rothman and S. Robert Lichter, "The Nuclear Energy Debate: Scientists, the Media and the Public," *Public Opinion,* August/September 1982, pp. 47–52.
[33] Michael Pertschuk, *Revolt Against Regulation: The Rise and Pause of the Consumer Movement* (Berkeley: University of California Press, 1982), p. 23.
[34] Paul H. Weaver, "Is Television News Biased?" *Public Interest,* Winter 1972, p. 69.
[35] Ranney, *Channels of Power,* pp. 54–55.

Michael Robinson's research supports the view that the press fosters a kind of political cynicism.

Has the press encouraged political cynicism?

> Events are frequently conveyed by television news through an inferential structure that often injects a negativistic, contentious, or anti-institutional bias. These biases, frequently dramatized by film portrayals of violence and aggression, evoke images of American politics and social life which are inordinately sinister and despairing.[36]

The effect of this, Robinson finds, is most substantial on viewers who approach politics without a great deal of political information or interest. Such viewers lack the political sophistication to reject the media depiction. As a result, they are apt to become themselves more cynical about political institutions and less confident that they can deal with such a political system.

Such findings may help us understand an important set of survey results. Public-opinion researchers have noted over the last two decades that Americans have become less confident than they were previously in the leadership of central institutions in the society, more distrustful politically, and more cynical. We have seen some decline in this cynicism, as part of the general recovery of public confidence in recent years; still, professed political cynicism is much higher now than it was a decade ago. According to one interpretation, the public simply reacted logically to a string of negative events and performances: the long Vietnam War and the domestic protests it engendered, the corruption of Watergate, double-digit inflation. These developments almost certainly were an important factor; but according to another

[36] Robinson, "Public Affairs Television," p. 430.

view, that work like Robinson's supports, increased public cynicism may have also resulted in part from an increasing cynicism in national news reporting, especially network television.

New Professional Norms

Some students of the press think it has become more negative in its portrayal of politics because an earlier set of professional norms has weakened and a newer set has become more prominent. John Johnstone and his colleagues identify the competing normative models as the "neutral" and the "participant." In the former, "the primary journalistic sins are sensationalism—overstatements of the natural reality of events, and bias—a violation of the observer's neutrality vis-à-vis information."[37] In contrast, the "participant" press model insists that journalists should give readers the interpretative background they need to put events in a proper perspective. "In this sense, the primary journalistic value is relevance, and the cardinal sins, news suppression and superficiality." Journalists are supposed to play a more active and, to some degree, creative part in developing what is newsworthy. Johnstone and his associates found sections of the press, especially younger and more highly educated journalists, swinging toward the participant model, which invites a more critical posture.

"Neutral" and "participant" journalism

Paul Weaver expanded on this distinction and came down harder in his evaluation. As Weaver sees it, there are two main traditions in American journalism. The one that has been dominant throughout most of the modern American experience he calls "liberal" journalism. It resembles Johnstone's "neutral" model. Liberal journalism "is characterized by a preoccupation with facts and events as such, and by an indifference to—indeed, a systematic effort to avoid—an explicitly ideological point of view."[38] In the late 1960s and 1970s, a new approach emerged that Weaver calls "partisan" journalism. To the degree that it triumphs, the press finds it harder to operate as a source of reliable factual, "neutral" information for the general citizenry. It becomes more of an advocate and critic.

The "participant," "partisan" critical approach seems to have reached its high tide in the mid-1970s, after Watergate and Vietnam. Today, there appears to be a swing back to the "liberal" model. Charles B. Seib of the *Washington Post* notes that "in the old days, when a reporter let his opinions show he was quickly brought to heel by an editor," and in time was turned into "what we call an objective reporter—meaning a reporter who stuck strictly to the raw, unvarnished facts." Now, Seib maintains, while it is good that the old search for "blind objectivity" is over, "too often the new permissiveness is

---

[37] John W. C. Johnstone et al., "The Professional Values of American Newsmen," *Public Opinion Quarterly*, Winter 1972–73, p. 523.
[38] Weaver, "The New Journalism and the Old," p. 69.

carried too far." The search for objectivity needs renewed emphasis.[39]

The public's commitment to fairness and objectivity

Time magazine notes that the highly critical "investigative" impulse of "participant" journalism worries many news executives. It quotes the editor of the *Oakland Tribune* as criticizing the trend of the 1960s and 1970s: "We are too hungry for blood—it sometimes seems to readers that we will not do the story unless we can do someone in." *Time* itself concludes that "the suspicious attitude among reporters leads to negativism in news coverage. The outlook of today's generation of journalists was formed during Watergate and Vietnam, when figures of authority seemed so often to be the proper adversary."[40] Work by John Immerwahr and John Doble suggests that most Americans think the press should hold to the "liberal" model. They want it to present the facts as objectively as possible. And they want it to be fair. The public believes that the general-news-dissemination segments of the press—television news and the daily papers—have an obligation not to be unduly partisan or critical, a constitutional responsibility to see to it that the populace has easy access to a balanced rendering of political happenings.[41]

What to Report: A Case Study

The debate over professional norms is not the only such issue occupying members of the press. An interesting case in 1983 that involved press handling of some missing State Department files illustrates another recurring issue in press ethics. The State Department sent a big collection of its file cabinets to the District of Columbia jail for refurbishing. Through a lapse of security at State, one drawer in one cabinet was not emptied. Prison inmates got hold of the files, which contained "telexes from embassies around the world, communications with CIA agents, sources in foreign embassies around the world." The classified files "dealt with Soviet missiles, the Druse in Lebanon, the border situation in Nicaragua [and the monitoring of a potential coup in the Third World]," among other things. The mistake was discovered, and most of the files were recovered and returned to the State Department. One set of files, however, was not found. The prisoner who had gotten hold of these called a reporter for a Washington television station and offered him the materials. The reporter picked them up, took them back to the station, and together with his editor perused them. The question was, Should the station put these classified materials on the air, or should it return them to the State Department without reporting on them?

[39] Charles B. Seib's observations are discussed by James Boylan, "News People," *Wilson Quarterly*, Special Issue, 1982, pp. 82–83.
[40] "Journalism Under Fire," *Time*, December 2, 1983, p. 79.
[41] John Immerwahr and John Doble, "Freedom of the Press," *Public Opinion Quarterly*, Summer 1982, p. 185.

The reporter who got the files, James Adams, and his editor, Betty Endicott, decided to return the materials without reporting on them. They called Senator Charles Mathias (Republican of Maryland), a member of the Foreign Relations Committee who was cleared to read such classified materials. On November 8, 1983, reporter Adams and Senator Mathias together brought the files back to State.

On what basis did Adams and Endicott reach their judgment? Endicott has stated that the key issue for her was that the documents

Responsibility to publish versus national security

contained no evidence that the government had lied. "If you find that the government is lying to the people, then I think you have a responsibility [to publish information revealing the lie]," she indicated. Adams has stated that "I didn't want to have a role in compromising national security. I kept asking myself the question, What good would it do?" Adams merely reported on the air that the files had been given to him and that he had returned them to the State Department. He did not divulge their substance.

This incident prompted a lively debate among journalists. Adams has stated that many news organizations called him asking for copies and refused to believe that he had not made copies before returning the documents. "You're giving gold away," they said. Staff for Jack Anderson, the syndicated columnist, were particularly insistent in prodding Adams to give them copies of the files.[42]

The deans of two major schools of journalism split on the issue. James Atwater, dean of the University of Missouri School of Journal-

The ethics of press reporting

ism, the oldest in the country, supported Adams's decision. Atwater carried Adams's position one step further, stating that he would not even have read the documents prior to returning them. "I would feel like I was prying in some sense in an area I should not be involved in," he stated. "It's a complicated ethical issue." By way of contrast, the dean of the Columbia University School of Journalism, Osborn Elliott, argued that "a reporter's responsibility is to report. I can conceive of instances where the materials are indeed so sensitive as to require great care in their publication. But I would feel impelled to publish them unless I found very strong reasons internally not to."

Who is right? The story has been told of Secretary of War Stimson, in the 1930s, coming into receipt of some correspondence addressed to another political figure, material that might have proved embarrassing to the latter if Stimson had read and used it. The Secretary refused even to read the material and returned it to its rightful owner. "Gentlemen do not read other gentlemen's mail," he reportedly stated. Is such an ethic outdated, not applicable to journalists? Dean Atwater of the University of Missouri School of Journalism clearly does not think so. Or was editor Endicott right: that journalists should, in

---

[42] For a thoughtful report on the State Department files and the journalistic debate over their disposition, see Jonathan Kwitny, "Returning State Department Files," *Wall Street Journal*, November 30, 1983, p. 28.

effect, read the government's mail but not report on it unless there is indication of clear governmental culpability? "Gentlemen can read other gentlemen's mail to see if the latter are lying and hence really not gentlemen." Or was Dean Elliott of Columbia University's School of Journalism on sound ground in stressing a journalistic responsibility to report everything relevant to politics, unless the gravest harm would be done? Journalists are not "gentlemen" at all, but rather "watchdogs for the people."

The debate goes on, and its importance extends far beyond one case involving State Department files. American journalists, with unparalleled access to governmental officials, and at times inadvertent access to various private communications, have to decide where their reportorial imperatives leave off and other values—such as the right of the government to private communication—begin. In many ways, this argument is too important to be left to journalists alone, because it has important implications for the way the business of government is conducted. Wouldn't the country generally be better off if both government and the press consistently acted toward one another as gentlemen? The debate over journalistic ethics must become a debate over political ethics in the broadest sense, in an era when the press is indeed a fourth branch of government.

SUMMARY

News reporting plays an important part in democratic governance. Without ample and reliable sources of information on political officials, policies, and events, the public cannot be in a position to determine where their interests and values should lead them.

But the press—all organizations, television and newspapers included, involved in the mass dissemination of news—can never be simply a neutral source of a vital substance, a river from which citizens drink as they see fit. It is a social, economic, and political institution that gets organized in a distinctive way, that has great resources and hence potentially great power, and that is composed of men and women whose outlooks shape how they do their jobs.

In the United States the press is primarily composed of private news businesses. Newspapers and magazines are privately owned and operated in most democracies, but radio and television are commonly government enterprises. The American electronic press is, however, largely privately owned and operated. Government regulation of the print media is minimal, but the regulatory reach of government is substantial in the case of radio and television. The airwaves are a finite public resource. The Federal Communications Commission grants and renews licenses to broadcast, and it imposes such regulatory standards as the equal-time rule and the fairness doctrine.

Contemporary technology for news dissemination—including radio and TV broadcasting, cable television, and the printing of newspapers in locales around the country by satellite transmissions—has contributed to a great concentration of news resources. To reach mass audiences, large-scale organizations and extensive physical facilities are required. We have come a long way from the situation of a century-and-a-half ago when the largest news medium in the country's biggest city (New York) reached only a few thousand readers and was capitalized with a few thousand dollars. With concentration has come, inevitably, greater attention to the power of the press and greater concern over its possible biases.

Though conservatives have often charged the national media, especially television news, with having a liberal bias in their reporting, the studies that have been conducted do not clearly substantiate this criticism. These studies do suggest, however, that journalists are now more likely to see themselves in an adversary relationship to other central institutions, including government, and to stress exposure of the latter's shortcomings and foibles. Some students of the press worry that its professional norms have contributed to the rise of an excessively cynical and manipulative view of political life.

The press and government are bound closely together in the United States. Journalists have unusually open access to government officials and they form an important part of the group with whom political figures have regular contact. Journalists are themselves part of the political community, not distant reporters on it. The press has come to play an especially extensive institutional role in the American electoral process. The news media, not the parties, are for most voters the main source of information about candidates and the shape of campaigns.

FOR FURTHER STUDY

Douglass Cater, *The Fourth Branch of Government* (New York: Vantage, 1965). Cater argues that the role of the press in contemporary government and politics has become so central that the press is appropriately seen as virtually a branch of government.

Doris A. Graber, *Mass Media and American Politics* (Washington, DC: Congressional Quarterly Press, 3rd ed., 1988). A useful review of the role of the contemporary mass media in American politics.

Ed Joyce, *Prime Times, Bad Times* (New York: Doubleday, 1988). A gossipy but nonetheless valuable account of the changing culture within one large television news organization, CBS News.

S. Robert Lichter, Stanley Rothman, and Linda S. Lichter, *The Media Elite* (Bethesda, MD: Adler and Adler, 1986). A study that uses survey research imaginatively to assess the social and political values of journalists, editors, and others who direct America's mass media of communication.

Frank Luther Mott, *American Journalism: A History of Newspapers in the United States through 250 years, 1690 to 1940* (New York: Macmillan, 1947). A definitive history of the evolution of the press in the United States.

Paul H. Weaver, "The New Journalism and the Old—Thoughts after Watergate," *The Public Interest*, Spring 1974. A classic essay on changing norms and standards among American journalists.

Part 5

Public Policy

Chapter 15

Civil Liberties and Civil Rights

What corrective measures should the United States take to remove as quickly as possible the vestiges of racial discrimination? Part of the answer seems clear and generates little debate: Where discrimination exists in law and formal practice, it should be ended. Governmental power should be used to prevent various private groups from continuing to block participation by blacks and other minorities. But is this all that is required? If a group has been subject to a pervasive pattern of discrimination over an extended period, is it enough simply to end legal discrimination? Or are additional positive steps needed, at least in the short run, to extend further opportunities to the deprived group and to increase its representation in various arenas of national life?

The issue of how the United States should respond to the fact of past discrimination has produced deep divisions. As is the case with most important controversies involving civil liberties and civil rights, this issue has been thrust heavily on the courts for resolution—and ultimately on the highest appellate court, the Supreme Court. Reflecting the complexity of the issue and the extent of differences in this country on how best to end discrimination, the Court itself has been sharply divided. Three recent cases illustrate these divisions very well.

One of the cases originated in a suit brought in 1971 by the Equal Employment Opportunity Commission (EEOC), an executive branch agency. The EEOC sued a local of the Sheet Metal Workers' International Union for discriminating against non-white candidates for membership. In 1975 a federal district court judge found the union local guilty and ordered it to increase its non-white membership to 29 percent of the total by July 1, 1981 (later extended, though with fines imposed on the local, to July 31, 1987). The case was appealed to the Second Circuit Court of Appeals and finally reached the Supreme Court in 1985.

Sheet Metal Workers' International v. *EEOC*. In the decision handed down in July 1986, Justice William J. Brennan, Jr., spoke for a closely divided (5–4) Court. The majority upheld the lower court rulings requiring the union to increase its non-white membership proportion to 29 percent.[1] Justice Brennan argued that "in most cases the Court need only order the employer or the union to cease engaging in discriminatory practices, and award make-whole relief to the individuals victimized by those practices." In some instances, however, it may be necessary to require the employer or union to take affirmative steps to end discrimination effectively. "If the company or the union has shown particularly long-standing or egregious discrimination," Brennan wrote, the requirement that it "hire and . . . admit qualified minorities roughly in proportion to the number of qualified minorities in the workforce may be the only effective way to ensure the full enjoyment of the rights protected by Title VII [of the 1964 Civil Rights Act]." In a dissenting opinion, Justice Byron R. White maintained that the lower court had ordered "not just a minority membership *goal* but also a strict racial *quota*. We have not heretofore approved this kind of racially discriminatory hiring practice and I would not do so now."[2]

Wygant v. *Jackson Board of Education*. The second case involved the question of whether a governmental agency—here the Board of Education of Jackson, Michigan—could in the absence of a judicial finding of discrimination adopt an affirmative action plan that protects black teachers from layoffs at the expense of whites with more seniority. Until the 1960s the schools of Jackson, Michigan, were segregated, not by law but as a result of housing patterns. The first black teacher was not hired in Jackson until 1953 and in 1968 only 4 percent of the system's teaching staff were black, although 15 percent of the students were black.

To create an integrated system, school officials began a concerted effort to hire black teachers; as part of this the 1972 contract with the teachers' union provided special protection for newly hired minority teachers. In the event of layoffs, white teachers would be dismissed instead of more junior black teachers if such action was needed to preserve the existing minority proportion in the teaching staff. This provision was to be continued until the percentage of minority *teachers* was as great as the percentage of minority *pupils*. Under this provision, when layoffs were required in 1981, a number of senior teachers,

---

[1] *Local #28 of the Sheet Metal Workers' International* v. *Equal Employment Opportunity Commission* (1986).
[2] Dissent by Justice Byron White. Emphasis added.

The 1963 march on Washington was in many ways the climactic event of the civil rights revolution.

including Wendy Wygant, were laid off while more junior black teachers were retained. Wygant and seven other white teachers sued, attacking the relevant section of the contract as unconstitutional.

Writing for a narrow 5–4 majority, Justice Lewis Powell agreed with the assertion of the Jackson Board of Education that, as Powell put it, "as part of this nation's dedication to eradicating racial discrimination, innocent persons may be called upon to bear some of the burden of the remedy."[3] But in this instance the remedy imposed an undue burden on the white teachers who were fired, in effect, because of their race. "In cases involving valid *hiring* goals," Powell wrote, "the burden to be borne by innocent individuals is diffused to a considerable extent among society generally." In contrast, "layoffs impose the entire burden of achieving racial equality on particular individuals, often resulting in serious disruption of their lives. That burden is too intrusive. We therefore hold that, as a means of accomplishing purposes that otherwise may be legitimate, the Board's layoff plan is not sufficiently narrowly tailored."

Concurring in the judgment, Justice White would have gone further: "The layoff policy in this case—laying off whites who would otherwise be retained in order to keep blacks on the job . . . is . . . violative of the Equal Protection Clause [of the U.S. Constitution]." In one of the dissents, Justice Thurgood Marshall maintained that "remedial use of race is permissible if it serves 'important governmental objectives. . . .'" He argued that "when an elected school board and a teachers' union collectively bargain a layoff provision designed to preserve the effects of a valid recruitment plan . . . that provision should not be upset by this Court on constitutional grounds."

In these two cases, then, the Supreme Court upheld enforcement of a minority membership percentage on a labor union, as part of an effort to eradicate past discrimination; but it struck down a layoff provision designed to maintain a racial balance achieved through the implementation of hiring goals. Both judgments saw the Court divided 5–4, and both produced a number of concurring and dissenting opinions.

The issue of affirmative action

Johnson v. Transportation Agency of Santa Clara County, CA. Though it has splintered on specific remedies, the Court has consistently produced a majority favoring the *principle* of remedial action for past discrimination. *Affirmative action*, carefully used, violates neither Title VII of the 1964 Civil Rights Act—which prohibits discrimination in employment based on race, sex, religion, or national origin—or the Constitution itself. In the *Johnson* case, decided in March 1987, the Supreme Court set aside any remaining doubts on this matter. By a 6–3 vote, it upheld the decision of the Transportation Agency of Santa

---

[3] *Wygant, et al, v. Jackson Board of Education, et al* (1986). Emphasis added.

Clara County to promote Diane Joyce to road dispatcher, a position not previously held by a woman, over Paul Johnson, who had scored marginally higher than Joyce on a qualifying interview. (Johnson had tied for second in the interview ratings, while Joyce had come in third; the person who got the highest rating did not bring action.) Justice William Brennan, for the majority, held that "our decision was grounded in the recognition that voluntary employer action can play a crucial role in furthering Title VII's purpose of eliminating the effects of discrimination in the work place. . . ."

A minority on the Court reject any form of affirmative action that suggests the continued application of racial standards in hiring. Chief Justice William H. Rehnquist and Justices Byron R. White and Antonin Scalia dissented in the *Johnson* case. Scalia strongly criticized the majority ruling for "effectively [replacing] the goal of a discrimination-free society with the quite incompatible goal of proportionate representation by race and sex in the workplace." He argued that it was "absurd to think" that road crew positions were "traditionally segregated" because of a systematic exclusion of women "eager to shoulder pick and shovel."

Part of the reason for the sharp divisions is the muddied distinction between *affirmative action* and *racial quotas*. The Court has held that taking positive measures to undo the effects of past discrimination—affirmative action—is valid. But many justices draw back from measures seen as imposing racial quotas. Setting quotas means that, in order to achieve more equitable racial representation, a certain number of positions—seats in an incoming university class or new job openings—will go to applicants from groups that have endured discrimination. Where does proper affirmative action leave off and the improper fixing of racial quotas begin? It is very hard for anyone to say—and "anyone" includes Supreme Court justices. The debate over this question—on which the Reagan administration has taken a strong stand, against quotas or affirmative action that it sees as the de facto imposition of quotas—has been going on for a long time. One of the most famous Court rulings involving this debate, the Bakke decision, was handed down in 1978.

Distinction between affirmative action and racial quotas

Regents of University of California v. *Bakke.* The efforts of the University of California at Davis Medical School to increase the number of black and Hispanic graduates produced the most publicized ruling on the use of quotas as part of affirmative action handed down to date. The Davis Medical School had developed a two-track system for applicants, with 84 of its 100 places in each year's entering class held for open competition, and the remaining 16 reserved for "disadvantaged" applicants, in practice, blacks and Mexican-Americans. This program, with its declared policy of preferential admission for ethnic minorities, was developed by personnel of the medical school without any specific outside intervention, but it was a response to general social pressure for affirmative action to hurry growth in the numbers of minority-group professionals.

Bakke's application

Allan Bakke is a white male who applied for admission to the medical school at Davis in 1972. While employed as an engineer for a space-agency laboratory near Palo Alto, California, Bakke came in contact with medical doctors who had been studying the effects of space on the human body. He was stimulated and encouraged to become a doctor. And, after night courses in science and voluntary work in hospitals, he applied for medical school at the age of 32. Bakke's credentials for application were generally very strong. He had impressed his medical school evaluators, receiving a score of 468 out of a possible 500 in the admissions office's summary compilation of all the measures it applied. But by the time Bakke completed his application (delayed because of family illness) most of the 84 places that had been set aside for open competition had already been filled. He was rejected—even though his scores were substantially higher than those of the minority applicants subsequently admitted.

In a July 1, 1972, letter to the medical school, Bakke stated that he was not prepared to accept his rejection as legitimate:

Bakke's rebuttal

> Applicants chosen to be our doctors should be those representing the best qualifications, both academic and personal. . . . I am convinced a significant fraction . . . is judged by a separate criterion. I am referring to quotas, open or covert, for racial minorities. . . . I realize that the rationale for these quotas is that they attempt to atone for past discrimination. But instituting a new racial bias in favor of minorities is not a just solution.

Bakke went on to state that it was his belief "that admissions quotas based on race are illegal," and he indicated that he might challenge the Davis Medical School quota system in the courts.[4]

Court appeal

Still, Bakke's next step was not to sue, but rather to reapply for admission to the Davis Medical School, in the next year's class. But he was again rejected, and this time he did file suit. The California court of original jurisdiction upheld his claim; when the University of California appealed, Bakke's position was again sustained by the highest state court. In a ruling joined by six of the seven justices, the California Supreme Court held that since the University had never discriminated *against* minorities, it could not now discriminate *for* them. It said that reserving sixteen places for minorities amounted to a quota based on race. The one dissenting justice attacked the decision of the court's majority: "Two centuries of slavery and racial discrimination have left our nation an awful legacy, a largely separated

[4] For this and other detailed information on the Bakke case, see Allan P. Sindler, *Bakke, DeFunis, and Minority Admissions: The Quest for Equal Opportunity* (New York: Longman, 1978).

society in which wealth, educational resources, employment opportunities—indeed all society's benefits—remain largely the preserve of the white-Anglo majority." It was high time that corrective measures like the preferential admissions program be instituted.

Having lost at the state level, the university carried its appeal to the U.S. Supreme Court. There, in a deeply divided opinion, Bakke's position was again sustained (and he was subsequently admitted to the Davis Medical School, graduating in 1982). The Supreme Court split in an unusual way: in effect, 4, 4, and 1. The one, Justice Lewis Powell, sided with one group of four in ruling that Bakke must be admitted. But he sided with the other four in rejecting the argument that the University of California could not consider race in any way in admissions. "The state certainly has a legitimate and substantial interest in ameliorating, or eliminating where feasible, the disabling effects of identified discrimination. . . . [This interest] may be served by a properly devised admissions program involving the competitive consideration of race and ethnic origin."

Justice Powell concluded that the minority-preferential admissions program of the Davis Medical School was unconstitutional, because the way it operated violated the equal-protection clause of the Fourteenth Amendment. That program, Powell held, "involves the use of an explicit racial classification never before countenanced by this Court. It tells applicants who are not Negro, Asian, or Chicano that they are totally excluded from a specific percentage of the seats in an entering class." The Constitution does not permit this. The other four judges who voted with Powell to admit Bakke wanted to strike down the Davis plan as in violation of Title VI of the Civil Rights Act of 1964. They presumably would have gone further than Powell would have in invalidating other preferential admissions programs.

"Both sides are right." Especially interesting, and what in his review of the case Allan Sindler calls a "mini-amicus brief," is the editorial of the *New York Times* on June 19, 1977. Entitled "Reparation, American Style," the editorial covered a full half-page in tiny print. The *Times* thought the Bakke case was not only important but complex in the clash of values it presented, and that "the law, without too much difficulty, could resolve this case either way." People who are equally "wise and generous," the *Times* argued, could be found on either side.

> Many grow anxious on the threshold of this case. They say we must not fight evil with evil, discrimination with "reverse discrimination." They say the entire society will suffer if it compromises standards of merit in education or employment and holds back competent people to promote the fortunes of the "less qualified." They say an America only recently liberated from official racism must require its institutions to be color-blind, to judge individuals without reference to race or ethnic origin.
>   Others argue, with equal passion, that there can be no remedy for inherited damage without transferring some opportunity from the

Supreme Court ruling

advantaged majority to injured minorities. They say we cannot claim equal rights and expect to achieve them without helping minorities to exercise those rights. They say the damage will endure if policy ignores the handicaps currently inherent in some racial and ethnic status—that color must be relevant today if it is to be irrelevant tomorrow.[5]

The *Times* concluded that "both sides are right. But it is in the national interest that Mr. Bakke should lose the case."

As noted, this controversy did not end with the *Bakke* decision. It continues to be a prominent part of the debate over civil rights policy. Supreme Court justices seem to be in much the same position as the *New York Times* editorial writer: They think both sides are right, so they try to give recognition to both positions in this clash of competing values. The goal is to be "color-blind": to assign jobs and other positions without regard to group membership. But recognizing the history of past discrimination, some forms of corrective or remedial action may be appropriate in some cases.

Continuing debate over civil rights policy

As we will see in this chapter and those that follow, public policy often involves the balancing of competing objectives—each of which is worthy. Achieving the proper balance is an especially demanding task in the area of civil liberties and civil rights.

THE CONSTITUTION, MAJORITY PREFERENCES, AND BASIC RIGHTS

Civil liberties and civil rights form the one major policy area where the Constitution makes detailed and explicit provisions. In other areas, it only outlines the institutional framework for decision making. For example, on foreign policy the Constitution sets important guidelines, but these reach only to *how it is to be made*, not *what it is to be*. The president is commander-in-chief of the armed forces; treaties do not take effect until they have secured the approval of at least two-thirds of the Senate. In the case of civil liberties and civil rights, however, the Constitution includes explicit policy statements.

Civil liberties and civil rights

Civil liberties and civil rights comprise the basic political tools and entitlements of the American people. When, for example, states deny some of their residents "the equal protection of the laws," they deny them a key element of their citizenship. Civil liberties and civil rights policies differ from those in other sectors in that they involve conditions without which democratic citizenship cannot exist. Because of this, we often assign civil liberties and civil rights issues entirely to another area: where *rights* are involved rather than legitimate *policy choices*.

The idea that a right of citizenship is at issue strongly suggests that there can be only one proper course of action: that which ensures or

[5]"Reparation, American Style," *New York Times*, June 19, 1977, p. E16.

guarantees the right. We debate what U.S. policy should be in Central America, or what government should do about the size of the federal deficit, because we assume that in these areas there is more than one valid choice. But if there is only one choice—a right to be fulfilled (even if it has at times been flagrantly denied)—the idea of policy is cast in a different light. Public policy becomes an effort to rectify present or past failings, or otherwise to ensure the proper realization of fundamental rights of American citizenship. No matter how weak its claimants are numerically, a right of citizenship must be honored.

Basic rights of citizenship

This brings us back to the basic idea of American democracy discussed in chapter 5: democracy encompasses both *majority rule* and *minority rights*. In many areas of public policy, Americans have long believed that the preferences of the majority should be followed. But in some areas fundamental rights of individuals are engaged, whose claim must take precedence over majority wishes. Civil liberties and civil rights are often discussed in these terms.

Race relations and civil rights

Race relations provide the most dramatic and pervasive instance where the proud claim of "unalienable Rights" of every person to "Life, Liberty, and the pursuit of Happiness" is at stake. Slavery flourished in the South in America's first century. And for the next century gross categorical discrimination survived as black Americans were denied the vote and access to equal education, barred from many public facilities or segregated within them, and abused by police and the courts. Although this was the result of conscious public policy, these policies were simply wrong, morally and constitutionally.

When should the majority prevail?

There are many other issues in civil liberties and civil rights, however, where policy differences are such that we should submit to majoritarian resolution, where "reasonable" men and women, all committed to the constitutional system, simply disagree as to which policy is best. In these cases, conditions similar to those in other policy sectors apply: (1) A general goal may be readily articulated, but there is great uncertainty as to how that goal is best achieved; and (2) the choice is not between accepting or rejecting a fundamental right, but rather involves the relative weight to be assigned two or more competing values, all of which are worthy and consistent with national political beliefs. This is true even in the case of First Amendment questions, where the language of the Constitution seems clear and absolute: "Congress shall make no law . . . abridging the freedom of speech, or of the press. . . ." Freedom of speech is, in the American system, a fundamental right of everyone, which even large majorities may not curtail—but not every policy issue or question that arises concerning First Amendment guarantees involves an absolute and unequivocal right that must be upheld without regard to competing values or majoritarian claims.

Because issues of civil liberties and civil rights often do involve fundamental considerations of citizenship, it is tempting politically for groups and individuals to insist that a fundamental right of theirs is being denied—of speech, of the press, of the accused—rather than that an arguable policy choice is being made. For if my dispute with a policy can be construed as my dispute with a policy that denies me a basic right, I have gone a long way toward carrying the day. Our language in this policy area is replete, sometimes misleadingly so, with references to "rights"; we need to remind ourselves that the more common conditions of public policy—where reasonable people can and should differ, and majorities should carry the day—frequently apply.

SECURING BASIC RIGHTS

For a long time, problems of **civil rights** were synonymous with segregation and discrimination against black Americans. The reference is now more inclusive. It encompasses other groups in the population that have encountered *categoric discrimination:* for example, other ethnic minorities and women. Membership in groups subject to this kind of discrimination is something over which one has no control. In contrast **civil liberties** problems typically involve the "rights of citizenship" of isolated individuals, such as persons accused of crimes, and groups made unpopular by their *beliefs*—religious, cultural, or political—rather than by attributes of birth like race or sex. Denying the right to vote to blacks is a *civil rights* issue; denying electoral participation to a small, unpopular political group is a *civil liberties* issue.

Extending Rights

All across the area of civil liberties and civil rights, one sees a clear progression or pattern of change, centered around *increasing expectations and demands,* and policy shifts that have come in response. This is especially noticeable in the years since World War II. The timing and magnitude of change varies from one sector to another. The political movement to advance the civil rights of black Americans was particularly strong in the 1960s; that for women's rights was more active in the late 1970s and in the 1980s. But heightened demands and important policy changes have been prominent in almost every sector of civil liberties and civil rights over the last forty years.

Curbing Racial Discrimination

Changes in expectations and demands with regard to rights of citizenship have been occurring since the early nineteenth century; they have been especially pronounced over the last half-century in the area of race relations. In the South, to which Negro GIs returned in 1945

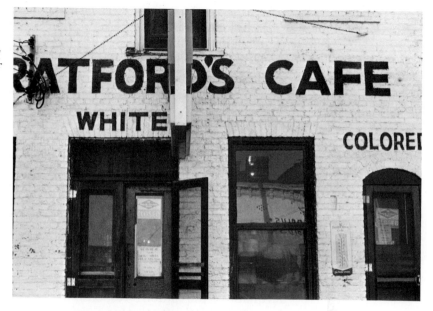

One face of the old "Jim Crow" system of racial segregation.

and 1946, the black population was almost totally excluded from decision making in all institutions that served the general, as opposed to solely the black, population. Nearly all public facilities in the region, including city parks and playgrounds, theater, hotels, and restaurants, were rigidly segregated. As one small example of the pervasiveness of segregation in public facilities, the Southern Political Science Association long held its annual meeting in the tiny mountain town of Gatlinburg, in eastern Tennessee, because it was one of the very few spots in the entire South where blacks and whites (in this case, as college teachers) could meet, eat, and reside together in a resort hotel. School systems across the South were totally segregated. And blacks were almost completely disenfranchised: In the early 1940s, only 5 percent of voting-age black citizens in the South were registered voters.[6]

Violence against blacks. The most reprehensible denial of basic citizenship rights was the vulnerability of blacks throughout much of the South to assaults on their personal safety and well-being. The Swedish social scientist Gunnar Myrdal observed in the 1940s that

> in the South the Negro's person and property are practically subject to the whim of any white person who wishes to take advantage of him or to punish him for any real or fancied wrong doing or "insult." A white man can steal from or maltreat a Negro in almost any way without fear of

[6] For further discussion of black political participation in the South, and of the changes that took place over the 1940s, 1950s, and 1960s, see Everett Ladd, *Negro Political Leadership in the South* (New York: Atheneum, 1969).

reprisal, because a Negro cannot claim the protection of the police or courts, and personal vengeance on the part of the offended Negro usually results in organized retaliation in the form of bodily injury (including lynching), home burning or banishment. . . . Physical violence and threats against personal security do not, of course, occur to every Negro every day. . . . But violence may occur at any time, and it is the fear of it as much as violence itself which creates the injustice and the insecurity.[7]

Myrdal was not exaggerating. At least 3,275 black Americans were lynched in the South between 1882 and 1936.[8] And, as Myrdal pointed out, even if violations, intimidations, and frauds occurred only sporadically, the threat was always present.

Racial discrimination was not exclusively southern. But the denial of equal citizenship to blacks was far more extreme in the South than elsewhere in the country. And, as late as 1950, two-thirds of all black Americans resided in the eleven states that had seceded in 1861 to form the Confederacy.

Assertion of American values. Today, although debate goes on over the adequacy of the nation's response in civil rights, there is no doubt that extraordinary changes have occurred over the last 40 years, greatly extending the rights of black citizens. The sources of this transformation are complex. Gunnar Myrdal identified one source when he pointed to the "ever-raging conflict" between the general principles of the American creed and the historic reality of American race relations—a conflict that could not persist forever. The average American is "more of a believer and defender of the faith in humanity than the rest of the Occidentals. It is a relatively important matter to him to be true to his own ideals and to carry them out in actual life."[9]

A "house divided" for over a century

The crucial question is not why the system of gross racial discrimination finally broke down in a rush in the 1950s and 1960s, but why this change was so slow in coming. The tensions between beliefs and practice were fundamental. A century earlier, Lincoln had seen clearly the extent and destructiveness of this contradiction. In his "House Divided" speech, delivered to the Republican state convention in Springfield, Illinois, on June 17, 1858, Lincoln cited the biblical passage "A house divided against itself cannot stand." He went on: "I believe this government cannot endure, permanently half *slave* and half *free*. I do not expect the Union to be *dissolved*—I do not expect the house to *fall*—but I do expect it will cease to be divided." But America's house was to remain divided for another century before the beliefs summoned sufficient action.

[7] Gunnar Myrdal, *An American Dilemma* (New York: McGraw-Hill, 1964; first published 1944), p. 530.
[8] E. Franklin Frazier, *The Negro in the United States* (New York: Macmillan, 1957), p. 160.
[9] Myrdal, *An American Dilemma*, p. lxx.

Effects of demographic changes. Another source of change has to do with population movement. Sweeping shifts of blacks from rural to urban areas, and from the South to a more national distribution, increased the political power of black Americans. On the eve of American entry in World War I, nearly 90 percent of the black population of the United States still resided in the South; most blacks lived in rural areas and worked in agriculture. But World War I, with its increased demand for labor in war industries, provided large numbers of blacks with the economic opportunity to leave southern agriculture. "They began one of the most massive internal migrations in the history of the United States. . . . Three-quarters of a million Negroes moved North within a four-year period during World War 1."[10] Migration continued after the war, and it expanded again during World War II. Between 1940 and 1970, the net migration of blacks from the South into northern states was more than 4.4 million (Figure 15.1). Note, however, that a dramatic change has occurred since 1970. More blacks are now moving into the South than are leaving it—reflecting in part the improved racial climate in the region.

An important shift has also taken place of blacks from rural areas

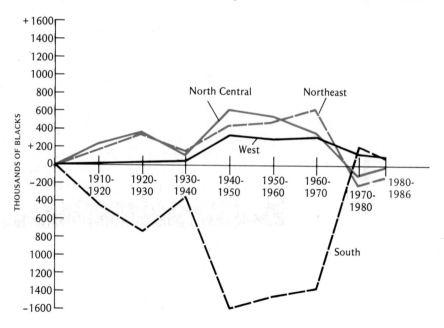

Figure 15.1
Net Migration of Blacks by Region since 1910 (in thousands)

Source: Population Reference Bureau, Inc., "Black America in the 1980s," *Population Bulletin,* vol. 37, No. 4, December 1982, p. 19, Bureau of the Census, Current Population Reports, *Geographic Mobility,* a series of annual reports from 1980 to 1986. In this graph, the minus numbers, below the "zero line," indicate a net *out-migration* from the region. Positive numbers represent a net in-migration.

[10]Thomas Sowell, *Race and Economics* (New York: McKay, 1975), p. 49.

to the cities, North and South alike. The 1960 census was the first to show a majority of southern blacks residing in urban areas. By 1980, a population that had been concentrated on farms and in small towns in the states of the old Confederacy was about evenly distributed between North and South, and overwhelmingly urban. According to the 1980 Census, only 15 percent of blacks nationally lived in rural areas, compared to 29 percent of whites. Some 57 percent of blacks, compared to just 25 percent of whites, lived in central cities.

How did this affect race relations? The system of gross discrimination and segregation (sometimes known as "Jim Crow") had been a product of the rural South. It reflected attitudes that derived from the historical experience of slavery and the extreme vulnerability of rural blacks to intimidation and violence. The movement of large numbers of blacks to the North brought them into environments where the traditions and institutions of segregation had never been firmly established. It made black votes of increasing concern to northern politicians. The movement of blacks from rural to urban areas, South as well as North, brought them into settings where political and social organization could proceed far more readily. And extralegal violence was far less pervasive among the concentrated black populations of southern cities than among the scattered populations of the rural South. Overall, the great demographic shifts of 1920–70 brought blacks into positions where political organization was easier and political influence much greater.

Effects of population shifts on race relations

Against this backdrop, a concerted political effort was mounted in the first two decades after World War II. It went on simultaneously in five different arenas: (1) in the courts, especially the federal courts; (2) through direct action by the civil rights movement, in marches, boycotts, sit-ins, and elsewhere; (3) within the legislative and executive branches of government, again especially at the federal level; (4) through voting and elections; and (5) in the "court" of American public opinion.

Sweeping changes in race relations since the 1950s

Brown v. Board of Education at Topeka. Many of the critical early steps were taken in the courts. Years of legal effort, led by the NAACP Legal Defense Fund, culminated in the Supreme Court's historic decision in *Brown v. Board of Education of Topeka* (and a series of companion cases) in 1954. (*Brown* is discussed in detail in chapter 9.) For the first time, segregated schools were declared in violation of the Equal Protection requirement of the Fourteenth Amendment. "Separate educational facilities are inherently unequal," wrote Chief Justice Earl Warren on behalf of a unanimous Court. *Brown* announced the end of "Jim Crow." It removed the aura of legitimacy and constitutionality from the entire system of racial exclusion. Although the case applied only to schools, and some recalcitrant judges tried to limit it to that arena, the Supreme Court followed up by citing *Brown* as authority for treating all official segregation as unconstitutional.[11]

Direct-action protests. The early direct-action protests in the South, notably those led by a young black clergyman, Martin Luther King, Jr., played a key role. King, the son of a distinguished clergyman in Atlanta, first came to national attention in 1955 when he led a bus boycott in Montgomery, Alabama. A black woman, Rosa Parks, had been arrested in Montgomery for refusing to move to the "colored" section in the back of the bus. The boycott focused national attention not only on bus segregation in Montgomery, but on the whole pattern of segregation in public facilities across the South. It was followed by an expanding stream of direct-action protests: against discriminatory treatment by law-enforcement officials, school segregation, laws, and practices that prevented blacks from eating with whites in restaurants and at lunch counters, and against almost all the forms of the old racial system.

Martin Luther King, Jr., was the single most influential black leader; he gave force and moral direction to the civil rights movement. Through his personal courage, eloquence as a speaker, strong commitment to nonviolence, and unflagging insistence that America honor its claim to the idea of equality, King helped shift the ground in race relations until his death at the hands of an assassin in 1968.

Gains in education and occupational status

Martin Luther King, Jr.

Dr. Martin Luther King, Jr. (second from right) stands on the motel balcony where he was slain, flanked by (from left) Hosea Williams, the Rev. Jesse L. Jackson, and the Rev. Ralph D. Abernathy.

[11] Richard Kluger, *Simple Justice: The History of Brown* v. *Board of Education and Black America's Struggle for Equality* (New York: Knopf, 1976).

Legislation and voting. New legislation strengthened the hand of the civil rights movement (Table 15.1). Title II of the Civil Rights Act of 1964 established the substantive right not to be discriminated against

Table 15.1
Major Civil Rights Laws and Court Decisions, 1948–70

Year	Policy shift	Major acts, landmark cases
1948	Executive branch decrees end to discrimination against blacks in the military.	*Executive Order #9981*, issued by President Truman
1954	"Separate but equal" doctrine struck down.	*Brown* v. *Board of Education of Topeka* (347 U.S. 483) and companion cases
1957, 1960	Acts signal the federal government to enter into a law enforcement role to protect voter rights. Actions take form of court injunctions.	*Civil Rights Act of 1957* (Public Law—PL—85-315) *Civil Rights Act of 1960* (PL 86-449)
1963	Employers required to pay equal wages to men and women for equal work.	*Equal Pay Act of 1963* (PL 88-38)
1964	Most significant policy departures in civil rights legislation since Reconstruction: guaranteeing blacks access to public accommodation, and equal employment opportunity.	*Civil Rights Act* (PL 88-352)
1964	Constitutionality of 1964 Civil Rights Act sustained.	*Heart of Atlanta Motel* v. *United States* (379 U.S. 241) *Katzenbach* v. *McClung* (379 U.S. 297)
1965	Major federal effort to guarantee voting rights to blacks.	*Voting Rights Act* (PL 89-110)
1968	Racially discriminatory housing practices made illegal. Constitutionality of 1968 fair housing policies sustained. Signals end to "officially sanctioned *de jure* racial segregation in housing," public as well as private.	*Civil Rights Act of 1968* *Jones* v. *Alfred H. Meyer Co.*

National guardsmen outside a Little Rock, Arkansas, high school in the 1950s, called by President Dwight Eisenhower to enforce a court order of integration.

in places of public accommodation. Titles III and IV authorized the Justice Department to bring suits to secure the desegregation of schools and other public facilities, upon the complaint of aggrieved parties who lacked the resources to pursue their own legal actions. The Civil Rights Acts of 1957 and 1960 were early efforts to extend the right of blacks to vote, but they had been badly watered down to get past filibusters by southern senators. The Voting Rights Act of 1965, however, put the federal government behind the full extension and free exercise of the vote by blacks.

Public opinion and race relations. Public attitudes on racial issues have become increasingly more liberal or tolerant over the last several decades. In 1956, only 51 percent of whites said they thought white and black students should attend the same rather than separate schools; by 1985, however, 93 percent endorsed the principle of integrated education (Figure 15.2). When the question was first asked of a national sample in 1958, just 42 percent said that if their party nominated a well-qualified black for president they would vote for him; the proportion reached 73 percent in 1969 and 87 percent in 1986. A survey taken by the National Opinion Research Center of the University of Chicago in the spring of 1988 put the proportion at 82 percent.

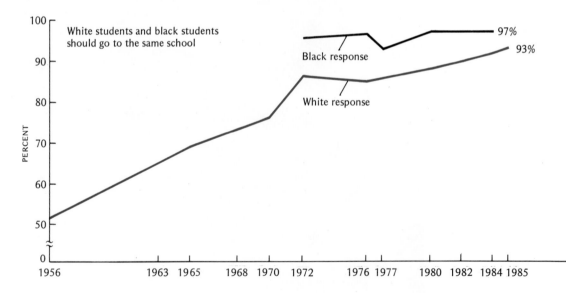

Figure 15.2
School Integration Meets with Greater Approval

Question: Do you think white students and Negro students should go to the same schools? Question not asked for blacks by NORC until 1972.
Source: Surveys by the National Opinion Research Center, 1956–70; National Opinion Research Center, General Social Surveys, 1972, 1976, 1977, 1980, 1982, 1984, 1985. Black response for 1985 not available due to insufficient number of cases in the small sample. The question has not been asked since 1985.

Answers to poll questions like the one asking people whether they would vote for a well-qualified black person for president are often viewed skeptically. Isn't the proportion who *say* they would back a black person for the highest office certain to be vastly higher than the proportion who *actually would vote* for him? Of course. For one thing, in an actual election, some would not vote for a specific black candidate because they would disagree with his stands on various issues. Others wouldn't support him because they would consider him less well suited for the office than his opponent for reasons of personality, character, or leadership ability. Such considerations as well lead voters to reject whites who in general are "well qualified." The real question is one that is hard to ask in an opinion survey, and impossible to get answered reliably: "If your party nominated a well-qualified black person for president, could you completely ignore the color of his skin and judge him just as you would judge a white candidate whose views and abilities were the same?"

Jesse Jackson's bid for the presidency

In 1988, Jesse Jackson made a spirited run for the Democratic nomination for president. He won a lot of votes in the primaries—29 percent of the total cast—and over 1,200 convention delegates. Still, his base was clearly in the black community, where he consistently won over 90 percent of the vote. According to surveys of Democrats leaving the polls on primary election days, Jackson never received as much as 25 percent of the white vote. (His 23 percent in the Wisconsin Democratic primary on April 5 was his highest.) We simply don't know how many white Democrats voted for someone other than Jackson largely because they were prejudiced against Jackson on grounds of race. In fact, most of those who voted for other Democratic contenders would find it very hard to sort out in their own minds the mix of considerations that influenced their vote.

We do know that surveys have shown large increases over the past several decades in the proportions of Americans stating their commitment to the ideal of racial justice. And we know that significant strides have been made in various areas of actual social experience or behavior. Polls don't give us accurate measures of the precise proportions holding various views, but they probably do show the real trend in public attitudes (Figure 15.3).

Gains in Civil Rights

De jure segregation

The net results of these several contributing factors are dramatic. Public accommodations throughout the country are now free of segregation. *De jure* segregation of the schools, based on law and enforced by government, has been eliminated. By the 1980s, black voter registration in the South was nearly as great proportionally as white registration (Figure 15.4). Blacks now have substantial electoral power in many cities, North and South, as the success of black candidates

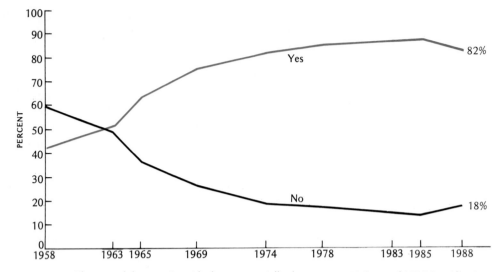

Figure 15.3
It Your Party Nominated a Well-Qualified Black Man for President, Would You Vote for Him?

The text of the question asked was essentially the same tor Gallup and NORC, with minor variations.

Source: Surveys for 1958–69 were conducted by the Gallup Organization, those for 1974–1988 by the National Opinion Research Center, University of Chicago.

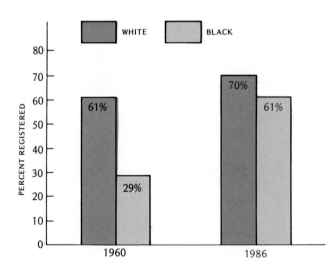

Figure 15.4
Voter Registration in the South by Race, 1960 and 1986

Source: U.S. Bureau of Census, *Statistical Abstract of the United States, 1986,* p. 257; 1988, p. 250.

attests. In 1988, a number of major U.S. cities, including Washington, Philadelphia, Chicago, Detroit, Los Angeles, and Atlanta, had black mayors. The number of blacks holding elective office climbed from just 1,500 in 1970 to nearly 6,400 in 1986 (Figure 15.5).

The proportion of blacks with at least a high school education grew from just 8 percent in 1940 to 62 percent in 1986. In 1940, the median

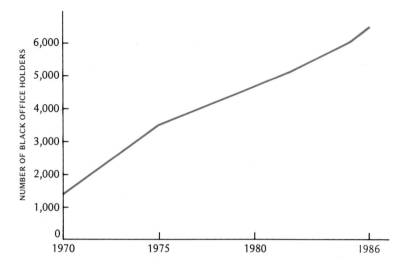

Source: U.S. Bureau of the Census, *Statistical Abstract of the United States, 1984,* p. 261; 1986, p. 252; 1988, p. 247

Figure 15.5
Blacks Holding Elective Office since 1970

Figure 15.6
Years of School Completed, by Race, since 1940 (persons 25 years old and over)

years of school completed among black Americans age 25 and older was just 5.8, compared to 8.6 for whites. As late as 1970, the gap was almost that great. By 1986, however, it had shrunk significantly as the median for blacks climbed to 12.3 years, compared to 12.6 years for whites (Figure 15.6). Similar advances can be seen in the occupational area, as the proportion of blacks in professional and managerial occupations has increased appreciably.

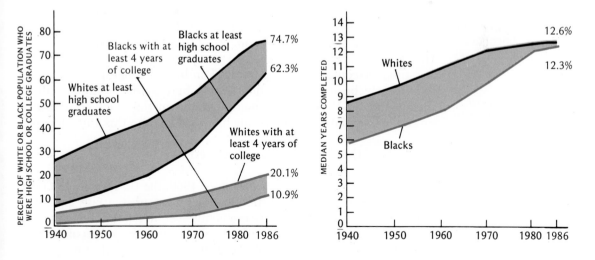

Source: Figures are based on computation of data listed in Tables 215 and 216 of *Statistical Abstract of the United States, 1986,* p. 133; Tables 201 and 202 of 1988 edition, p. 125; and *Historical Statistics,* part 1, p. 380.

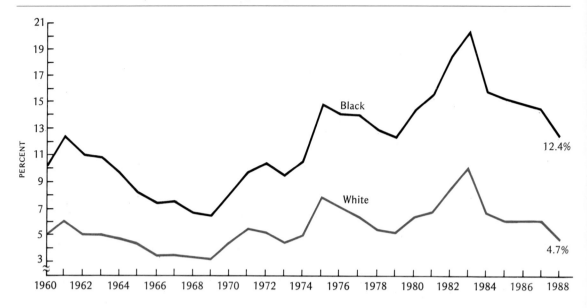

Figure 15.7
Black and White Unemployment Rates since 1960

Black data for 1960–71 are for "Blacks and other races."
Source: Population Reference Bureau, Inc., "Black America in the 1980s," *Population Bulletin,* vol. 37, no. 4, December 1982; U.S. Department of Labor, Bureau of Labor Statistics, *Employment and Earnings,* July 1984, p. 46; October 1985, p. 5; and *Statistical Abstract of the United States, 1988,* p. 382. (March 1987 date). The 1988 data are for May 1988 only, the latest month available when this figure was prepared. For all of the other years the figures are annual averages. The 1988 data are taken from *Economic Indicator,* June 1988 (Washington, DC: U.S. Government Printing Office), p. 12.

In two other critical areas, however, the experience of the last decade is far less encouraging. The income of black families continues to lag substantially behind that of white families: In 1986 the median income of black families was $17,600 compared to $30,800 for white families. The ratio of the incomes of the two groups has changed little over the last quarter-century. As Figure 15.7 indicates, unemployment has consistently been much higher among blacks than among whites. During the 1982 recession, unemployment in the black community surged, particularly among young black males, and this gap widened.

Less improvement in income and employment levels

Extending the Rights of the Accused

Since World War II and especially since 1960, the U.S. Supreme Court has issued a series of opinions that together have substantially extended constitutional guarantees to persons involved in legal proceedings. A key element in these rulings is the application to the states of the full force and specificity of the Bill of Rights requirements that were originally intended to apply only to federal action.

The central role of the federal courts

Selective incorporation. Many Americans in the late 1780s and 1790s worried that the new national government might prove too strong and threaten individual liberty. The Bill of Rights was an important response to these concerns. It contained a set of specific prohibitions on national government action: *"Congress* shall make no law . . ." the First Amendment begins its famous stipulation of guarantees of freedom of religion, speech, press, and assembly. By the time of the Civil War, however, the context had changed greatly. Outside the South the concern was not with federal action abridging individual liberty, but rather with denials of freedom by southern state governments. Against this backdrop the Fourteenth Amendment, ratified July 9, 1868, specified that "no *State* shall make or enforce any law which shall abridge the privileges or immunities of citizens of the United States; nor shall any State deprive any person of life, liberty, or property, without due process of law; nor deny to any person within its jurisdiction the equal protection of the laws."

The Fourteenth Amendment was obviously intended to provide federal guarantees to black Americans against southern state denial

Extension of guarantees under the Fourteenth Amendment

of equality before the law. But the amendment's sweeping language has a broader reach. It does not refer just to blacks. No state government may deny *any person* "life, liberty, or property, without due process of law." The spirit is clear, but what specific requirements does it entail? Near the end of the nineteenth century, the Supreme Court began a process of **selective incorporation,** holding that specific limitations imposed on the national government by the Bill of Rights are similarly applied to state governments through the due-process clause of the Fourteenth Amendment. In *Chicago, Burlington, and Quincy Railroad Co.* v. *City of Chicago* (1897), the Court incorporated the Fifth Amendment guarantee against the taking of private property for public use without just compensation within the Fourteenth Amendment's due-process protections. Ever since that decision, as Table 15.2 shows, the Supreme Court has extended, one at a time, the range of Bill of Rights protections.

Right to counsel. In a 1938 decision *(Johnson* v. *Zerbst),* the Supreme Court ruled that the right to be represented by counsel is an absolute constitutional requirement in federal trials, under the terms of the Sixth Amendment. It wasn't until *Gideon* v. *Wainwright* in 1963, however, that the Court incorporated this guarantee of appointed counsel into the Fourteenth Amendment, making it applicable to state courts, where the bulk of criminal proceedings occur. Clarence Earl Gideon had been convicted in a Florida court of breaking and entering. Since he had no funds, he asked that the court furnish him with an attorney. The Florida judge replied:

> Mr. Gideon, I am sorry, but I cannot appoint counsel to represent you in this case. Under the laws of the state of Florida, the only time the court can appoint [in effect, pay for] counsel to represent a defendant is when that person is charged with a capital offense. I am sorry, but I will have to deny your request to appoint counsel to defend you in this case.

Table 15.2
Major Cases Involving Selective Incorporation of the Bill of Rights into the
Fourteenth Amendment

1897	*Chicago, Burlington, and Quincy Railroad Co. v. Chicago*	Fifth Amendment guarantee against taking of private property for public use without just compensation
1925	*Gitlow v. New York*	First Amendment guarantee of freedom of speech and press
1932	*Powell v. Alabama*	Sixth Amendment right to employ counsel
1934	*Hamilton v. University of California*	First Amendment guarantee of free exercise of religion
1937	*Palko v. Connecticut*	Concept of "selective incorporation" articulated
1942	*Betts v. Brady*	Sixth Amendment guarantee of appointed counsel denied
1947	*Everson v. Board of Education*	First Amendment prohibition of laws respecting an establishment of religion
1948	*In re Oliver*	Sixth Amendment right to a public trial
1949	*Wolf v. Colorado*	Fourth Amendment guarantee against unreasonable searches and seizures, but not the exclusionary rule
1961	*Mapp v. Ohio*	Exclusionary rule
1962	*Robinson v. California*	Eighth Amendment guarantee against cruel and unusual punishment
1963	*Gideon v. Wainwright*	Sixth Amendment guarantee of appointed counsel
1964	*Malloy v. Hogan*	Fifth Amendment guarantee against compulsory self-incrimination
1965	*Pointer v. Texas*	Sixth Amendment right to confront opposing witnesses
1966	*Parker v. Gladden*	Sixth Amendment right to an impartial jury
1967	*Klopfer v. North Carolina*	Sixth Amendment guarantee of speedy trial
1967	*Washington v. Texas*	Sixth Amendment guarantee of compulsory process for obtaining witnesses
1968	*Duncan v. Louisiana*	Sixth Amendment guarantee of trial by jury
1969	*Benton v. Maryland*	Fifth Amendment guarantee against double jeopardy

Right to counsel

If you want a lawyer, Mr. Gideon, you will have to find the funds to pay for him yourself. The Supreme Court disagreed. It accepted Gideon's claim that he was entitled to be represented by counsel, and that Florida was required to provide him with one. The Court overturned Gideon's conviction. What had been simply a right to be represented by an attorney during a trial if the defendant wanted such counsel and could afford to pay for it, became a positive obligation upon state as well as federal courts to make certain that *all individuals* accused of crimes be represented by attorneys. The Court concluded that

> in our adversary system of criminal justice, any person hauled into court, who is too poor to hire a lawyer, cannot be assured a fair trial unless counsel is provided for him. . . . From the very beginning, our state and national constitutions and laws have laid great emphasis on procedural and substantive safeguards designed to assure fair trials before impartial tribunals in which every defendant stands equal before the law. This noble ideal cannot be realized if the poor man charged with crime has to face his accusers without a lawyer to assist him.[12]

The exclusionary rule. In *Mapp* v. *Ohio* (1961), the Court enlarged the Fourth Amendment guarantee of "the right of the people to be secure in their persons, houses, papers, and effects, against unreasonable searches and seizures . . . ," by requiring that the states do what the federal government had been required to do since 1914: exclude from criminal trials evidence that had been unconstitutionally obtained.

Mapp v. *Ohio*

Police officers in Cleveland, Ohio, had forced their way into the residence of one Dolly Mapp, searched her dwelling, and seized "certain lewd and lascivious books, pictures, and photographs. . . ." This resulted in Mapp's conviction under an Ohio obscenity statute. The Supreme Court reversed her conviction, ruling that the Fourth Amendment guarantee is enforceable against the states "by the same sanction of exclusion as is used against the federal government." Since the evidence against Dolly Mapp had been obtained in violation of her right to privacy, it could not be used in a trial as part of the government's case against her. This is known as the *exclusionary rule.* In *Mapp,* the Supreme Court put the states on notice that if they convicted people on the basis of evidence unconstitutionally obtained, they could find the convictions overturned.

The "Miranda rules." In *Miranda* v. *Arizona* (1966), the Supreme Court ruled that no conviction, whether in federal or state court, could stand if evidence introduced at the trial had been obtained by law-enforcement officers in interrogations where the accused had not been spe-

---

[12] *Gideon* v. *Wainwright,* 372 U.S. 335 (1963). For an interesting account of the *Gideon* case and its implications, see Anthony Lewis, *Gideon's Trumpet* (New York: Vintage Books, 1966).

cifically advised, prior to any questioning, of his constitutional rights to remain silent and to be represented by an attorney. Ernesto A. Miranda had been convicted in a state court in Arizona of kidnapping and rape, on the basis of a confession obtained after two hours of questioning in which he was not told of his rights to counsel and to silence.

Chief Justice Earl Warren delivered the majority opinion that laid out what have come to be known as the ***"Miranda Rules."*** These rules have affected the way police officials all across the country handle the questioning of persons accused of crimes. A specific set of procedures must be followed, Warren wrote, in all cases of "custodial interrogation," which he defined as "questioning initiated by law-enforcement officers after a person has been taken into custody or otherwise deprived of his freedom of action in any significant way." Before any questioning,

The "Miranda Rules"

> the person must be warned that he has a right to remain silent, that any statement he does make may be used as evidence against him, and that he has a right to the presence of an attorney, either retained or appointed. The defendant may waive effectuation of these rights, provided the waiver is made voluntarily, knowingly, and intelligently. If, however, he indicates in any manner and at any stage of the process that he wishes to consult with an attorney before speaking there can be no questioning. Likewise, if the individual is alone and indicates in any manner that he does not wish to be interrogated, the police may not question him.[13]

Police officers are now routinely provided with a "Miranda Card," containing a statement of the rules Warren set forth, which the officer can refer to in reading the defendant his rights.

The Miranda requirement is now well-established. In 1984, however, the Supreme Court for the first time established a "public safety exception." A woman in Queens, New York, had hailed a police car and told the officers that a gunman had just raped her. She said that her assailant had fled into a nearby supermarket. The police entered the store, sighted a man who fitted the woman's description, chased him down an aisle and caught him. One of the officers noticed that the suspect was wearing an empty shoulder holster and asked where the gun was. The man nodded toward a pile of boxes and said, "The gun is over there." The officer had not informed the suspect of his right to remain silent before he asked about the gun, and for this reason the New York courts subsequently granted motions filed by defense attorneys to prevent the suspect's statement and the gun from being admitted as evidence. In *New York* v. *Quarles* (1984), a closely divided Supreme Court held that while the New York courts had been correct under the prevailing interpretation of the Miranda Rule, an exception had to be established. "We believe that this case presents

New York v. *Quarles*

[13]*Miranda* v. *Arizona*, 384 U.S. 436 (1966).

a situation where concern for public safety must be paramount to adherence to the literal language of the prophylactic rules enunciated in Miranda," Justice William Rehnquist (now Chief Justice) stated for the 5–4 majority.

Oregon v. *Elstad*

In 1985, the Supreme Court continued its adjustments of the Miranda requirement in *Oregon* v. *Elstad*. Eighteen-year old Michael James Elstad, a suspect in the burglary of a neighbor's home, voluntarily and in the presence of his mother, admitted being in the neighbor's home at the time of the burglary. Taken to the sheriff's office where he was warned of his rights, Elstad waived them and confessed his involvement in the crime. Convicted of first-degree burglary, Elstad appealed, arguing that his initial admission of guilt—made before he had been formally apprised of his rights—predisposed him to make the second, and that in spite of the reading of his rights, the second confession was involuntary, coerced, and therefore inadmissible. The Supreme Court held 6–3 that a voluntary admission of guilt made "in a non-coercive environment" prior to the Miranda warning does not "taint" a later confession made *after* the suspect has been warned of his right to remain silent. While the earlier confession is inadmissible as evidence, the later one is admissible and cannot be excluded. In the majority opinion, Justice Sandra Day O'Connor argued that the decision "in no way retreats from the bright line rule of Miranda." The dissenters, Justices Brennan, Marshall, and Stevens, argued that it did.

COMPETING VALUES COLLIDE

One of the greatest complexities of public policy making is the frequency with which the pursuit of one value creates problems for other worthy objectives. Would it be desirable, for instance, to increase retirement benefits paid to elderly Americans under social security? Of course it would, especially for that segment of the populace that depends on social security for its sustenance. Any large increase in social security benefits requires large tax increases, however—increases that would be resented by many taxpayers. It would cause discomforts for some as great as the comforts higher benefits would confer on others. Increasing benefits is a worthy goal, but so is keeping taxes down. There does not seem to be a single, clear-cut "right" answer; rather there is a need to compromise and adjust among competing objectives, where no one can be sure just what balance is best.

This is the situation facing the Supreme Court and the country in large areas of civil liberties and rights policy. A new plateau was reached in the 1960s, defined by greater attentiveness to individual rights than obtained previously. But on this new plateau the old need to strike appropriate balances among competing objectives has inevitably asserted itself.

The exclusionary rule revisited. We noted above that the principle of the exclusionary rule's application to the states—as a deterrent to impermissible police conduct—was established in the 1960s. This does not mean that judicial policy in this area has become a consensual matter where a straightforward provision is easily followed. As it has tried to apply the exclusionary rule, the Supreme Court has run into some thorny problems, and has found itself engulfed in a vigorous debate.

A highly controversial case that reached the Supreme Court in 1976 and was decided the next year involved a man, Robert Williams, who was convicted by an Iowa court for the murder on Christmas Eve, 1968, of a ten-year-old girl. While being returned by police to Des Moines, Iowa, where the crime was committed, and without his attorney present, Williams was told by a detective: "I feel that you yourself are the only person that knows where this little girl's body is. . . . And, since we will be going right past the area on the way into Des Moines, I feel we should stop and locate the body, that the parents of this little girl should be entitled to a Christian burial for the little girl. . . ." No violence or compulsion was employed. After thinking about the matter for some time, Williams directed the officers to the victim's body. He was subsequently convicted of the murder.

Brewer v. *Williams*

A Court divided

In *Brewer* v. *Williams* (1977), a deeply divided Court set aside Williams's conviction. It held that the right to the assistance of counsel, "guaranteed by the Sixth and Fourteenth Amendments, is indispensable to the fair administration of our adversary system of criminal justice." Williams's incriminating statements, made in response to police conduct that violated his constitutional right to counsel, should have been excluded, the Court ruled by a narrow 5–4 majority. Williams's attorney had been promised that no questioning would be attempted on the trip back to Des Moines. Yet the police officer had persisted. "The crime of which Williams was convicted," Justice Potter Stewart wrote for the majority,

> was senseless and brutal, calling for swift and energetic action by the police to apprehend the perpetrator and gather evidence with which he could be convicted. No mission of law enforcement is more important. Yet "disinterested zeal for the public good does not assure either wisdom or right in the methods it pursues." . . . The pressures on state executive and judicial officers charged with the administration of the criminal law are great, especially when the crime is murder and the victim a small child. But it is precisely the predictability of those pressures that makes imperative a resolute loyalty to the guarantees that the Constitution extends to us all.

This ruling drew strong criticism, including a bitter dissent by then Chief Justice Warren Burger.

> The result in this case ought to be intolerable in any society which purports to call itself an organized society. . . . Williams is guilty of the sav-

Criticism of
Brewer v. *Williams*

age murder of a small child; no member of the Court contends he is not. While in custody, and after no fewer than *five* warnings of his rights to silence and to counsel, he led police to the concealed body of his victim. The Court concedes Williams was not threatened or coerced and that he spoke and acted voluntarily and with full awareness of his constitutional rights. In the face of all this, the Court now holds that because Williams was prompted by the detective's statement—not interrogation but a statement—the jury must not be told how the police found the body.

Feelings run high, even among professional jurists in the lofty setting of the U.S. Supreme Court, when key values compete for recognition in a context where something has to give. In *Brewer* v. *Williams*, the justices did not disagree on the high worth of both sets of contending objectives: protecting the rights of the accused and ensuring the prompt apprehension and conviction of those who commit crimes against society. But they were sharply at odds over how to balance these values in the immediate case. They disagreed on two major questions. (1) Did the police officer deny Williams his constitutional rights? The majority emphasized that the officer persisted in a kind of interrogation, even though a specific promise had been made that no questioning would take place in the absence of counsel. The minority stressed that a gentle appeal to the suspect's conscience is hardly equivalent to police brutality or coercion. (2) If the police did act improperly, should the evidence that resulted be excluded? Here, some justices opted for a more sweeping application of the exclusionary rule, while others felt it should not be applied to "non-egregious" police conduct—in other words, to behavior that, if technically wrong, did not threaten the "individual dignity or free will" of the suspect.

The Court has continued to search for the right balance in its use

*One view of the
exclusionary rule.*

Reprinted by permission of UFS, Inc.

of the exclusionary rule. In *Stone* v. *Powell* (1976), for example, it ruled that federal courts need not require the exclusion of evidence acquired in violation of Fourth Amendment ("unreasonable searches and seizures") guarantees, unless the prisoner could show that he was denied "a full and fair" litigation of his Fourth Amendment claim in state courts. Another exception, the so-called inevitable discovery doctrine, was issued in a case that resulted from the retrial of Robert Williams, whose first appeal we have just discussed.

Stone v. *Powell*

After the Court overturned Williams's conviction in *Brewer* v. *Williams*, the state of Iowa brought him to trial a second time in state court on the "inevitable discovery" doctrine. Williams had never been found innocent, so there was no question of double jeopardy (trying a person a second time, after he had been found not guilty). Williams's conviction had simply been set aside on the grounds that some of the evidence introduced should not have been admitted. Two hundred volunteers had been combing the area and were nearing the spot where the body was discovered, when Williams led the police to it. In the second trial, the Iowa court concluded that even without Williams's statement, the body would have been discovered anyway. In *Nix* v. *Williams* (1984), the Supreme Court accepted the state's argument. The majority opinion—written by Chief Justice Burger, author of the angry dissent in the Court's consideration of the case seven years earlier—held that the point of the "inevitable discovery" doctrine was to put the police "in the same, not a worse, position than they would have been if no police error or misconduct had occurred."

Nix v. *Williams*

In another 1984 ruling, *United States* v. *Leon*, the Supreme Court partially adopted the "good faith" exception to the exclusionary rule. This provision follows from an argument some justices, including the chief justice, had advanced in earlier cases concerning "non-egregious" police conduct. The "good faith" exception permits the use of improperly obtained evidence as long as the police had a reasonable belief that they were acting lawfully. Writing for the majority in the *Leon* case, Justice Byron White for the present limited the application of the "good faith" exception to situations in which the police obtained a search warrant and executed a search in accord with it, only later to have the warrant found defective. The evidence obtained through such searches need not be excluded, the Court held.

United States v. *Leon*

Where the Court finds the proper balance of conflicting values or claims depends on the outlooks of the sitting justices and the national climate of opinion in which the Court is operating. In the 1980s majorities on the Burger Court were somewhat more inclined to lean toward the claims of police officials and state court decisions than the Warren Court's majorities had been in the 1960s. Still, the process of sorting out contending claims in occurring within a general structure set down in the 1960s in such decisions as *Mapp, Gideon,* and *Miranda.*

Balancing conflicting values

Other policy issues in the area of civil liberties and rights—including affirmative action and equality of opportunity, as we saw at the beginning of this chapter—are experiencing this same sort of search for the right balance of competing objectives, within the new climate of opinion and expectations that appeared in the quarter-century after World War II.

From *de Jure* to *de Facto* Segregation

The Supreme Court ruled in *Brown* and its companion cases that governmental operation of a segregated school system violates the Fourteenth Amendment of the U.S. Constitution. That issue has been settled. *De jure* (arising out of law) segregation is no longer countenanced anywhere in the United States. But what about *de facto* segregation: the kind that results from residential patterns? For example, large sections of cities, or even entire cities, are sometimes so disproportionately black, at least among the public-school-attending population, that most black pupils attend schools that are not integrated, even though school authorities do not require or encourage this situation.

De facto segregation and busing

In the late 1960s, the argument over *de facto* segregation centered on the issue of busing. If urban schools located in the center of black or white neighborhoods were to be racially integrated, it would be necessary to transport students out of their home neighborhoods. Was such busing desirable? Should it be required by law? And if required by law, how far should busing extend? Within the bounds of the city, or across an entire metropolitan area?

Swann v. *Charlotte-Mecklenburg County Board of Education*

Federal district courts increasingly ordered busing because it seemed in many cases the only way to achieve genuine desegregation. In an important 1971 decision, *Swann* v. *Charlotte-Mecklenburg County Board of Education*, the Supreme Court reviewed one district court order, in which the Charlotte-Mecklenburg (North Carolina) Board of Education was required to bus pupils to increase integration. Considering the school authorities in default of their "affirmative obligation" to advance integration, the district court had fashioned its own busing plan, the specifics of which were worked out by a court-appointed expert.

In his opinion written for a unanimous Supreme Court, Chief Justice Burger held that the requirement of extensive busing within the school district—one key feature of which involved transporting black students, grades one through four, to outlying white schools, and transporting white students from the fifth and sixth grades into inner-city black schools—was a constitutionally defensible remedy. It was constitutional in this instance, Burger argued, because it was needed as part of the dismantling of the old system, common throughout the South, of *de jure* segregation.

Busing was not authorized, the chief justice maintained, to deal with *de facto* segregation. Three years after the Charlotte-Mecklenburg decision, Burger wrote the majority opinion for a sharply (5–4) divided court, overturning a district court's order of metropolitan-area-wide busing, involving the city of Detroit and the surrounding suburban school districts. There was no "substantive constitutional right," Burger held, to "any particular degree of racial balance or mixing," and the lower court's requirement of a metropolitan plan to achieve a uniform mix of black and white students throughout the area was not constitutionally authorized because it involved school districts where no official segregation had ever been shown to have occurred. The district-court ruling in this case, *Milliken* v. *Bradley*, is reviewed in chapter 9.

Is the busing of pupils from schools in the geographic areas where they reside, so as to advance school integration, good public policy? Many experts continue to defend it. Certainly large numbers of black and white pupils will continue to attend schools largely of one race unless busing is used extensively, given prevailing residential patterns. On the other hand, court-ordered busing seems to encourage "white flight": the exodus of whites out to the suburbs. "White flight" only increases the percentage of blacks in central-city school districts, making it virtually impossible to achieve school desegregation there. The 1980 Census found nine central cities in the United States with populations 50 percent or more black. As Table 15.3 shows, the public-school-attending populations of these cities are overwhelmingly black, such that even extensive intracity busing would do little to remove *de facto* segregation. Is metropolitan-area-wide busing

Is busing good policy?

Table 15.3

Black Public School Enrollment (Grades 1–12) in Large U.S. Cities (100,000 and more) with Populations More Than 50 Percent Black

Cities	Total population (thousands)	Percent black	Black public school enrollment as percentage of total public school enrollment
Atlanta, GA	495	67	93
Baltimore, MD	905	55	81
Birmingham, AL	301	56	76
Detroit, MI	1,514	63	91
Gary, IN	175	71	85
New Orleans, LA	593	55	97
Newark, NJ	382	58	76
Richmond, VA	249	51	85
Washington, DC	757	70	99

Source: U.S. Bureau of the Census, *Statistical Abstract of the United States, 1984*, pp. 28–30; idem, *1980 Census of Population* 1 (Washington, D.C.: Government Printing Office, 1983), chap. C.

needed? The Supreme Court overturned a district court's order of such busing in *Milliken* v. *Bradley*.

Public opinion on busing

A large majority of whites have consistently opposed busing. When, in the spring of 1988, the National Opinion Research Center asked a national sample whether "in general . . . you favor or oppose the busing of black and white school children from one district to another" 71 percent of whites said they were against it. Forty-three percent of blacks opposed busing. The courts have struggled with this issue, and the debate over busing goes on, because there is no simple answer. Contending interests and objectives on both sides are valid ones. America has a strong national interest in seeing school integration advanced. But just how much busing should be required, in what instances? Or what are the alternatives to busing? These questions require a search for subtle balances, rather than the easy assertion of a basic "right."

Freedom of Expression

Democracy is impossible without freedom of expression—impossible if citizens are prevented from speaking and writing, meeting and organizing on behalf of their social aims. Although we draw many other satisfactions from free expression, we recognize its special importance to the operation of a democratic polity. Freedom of expression has always been given a high position in American law, from the First Amendment's insistence that Congress shall make no law curtailing the freedom of religion, speech, press, and assembly.

Schenck v. *United States*

Despite the language of the First Amendment, the rights of free speech and other forms of expression have not been seen by most people or by American law as absolute. We recognize instances where uncurbed expression does violence to other worthy ends. Libelous and obscene speech have been held subject to restrictions. In his famous opinion in the case of *Schenck* v. *United States* (1919), Justice Oliver Wendall Holmes, Jr., offered this example of why curbs are sometimes valid: "The most stringent protection of free speech," Holmes wrote, "would not protect a man in falsely shouting fire in a theater and causing a panic." But Holmes's example is too easy. When are restrictions on political expression justified, and when do they have a "chilling effect" on a free society? This question has been debated in many different contexts, and the Supreme Court has struggled to provide coherent answers.

Curbs on freedom of expression

When the United States has faced a serious threat, notably during a war, governmental authorities have generally been more willing to enact and countenance restrictions on political speech than in less threatening times. For example, during the Civil War military officials imposed curbs on speech and press under the sanction of martial law. No question of the validity of these acts was ever brought to the Supreme Court. Curbs were also enacted during World War I. The Espionage Act of 1917 penalized any circulation of false statements made with intent to interfere with military success. The Sedition Act of 1918 made it a crime to say (or do) anything that might obstruct the sale of government bonds needed to finance the war effort, or to speak or publish words intended to bring into contempt the government of the United States, or to invite resistance to its lawful acts. The legality of these two pieces of legislation, under which almost a thousand persons were convicted, was upheld in six cases decided by the Supreme Court after the war.

Dennis v. United States

In 1940, against the backdrop of the rise of fascism and communism, and the outbreak of World War II, Congress enacted the Alien Registration Act (Smith Act). It provided for punishment of anyone who "knowingly or willfully advocates . . . or teaches the duty . . . or propriety of overthrowing . . . the government of the United States . . . by force or violence. . . ." It further provided for punishment of those disseminating literature advocating such overthrow, those organizing any group "to teach, advocate or encourage" such overthrow, and those who knowingly became members of any group advocating the violent overthrow of American government. In 1948 amid fear (some say hysteria) over domestic communism, 11 top leaders of the Communist Party of the United States were indicted under the Smith Act; they were convicted in federal district court in 1949, and their conviction was subsequently upheld by the Court of Appeals and by the Supreme Court (*Dennis v. United States*, 1951).

In the majority opinion, Chief Justice Frederick Vinson observed that

How much information the government should "classify" as secret is still debated.

the obvious purpose of the statute is to protect existing Government, not from change by peaceable, lawful constitutional means, but from change by violence, revolution and terrorism. That it is within the power of the Congress to protect the Government of the United States from armed rebellion is a proposition which requires little discussion. . . . We reject any principle of governmental helplessness in the face of preparation for revolution, which principle, carried to its logical conclusion, must lead to anarchy.[14]

The chief justice argued that the conviction of Eugene Dennis and the other Communist leaders represented a lawful restriction of freedom of expression under a test that the courts had applied, with varying emphases, in a number of earlier cases: the "clear and present danger" rule. A highly regarded federal judge, Learned Hand (1872–1961), expressed the rule this way in his opinion for the Court of Appeals in Dennis: "In each case [courts] must ask whether the gravity of the 'evil,' discounted by its improbability, justifies such invasion of free speech as is necessary to avoid the danger." Is there a compelling case that political expression in a given instance might be so intertwined with action as to threaten constitutional government? The Court upheld the conviction of Dennis and his associates on the ground that there was.

Six years later, however, in *Yates* v. *United States* (1957), the Supreme Court reversed the conviction of 14 middle-level Communist party officials under the Smith Act. While the Court insisted that its Yates ruling was consistent with that in Dennis, it in fact was moving to restrict prosecution of Communist party officials. Where in 1951 a court majority had felt that the threats posed by the party were sufficient to justify the Smith Act curtailment of its political freedom, by 1957 a majority no longer felt that way.

By the 1960s, with new appointees and a changed climate of national opinion, the Supreme Court was ready to swing more fully and consistently from the perspective that guided it in *Dennis*. It took a more expansive view of the guarantee of the First Amendment for the right of individual expression, and it was much less worried about the threat of domestic communism. In *United States* v. *Robel* (1967), the Court upheld the right of Eugene Frank Robel, an admitted member of the Communist party, to work in a shipyard, despite a federal statute forbidding such employment to a party member. The Court declared the statute unconstitutional. While Congress is entitled to protect sensitive activities from spies and saboteurs, the Court held that it "must achieve its goal by means which have a 'less drastic' impact on the continued vitality of First Amendment freedoms." The law, it was ruled, was much broader than necessary to achieve its stated purpose, since it restricted the employment opportunities of all mem-

"Clear and present danger"

Yates v. United States

United States v. Robel

[14] *Dennis v. United States*, 341 U.S. 494 (1951).

bers of the Communist party, not merely those active in the unlawful aims of the party and thus most likely to engage in sabotage.

Brandenburg v. Ohio

The Court moved in the 1960s to fashion a conception of the clear and present danger rule very different from the one it offered in *Dennis. Brandenburg* v. *Ohio* (1969) grew out of the prosecution of a Ku Klux Klan leader under Ohio's criminal syndicalism statute. A unanimous Court overturned the Klansman's conviction and declared the statute unconstitutional. Because the law purported to punish "mere advocacy" and to prevent assembly with others for such advocacy, it violated the requirement of the First and Fourteenth Amendments. The Court held that "the constitutional guarantees of free speech and free press do not permit a state to forbid or proscribe advocacy of the use of force or of law violation except *where such advocacy is directed to inciting or producing imminent lawless action and is likely to incite or produce such action"* (emphasis added). This requirement of imminency represented a fundamental shift from the Court's construction of the clear and present danger rule in *Dennis* and earlier decisions.

Obscenity and Community Standards

Political speech bears a special relationship to democratic governance. Not all forms of expression can make this claim. The Supreme Court has repeatedly ruled, for instance, that obscene material is not protected by the First Amendment. Of course, even if this is accepted, it still leaves unresolved the question of what is obscene. The Court has found it hard to fashion satisfactory formulations as to when curbs are permitted and what kinds of restrictions are valid.

Obscenity and constitutional rights

A few justices have dissented from the basic Court position that obscene and pornographic expression may be curbed; they have wanted to see all expression absolutely protected. Justice William O. Douglas (1898–1980) was prominent in this small camp. He argued that the First and Fourteenth Amendments absolutely protect obscene and nonobscene material alike. In one opinion, Douglas concluded that

> the First Amendment allows all ideas to be expressed—whether orthodox, popular, off-beat, or repulsive. I do not think it permissible to draw lines between the "good" and the "bad" and be true to the constitutional mandate to let all ideas alone. . . . The theory is that people are mature enough to pick and choose, to recognize trash when they see it, to be attracted to the literature that satisfies their deepest needs, and, hopefully, to move from plateau to plateau and finally reach the world of enduring ideas. I think this is the ideal of the Free Society written into our Constitution.[15]

---

[15] Dissent by Justice William O. Douglas in *Ginzburg, et al.,* v. *United States*, 383 U.S. 492 (1966).

As Douglas saw it, the constitutional claim of any one form of expression is equal to that of any other. "Some like Chopin, others like 'Rock and Roll.' Some are 'normal,' some are masochistic, some deviant in other respects, such as homosexual." Individuals choose as they see fit; the Constitution mandates governmental "hands off" from all curbs. On the present Court, Justices William J. Brennan, Jr., Thurgood Marshall, and John Paul Stevens argue that the First Amendment does not permit a state to make it a crime for consenting adults to sell or buy obscene magazines, unless the transaction involves children or an "obtrusive display to unconsenting adults."

Regulating obscene speech

Most justices have looked for formulas that give more scope to governmental officials in regulating obscene speech. There have been efforts to give at least partial recognition to the contrasting ideas of different groups of people in different parts of the United States about what is unacceptably obscene or pornographic. When citizens, acting through duly constituted governmental bodies such as state legislatures or city councils, impose certain restrictions to uphold community sensibilities, the courts should not sweep these aside in the name of an absolute right of expression. Justice John Marshall Harlan (1899–1971) shared this perspective.

> The varying conditions across the country, the range of views on the need and reasons for curbing obscenity, and the traditions of local self-government in matters of public welfare all favor a far more flexible attitude in defining the bounds for the states. From any standpoint, the Fourteenth Amendment requires of a state only that it apply criteria rationally related to the accepted notion of obscenity and that it reach results not wholly out of step with current American standards.[16]

At the same time, Harlan and many other observers have been concerned lest narrow community standards censor even major works of literature and art in the name of obscenity. How is the balance to be struck?

Miller v. California

In *Miller* v. *California* (1973), the Supreme Court issued an important obscenity ruling to which it still broadly adheres. Miller was convicted in a California court of mailing unsolicited sexually explicit material in violation of a state statute. The Supreme Court upheld his conviction, maintaining that it would be guided by three related tests in obscenity cases:

> (a) whether "the average person, applying contemporary community standards" would find that the work, taken as a whole, appeals to the prurient interest . . . ; (b) whether the work depicts or describes, in a patently offensive way, sexual conduct specifically defined by the appli-

[16] The dissenting opinion of Justice Harlan in the case *A book named "John Cleland's Memoirs of a Woman of Pleasure," et al.,* v. *Attorney General of Massachusetts,* 383 U.S. 458 (1966).

cable state law; and (c) whether the work, taken as a whole, lacks serious literary, artistic, political, or scientific value.[17]

States may curtail material that meets this obscenity test.

The argument over what restrictions society may—or should—impose on obscenity or pornography continues. In July 1986, a commission appointed by the U.S. attorney general to assess the effects of pornography issued its report—and created considerable controversy. The report urged Congress and state legislatures to strengthen provisions of obscenity laws. It advised community groups to monitor conditions in their locales, boycott merchants selling pornographic materials, put pressure on law enforcement agencies, and more.

Men and Women in the Labor Market: The Issue of "Comparable Worth"

The movement for women's rights over the last decade has produced important changes in many areas of American society and politics. Women's rights have become an important component of civil rights. The economic dimension has been especially prominent and seems certain to become more so. At issue here is ensuring nondiscrimination and equal opportunity in hiring, promoting, and compensation. With regard to the latter, especially, women's groups and others argue that a historic pattern of discrimination against women is evident in the area of compensation and that new initiatives are needed to end it.

Some of the pertinent facts are readily determined, others not so. It is apparent that women who are full-time workers on the whole make much less than their male counterparts. As Figure 15.8 indicates, the average pay of full-time female workers has been only about 60 to 65 percent that of male workers over the last decade. As more and more women take jobs outside the home, many as the prime wage earners in their households (rather than providing supplementary earnings), and as the women's movement gives greater emphasis to the claims of equal status generally, these basic wage differences have spurred protest and action.

Several different factors contribute to the overall pay differential, and the precise weight of any one of them is not known. (1) Women

Pay differential between men and women

---

[17] *Miller* v. *California*, 413 U.S. 24 (1973). In 1987 the Court issued another in a series of modifications of the basic rule laid down in *Miller*. It held by a 6–3 majority in *Pope* v. *Illinois* that while the contemporary standards of the local community may be employed in the first two prongs of the obscenity test, they may not be followed in deciding whether allegedly obscene materials have scientific, literary, or artistic value. Instead, a more objective national standard should be used. The value of a work does not "vary from community to community," Justice Byron White wrote for the majority, "based on the degree of local acceptance it has won."

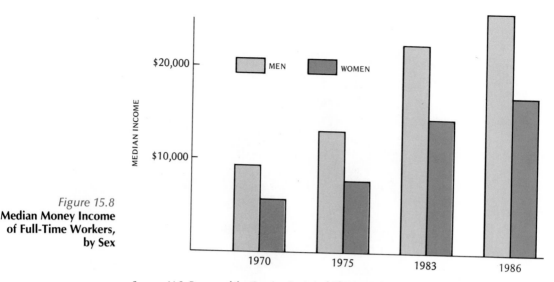

Figure 15.8
Median Money Income of Full-Time Workers, by Sex

Source: U.S. Bureau of the Census, *Statistical Abstract, 1986,* p. 456; 1988, p. 432.

Contributing factors

have been subject to conscious, intentional wage discrimination. (2) Cultural values and norms pervailing in the past have "assigned" disproportionate numbers of higher-status jobs to male workers. (3) The recent surge of women into the labor force has produced a situation where many female workers have relatively little seniority. (4) The employment of many women has been broken by periods of childbearing and child-rearing, which has had some cumulative impact on overall job and compensation progress. (5) Market forces deriving from the above and other factors mean that employers can in many instances hire female employees for less than they pay men. And (6) many of the occupational sectors where labor unions have since World War II achieved relatively high rates of compensation are occupations where women are substantially underrepresented.

Comparable skills, less pay

Younger women in the labor force, such as those 20–24 years of age, lag much less behind their male age counterparts than is the case for older groups. This suggests that significant changes are occurring, such as the entry of more women into jobs that traditionally are higher paying. Still, even among workers 20–24 years of age, the average pay in 1980 for female workers was only 78 percent that of male workers. Further, studies of the pay of men and women in specific occupations where comparability of skills and training is required suggest that the women still make less than the men. For example, female faculty members, at the rank of full professor, on average earn less than male full professors.[18]

[18] "Average Faculty Salaries by Rank and Sex at Institutions," *Chronicle of Higher Education,* February 8, 1984, pp. 21–30.

In the 1970s and 1980s, women have entered the labor force and the military in increasing numbers.

Women employees and some labor unions are turning increasingly to the courts to find remedies for these pay differentials. One critical area in this litigation involves the distinction between "equal work" and "comparable work." While at first glance this might seem to be a minor semantic quibble, it is emerging as the hub of the controversy. In 1962, legislation was introduced into the U.S. House of Representatives to implement the Kennedy administration's commitment to equal-pay legislation. One section of the bill provided that

"Equal work" versus "comparable work"

> no employer . . . shall discriminate . . . between employees on the basis of sex by paying wages to any employee at any rate less than the rate at which he pays wages to an employee of the opposite sex for work of comparable character on jobs the performance of which requires comparable skills, except where such payment is made pursuant to a seniority or merit increase system which does not discriminate on the basis of sex.

In hearings on this proposed legislation, debate broke out over the "comparable character" provision. Representative Katherine St. George objected to the language and offered an amendment that limited equal pay claims to those "for *equal work* on jobs, the performance of which requires *equal skills*." She explained that her purpose was to limit wage discrimination claims to situations where men and women are paid differently for performing *the same job*.

The St. George amendment

> What we want to do in this bill is to make it exactly what it says. It is called equal pay for equal work in some of the committee hearings. There is a great difference between the word "comparable" and the word "equal." . . . The word "comparable" opens up great vistas. It gives tremendous latitude to whoever are the arbitrators in these disputes.

The House adopted the St. George amendment; the Senate, too, rejected the "comparable work" wording in favor of the "equal work" standard.

The matter did not end there, however, even though no subsequent congressional legislation has changed the "equal work" language. Job-classification procedures and standards have been sought, and in some instances applied, in which very different types of jobs are assessed as to their *intrinsic worth* or *difficulty*, compared to other types of jobs. Under these classifications, otherwise dissimilar jobs are grouped, with the stipulation that compensation should be equal for all of the different but comparable positions within a class.[19]

"Comparable worth" ruling

The issue of "comparable worth" burst forth front and center on the national political agenda following a December 1983 ruling by a federal district judge in Washington. In a suit brought by the American Federation of State, County, and Municipal Employees (AFSCME) against the state of Washington, the judge ruled that the state had failed to provide equal pay for jobs of comparable worth, as determined by classification studies. He ordered the state not only to "forthwith pay each and every individual plaintiff herein, the amount of compensation that they are entitled to receive as evaluated under [the] 'comparable worth' plan as adopted in May 1983," but to pay back pay, commencing from September 1979. The judge appointed a "special master" to monitor compliance. If sustained, his ruling would have raised the wages and provided back pay to thousands of state employees in female-dominated job classifications in the state of Washington. The state had argued that the burden would be too severe because of the tremendous costs involved, a severe lack of revenue given the state's depressed economy, and the serious impact on the state's work force. Besides, the state legislature was already attempting to work out a gradual long-term solution. The court found these arguments "without merit and unpersuasive."

The district court ruling was reversed by the U.S. Court of Appeals for the Ninth Circuit. Before the rehearing that the circuit court ordered could take place, however, state and union negotiations agreed on a settlement. Beginning in 1986 and continuing through 1992, the state agreed to add $10 million annually to the funding base available for eradicating wage differentials between jobs often held by women and those more highly paid and usually held by men that require comparable skill, effort, and responsibility. The settlement did not provide for any back pay, which was stipulated in the original district court ruling.

---

[19] See Elaine Johansen, "From Social Doctrine to Implementation: Agenda Setting in Comparable Worth," *Policy Studies Review,* vol. 4, no. 1, August, 1984, pp. 71–85.

SUMMARY

Policy on civil liberties and rights differs from that in other sectors because many of its claims are presented on basic constitutional rights rather than simple group preferences. The courts try to differentiate between instances where fundamental rights of citizenship are engaged, which even large popular majorities must not infringe upon, and those where majority preferences should be respected.

The progression of public policy in any area does not follow a simple straight-line course; zigs and zags respond to the change of political leadership and events. But a clear direction is often evident. With regard to policy on civil liberties and rights, that direction involves more extensive recognition and guarantees of individual rights since World War II than obtained in earlier periods of American history. Characteristics of postindustrial society, including its affluence and high levels of education, seem linked to generally enlarged expectations concerning individuals and their entitlements.

Since World War II the system of discrimination and segregation, that had been entrenched in the South and known as "Jim Crow," has been dismantled. This is not to say that America's racial problems have been solved. But it is to say that clear and profound changes are evident in civil rights, which have promoted the principle of equality.

Other components of civil liberties and rights policy show a similar progression. Judicial guarantees of the rights of the accused have been expanded. A prime instance is the Supreme Court's extension of the range of Bill of Rights protections incorporated within the Fourteenth Amendment's due-process clause and thus made specifically binding on the states. Fourth, Fifth, and Sixth Amendment guarantees have been enforced on state courts and law-enforcement officials, as on their federal counterparts, by excluding from criminal proceedings evidence unconstitutionally obtained.

A new plateau was reached in the first quarter-century after World War II, defined by greater attentiveness to individual rights. But on this new plateau the familiar policy need to strike appropriate balances among competing objectives has asserted itself, with the Supreme Court at the center of this balancing act. The Court has in the case of the exclusionary rule tried to adjust the contending objectives of protecting the rights of the accused and ensuring the prompt apprehension and conviction of those who commit crimes.

In the controversy over affirmative action and quotas, the Court has recognized the importance of being "color-blind," more generally assigning jobs and other positions without regard to group identity or membership. But it has also recognized that the history of past discrimination cannot be ignored, and that some forms of special remedial action may be required. Many of the great contemporary arguments over civil liberties and civil rights policy stem from differences over how the claims of worthy goals and values, at times in contention one with another, are best adjusted and balanced.

FOR FURTHER STUDY

Nat Hentoff, *The First Freedom: The Tumultuous History of Free Speech in America* (New York: Dell, 1981). A spritely, well-written review of court decisions made under the First Amendment to the U.S. Constitution.

Richard Kluger, *Simple Justice: A History of Brown* v. *Board of Education and Black America's Struggle for Equality* (New York: Knopf, 1976). A superb description of the legal struggle for school integration.

Anthony Lewis, *Gideon's Trumpet* (New York: Vintage Books, 1966). A fascinating account of a Supreme Court case that established the right of defendants in state courts to have competent legal counsel made available to them in felony cases, even when they cannot themselves pay for such counsel.

Gunnar Myrdal, *An American Dilemma* (New York: McGraw-Hill, 1964; first published 1944). A major study of American race relations in the 1930s and 1940s, before the civil rights revolution of the postwar years.

Allen P. Sindler, *Bakke, DeFunis, and Minority Admissions: The Quest for Equal Opportunity* (New York: Longman, 1978). A brilliant examination of a major Supreme Court decision involving remedial efforts (affirmative action) to deal with past discrimination.

Chapter 16

Political Economy

Use of governmental power to secure economic objectives comprises *political economy.* There are severe limits on what any official of the U.S. government can do to promote desired economic results, so dispersed is authority across the executive branch and Congress. And there are severe limits on what American government at large can accomplish, so great is the role played by individuals and groups in the private sector, by international developments like those affecting oil supply and price, by foreign governments, and other elements. Still, the U.S. government does seek to promote a variety of economic objectives, including economic growth. One of its principal means of doing this involves *tax policy.*

In the mid-1980s, the administration and the Congress went through a long, elaborate review of existing tax policy and how it might be changed. To the surprise of most pundits who had thought that the plethora of competing groups and interests would be able to block any sweeping or coherent change in tax policy, major new tax legislation emerged from the House in December 1985 and from the Senate in June 1986. In mid-August a Senate-House conference committee adjusted differences between the two chambers and in late September both houses gave the bill final passage. The president signed it into law on October 22, 1986. The substance of the sweeping changes made in U.S. tax policy, and how agreement was reached on such a major policy shift, provide a good introduction to current directions in the political economy.

The Intellectual Case for Tax Reform

The tax reform effort was replete with political calculations and compromises, but it also reflected considerable intellectual agreement on the need for change. Over the years many provisions were put into federal tax laws that in effect exempted certain types and amounts of income from taxation. Before the 1986 tax reform was enacted, this meant for businesses provisions for depreciating plant and equipment, for investment credits, and for other measures to encourage particular forms of investment, such as investment in oil and natural gas. The net result was a system highly discriminatory among various kinds of business investments and types of industries. Some wound up being more subject to taxation than others. For example, the Joint Congressional Committee on Taxation estimated that the real effective tax rate in 1985 was 35.6 percent for companies manufacturing soaps and cosmetics and 26.3 percent for computer and office equipment firms, compared to 9.9 percent for the insurance industry and 3.5 percent for automobile manufacturers. It was far from a level playing field.

Tax deductions on personal income were permitted for those portions of income devoted to paying interest charges: mortgage interest not only for one's residence but for all other dwellings, including vacation houses; interest on loans for automobiles, up to the most luxurious; and interest on all other loans, including credit card purchases. Deductions were also allowed for all state and local property, income, and sales taxes; and for the full range of charitable contributions. Many benefits paid to workers that undeniably have economic value, such as the provision of health and life insurance, were not taxed. Deductions could be taken by virtually all wage earners for funds put into Independent Retirement Accounts (IRAs) up to $2,000 per taxpayer each year; and other income placed in various retirement accounts were deferred from taxation in the years when the income was earned. Interest from all types of municipal bonds was exempted from federal taxation. A great number of provisions were put in the tax code under which individuals investing in certain areas— apartments and other commercial construction, oil and natural gas drilling, etc.—might receive tax write-offs that were often of greater value than the direct returns of the investment itself.

Inevitably, there was a two-way interaction between these deductions, exemptions, deferrals, and write-offs on the one hand, and the rates of taxation on the other. High marginal tax rates encouraged individuals and groups to push for exemptions and deductions; at the same time, the latter's presence in the tax laws required the tax rates to be much higher than they otherwise would have to be, to realize a given amount of revenue.

The abundance of tax exemptions and loopholes made the tax code enormously complicated. It was a delight to attorneys, accountants, and investment counselors—and a nightmare for almost everyone else. What was worse, the layers of complex provisions for deductions and exemptions contributed to the prevailing sense that the tax code was

Hosefros

President Reagan sign-
ing the new tax bill on
October 22, 1986.

unfair. Two taxpayers with the same real income often wound up with different tax bills: One was positioned to play the exemptions and loopholes for all they were worth; the other was not.

Given these conditions, many specialists in economic policy came to believe that the United States should revise its tax laws so as to tax people on their actual income, from whatever source derived and regardless of the goods and investments to which it is committed. These experts also developed a consensus that the present system was *economically inefficient*. It pushed people toward investments and economic activities that they otherwise would not engage in, simply because the tax laws rewarded these activities. Fairness, simplicity, and economic efficiency were all served by *broadening* the *base* of taxation, which would then permit cuts in the *rates* of taxation.

The Tax Reform Act of 1986

In the push and pull for tax reform in the House and Senate, many compromises were made among contending interests. Still, what is striking is the extent to which the legislation finally enacted followed the line set forth in the intellectual case for tax reform: The base was broadened and the rates were lowered. Put another way, the policy change was achieved because large numbers of leaders in both parties became convinced of its soundness.

The Tax Reform Act of 1986 established two rates for individual taxes, 15 and 28 percent, replacing the old system of 14 tax brackets with marginal rates (those paid on the last dollar earned) of 11 to 50 percent. The corporate tax rate was cut to 34 percent. Some six mil-

Three Democratic proponents of the 1986 tax reform: (left to right) Senator Bill Bradley of New Jersey, Representative Dan Rostenkowski of Illinois, and Representative Richard Gephardt of Missouri.

Lopez

lion working poor who had previously paid at least some income tax were taken off the tax rolls. On the other side, a great many exemptions and deductions were eliminated. Unemployment compensation is now taxed in full, like any other income. The exclusion from taxation of the first $100 in dividend income ($200 for a married couple) was ended. Unlimited deductions were retained for mortgages on first and second residences, but deduction of interest is no longer allowed on consumer loans. State income and real estate taxes can still be deducted, but not state sales tax payments. The deductibility of payments into Independent Retirement Accounts (IRAs) was retained only for persons not covered by pension plans and those with low incomes. Only 80 percent of the cost of business meals and entertainment is now deductible—compared to the 100 percent previously. The investment tax credit on business purchases of machinery and equipment was repealed, retroactive to January 1, 1986.[1]

The 1986 changes to the tax system

Democrats and Republicans have each attempted to claim special credit for the Tax Reform Act of 1986. And, in fact, each deserves credit for an unusually bipartisan policy shift. If President Reagan had not committed himself firmly to reform after the 1984 election and had not continuously lent his personal prestige and the resources of his administration to the effort, the new tax legislation would surely never have emerged. But the Democrats, too, made major contributions. Not the least of them was the intellectual leadership provided

Major figures behind the Tax Reform Act

[1]See "Congress Expected to OK Tax Overhaul Bill," *Congressional Quarterly,* August 23, 1986, pp. 1947–59, for a detailed review of provisions of the Tax Reform Act of 1986.

by two young Democrats—Senator Bill Bradley of New Jersey and Congressman Richard Gephardt of Missouri. Gephardt was a contender for the Democratic presidential nomination in 1988. Bradley's contribution to tax reform was especially large; in many ways he and Ronald Reagan were the fathers of the 1986 legislation. Together with Gephardt, Bradley wrote the first major tax reform bill (in 1983) to embody the approach finally adopted in 1986; and he tirelessly urged reform in Congress, in speeches around the country, in articles and a book on the subject. He was a driving force behind the legislation not only in the Senate but in the House as well—where Ways and Means Chairman Dan Rostenkowski (D- Illinois) used him extensively to help persuade wavering Democrats to support the measure.

Politics and Economics

As more experience with it accumulates, economists will offer their assessments of the lasting consequences of the 1986 tax legislation. Apart from the matter of its pluses and minuses, they are likely to conclude that its impact was considerably less than its sponsors had hoped for or claimed. Policies initiated by government usually have only limited influence on the achievement of economic goals.

Tax reform and public opinion

Government actions like tax reform are, though, far from inconsequential. They are, moreover, much more responsive to the wishes and sanctions of the general public through the political process than other factors determining economic outcomes, so they are properly the focus of political attention and debate. Current economic performance is taken, often to a greater extent than is justified, to reflect upon the wisdom or folly of policies emanating from Washington. The electoral fate of presidents and their administrations rests in substantial part on the perceived link between their economic policies and the behavior of the national economy.

GNP and the 1982 recession

During the 1982 elections, for example, the U.S. economy was deep in recession. The **gross national product** (GNP)—the measure of the total market value of all goods and services produced in a given year—was falling in real terms, and the unemployment rate had climbed to over 10 percent for the first time since 1940. Reagan administration policies were attacked as responsible for collapse and privation. Democrats made gains in voting for the House of Representatives and in gubernatorial races across the country. Just after the 1982 elections, the *New York Times* editorially branded the administration as a failure.

By his own reckoning, Mr. Reagan became president for one basic reason: to restore the morale and power of America. By his own analysis, that meant above all "the rejuvenation of our economy" so that America could regain industrial strength, put all its people to work and defend its interests around the world. But the economy totters, dragging down the West and eroding American influence everywhere.[2]

The 1984 recovery

By the 1984 elections, however, the country was in the midst of a vigorous economic recovery. GNP grew at a 10.1 percent rate in real terms (controlling for inflation) in the first quarter of 1984 and 7.1 percent in the second quarter; although there was a slowdown in the third quarter, the overall rate for the year was vigorous, especially for an economy in the second year of a recovery. As the GNP soared, the rate of inflation declined, to the 3 to 4 percent range (depending on the measure used). Job creation was at record high levels; about 105 million Americans were employed in mid-1984, compared to 99 million a year and a half earlier. In this same period unemployment dropped from over 10 percent to 7.4 percent. "To many analysts and to the Europeans," the *New York Times* concluded, "that makes the United States a remarkable job machine—the world's most remarkable."[3] The economic news was not all favorable in 1984; interest rates were high, and the federal deficit was higher than it had ever been in peacetime. But overall the economy's performance was robust. How much Reagan-administration economic policies deserved credit for this was vigorously debated. How much developments in the economy influenced the final outcome of the presidential election cannot be precisely determined, but most observers believe the link was strong.

The economy in 1988

The 1988 elections were held in an interesting and quite complex economic environment. The public was clearly less confident that things were on track economically than it had been four years earlier. The twin deficits—in the federal budget and in the U.S. international balance of payments—prompted concern. Growth was slower than it had been in 1984–85. Inevitably, some parts of the country, and some groups, were faring much less well than others—a condition that Democratic presidential nominee Michael Dukakis referred to as the "Swiss cheese economy."

Nonetheless, overall economic performance was quite strong. Total civilian employment had climbed from 99.3 million in 1980 to 115.3 million in September of 1988, and the unemployment rate stood at 5.4 percent. The country's gross national product, measured in "constant" dollars (of 1982 purchasing power), had risen by 25 percent over the 1980s. The long recovery, which had begun early in 1983, was still continuing at the time of the 1988 balloting—defying many earlier predictions.

Views on the economy are bound to influence the electorate's conclusions on whether it's time for a change. Overall, these views were

---

[2]"The Failing Presidency," *New York Times* editorial, January 9, 1983, p. E22.
[3]Leslie Wayne, "America's Astounding Job Machine," *New York Times*, June 17, 1984, pp. F1, 25.

positive in 1988. The University of Michigan's Index of Consumer Sentiment was 97.4 in August 1988—not the highest figure in the last 35 years but near the high end of modern experience and the highest in more than two years. By a margin of 69 to 26 percent, respondents to an early August CBS News/*New York Times* poll said they considered themselves better off than they were *eight years* earlier. By 40 to 16 percent in an early September Roper Organization survey, respondents declared themselves better off than they had been *four years* previously. Fifty-seven percent in this latter poll expected to be better off four years hence than they are now, just 6 percent worse off. A survey taken September 8–11 by CBS News and the *New York Times* found 68 percent describing the nation's economy as good, 31 percent as bad. Seventy-four percent said their family's financial position was good, just 15 percent bad.

In a question favored by many analysts, respondents were asked whether they think things in general are moving in the "right direction" or are off on the "wrong track." Surveys showed the former response increasing over the summer and fall of 1988. Stanley Greenberg, who polls for many Democratic candidates, told the presidential campaign *Hotline* in early September that "in every statewide and every congressional poll that we've done in the last two weeks, more people thought the country was moving in the right direction than off on the wrong track, whereas two months ago we barely had a district or state—including ones with low unemployment like Delaware and Connecticut—where the right direction exceeded the wrong track." Greenberg concluded that the shift "is part of a general mood in which people are reevaluating where the economy is—beginning to believe that the Reagan years brought positive gains at the economic level that are real. . . ."

Disputes over Economic Theory

Presidents and other party leaders engage in a lot of *ad hoc* improvisation in their search for policies to advance such desired ends as economic growth and high employment, and to minimize such evils as inflation. But leaders are also guided by underlying economic philosophies. Although never consistently followed, these philosophies are rarely absent. The roots of the present debate over national economic policy go back more than half a century. To understand it we need to look first at how the argument was joined by the response of Franklin Roosevelt's New Deal to the challenge of the Great Depression, and how it has evolved in the face of changing economic conditions. In the second section of this chapter, we will look more closely at specific developments and arguments in contemporary economic policy.

ECONOMIC POLICY: 1930s THROUGH THE 1980s

Debates over economic policy often involve two entirely different questions: (1) What *goals and objectives* are to be advanced through governmental intervention? (2) How does the economy really work, and *how can a given economic objective best be achieved*? To some extent, differences over desired *ends*, and over the best *means* to attain these ends, get scrambled together in the policy debates in every nation. But the relative weight of these two dimensions varies greatly.

In some countries, differences over basic objectives dominate economic policy arguments. For example, in many Western democracies throughout much of this century, including France, Italy, and England, lines have been drawn between those who want more governmental control of the economy and less control by private business interests, and those who favor private ownership with reduced government influence. With the election of Socialist party leader François Mitterrand as president in 1981, France took an ideological turn toward more government ownership of industries. In England, the Conservative government of Prime Minister Margaret Thatcher cut back on government ownership; its Labour party opponents vow to expand socialism when they next form the government.

In the United States, although there are differences over the goals of economic policy, the main disagreements concern how particular goals are best obtained. We want strong economic growth, high levels of employment, and low inflation—all within the general structure of a private-property-based economy. At issue are the steps the country should be taking to promote these shared objectives. Issues of economic policy often loom large in U.S. politics, but they usually encompass contending partisan claims that "we can do it better."

Americans turn to economists much as to medical doctors: We do not want them to make the patient *different*, only *well*. This "how-to-do-it" emphasis means that technical and scientific assessments offered by economists are often very important politically. While in the complex, highly pluralistic push and pull of American politics no set of economic prescriptions ever gets fully or neatly applied, politicians look to economists for general guidance on how to most effectively advance shared goals.

Margin notes:
- Economic policies in other countries
- America: conflicting means to a common end

John Maynard Keynes and Keynesian Economics

The "how-to-do-it" prescriptions of a distinguished British economist, John Maynard Keynes (1883–1946), entered into the American debate over economic policy in the 1930s, against the backdrop of the Great Depression. The **Keynesian** approach came to dominate the thinking of professional economists in the United States and helped shape the policies of the Roosevelt administration and its successors.

Keynesian economics

What made Keynes so influential was the force of his argument that the ideas on which politicians had been leaning had ceased to fit actual economic conditions. Since the "old economics" no longer pointed government in the right direction, a "new economics" and new answers to problems of political economy were needed. In his celebrated *The General Theory of Employment, Interest, and Money*, Keynes provided them.[4]

Keynesian prescriptions. Keynes offered capitalist economies a way out of the crisis they faced in the 1930s, without abandoning capitalism. He rejected the centralization and collectivization inherent in state socialism. "I come not to bury capitalism," Keynes might have said, "but to save it." A private-property-based economy, he wrote, "if it can be purged of its defects and its abuses, is the best safeguard of personal liberty in the sense that, compared with any other system, it greatly widens the field for the exercise of personal choice."[5]

Focus on consumption and investment

What were the key elements of Keynes's primer for American and British politicians wanting tools to make their capitalist economies work better? Keynes maintained that full employment and high economic growth are best advanced by promoting *consumption* rather than *savings*. Savings tend to be hoarded rather than applied to productive investments. In contrast, the demand generated by increased consumption stimulates greater investment and promotes the best utilization of society's resources. The richer a society becomes—and by the late 1920s both Britain and the United States were, by any historical comparison, very rich societies—"the wider will tend to be the gap between its actual and its potential production. . . ." Such a society "will have to discover much ampler opportunities for investment if the saving propensities of its wealthier members are to be compatible with the employment of its poorer members."[6]

"Priming the pump"

Rather than encouraging individual thrift, then, government should help generate consumption through such means as public-works programs. "Priming the pump" was the analogy that best conveyed the idea that government spending would lead to greater activity in the private sector. These programs would put money into the hands of poorer citizens, who would then use the money to buy goods. Furthermore, government spending should not be paid for by economizing in other areas. When demand lags, because people lack money to buy the things they need, government should run a deficit—that is, spend more than it takes in from taxes—to provide economic stimulus.

These increased expenditures need not even be productive in the usual sense. Keynes contended that unemployment could be reduced

[4] John Maynard Keynes, *The General Theory of Employment, Interest, and Money* (New York: Harcourt, Brace, 1965; first published 1936), p. 383.
[5] Ibid., p. 380.
[6] Ibid., p. 31.

John Maynard Keynes.

even "if the Treasury were to fill old bottles with bank notes, bury them at suitable depths in disused coal mines which are then filled up to the surface with town rubbish, and leave it to private enterprise . . . to dig the notes up again."[7] This remark was in part facetious, but its main message was serious. Unemployment was high and production was down because many people lacked the money required to buy necessities. If only government would pump money to those who needed it, increased consumption would occur, more jobs would be created to produce goods to meet this demand, and investment in new plant facilities would become attractive again.

It sounded almost too good to be true. Politicians who created new social programs, especially to help those in need, and who spent for such programs more than they asked people to pay in taxes, were not being profligate or crassly buying votes; they were stimulating the economy, increasing productivity, lowering unemployment, and generally making everyone more prosperous. Many politicians were understandably happy to receive this advice. But what made Keynesianism so unassailably alluring was the fact that, in the economic context in which Keynes wrote, it was right.

Economic Conditions in the 1930s

To understand why Keynes was correct in telling the governments of Western democracies that they should forget about budget-balancing

[7] Ibid., p. 247.

and start spending, one needs to look at the economic conditions that prevailed when *The General Theory* was written. All of the western nations, the United States included, were experiencing in the 1930s a vast economic crisis distinguished by (1) unemployment, (2) under-consumption, and (3) deflation. The three went hand in hand.

Unemployment. In 1900 in the United States, the rate of **unemployment** (the number of people unemployed as a percentage of the total civilian labor force) stood at just 5 percent. It hovered around that mark for most of the ensuing three decades: 5.9 percent in 1910, 5.2 percent in 1920, and just 3.2 percent in 1925. With the onset of the Depression, however, unemployment soared: It reached 8.7 percent in 1930 and by 1935 had climbed to *20.1 percent.* Even as late as 1940 it stood at 14.6 percent. Never had so many people been out of work in America. Conditions were much the same in Europe.

Unemployment

Massive drop in the GNP. With people unemployed, productivity, income, and consumption fell off drastically. In 1922, the GNP of the United States totaled $74.1 billion; over the next several years it rose further, reaching a high of $103.1 billion in 1929. During the Depression, however, it plummeted, bottoming out at just $55.6 billion in 1933—a drop of *nearly 50 percent from the level of just four years earlier.* We can scarcely imagine what the impact would be today if the GNP were to be cut in half in the space of a few years.

Low GNP

The basic productive capacities of the United States (and the other Western democracies) were as great in the mid-1930s as they had been in the late 1920s; the skills of the people, the technology, and the output possible from the factories and farms were undiminished. But, in a vicious circle, unemployment and falling income meant falling consumption, and that meant lower production, and so on, round and round.

Deflation. Today, *inflation* is so prominent a feature of American economic life that we sometimes find it hard to appreciate that throughout much of U.S. history **deflation**—falling prices—was the more common problem. In the 1920s and 1930s, because of unemployment and low consumption, prices fell dramatically. Unable to find markets for their products, manufacturers, farmers, and merchants had to cut what they were charging. According to one index, producer prices stood at 79.6 in 1920. This composite index of prices at the wholesale level fell to 50.0 in 1928, to 44.6 in 1930, and to just 33.6 in 1932. This deflationary experience was so prolonged and deep that it was not until 1948 that the composite index of wholesale prices had climbed back to its 1920 level.

Deflation

Why are falling prices an economic problem? Price deflation creates a disincentive to invest in new plant facilities. The return that can be expected will lag behind current costs. Keynes noted:

If, for any reason right or wrong, the business world *expects* that prices will fall, the processes of production tend to be inhibited. . . . The deflation which causes falling prices means impoverishment to labor and to enterprise by leading entrepreneurs to restrict production, in their endeavor to avoid losses to themselves; and is therefore disastrous to employment.[8]

Limited government involvement

Limited government. Keynes's call for expanded governmental management of the economy came when government was still small, with limited responsibilities. When FDR first won election in November 1932, the total budget of the national government was just $4.7 billion, or about $37 per person. Over the 1930s, under the Roosevelt administration, expenditures rose significantly, but in 1940 they were still only $9.1 billion, less than $69 a citizen. Contrast these figures to the fiscal 1986 federal budget of just under one trillion dollars, or about $4,150 per person. Keynes's call in 1936 for a broadened governmental role appeared to many to be a measured, sensible, prudent response. And it was.

In the 1930s, then, the United States and other industrial democracies found themselves with a massive economic problem. Unemployment was up, production and consumption down. The standard

"*Yes, You Remembered Me*"

[8] John Maynard Keynes, *A Tract on Monetary Reform*, in *The Collected Writings of John Maynard Keynes* (London: Macmillan, 1971), pp. 30, 35–36. The first edition of this work appeared in 1923.

Triumph of
Keynesianism

of living for many citizens had fallen drastically. Deflation was a prime obstacle, as it provided incentives *not* to invest in productive plant facilities. The call for more governmental intervention, in a setting where government did relatively little, seemed excessive only to those ideologically opposed to the very idea of governmental responsibility for promoting prosperity. The triumph of Keynesianism was fundamentally empirical or practical: It read and responded better to prevailing needs than any available alternative.

Post–World War II
Keynesianism

The Roosevelt administration did not immediately seize upon and implement Keynesian prescriptions. Many contradictory perspectives and pressures continued to be felt. The amount of stimulus given the economy in the latter half of the 1930s was modest—much too modest, most economists now agree. Only the massive government spending made necessary by America's entry into World War II finally ended the decade-long depression and brought unemployment down to stay. But the national leadership of the Democratic party gradually converted to the "new economics," and from World War II through the 1960s, Keynesianism exerted great influence over the American approach to issues of political economy. By 1971, even a conservative Republican president, Richard Nixon, was moved to proclaim that "now I am a Keynesian."[9]

Shifts in the Political Economy: The Post-Keynesian Era

The "new economics" spurred by John Maynard Keynes proved to be a generally successful response to the needs of one particular period and its economic conditions. But conditions change. The shifts were gradual, but by the 1970s enough had occurred to stimulate vast rethinking of economic issues and government's position in national economic life. First economists and then politicians joined in the search for another new economics.

Big government. When the New Deal expansion of government's role in the U.S. economy began, government was a modest presence. By the 1970s, it had become a major one, and it became increasingly difficult to argue that "more government" was the answer.

Table 16.1 shows the level of federal taxation from 1922 to the present. One is struck by how small the federal tax burden was in the early part of this century: just over $15 per person as late as 1932. After 1960, however, federal taxes rose sharply, from $512 per capita in 1960 to about $3,700 in 1988. Some of this apparent growth is illusory, accruing simply because of inflation. A 1988 dollar pur-

[9]Richard Nixon, remarks made to Howard K. Smith following a nationally televised interview with Smith and three other network correspondents on January 4, 1971. Rowland Evans, Jr., and Robert D. Novak, *Nixon in the White House: The Frustration of Power* (New York: Random House, 1971), p. 372.

Table 16.1

Federal Taxation from the 1920s through the 1980s

Year	Total budget receipts (in thousands of dollars)	Per capita federal taxes (in dollars)
1922	4,025,901	37
1932	1,923,892	15
1940	6,879,000	52
1950	40,940,000	270
1960	92,492,000	512
1970	193,743,000	946
1980	517,100,000	2,271
1985	734,100,000	3,074
1988	909,200,000 (est.)	3,703

Source: 1922–70: Bureau of the Census, *Historical Statistics of the United States: Colonial Times to 1970*, parts 1 and 2, pp. 8, 1105–6. 1980–88: *Economic Indicators*, June, 1988, p. 32; Bureau of the Census, *Statistical Abstract of the United States*, 1988, p. 7.

chases less than a 1960 dollar. But even when inflation is controlled for, a major increase has occurred. Public opposition to tax hikes, while sometimes exaggerated, is now substantial, and some economists worry about a drag on the economy from high taxation.

Data on governmental spending show the same progression (Table 16.2). As late as 1950, total federal expenditures in the United States averaged out to just $260 per person. By 1970, however, the figure had reached almost $960 and in 1988 it stood at $4,300. Again, a significant part of this rise is not real—inflation enters the picture—but much of it *is* real. Over the last quarter-century, the rate of growth of

Increased government spending

Table 16.2

Federal Expenditures from the 1920s through the 1980s

Year	Total federal expenditures (in thousands of dollars)	Per capita federal expenditures (in dollars)
1922	3,289,404	30
1932	4,659,000	37
1940	9,055,269	69
1950	39,544,037	261
1960	92,223,354	510
1970	196,587,786	960
1980	590,920,000	2,595
1985	946,316,000	3,955
1988	1,055,904,000 (est.)	4,301

Source: 1922–70: Bureau of the Census, *Historical Statistics of the United States: Colonial Times to 1970*, parts 1 and 2, pp. 8, 1114–15, 1120. 1980–87: Executive Office of the President, OMB, *Budget of the U.S. Government, FY 1989*, p. 6g–45.

government spending has substantially outstripped the growth of the overall economy.

The federal debt. Not surprisingly, politicians have found it easier politically to increase expenditures than taxation—especially at the national level where there are no legal requirements that the budget be balanced, and where under sluggish economic conditions there is a good case for spending beyond revenues. During the 1930s, the Roosevelt administration expended more than it collected in taxes, to provide economic stimulus. Still, over the entire decade the cumulative federal debt rose by what now appears as a modest $26.8 billion. The total debt climbed sharply during World War II, reflecting the heavy costs of the war. After 1945, however, it remained rather stable in absolute terms for the next quarter-century; as a proportion of the GNP the federal debt actually declined substantially during this period. Since 1970, though, and especially since 1980, the debt has soared: from $371 billion in 1970, to $544 billion in 1975, $914 billion in 1980, and $2.6 _trillion_ in 1988 (Table 16.3). The latter works out to roughly $10,500 per person. Annual interest payments on total federal borrowing has become a large factor: over $210 billion in FY 1988 alone. Thirty-three percent of the current annual GNP in 1980, the gross federal debt rose to 53 percent of the 1988 GNP. The federal government has run a deficit every year since 1964, regardless of whether the nation's economy was booming or in recession.

According to Keynesianism, the central government should spend

Table 16.3
Federal Debt from the 1920s through the 1980s

Year	Total (in thousands)	Per capita
1920	24,299,321	228
1930	16,185,310	132
1940	42,967,531	325
1945	258,682,187	1,849
1950	257,357,352	1,697
1960	286,330,761	1,585
1970	370,981,707	1,811
1975	544,100,000	2,519
1980	914,300,000	4,230
1985	1,827,500,000	7,654
1988	2,581,600,000 (est.)	10,514

Source: 1920–70: Bureau of the Census, _Historical Statistics of the U.S.: Colonial Times to 1970,_ parts 1 and 2, pp. 8, 1117–18. 1975–80: idem, _Statistical Abstract of the U.S., 1984,_ pp. 6, 315. 1985–88: Executive Office of the President, OMB, _Budget of the United States Government,_ FY 1987, p. 6e–7, and FY 1989, p. 6g–7.

more than it takes in when the economy is in recession, so as to stimulate demand, but it should tax more than it spends in periods when the economy is booming, to temper inflationary pressures and sustain even growth. This adjusting of taxing and spending levels is known as **fiscal policy.** But in recent years American politicians have found fiscal policy exceedingly hard to manage. No body of economic theory justifies the federal government's running deficits each year, as it has for two decades now. The cuts in federal income tax rates pushed by the Reagan administration in 1981 and enacted by Congress added to the size of the deficit by reducing revenues while expenditures continued to climb. But the scope and persistence of the deficit are hardly the result of any one administration's actions or any single set of economic circumstances. They are structural problems of the contemporary political economy.

Inflation. Unemployment was an overwhelming problem in the 1930s. Since World War II, however, it has not been as out of control, and governmental programs, notably payments to workers who have been laid off, under Unemployment Compensation, have at least somewhat cushioned the impact of being out of work. But while this happened, inflation climbed to record levels and came to dominate the public's concerns. Looking at consumer prices expressed in an index where the 1967 level is set equal to 1.00, we see that price increases were modest over the 1950s and 1960s. There was inflation, but not much. Since the late sixties, though, inflation has been formidable, moderating only since 1982. There has been a sharp decline in the dollar's purchasing power: In 1983 it would buy only one-third as much as it had just sixteen years earlier. In the early 1960s, the annual rate of increase in consumer prices averaged just one percent. Then it began climbing. Despite ups and downs, the trend from 1960 to 1980 is unmistakable: Inflationary peaks rose even higher. Figure 16.1 shows that the valley reached in the mid-1980s was lower than any had been in more than a decade.

All of the industrialized countries found themselves with reduced inflation in the mid-1980s. The fall of oil prices was an important factor here—just as the big oil price increases of the 1970s had fueled runaway inflation in that decade. Commodity prices in general were weak in the mid-1980s, though, and this, coupled with the success of anti-inflation policies that many western governments, including the United States, had introduced, brought inflation to a halt. In the first six months of 1986, for example, consumer prices in the United States actually fell by two-tenths of one percent—the first such decline in over thirty years.

John Maynard Keynes himself had once shown ample appreciation of the problem of inflation. In 1920 he commented on the harm high inflation can do:

Problems in formulating sound fiscal policy

Reduced inflation in the 1980s

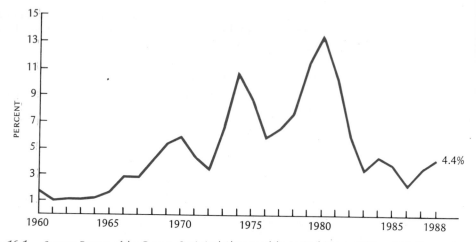

Figure 16.1
Annual Rate of Increase
of Consumer Prices
since 1960

Source: Bureau of the Census, *Statistical Abstract of the United States, 1986,* p. 469; *Economic Indicators,* June 1986, p. 24; June, 1988, p. 24. All data on changes in consumer prices reflect the percentage change from the preceding year or, in the case of 1988, a third quarter estimate.

> As the inflation proceeds and the real value of the currency fluctuates wildly from month to month, all permanent relations between debtors and creditors, which form the ultimate foundation of capitalism, become so utterly disordered as to be almost meaningless; and so the process of wealth-getting degenerates into a gamble and a lottery. . . . Lenin was certainly right. There is no subtler, no surer means of overturning the existing basis of society than to debauch the currency.[10]

By the time *The General Theory* was published in 1936, Keynes had shifted his emphasis—not surprising, given the extreme deflation of the 1920s and 1930s. In recent years, though, the earlier Keynes has again made good reading. For, as Professor David Calleo has written, "this is no longer an age of underconsumption, but of inflation."[11]

Gains as well as problems. Changing conditions are often depicted in terms of the new problems they entail. Big and sometimes clumsy government efforts, political difficulties in keeping revenues in line with expenditures, and strong underlying inflationary pressures are persisting problems of the contemporary political economy, just as deflation, underconsumption, and unemployment dominated a half-century earlier. But no era, economic or otherwise, is defined simply by problems. Although discussions of the nation's economic position and performance over the last decade and a half have often been couched in the language of failings, many things have performed well.

[10] Keynes, *The Economic Consequences of the Peace* (1920), reprinted in *Collected Works.*
[11] David P. Calleo, *The Imperious Economy* (Cambridge, Mass.: Harvard University Press, 1982), p. 176.

GNP growth. Looking back on the last fifteen or so years, we see an economy that has had to confront a host of severe problems—and that has still managed to perform pretty well. Many key industries, including autos and steel, have gone through a painful adjustment involving high domestic wage rates and intense foreign competition. The economy had to absorb massive "oil shocks" in 1973–74 and 1979: huge, rapid price hikes. Despite this, the GNP rose impressively over the span. Between 1978 and 1988, for example, real GNP rose about $825 billion (measured in constant dollars)—a gain of 26 percent.[12]

Creation of jobs. The idea that there was stagnation is contradicted even more forcefully by the national experience in job creation. The U.S. economy confronted conditions in the 1960s and 1970s that could easily have led to massively high rates of unemployment: An unprecedentedly large number of people were entering the labor force. After World War II birth rates rose dramatically and stayed high until the 1960s. By the 1970s large numbers of this "baby boom" generation were looking for jobs. Between 1946 and 1955 alone, more than 34 million people were born in the United States; by 1980 the youngest among them were 25 years old and most were in the labor force.

A second reason for the rise in the number of people seeking jobs was the jump in what economists call the "labor-force participation rate" of women. In 1960 there were 62.4 million women in the United States 16 years of age and older; 36.5 percent of them were in the labor force—employed or actively seeking paid employment outside the home. Just 26 years later, in 1986, the female population 16 years and older totaled 96.5 million, 54.3 percent of whom were in the labor force. This translates into a total increase of 29.6 million women employed or seeking work.

These statistics tell a simple story: If the United States had not created millions of new jobs in a short span of time, the unemployment rate would have gone up like a rocket. Jobs *were* rapidly created, however—created at a rate high even by America's historical standards. Between 1975 and 1987 the United States produced over 26 million new jobs, while the industrial nations of Western Europe produced only about 5.7 million (Figure 16.2). Though Japan's "economic miracle" is often remarked upon, American job creation was at approximately twice the rate or proportion of Japan's over this span. Job creation in the United States has continued strong since the 1982–83 recession. From a low of 99.5 million in 1982, total civilian employment climbed to just under 101 million in 1983, 105 million in 1985, and over 115 million in the fall of 1988.

Women in the labor force

American job creation

[12]*Economic Indicators*, report prepared for the Joint Economic Committee of Congress by the Council of Economic Advisers, June, 1986, p. 2; June, 1988, p. 2.

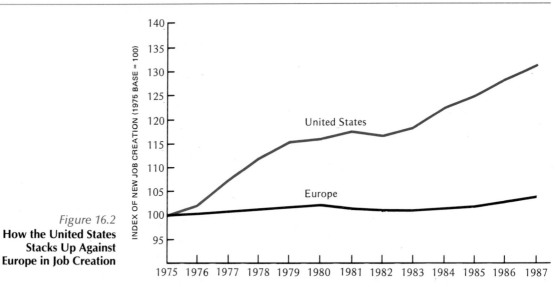

Figures for Europe are composite of all European members of OECD, with the exception of Yugoslavia.
Source: U.S. Bureau of the Census, *Statistical Abstract of the United States, 1988*, p. 364. U.S. Bureau of Labor statistics, Office of Current Employment Analysis, unpublished date.

Affluence. We noted in chapter 2 that the United States, a comparatively wealthy country before World War II, enjoyed a great spurt in national wealth in the first quarter-century after the war. Since the early 1970s per capita income has continued to rise in real terms. We can understand this recent performance by comparing the income growth in the United States to that in other successful industrial nations. The United States had the highest per capita income in the industrial world in 1970 and retained the position 15 years later. In 1986, per capita GNP in the United States was $17,324, according to calculations of the Organization for Economic Cooperation and Development (OECD).[13] By comparison, per capita GNP that year was $12,741 in West Germany, $12,218 in France, $12,339 in Japan, $11,498 in Britain, and $11,406 in Italy. Japan increased its share of the total income of all OECD countries, while the United States's share declined very slightly, but on the whole income shares of the wealthy nations were stable. The United States had moved ahead proportionately.

Many factors account for recent American economic performance; and the fact that economic growth has been achieved does not mean

[13] The countries of the Organization for Economic Cooperation and Development (OECD) are the United States, Belgium, Denmark, France, West Germany, Greece, Ireland, Italy, Luxembourg, the Netherlands, United Kingdom, Austria, Finland, Iceland, Norway, Portugal, Spain, Sweden, Switzerland, Turkey, Canada, Japan, Australia, and New Zealand. For an explanation of how the OECD calculates income in the various countries for comparative purposes, see the note to Table 2.2.

that economic policy has been generally sound. The point is that the movement of the United States into the new economic era is not all gloom and doom. The record shows bright spots as well as problems.

Public Attitudes on Political Economy

Americans seem to recognize that their nation's economy has strong features as well as weak points. But looking just at the problem side, major shifts have occurred. The level of unemployment was the litmus test of prosperity in the New Deal era; now the rate of inflation commands at least equal billing. Public anxiety has paralleled movement of the inflation rate, becoming most acute in times of double-digit inflation, and diminishing when the rate fell back, as it did in the mid-1980s. Throughout these ups and downs, the problem of inflation has remained prominent in voters' thinking. For a people who historically did not have to grapple with the problem, recent experience with steadily rising prices—eroding savings, wiping out apparent pay increases, making financial planning difficult—was terribly upsetting. Moreover, the persistence of high inflation raised questions about the capability of the national government to manage economic life effectively.

Recent elections have shown how much the new public concerns over the economy can disrupt traditional political calculations. The 1982 congressional elections were conducted at a time of major recession, with unemployment having climbed to over 10 percent. Double-digit unemployment dominated economic news all during the campaign, and many observers expected it to dominate the election results. It didn't. When, on election day, NBC News asked in a national poll whether it was more important to the nation's economy for the federal government to control unemployment or control inflation, the electorate split down the middle, 46 percent to 44 percent, respectively. And when voters were asked a companion question on their own financial concerns—"In terms of your own personal finances, would you rather see the federal government control inflation or unemployment?"—the results affirmed inflation's continuing centrality. By 59 to 33 percent nationally, and by solid majorities in every state surveyed—including those especially hard hit by unemployment—voters said that government's success in fighting inflation was more important to them personally.[14] Moreover, clear majorities of every occupational group (except for the unemployed), of union members as well as those not in unions, and of every income group except the poor stressed inflation.

Not only was concern over inflation salient, but the public shifted its sense of who and what are responsible for inflation. Before 1965,

Public opinion and the political economy

[14] Election-day polls by NBC News, November 2, 1982.

Who is responsible for inflation?

when Gallup interviewers asked Americans whether they thought government, business, or labor was most responsible, Republicans tended to say "labor" while Democrats answered "business." By 1968, however, large and equivalent majorities of both Democrats and Republicans said "government." In a poll taken by ABC News/*Washington Post* in January 1982, 57 percent held government responsible, while just 19 percent blamed labor and 13 percent business.[15]

In the late 1960s and 1970s, governmental actions came increasingly to be seen widely as problems, not just as solutions to problems. "Government causes inflation" is one part of this. "Government taxes too much" is another part. The actual tax burden on most citizens increased dramatically after the 1950s. In 1953 families with incomes around the national average paid 11.8 percent of their income in taxes; in 1966 they paid 17.8 percent, and in 1980 22.7 percent. Incomes rose, but the proportion paid out in taxes rose much faster—and took about twice as much of the average family's earnings (see Figure 16.3).

Ambivalence about government

These developments contributed to a loud chorus of criticism of American government and resistance to its further expansion. They did not lead, though, to any broad public sentiment to cut back. Americans continue to want a lot by way of protections and services. As we saw in chapter 10, the end result is a public highly ambivalent about the contemporary state. "Big government" is no longer in, although almost no one wants to dismantle the governmental edifice already built. Economic growth is in, and both parties recognize that the terms of the debate over how best to achieve it have shifted. Which one will be the "party of prosperity"?

Political Implications

In the New Deal era the Democrats had much more electoral success than the Republicans. Perhaps most important was their success in convincing people that they were the party of prosperity. But as we have seen, recent economic changes have affected this perception. Ronald Reagan received generally high economic marks from voters in 1984. Neither the Republicans nor the Democrats have yet established a firm contemporary hold on the title "party of prosperity."

Republicans' approach. In the 1980s, the Republicans staked their claim to effective handling of the political economy on four related commitments. First, they said that the overall growth of government should be curtailed and the steady growth of federal domestic spending curbed. Second, governmental regulation of private business should be cut back. Third, federal taxes are too high and, at a minimum, their continuing growth as a proportion of personal income should

[15] Survey by ABC News/*Washington Post*, January 22–30, 1982.

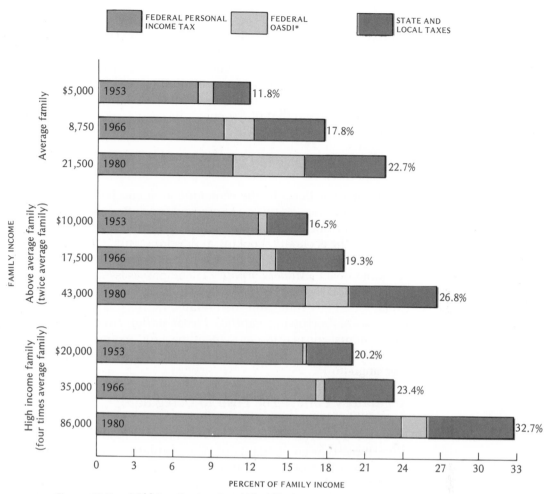

Figure 16.3
Comparing Tax Burden Borne by Families by Year and Income

*Old Age, Survivors', and Disability Insurance taxes.
Source: Significant Features of Fiscal Federalism, 1980–81 Edition (Washington, D.C.: Advisory Commission on Intergovernmental Relations, December 1981), p. 48.

be arrested. Fourth, inflation can and should be kept under control by a growing and competitive private economy, and through increases in the nation's money supply (see below) that are both steady and proportional to overall economic growth.

Democrats' approach. In contrast, Democratic leaders have insisted that while big government is indeed a problem, it is the growth of military spending that is especially troublesome and that must be curbed. Second, they have endorsed deregulation in a number of areas of the economy but maintained that more vigorous federal regulation is needed in others, especially those involving the environment and consumer protection. Third, they argue that the Reagan-backed tax cuts were excessive and fueled an unacceptably large deficit that carries strong pressures for high interest rates and future inflation. Fourth, they believe that sustained economic growth and national prosperity will require a greater measure of intelligent federal planning and management than the Republicans favored, although management very different from that of the past.

TOOLS OF ECONOMIC POLICY

Regulatory policy, monetary policy, fiscal policy

Government policies in the economic area can be sorted into three broad groups: *regulatory, monetary,* and *fiscal.* **Regulatory policy** comprises governmental standard setting and rule making for different sectors of the economy. Looking at developments in this area gives us a good sense of the scope of recent efforts to cut back on government's economic reach. **Monetary policy** encompasses issues of management of the nation's money supply: decisions on how much it should be expanded at any time, and such related matters as interest rates and the ease of borrowing capital. **Fiscal policy** covers governmental adjustments in taxing and spending: for example, determining whether, and by how much, overall federal spending should exceed revenues.

Regulatory Policy: The Push to Deregulate

Deregulation

From the time Franklin Roosevelt took office in 1933 to the early 1970s, there were two great bursts of new regulatory activity, one in the 1930s, the other beginning in the mid-1960s and extending into the early 1970s. Against this backdrop, recent developments are distinguished by efforts to cut back on governmental regulations. **Deregulation** has been the watchword of the late 1970s and the 1980s. A distinction must be made between two types of regulation: One involves the regulation of prices charged by businesses and the entry of firms into various industrial sectors; the other comprises regulations aimed at health, safety, and consumer protection. Since the early 1970s there has been extensive deregulation in the former area, but little in the latter.

Prices and entry. By the 1970s an enormous array of regulations setting prices and determining which firms could enter certain markets were in place—governing airlines, trucking, railroads, oil and natural gas, banks and other financial institutions. Regulations were imposed early in the development of these industries to promote orderly growth. Airlines are a good case in point: The federal Civil Aeronautics Board (CAB) determined the prices airlines could charge for tickets, and which airlines could service which routes, in an effort to achieve a stable system of air transportation linking cities large and small across the country. The industry was seen as a kind of public utility, much like telephone service and electric power. Under the CAB's rigid controls on prices and entry, the infant air industry developed impressively.

By the 1970s, however, economists and other observers felt that much of this regulation was no longer needed and that its principal continuing effect was to limit competition. In this view, governmental control over prices and entry simply preserved comfortable niches in which businesses could operate free from competitive challenge. The regulatory barriers should be removed, and free-market controls substituted. The essential element of free markets is the right to compete without permission from any governmental agency. Under open competition, firms would have greater incentive to offer better prices and services. Poorly managed firms would be driven from the market by consumer choice.

Economist Alfred Kahn played a leading role in deregulation efforts in the 1970s through both his writings and his chairmanship of the Civil Aeronautics Board when airline deregulation was rushing along.

Deregulation in the 1970s

> Whenever the government intervenes in the economy in one way or another . . . it typically confers benefits on some groups of people and, directly or indirectly, burdens on others. In so doing, it necessarily creates vested private interests in a continuation of that particular activity. The interests usually antedate the government action and provide part of the political motivation for the government's undertaking it in the first place; but the explicit intervention by the government then validates those

"All those in favor of establishing government regulatory agencies say 'Aye.'"

Drawing by H. Martin; © 1983 The New Yorker Magazine, Inc.

interests, confers those benefits, and makes the beneficiaries eager to see the activity continue.[16]

The position of regulated businesses was often at odds with what a superficial reading might lead one to expect: Industries often profited from and strongly defended the control government imposed. For example, many more airlines opposed legislation deregulating that industry than favored it.

The liberal-conservative alliance. Economists do not enact national legislation. To understand how a political majority in Congress and the executive branch emerged behind deregulation, one needs to see how liberals and conservatives found reason to join forces. For conservatives, deregulation was an opportunity to "help get government off our backs." Through deregulation, market forces would be permitted to work, replacing burdensome governmental restraints, and improving productivity. But many liberal politicians, among them Senator Edward Kennedy, also enthusiastically supported deregulation of airlines, railroads, and trucking. The liberals were responding to consumer groups who had come to believe that regulations were keeping prices unnecessarily high and services poorer than they could be. To the extent that regulation was an unwarranted aid to business, liberals had every incentive to oppose it. Beyond this, as Michael Pertschuk notes, the clamor to cut back on the growth of government had grown loud by the late 1970s, and many politicians were looking for ways to show voters that they were responsive.

Rapid deregulation. With broad agreement among economists, and with liberals and conservatives making common cause, deregulation was almost irresistible. The result was a surge of well over twenty-five pieces of major new legislation and administrative rulings in this area in the late 1970s and early 1980s. What specifically has it meant?

Airline deregulation

In the airline industry, the Civil Aeronautics Board began in 1976 allowing airlines to engage in competitive pricing, and in 1978 it became much more flexible in awarding new routes. The Airline Deregulation Act of 1978 carried these developments ahead. Airlines are now free to enter and leave routes as they see fit, and to determine by themselves, subject to market pressures, what they will charge. In 1978, only 36 airlines serviced interstate markets; in 1984 more than 100 firms competed interstate. Deregulation spurred competition and decreased the market shares of the airlines that had previously been the major trunk carriers. Its regulatory role ended, the CAB ceased to operate on January 1, 1985.

In the old regulatory environment, employees, such as pilots, had

[16] Alfred E. Kahn, "Deregulation and Vested Interests: The Case of Airlines," in Roger G. Noll and Bruce M. Owen, *The Political Economy of Deregulation* (Washington, D.C.: American Enterprise Institute, 1983), p. 132.

been able to capture for themselves a significant part of the economic gains that accrued from technological advances, in the form of high salaries. Now, faced with competition, carriers with large numbers of high-priced employees are struggling to adapt. Airline ticket prices under deregulation, it is generally agreed, have come to reflect much more closely actual costs of doing business. Fares in longer-haul markets and in heavily traveled routes have fallen substantially, relative to fares in short-haul and lightly traveled routes.

Rail and trucking deregulation

On the ground, the Motor Carrier Act of 1980 and the Staggers Rail Act of 1980 similarly extended trucking and rail deregulation, which had been initiated in the mid-1970s by the regulatory body with jurisdiction in the area, the Interstate Commerce Commission (ICC). While the ICC still imposes some rate and entry regulations, it now leaves much more room for market forces. Carriers can now operate in an integrated fashion across all transportation sectors. Whereas railroads had been prohibited from operating trucking companies, they are now free to do so. The old separation of ship, railroad, and truck carriers is coming to an end; firms are offering packages of transportation services which take advantage of the relative efficiencies of each of the three means.

Is deregulation working? Results are complicated and by no means uniform. But the conclusion of most observers seems to be a tentative yes. Perhaps the most striking confirmation is that, after a decade of change and experimentation, almost no one advocates a return to the more highly regulated environment that had previously existed.

Health, safety, and consumer protection. Other types of governmental regulation set health and safety standards and seek to protect consumer interests. From roughly 1965 through 1975, there was an extraordinary increase in this type of regulation. For example, the Clean Water and Clean Air Acts, together with their various amendments, imposed standards and restrictions on industry relating to the emission of pollutants into the atmosphere and into the nation's lakes and rivers. In all, more than 50 major pieces of regulatory legislation were passed by Congress from the mid-1960s through the mid-1970s—including the Federal Cigarette and Labeling Advertising Act (1965), the National Traffic and Motor Vehicle Safety Act (1966), the Child Protection Act (1966), and the Flammable Fabrics Act Amendments (1967).

Earlier government regulation of business focused on a limited number of industries and was primarily concerned with prices and with the allocation of market shares. In contrast, the new legislation of the 1960s and 1970s was directed at "ameliorating the social impact of businesses, not their economic behavior."[17] As American society

[17] Michael Pertschuk, *Revolt Against Regulation* (Berkeley, Calif.: University of California Press, 1982), p. 23.

A foreman instructs miners on safety rules.

became wealthier in the post–World War II years, public expectations rose in such areas as environmental cleanliness and consumer protection. Various policy entrepreneurs, in Congress and in public-interest groups, responded to this new climate of opinion.

By the latter half of the 1970s, a backlash had set in against this surge of regulation. But the liberal-conservative (or Democratic-Republican) alliance evident in the campaign for airline and trucking deregulation was nowhere to be seen in the environmental, consumer-protection, and health and safety areas. Instead, there was a fairly clear-cut liberal vs. conservative split. Liberals continued to defend the new regulation and often to seek its extension, while conservatives favored a rollback or at least an end to the rush to pass new laws. A political equilibrium has largely been reached, in that business and conservative interests have for the most part blocked new regulation but liberal, consumer, and environmental interests have prevented a rollback.

Liberal / conservative split over regulation

Fiscal and Monetary Policy: Contending Approaches Among Economists

Broad changes in the economy and in thinking about how it is best managed are now reflected in a number of competing schools of opinion among economists. In the real world, the lines separating these positions are often blurred—and, indeed, now seem increasingly blurred, as economists of all persuasions grapple with the often confounding changes and new problems evident at the end of the 1980s.

Still, elements of the following positions are evident in the ongoing debate over how to manage the U.S. economy through fiscal and monetary policies.

Monetarism. As a pure form of economic theory, **monetarism** puts a singular emphasis on controlling the money supply and the price of money (the interest rate) to secure a growing and inflation-free economy. While every economist recognizes that monetary policy is important, only monetarists make it their keystone. Monetarism's leading theorist is Milton Friedman, a Nobel Laureate in economics (1976) with a long and distinguished career at the University of Chicago.

Monetarism

Friedman and other monetarists start from the straightforward and, to a degree, unassailable proposition that inflation occurs as the result of "too much money chasing too few goods." For a variety of reasons—including the desire of politicians to "heat up the economy" so that they can go into election years with unemployment down and the GNP up—the money supply in the United States over the last quarter-century has been expanded in excess of what would be justified given actual increases in productivity. The inevitable result has been a reduction in the purchasing power of the dollar—inflation.

Monetarist policies

At various times when the economy has been beset by inflation, there have been short-term efforts to curtail it by sharply cutting back monetary growth. Temporary monetary tightness has indeed temporarily reduced inflation, but at substantial cost: increased unemployment and diminished productivity growth. So, after a while, expansionist policies have been resumed. What is needed, monetarists maintain, is not a lurching between overexpansion and sharp contraction, but a stable, steady growth of the money supply corresponding to and sustaining real growth. The absence of such a policy has been the main source of the country's erratic economic performance. As a remedy, Friedman advocates legislating the monetary rule—that the money supply be expanded each year at the same annual rate as the potential growth of the country's real GNP, or at 3 to 5 percent per year. As long as this happens, any decline into recession will be modest and only temporary, and any inflationary increase in spending will burn itself out for lack of fuel.

Supply-side economics

Supply-side economics. Monetarists are usually catalogued as political conservatives because they stress the capacity of the competitive market system to allocate resources efficiently. Not all conservative private-market economists are monetarists, however. In the 1970s, a new emphasis took shape among some younger conservatives that was christened **supply-side economics.** In contrast to monetarists, supply-siders put great weight on fiscal policy. In particular, they argue for large across-the-board tax cuts, to encourage many people

(1) to work harder, since the "tax penalty" on additional earnings would be reduced; and (2) to invest more in productive enterprises, rather than trying to find economically unproductive tax shelters to escape high marginal tax rates. (The "marginal" tax rate is what a taxpayer gives the government on the last dollars he earns.) Growth resulting from the immediate stimulus of a large across-the-board tax cut and from long-term encouragement of greater work efforts means there will be a much larger base of national wealth to be taxed—hence, in the supply-side view, *reduction of the tax rate* can actually culminate in an *increase in total tax revenues.*

Controversy over supply-side policies

The most controversial aspect of the supply-side diagnosis has been the notion that a large cut in the tax rate would not lead to big federal deficits that would accelerate the rate of inflation. In defense, proponents of the supply-side approach argue that their position here has been misstated. "The idea that supply-side economics would provide an instant, large increase in government tax revenue by reducing tax rates was simply not true to begin with...."[18] What *was* valid, in this view, was the general idea that reducing high marginal tax rates contributes to overall economic growth—benefiting everyone, including government in its need for tax revenues.

Did the Reagan administration try and test supply-side prescriptions? Answers to this vary. The centerpiece of the early Reagan program was a substantial cut in income tax rates: a 23 percent cut over 3 years. But the overall mix of federal taxes under Reagan shows something quite different than a determined test of supply-side theory. While income tax rates were in fact reduced, other taxes rose—notably social security payroll taxes. In addition, much of the reduction in income tax rates merely offset the earlier effects of "bracket creep," which occurred as inflation pushed people into higher income tax brackets. Nonetheless, the Reagan administration has been guided by a mix of supply-side and monetarist ideas. Supply-siders hail the length and strength of the recovery in the 1980s, and the low rate of inflation, as at least partial confirmation of the validity of their approach.

"Mainstream" conservative economics. Neither monetarism nor the supply-side approach is the traditional "mainstream" economics of American conservatives—which emphasizes curbing government spending and keeping tight checks on inflation. Mainstream conservatives, whose ranks include Harvard economist Martin Feldstein and Stanford economist Michael Boskin, both of whom advised George Bush in the 1988 campaign, have been especially unhappy with the size of federal deficits in the Reagan era.

What is conventionally called conservative economics has, then,

---

[18] Martin Anderson, "Is Supply-Side Economics Dead?" *The American Spectator,* November 1983, p. 10.

been torn three different ways in recent years: supply-siders, for whom the very idea of a tax increase is anathema; monetarists, who are primarily concerned with the failure of the Federal Reserve to follow their prescription for slow, steady monetary growth; and traditional conservatives who feel that large budget deficits carry unacceptable threats to the long-term health of the economy. Somewhat eclipsed early in the Reagan administration, the latter position has made something of a comeback at the end of the 1980s. But the traditional mainstream position has been modified as its supporters have accepted significant elements of the supply-side emphasis.

Industrial policy. The other main approaches that vie for attention have liberals as their proponents. One goes under the label **industrial policy.** This approach blends an emphasis on stimulating economic growth—which liberals and conservatives alike can agree on—with an enlarged role for government in promoting the conditions for growth. Tensions in American society will rise, proponents of an industrial policy approach argue, unless ways are found to strengthen America's competitive position in the world economy, especially vis-à-vis Japan. Government must take the lead here, generally in finding new means of promoting growth.

How are productivity gains and more rapid growth to be achieved? The answer, according to economists such as Lester Thurow of MIT and Dukakis adviser Robert Reich of the Harvard Business School, is in part to copy those nations like Japan that have been doing especially well of late. The Japanese government has provided major support for the development of industries with high growth potential—sometimes called "sunrise industries." Thurow gives as an example of this encouragement Japan's great success in robotics: the use of robots to assist in manufacturing.

> The problem for the robotics industry [in Japan] was that the seller couldn't get economics of scale to sell a lot of robots so he could sell them cheaply. Buyers wanted only one or two. So JDB [the Japanese Development Bank] stepped in and financed a short-term leasing company. They didn't subsidize anyone, but they bought the robots, guaranteed producers a market of so many robots a year, and then leased the robots to industry. Now if robots had been a failure, the leasing company would have taken a bath. But they were a great success, and the Japanese conquered robots before the rest of us got started. [Today] they have 14,000; we have 4,000.[19]

In the United States, the federal government needs to step in, industrial policy proponents insist, with new programs to encourage productivity gains and economic growth along the lines of the Japa-

Margin notes:
Traditional conservative economics

Industrial policy

Achieving productivity growth

---

[19] Interview by the author with Lester Thurow, *Public Opinion*, August/September 1983, pp. 7, 58.

New industrial policy

nese model. As one such means, Thurow advocates a kind of National Science Foundation for American industry, providing funding for the development and introduction of important new technologies. He also favors "industrial triage" as the companion approach to "sunset industries." Just as "sunrise industries" need economic encouragement from government, so industries in decline need to be put out of business faster so that the economy can adapt to new opportunities.

> The Japanese are currently doing this in the aluminum industry, forcing reductions in the business. The Japanese Development Bank plays a role by buying obsolete facilities, then tearing them down. They don't get full value but they get something. Something similar should be done for [American firms like] International Harvester so that they get out of the tractor business and into trucks, which they do well.[20]

Keynesian economics revisited. While having lost the intellectual and political preeminence they enjoyed from the late 1930s to the 1960s, Keynesians and the economic policies they favor still figure prominently in America's economic debates. At the core of Keynesianism are two basic elements: expansionism and the welfare state. Full employment is a central goal, one that both requires and makes possible high and rapid growth of the GNP. To ensure growth, government must manage the level of demand: When demand is insufficient, government should provide economic stimulus, by spending more than it takes in; conversely, when demand is excessive, government should put the brakes on through fiscal policy.

Support for an expanding welfare state

A rapidly growing economy provides, Keynesians maintain, a "growth divided": additional revenues that can be expended to enlarge social programs. As in earlier decades, the Keynesian emphasis now includes an expansive, growing federal responsibility for public welfare through antipoverty programs, Social Security, Medicare, and more. Keynesian economists such as Paul Samuelson of MIT and James Tobin of Yale remain strong advocates of an expanding welfare state.

The Bush economic team. The key economic policy makers appointed by George Bush—Nicholas Brady as secretary of the Treasury, Richard Darman as director of the Office of Management and Budget (OMB), and Michael Boskin as chairman of the Council of Economic Advisers—on the whole reflect what have become mainstream conservative economic assumptions. As noted above, though, the mainstream has moved during the Reagan years. Look for the Bush team to strongly resist any significant increase in federal income taxes.

---

[20] Ibid.

MAKING ECONOMIC POLICY

In 1928, Republican Herbert Hoover was elected president by a massive majority (58.1 percent to 40.8 percent) over his Democratic opponent, Alfred E. Smith. Considered part of the "progressive" wing of the Republican party, Hoover was hailed for his achievements in business, government, and humanitarian assistance. Just four years later, however, Hoover lay buried under an electoral landslide that brought to power Franklin Roosevelt and big Democratic majorities in both houses of Congress. What had so drastically changed Hoover's fortunes was the Great Depression.

Republican policies were hardly the sole cause of the worldwide economic collapse, and Hoover's own responsibility for the Depression was more limited still. Few experts would argue that the Depression would have occurred with any less severity had Al Smith and the Democrats taken office in 1929. But Hoover became president, and his administration was the Depression's main political victim. Again and again since the 1930s, we have seen presidential popularity substantially affected by how the economy is doing.

All U.S. politicians want to see their country as prosperous as possible, and believe sincerely that the policies they espouse will contribute to that end in the long run. Elections are not held "in the long run," however, and political leaders also pursue short-term policies to encourage an upbeat economy for the next election campaign. The result, political scientist Edward Tufte has found, is

Making economic policy at the international level: from left to right, Prime Minister Margaret Thatcher (U.K.), President Ronald Reagan (U.S.), Prime Minister Brian Mulroney (Canada), and President François Mitterand (France), attending the 1988 economic summit meeting in Toronto.

an electoral rhythm to the national economic performance of many capitalist democracies. . . . In the United States, the electoral, economic cycle from 1948 to 1976 (other than the Eisenhower years) has consisted of . . . a four-year presidential cycle in the unemployment rate, with downturns in unemployment in the months before the presidential election and upturns in the unemployment rate usually beginning from 12 to 18 months after the election.[21]

Tufte notes, too, that personal income tends to grow faster in election years than in years without elections. He concludes that "these patterns are consistent with the character of the economic tools available to control real disposable income and unemployment. . . . Further, the greater the electoral stakes, the greater the economic stimulation. In particular, those years when incumbent presidents sought re-election enjoyed the most favorable short-run economic conditions."[22]

Monetary policy can have the greatest impact on short-term economic performance. The president has, however, little direct control over monetary policy. That authority resides largely in a unit of the national government that has been given substantial formal independence from both president and Congress: the *Federal Reserve System*. A president's influence over monetary decisions must come indirectly, then, from persuading and/or pressuring the Federal Reserve to take steps he favors.

Monetary policy and the Federal Reserve

The Federal Reserve System

The Federal Reserve

The U.S. Constitution confers upon Congress the power "to coin money" and to "regulate the value thereof" (Article I, Section 8). For all practical purposes, however, this authority has been delegated to the **Federal Reserve.** The Fed is the central bank of the United States. Every major democracy has a central bank, because each needs a publicly controlled financial institution capable of conducting its monetary affairs.

Established in 1913, the Federal Reserve combines centralization and decentralization, and private as well as public involvement, in the U.S. central bank. The system has four main elements: (1) the Board of Governors, which has its headquarters in Washington; (2) the Federal Open Market Committee; (3) twelve Federal Reserve banks, together with their 25 branches and other facilities located throughout the United States; and (4) all of the member commercial banks, including all national banks and those state-chartered banks that have elected to join the system (see Figure 16.4).

---

[21] Edward R. Tufte, *Political Control of the Economy* (Princeton, N.J.: Princeton University Press, 1978), pp. 26–27.

[22] Ibid., pp. 12, 27.

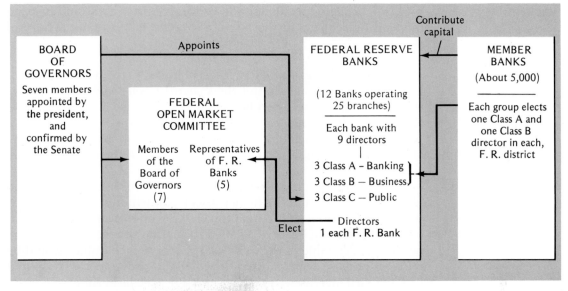

Figure 16.4
Organization of the Federal Reserve System

Source; Board of Governors, *The Federal Reserve System*, Organizational Chart, 1985; *United States Government Manual, 1987–88*, pp. 563–67.

Board of Governors

The Boards of Governors. The **Board of Governors** is at the apex of the system. Its seven members are appointed for long (14-year) staggered terms, to insulate them from political pressure. Terms of board members are also so arranged that one expires every two years, which means that no president, even if he served eight years in office, could appoint more than four members. These provisions prevent a president from exerting the kind of control over the Federal Reserve that he can over the Cabinet departments. The chairman and vice chairman of the Federal Reserve Board are named by the president for four-year terms. The position of chairman—occupied by Paul Volcker from August 1979 through August 1987 and by Alan Greenspan since then—has become enormously influential in policy making.

The discount rate

The Board of Governors and its chairman have broad policy-making and supervisory authority. They establish the reserve requirements for member banks, which help determine how much money the latter will have available for loans and thus expand or contract available credit. They review and approach **discount-rate** actions of the Federal Reserve banks. The discount rate is the rate of interest charged to member banks when they borrow from the Reserve banks. The higher the discount rate, the higher the interest rates banks will have to charge their customers for home mortgages, car loans, and the like. In addition, the Board of Governors conducts examinations of the Federal Reserve banks, requires reports from them, supervises the issue and retirement of Federal Reserve notes (the nation's paper money), and exercises jurisdiction over the admission of state banks into the Federal Reserve System. If the board finds malperformance or illegal behavior, it can issue "cease and desist orders" and suspend member banks from further use of the credit facilities of the Federal Reserve.

Federal Open-Market Committee. Closely linked to the work of the Federal Reserve Board is that of the **Federal Open-Market Committee** (FOMC). Each of the seven board members is also a member of the FOMC, which includes, as well, five representatives of the Reserve banks (elected annually). The "open-market operations" are the prime vehicles used by the Fed to determine the size of the nation's money supply.

The basic rules in money-supply regulation are simple enough. Too rapid an expansion of the money supply contributes to an overheating of the economy and to inflation. To take an extreme hypothetical case, if the Federal Reserve doubled the nation's money supply in the next year, the value of each monetary unit, of each dollar, would be reduced, because such an expansion would not be supported by actual productivity increases. On the other hand, if Federal Reserve restrictions on the growth of the money supply are too tight, demand is curbed and the economy is put into recession. The task of the FOMC interventions is to avoid these extremes.

This is easier said than done. Regulating the money supply of the United States is enormously complicated. There is no general agreement on how the money supply is understood and calculated, given current economic realities. Gone are the days when money was simply the coins or paper currency people carried in their pockets. Today, the majority of "money" takes the form of electronic bytes of information within the computers of financial institutions: the balances of various personal and business accounts. When the Federal Reserve acts to increase the money supply, it does not literally run the printing presses and produce more pieces of paper currency. Rather, it does things such as buy back government securities—for example, bonds that the federal government issued to help finance the national debt. When the Fed buys back bonds, it pays for them by checks drawn on its accounts, and these checks are in turn deposited into various bank accounts around the country. The money supply is thus increased because these banks can lend more money.

The Federal Reserve banks. The Federal Reserve Board and the FOMC are agencies of the federal government. This is not the case for the twelve **Federal Reserve banks** and their branches, often called "quasi-public" banks, for they reflect an interesting blend of private ownership and public control. Each Reserve bank is owned by the member commercial banks in its district. Upon joining the Federal Reserve System, commercial banks are required to purchase shares of stock in the Reserve bank that serves this area. Reserve banks are incorporated institutions with their own boards of directors. But despite their private ownership, Reserve banks are fundamentally public institutions. They are not motivated by profits as private businesses must be. All of their earnings, after operating expenses have been met, are paid into the U.S. Treasury. These central banks are supposed to promote the growth and well-being of the economy as a whole.

The Reserve banks are sometimes referred to as "bankers' banks," meaning that they perform functions for commercial banks much as the latter do for the general public. Just as commercial banks receive deposits from the public and make loans to the public, so the Reserve banks receive deposits and extend loans to commercial banks. The Reserve banks also have a third main function that commercial banks no longer perform (although they once did): issuing currency. Congress has provided that the Reserve banks alone put into circulation the country's paper money. Look at a one-dollar bill; right above the portrait of Washington you will see imprinted "Federal Reserve Note."

Political pressures on the Fed. Monetary policy is critically important, and the Federal Reserve makes it. This puts the Fed in a political storm center. For example, if the Fed has been restricting the growth of the money supply in an effort to check inflation, the demand for available money is likely to be very high. This means interest rates are likely to be high. If home mortgages are at annual rates of 17 percent interest, and automobile loans are at 14 percent, large numbers of people who need such loans to make their purchases are not going to be able to afford them. The housing and automobile industries are especially vulnerable to high interest rates, so naturally they press for lower rates. An attempt was made to insulate the Fed from such pressures, which was partly successful. But only partly so. No institution like the Federal Reserve can operate in a democratic nation in disregard of the policy demands made on it.

Given the pressure, the position of the president and his administration becomes critical. When the president strongly backs the Fed in its current approach to monetary policy, this usually gives it enough support to persist. Without the president's backing, however, the Fed is terribly vulnerable, given the other pressures almost certain to be placed on it. Thus we have a situation where, in formal institutional terms, the Fed is separate from the president and his administration but where, in a practical sense, it is sensitive to the suggestions for monetary policy that emanate from the White House. The president and the Federal Reserve need each other. The Fed needs the president's political backing and sustenance. And the monetary policies that the Fed conducts are extremely important to national economic performance, on which the success of any administration hinges.

Signals coming from the president in the first years of his term are much more likely to encourage the Federal Reserve to pursue a restrictive, inflation-checking approach to currency expansion than those received in the months preceding the next presidential election.

Margin notes:

"Bankers' banks"

The executive branch and the Federal Reserve

No party wants to run for re-election in an economic environment where productivity is down and unemployment up. Signals sent to the Fed from the White House, when thoughts there turn to the next presidential election, have tended to encourage the expansion of the money supply.[23] This may be changing. The nation's experience with high inflation during the 1970s has produced a climate of great sensitivity about anything that looks as though it might encourage a renewal of inflation.

The Council of Economic Advisers

Recognizing the president's need for more economic expertise in the White House, the Employment Act of 1946 established the **Council of Economic Advisers** (CEA). The council consists of three members appointed by the president, with confirmation by the Senate. The president designates one of the three as chairman. For the last three decades, the chairman of the CEA has been a key figure in federal economic policy. He is one of a small group of high-level economic officials who interact regularly with the president, advising him on what economic issues need his attention and what his options are. Other members of this informal economic policy committee are the secretary of the Treasury and the director of the Office of Management and Budget (OMB). The Council of Economic Advisers does not make and execute policy; rather, it advises the president.[24]

The Treasury Department

Established in 1789, the **Treasury Department** is one of the original executive departments. Today it is by far the most influential Cabinet department in economic policy. The Treasury is in the middle of economic planning and policy management. Its secretary serves with the head of the OMB and the chairman of the Council of Economic Advisers in what has developed over successive administrations to be an informal economic central committee. One of the secretary's principal associates, the undersecretary for monetary affairs, is the administration's chief liaison person with the Federal Reserve Board of Governors and the FOMC. The government's agency for tax administration, the Internal Revenue Service, is located within the Treasury Department. So, too, is the Office of the Comptroller of the Currency; the comptroller shares with the Federal Reserve broad responsibilities for supervising and regulating commercial banks.

[23] Robert J. Shapiro, "Politics and the Federal Reserve," *The Public Interest*, Winter 1982, p. 119.
[24] For a thoughtful discussion of the advisory responsibilities of the Council of Economic Advisers, and its interaction with other units of the executive branch, see Herbert Stein, "The Chief Executive as Chief Economist," in William Fellner, ed., *Essays in Contemporary Economic Problems* (Washington, D.C.: American Enterprise Institute, 1981), pp. 53–78.

Office of Management and Budget

Office of Management
and Budget

Located in the Executive Office of the President, the **Office of Management and Budget** (OMB) was established in 1970 as a successor to the old Bureau of the Budget. Among its various activities, the OMB assists the president in preparing the budget he submits each year to Congress and, more generally, in formulating a fiscal program for the U.S. government. It is also responsible for overseeing executive branch expenditures.

The OMB was created on the premise that the executive budget cannot be left to the separate acts of the various departments and agencies. It is concerned with the budget's overall impact. It adjusts the "wish lists" of all the executive agencies, producing a reasonably unified budget that reflects at least in part an administration's fiscal policy judgments and objectives. It then presents this budget before Congress. In the Reagan administration, OMB directors David Stockman (1981–85) and his successor, James C. Miller III, played major economic policy roles. After the November 1988 election, President-elect George Bush picked former White House aide and Treasury Deputy Secretary Richard Darman for this key post.

SUMMARY

Political economy involves the uses of governmental power to effect economic goals. The areas of economic policies attempted by American government include *regulation* of the private economy; controls over the supply of money and credit, which is the field of *monetary policy;* and efforts to adjust levels of taxation and expenditures, which is *fiscal policy.* In 1986, with the passage of the Tax Reform Act, the United States decided upon a substantial shift of fiscal policy that involves dramatically lower marginal tax rates coupled with a broader tax base.

Committed to the general ideal of a growing private-property-based, individual-serving economy, Americans have not engaged much in debates over basic ends; questions of what are the best means, of *"how to do it,"* have predominated. Prompted by the conditions of the Great Depression, leaders and citizens alike swung to a new view of what arrangements of the political economy would best effectuate growing prosperity. A much-expanded role for government figured prominently in the new perspective. *John Maynard Keynes,* a distinguished English economist, offered prescriptions that proved enormously influential and that, in the incomplete and imperfect way of democratic politics, came to underlay the claim of the Democrats as the "party of prosperity."

By the late 1960s, however, a new set of economic conditions had begun to disrupt the Keynesian view of the world. *Inflation* had replaced *deflation* as the predominant challenge to sustained economic prosperity. Excessive growth of government and excessive governmental intervention in economic life—as in the area of *regulation*—appeared to require new responses. The mainstream of economic thinking shifted. This shift is evident in the work of professional economists and, as well, in the outlook and expectations of the general public. In this new environment, Republicans and Democrats find themselves in a contest to claim the title of "party of prosperity" that had been won by the Democrats in the New Deal era.

Shifts in the economy and in thinking about how it is best managed are now reflected in the debates among five schools of professional economic opinion. *Monetarists* put a singular emphasis on controlling the money supply and the price of money (interest rates) to secure a growing, inflation-free economy. *Supply-siders* emphasize the importance of fiscal policy, especially the stimulation of work incentives and economic growth through large cuts in the marginal tax rates: what proportion taxpayers give the government of the last dollars they earn. *"Mainstream"* conservatives stress balanced budgets and restraints on federal spending.

Advocates of *industrial policy* share the traditional liberal view that a large measure of governmental intervention in the economy is desirable; but they want government to pursue new means of stimulating economic growth, borrowing on the successes Japan has had. *Keynesians* continue to emphasize fiscal policy answers to achieve the economic expansion that can sustain an enlargement of social welfare programs.

Among the governmental agencies that play key roles in formulating and executing economic policy, the *Federal Reserve System* is especially important. The Fed is the central bank of the United States. Its *Federal Open Market Committee* is charged with taking actions that determine the size and rate of expansion of the nation's money supply.

FOR FURTHER STUDY

John Maynard Keynes, *The General Theory of Employment, Interest, and Money* (New York: Harcourt, Brace, 1965; first published 1936). The enormously influential study that provided the intellectual underpinnings for an expanded governmental role in economic life in the United States and other democracies in the years following the Great Depression.

Michael Pertschuk, *Revolt Against Regulation* (Berkeley, CA: University of California Press, 1982). A fascinating analysis of the development of policies involving governmental regulation of the economy, and how these policies have changed.

Edward R. Tufte, *Political Control of the Economy* (Princeton, NJ: Princeton University Press, 1978). An analysis arguing that American politicians have sought repeatedly to manipulate the economy to their electoral advantage.

Economic Indicators, prepared for the Joint Economic Committee of Congress by the Council of Economic Advisers (Washington, DC: U.S. Government Printing Office, published monthly). Contains the latest monthly statistics on the gross national product, national income, personal consumption, corporate profits; employment and wages, industrial production, and business activities; prices; money, credit, and security markets; federal finance, international finance, and business transactions.

Executive Office of the President, Office of Management and Budget (OMB), *Budget of the United States Government* (latest fiscal year) (Washington, DC: U.S. Government Printing Office). Appearing in about six volumes annually, these documents contain the yearly budget message of the president to Congress, with summary and detailed tables setting forth the administration's budget proposals for the entire federal government for the next fiscal year.

Chapter 17

Public Welfare

Welfare policies are often understood as those that assist the poor. Some welfare programs are indeed for that purpose, and we will be examining them later in this chapter. But the idea of public welfare is broader than just helping the needy, and the U.S. government now operates a great variety of programs designed to enhance the well-being of groups throughout the population. *Farm assistance* programs provide a good example of the reach of contemporary efforts in using government to improve the public welfare—and of the difficulty often encountered by these programs in achieving their intended objectives.

The U.S. Department of Agriculture (USDA) might well be considered the first welfare agency of the federal government. Over the century and a quarter since its creation in 1862, the Department of Agriculture has helped develop and has administered many programs to improve rural life, agricultural production, and farm prosperity. Through its farm extension services, USDA has been the prime disseminator of information on scientific agriculture—such as how to improve crop yields and the productivity of farm animals. Its Rural Electrification Administration has provided rural electric utilities with financing needed to bring electricity into sparsely settled areas, where the per household costs would have been prohibitive without government help. USDA programs are seen as affecting broad national interests. For example, the loans that the USDA makes to farm and ranch owners for soil and water conservation contribute to clear national objectives. In general, farm prosperity is seen tied closely to national prosperity. Still, farmers are the immediate beneficiaries of USDA programs. The drought relief provided to farmers in 1988 is another example of the importance to the farm community of these federal welfare efforts.

Farm subsidies. The most expensive, and controversial, farm assistance programs have been those established to help farmers receive what is considered a fair price for their crops. Farming has long been subject to alternating periods of boom and bust. In years of high output of crops like wheat and corn, flooded markets have often responded with declines in commodity prices so great that the return to farmers does not even cover their expenses—such as meeting their payments on loans taken out to buy costly farm machinery. Over the last fifty years many different assistance programs have been implemented to try to solve these problems. These include the payment to farmers of government subsidies that make up the difference between the market prices for certain crops and what is considered a fair return; and mandatory production controls in which individual farmers are given limits on the number of acres they can plant of a particular crop, and in turn are granted subsidies that compensate them for not planting, according to a specific formula.

The 1985 farm law. In the 1980s, reflecting both Reagan administration views and a general shift of philosophy among farm experts, mandatory crop controls have been out of favor. Market forces, not USDA regulations, should determine what farmers produce. Agricultural prosperity should be attained by having American farmers compete effectively in selling their immense production on the national and world markets.

These objectives have been hard to meet, however, in large part due to an enormous increase in farm production around the world—an increase to which agricultural science in the United States has contributed greatly. American farmers have faced growing competition from producers abroad. As a result, exports of farm commodities dropped from $43.8 billion in 1981 to $31.5 billion in 1984, to just $24.3 billion in 1987. As their exports have fallen, farmers have faced strong pressure from imported commodities, with the result that the once-large U.S. balance of farm exports over imports has shrunk, from a $26.6 billion surplus in 1981 to 0—no surplus of exports over imports at all—in May 1987. "Something is radically wrong when the greatest food producer in the world is buying more agricultural commodities than it is selling," Senate Republican Leader Robert Dole (Kansas) told President Reagan in June 1986, in warning him that political pressure was building for new action.

Major sections of the 1985 farm bill were designed to try to address this problem in the long run by changing the way the government underwrites the prices farmers receive for some key crops. The bill allowed the administration to reduce drastically government price guarantees to farmers on various crops, in the hope that U.S. commodity prices would fall to a level more competitive with foreign crops. The guarantees are in the form of government loans to farmers producing wheat, corn, soybeans, rice, and cotton. Under the law,

Falling exports, rising imports

Farm price guarantees

The productivity of American agriculture has long been a source of pride, but it has also been a source of problems as farm production has exceeded market demand.

farmers can forfeit their crops to the government rather than sell at a price below the loan rate—which means that the loan price effectively becomes the domestic market price.

Again, things did not work out as planned. Under the 1985 farm law, the secretary of agriculture cut the loan rate for 1986 on wheat to $2.40 a bushel from its 1985 rate of $3.30—a 30 percent reduction. But world wheat prices remain substantially lower than even the new U.S. price floors, which means that many farmers found it more profitable to default on their loans—in effect, selling their crops to the USDA—than selling to private buyers. The result: U.S. exports were not encouraged; the U.S. government was left to store more wheat than it knew what to do with (although this surplus proved a boon in 1988 when the drought cut sharply into grain production); and the costs of farm subsidies skyrocketed. A record $26 billion was expended on the subsidies in FY 1986, up from the $16.6 billion that was estimated when the farm bill was enacted just a year earlier.

Results of the 1985 bill

What we have seen in this brief review of farm assistance programs is common to many other welfare efforts. Government assistance is provided to a group to enhance their immediate well-being and to contribute to large national interests. The objectives are worthy but accomplishing them proves exceedingly hard. Programs often have many unforeseen or unintended consequences. Experimentation goes on with new approaches, in hopes of finding a better means of attaining the desired results, in a world where economic complexities and other factors just don't cooperate.

Public Opinion and Welfare

We have noted that some welfare programs are designed to help the needy, but that others are seen helping the great majority of citizens or have beneficiaries, like farmers, who are not designated primarily because they are poor. The politics of these two broad sectors of welfare programs are different.

Public opinion and welfare

Even when we look only at the first sector, however, we encounter confusion as to what the public thinks and expects. Americans in recent years are supposed to have been in an antigovernment mood, frustrated by the rising costs of welfare programs for the needy. Public opinion polls have shown repeatedly that large majorities resent the growth of "welfare." At the same time, though, equally large majorities have declared themselves firmly committed to increasing governmental efforts to "help the poor." Cut "welfare"—but do more to aid the poor.

For example, the University of Chicago's National Opinion Research Center (NORC) has periodically asked some of its respondents whether they think we are spending too much, too little, or about the right amount on "welfare," and asked other respondents with the same general characteristics the same question about "assistance to the poor." See how differently people answered, depending on which of these two wordings were used.[1]

	"Welfare"	"Assistance to the poor"
Too much	43%	9%
Too little	22%	65%
About right	34%	25%

These polls capture a fundamental contradiction in popular beliefs and expectations. Over the last half-century, the American public has shown itself troubled by much of what "welfare" has come to connote, but at the same time it is committed to governmental help for those in need. This is not a minor semantic distinction but rather a matter of deep-seated philosophy.

THE AMERICAN APPROACH TO WELFARE

Increased spending for public welfare

As nations become wealthier and thus better able to finance welfare programs, these programs increase. In every Western democracy in this century, government's role in welfare has steadily expanded (as indicated by major real increases in public-welfare spending). Expenditures for welfare programs were low when the absolute need for such programs was greatest—and have reached their highest historic levels precisely when absolute need is the least severe. This does not diminish the importance of current efforts or the need for spending; but welfare spending is in significant measure "the art of the possible."

To take just one example, total social-welfare expenditures by local, state, and federal governments in the United States were $6.5 billion

[1] These data are from the 1986 and 1987 General Social Surveys, conducted by the National Opinion Research Center.

in 1935, in the face of overwhelming need resulting from the Great Depression. This averaged about $51 per person. In contrast, total public welfare spending in 1985 was roughly $729 billion, or approximately $3,050 per capita. Even when the effects of inflation are taken into account, the increase is enormous. It has resulted not so much from the efforts of individual political leaders and parties as from the changing capacities and expectations made possible by modern industrial development. Other countries show the same progression, starting from different bases.

Two Approaches to Welfare

Despite similarities, each country approaches welfare issues in its own distinctive manner, reflecting its history and values. Two hypothetical contrasting national philosophies on welfare policy help us see the range and importance of these variations.

Country A has long shown a strong preference for a collectivist rather than individualistic approach. The majority of its citizens concluded from their country's historical experience that individual efforts were insufficient in the absence of major governmental efforts to extend economic security and well-being. Centralized governmental welfare programs in health, unemployment insurance, and pensions for the aged were developed in the late nineteenth century and, with strong public backing, were expanded in the twentieth century. The public sees governmental intervention as a desirable response to community needs. National values also strongly support governmental efforts to reduce economic inequality: redistributing wealth through progressive taxation and public-benefits programs.

Country B prefers an individualistic approach. Its public has concluded from national experience that great opportunities for advancement are present if individual effort is made to realize them. The public strongly backs equality of opportunity. But it rejects equality of result—where government redistributes income and other values to minimize differences in socioeconomic status. It finds governmental intervention often more problem-causing than helpful. It wants to see individual citizens given the widest freedom to make their own way and to enjoy what they earn.

Few observers would confuse the United States with the model of Country A. As we noted elsewhere (especially chapter 3), American political ideology enshrined many of the central assumptions of classical liberalism, and it is notably attentive to assertions of individual rights and interests. Political philosophies representing collectivist goals have foundered on America's singular individualism. Citizens believe that their society gives unusual opportunities to the individual and have been less inclined than their counterparts in many other countries to back collective action through the state. The American idea of equality aims at equal opportunity, not equal results.

The American approach

Still, it would be a mistake to see the United States as a pure embodiment of Country B. Americans have not been hostile to government. Two types of governmental action in the welfare area have found fertile soil in the United States: (1) to provide a general climate where individual interests and pursuits can be more fully realized; and (2) to help people who through no lack of effort find themselves in need. Modern United States welfare policies have been shaped by the public's insistence that the policies extend social and political individualism rather than restrict it.

"Helping the Poor" versus "Welfare"

Equality of opportunity

What about the distinction the polls show? As noted, Americans back governmental efforts to help the needy but are uncomfortable with "welfare." American egalitarianism stresses giving individuals an equal opportunity to compete. We back the claims of deserving individuals who find themselves in need: the ill, the elderly, those unable to find work, children whose families cannot provide for them. We support job-training programs, programs that extend access to college education through government grants and loans, and more.

Emphasis on individual effort

What about individuals who are able-bodied but unwilling to make the effort to support themselves and their families? An ideology that emphasizes individual responsibility, and insists that American society offers unusual opportunities to those who try, is much less sympathetic. "The opportunity is there; I make the effort; you should too if you are not too old, too young, or too infirm." Many Americans, sympathetic to programs that extend opportunity to those whom they see as the deserving poor, are unhappy about "welfare." In the informal shorthand of American politics, "welfare" has come to connote the avoidance of individual responsibility and effort.

Belief in the importance of individual effort depends, of course, on the belief that society offers great opportunities for advancement to those willing and able to work for it. Asked in a 1986 survey whether they believe it is true that in the United States "if you work hard, eventually you will get ahead?," 73 percent said they thought work is so rewarded, only 27 percent that it is not.[2] Majorities of the lowest income groups as well as of the highest gave this assessment.

American ambivalence about welfare. Americans believe that government should help the deserving poor, but able individuals should help themselves. They also believe that existing welfare programs reach large numbers who really need them but are, at the same time, exploited by those unwilling to do what they can for themselves. This mix of values and assessments generates ambivalence about the practical operations of welfare programs. Eighty-five percent of those

[2] Poll by ABC News / *Washington Post*, September 2–8, 1986.

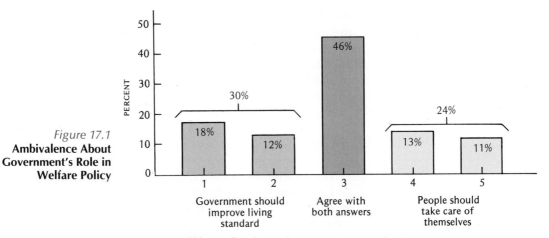

Figure 17.1
Ambivalence About Government's Role in Welfare Policy

Question: "I'd like to talk with you about issues some people tell us are important. Some people think that the government in Washington should do everything possible to improve the standard of living of all poor Americans; they are at Point 1. Other people think it is not the government's responsibility, and that each person should take care of himself; they are at Point 5." Where would you place yourself on this scale, or haven't you made up your mind on this?"
Source: Survey by National Opinion Research Center, General Social Survey, Spring, 1987.

interviewed in the National Opinion Research Center's General Social Survey in 1986 agreed with the criticism of welfare that it encourages people to work less; but 84 percent agreed with the defense of welfare that it helps people overcome difficult times. In a question posed by interviewers from NORC in the spring of 1987, respondents were asked to locate themselves on a five-point scale (Figure 17.1). By picking point 1, a respondent was indicating strong agreement that "the government in Washington should do everything possible to improve the standard of living of all poor Americans"; by selecting point 5, he was agreeing strongly that "it is not the government's responsibility and each person should take care of himself." The midpoint on the scale was identified as "I agree with both answers." By far the largest proportion—46 percent of all respondents—put themselves at the midpoint. The contradiction here results from the pull of contending social and political values.

Americans have tried to reconcile these contrasting perspectives. One result is the judgment that welfare programs should require those

Workfare and in-kind benefits

able to work to do so, as a condition for receiving public assistance; this is sometimes called "workfare." Whenever administrators have sought to implement such a rule, they have encountered serious practical difficulties. Jobs that able-bodied welfare recipients are trained to perform may not be available in significant numbers, in the right geographic areas. But Americans continue to endorse this requirement. Another response is to provide *in-kind benefits* rather than cash payments. People in need are given government-supported medical care, subsidized housing, and food stamps rather than simply bigger welfare checks. The idea is that need will be more directly targeted, and recipients will be less likely to be discouraged from learning to help themselves. In 1980, local, state, and national governments in the United States expended $61.3 billion in means-tested welfare benefits: benefits available only to persons meeting certain standards of financial need. Of this total, $42.4 billion were in-kind, while only $18.9 billion were cash payments.[3]

Extending Individual Security and Opportunity

The strong commitments in American ideology to individual responsibility, and equality of opportunity rather than results, have slowed the development of the "welfare state" here. When the U.S. Congress first passed comprehensive Social Security legislation in 1935, most European countries had long since enacted similar programs: Germany in 1889, England in 1908, and Sweden in 1913. And throughout the twentieth century, U.S. governmental expenditures for public-welfare programs have been a significantly smaller proportion of the country's GNP than comparable programs have been of the GNPs of the European democracies. Despite this overall experience, in some areas American spending for public welfare is proportionally greater than in Europe. Education is a case in point.

Education. In the latter half of the nineteenth century, primary and secondary education became free, public, and virtually universal in the United States—long before it was thus extended in any other country. Government-assisted mass higher education also came sooner to the United States; today a higher proportion of Americans are enrolled in colleges and universities, many with substantial government assistance, than in other wealthy nations such as West Germany, France, Britain, or Japan. America's educational expenditures, on a per capita basis, have consistently surpassed those of other industrial nations.

Is education a public-welfare program? It is closely linked to the idea of public welfare. Through public schools the authority and resources of government are used to make generally available a resource considered essential to personal opportunity and national well-being. Why are Americans less inclined than citizens of other industrial nations to support many governmental welfare initiatives, yet so supportive of programs in education? Public education historically has been an attractive value in the United States because of its close link to individual opportunity. Through access to education, people obtain the means of developing their talents and moving ahead

Education and public welfare

[3]Timothy M. Smeeding, "Alternate Methods for Valuing Selected In-Kind Transfer Benefits and Measuring Their Effect on Poverty," *Technical Paper* 50 (Washington, D.C.: U.S. Bureau of the Census, 1982), p. 2.

socially and economically. Public spending for education extends the opportunity for individual initiative.

Social Security. During the 1930s, partly as a result of the Great Depression and partly as a more gradual response to new needs attendant upon industrialization and urbanization, many Americans came to feel that expanded governmental welfare efforts were needed and would complement individual efforts. Passage of the Social Security Act in 1935, with such key provisions as Old Age and Survivors Insurance, and Unemployment Compensation, became possible as a result of this shift in public thinking. When Gallup asked a cross-section of Americans nationally in November 1936 whether they favored "the compulsory Old Age Insurance plan, starting in January, which requires employers and workers to make equal contributions to worker's pensions?", 68 percent said they did.[4] From this high base, support grew rapidly.

Continuing public support for Social Security

In recent years, Social Security taxes have risen dramatically, because benefit levels have been raised and the proportion of currently employed workers paying into the system has declined relative to the proportion currently drawing benefits. In light of this, questions have been raised as to whether public support might erode. But it has not. The increases in Social Security benefits have been substantial, but few Americans describe them as too high. What is even more striking, given the sharp rise in employee payroll taxes for the program, is that most people do not claim that Social Security taxes are too high. During the debate in the early 1980s over what changes should be made to solve the growing financial problems of the Social Security system, polls repeatedly asked the public which way they wanted to go to bring receipts and expenditures into balance: raising taxes or reducing benefits. The response was always the same: If a choice must be made, raise taxes rather than cut benefits.

Recently, Americans by margins of roughly 3 to 1 have said they opposed reducing the cost-of-living adjustments for Social Security recipients to lower the federal budget deficits (Figure 17.2).

Social Security versus "welfare"

These responses attest to the prophetic character of President Franklin Roosevelt's observations at the time Social Security was enacted. Responding to the argument that the Social Security tax was relatively regressive compared to the graduated income tax, because many working-class families paid in the same amount as those in high-income brackets, the president observed:

> I guess you're right on the economics, but those taxes [payroll deductions] were never a problem of economics. They are politics all the way through. We put those payroll contributions there so as to give the con-

[4]Michael E. Schiltz, "Public Attitudes toward Social Security, 1935–1965," *Research Report 33* of the Social Security Administration (Washington, D.C.: U.S. Government Printing Office, 1970), p. 18.

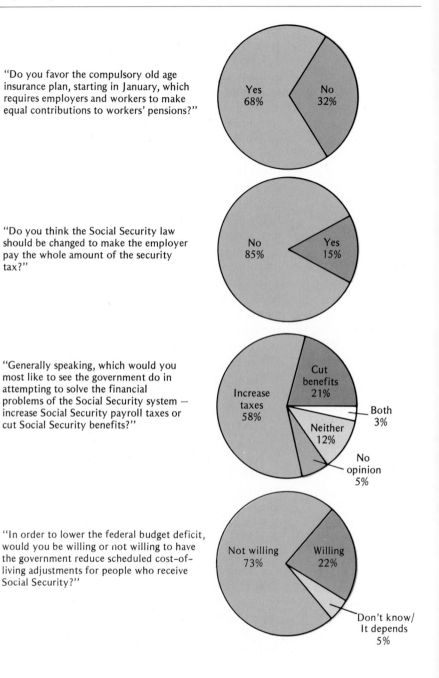

"Do you favor the compulsory old age insurance plan, starting in January, which requires employers and workers to make equal contributions to workers' pensions?"

Yes 68%
No 32%

"Do you think the Social Security law should be changed to make the employer pay the whole amount of the security tax?"

No 85%
Yes 15%

"Generally speaking, which would you most like to see the government do in attempting to solve the financial problems of the Social Security system — increase Social Security payroll taxes or cut Social Security benefits?"

Increase taxes 58%
Cut benefits 21%
Both 3%
Neither 12%
No opinion 5%

"In order to lower the federal budget deficit, would you be willing or not willing to have the government reduce scheduled cost-of-living adjustments for people who receive Social Security?"

Not willing 73%
Willing 22%
Don't know/ It depends 5%

Figure 17.2
Public Attitudes toward Social Security

Source: 1936: Survey by the Gallup Organization, November 6–11, 1936. *1938:* Survey by the Gallup Organization, December 30, 1937—January 4, 1938. *1983:* Survey by ABC News / *Washington Post,* January 18–22, 1983. *1987:* Survey by CBS News / *New York Times,* November 20–24, 1987.

tributors a legal, moral, and political right to collect their pensions and their unemployment benefits. With those taxes in there, no damn politician can ever scrap my Social Security program.[5]

Social Security was not "welfare." Its benefits were to be bought and paid for by individuals to provide for their economic security and well-being.

Social Security has never operated like a private annuity or pension program, where the benefits derived are a direct function of contributions made; but Roosevelt's initial idea of setting the system up on the theme of individuals' earning future benefits through regular payroll deductions was a shrewd reading of American values. Workers *wanted* to "pay their share." In 1938 Gallup asked whether the Social Security law should be changed so that *employers* pay the whole amount. The idea might have seemed attractive; the prestige of American business was low after the Great Depression, and what workers would not want to be freed from having to make payments and have employers foot the whole bill? But only 15 percent of those surveyed favored changing the law to eliminate the tax on individual workers.

Social Security is now a broadly supported program for which most Americans are prepared to make sacrifices (in the form of higher payroll taxes) so that a rise in benefits can be sustained. It is seen as essential in providing a measure of security for individuals, such that they can look forward to a retirement income at least sufficient for a basic standard of living. The health-care components of Social Security, added in the 1960s as medical benefits for the elderly (Medicare) and the needy (Medicaid), have found the same high measure of public backing that the Old Age Pension and Assistance programs attained earlier. The possibility of being denied adequate health care because one lacked the money to pay for it, or of finding one's retirement savings wiped out through catastrophic illness, seems incompatible with the sense most Americans now have of their needs and entitlements.

Support for Social Security's health-care programs

Minority versus Majority Welfare

Public welfare connotes two different kinds of programs: (1) means-tested programs, such as Aid for Families with Dependent Children (AFDC) and Medicaid, targeted to help the poor; and (2) those for which no means tests are applied, like the Old Age, Survivors', and Disability Insurance (OASDI) and the Medicare components of Social Security, which in effect apply to the entire population.

At first glance, the politics of these two components of welfare would seem to be entirely different. In the first case, a majority who are not poor are asked to assist a minority who are. The majority pay, but

[5] Quoted in Arthur M. Schlesinger, Jr., *The Coming of the New Deal* (Boston: Houghton Mifflin, 1958), pp. 308–9.

only a distinct minority of the total population draw direct material benefits. In contrast, the second set of welfare programs, like OASDI and Medicare (and public education), ask the majority to support measures to help themselves. All who contribute to OASDI can expect to collect benefits. We might expect the latter programs to have easier sledding politically than the first set.

This is not the case. While spending for welfare programs for the benefit of the majority of the population has expanded greatly over the last twenty years, the *rate of increase* of all means-tested benefits has been as great. There has been much discussion about the impact of Reagan-administration policy changes on this relationship, and some argue that recent cuts have fallen disproportionately on the poor. From the early 1960s through the early 1980s, though, the contrasting political dynamics of majoritarian and minoritarian beneficiary programs did not produce less growth among the latter. We will review data pertinent to this issue in greater detail below. One reason is that U.S. public opinion tends to apply one set of standards to both sectors. If a program is seen to enlarge the opportunity for constructive individualism, it gets support. This is true of programs to help the "deserving poor" as well as those conferring benefits on the many. The decisive consideration often seems to be whether a program squares with the country's special mix of liberal individualism—a standard not inherently stacked against persons in economic need.

Federalism and Public Welfare

Another distinctive aspect of the American approach to welfare policy involves the extent to which states and municipalities participate in financing and managing welfare programs. Federalism is enormously important in the American welfare system. Prior to the Great Depression, the national government had a modest role in public welfare; veterans' benefits were the one big program. But when the nationwide depression crisis brought Washington into the welfare picture in a big way, nationally inspired and funded programs were frequently grafted onto an existing system of state-centered management. A few key public-welfare programs are funded and administered exclusively through national agencies—notably, OASDI and Medicare—but many of the most important programs are federal-state partnerships: Medicaid, AFDC, Food Stamps, and Unemployment Compensation. Public-welfare programs throughout much of Europe are run by national agencies with centralized standards and uniform benefits, but the American programs are often decentralized and vary substantially from state to state.

Aid to Families with Dependent Children is a case in point. AFDC is a means-tested program developed to provide assistance for children whose parents are unable to provide properly for them. In 1950 it was

The food stamp program is a joint federal and state venture, funded largely by the federal government.

Aid to Families with Dependent Children

expanded to give support to adults in such families, as well as to their dependent children. Today, a large proportion of AFDC recipient families are female-headed: the father either is not present or is not providing support. AFDC is administered at the state level, subject to some federal regulations, with funding provided jointly by Washington and the states. There are large variations in benefits from one state to another. Individual states have the authority to set benefit levels, and they have made different choices. The average monthly payment per family in 1985 ranged from $514 in California to just $104 in Mississippi. Whether such differences should be permitted, or, instead, uniform benefits provided across the country has been hotly debated. AFDC is an extreme case. In other programs, such as Food Stamps, national benefit levels *have* been applied.

WELFARE PROGRAMS AND POLICIES

Welfare programs in which the federal government participates may be distinguished by several different dimensions: (1) whether benefits are targeted just to the poor or to the general population; (2) whether programs are run exclusively by the national government or have state participation; (3) among the latter, whether the state role extends to financing the program, administering it, or both. Table 17.1 pro-

Table 17.1

Major Public-Welfare Programs

Program and program costs (1988)	Key legislation	Tax source	Funding	Administration	Function
1. Old Age, Survivors, and Disability Insurance (OASDI); $219.7 billion	Social Security Act of 1935, extensively amended	Payroll tax with shares paid by employers and employees.	Federal; trust funds set up in U.S. Treasury.	Federal: HHS/Social Security Adm.	National pension system for the retired, the bereaved, the orphaned, and the disabled.
2. Federal Supplemental Security Income (SSI); $12.6 billion	Social Security Amendments of 1972	General revenue	Federal; states are "encouraged to provide optional supplements."	Federal: Social Security Adm.	Assistance to the aged poor. Need, the sole criterion, is established by a means test.
3. Medicare; $78.8 billion	Social Security Amendments of 1965	For part A of program, basic health insurance: payroll tax, shares paid by employers and employees. For part B, supplementary medical care, general revenue and premiums paid by beneficiaries.	(Part A) Federal: Hospital insurance trust fund is repository for payroll tax revenues. (Part B) Federal and client funded.	Federal: HHS/Health Care Financing Adm.	Health insurance for the aged. (Part A) Basic inpatient hospital services, and post-hospital care for persons 65 and older. (Part B) Payments of 80% of patient's costs for physicians and various medical specialists, regardless of where services are performed.
4. Medicaid; $54.8 billion	Social Security Amendments of 1965	General revenue	Federal matching grants provided to states according to state per-capita income.	Federal and state. Federal: HHS/Health Care Financing Adm. State: basic provider of health care—according to federal standards—to those who qualify. State may set ceiling on benefits and may exercise options on choice of physicians and facilities.	Health care to the poor through payments to health-care providers—hospitals, doctors, nursing facilities, rural health clinics.
5. Aid to Families with Dependent Children (AFDC); $17.5 billion	Social Security Act of 1935, amended over 100 times	General revenue	Federal government reimburses states for about half of	State. Set criteria for eligibility and benefit level "within broad	Financial assistance for poor families, pegged to the care of dependent

6. Food Stamp Program; $13.4 billion	Food Stamp Act of 1964	General revenue	Federal, except for state share of administrative expenses.	Jointly federal, state, and local. *Federal:* USDA/Consumer Services, Family Nutrition program. *State and local:* welfare agencies.	"Help lower-income Americans maintain a nutritious diet."
7. Unemployment Compensation; $15.8 billion	Social Security Act of 1935; extensively amended	Payroll tax on employers	State tax on employers funds regular benefits; state and federal taxes (in equal portions) on employers funds extended benefits.	Federal by U.S. Employment and Training Adm. (Dept. of Labor), and state by employment security agency of each state. Each state administers its Unemployment Compensation program according to a "certified state plan." States provide benefits schedule (benefit ceilings, duration, etc.), following federal guidelines. States collect employer taxes and disburse benefits "payable under the laws of individual states."	Unemployment insurance for persons temporarily unable to find a job.
8. Veterans' Benefits; $27.8 billion	Many statutes, including Serviceman's Readjustment Act of 1944—GI Bill of Rights	General revenue	Federal	Federal, through Veterans Administration	Benefits for U.S. war veterans and dependents, including: compensation for loss due to disabilities or death resulting from military service; pensions for the disabled; education benefits, home loan guarantees; burial expenses; medical services and care.

vides information on these dimensions for eight of the largest U.S. welfare programs. It does not include all federal welfare programs; even some large ones have been omitted—such as housing subsidies, and educational assistance for needy or disadvantaged students. But these eight programs are the core of U.S. public welfare efforts and account for a very large slice of all welfare spending—about $440 billion in 1988.

Four of these eight programs are targeted to persons in financial need: federal Supplemental Security Income (SSI); Medicaid; Aid to Families with Dependent Children (AFDC); and Food Stamps. Two programs serve the general population without regard to economic status: Old Age Survivors', and Disability Insurance (OASDI); and Medicare. The two remaining programs, Veterans' Benefits and Unemployment Compensation, are not located effectively by this distinction. Most veterans' benefits do not have means tests, but some do. One has to have served in the country's armed services (or in certain instances be a member of a veteran's family) to qualify. Unemployment Compensation does not have any means test; yet it has an obvious economic requirement: one must be out of work to qualify.

Attesting to the federalized character of American welfare programs, only three of the eight programs described in Table 17.1 are financed and operated exclusively by the national government: OASDI, Medicare, and Veterans' Benefits. The other five involve some form of joint federal-state financing or management.

The Social Security Administration administers SSI. Uniform national eligibility standards are imposed. But there is state financial participation. Congress requires all states to supplement the federal minimums in the SSI program to the extent necessary so that persons who had previously been receiving state-administered assistance at higher levels would not suffer a reduction of benefits in the shift to a federally administered program. These mandatory supplements are strictly transitional. But the states are also encouraged under SSI to provide optional supplements above the federal minimums. The federal government pays all costs of administering the supplements when the states opt to have the Social Security Administration handle all the paperwork.

Medicaid uses a combination of federal and state funds in providing medical assistance to the poor. About half of the program costs are borne by Washington. The states are required to provide health benefits, according to federal standards, to all who qualify for public assistance, but the states set the benefit levels and administer the program. *AFDC* involves a federal-state mix similar to that of Medicaid. The national government reimburses the states for about half of the total benefit costs. The states administer the program and set criteria for eligibility, as well as benefit levels, subject to a variety of federal requirements. The *Food Stamp* program is totally federally

Eight core welfare programs

State involvement in Social Security

Medicaid, AFDC, Food Stamps

funded, and uniform eligibility standards are required of all states. At the same time, state welfare agencies actually administer the program.

Under **Unemployment Compensation** the states collect from employers (all those employing eight or more workers) according to a federally determined wage base, but they must place these tax receipts in the federally administered Unemployment Trust Fund (where separate accounts are maintained for each state). The federal government shares in the costs of extended benefits. When a state is overdrawn, as happens quite often in periods of high unemployment, it can borrow from the federal government to ensure a continuation of prescribed benefits. Unemployment Compensation is managed by the states subject to federal standards.

Unemployment Compensation

Spending on Welfare

Whether the United States is spending more or less than it should for social-welfare programs is a matter on which party and interest-group leaders, social scientists, and others disagree. Differing political values determine "How much is enough?" But it is clear what expenditures are and how they have changed over the last few decades. The rate of increase in welfare expenditures has by any measure been substantial.

Figure 17.3 shows that in 1950 OASDI disbursed about $1 billion; nearly five decades later, in 1988, expenditures were $219.7 billion. Obviously, the increase is enormous. But how much of it is simply a product of inflation, and how much is real? How have expenditures changed in comparison to the overall performance of the economy? Does welfare now claim a larger or smaller proportion of overall public outlays?

Growth of welfare spending

Look at Table 17.2 in answer to these questions: If spending is expressed in 1980 purchasing power (constant 1980 dollars), all social-welfare expenditures by government—local, state, and national—have climbed from just under $74 billion in 1950 to just over $492 billion in 1980. Included in these totals are expenditures for Social Security, education, help for the poor, medical care, and veterans' benefits. Real per-capita welfare spending increased by more than 400 percent over this thirty-year span. Veterans' benefits were the one area where inflation-controlled expenditures were lower in 1980 than they had been three decades before. There were unusually heavy benefit requirements in the years immediately following World War II.

Social-welfare spending has also been increasing at a rate much greater than the overall economy. In 1950 government welfare expenditures were only 8 percent of the GNP; thirty years later the proportion had more than doubled, to just under 19 percent. As the country got wealthier, welfare spending by government became a bigger pro-

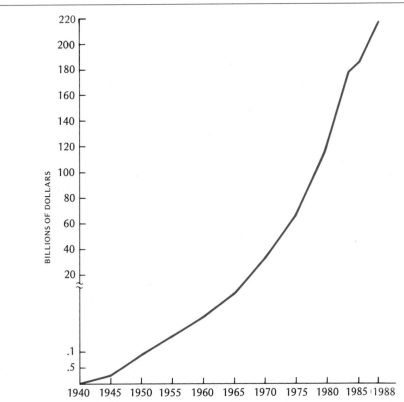

Source: 1937–55: U.S. Bureau of the Census, *Historical Statistics: Colonial Times to 1970*, part 1, p. 347. 1960–80: Idem, *Statistical Abstract*, 1984, p. 379. 1984 estimate: Executive Office of the President, OMB, *Budget of the United States Government, Fiscal Year 1986*, p. 5–111; *1987*, p. 5–127; *1989*, p. 5–133.

Figure 17.3
Benefits Paid under Social Security (OASDI) since 1940

portion of the total. This increase was especially pronounced at the federal level, where welfare spending was just 3.7 percent of the GNP in 1950 but rose to 11.5 percent of the GNP in 1980.[6] Social-welfare spending has claimed a steadily increasing share of government's expenditures. In 1950, just 26 percent of all federal spending went for social welfare; thirty years later, the proportion had climbed to 54 percent.

The big jump in welfare spending reflects increases in both the number of beneficiaries and the amount of benefits provided to individual recipients. The most dramatic increase in the former has come in the Social Security program. In 1960 14.8 million people received benefits under OASDI; twenty-five years later, in 1985, the number was 36.8 million. Some of this increase resulted from policy changes expanding coverage. Another large part resulted from demographic shifts: the simple expansion of the number of older people.

Increase in Social
Security benefits

[6] *Social Security Bulletin* 46 (8), August 1983.

Table 17.2

Social-Welfare Spending under Public Programs, 1950–80
(in constant 1980 dollars)

FY	Total spending (in millions of dollars)	Per capita spending					All health and medical care
		All programs	Social insurance	Public aid	Veterans' programs	Education	
1950	$ 73,650.3	$ 479.75	$101.23	$ 51.13	$138.93	$136.70	$ 62.80
1960	129,940.9	711.77	262.72	56.01	73.62	240.47	87.36
1970	281,945.5	1,354.46	507.27	153.60	83.64	473.95	235.12
1980	492,231.7	2,140.08	994.15	314.15	92.50	524.10	437.81

"Total spending" excludes expenditures within foreign countries for OASDI and Civil Service retirement benefits, veterans' programs, and education. "All programs" includes housing, not shown separately here. "All health and medical care" combines health and medical care with medical services provided in connection with social insurance, public aid, veterans', and vocational rehabilitation programs.

Source: Social Security Bulletin, 46 (8), August 1983.

Reducing the Rate of Increase

In response to the steep climb in welfare spending, the leaders of both parties and the general public began to feel that checks had to be imposed. Around 1975, as a result of this new bipartisan consensus, welfare expenditures began to level off. As a proportion of all federal spending, welfare spending actually dropped between 1975 and 1980.

This was the setting when Ronald Reagan assumed the presidency in January 1981. He had campaigned on the theme that the national

Modest cuts by the Reagan administration

government had become too big and too intrusive, and that the rate of domestic welfare spending had been climbing too precipitously. Once in office, the Reagan administration sought to cut back on some components of domestic welfare programs.[7] But the result has been only a modest overall extension of the leveling-off trend that began during the Carter years. This belies the ringing rhetoric on the "Reagan revolution" in domestic welfare spending. "All in all," writes economist John Weicher after a careful review of the data, "both the budget and the program changes turn out to be smaller than much of the public discussion would suggest. . . ."[8]

Social Security and Medicare. Early in 1984, the Reagan administration proposed changes in future Social Security benefits that, if implemented, would have reduced the rate of future cost increases. But when floated, these proposals generated furious attacks from interest groups representing the elderly and some leaders in both

[7] For an early effort to assess the impacts of Reagan-administration program changes more analytically and dispassionately, see John L. Palmer and Isabel V. Sawhill, eds., *The Reagan Experiment* (Washington, D.C.: Urban Institute Press, 1982).

[8] John C. Weicher, "The Safety Net after Three Years," in *Maintaining the Safety Net* (Washington, D.C.: American Enterprise Institute, 1984), p. 17.

Medicare, a program of health insurance for the elderly, is run wholly by the federal government.

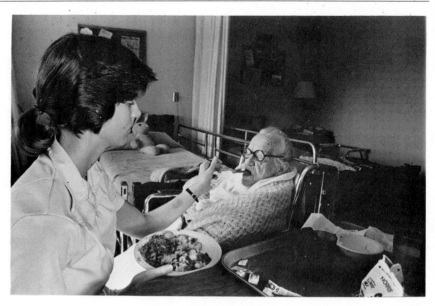

parties, and the administration quickly backed away from them. The president subsequently charged a bipartisan commission with the task of proposing changes to meet the immediate financial problems of Social Security. The commission was successful in the sense that its limited proposals secured legislative enactment and produced additional revenue.[9] But only the most modest cuts were made in projected future increases in program costs, and expenditures continued their rapid climb. In 1980, $119 billion were paid out through OASDI; in 1988, $219 billion—an increase of more than 80 percent in the space of eight years. The progression is the same in Medicare. In fiscal year 1980, Medicare expenditures were about $36 billion; eight years later, they had risen by over $42 billion or about 115 percent.

Social Security and Medicare are what is known as "entitlement programs." This means that outlays expand automatically with infla-

Entitlement programs

tion and with the growth of eligible populations. Congress does not appropriate a fixed sum of money, but rather all that is needed to cover all who are entitled to specified benefits. Finding the political agreement needed to change the entitlement formulas—to reduce the amount benefits increase or to cut back on eligibility—is exceedingly difficult. These programs receive strong, widespread public support.

Unemployment Compensation. The Reagan administration did not try to cut unemployment compensation. The main factor producing year-to-year variations in unemployment costs is the unemployment rate itself: In the latter half of 1982, and early 1983, when unemployment climbed to over 10 percent, program costs naturally soared—to $25.7

[9] See "Report of the National Commission on Social Security Reform," Alan Greenspan, chairman (Washington, D.C.: U.S. Government Printing Office, January 1983).

billion. They declined in the mid- to late 1980s, as unemployment dropped. Even so, expenditures for unemployment compensation were $15.8 billion in 1988, compared to $9.4 billion in 1979.

Helping the poor. Federal spending for the poor during the Reagan years has been the subject of vigorous debate. Democrats at times accused the Reagan administration of unfairness and insensitivity to the needy, while the administration argued that it was maintaining, even strengthening, the "safety net." "Safety net" refers to assistance programs providing for the poor, which are supposed to prevent anyone from falling too far economically. What do the data show has happened? Federal spending for low-income benefit programs totaled $52.5 billion in 1980, and it rose to $91.4 in 1988, a gain of about 75 percent (Table 17.3). This rise is less than that for Social Security and Medicare, but it indicates that low-income assistance was far from demolished. Controlling for the effects of inflation, federal spending for the poor increased modestly during Reagan's eight years in office.[10]

Table 17.3

Federal Spending for Benefit Programs for Low-Income Persons, 1980 and 1988 (billions of dollars)

	1980	1988
Aid to Families with Dependent Children (AFDC)	7.2	10.8
Supplemental Security Income (SSI)	6.4	12.6
Housing assistance	8.4	11.8
Food and nutrition assistance (including food stamps)	13.0	20.5
Medicaid	14.5	30.7
Total	52.5	91.5

Source: Statistical Abstract of the United States 1982–83, p. 319. *Budget of the United States Government*, FY 1987, pp. 6d–124, 6d–134, FY 1989, pp. 5–120, 5–129, 6f–81, 6f–84, 6f–87. The figures for AFDC and Medicaid do not include the state government shares, which are about 50 percent of the total costs of these programs.

Welfare spending levels under Reagan

Spending for the poor *is* increasing more slowly now than it did over the preceding two decades. Whether this is a positive or negative accomplishment is arguable. In one area, subsidized housing construction, the administration succeeded in getting changes greater than the data in Table 17.3 suggest; it managed to stop almost all new subsidized construction. Current spending also reflects interest and subsidy payments on *past* long-term bonds and contracts, so it does not reveal the full magnitude of a reduction that will be evident in future budgets. Moreover, these basic budgetary data do not clearly reflect major administration efforts to direct benefits more precisely

[10] Weicher, "The Safety Net after Three Years," pp. 8–13.

to low-income people and to cut assistance to persons above the poverty line. For example, the income limit for receiving food stamps was reduced from 60 percent to just 30 percent above the poverty line. The Reagan administration argued that help for those who are most needy was thus increased more than overall spending suggests, because assistance was better targeted. Critics charged that important segments of the working poor have suffered. Overall, though, the level of welfare spending that resulted from the Reagan efforts in the 1980s represents only modest reductions from what was established during the preceding Democratic administration.

The effects of Gramm-Rudman-Hollings. Frustrated by its inability to reduce the huge federal deficit and prodded by the Reagan administration to take action, Congress passed in December 1985 the Balanced Budget and Emergency Deficit Control Act of 1985, better known by the names of its three principal Senate sponsors, Phil Gramm (R-Texas), Warren Rudman (R-New Hampshire), and Ernest Hollings (D-South Carolina). The president signed the Gramm-Rudman-Hollings bill into law on December 12, 1985. It required that the federal budget not be in deficit by more than $171.9 billion in FY 1986, $144 billion in FY 1987, $108 billion in FY 1988, $72 billion in FY 1989, $36 billion in FY 1990, and that the budget be balanced in FY 1991. To achieve these budget goals, the measure required across-the-board cuts of nonexempt programs by a uniform percentage to meet the deficit targets, if regular budget and appropriations actions failed to reach the goals.

The Gramm-Rudman-Hollings bill

Gramm-Rudman-Hollings has had very limited implications for federal welfare spending. A great many welfare programs were *excluded* from automatic cuts. Among the programs exempted: Social Security, veterans' compensation and pensions. Medicaid, Aid to Families with Dependent Children, Supplemental Security Income, Food Stamps, and Child Nutrition. In addition the cuts were limited in five health programs including Medicare.

Limited impact on welfare spending

Even the limited potential impact of Gramm-Rudman-Hollings in the welfare area was put in doubt in mid-1986, following the Supreme Court's decision in *Bowsher* v. *Synar, United States Senate* v. *Synar, O'Neill* v. *Synar*, which struck down a key element of the law. The invalidated section provided that if the president and Congress failed to meet a prescribed deficit target through the regular legislative process, the Congressional Budget Office (CBO) and the Office of Management and Budget (OMB) were to calculate across-the-board reductions needed to bring the deficit down to target. Then, the U.S. comptroller general, head of the General Accounting Office, was to review, reconcile as needed, and transmit to the president the proposed reductions. The president in turn *was required* to issue an executive order implementing these spending cuts, without change.

This provision made the comptroller general the key executive figure; the president had to do what he decided upon. Mike Synar (D-Oklahoma) immediately brought a legal challenge to this provision, in which the Reagan administration joined. The Supreme Court subsequently struck down this part of the statute, by a 7–2 vote, on the grounds that it violated separation of powers. Because Congress can initiate removal of the comptroller general, he is subordinate to Congress. An agent of Congress may not exercise executive powers of the type given the comptroller general under Gramm-Rudman-Hollings.

Following the Court's decision, Congress debated alternative means of achieving the implementation of cuts originally provided for through the comptroller general. In September 1987, it finally passed a revised version of the deficit reduction law. Under it, the CBO and OMB issue separate reports on the size of the estimated deficit for the coming year, and the uniform percentage cut in each affected program needed to get a sufficient overall deficit reduction. OMB then must explain the source of any differences between its and CBO's estimates, which must follow common assumptions on performance of the economy, and *the president* then issues the OMB reports as an order imposing the spending cuts. Recognizing that they could not meet the original deficit targets, the president and Congress agreed on higher ceilings. As in the original act, any cuts imposed under the amended law must come half from defense and half from non-military programs. Most welfare spending is still exempted from automatic cuts. For all the complaining about the law, and its obvious flaws, executive and legislature alike have considered it better than nothing. At the least, it provides some mechanism for reducing the federal deficit.

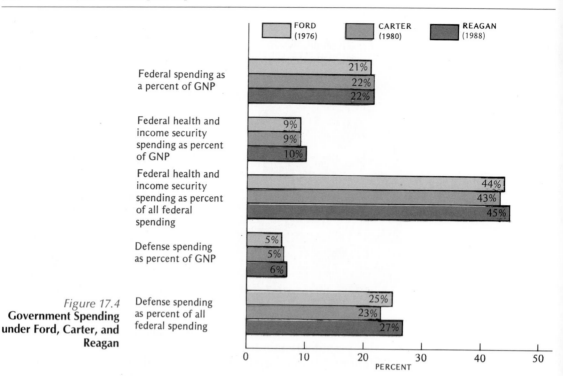

Source: Economic Indicators, June 1988, pp. 32–33.

Figure 17.4
Government Spending under Ford, Carter, and Reagan

Boundaries for change. At every stage in American history, needs dictated by the socioeconomic setting, together with expectations of the populace, have established basic levels of governmental action. Politicians operate within the boundaries set; their actions can be very important but are usually less than partisan rhetoric suggests. Ronald Reagan came to office seeking to reduce the rate of increase of domestic welfare spending and, as we discuss in chapter 19, to increase the effort in national defense. By the end of his first term he could claim some success in both pursuits. But, as Figure 17.4 shows, the Reagan shifts were within boundaries established by national needs, resources, and expectations. Federal spending was exactly the same proportion of the GNP at the end of Reagan's first term as it was when he took office. Health and income-security spending rose slightly as a proportion of both the GNP and total federal spending. Defense spending also rose, but it remained within the boundaries of recent U.S. commitments.

"How to Do It"?

Over the last half-century, Democrats have given stronger backing than Republicans to the expansion of government welfare programs. They can be credited with, or blamed for, the overall design and levels of American public welfare. Today, the parties remain divided philosophically over how much government should be doing in the welfare area—with the Democrats still inclined to turn more to the government and the Republicans more to private-sector solutions. While important, this partisan split is often overshadowed by complex "how to do it" issues that arise in the administration of the national welfare system.

Restraining medical costs. Many Republicans and Democrats agree that mechanisms must be found to restrict the escalating growth of medical costs, without denying people the medical care they need. Expenditure increases under Medicare and Medicaid are so substantial that liberals and conservatives alike worry they will crowd out other programs. Since there are political limits on how much taxes can be raised, the rapid escalation of medical costs will be borne by relative reductions in other areas of welfare spending. David Swoap, who served as under secretary in the Department of Health and Human Services in the Reagan administration, has argued that

> any real solution [to the problems of Medicare and Medicaid] must affect our entire health-care delivery system and must attack the primary reason costs are out of control: a health-care industry in this country immune from the forces of the marketplace. Government and insurance coverage insulates consumers and providers from the true cost of care; an open-ended reimbursement system rewards excessive admissions, excessive services and inefficient use of high technology; and a mass of regulations stifles the entrepreneurship and innovation the industry so badly needs to cut waste and create efficiency.[11]

[11] David B. Swoap, "Medicare Crisis Is Only a Symptom," *Wall Street Journal*, January 3, 1984, p. 30.

Swoap is a Republican and a conservative; many who are Democrats and liberals make virtually identical assessments.

Assisting the needy without discouraging work. How does one go about setting benefits for the poor that are sufficiently generous, but at the same time will not encourage people to stop work and "go on welfare"? Over the last quarter-century, this question has been endlessly debated and various reforms proposed—with results that are to almost no one's satisfaction.

Family Assistance Plan

One of the most comprehensive and innovative reform proposals was made during the Nixon administration, under the initiative of presidential adviser Daniel P. Moynihan. Known as the Family Assistance Plan (FAP), it was designed to replace AFDC and provide a basic income for all families, where the head of the household was working as well as where that individual was unemployed, and single-parent and two-parent families alike. It would have established a national minimum income below which no family would fall. All FAP recipients who were able to work would be required to do so, or enter job training programs. Their earnings would be offset against their FAP benefits, but in such a way that, as their job income rose, they would be better off overall than if they were receiving FAP benefits only. Family Assistance was supposed to help reduce the "notch" problem, which involves families with incomes just over the level qualifying them for aid. A family whose income falls below a specific level qualifies for certain cash welfare benefits and for a great variety of in-kind assistance, such as subsidized housing, free medical care, and food stamps. Families with incomes just above the qualifying levels are sometimes worse off than many families who are on welfare and who receive the full mix of cash and in-kind assistance. FAP would help these families just above the "notch" (the working poor) by giving them additional assistance.

But Family Assistance had its own deficiencies, as Moynihan himself subsequently acknowledged.

> The Administration might seriously have hoped that Family Assistance would, subtly but powerfully, so alter incentive structures that the incidence of female-dependent families would decline, but conservatives could point out that under FAP, no less than under AFDC, any low-income family with an employed head could substantially increase the "cash flow" through its various pockets and pocketbooks by the simple expedient of breaking up and putting the women and children on welfare. Reform indeed![12]

Welfare reform in 1988. The House and Senate reached agreement in September 1988 on legislation overhauling important elements of the nation's welfare system. Signed by the president on October 13, 1988,

[12] Daniel P. Moynihan, *The Politics of a Guaranteed Income: The Nixon Administration and the Family Assistance Plan* (New York: Random House, 1973), p. 446.

the key provision of the new statute (PL100-485) would replace Aid to Families with Dependent Children (AFDC) with a program offering basic education, job training, and skills improvement for welfare recipients. The legislation was pushed along through House-Senate and Republican-Democratic disputes by a general consensus that welfare recipients should be given sufficient education and training to help them move off public assistance and into paying jobs. Under the new law, each state is required to establish an education, training, and employment program for adult welfare recipients. The states must, by 1995, enroll at least 20 percent of those on their welfare rolls in this program, and they must as well guarantee the child care and transportation that welfare recipients need to participate.

Measuring Poverty and "Income"

Not only is it hard to figure out how to achieve various goals that we bring to welfare programs, it is difficult even to describe accurately the needs to be met and the extent of the contributions that existing programs make. *Poverty* in a country like the United States, as we have seen, involves relative as well as absolute deprivation. People are poor when their incomes are well below the average, even when their living standards do not involve absolute privation. When children are growing up, they draw their sense of what is an acceptable standard of living from what they see around them. If they are denied what is available to most of their friends, they are likely to think of themselves as deprived.

The "relative" dimension of poverty

Attempts to measure the number of people below the poverty level in the United States, while of some merit in assessing social need and performance, founder on this "relative" dimension of poverty. According to widely used Bureau of the Census calculations, 32 million Americans, out of a population of some 242 million, were "below the poverty line" in 1986. About 22 million of them were whites, 9 million blacks. Just over 5 million were of Hispanic background.[13] Reflecting the changing age makeup of the poor, nearly 13 million were under 18 years of age, just 3.5 million 65 years and older. These statistics are a mixture of absolute and relative criteria relating to poverty. Relative criteria simply cannot be excluded entirely, yet there can be no agreement on precisely how they should be included. Poverty exists in the United States. Part of it involves absolute deprivation; another very large part stems simply from the fact that some have much less than others.

We need the best possible information on income distribution and standards of living if we are to assess the adequacy of existing welfare programs. Since, however, the claim is made that poverty is a quan-

[13] Bureau of the Census, *Poverty in the United States, 1986* (Washington, D.C.: U.S. Government Printing Office, 1988), pp. 5–7.

Measuring welfare
benefits

tifiable condition, the statistics that go into the poverty calculations have become political footballs. One result of the political sensitivity surrounding poverty statistics has been a reluctance to change the way they are computed, even after it has become apparent that the formula has become grossly inadequate. At present a prime deficiency of the poverty statistics is their failure to include in-kind transfer benefits—their reliance simply on *money income* data. As we noted earlier in this chapter, in-kind transfers involve such benefits as subsidized housing, food stamps, and the provision of medical care. A Bureau of the Census study in 1982 documented the fact that from the early to mid-1960s, as overall public-welfare expenditures climbed in the United States, the growth was far greater among in-kind benefits than cash payments.[14] In 1965 two-thirds of all the major means-tested welfare benefits conferred in the United States were in the form of cash; in-kind benefits amounted to one-third, or less than $2 billion. By 1980, however, the proportions were completely reversed: Nearly 70 percent of all means-tested welfare benefits were of the in-kind variety—about $42.5 billion worth (Table 17.4).

Money income versus
in-kind benefits

These data have important implications for the adequacy of statistics on income and poverty, because as noted the most widely used income statistics *exclude in-kind benefits entirely.* Poverty and income statistics in the United States are for the most part based on *money income only:* cash received from employment, Social Security, public

Table 17.4
Major Transfer Benefits since 1965 (market value of benefits in billions of dollars)

Type of benefit	1965	1970	1975	1980
Major in-kind transfers (means-tested and non-means-tested)* Total food, housing and medical care	$2.166	$15.014	$36.685	$72.527
Major means-tested transfer benefits only				
Cash public assistance	4.025	8.864	16.312	18.863
In-kind benefits	1.954	8.628	22.197	42.436
Percent of total means-tested benefits which are in-kind	32.7	49.3	57.5	69.2

*Means-tested income-transfer programs are those that benefit only families with low enough incomes and resources (assets) to qualify. Non-means-tested benefits have no income or resource test.

Source: Timothy M. Smeeding, *Alternate Methods for Valuing Selected In-Kind Transfer Benefits and Measuring Their Effect on Poverty* (Washington, D.C.: U.S. Government Printing Office, 1982), p. 3.

[14] The study was done under the direction of Timothy M. Smeeding: *Alternate Methods for Valuing Selected In-Kind Transfer Benefits and Measuring Their Effect on Poverty*, Technical Paper 50 (Washington, D.C.: U.S. Government Printing Office, 1982).

assistance and welfare, interest, property. Computing *income* exclusively in terms of *money income* mattered little prior to the 1960s because for most people, and the poor in particular, in-kind transfers were not substantial. But as in-kind transfers have expanded greatly in the last quarter-century, methods of computing economic positions that limit themselves to money income have become increasingly inadequate. With regard to the poverty issue, the Census Bureau is now using various calculations that value noncash or in-kind benefits that provide food, housing, and medical assistance. These data are still rarely cited in the press.[15]

It should be noted that the distortion resulting from omitting in-kind transfers is not limited to income data on the poor. Census Bureau studies have not attempted to measure all of the in-kind benefits received by middle- and upper-income families, but they have documented that these are enormous. Even the incomplete Census calculations showed $167.4 billion in non-means-tested, in-kind transfers in 1980. For example, many companies pay all or part of the health insurance premiums of their employees, thus conferring substantial in-kind medical benefits. By excluding in-kind transfers, income statistics for all groups of Americans are made seriously incomplete.

ADMINISTERING FEDERAL WELFARE PROGRAMS

Department of Health and Human Services

The largest federal welfare agency is the **Department of Health and Human Services** (HHS). It was created in 1953 as the Department of Health, Education, and Welfare (HEW) but was redesignated in 1979. At that time Education was made a separate department. HHS describes itself as "the Cabinet-level department of the federal Executive Branch most concerned with people and most involved with the nation's human concerns." It doesn't exaggerate when it asserts that "in one way or another—whether it is mailing out Social Security checks or making health services more widely available—HHS touches the lives of more Americans than any other Federal agency."[16] HHS is the principal welfare agency of the national government (Figure 17.5).

The Scope of HHS Programs

Budget data alone give a good indication of the scope of HHS-administered programs. In 1973, the department (then HEW) became the largest in the federal government, surpassing Defense in total expen-

[15] U.S. Bureau of the Census, *Estimates of Poverty Including the Value of Noncash Benefits*, Technical Paper II, p. 57.

[16] This description of HHS is taken from its description in the *United States Government Manual*, 1987 / 88, p. 290.

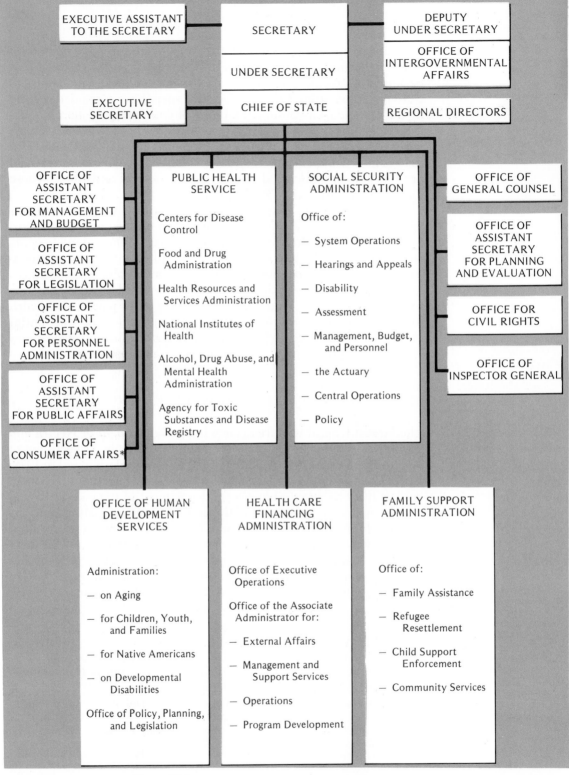

Figure 17.5

Department of Health and Human Services

Located administratively in HHS but reports to the President.
Source: The United States Government Manual, 1987 / 88, p. 291.

ditures. Its 1988 budget of $375 billion was easily the largest, even with its education component now separate.

Social Security Administration

Within HHS the biggest unit is the Social Security Administration (SSA), created in 1946 as a successor to the original Social Security Board. SSA's 1988 outlays of just under $215 billion would make it the second largest department in the U.S. government (exceeded only by Defense) were it free-standing. Under the direction of a commissioner, the Social Security Administration is responsible for managing the contributory social-insurance program covering pensions for retired workers, benefits for those disabled, and cash payments made to surviving members of workers' families. By one measure, it is among the most "efficient" of all federal agencies: It takes a relatively small staff to dispose of a very large amount of money. SSA is a medium-size federal agency, with only about 75,000 employees. Its tasks are highly routinized: dispensing Social Security checks and resolving questions of eligibility.

Health Care Financing Administration

The budget of the Social Security Administration would be even more imposing if SSA had financial and management responsibilities for all of the basic Social Security programs. Medicare and Medicaid have been transferred, however, to another unit of HHS, the Health Care Financing Administration (HCFA). HCFA was created in 1977. Wholly a program of the federal government, Medicare is directly administered by HCFA. Medicaid, in contrast, is a joint federal- and state-financed program administered by state welfare agencies. HCFA processes federal grants to the states. Total budget outlays of the Health Care Financing Administration in 1988 were about $88 billion.

Public Health Service

Another important agency within the Department of Health and Human Services is the Public Health Service (PHS). It began a long time ago, through an act of Congress of July 1798 that authorized hospitals to provide care for American merchant seamen. The Public Health Service Act of 1944 gave the PHS its present institutional form, although its responsibilities have since been substantially expanded. Among its principal units are the Alcohol, Drug Abuse, and Mental Health Administration; the Centers for Disease Control; the Food and Drug Administration; the Health Resources and Services Administration; and the National Institutes of Health. The latter conduct and support biomedical research into various diseases, including cancer, heart and lung diseases, arthritis, allergies, and infectious diseases. The 1988 budget of the National Institutes of Health was about $6.7 billion—making it the largest federal government sponsor of academic research. Total 1988 spending of the Public Health Service was about $11 billion.

Agriculture

As noted at the beginning of this chapter, the **Department of Agriculture** (USDA) operates a number of programs, including crop subsi-

Department of
Agriculture

dies, of direct benefit to the farm community. In addition, the USDA operates food-related welfare programs—the largest of which is Food Stamps. The Food Stamps program provides food coupons to needy persons to increase their resources for food purchases. Entirely funded through the Food and Nutrition Service (FNS), and with uniform eligibility standards required of all states, food stamps are actually administered by state and local welfare agencies. Other FNS programs are the National School Lunch Program, the Child Care Food Program, the Special Milk Program for Children, and the Special Supplemental Food Program for Women, Infants and Children.

Housing and Urban Development

Department of
Housing and Urban
Development

With a 1988 budget of about $15.4 billion the **Department of Housing and Urban Development** (HUD) has a number of housing-related responsibilities; the biggest involves housing assistance for the needy. Together with state agencies, HUD provides partial financing for low-rent public housing projects owned, managed, and administered by local housing authorities. Income standards for occupancy are set by the local agencies, subject to HUD guidelines. Rental charges cannot exceed 25 percent of the net monthly money income of recipients.

HUD funding also subsidizes rentals by low-income families in the private sector. Under *rent-supplement plans*, the difference between the "fair market rent" of a dwelling and the rent charged to the tenant is paid to the owner by the government. Under *interest-reduction programs*, the amount of interest paid on a mortgage by the owner of a property is reduced, with the requirement that the subsequent savings be passed along to low-income tenants through lower rent charges.

HUD administers the Community Development Block Grants (CDBG). These grants go largely to medium-size and large cities for community development, including neighborhood revitalization and increased community services.

Education

Department of
Education

The **Department of Education** administers two large programs of educational assistance for low-income persons. One, aimed at the primary and secondary school population, supports compensatory education for the disadvantaged. Its 1988 budget was about $20.0 billion. The department also assists needy students in higher education. Key programs here are the Basic and Supplemental Educational Opportunity Grants (Pell Grants), which are restricted to students from low-income families attending institutions of higher education. As grants, these funds need not be repaid. The department also administers a program of guaranteed loans for students from lower-middle-income as well as low-income families. These loans are interest-free while the student is enrolled in undergraduate or graduate education and need not be repaid during this period; the loans must be repaid over a ten-year span after graduation. The rate of default on student loans has become a subject of concern, and what to do about it has become a hot political issue in the late 1980s.

Veterans

Veterans
Administration

The **Department of Veterans Affairs** (prior to March 1989, the Veterans Administration) is the last of the principal federal agencies administering welfare programs. It was established in its present form as an independent executive-branch agency in 1930, with the consolidation of several federal bureaus then handling veterans' affairs. Operating with FY 1988 outlays of about $27.6 billion, the Veterans Department is a major federal welfare agency. Its beneficiaries are, of course, veterans of U.S. military service: for some programs, all veterans; for others, veterans of particular wars, needy veterans, those who suffered disabilities as a result of their military service, and surviving family members of veterans who lost their lives while performing military duties.

The largest veterans programs are those covering disability compensation and pensions based on financial need. These programs expended about $15 billion in 1988. The next largest group provides medical benefits for veterans. The Department of Medicine and Surgery operates 172 medical centers, 228 clinics, and 116 nursing homes, as well as other facilities. Government-provided medical benefits cost about $10.8 billion in 1988. Life insurance, subsidized loans for housing, and education assistance are also provided by the department.

SUMMARY

Welfare policy is sometimes taken to include only governmental efforts to help the needy. But the majority of public-welfare programs, including Social Security and Medicare, are directed to all economic groups, not just the poor. A great variety of programs assist farmers, for example. The main impetus for the expansion of welfare spending in the United States and every other industrial democracy over the last half-century is the heightened expectations of citizens for greater protection and security. Present-day affluence means that most people expect more consumer goods than preceding generations did; it also means they expect more help from government, such as the assurance through Social Security and Medicare of basic retirement income and health care.

American ideology puts special emphasis on individual responsibility and insists that American society offers unusual opportunities to those who apply themselves. Because of this, the United States has been less inclined than other industrial democracies to back collective governmental efforts at promoting public welfare. But two types of government action have found strong support in the United States: to create a climate where individual opportunity is expanded and individual interests are more fully realized, and to help people who through no lack of individual effort find themselves in need. Public education is a collective welfare program whose primary function is to extend individual opportunity, and education has received more governmental support in the United States than in any other country.

Federalism exerts major influence on American welfare programs. Though some of the big programs are funded and administered exclusively through national agencies—veterans' benefits, Social Security, and Medicare—many others involve partnership of the federal and state governments. This is true of Medicaid, AFDC, Food Stamps, and Unemployment Compensation. In most other democracies public-welfare programs are run by national agencies which impose uniform standards and benefits, but in the United States their administration is often decentralized and their provisions vary from state to state.

Since the New Deal, the rate of welfare spending has risen rapidly in the United States, far faster than the overall economy has expanded. Thus welfare expenditures have accounted for a steadily expanding share of the nation's GNP. Between 1950 and 1980, for instance, all social welfare expenditures by local, state, and national government climbed from about $74 billion to $492 billion (expressed in dollars of 1980 purchasing power).

In response to this steep rise, many leaders in both parties, and the general public, swung to the view that some curbs should be imposed. As a result, the *rate of increase* of welfare expenditures was reduced. At the federal level, the Reagan administration pushed for reduction further than a majority of Democratic leaders want or support, and a major political battle was joined. The net result of this partisan struggle was some significant slowing of the overall rise—although welfare spending is still rising in real terms.

Not all pressing issues in the area of public welfare involve sharp partisan conflict. In many instances the key question is how to accomplish goals that leaders of both parties want but do not know how to accomplish. There is general agreement that expenditure increases in the health-care programs, Medicare and Medicaid, need to be curbed lest they crowd out spending in other important areas. There is also agreement that the existing levels of real health benefits to individuals should not be reduced. The search, then, transcending party ideology, is for changes in the health-care delivery system that can achieve discipline over cost escalation without cutting benefits. It is as difficult as it sounds.

FOR FURTHER STUDY

Martha Derthick, *Policymaking of Social Security* (Washington, DC: Brookings Institution, 1979). The best available study of the political influences on the Social Security system in the United States and how Social Security policy has evolved.

Michael Harrington, *The Other America* (Baltimore, MD: Penguin Books, 1981; first published 1962). An important and influential analysis of the nature of poverty in the United States in the early 1960s.

Daniel P. Moynihan, *The Politics of a Guaranteed Income: The Nixon Administration and the Family Assistance Plan* (New York: Random House, 1973). A brilliant account of efforts at welfare reform in the Nixon administration, in which the author played a leading role.

John L. Palmer and Isabel V. Sawhill, eds., *The Reagan Record: An Assessment of America's Changing Domestic Priorities* (Cambridge, MA: Ballinger Publishing, 1984); and John L. Palmer, editor, *Perspectives on the Reagan Years* (Washington, DC: The Urban Institute Press, 1986). Two collections of essays reviewing a range of Reagan administration initiatives in welfare policy.

John C. Weicher, "The Safety Net after Three Years," in *Maintaining the Safety Net* (Washington, DC: American Enterprise Institute, 1984). Assesses Reagan administration initiatives in terms of their impact on basic protection of the poor, the so-called "safety net."

Chapter 18

State Government and Public Policy

We saw in Chapter 5 that the states have a huge, constitutionally defined place in American government. Our federal system elaborately divides power between national and state governments. State involvement does not stop, though, with these matters of organization and structure; it extends throughout the processes of deciding what government will and will not do—the making of public policy. While our examination of public policy in this text focuses largely on that made at the national level, it is important to see that the whole of policy in the United States includes vast sectors that are substantially the province of the states and their constituent units—counties, towns and cities, school districts, and other subdivisions.

In the two centuries since the Constitution was ratified, government at every level in the United States has grown enormously in the scope of programs and services. Within this overall expansion, however, the balance between the states and the national government has shifted. Especially in this century as our increasingly nationalized society has confronted problems that reach across state boundaries, we have looked more and more to the national government for solutions. There are exceptions to this overall drift. During Ronald Reagan's presidency, under the pressure of large federal deficits, what had been a steady growth of federal grants to the states from the 1950s through the 1970s was reversed. In 1978, nearly 27 percent of all state and local spending was supported by federal grants; by 1987, it was down to 19 percent. Still, the regulatory reach of the federal government—setting standards for state action—has seen no such cutback. The twentieth-century experience has been a major augmentation of the national role. And, it is hard to envision a future in which the press of national and international problems does not continue to enhance the national government's position compared to that of the states.

The theme of this chapter is a different one, however. If the growth of national responsibility is clear and in the main irreversible, the policy role of state and local government remains enormous. Although there are areas—from school integration to the 55 mph highway speed limit—where federal action has set common standards for the states, there are many other areas where the states are free to choose among policy alternatives—and where their differing choices yield rich variety. *American* public policy is indeed something distinct—compared to that of France, Italy, or Japan. But the fifty states define fifty policy systems that differ one from another in many important ways. (Also, their institutional structures vary, though many correspond to those of the California state government, see pp. 672–73.)

THE EVOLVING STATE ROLE: DIFFERENCES BY SECTOR

Table 18.1 summarizes some of the key changes that have occurred in the relative size of state and national program responsibilities. At the turn of the century, state and local governments accounted for over two-thirds of all public spending; now they account for just two-fifths. The big change in the overall proportions came in the New Deal years. Since 1950 the respective shares have been remarkably constant.

Note that the proportional shifts in governmental spending after 1930 produced no such change in government employment. Quite the contrary: Most of the big increase in government workers since the New Deal has occurred in the states and municipalities. In 1985, over 80 percent of all public employees worked for state and local governments—the highest proportion in American history. These contrasting progressions—more federal spending, more state employment—are explained in part by the fact that the two areas of the greatest federal spending gains—defense and Social Security—employ relatively few civilian workers directly. The defense budget goes largely to pay salaries of members of the armed forces and to buy weapons—most of which are manufactured under contract by private businesses. But the contrast also tells us something important about how public policy is managed in the contemporary United States. In many areas, including assistance for the needy, the federal government's role involves setting program rules and standards and providing funding, while the states handle actual program administration.

The federal-state relationship varies greatly from one program area to the next. For example, Table 18.1 shows that state and local governments raise and spend most of the funds for public education—nearly nine out of every ten dollars. The one period of federal expansion came not in the 1930s but in the 1950s and 1960s, when increased support to states and to individual students—Pell grants, student loans, etc.—raised the total federal share from almost nothing to 12 percent.

More federal spending, more state employment

State and federal involvement in education and highway maintenance

Table 18.1
State and National Government: Employment and Expenditures

	1929	1950	1970	1985
Total government employees	2.1 mil.	6.0 mil.	12.8 mil.	16.7 mil.
% state and local	71	68	77	82
% national	29	32	23	18
Total government spending	9.0 bil.*	70.5 bil.	343.7 bil.	1.6 tril.
% state and local	63	40	43	41
% national	37	60	57	59
Total government welfare spending (excluding education)**	1.5 bil.	16.7 bil.	95.1 bil.	563.1 bil.
% state and local	49	38	25	22
% national	51	62	75	78
Total government spending for education	2.4 bil.	6.5 bil.	50.8 bil.	180.2 bil.
% state and local	99.85	98	88	88
% national	.15	2	12	12
Total government spending for highways	1.3 bil.*	3.9 bil.	16.7 bil.	45.9 bil.
% state and local	99.8	97	72	67
% national	.2	2	28	33

*1922. **There are two ways in which state and local spending for public education can be computed: (1) As shown here, to include only spending derived from state and local taxes, or (2) as sometimes cited, to include fees paid by users of school systems, e.g., tuition and room and board paid by students at public colleges and universities. In 1985, using the latter method, the total state and local spending figure for education would have been about 185 billion.

Source: U.S. Bureau of the Census, *Statistical Abstract of the United States, 1988*, pp. 119, 258, 262, 265, 285, 291, 295; and 1986, p. 263; idem, *Historical Statistics of the United States, Colonial Times to 1970*, pp. 340, 341, 374, 1102, 1104, 1114, 1120, 1124, 1127.

The pattern is quite different in roadway building and maintenance. State and local governments still play the leading role in this area, but the federal share has risen much more since the 1950s than it has in education. Though the national government has supported state highway construction since 1916, a really large federal funding role awaited passage of the Federal Highway Act of 1956, which provided for the national interstate highway system. This and later legislation have provided large grants to the states for road and bridge construction; the money comes from federal trust funds that receive federal taxes on trucks, tires, and gasoline.

Welfare spending outside the area of education—for health, pensions, aid to the needy, and other social services—shows yet another pattern. Prior to the New Deal, when total spending was limited, the overall state and national shares appear to have been roughly equivalent. Actually, though, the national government did almost nothing in the area of social welfare except for veterans' pensions, which after the Civil War and again after World War I were costly. In every other welfare sector, whatever was done by government was done by the states and municipalities. With the passage of Social Security and other welfare legislation in the 1930s, however, the federal role expanded across the board. By the 1980s, only one dollar in every five spent for social welfare programs outside of education came from state and local funds (Table 18.1).

Increased federal role in welfare

EDUCATION

Education claims a larger share of state and local tax dollars—about a quarter of the total—than any other activity. Public higher education in the United States is funded and managed largely at the state level. Statewide boards of higher education, in conjunction with the trustees and administrations of state colleges and universities, provide day-to-day management. Governors and state legislatures shape many of the larger policy decisions through the levels of funding they provide. Elementary and secondary education is still substantially a function of local government. School districts, numbering over 15,000, elect boards of education, which in turn set school tax rates, appoint

Education in the post-industrial era.

McCarthy

local school officials, and generally oversee public education from kindergarten through the twelfth grade.

Today as in the past, states and localities make most of the decisions about directions in American public education. For example, rising concern about school performance in equipping young Americans for jobs in a new economic era has led many states to increase teachers' salaries substantially, in an effort to attract more able people into the teaching corps and then to keep them there. It also has prompted vigorous debates in many states over whether to test certified teachers to determine their competency to teach their subjects—and if they are to be tested, through what means. Teachers' unions have generally opposed competency examinations, arguing that standardized tests simply can't measure many of the things—like caring and dedication—that contribute most to good classroom performance. Nonetheless, more and more states are turning to teacher testing as one means of trying to raise educational standards.

Supreme Court Justice Louis Brandeis once observed that "it is one of the happy incidents of the federal system that a single courageous state may, if its citizens choose, serve as a laboratory; and try novel social and economic experiments without risk to the rest of the country."[1] Concern over the job the schools are doing is leading to much experimentation with new approaches in states across the country. It would be naive to assume that these experiments in our fifty state "laboratories" must all have the happy end result of being proved successful and then widely implemented. But in a case like this one, where it's very hard to know just what steps can improve the quality of public education, it's far from naive to welcome the vigorous educational experimentation that a state-and-local-centered system encourages.

The states are now taking advantage of lessons learned from the diversity of their policies. The work of the National Governors' Association is a good example of these efforts. Founded in 1908, the NGA represents the governors of all 50 states. It operates a Center for Policy Research to share knowledge of innovative programs among the states and to provide technical assistance for governors. Working through the Center, the governors defined in 1986 a five-year program for strengthening education. In work done for this large, on-going project, the governors found that only nine states as of 1987 provided any concrete recognition (nonmonetary awards, such as teacher recognition, etc.) to school districts displaying high achievement. In only five states were highly performing schools rewarded with increased financial resources. The governors concluded that much more needs to be done to link results to rewards and sanctions.[2]

Raising standards for education at the state level

State "laboratories" for educational experimentation

NGA programs to strengthen educational standards

[1] *New State Ice Co.* v. *Liebmann*, 1932, dissent by Justice Brandeis.
[2] National Governors' Association, *Results in Education: 1988* (Washington, DC: National Governors' Association, 1988), p. 5.

Massachusetts Governor Michael Dukakis signs the first universal health insurance bill to be enacted by any state.

HEALTH CARE FOR ALL

One important element of the governors' project on improving public education involves identifying and publicizing new programs being tried around the country, and monitoring their results. Among the state programs identified in the 1988 report are:

Five experimental state programs

Rhode Island's funding scholarships to attract outstanding students to teaching;

Indiana's providing scholarships for minority teachers;

Georgia's developing alternate routes whereby liberal arts graduates can enter critically short teaching fields;

Texas's requiring internships for new teachers;

Washington's establishing testing standards for entry into and exit from the state's professional teacher preparation programs.[3]

Effect of differing state resources

Many observers are inclined to applaud differences in state educational programs that result from their having the opportunity to *choose*—to experiment with new policies, to tailor programs to fit local preferences and values, and the like. Less attractive, though, are differences that result from some states having greater resources than others. The wide gap in state per-pupil spending is a case in point. This gap in part reflects such local conditions as differences in costs of living and citizen preferences. But there can be little doubt that the gap is also due to some states being richer than others.

Table 18.2 gives us a sense of how hard it is to determine what

[3] Ibid, pp. 49–67.

Table 18.2
State Wealth and Spending for Education, 1987

State	Per capita personal income	Average expenditure per pupil
CT	$20,980	$5,552
NJ	20,067	6,120
MA	18,926	4,856
NY	18,055	6,299
AK	17,886	8,842
MD	17,722	4,659
CA	17,661	3,751
NH	17,133	3,386
IL	16,347	3,980
VA	16,322	3,808
DE	16,238	4,776
NV	15,958	3,768
CO	15,862	4,129
MN	15,783	4,241
WA	15,444	3,808
HI	15,366	4,372
RI	15,355	4,574
MI	15,330	3,954
FL	15,241	4,056
PA	14,997	4,752
KS	14,952	4,137
WI	14,659	4,701
OH	14,543	3,769
MO	14,537	3,345
NE	14,341	3,437
IA	14,191	3,740
GA	14,098	3,167
VT	14,061	4,459
AZ	14,030	2,784
OR	13,887	4,236
IN	13,834	3,379
TX	13,764	3,584
ME	13,720	3,650
NC	13,155	3,473
ND	13,061	3,209
WY	12,759	2,842
TN	12,738	6,229
OK	12,520	2,701
SD	12,511	3,190
MT	12,255	4,070
KY	11,950	3,107
SC	11,858	3,005
ID	11,820	2,555
AL	11,780	2,610
NM	11,673	3,537
LA	11,362	3,237
AR	11,343	2,795
UT	11,246	2,455
WV	10,959	2,959
MS	10,204	2,534
U.S. average	15,340	3,970

Source: ACIR, *Significant Features of Fiscal Federalism,* 1988 Edition, Vol. II, p. 98; U.S. Bureau of the Census, *Statistical Abstract of the United States, 1988,* p. 133.

causes what in the case of differences in state policy outcomes such as per-pupil spending. The tau a—which is here a coefficient of correlation between state wealth, measured by per capita personal income, and average state educational expenditures per pupil, .56 in 1987—was moderately high for data like these. This means that, by knowing a state's relative standing in personal income, we improve our capacity to predict its position in school spending by about 55 percent over what it would be if we just guessed. But in many cases factors other than a state's wealth help determine its relative position in school expenditures. Arizona and Vermont have almost identical levels of personal income, but Arizona spends only 60 percent as much per pupil as Vermont does. Tennessee is a relatively poor state, but in 1987 it spent more per pupil than any state except Alaska and New York—a high ranking that probably results in large part from the fact that recent governors in the state have made notably strong commitments to education.

Correlation of state wealth and spending for education

SOCIAL WELFARE

We noted in chapter 17 that social welfare and welfare programs are much broader than just helping the needy. In fact, the two largest welfare programs in the United States—Social Security and public education—are designed to benefit the entire population. Social Security is wholly a program of the national government. As we have just seen, public education is, in contrast, still largely the province of state and local government, and it is their largest welfare activity.

However, the state and local role in other areas of social welfare is far-reaching. Many thousands of local governments operate public health programs. California, New York, and Pennsylvania developed strong programs in environmental health—clean air, etc.—before the federal government acted. Along with federal agencies such as the Occupational Safety and Health Administration (OSHA), states set rules governing health and safety in the workplace—requiring adequate ventilation, heat and lighting, fire escapes, and the like. They employ staffs of inspectors to ensure compliance with these requirements. State departments of agriculture inspect dairy herds, to see that they are free from communicable diseases and to ensure proper sanitation. State departments of consumer protection monitor various sales practices and provide whatever governmental redress is available in areas of persistent consumer dissatisfaction—such as auto repairs.

State and local role in social welfare

As we saw in chapter 17, programs assisting the poor in the United States are distinguished by complex federal-state partnerships. Medicaid, Supplemental Security Income, Aid for Families with Dependent Children, and food stamps all provide for large state *and* national roles. The federal government pays most of the cost of food stamps, but AFDC and Medicaid have joint funding. Eligibility standards for the food stamp program are set nationally and are the same in every state, but both state and federal government are heavily involved in setting rules for AFDC and Medicaid.

The variation in benefits from state to state in programs such as AFDC has been much criticized. States where benefit levels are relatively high, such as California and New York, see themselves unfairly burdened as needy persons in low-benefit states are given an incentive to move to higher-benefit areas. The extent of interstate differences shown by Figure 18.1 is hard to justify, when set against the idea of basic individual rights and entitlements of all Americans.

The Advisory Commission on Intergovernmental Relations (ACIR) has long argued that there are areas involving the rights of national

Figure 18.1
State Differences in AFDC Payments
This figure shows the levels of average monthly AFDC payments per family by state. See Legend.

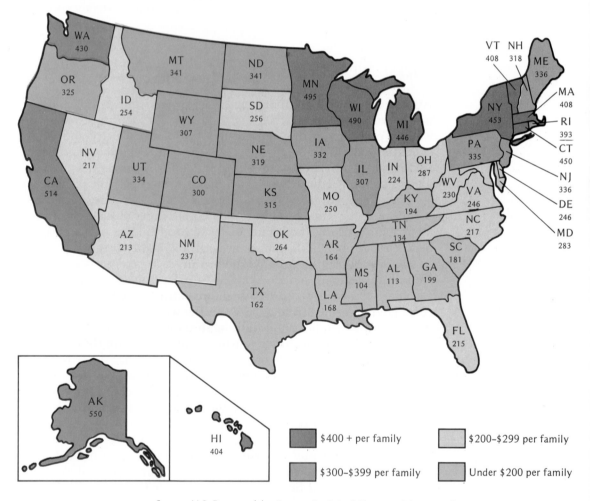

Source: U.S. Bureau of the Census, *Statistical Abstract of the United States, 1988*, p. 354.

citizens—including basic benefits for the poor—where more uniform national standards should apply. But, the ACIR insists, there are many other areas where interstate differences, reflecting local preferences, needs, and choice, are desirable and essential if a vital state role is to be maintained. Thinking through this question of where uniformity is needed on the one hand, and where variety should be permitted and even encouraged on the other, should be a key part of public policy discussions in the years ahead.

State experimentation in aid to the poor

Political writer David Osborne argues that Justice Brandeis's idea of the states as laboratories in American democracy continues to be apt and vital.[4] He cites recent state programs for assisting people in need as an example of valuable state experimentation and innovation. In the 1960s, Osborne argues, the primary focus was on bringing the poor into the *political* process, through civil rights legislation and community organizing. Now, in contrast, the primary needs involve bringing the poor into the *economic* process. Liberals in the 1960s sought primarily to increase the *incomes* of the poor; in the 1980s a new generation of liberals and conservatives alike have sought means for increasing their *economic activity*—means such as improved education and training, and investment in businesses that can yield jobs for the poor once proper training has been acquired. Osborne believes that, while the private sector has a key role to play in increasing the economic activity of the poor, government's role is important too. He sees the states taking the lead here, as they begin to work out small-scale, decentralized approaches to revitalizing poor communities.[5]

LAW ENFORCEMENT

State and local role in criminal justice

In no policy area is the state and local role proportionately greater than in criminal justice. Law enforcement in the United States is enormously decentralized. The states, counties, and municipalities raise most of the funds for law enforcement. They hire most of the personnel who operate the programs, including most of the police. States enact most of the relevant legislation.

Federal policing functions

This is not to say that the national role on matters of crime and punishment is trivial. The Supreme Court of the United States, as we saw in chapter 15, is the leading "standards setting" agency. It is the ultimate arbiter of what the Constitution requires respecting the rights of the accused. Its decisions on these matters—such as its famous ruling in *Miranda* v. *Arizona* (1966) that no conviction could stand if evidence introduced had been obtained through interrogation without the accused being properly advised of his rights—are binding in

[4] David Osborne, *Laboratories of Democracy* (Boston, MA: Harvard Business School Press, 1988).
[5] Ibid, especially pp. 11–14.

Citizens march against drug crime.

Zale

state courts and for state and local police. Responsible for enforcing federal laws, approximately fifty agencies of the national government have policing functions. The Federal Bureau of Investigation of the Department of Justice has the broadest law enforcement mandate of any federal agency. Units of the Treasury Department police laws governing the collection of income taxes (Internal Revenue Service), customs (Customs Service), and tobacco and alcohol taxes and gun control (Bureau of Alcohol, Tobacco and Firearms). The Drug Enforcement Administration of the Department of Justice is being thrust more and more into national attention by an escalating drug problem. The Secret Service Division of the Treasury Department enforces laws on forgery and counterfeiting, in addition to protecting the president.

Still, crime and punishment are largely the province of the states and their subdivisions (Figure 18.2). Unlike most other countries, the United States has never had a national police force—although 50 federal agencies have some policing responsibilities, with those of the FBI the broadest. Most criminal law in the United States is state law, written by state legislatures and managed by state executive and judicial agencies. The major policy choices are made at the state and local level. One of the most important of these choices is how much police protection we need. Police protection is overwhelmingly at the state and local level. Persons arrested by state and local police are charged by state prosecutorial officials, tried in state courts, and if convicted are sent to state prisons. They are subject to release under state parole laws.

Law enforcement: the province of states and municipalities

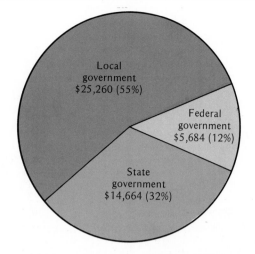

Figure 18.2
Public Spending on Criminal Justice, 1985 (in billions of dollars)

Source: U.S. Bureau of the Census, *Statistical Abstract of the United States, 1988,* p. 168.

State spending on law enforcement

States confront vastly different types of problems in law enforcement. For one thing, crime rates are much higher in New York and California than in Maine and North Dakota. States have to respond to these conditions. In 1985 New York and its local governments spent $294 per person on criminal justice activities, California $248 per person. Maine spent just $110, North Dakota $109. New Jersey employed an average of 36 policemen for every 10,000 of its residents; at the other end of the continuum, West Virginia employed just 17 per 10,000 of its inhabitants (Figure 18.3).

State differences on the death penalty

The U.S. Supreme Court has ruled that the death penalty may be constitutionally employed by the states under carefully defined conditions, and most states have statutes providing for it in the case of murder. Eighteen specify electrocution as the method of execution, 13 lethal injection, 8 lethal gas, 4 hanging, and 2 firing squad.[6] In practice, though, most of the small number of executions carried out in the United States in recent years have been in just a few states. Of the 65 executions between 1980 and 1986, 20 were carried out by Texas, 15 by Florida, 7 each by Georgia and Louisiana, 5 by Virginia, and 3 by North Carolina. Only two states outside the South—Indiana and Nevada—executed anyone in this period.

ECONOMIC DEVELOPMENT

In chapter 16 we reviewed the broad federal responsibilities in economic management. Through taxing and spending, the national gov-

[6] In all, 38 states have the death penalty on the books. Seven states provide for two possible methods of execution, which is why the numbers cited in the text above add up to more than 38.

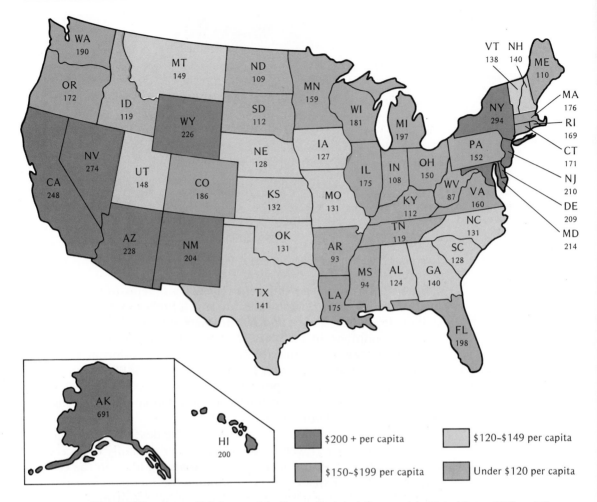

WA 190	
OR 172	
MT 149	
ND 109	
MN 159	
ID 119	
WY 226	
SD 112	
WI 181	
MI 197	
NV 274	
UT 148	
NE 128	
IA 127	
CA 248	
CO 186	
IL 175	
IN 108	
OH 150	
NY 294	
PA 152	
VT 138	NH 140
ME 110	
MA 176	
RI 169	
CT 171	
NJ 210	
DE 209	
MD 214	
AZ 228	
NM 204	
KS 132	
MO 131	
KY 112	
WV 87	VA 160
NC 131	
OK 131	
AR 93	
TN 119	
SC 128	
TX 141	
LA 175	
MS 94	AL 124	GA 140
FL 198	
AK 691	
HI 200	

■ $200 + per capita
□ $120–$149 per capita
▨ $150–$199 per capita
▨ Under $120 per capita

Figure 18.3
State Differences in Criminal Justice Expenditures, 1985
This figure shows the levels of per capita spending for all criminal justice activities by state. See Legend.

Source: U.S. Bureau of the Census, *Statistical Abstract of the United States, 1988,* p. 169.

ernment influences the economy in what is known as *fiscal policy.* Through regulation of the money supply and interest rates, the Federal Reserve is the major governmental player in *monetary policy.* Economists don't agree on the effects of various types of fiscal and monetary policy, but they do agree that these policies have major impact on U.S. economic growth and development.

State government's role in economic development, while more modest than the federal government's, is substantial. Collectively, state action has important implications of the overall American economy. Individually, the fifty states compete to advance their own economies over—and to some extent even at the expense of—other states.

The United States in the postindustrial era has an almost insatiable appetite for higher education, science, and technological innova-

Education and economic development

tion for its economic development. Federal agencies such as the National Science Foundation and the National Institutes of Health provide major science funding. The Department of Defense and the National Aeronautics and Space Administration support research and development that has impact far beyond the defense and space programs. But the states are also key actors. Indeed, one of their agencies, the public university, is the country's single most important vehicle for advanced training and scientific research. Through their support of higher education and other educational activities, the states exercise their greatest influence on the nation's economic development.

Economic competition between states

States and cities have long competed economically with one another—for example, by offering tax concessions to businesses to induce them to locate within their boundaries. Periodically, New York City finds itself competing with New Jersey and Connecticut, as a large corporation headquartered in the city decides whether to stay put or move to the suburbs. Property tax relief is often a factor in the ultimate decision. From the 1950s through the 1970s, as the South belatedly industrialized, southern state governments often engaged in bidding wars with states outside the region where industrial development had come much earlier and where aging plants and high labor costs provided incentives to move.

States still make substantial efforts, through tax abatements and other incentives, to attract industry from other parts of the country. But by the 1980s "smokestack chasing" had come increasingly to be seen as an unsatisfactory means of state economic development. Cit-

The states attempt to attract modern technological industries.

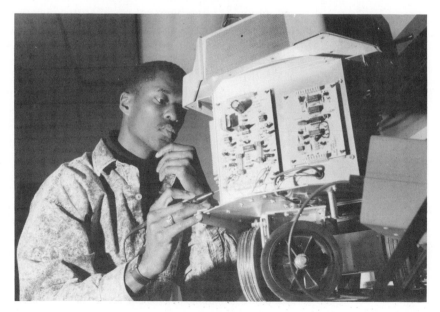

ies found in some cases that they had given away so much in tax relief that they had crippled their capacity to raise needed revenue. More importantly, many of the factors leading to a business's decision to locate in a given area are really not susceptible to influence by state action. Labor costs are often a prime factor. Textile mills long ago began their treck from Maine and Massachusetts to South Carolina and Georgia because the latter had large underemployed labor forces available for relatively low wages. The state governments had little influence over these conditions. As this pattern was repeated in the subsequent waves of plant relocations, the idea gradually took shape that states should concentrate more on the things they could influence. In particular, they should try to nurture climates for economic development that accepted and indeed built upon such basic givens as their location and labor force makeup.

Attracting industry

In the 1980s, state policy efforts in economic development have shifted significantly in the direction of industrial policy. States have created new agencies to foster technological innovation, loan money to new businesses that find it hard to attract the capital they need through private financial markets, provide management assistance to infant firms longer on product ideas than on managerial talent, and so on.

The shift to an "industrial policy"

During the New Deal, a whole series of federal agencies were created to deal with national economic development. Identified by their initials rather than their full names, these agencies, such as the AAA (Agricultural Adjustment Administration), the TVA (Tennessee Valley Authority), and the WPA (Works Progress Administration), came to be known as "alphabet agencies." In the 1980s a slew of new alphabet agencies have been set up in states across the country to encourage new business formation and development. Michigan alone has created in this area such organizations as the ONES (Office of New Enterprise Services), the TDS (Technology Development Service), the MMS (Michigan Modernization Service), the ITI (Industrial Technology Institute), and the MBI (Michigan Biotechnology Institute).

State agencies for economic development

During the New Deal, emphasis on the states' role in public policy came to be associated with political conservatism. Liberals generally looked to the national government for new initiatives. Inherently, though, states are no more vehicles for conservative policies than for liberal ones. In the Reagan years, with the national government pushing for restraint in federal services, liberal Democratic governors in a number of states—including Michael Dukakis in Massachusetts, Mario Cuomo in New York, and James Blanchard in Michigan—took the lead in pushing for an expanded state role in the economy. Governmental stimulus for new business development and expansion emanated more from the state capitals than from Washington.[7]

[7] Osborne, *Laboratories of Democracy*, especially pp. 145–210.

TAXES: HOW MUCH AND WHICH ONES?

States differ considerably as to the levels of public services they choose to provide—which means, of course, that they must differ significantly in how much they tax their citizens. In 1986, state and local government in New York received through taxes and user fees an amount that worked out to just over $3250 per person. At the same time, state and local revenue per capita was just over $1525 in Mississippi, just under $1450 in Arkansas. As in virtually all areas, the differences here result from a range of factors from state costs of living and wealth to state political choices and preferences. Mississippi is at once a relatively poor state and a conservative state; New York is both fairly wealthy and fairly liberal.[8]

Interstate differences in the *means* of taxation are as striking as in the amounts. Some states, such as New York, Delaware, Maryland, Massachusetts, and California, rely heavily on personal income taxes. A number of others—including Florida, South Dakota, Texas, and Wyoming—have no personal income tax. Connecticut, which has a very low and limited (to interest and dividends) personal income tax has very high corporate income taxes, and high property and sales taxes. Delaware, which has the second highest personal income taxes per capita has low property taxes and no sales tax. A few states tax their citizens heavily through just about all of the principal means. In 1986, for example, New York ranked highest in the country in per capita personal income tax collection, third in corporate income taxes, fourth in per capita property taxes, eighth in sales taxes. Hold on to your pocketbooks, New Yorkers!

State differences in taxation policy

EXPLAINING STATE POLICY DIFFERENCES

We have noted some of the factors that account for interstate differences in public policy. Wealthy states tend to spend more for social services than do poor states—because they can afford to spend more. States facing high rates of crime are likely to hire more police than states where crime rates are low. And where interest group pressures and public opinion favor liberal causes, a whole range of liberal policy outcomes, including greater government assistance for the poor, get relatively far advanced. (Pages 672–73 show the structure of a state government, in this case, that of California.)

Underlying these observations on the sources of state policy differences are three basic generalizations. State policy outcomes are influ-

[8] Detailed data on levels of state and local taxation may be found in the Advisory Commission on Intergovernmental Relations, *Significant Features of Fiscal Federalism, 1988 edition*, volume II (Washington, DC: ACIR, 1988), pp. 114–21.

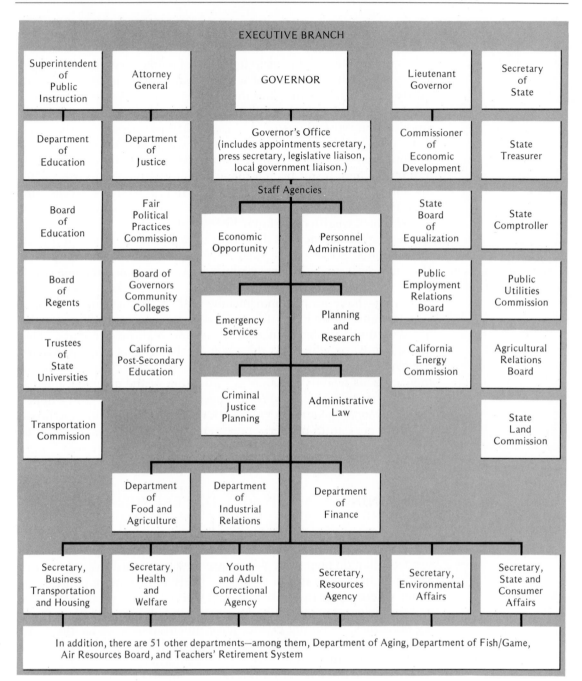

EXECUTIVE BRANCH

| Superintendent of Public Instruction | Attorney General | GOVERNOR | | Lieutenant Governor | Secretary of State |

Governor's Office
(includes appointments secretary, press secretary, legislative liaison, local government liaison.)

| Department of Education | Department of Justice | | Commissioner of Economic Development | State Treasurer |

Staff Agencies

| Board of Education | Fair Political Practices Commission | Economic Opportunity | Personnel Administration | State Board of Equalization | State Comptroller |

| Board of Regents | Board of Governors Community Colleges | Emergency Services | Planning and Research | Public Employment Relations Board | Public Utilities Commission |

| Trustees of State Universities | California Post-Secondary Education | Criminal Justice Planning | Administrative Law | California Energy Commission | Agricultural Relations Board |

| Transportation Commission | | | | | State Land Commission |

| Department of Food and Agriculture | Department of Industrial Relations | Department of Finance |

| Secretary, Business Transportation and Housing | Secretary, Health and Welfare | Youth and Adult Correctional Agency | Secretary, Resources Agency | Secretary, Environmental Affairs | Secretary, State and Consumer Affairs |

In addition, there are 51 other departments—among them, Department of Aging, Department of Fish/Game, Air Resources Board, and Teachers' Retirement System

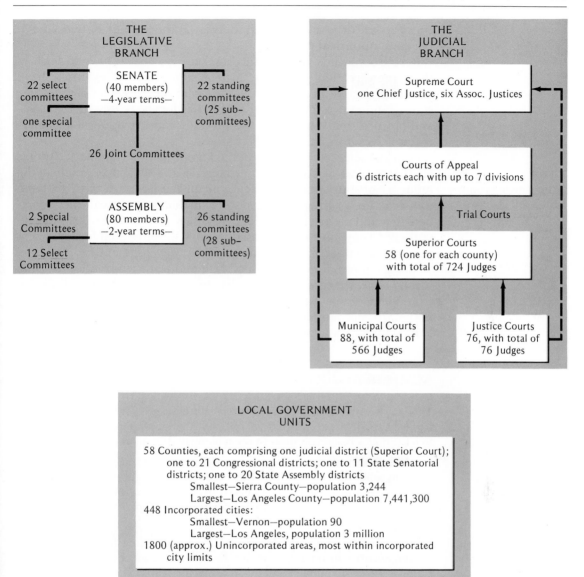

Figure 18.4
**California State
Government**

Source: For legislative branch: *Pocket Directory of the California Legislature* (Sacramento, CA: Capital Enquiry, 1988). For judicial branch: Judicial Council of California, 1988 data. For executive branch and local government: California State Government, Secretary of State, *Roster, California State, County, City Township Officials, State Officials of the United States,* 1988, p. 20, pp. 79–186, passim.

enced by 1) the level of state resources; 2) the level of state needs; 3) the state's political makeup.

Resources, needs, and political makeup do not all have to push in the same direction, of course. A poor state may, for example, have greater objective needs for certain public services than a wealthier state—but fewer resources available to pay for them. Resources, needs, and political makeup interact to produce varying patterns in different policy sectors across the fifty states.

Political scientists have conducted a number of systematic studies on the sources of state policy differences. They have weighed the influence of state social and economic makeup, of variables involving the structure of the political system, including political party competition, and of general political variables such as voter interest and outlook.[9] They have also stressed the role of individual leadership. A governor deeply committed to economic development for his state, or to education, can often through skill and persistence move his state much further in these areas than structural variables like overall wealth would lead one to expect. At the state and local level, even more than nationally because things are of more manageable size, individual leadership can make a large difference.[10]

Studying the sources of state policy differences

SUMMARY

Though the governmental balance has shifted significantly in this century toward a relatively greater federal role, state and local governments continue to have major responsibilities in the making of American public policy.

Education claims about 25 percent of state and local tax dollars—more than any other activity; decisions bearing on public education are made mostly at the state and local levels. Concern over inadequacies in school performance is now prompting extensive evaluation and experimentation in states across the country.

Most programs for assistance to the poor—including Medicaid, Supplemental Security Income, Aid for Families with Dependent Children, and food stamps—involve complex federal-state partnerships. The national government provides substantial funding—all of it in the case of food stamps—and sets some program standards. States are responsible for the bulk of program administration. Benefit levels vary significantly from state to state in all of

---

[9] See, for example, John C. Kincaid, *Political Culture, Public Policy and the American States* (Institute for the Study of Human Issues, 1982); David Klingman and William W. Lammers, "The 'General Policy Liberalism' Factor in American State Politics," *American Journal of Political Science* (August 1984), pp. 598–610; and Thomas R. Dye and Virginia Gray, *The Determinants of Public Policy* (Boston, MA: D.C. Heath, 1980).

[10] For a study stressing the role of individual political leadership in shaping policy outcomes, see Herbert Jacob, "Public Policy in the American States," in Virginia Gray, Herbert Jacob, and Kenneth Vines (eds.), *Politics in the American States*, 4th ed. (New York: Harper and Row, 1983).

the principal programs assisting the needy except for food stamps, where standards are set nationally.

Like education, law enforcement remains an area of predominantly state and local decision making. States, counties, and municipalities raise most of the tax dollars going for criminal justice, and they employ most of the personnel, including most police. Unlike most other countries, the United States has never had a national police force—although 50 federal agencies have some policing responsibilities, with those of the FBI the broadest.

States have long been concerned with promoting their own economic development, especially by attracting already established industries. In recent years, though, many states have moved into a relatively new area, industrial policy. It involves programs to foster technological innovation and stimulates new business development by providing "seed money" and management expertise.

States vary greatly in what is perhaps their most visible and controversial set of policy choices: those involving how much to tax their citizens and through what means. Per capita taxes and user fees are more than twice as high in states that tax most heavily, such as New York, as in the lowest tax states, Mississippi and Arkansas. States make different choices among the principal types of taxes: sales, income, and property. New York has, for example, the highest personal income taxes of any state in the country, while Connecticut, its next-door neighbor, has no personal income tax.

FOR FURTHER STUDY

David Osborn, *Laboratories of Democracy* (Boston, MA: Harvard Business School Press, 1988). A major new study that stresses the need for innovations by state government to advance U.S. economic development.

Jack Treadway, *Public Policymaking in the American States* (New York: Praeger, 1985). A useful review and comparison of interstate differences in public policy and policy making.

Advisory Commission on Intergovernmental Relations, *Significant Features of Fiscal Federalism, 1988 Edition* (Washington, DC: ACIR, 1988). A valuable summary of statistical information on state taxation and expenditures.

Neil R. Peirce and Jerry Hagstrom, *The Book of America: Inside 50 States Today* (New York: W. W. Norton, 1983). Careful reporting on the people and events that shape current state politics by two journalists who have specialized in covering the state scene.

V. O. Key, Jr., *Southern Politics in State and Nation* (New York: Alfred A. Knopf, 1949). A classic study of parties and politics in the states of the Old Confederacy—still a model for comparative state political research.

The Council of State Governments, *The Book of the States, 1988–89 Edition* (Lexington, KY: Council of State Governments, 1988). A basic sourcebook of information on governmental organization, finance, and policy outcomes in the fifty states.

Chapter 19

Foreign and Defense Policy

By the mid-1980s, South Africa's system of racial segregation and discrimination, known as *apartheid*, under which the rule and privilege of the white minority is maintained, had come under increasing challenge at home and abroad. The manner in which the transition from apartheid proceeds—and even most white South African leaders now seem to recognize that the end of apartheid is inevitable—obviously is of enormous importance to all the people of South Africa. It is also a key issue in contemporary U.S. foreign policy.

Discussions of factors influencing American foreign policy sometimes focus on the tension between doing what is "right" and what is in "our interest." We see aspects of this tension at play in the debate over what U.S. policy should be toward South Africa. But at other times the main arguments in the foreign policy debate are over what in fact is the morally right approach for the country to adopt, and how the national interest is best served.

Morality Versus Interests

In 1986 Congress passed legislation imposing limited economic sanctions on the Union of South Africa. These sanctions included prohibiting imports of that country's agricultural products, textiles, and steel into the United States. In 1988, Congress debated a new bill that would expand the sanctions. Proponents argued that greater pressure was needed to force the South African government to end apartheid. A number of Democrats in the House of Representatives, including Ronald V. Dellums of California and Robert E. Wise, Jr., of West Virginia, took the lead in pushing the new legislation.

House Democrats were generally in support of broader sanctions, but one key provision divided them. This provision took aim at one of South Africa's greatest economic weaknesses, its heavy dependence on imported oil, by prohibiting foreign oil companies from gaining U.S. oil, gas, and coal leases so long as they continued to operate in South Africa. The measure would have a big impact on two petroleum giants, British Petroleum and Royal Dutch Shell, which are active in South Africa and which bid extensively for oil and gas leases here in the United States. If it became law, the provision would force them out of either South Africa or the United States.

This issue split the Democrats. Those from oil producing states especially were fearful that BP and Shell might *not* leave South Africa and would thus be shut out of the United States—costing their American workers their jobs. A pull-out by Shell raised special concern because it is the largest wildcat driller in the United States. A wildcat driller is one that is willing to drill wells in unproved territory. Shell has developed techniques for drilling deeper and farther from shore than its competitors, and it has bid on leases that no other company has sought.

Some Democrats were saying: We will support further sanctions on South Africa, to try to force that country to end apartheid—but not this sanction, because it might cost some of our constituents their jobs and otherwise jeopardize American economic interests.[1]

What Policy Is in America's Interest?

Often, though, in the ongoing debate over U.S. policy toward South Africa, the division hasn't been over how much we should be bound

Protests against apartheid in South Africa grew stronger in the mid-1980s.

[1] For a useful summary of the debate over new economic sanctions in 1988, see John Felton, "In Partisan Drama, Sanctions Bill Waits in Wings," *Congressional Quarterly*, August 6, 1988, pp. 2149–51.

by concrete self-interests—how much we should worry about the economic price we would pay by imposing certain sanctions—but instead, over what our interests actually require.

Assume for a moment that you are a key figure in American foreign policy making, and you have decided to be guided in your actions on South Africa solely by your judgments of what American interests demand. Where does this lead you on the issue of tough U.S. sanctions? You conclude that, if the present South African regime were to collapse amid turmoil and violence and be replaced by a government oriented toward Moscow, much like Fidel Castro's in Cuba, that would greatly strengthen the Soviet position throughout the whole southern part of the African continent and be an enormous setback to American interests. Your judgment, then, is that the United States should do what it can to make sure that a government allied with the Soviet Union does not emerge in the Union of South Africa.

The effect of imposing sanctions

But, again, what does this tell you about whether the United States should adopt tough sanctions? If the sanctions are effective—and there is debate about how effective sanctions like import and export curbs really are—they might weaken the South African government and hasten its demise. The collapse of a long-standing social and political system—even a bad one—is far from casual and cannot easily be managed. Extreme violence and near-anarchy could result, and in this maelstrom a lot of innocent people could suffer. In addition, a pro-Soviet dictatorship could establish itself in Pretoria (the South Africa capital). The Reagan administration's opposition to sanctions was prompted in part by such fears.

On the other hand, if the United States does not take strong measures, like economic sanctions with real bite, it could hopelessly alienate non-Communist black leaders like Anglican Bishop Desmond Tutu and thereby increase the likelihood that the regime replacing the present one in South Africa is pro-Moscow. Former Australian Prime Minister Malcolm Fraser made this argument forcefully: "If the United States and the United Kingdom persist in policies that have patently failed over the past five or six years, the black South Africans will make irreversible decisions to fight for political participation and freedom. The emerging government would be pro-Soviet and anti-West." Many Democrats have been guided by similar views in calling for strong sanctions, and Republicans like Richard Lugar (Indiana) of the Senate Foreign Relations Committee broke with Reagan in supporting limited economic sanctions in 1986 in part because they shared this concern.

Even a firm determination to be guided solely by calculations of American national interest doesn't make clear what the United States should do vis-à-vis South Africa, or in many other complex foreign policy situations. Capable people reach different conclusions about where national self-interest leads.

What Is a Moral Foreign Policy?

You might decide, of course, that as a foreign policy leader you will place moral concerns before national self-interest. "America must do what is right in South Africa. We must exert the proper moral leadership, however this impacts on our own special interests." Very well—what does morality require?

Most Americans believe in the ideals of individual freedom and equality. Apartheid is based on a gross denial of the ideal of equality and rejects freedom for the majority. It is a system that conflicts with much that is best in the American political tradition. The imposition of strong economic sanctions is one of the few concrete things the United States can do to declare its moral objections to apartheid.

Moral objections to apartheid

On the other hand, some argue that U.S. policy can be truly moral only if it follows toward South Africa the ancient admonition of Hippocrates to physicians: "First, do no harm." American influence in South Africa, such as it is, should be used to help white and black South Africans along the difficult road to a peaceful, prospering, multi-racial society. It is by no means clear that strong sanctions would serve this end. For example, might not the total withdrawal of U.S. businesses from South Africa and the ending of all economic ties weaken prospects for a moderate center and leave extremists—white and black alike—stronger? In defending its policy of trying to persuade Pretoria to abandon apartheid, rather than employing strong sanctions to pressure it, the Reagan administration argued that the net impact of some of the proposed sanctions would be harsher on the majority of black workers in South Africa than on the white minority. Some black South Africans agree; others disagree, or support sanctions anyway.

Arguments against apartheid

Issues of morality and national interest can be read both ways by honest people trying to follow their dictates. Is this a counsel of inaction? "I can't be sure what steps are really in U.S. interests, and I don't know with certainty what action will produce the larger good I seek—so I had better do nothing." Of course it is not. It is, though, a reminder of the complex challenges confronting those who want to frame an American foreign policy for the 1990s that is both rationally self-interested and morally defensible. It also leads to practical conclusions. For example, the proper question of U.S. policy toward South Africa may not be, "Are you for sanctions?" Instead it might be, "What steps, economic sanctions and others, can the United States take to encourage in South Africa the emergence of a truly democratic and humane society?" Answers aren't always easy to come by—but it always helps to ask the right question.

Caution in U.S. foreign policy

The Republican and Democratic parties differ sharply in their approach to South Africa. Both denounce apartheid as morally repugnant. But the Republicans stress that sanctions can easily do more harm than good to the long-term needs of South Africa's black population as well as to U.S. political and economic interests. Democrats tend to defend stronger sanctions, again for reasons both of morality in American foreign policy—committing it securely to the side of human rights—and of long-term national interests. Planks in the parties' 1988 national platforms reflect these contending views.

> *Republicans' platform:* Republicans deplore the apartheid system of South Africa and consider it morally repugnant. . . . We believe firmly that one element in the evolution of black political progress must be black economic progress; actions designed to pressure the government of South Africa must not have the effect of adversely affecting the rising aspirations and achievement of black South African entrepreneurs and workers and their families.

> *Democrats' platform:* We believe that the time has come to end all vestiges of the failed policy of constructive engagement, to declare South Africa a terrorist state, to impose comprehensive sanctions upon its economy, to lead the international community in participation in these actions, and to determine a date certain by which United States corporations must leave South Africa.

Foreign and defense policy comprises the agreements, alliances, military and economic intervention, and the like, that nations undertake for dealing with the world outside—guided by whatever standards of morality and self-interest they establish. A country formulates its particular foreign policy in a setting determined by its own needs, resources, values and aspirations, and political institutions. In this chapter we will look at aspects of the setting for American foreign policy. Then we will review U.S. foreign and defense policies in the years since World War II. Finally we will discuss the governmental institutions and interest groups that play key roles in the foreign policy and defense spheres.

DEMOCRACIES AND FOREIGN AFFAIRS

Reviewing foreign policy in *Democracy in America*, Alexis de Tocqueville praised the course the United States followed in its first half-century after independence. It had, rather effectively, held to the position laid down by George Washington in his Farewell Address: Washington counseled his countrymen to take advantage of "our [geologically] detached and distant situation." "Why quit," the president had asked, "our own to stand upon foreign ground? Why, by interweaving our destiny with that of any part of Europe, entangle our peace and prosperity in the toils of European ambition, rivalship, interest, humor, or caprice?" Tocqueville thought Washington was right for the time, but he wondered what would happen when more was required of American policy than avoiding entangling alliances.

Tocqueville on foreign policy

"As for myself," Tocqueville wrote, "I do not hesitate to say that it is especially in the conduct of their foreign relations that democracies appear to me decidedly inferior to other governments." Problems will arise, he argued, because

> foreign politics demand scarcely any of those qualities which are peculiar to a democracy; they require, on the contrary, the perfect use of almost all those in which it is deficient. Democracy is favorable to the increase of the internal resources of a state; it diffuses wealth and comfort, promotes public spirit, and fortifies the respect for law in all classes of society: All these are advantages which have only an indirect influence on the relations which one people bears to another. But a democracy can only with great difficulty regulate the details of an important undertaking, persevere in a fixed design, and work out its execution in spite of serious obstacles. It cannot combine its measures with secrecy or await their consequences with patience.[2]

Special constraints on democratic governments

In our own time, politicians and scholars have often reached the similar conclusion that democracies face special problems in foreign affairs. One basic theme keeps recurring: Stable authoritarian governments, despite their many social, economic, and political weaknesses, can ignore divergent interests, set a coherent course of foreign policy action, pour resources disproportionately into the means (notably military) for advancing foreign objectives, indulge in whatever secrecy is needed, and persevere in a foreign policy over long periods of time. Given their contrasting commitments and organization, democracies find it hard to respond with comparable coherence, persistence, and dispatch. Among contemporary leaders sharing Tocqueville's concern is Henry Kissinger, who left teaching political science at Harvard to become national security adviser under Richard Nixon and then secretary of state under Nixon and Gerald Ford. Kissinger believes that the U.S.S.R. has been able to concentrate its resources in such a way as to make it a formidable adversary of the otherwise much stronger industrial democracies.[3]

The democracies before World War II

Perhaps the most vivid memory of many twentieth-century students of foreign affairs comes from the experience leading up to World War II. The industrial democracies of that time—including the United States, Great Britain, and France—had resources that outstripped those of the dictatorships aligned against them. But the democracies found it hard to act coherently in employing their social and economic strengths to meet the challenge. It seemed that so many of the things that made the democracies vastly preferable places in which to live—their openness, freedom for debate and dissent, responsiveness to popular demands for consumer spending rather than preparations for war, ease with which governments were changed, and possibility

---

[2] Tocqueville, *Democracy in America*, pp. 243–45.
[3] See Henry Kissinger, "The Footsteps of History," in *For the Record* (Boston: Little, Brown, 1981), p. 264.

of debate within government over what actions should be pursued—made it hard for them to handle the single-minded ruthlessness of Hitler's Germany.

The experience of the 1930s may indeed be an extreme case. But, even so, was it not a tragic example of *a recurring problem that free and open societies confront* in conducting foreign relations with countries that are not free and not open? Democracy demands freedom and openness; if these characteristics impose problems, the problems must be borne. Still, the question does remind us that differences in type of government do affect the conduct of foreign policy. In the United States, administrations change regularly through free elections; this virtually mandates periodic shifts in foreign policy. Such oscillations frequently frustrate other nations that must do business with us.

FOREIGN AND DEFENSE POLICY SINCE WORLD WAR II

Our study of the American party system and other political institutions has revealed long periods of continuity, interrupted on occasion by some fundamental change that initiates a new course. Foreign policy can be similarly marked off into a few periods. World War II was a great watershed; U.S. policy after the war has been significantly different than it was before.

Emergence as a World Power

The most important factors changing the course of U.S. foreign policy after World War II involve *national power*—specifically, the major increases in U.S. power and the sharp decline in the position of the three principal international powers of the prewar era: Germany, France, and Great Britain. The bases of American influence in international affairs were not all suddenly erected in the 1940s. After the Civil War, the United States rapidly industrialized; by 1900 its industrial economy was the world's largest. These productive capabilities did not automatically mandate an expanded international role, but they were an important resource for it. For one thing, American productivity could be harnessed for military production.

In 1946, the major European states were grappling with political problems resulting from their having been ravaged by two major wars in just three decades. Quite apart from their economic capacity, their resolve to sustain world leadership had weakened. All of the European nations needed desperately to turn inward and reconstruct their own societies. While large, the American losses in World War II did not begin to approach those of the European powers. With its econ-

President Truman (middle), Joseph Stalin of the U.S.S.R. (left, uniformed), and Britain's prime minister Winston Churchill meet after World War II.

omy now dominant and its political will sustained, the United States was thrust into the power vacuum left by the European collapse.

The guiding approach to U.S. foreign policy prior to World War II has often been called **isolationist.** The term is misleading, however. As we noted at the beginning of this chapter, America was never truly isolated from world affairs. **Unilateralist** is a more accurate description. George Washington thought we could and should avoid getting drawn into the European system of alliances, and for a long time American foreign policy adhered to this plan. Given the technology of the nineteenth and early twentieth centuries, the physical distance of the United States from Europe permitted it to "go it alone." But more than anything else, American unilateralism was sustained by the vast commitment Great Britain made to maintaining a world balance of power.[4] After World War II, however, Britain was no longer able to play this role. Among the Western democracies, only the United States could sustain a new balance in the postwar world.

The new course of American foreign policy after World War II, then, was not simply a position taken by leaders who happened to be in power at the time. It reflected the structural position the United States had assumed in the international community. While much has happened since 1946 to affect it—for example, the revival of the European and Japanese economies—the position of the United States has not changed fundamentally. Through eight postwar administrations and kaleidoscopic shifts in international problems and crises, powerful continuities are evident in American foreign and defense policy.

America's historic commitment to unilateralism

Shift in American policy after World War II

[4] John Spanier, *American Foreign Policy since World War II*, 11th ed. (Washington, D.C.: Congressional Quarterly Press, 1988), p. 3.

Containment

The words "balance of power" have a ring of nineteenth-century Europe, conjuring up a picture of nations forming elaborate alliance systems to prevent their opponents from getting too strong and threatening their interests. The words also suggest a kind of international amorality: "power politics" rather than a commitment to moral purposes. Yet, early efforts to maintain a balance of power were by no means without large moral objectives. When Great Britain maintained the European balance for a century after Napolean's defeat at Waterloo in 1815, it provided the basis for an extended period of peace.

After World War II, the United States set about performing, in its own way, the balance-of-power role that had been Britain's. America's effort was called ***containment.*** The United States was "containing" the Soviet Union and communist expansion. If one had to pick a date for the beginning of U.S. containment policy, February 21, 1947, would be a good choice. On that date the first secretary of the British

Containment

Prior to World War II, those who wanted to keep the U.S. out of "Europe's war" had much support, as this Madison Square Garden rally suggests.

President Truman urging Congress to appropriate money for economic and military aid to Greece and Turkey.

embassy in Washington handed American officials two notes from his government, one concerning Greece, the other Turkey. They both stated that Britain could no longer meet its traditional responsibilities in those two countries. Since Greece and Turkey were on the verge of collapse, Britain's decision meant that a Soviet breakthrough in the area could be stopped only by a major American commitment.

The Truman Doctrine

American leaders felt that they had to act. President Harry Truman appeared before a joint session of Congress on March 12, 1947, to announce a major departure from historic American foreign policy. Setting forth what came to be known as the Truman Doctrine, the president argued that the United States must be "willing to help free peoples to maintain their institutions and their national integrity against aggressive movements that seek to impose upon them totalitarian regimes." To meet the immediate need, he urged Congress to appropriate $400 million for economic and military assistance to Greece and Turkey. He also asked authorization to send both American civilian and military personnel to help those two countries rebuild their domestic economies and strengthen their armies.

America's view of the Soviet Union

The intellectual case for the new containment policy was made impressively by George Kennan, then a State Department official and its leading Soviet expert. Kennan argued that "the main element of any United States policy toward the Soviet Union must be that of a long-term, patient but firm and vigilant containment of Russian expansive tendencies." To block Soviet thrusts, counterforce must be applied "at a series of constantly shifting geographical and political points, corresponding to the shifts and maneuvers of Soviet policy. . . ."[5]

The Marshall Plan and NATO

In the wake of World War II, misery was widespread throughout devastated Europe. On humanitarian grounds alone, there was a strong case for a program of American assistance. But America's preference for a democratic Europe, and its security needs in the area, also demanded action. Democratic governments able to resist communist advances could hardly survive in the absence of rapid economic recovery. The most important U.S. response was the initiation of a recovery program commonly known as the Marshall Plan. It was first set forth in 1947 and named for the man who announced it, Secretary of State George C. Marshall. Through the Marshall Plan, the United States gave West European nations over $12 billion dollars—more than half of which went to Britain, France, and West Germany. The effort was extraordinarily successful; by 1950, Europe was already exceeding its prewar levels of production.

As the economic program proceeded, so did the promotion of a military alliance, spurred by Soviet actions. In February 1948, the Soviets engineered the overthrow of an independent democratic

In response to the 1948 blockade on Berlin, the U.S. airlifted supplies to Berlin.

[5] George Kennan, "The Sources of Soviet Conduct," *Foreign Affairs*, July 1947, pp. 575–76. Because Kennan was at the time an official of the Truman administration, he signed the piece simply "by X."

The birth of NATO

government in Czechoslovakia, putting that country under communist domination. In July 1948, the Soviets imposed a blockade on Berlin, seeking to drive the Western powers out of that city. In response to such military acts, the United States and the democracies of Western Europe established a military alliance, the North Atlantic Treaty Organization (NATO). The North Atlantic Treaty was signed in April 1949, and ratified by the U.S. Senate three months later.

Strong Rhetoric, Cautious Policy

At times in the late 1940s and 1950s, some American political leaders sounded a call for something more than simply "containing" Soviet expansion. In the 1952 presidential campaign, the out-of-power Republicans attacked the Democrats on the issue of containment, arguing that it conceded the initiative to the Soviet Union. As John Foster Dulles—then the leading Republican foreign policy spokesman—saw it, containment aimed only at preserving the status quo and thus was "negative, futile, and immoral." The objective of American foreign policy, Dulles argued, should be not to coexist indefinitely with a communist threat but rather to eliminate the threat. American power should be committed to a rollback of Soviet power.

Cautious containment in Korea and Eastern Europe

In fact, however, the Republican administration of Dwight Eisenhower, elected in 1952, continued for the most part the basic approach developed in 1947–49. The Korean War was concluded with a peace agreement that left in place the situation that prevailed before North Korea's 1950 attack on South Korea: A communist regime allied with the Soviet Union remained in power north of the 38th parallel, while a noncommunist regime allied to the United States existed in the south. More importantly, the Eisenhower administration did almost nothing to challenge Soviet control in Eastern Europe, not even in the face of the brutal use of Soviet military power in crushing the October-November 1956 revolt in Hungary against that country's Soviet-dominated regime. The United States stuck to a cautious policy of containment even though its rhetoric at times suggested an anticommunist crusade.

Public opinion on U.S. foreign policy

One reason for this was that the American people never wanted a crusade. The public was frustrated by the Soviet Union's behavior, as in stifling national independence in Eastern Europe, but it resisted measures that would lead to war.[6] This posture seems to have characterized American opinion since World War II.

---

[6] See William Schneider, "Conservatism, Not Interventionism: Trends in Foreign Policy Opinion, 1974–1982," in Kenneth Dye, et al., *Eagle Defiant: United States Foreign Policy in the 1980s* (Boston: Little Brown, 1983), p. 34.

Vietnam: The Misapplication of Containment

Though a great power with far-reaching international interests, the United States was far from omnipotent. American power had to be carefully and selectively applied, distinguishing between cases vital to national security and cases not so, and taking into account the human and material costs that would be incurred in any intervention. These strictures on costs were observed fairly carefully until the mid-1960s, when the administration of Lyndon Johnson committed a half-million American soldiers to a land war 9,000 miles from the continental United States, in an area (Indochina) that was undeveloped economically, without resources that mattered to the industrial world, and that lacked strategic location. Lasting longer than any other military conflict in U.S. history, the Vietnam War claimed the lives of some 50,000 American soldiers, as well as hundreds of thousands of Vietnamese, and it drained billions of dollars in economic and military resources. The United States did not start this war; it did not seek to subjugate anyone, but rather sought to prevent the regime in North Vietnam from toppling the regime in South Vietnam.

But the question of costs had not been carefully considered. Even with the best motives, democracies cannot fight ten-year wars in which they are party to great destruction in areas remote from their immediate national interests. In the United States, the Vietnam War sparked bitter domestic divisions, including massive protests on American college and university campuses. It created a domestic political situ-

Division and protest

People of Vietnam were forced to leave their homes under the siege of Saigon.

ation that preoccupied and crippled two presidencies, Lyndon Johnson's and Richard Nixon's. Begun to attest to the strength of American resolve in containing communist aggression, the Vietnam War shook that resolve more fundamentally than any other event since World War II.

Public opinion on
Vietnam

Even now, a decade and a half after the United States withdrew from Indochina, the debate continues over why we intervened and what the lessons of the war for future American policy actually are. The debate has been a three-way rather than a two-way division. Two separate questions were at issue: (1) whether the objectives and view of the world that led American officials to bring the country into the war were sound; and (2) whether the immediate action and strategy were appropriate. The position defended by Lyndon Johnson's administration held that the long-standing policy of containment was correct, and that the U.S. military intervention in Vietnam was a necessary application of it. A second position objected both to the general vision and to the specific action. For those who held this view, containment was a flawed idea. It relied too much on the use of American military power, and it was too inclined to fix responsibility for international tensions on the Soviet Union and to overlook U.S. responsibility. The American engagement in Vietnam represented a bad application of a bad general policy. But from the beginning of heavy U.S. involvement in Vietnam, some held a third position: the containment policy was generally sound, but Vietnam was a misapplication of it because the human and material costs were excessive. It was just such a calculation that had led the United States not to intervene in Hungary in 1956 and Czechoslovakia in 1968, when Soviet troops crushed popular independence movements in those countries. The numbers holding to this third position grew as the Vietnam War continued.

Reassertion

De-emphasizing the military aspects of containment fitted the American mood after the disappointment and disillusionment of Vietnam. But it did not lead to the results that the new administration of President Jimmy Carter had hoped for. The Soviet Union asserted itself aggressively in a number of areas. The invasion of Afghanistan by Soviet soldiers in late 1979 indicated to many Americans that a de-emphasis by this country on the application of its military power would not encourage comparable restraint on the Soviets' part. The invasion of Afghanistan followed closely on the heels of the seizure by Iranians of the U.S. embassy and staff in Teheran, Iran, which added to a sense of frustration over national weakness. American public opinion soon reflected a new assertiveness. By the spring of 1980, the National Opinion Research Center found in its national survey of

American attitudes that 60 percent of the public believed the United States was spending too little for defense.[7]

The Carter administration shifted its emphasis. In a speech at the U.S. Naval Academy in June 1978, the president reaffirmed the country's long-standing commitment to containment, charging that the Soviet Union had exploited *détente* to cover "a continuing aggressive struggle for political advantage and increased influence in a variety of ways." More importantly, the Carter administration took such concrete steps as urging substantial increases in defense spending and a modernization of nuclear forces based in Western Europe for that region's defense. In his January 1980 State of the Union Address, the president announced an extension of American military commitments, in what came to be known as the Carter Doctrine: "An attempt by any outside force to gain control of the Persian Gulf region [important in the flow of petroleum to the United States, Europe, and Japan] will be regarded as an assault on the vital interests of the United States of America, and such an assault will be repelled by any means necessary, including military force."

The Carter Doctrine

Foreign Policy in the Reagan Years

The post-Vietnam reaction in U.S. foreign policy had been greatly tempered. When the Reagan administration took office in January 1981, it placed even more emphasis on strengthening American military forces and containing the Soviet Union. As Robert Osgood noted, "The dominant theme of President Reagan's foreign policy, to which all major policies were subordinated, was revitalizing the containment of Soviet expansion."[8]

To this end, the Reagan administration pushed hard for and won congressional approval for substantial real increases in defense spending (discussed below, pp. 691–94). It worked to strengthen the Central Intelligence Agency, rebuilding its capacity to conduct covert operations abroad. It supported groups fighting against Soviet-backed regimes in Central America and Africa, and against the Soviet forces in Afghanistan. The latter effort, which included more than $2 billion in U.S. military aid for the Mujahedeen rebels, delivered through Pakistan, spurred the decision by the U.S.S.R. in 1988 to withdraw its army from Afghanistan. In his 1985 State of the Union address, the president articulated, in support of these commitments, what became known as the Reagan Doctrine. "Freedom is not," he said, "the sole prerogative of a chosen few; it is the universal right of all of God's children. . . . Our mission is to nourish and defend freedom and

Reagan's push for increased defense spending

[7] National Opinion Research Center, *General Social Survey*, Spring 1980.
[8] Robert E. Osgood, "The Revitalization of Containment," *Foreign Affairs* 60 (3), 1982, p. 472.

democracy, and to communicate these ideals whenever we can. . . . Support for freedom fighters is self-defense."

Some elements of Reagan's foreign policy were strongly criticized. Many Republicans joined Democrats in late 1986 and 1987, after the effort had come to light, in attacking the Reagan administration's decision to sell arms to Iran. This initiative had begun, over opposition within the administration itself, in hopes of improving U.S. relations with certain factions of the Iranian government and securing the release of Americans held hostage in Lebanon by groups linked to Iran.

In May 1987, the Reagan administration announced that it would increase its naval forces in the Persian Gulf to protect Kuwaiti oil tankers flying the American flag. To some critics, the Persian Gulf policy seemed something hastily tossed together in a crisis, largely as a reaction to attempts by the Soviet Union to widen its role in the region. Others pointed to the vulnerability of U.S. surface ships to Iranian mines and missile attacks. Defenders of the administration's Gulf policy argued that it was essential in rebuilding American credibility among moderate Arab states in the region. The agreement by Iran and Iraq in the summer of 1988 to a cease-fire in their long and

Reagan's policy in the Persian Gulf

"APPARENTLY, SOMEONE TOLD REAGAN THERE WERE REDS IN CINCINNATI..."

costly war promised to defuse the explosive situation in the Gulf. Administration supporters argued that the cease-fire resulted in part from the strong U.S. military presence in the Gulf.

Controversy over the U.S.'s policy toward Central America

The most bitter, sustained foreign policy controversy in the Reagan years revolved around Central America. Democrats and Republicans have divided sharply over what response the United States should take, first to the communist insurgency in El Salvador, and then to the Sandinista government in Nicaragua. After big political battles with congressional Democrats in its first two years, the Reagan administration had considerable success getting the support it wanted for the Salvadoran government. Having received nearly $3 billion in U.S. military and economic assistance between 1981 and 1988, El Salvador is tenuously a democracy. But the presence of a still-strong leftist insurgency, coupled with the resurgence of right-wing political forces, leaves the position of democratic center highly precarious.

Aid to the Contras in Nicaragua

The Reagan administration had far greater problems advancing its policy toward Nicaragua. With few exceptions, the administration and congressional Republicans were unable to reach agreement with congressional Democrats. The Republicans have strongly supported both military and economic assistance for the Contras: the rebels fighting against the Sandinista government of Nicaragua. In doing so they have argued that the Sandinistas seek to impose a full-fledged communist dictatorship on their country, allied with Cuba and the Soviet Union, that would threaten U.S. interests and democratic governments in Central America. The Democrats, less united on the issue than the Republicans but still substantially united, have opposed aid

Nicaragua.

Juan Carlos Piovano

to the Contras, arguing that the latter's human rights violations make them unworthy of U.S. support, and that the United States runs the risk of being drawn into a protracted military conflict in Nicaragua, with all too familiar echoes of Vietnam.

After a series of bruising battles, Congress appropriated $100 million for the Contras in 1986, which included military assistance. But the division on this vote, as on virtually every other on aid issues, was extremely close, especially in the House of Representatives. The revelation at the end of 1986 of the diversion of aid to the Contras of profits from the Iranian arms sales put the administration on the defensive and further heightened partisan feelings. In February 1988, by a vote of 219 to 211, the House killed administration efforts to continue military aid. The vote followed agreement by the governments of Guatemala, Honduras, El Salvador, Costa Rica, and Nicaragua on a plan for peace in the region, which included provisions for negotiations between the Sandinista government and the Contras. The administration argued that provisions for renewed military aid, to keep the Contras a credible challenge, were needed to pressure the Sandinistas to permit peaceful domestic opposition to their rule. Democrats insisted that other forms of pressure, including international opinion, held the promise of doing the job. In any case, a majority of Democrats continued to view the Contras both as undeserving of U.S. backing and having little chance to win, even with aid.

The argument over what U.S. policy toward Nicaragua should be is certain to continue in the new administration. The two parties are deeply divided on what is the morally correct course and what is in American interests. In the Congress, just enough Democrats back Contra aid to leave the two sides evenly balanced. Throughout the prolonged partisan argument on the issue, a large segment of the general public has clearly been of mixed minds. They fear communist expansion in Central America, but they also fear the United States being drawn into a widening military struggle.

Sources of Differences on Foreign Policy

Underlying many specific Democratic-Republican disagreements over foreign policy is a general liberal-conservative split. It was deepened by the bitterness and distrust of the Vietnam War years. William Schneider identifies both sides in this policy conflict as internationalists, because both accept the idea that the United States must be actively involved in world affairs. Liberal internationalists, Schneider argues, stress economic and humanitarian issues over security issues and containing Soviet expansion. "They . . . regard the common problems facing all of humanity as more urgent than the ideological differences between East and West." In contrast, conservative internationalists see Soviet (or Soviet-encouraged) expansionism as

[margin note: Congress cuts off aid to the Contras]

[margin note: A continuing controversy]

[margin note: Liberal versus conservative internationalists]

The question of
"Soviet psychology"

the main threat to the world community. They stress military preparedness and the importance of clearly signaling Western resolve.[9]

This debate involves contrasting views of the essential character of the Soviet Union as a political system and of the psychology of its leaders. With or without acknowledging it, American foreign policy makers play psychologist to the Soviet leadership. What are those leaders really like? What are their motivations? What kinds of American actions in the international sphere are most likely to advance world peace and discourage Soviet expansion? As vice president from 1953 to 1961, and then as president from 1969 to 1974, Richard Nixon had extensive contact with Soviet officials. From this he developed a reading of Soviet psychology that he applied fairly consistently in shaping his policy approach. "The basic rule of Soviet behavior was laid down years ago by Lenin," Nixon writes. "Probe with bayonets. If you encounter steel, withdraw. If you encounter mush, continue. . . . Ruling out force is considered an act of virtue in the West: The Soviets and other potential aggressors consider it a sign of weakness. Ruling out American use of force provokes the use of force against us."[10] Conservative internationalists generally would agree with these assessments. Liberal internationalists are more confident that there is a mutuality of interests that can be recognized and acted upon by the U.S. and the U.S.S.R. Will the Soviet Union under Gorbachev change in ways that will reshape the views of these two groups and shift the base of their disagreement?

Military Balance: How Much Is Enough?

There is widespread agreement that American military forces are a necessary instrument of the nation's foreign policy. But there is disagreement on the issue of, militarily, how much is enough. If the object of a strong American defense is to convince the Soviet Union not to take certain aggressive acts, how much military capability is required? This complicated question involves objective facts on the relative capabilities of Soviet and American weaponry, facts not easily determined. It also involves issues of what Soviet reactions are likely to be, based upon their perceptions of American preparedness. And it is made even more complicated because America's defense capabilities are determined not just by numbers and types of weapons, but also by the country's political readiness to employ its military strength in various circumstances. "[M]ilitary capabilities reveal nothing about resolve. Resolve is a function of leadership, a people's traditions and expectations, and their perceptions of what is at stake."[11]

[9] Schneider, "Conservatism," p. 40.
[10] Richard M. Nixon, *The Real War* (New York: Warner Books, 1980), pp. 2, 4, 293–94.
[11] Richard Ned Lebow, "Misconceptions in American Strategic Assessment," *Political Science Quarterly*, Summer 1983, p. 206.

Soviet missile on display during May Day parade.

<u>*U.S. military expenditures.*</u> America is spending more at present for military purposes in absolute dollar terms than at any other time in its history. By itself this finding does not tell us very much. The United States is also spending much more today for education, Social Security, various welfare programs, protecting the environment, preventing crime, and so on, than ever before. Because of the substantial inflation since World War II, a dollar had only one-fourth the purchasing power in 1988 that it had in 1945. We need to examine expenditures in constant dollar terms, adjusting for inflation to show actual purchasing power. When this is done, we see that the level of U.S. military spending increased in the 1960s and then, even while the Vietnam War was still going on, began to decline. By the mid-1960s, the United States was spending much less in real terms than it had spent a decade earlier. After 1978, however, the level of real military spending increased substantially, reaching about the same level in the late 1980s as that of the late 1960s (see Figure 19.1).

In the last full year of World War II (1944), roughly one-third of the total American GNP and three-fourths of all federal government expenditures were assigned to the military effort. In the demobilization that followed the war, there was a vast reduction in these proportions: In 1950, just 4 percent of the GNP and 27 percent of the federal budget went for military purposes. The proportions then rose sharply, spurred in part by the Korean War, and reached their postwar highs of 9 percent of the GNP and 49 percent of the federal budget in 1955. During the 1970s, reflecting the national frustration with the war in Vietnam, they fell sharply: The military's share of the GNP dropped from 8 percent in 1970 to 5 percent in 1979. Having claimed

Defense spending as a proportion of the GNP

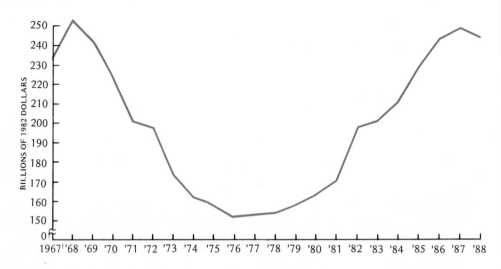

Figure 19.1
U.S. Defense Spending since 1967 (constant 1982 dollars)

Source: Executive Office of the President, OMB, *Budget of the United States Government,* FY 1987, p. 6e–44; FY 1989, p. 6g–42.

nearly half of the federal budget in the 1950s, defense spending accounted for less than a fourth by the end of the 1970s. Under the defense buildup begun late in the Carter administration and accelerated under Reagan, this decline was reversed. In 1985, defense spending was 6.7 percent of the American GNP and 28 percent of all federal expenditures. By 1988, however, under budget pressures and the sense that the buildup had accomplished its purposes, defense expenditures had again declined—to 6 percent of GNP and 27 percent of all federal spending.

U.S.–U.S.S.R. expenditures. Defense efforts are not made in a vacuum. How do the United States and the Soviet Union compare in the extent of their efforts? This comparison is critical, but not easily made. The Soviet Union does not share its defense data with the United States. Intelligence efforts yield some of the needed information, but not all of it and not all reliably. The problem of comparison is compounded by the difficulty of translating Soviet expenditures into terms resembling those used in the West. The American and Soviet economies are fundamentally different. As the International Institute for Strategic Studies pointed out:

Problems in comparing U.S./ U.S.S.R. spending

Soviet pricing practices are quite different from those in the West. Objectives are set in real terms with no requirement for money prices to coincide with the real costs of goods and services. The ruble [the Russian currency] cost of the defense effort may thus not reflect the real cost of alternate production forgone. . . . If ruble estimates are then converted into dollars to facilitate international comparison, the difficulties are compounded, because the exchange rate chosen should relate the purchasing power of a ruble in the Soviet Union to that of a dollar in the U.S.A. The official exchange rate is considered inadequate for this purpose, and there is no consensus on an alternative.[12]

Western experts have sought to meet these problems by estimating how much it would cost to *produce and man the equivalent of the Soviet defense effort in the United States.* Even this is fraught with difficulties, though, because if it were confronted with the American price structure, the Soviet Union might well resort to a pattern of spending different from its present one. For example, the Soviet Union might well not maintain as large an army as it does if it had to pay its soldiers the wages the United States must pay.

Current Soviet defense spending

We know that Soviet defense spending rose significantly over the last two decades and that the Soviet Union is now spending somewhat more than the United States—although we don't know precisely how much more. A study done by the Library of Congress for the Senate Armed Services Committee in 1976 concluded that "the quantitative military balance since 1965 had shifted substantially in favor of the Soviet Union."[13] The Defense Department concluded that from 1977 to 1987 Soviet defense outlays exceeded those of the United States by nearly 20 percent. In 1987, though, after the U.S. buildup, "the annual difference in the cost of the military programs was virtually eliminated."[14] The U.S. Arms Control and Disarmament Agency also put Soviet expenditures for 1985 just slightly ahead of those of the United States—31.2 and 30.2 percent, respectively, of the world's total.[15]

NATO versus the Warsaw Pact. A more complete comparison requires consideration of the military expenditures not only of the U.S. and the U.S.S.R. but of their principal allies. This shows the Soviet side in a weaker relative position. Figure 19.2 compares the expenditures of all the countries in NATO to those of the Warsaw Pact nations—which include the U.S.S.R. and the East European countries bound to it. Outside of what the Soviet Union itself spends, Warsaw Pact expenditures are modest. But other NATO countries make quite substantial military expenditures. The western alliance outspent the Soviet bloc by an estimated $50 billion in 1986. NATO spending exceeded that of the Warsaw Pact by about $10 billion in 1972, fell behind in the mid-1970s, then pulled ahead again in the 1980s. The Warsaw

[12]*The Military Balance 1982–1983* (London: International Institute for Strategic Studies, 1982), pp. 12–13.
[13]Congressional Quarterly, *U.S. Defense Policy* (Washington, D.C.: Congressional Quarterly, 1983), p. 13
[14]Department of Defense, *Soviet Military Power* (Washington, D.C., Government Printing Office, 1988), p. 32.
[15]U.S. Arms Control and Disarmament Agency, *World Military Expenditures and Arms Transfers 1987* (Washington, D.C.: Government Printing Office, 1988), p. 2.

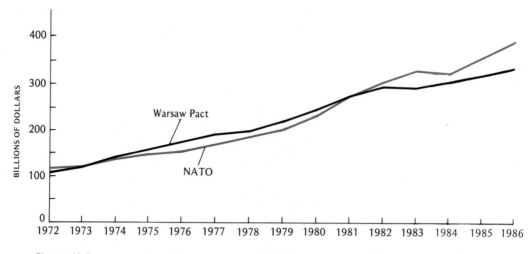

Figure 19.2
NATO and Warsaw Pact Military Expenditures since 1972

Source: The 1986 data are from the U.S. Arms Control and Disarmament Agency, *World Military Expenditures and Arms Transfers 1987* (Washington, D.C.: Government Printing Office, 1988), pp. 1, 14, 44, 45, 77, and 81. Data for the previous years are from earlier editions of this same publication.

Pact countries expend a much higher proportion of their total GNP on the military, but since their economies are smaller than those of the NATO states, even their higher proportional commitment still leaves them behind.

Arms Control

The SALT II agreement

An alternative exists to the competition in armaments in which the U.S. seeks to match the U.S.S.R., and vice versa. That is *arms control*, in which the two superpowers agree to steps to cut back in a way that each considers acceptable to its security and other interests, or agree not to go ahead with new weapons deployment. Ronald Reagan came to the presidency in 1981 believing that the arms control agreements of the 1970s—such as the Strategic Arms Limitation Treaty (SALT II), which was not ratified by the U.S. Senate but was still observed—were on the whole not in the best interest of the United States. First, the Soviet Union violated the agreements. Second, the Soviet Union proceeded with a massive military buildup in other areas. Reagan maintained that agreements like SALT II only encouraged a false sense of real accomplishment among some Americans while the balance of power shifted against the United States. By the mid-1980s, however, with his own defense buildup substantially complete and facing huge budget deficits, Reagan began to explore the outlines of new arms agreements with the Soviet Union. For their part, having tried unsuccessfully to stop American defense initiatives—including the placement of new missiles in NATO countries—and confronting an enormous

President Reagan and Mikhail S. Gorbachev signing ratification documents of treaty on intermediate and shorter-range missiles.

need to reform and invigorate their ailing economy, the Soviets began to look for a possible new *modus vivendi* on arms with the American leader.

The first major result of the renewed search by the two major powers for arms limitation was the INF (intermediate-range nuclear-force missiles) treaty. It was signed by President Reagan and General Secretary Gorbachev on December 8, 1987, and was ratified by the U.S. Senate on May 27, 1988. The INF treaty provides for the complete elimination of an entire class (the intermediate-range) of missiles and establishes stringent procedures, including on-site inspection, for verifying that the missiles are in fact destroyed.

The INF treaty

"North-South" Issues

American foreign policy since World War II has been occupied primarily with East-West relations—involving relations with the Soviet Union and related defense and security issues. But the U.S. and the U.S.S.R., and their immediate allies, make up only a small part of the world's population. For most people outside the industrial West and the Soviet orbit—for most countries of the Third World—the problem of poverty and its effects is of the most compelling importance. However the conflict between the West and the communist bloc is explained and justified, it so absorbs attention and, through the arms race, economic resources that it greatly restricts efforts to combat world poverty.

Because the more developed countries are located disproportionately in temperate parts of the northern hemisphere, while the less developed countries lie largely to the south, questions of international economic development are now referred to as "north-south" issues. North-south issues reach beyond the immediate needs of the

Huge population
increases

less-developed countries and involve every nation. In 1987, the planet's population was just over five billion, up almost two billion since 1960. While the more developed countries have curbed rapid population growth, the less-developed regions have not. Mexico's population alone has increased by almost 30 million since 1970, India's by almost 250 million. The implications of this population growth—political, economic, environmental—are enormous.

Economic assistance

The U.S. government is currently spending about $5 billion a year in assistance to Third World countries to alleviate poverty and promote economic growth. In 1985, $1 billion went in the form of emergency famine assistance to Africa alone. Over $2 billion were expended in 1988 through the U.S. Agency for International Development (AID) in bilateral development programs in some sixty countries. The United States also contributes to the World Bank and three regional banks for Latin America, Asia, and Africa. These institutions make loans for economic development in Third World countries through direct contributions of the United States and other developed countries, and by borrowing in world capital markets backed by "callable capital": a means by which contributing governments guarantee loan repayments. In 1985 the United States contributed $1.41 billion directly and guaranteed another $3 billion in loans through the callable capital provision.

Figure 19.3 shows total U.S. foreign aid over the 1980s by the principal categories to which it was applied. Note that aid to two countries, Israel and Egypt, has accounted for between 31 and 38 percent of the total each year in this span. While strong U.S. ties and interests in the Middle East explain this heavy commitment, its size does serve to reduce funds for other aid purposes—given Congress's refusal to increase overall foreign assistance.

Debt burdens and
repayment

Experts believe that the present level of U.S. assistance is insufficient. The economic plight of many developing countries is compounded by their accumulation of a staggering debt to industrial nations like the United States, West Germany, and France, to the point where debt repayment and interest exceed the amount of all new assistance. For example, in 1983 the developing countries were net exporters of capital; their interest payments totaled $52 billion (on all loans to all countries), while their new loans from all sources like the World Bank amounted to just $35 billion. Richard Feinberg of the Overseas Development Council, a research facility that examines problems of developing countries, argues that there is doubt both that some of these Third World nations can in simple economic terms squeeze enough capital from their economies to service their debts, and that they can pay the domestic political costs of doing so.[16] In

[16] As cited by Christopher Madison, "Economic Focus" *National Journal*, 23 (June 9, 1984):1145.

Categories of aid as percentages of total U.S. foreign aid:

	1981	1983	1985	1987	1989*
Bilateral development	18	15	15	17	17
Food for Peace	13	9	12	10	10
Multilateral aid	13	13	11	10	11
Economic support fund	4	8	11	12	8
Military aid	7	10	8	7	6
Egypt and Israel	36	34	31	36	38
Greece, Portugal, Spain, and Turkey	9	11	11	8	9

*estimate

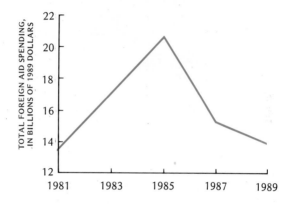

Figure 19.3
Where American Foreign Aid Goes

Source: Joel Johnson for the Overseas Development Council, as cited by Christopher Madison and David C. Morrison, "The Cautious Warrior," *National Journal,* May 14, 1988, p. 1272.

May 1984 the presidents of Mexico, Colombia, Brazil, and Argentina issued a joint statement that their capacity to handle their debt burdens was strained to the breaking point: "We do not accept seeing ourselves forced into a situation of insolvency and continuous economic crisis. Our nations cannot indefinitely accept these hazards."

Some Third World countries have made proposals for rescheduling their debt repayments. Common to these proposals is the idea of a grace period, during which these countries would make no debt payments or greatly reduce them—giving them time to get back on their feet economically. Many western experts agree that major action is needed. They suggest, for example, that interest rates might be reduced to the actual cost of the funds being loaned, with the Western banks forgoing their normal margin of profit. Whatever steps are taken, the problem of Third World debt will remain a large one. And it reflects an even bigger problem: the gap between the financial resources of rich and poor countries.

The economic difficulties of the Third World, exacerbated by rapidly expanding populations, are made even more difficult to solve by their being caught up in East-West conflict. Conditions in Central

Many Third World countries are the scene of guerilla warfare against the established governments; here, Indians in Peru walk past political slogans.

America are a good case in point. Sometimes, in the debate over what U.S. policy in that troubled region should be, the argument is joined as to whether the region's problems are primarily in the form of domestic poverty and injustice, or instead are caused by Soviet, Cuban, and Nicaraguan-backed efforts to undermine established governments through force of arms. But in fact both sides have a point, and the interaction of these two realities compounds the overall problem. Oppressive poverty creates dissatisfactions that can be exploited by outside forces, and the conflict that results makes it harder, not easier, to address some of the underlying economic problems. It is tempting to conclude simply that Third World countries should be disengaged from the conflict of East and West. But the real issue is how that disengagement can be achieved.

MANAGING FOREIGN AND DEFENSE POLICY

Each American policy system has its own distinctive mix of governmental agencies and interest groups. Foreign policy has one special ingredient that separates it from every other policy area: It is the only one in which *foreign governments* are active participants. The United States has established alliances with various foreign countries, the most important of which is NATO. These governments affect aspects of American foreign and defense policy, because the alliances require a common approach and shared responsibilities. Our allies are not the only nations that try to shape American foreign relations. Because the United States plays such a large role in world affairs, what it does or does not do is often of great consequence to many nations, friend and foe alike. And because of the openness of America's democratic decision making, the world has learned that there are many avenues to influence. Foreign governments have become sophisticated actors in the complex process of American foreign policy formation.

The President: Chief Foreign Policy Maker

In no other area of U.S. public policy does the scope of the president's formal authority or the extent of his day-to-day influence approach what it is in the foreign and defense sphere. As we have seen in this chapter, separation of powers is alive and well in foreign policy making, as in all areas of American governance. On such issues as sanctions against South Africa and aid to the Contras in Nicaragua, the Reagan administration often saw Congress prevail. Still, the president's resources for shaping foreign and defense policy are enormous. First, the grant of power given him by the Constitution is greater in foreign policy than elsewhere. Second, there is a special practical need for the president to represent the United States in dealing with other countries and in response to international challenges. Third, while the president must share the foreign policy stage with other actors, the contending agency and group pressures he encounters are less formidable than in any sector of domestic policy.

The first among equals

In debates over government's role in managing the economy, or over new social-welfare proposals, the president can hardly claim to embody the needs and interests of the United States. As the popularly elected head of the executive branch, he has a claim to substantial influence. But each of his domestic policy initiatives is only one effort among many; the president can never hope to be more than *primus inter pares*, first among equals. When a foreign crisis occurs, however, or negotiations proceed on an arms limitation treaty, a president can and often does plausibly claim to articulate transcending national interests. Critics of his approach usually grant him greater room to maneuver than they would on any domestic issue.

The power to act in military crises

The contemporary importance of the American military establishment in the country's foreign relations has made the president's constitutional position as commander-in-chief unusually influential. Congress has taken steps over the last decade to reassert its authority in questions of war and peace, but when a military crisis ensues the president alone has a mandate to act with the dispatch and force that national security requires. President Kennedy acted forcefully, imposing a military blockade on Cuba, during the missile crisis of 1962 when the Soviet Union placed offensive missiles in Cuba, just

90 miles from the U.S. mainland. And President Reagan sent U.S. troops to the Caribbean island of Grenada in October 1983 to prevent the establishment of a Soviet-bloc military base on the island and to protect 1,000 Americans, mostly students, who were in residence there. Reagan also authorized a U.S. air attack on targets in Libya in April 1986, in retaliation for Libyan support of international terrorism. Much less stands between the president and decisive action in foreign policy than elsewhere. Executive agencies and Congress play key roles, but they typically lack the capacity to block determined presidential initiatives as they can in the domestic policy spheres. Interest groups try to shape foreign policy, but they are far less numerous or muscular than their counterparts in the fields of social welfare or economic management. In part the idea of a "national interest," as distinct from contending group interests, is in reality more imposing in foreign policy than anywhere else.

The National Security Council

The most important institutional change made since World War II to provide the president with more assistance in discharging his foreign policy responsibilities was the creation of the National Security Council (NSC). Established by the National Security Act of 1947, the NSC is charged with advising the president "with respect to the integration of domestic, foreign, and military policies relating to the national security." Its membership includes the president as chairman, the vice president, and the secretaries of state and defense. The director of the Central Intelligence Agency and the chairman of the Joint Chiefs of Staff are statutory advisers to the NSC. Heads of other international agencies, such as the United States Information Agency and the Agency for International Development, also participate at times in council activities. So does the president's personal staff; one of these staff positions—the assistant for national security affairs—has become exceptionally prominent, as described below.

NSC as presidential adviser

How its members participate, and how the council operates generally, are strictly at the president's discretion. The NSC's deliberations and decisions are only advisory to him. Every president since Truman has, however, chosen to make the NSC an important instrument of presidential foreign policy management. As political scientists Charles Kegley, Jr., and Eugene Wittkopf have noted presidents turn to the council for help in tackling persisting problems confronting presidential leadership in foreign policy: "acquiring information; identifying issues; coping with crisis; making decisions; coordinating actions; and assuring agency performance in accordance with presidential wishes."[17]

[17] Charles W. Kegley, Jr., and Eugene R. Wittkopf, *American Foreign Policy: Pattern and Process* (New York: St. Martin's Press, 1982), p. 329.

Since 1961, in John Kennedy's presidency, the National Security Council has been less important as a formal mechanism than as the locus of an enlarged corps of presidential advisers. The impetus for expanding the number and influence of the president's personal foreign policy staff has been basically the same as for augmenting the role of his domestic assistants. The executive establishment has grown so large that if a president confines himself to making the big decisions, then leaves their implementation to the departmental bureaucracies, he is apt to lose effective control over his administration's policy. Key to the expanded role of the NSC staff was the elevation of the president's special assistant for national security affairs, who directs the staff of the NSC. Some NSC chiefs, such as Henry Kissinger (under Richard Nixon) and Zbigniew Brzezinski (under Jimmy Carter) have played decisive roles in managing foreign policy, rivaling and even surpassing that of the secretary of state. The security adviser and his NSC staff have been "the president's men" in White House management of American foreign relations.

The national security adviser

Under John Kennedy, the NSC staff moved to fill what the president believed was a persisting deficiency of the State Department. As Theodore Sorensen, one of Kennedy's top aides, put it:

The NSC and the State Department

> The President was discouraged with the State Department almost as soon as he took office. He felt that it too often seemed to have a built-in inertia which deadened initiative and that its tendency toward excessive delay obscured determination. It spoke with too many voices and too little vigor. It was never clear to the President . . . who was in charge, who was clearly delegated to do what, and why his own policy line seemed consistently to be altered or evaded [at the State Department].[18]

Bundy and his NSC staff became Kennedy's personal foreign policy team.

Under Richard Nixon and his national security adviser, Henry Kissinger, many of the characteristic developments of the Kennedy era were extended further. Providing personal assistance to the president, the NSC staff was enlarged and its day-to-day managerial authority increased. It was the White House, far more than the established departmental bureaucracies of State and Defense, that was shaping, down to considerable detail, U.S. activities in the foreign sphere. When Kissinger became secretary of state and gave up the post of national security adviser, influence shifted back to the State Department.

The underlying *raison d'être* for a strong assistant for national security affairs and his White House bureaucracy—modern presidents' belief that they need personal staff machinery for managing America's far-flung foreign commitments—has proved to be enduring. Controversy over the role of the NSC has also persisted. Ronald Reagan's

[18] Theodore Sorensen, *Kennedy* (New York: Harper and Row, 1965), p. 287.

Henry Kissinger, secretary of state under Richard Nixon, played a pivotal role in American foreign policy.

use of the NSC to manage delicate negotiations with Iran involving future relations and U.S. hostages held in Lebanon by pro-Iranian factions, by-passing the State Department, led to errors that shook his administration in late 1986 and 1987.

The Department of State

Among the many departments and agencies of the "foreign affairs government" of the United States, the Department of State bears the broadest formal responsibilities. Its work includes representing the United States in roughly 50 different international organizations, conducting bilateral negotiations on matters large and small with other countries, and formulating policy recommendations in virtually every facet of U.S. foreign relations. To discharge these responsibilities, the department operated (as of January 1988) a network of 300 posts throughout the world—including 141 embassies, 11 missions, 73 consulates general, and 29 consulates.[19] Extensive though this seems, the State Department is actually quite small compared to most of the other departmental bureaucracies of the executive branch. It has a staff of roughly 25,000 worldwide, as against 211,600 for Health and Human Services, and it has an annual budget (in 1988) of about

[19] For detailed information on the internal organization of the Department of State, see the *United States Government Manual, 1988–89* (Washington, D.C.: Government Printing Office, 1988), p. 428.

$3.3 billion. Figure 19.4 shows the State Department's principal operating units.

Three other agencies involved in foreign affairs are loosely attached to the State Department: the Arms Control and Disarmament Agency

Figure 19.4
Department of State

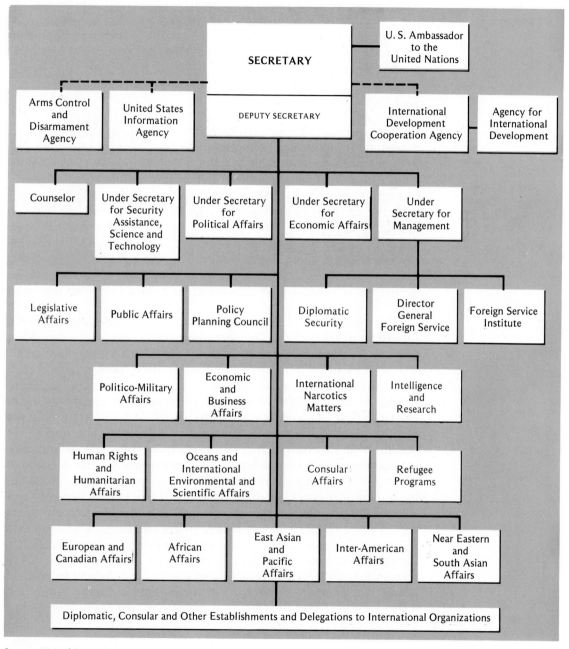

Source: *United States Government Manual 1988–89,* p. 423.

(ACDA), which conducts research on arms control and disarmament policy and negotiates on these subjects with other countries; the United States Information Agency (USIA), which handles cultural and informational activities directed at overseas audiences; and the International Development Cooperation Agency (IDCA), which is responsible for coordinating U.S. economic assistance to developing countries. The Agency for International Development (AID) is the principal operating arm of the IDCA, administering the country's major bilateral aid programs.

The Department of Defense

The Department of Defense (DOD) has the biggest payroll in the United States, with more than two million men and women on active duty in the armed forces and about one million civilian employees (Figure 19.5). The DOD expended about $300 billion in 1988. Even the physical dimensions of the DOD's headquarters seem to affirm symbolically the department's massive governmental presence. The Pentagon "is one of the largest office buildings in the world, covering, under one roof, 17½ miles of corridors running into and around 83 acres of offices, drafting rooms, . . . restaurants, auditoriums, dispensaries, banks, a shopping center, a printing plant, and even its own fire department."[20] Even so, the DOD has long since outgrown the building.

Critics worry about the overall role of the Defense Department in American public policy. The sheer number of employees dependent upon the department for their livelihood is itself a source of influence.

Controlling the defense establishment

The total includes not only active-duty military personnel and regular civilian employees, but also millions of other workers indirectly employed through DOD expenditures for weapons, construction, and more. In 1987, the department spent almost $83 billion for weapons procurement, $34 billion for research and development, and $5 billion for military construction. Many business corporations and other private organizations are heavily dependent upon DOD decisions—and try to shape them, on matters like what weapons to purchase and from whom to purchase them. One result has been a series of procurement scandals, with corporations accused of overcharging the department, or using illegal means to get contracts. The size of the American defense establishment makes policing it very difficult. The foreign affairs role of the department is not simply a product of its economic muscle. It also results from the fact that American military power is a primary instrument of the country's foreign policy and international leadership. Adam Yarmolinksy, who served as deputy assistant secretary of defense for international security affairs under

[20]C. W. Borklund, *The Department of Defense* (New York: Praeger, 1968), pp. 95–97.

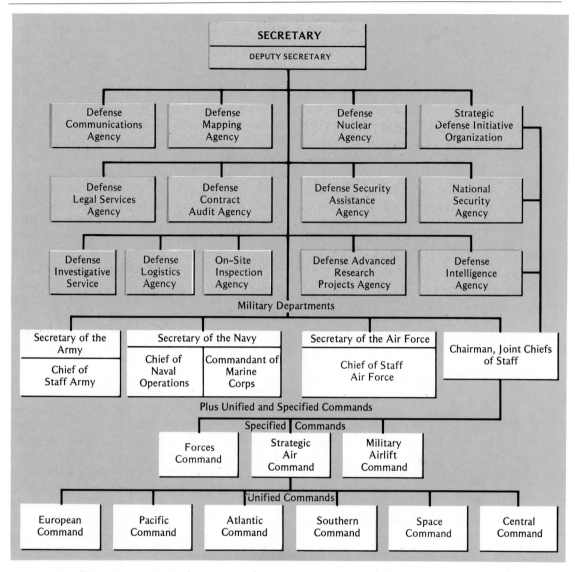

| SECRETARY |
| DEPUTY SECRETARY |

| Defense Communications Agency | Defense Mapping Agency | Defense Nuclear Agency | Strategic Defense Initiative Organization |

| Defense Legal Services Agency | Defense Contract Audit Agency | Defense Security Assistance Agency | National Security Agency |

| Defense Investigative Service | Defense Logistics Agency | On-Site Inspection Agency | Defense Advanced Research Projects Agency | Defense Intelligence Agency |

Military Departments

| Secretary of the Army | Secretary of the Navy | Secretary of the Air Force | Chairman, Joint Chiefs of Staff |
| Chief of Staff Army | Chief of Naval Operations | Commandant of Marine Corps | Chief of Staff Air Force | |

Plus Unified and Specified Commands

Specified Commands

| Forces Command | Strategic Air Command | Military Airlift Command |

Unified Commands

| European Command | Pacific Command | Atlantic Command | Southern Command | Space Command | Central Command |

Figure 19.5
Department of Defense

Source: The United States Government Manual 1988–89, p. 173; and other DOD published charts.

Kennedy and Johnson, argued that the central place of military calculations in U.S. foreign policy extends well beyond the intervention of military officials themselves.

Civilians like [secretaries of state] Dean Acheson, [John Foster] Dulles, and Dean Rusk did not speak lines written for them by the Joint Chiefs or by secretaries of defense. They spoke their convictions in the language most likely to persuade Congress and the public. They framed their proposals in such a way as to justify open support by military men. It is fair to say that if American foreign policy became partially militarized, the blame should not be laid primarily on the military establishment, but on presidents, civilian policymakers, the Congress, and the American people—and on the situation in which they found themselves.[21]

Within each military service, the senior officer is responsible for advising his civilian secretary (the secretaries of the Army, Navy, and Air Force) on military issues and for maintaining the effectiveness of the armed forces under his authority. These military officials—the chief of staff of the Army, the chief of staff of the Air Force, the chief of naval operations, and the commandant of the Marine Corps—constitute collectively the Joint Chiefs of Staff (JCS). The chairman of the JCS is appointed by the president, subject to Senate confirmation, from among the officers of one of the military departments. Drawing on its own staff of some 400 officers, and the ideas and recommendations developed by each branch of the armed forces, the JCS advises the secretary of defense and the president on all military matters relating to national security, such as what weapons systems are needed, military assistance to countries allied to the United States, and plans for industrial mobilization. The service chiefs have not been reluctant to take their views on national security directly to influential members of Congress.

The joint chiefs of staff

Intelligence Services

The beginnings of a major U.S. effort in foreign intelligence may be traced to the Japanese bombing of Pearl Harbor. The success of that attack revealed gross deficiencies in the country's intelligence gathering and spurred a new emphasis. Today, the United States has a vast and complex network of intelligence agencies that play a large part in foreign affairs. "Intelligence" covers many different activities. While the first image is often that of the spy or covert operator—whether Ian Fleming's daring "007" or John Le Carré's introspective "Smiley"—most intelligence work is highly technical and done far from enemy lines. Whether they are monitoring Russian newspapers and magazines, or analyzing photographs taken by reconnaissance satellites, intelligence agency staffers are usually very different from the stereotypical spy. Popular folklore has it that American intelligence activity is centered in the Central Intelligence Agency (CIA). This is inaccurate. The CIA is an important part of the intelligence community, but it is by no means the largest, either in staff or in budget.

DOD intelligence agencies. The Defense Department does more in the intelligence-gathering area than any other executive agency. Units of

[21]Adam Yarmolinsky, *The Military Establishment: Its Impact on American Society* (New York: Harper and Row, 1971), p. 37.

the DOD expend over 80 percent of the total intelligence budget, with Air Force Intelligence the biggest single unit. Including the National Reconnaissance Office, Air Force Intelligence is responsible for the extremely costly and highly effective surveillance carried out through orbiting satellites.With their sophisticated photographic and electronic equipment, the reconnaissance satellites have become the most basic U.S. source of technical intelligence data.

The National Security Agency (NSA), also in the DOD, is the second largest in the U.S. intelligence community in total budget. It handles "signal intelligence" and "cryptology": code breaking and code making. Utilizing highly advanced technology, including elaborate computer systems, the NSA intercepts and interprets messages sent by other countries; it also tries to ensure the security of messages sent by the United States. It does technical work for codes used by the CIA, the FBI, the military services, the State Department, and other federal agencies.

The Central Intelligence Agency. Only about 10 percent of the staff involved in U.S. intelligence activities is in the employ of the Central Intelligence Agency. When the CIA was established in 1947 as the successor to the World War II Office of Strategic Services (OSS), it was intended to integrate many separate pieces of national intelligence gathering. Over the ensuing years, its coordinating function has diminished. The CIA carries on its major activities within three operating units: the directorates of Intelligence, Science and Technology, and Operations. The first two are devoted principally to intelligence processing and assessment, and the third to clandestine activities abroad.

The preponderance of intelligence gathering conducted under CIA auspices involves the straightforward compilation of available information from already-published sources throughout the world. Much of the CIA's expertise is devoted to selecting, translating, interpreting, and assessing this vast accumulation of data. Experts have questioned the quality of the CIA's foreign evaluations. The agency has done its share to contribute to this lack of confidence—as, for example, in 1976, when it dramatically reversed its assessment of the rate of the Soviet Union's military buildup, saying, in effect, that it had been wrong in its calculations of the preceding years, and that the U.S.S.R. was in fact strengthening its military capabilities much faster than had been thought.

Spying and covert operations. It is not, however, the foreign data assessments as much as the clandestine activities that got the CIA into political trouble in the United States and made it a source of public concern. *Clandestine activities* include two different activities: spying of the type that must be done with agents rather than satel-

The National Security Agency

Intelligence gathering

lites or electronic equipment; and covert operations conducted for or against foreign governments. The CIA's notably unsuccessful orchestration of the "Bay of Pigs" invasion by anti-Castro Cuban exiles in 1961, and the agency's intervention in Iran on behalf of the Shah prior to his downfall in 1979, are much-debated examples of covert operations.

Many Americans have ambivalent feelings about foreign intelligence gathering. On the one hand, they grant its necessity, given world conditions—and as long as it is carried out through such "antiseptic" technology as reconnaissance satellites, their political objections are moderate. But when it extends to clandestine activities, especially operations against foreign governments, objections mount. Too much of such activity seems undemocratic—but too little seems incautious, imperiling the country's defenses against foreign adversaries.

In the mid-1970s, Congress sought to exert greater control over covert interventions and to reduce their scope. The Hughes-Ryan Amendment to the 1974 Foreign Assistance Act required that the president certify to Congress that he had approved any covert intervention as "important to the national interests of the United States." Congress was to be informed in a "timely manner." In practice, this meant informing House and Senate committees on foreign affairs and foreign relations, appropriations, armed services, and intelligence—so that as many as 200 members of Congress and their staffs could be knowledgeable about impending *secret* operations in foreign countries. By 1980, the pendulum had swung back; the Hughes-Ryan Amendment was repealed, and congressional oversight in the intelligence area was restricted in response to the feeling that in the previous six years the United States had gone too far and had put a "straitjacket" on its covert capabilities. Under the Reagan administration and CIA Director William Casey, the CIA resumed covert operations. Its support in 1983 and 1984 of Nicaraguan rebels brought the agency back into the limelight and prompted renewed criticism. In particular, CIA participation in the mining of Nicaraguan ports to put pressure on the Sandinista government led to charges that the agency was not keeping Congress properly informed about its covert operations, and to a debate over whether the mining was justified. In April 1984, Congress passed a non-binding resolution that no U.S. funds should be used to mine Nicaraguan waters, after administration officials said the mining operation had been stopped.

The director of Central Intelligence is not only the head of the Central Intelligence Agency; he also has general responsibility for coordinating the entire U.S. intelligence community. His considerable authority over all intelligence expenditures adds muscle to this role. He is responsible to the National Security Council, and through the NSC to the president.

Public opinion on covert intelligence operations

Congressional oversight in intelligence operations

SUMMARY

At every point in American history, the country has found itself affected by developments beyond its shores. The demands of foreign and defense policy have been unavoidable; the only question has been what policy should be. As in the argument over what contemporary U.S. policy should be toward South Africa, neither the view that foreign policy should serve the national interest nor the argument that it should conform to high moral standards avoids deep divisions over the proper shape of U.S. policy. Some observers, from Tocqueville on, have felt that from a purely tactical standpoint democracies are put at some disadvantage in their relations with authoritarian governments. The latter can set a course of foreign policy action, commit resources disproportionately to its attainment, be as secretive as is necessary, and persevere in the policy over long periods of time.

The basic approach of the United States to foreign affairs shifted after World War II. The major European powers of the prewar world—Britain, France, and Germany—had been devastated, and they needed to turn inward to reconstruct their own societies. No Western nation besides the United States had the resources to maintain an international balance of power, counter balancing the Soviet Union, which emerged in 1945 as the dominant power on the Eurasian land mass.

The name attached to the American balance-of-power effort is *containment:* containing the Soviet Union and communist expansion. Pursuing this policy, the United States assisted in the rapid postwar reconstruction of the European democracies, assumed leadership of various military alliances including NATO, maintained a large defense establishment, and committed U.S. troops in response to communist-bloc expansion, as in the invasion of South Korea. Yet while it engaged in these ambitious undertakings, the United States's implementation of containment was on the whole cautious and restrained. American public opinion never supported a crusading stance against the U.S.S.R.

The one major exception in a record of generally cautious and prudent balance-of-power politics came in Vietnam, when the United States committed a half-million troops to a prolonged military effort to block the communist takeover of South Vietnam. As the war proceeded, growing proportions of the American public concluded that the human and material costs of the conflict were excessive. Domestic divisions resulting from the war dominated U.S. politics from the mid-1960s through the mid-1970s.

Among political leaders three different interpretations found substantial support: (1) that the postwar containment policy is sound, and the Vietnam intervention was a necessary if painful application of it; (2) that containment is flawed as a basic policy approach, and Vietnam was a bad application of a bad policy; and (3) that the rationale for containment is sound, but the massive U.S. intervention in Vietnam was ill-conceived.

There is little disagreement in the United States on the need to maintain a strong defense, but there is disagreement on how much is enough. U.S. military spending declined significantly during the 1970s, partly as a result of widespread public dissatisfaction with the U.S. role in Vietnam. This decline is evident when military expenditures are calculated with controls for the effect of inflation, and when they are expressed as proportions of the GNP and all federal spending. It is also evident when U.S. military spending is compared to that of the U.S.S.R.

After the late 1970s, however, the pendulum swung the other way. Concern prompted by the perception of U.S. weakness compared to the U.S.S.R. led to new bipartisan efforts to expand real defense spending. The Reagan administration strongly supported a defense buildup, and received the support of Congress for much of what it proposed. In the mid-1980s, interest in both the U.S. and the U.S.S.R. swung back to arms control agreements that might at least in part dampen the arms race.

The National Security Act of 1947 established the National Security Council (NSC) as a key advisory body assisting the president in the conduct of American foreign and defense policy. Besides the president, NSC membership includes the vice president and the secretaries of state and defense. The director of Central Intelligence and the chairman of the Joint Chiefs of Staff are statutory advisers to the NSC. The assistant to the president for national security affairs manages the NSC staff and operates as an influential presidential adviser in foreign policy making.

FOR FURTHER STUDY

Kenneth A. Oye, et al, *Eagle Defiant: United States Foreign Policy in the 1980s* (Boston: Little Brown, 1983). A useful collection of essays on issues of American foreign policy in the 1980s, with attention to all the principal geographic regions.

Charles W. Kegley, Jr., and Eugene R. Wittkopf, *American Foreign Policy: Pattern and Process*, 3rd ed. (New York: St. Martin's Press, 1987). A comprehensive, balanced account of contemporary decision making in American foreign policy.

George Kennan, "The Sources of Soviet Conduct," *Foreign Affairs*, July 1947. This article, published anonymously by Kennan, set forth the rationale for a U.S. "containment" policy toward the Soviet Union.

The Military Balance 1987–1988 (London: International Institute for Strategic Studies, 1988). The best comparative review of the military commitments and strengths of the United States and the NATO countries, and of the Soviet Union and its Warsaw Pact allies.

John Spanier, *American Foreign Policy since World War II*, 11th ed. (Washington, D.C.: Congressional Quarterly Press, 1988). A well-written account of the major decisions and events involving American foreign policy over the last forty years.

Appendix 1

The Declaration of Independence

When in the course of human events, it becomes necessary for one people to dissolve the political bands which have connected them with another, and to assume among the Powers of the earth, the separate and equal station to which the Laws of Nature and of Nature's God entitle them, a decent respect to the opinions of mankind requires that they should declare the causes which impel them to the separation.

We hold these truths to be self-evident, that all men are created equal, that they are endowed by their Creator with certain unalienable rights, that among these are Life, Liberty, and the pursuit of Happiness. That to secure these rights, Governments are instituted among Men, deriving their just powers from the consent of the governed. That whenever any Form of Government becomes destructive of these ends, it is the Right of the People to alter or to abolish it, and to institute new Government, laying its foundation on such principles and organizing its powers in such form, as to them shall seem most likely to effect their Safety and Happiness. Prudence, indeed, will dictate that Governments long established should not be changed for light and transient causes; and accordingly all experience hath shown, that mankind are more disposed to suffer, while evils are sufferable, than to right themselves by abolishing the forms to which they are accustomed. But when a long train of abuses and usurpations, pursuing invariably the same Object evinces a design to reduce them under absolute Despotism, it is their right, it is their duty, to throw off such Government, and to provide new Guards for their future security.—Such has been the patient sufferance of these Colonies; and such is now the necessity which constrains them to alter their former Systems of Government. The history of the present King of Great Britain is a history of repeated injuries and usurpations, all having in direct object the establishment of an absolute Tyranny over these States. To prove this, let Facts be submitted to a candid world.

He has refused his Assent to Laws, the most wholesome and necessary for the public good.

He has forbidden his Governors to pass Laws of immediate and pressing importance, unless suspended in their operation till his Assent should be obtained; and when so suspended, he has utterly neglected to attend to them.

He has refused to pass other Laws for the accommodation of large districts of people, unless those people would relinquish the right of Representation in the Legislature, a right inestimable to them and formidable to tyrants only.

He has called together legislative bodies at places unusual, uncomfortable, and distant from the depository of their public Records, for the sole purpose of fatiguing them into compliance with his measures.

He has dissolved Representative Houses repeatedly, for opposing with manly firmness his invasions on the rights of the people.

He has refused for a long time, after such dissolutions, to cause others to be elected; whereby the Legislative powers, incapable of Annihilation, have returned to the People at large for their exercise; the State remaining in the mean time exposed to all dangers of invasion from without, and convulsions within.

He has endeavoured to prevent the population of these States; for that purpose obstructing the Laws of Naturalization of Foreigners; refusing to pass others to encourage their migrations hither, and raising the conditions of new Appropriations of Lands.

He has obstructed the Administration of Justice, by refusing his Assent to Laws for establishing Judiciative powers.

He has made Judges dependent on his Will alone, for the tenure of their offices, and the amount and payment of their salaries.

He has erected a multitude of New Offices, and sent hither swarms of Officers to harass our People, and eat out their substance.

He has kept among us, in times of peace, Standing Armies without the Consent of our legislature.

He has affected to render the Military independent of and superior to the Civil Power.

He has combined with others to subject us to a jurisdiction foreign to our constitution, and unacknowledged by our laws; giving his Assent to their Acts of pretended Legislation:

For quartering large bodies of armed troops among us:

For protecting them, by a mock Trial, from Punishment for any Murders which they should commit on the Inhabitants of these States:

For cutting off our Trade with all parts of the world:

For imposing taxes on us without our Consent:

For depriving us of many cases, of the benefits of Trial by jury:

For transporting us beyond Seas to be tried for pretended offences:

For abolishing the free System of English Laws in a neighbouring Province, establishing therein an Arbitrary government, and enlarging its Boundaries so as to render it at once an example and fit instrument for introducing the same absolute rule into these Colonies:

For taking away our Charters, abolishing our most valuable Laws, and altering fundamentally the Forms of our Governments:

For suspending our own Legislatures, and declaring themselves invested with Power to legislate for us in all cases whatsoever.

He has abdicated Government here, by declaring us out of his Protection and waging War against us.

He has plundered our seas, ravaged our Coasts, burnt our towns, and destroyed the lives of our people.

He is at this time transporting large armies of foreign mercenaries to compleat the works of death, desolation, and tyranny, already begun with circumstances of Cruelty & perfidy scarcely paralleled in the most barbarous ages, and totally unworthy the Head of a civilized nation.

He has constrained our fellow Citizens taken Captive on the high Seas to bear Arms against their Country, to become the executioners of their friends and Brethren, or to fall themselves by their Hands.

He has excited domestic insurrections amongst us, and has endeavoured to bring on the inhabitants of our frontiers, the merciless Indian Savages, whose known rule of warfare, is an undistinguished destruction of all ages, sexes, and conditions.

In every stage of these Oppressions We have Petitioned for Redress in the most humble terms: Our repeated Petitions have been answered only by repeated injury. A Prince, whose character is thus marked by every act which may define a Tyrant, is unfit to be the ruler of a free people.

Nor have We been wanting in attention to our British brethren. We have warned them from time to time of attempts by their legislature to extend an unwarrantable jurisdiction over us. We have reminded them of the circumstances of our emigration and settlement here. We have appealed to their native justice and magnanimity, and we have conjured them by the ties of our common kindred to disavow these usurpations, which, would inevitably interrupt our connections and correspondence. They too must have been deaf to the voice of justice and of consanguinity. We must, therefore, acquiesce in the necessity, which denounces our Separation, and hold them, as we hold the rest of mankind, Enemies in War, in Peace Friends.

WE, THEREFORE, the Representatives of the UNITED STATES OF AMERICA, in General Congress, Assembled, appealing to the Supreme Judge of the world for the rectitude of our intentions, do, in the Name, and by Authority of the good People of these Colonies, solemnly publish and declare, That these United Colonies are, and of Right ought to be FREE AND INDEPENDENT STATES; that they are Absolved from all Allegiance to the British Crown, and that all political connection between them and the State of Great Britain, is and ought to be totally dissolved; and that as Free and Independent States, they have full Power to levy War, conclude Peace, contract Alliances, establish Commerce, and to do all other Acts and Things which Independent States may of right do. And for the support of this Declaration, with a firm reliance on the Protection of Divine Providence, we mutually pledge to each other our Lives, our Fortunes, and our sacred Honor.

The foregoing Declaration was, by order of Congress, engrossed, and signed by the following members:

John Hancock

NEW HAMPSHIRE
Josiah Bartlett
William Whipple
Matthew Thornton

MASSACHUSETTS BAY
Samuel Adams
John Adams
Robert Treat Paine
Elbridge Gerry

RHODE ISLAND
Stephen Hopkins
William Ellery

CONNECTICUT
Roger Sherman
Samuel Huntington
William Williams
Oliver Wolcott

NEW YORK
William Floyd
Philip Livingston
Francis Lewis
Lewis Morris

NEW JERSEY
Richard Stockton
John Witherspoon
Francis Hopkinson
John Hart
Abraham Clark

PENNSYLVANIA
Robert Morris
Benjamin Rush
Benjamin Franklin
John Morton
George Clymer

James Smith
George Taylor
James Wilson
George Ross

DELAWARE
Caesar Rodney
George Read
Thomas M'Kean

MARYLAND
Samuel Chase
William Paca
Thomas Stone
Charles Carroll,
of Carrollton

VIRGINIA
George Wythe
Richard Henry Lee

Thomas Jefferson
Benjamin Harrison
Thomas Nelson, Jr.
Francis Lightfoot Lee
Carter Braxton

NORTH CAROLINA
William Hooper
Joseph Hewes
John Penn

SOUTH CAROLINA
Edward Rutledge
Thomas Heyward, Jr.

Thomas Lynch, Jr.
Arthur Middleton

GEORGIA
Button Gwinnett
Lyman Hall
George Walton

Resolved, That copies of the Declaration be sent to the several assemblies, conventions, and committees, or councils of safety, and to the several commanding officers of the continental troops; that it be proclaimed in each of the United States, at the head of the army.

Appendix 2

The Constitution of the United States

We the People of the United States, in order to form a more perfect Union, establish Justice, insure domestic Tranquility, provide for the common defence, promote the general Welfare, and secure the Blessings of Liberty to ourselves and our Posterity, do ordain and establish this Constitution for the United States of America.

ARTICLE I.

Section 1. All legislative Powers herein granted shall be vested in a Congress of the United States, which shall consist of a Senate and House of Representatives.

Section 2. The House of Representatives shall be composed of Members chosen every second Year by the People of the several States, and the Electors in each State shall have the Qualifications requisite for Electors of the most numerous Branch of the State Legislature.

No Person shall be a Representative who shall not have attained to the Age of twenty five Years, and been seven Years a Citizen of the United States, and who shall not, when elected, be an Inhabitant of that State in which he shall be chosen.

Representatives and direct Taxes shall be apportioned among the several States which may be included within this Union, according to their respective Numbers, which shall be determined by adding to the whole Number of free Persons, including those bound to Service for a Term of Years, and excluding Indians not taxed, three fifths of all other Persons. The actual Enumeration shall be made within three Years after the first Meeting of the Congress of the United States, and within every subsequent Term of ten Years, in such Manner as they shall by Law direct. The Number of Representatives shall not exceed one for every thirty Thousand, but each State shall have at Least one Representative; and until such enumeration shall be made, the State of New Hampshire shall be entitled to chuse three, Massachusetts eight,

Rhode-Island and Providence Plantations one, Connecticut five, New-York six, New Jersey four, Pennsylvania eight, Delaware one, Maryland six, Virginia ten, North Carolina five, South Carolina five, and Georgia three.

When vacancies happen in the Representation from any State, the Executive Authority thereof shall issue Writs of Election to fill such Vacancies.

The House of Representatives shall chuse their Speaker and other Officers; and shall have the sole Power of Impeachment.

Section 3. The Senate of the United States shall be composed of two Senators from each State, chosen by the Legislature thereof, for six Years; and each Senator shall have one Vote.

Immediately after they shall be assembled in Consequence of the first Election, they shall be divided as equally as may be into three Classes. The Seats of the Senators of the first Class shall be vacated at the Expiration of the **second Year, of the second Class at the Expiration of the fourth Year, and of** the third Class at the Expiration of the sixth Year, so that one third may be chosen every second Year; and if Vacancies happen by Resignation, or otherwise, during the Recess of the Legislature of any State, the Executive thereof may make temporary Appointments until the next Meeting of the Legislature, which shall then fill such Vacancies.

No Person shall be a Senator who shall not have attained to the Age of thirty Years, and been nine Years a Citizen of the United States, and who shall not, when elected, be an Inhabitant of that State for which he shall be chosen.

The Vice President of the United States shall be President of the Senate, but shall have no Vote, unless they be equally divided.

The Senate shall chuse their other Officers, and also a President pro tempore, in the Absence of the Vice President, or when he shall exercise the Office of President of the United States.

The Senate shall have the sole Power to try all Impeachments. When sitting for that Purpose, they shall be on Oath or Affirmation. When the President of the United States is tried, the Chief Justice shall preside: And no Person shall be convicted without the Concurrence of two thirds of the Members present.

Judgment in Cases of Impeachment shall not extend further than to removal from Office, and disqualification to hold and enjoy any Office of honor, Trust or Profit under the United States: but the Party convicted shall nevertheless be liable and subject to Indictment, Trial, Judgment and Punishment, according to Law.

Section 4. The Times, Places and Manner of holding Elections for Senators and Representatives, shall be prescribed in each State by the Legislature thereof, but the Congress may at any time by Law make or alter such Regulations, except as to the Places of chusing Senators.

The Congress shall assemble at least once in every Year, and such Meeting shall be on the first Monday in December, unless they shall by Law appoint a different Day.

Section 5. Each House shall be the Judge of the Elections, Returns and Qualifications of its own Members, and a Majority of each shall constitute a Quorum to do Business; but a smaller Number may adjourn from day to day, and may be authorized to compel the Attendance of absent Members, in such Manner, and under such Penalties as each House may provide.

Each House may determine the Rules of its Proceedings, punish its Members for disorderly Behaviour, and, with the Concurrence of two thirds, expel a Member.

Each House shall keep a Journal of its Proceedings, and from time to time publish the same, excepting such Parts as may in their Judgment require Secrecy; and the Yeas and Nays of the Members of either House on any question shall, at the Desire of one fifth of those Present, be entered on the Journal.

Neither House, during the Session of Congress, shall, without the Consent of the other, adjourn for more than three days, nor to any other Place than that in which the two Houses shall be sitting.

Section 6. The Senators and Representatives shall receive a Compensation for their Services, to be ascertained by Law, and paid out of the Treasury of the United States. They shall in all Cases, except Treason, Felony and Breach of the Peace, be privileged from Arrest during their Attendance at the Session of their respective Houses, and in going to and returning from the same; and for any Speech or Debate in either House, they shall not be questioned in any other Place.

No Senator or Representative shall, during the Time for which he was elected, be appointed to any civil Office under the Authority of the United States, which shall have been created, or the Emoluments whereof shall have been encreased during such time; and no Person holding any Office under the United States, shall be a Member of either House during his Continuance in Office.

Section 7. All Bills for raising Revenue shall originate in the House of Representatives; but the Senate may propose or concur with Amendments as on other Bills.

Every Bill which shall have passed the House of Representatives and the Senate shall, before it becomes a Law, be presented to the President of the United States; If he approve he shall sign it, but if not he shall return it, with his Objections to that House in which it shall have originated, who shall enter the Objections at large on their Journal, and proceed to reconsider it. If after such Reconsideration two thirds of that House shall agree to pass the Bill, it shall be sent, together with the Objections, to the other House, by which it shall likewise be reconsidered, and if approved by two thirds of that House, it shall become a Law. But in all such Cases the Votes of both Houses shall be determined by yeas and Nays, and the Names of the Persons voting for and against the Bill shall be entered on the Journal of each House respectively. If any Bill shall not be returned by the President within ten Days (Sundays excepted) after it shall have been presented to him, the Same shall be a Law, in like Manner as if he had signed it, unless the Congress by their Adjournment prevent its Return, in which Case it shall not be a Law.

Every Order, Resolution, or Vote to which the Concurrence of the Senate and House of Representatives may be necessary (except on a question of Adjournment) shall be presented to the President of the United States; and before the Same shall take Effect, shall be approved by him, or being disapproved by him, shall be repassed by two thirds of the Senate and House or Representatives, according to the Rules and Limitations prescribed in the Case of a Bill.

Section 8. The Congress shall have Power To lay and collect Taxes, Duties, Imposts and Excises, to pay the Debts and provide for the common Defence and general Welfare of the United States; but all Duties, Imposts and Excises shall be uniform throughout the United States.

To borrow Money on the credit of the United States;

To regulate Commerce with foreign Nations, and among the several States, and with the Indian Tribes;

To establish an uniform Rule of Naturalization, and uniform Laws on the subject of Bankruptcies throughout the United States;

To coin Money, regulate the Value thereof, and of foreign Coin, and fix the Standard of Weights and Measures;

To provide for the Punishment of counterfeiting the Securities and current Coin of the United States;

To establish Post Offices and Post Roads;

To promote the Progress of Science and useful Arts, by securing for limited Times to Authors and Inventors the exclusive Right to their respective Writings and Discoveries;

To constitute Tribunals inferior to the supreme Court;

To define and punish Piracies and Felonies committed on the high Seas, and Offences against the Law of Nations;

To declare War, grant Letters of Marque and Reprisal, and make Rules concerning Captures on Land and Water;

To raise and support Armies, but no Appropriation of Money to that Use shall be for a longer Term than two Years;

To provide and maintain a Navy;

To make Rules for the Government and Regulation of the land and naval Forces;

To provide for calling forth the Militia to execute the Laws of the Union, suppress Insurrections and repel Invasions;

To provide for organizing, arming, and disciplining, the Militia, and for governing such Part of them as may be employed in the Service of the United States, reserving to the States respectively, the Appointment of the Officers, and the Authority of training the Militia according to the discipline prescribed by Congress;

To exercise exclusive Legislation in all Cases whatsoever, over such District (not exceeding ten Miles square) as may, by Cession of particular States, and the Acceptance of Congress, become the Seat of the Government of the United States, and to exercise like Authority over all Places purchased by the Consent of the Legislature of the State in which the Same shall be, for the Erection of Forts, Magazines, Arsenals, dock-Yards, and other needful Buildings;—And

To make all Laws which shall be necessary and proper for carrying into Execution the foregoing Powers, and all other Powers vested by this Constitution in the Government of the United States, or in any Department or Officer thereof.

Section 9. The Migration or Importation of such Persons as any of the States now existing shall think proper to admit, shall not be prohibited by the Congress prior to the Year one thousand eight hundred and eight, but a Tax or duty may be imposed on such Importation, not exceeding ten dollars for each Person.

The Privilege of the Writ of Habeas Corpus shall not be suspended, unless when in Cases of Rebellion or Invasion the public Safety may require it.

No Bill of Attainder or ex post facto Law shall be passed.

No Capitation, or other direct, Tax shall be laid, unless in Proportion to the Census or Enumeration herein before directed to be taken.

No Tax or Duty shall be laid on Articles exported from any State.

No Preference shall be given by any Regulation of Commerce or Revenue to the Ports of one State over those of another; nor shall Vessels bound to, or from, one State, be obliged to enter, clear, or pay Duties in another.

No Money shall be drawn from the Treasury, but in Consequence of Appropriations made by Law, and a regular Statement and Account of the Receipts and Expenditures of all public Money shall be published from time to time.

No Title of Nobility shall be granted by the United States: And no Person holding any Office of Profit or trust under them, shall, without the Consent of the Congress, accept of any present, Emolument, Office, or Title, of any kind whatever, from any King, Prince, or foreign State.

Section 10. No State shall enter into any Treaty, Alliance, or Confederation; grant Letters of Marque and Reprisal; coin Money; emit Bills of Credit; make any Thing but gold and silver Coin a Tender in Payment of Debts; pass any Bill of Attainder, ex post facto Law, or Law impairing the Obligation of Contracts, or grant any Title of Nobility.

No State shall, without the Consent of the Congress, lay any Imposts or Duties on Imports or Exports, except what may be absolutely necessary for executing its inspection Laws: and the net Produce of all Duties and Imposts, laid by any State on Imports or Exports, shall be for the Use of the Treasury of the United States; and all such Laws shall be subject to the Revision and Controul of the Congress.

No State shall, without the Consent of Congress, lay any Duty of Tonnage, keep Troops, or Ships of War in time of Peace, enter into any Agreement or Compact with another State, or with a foreign Power, or engage in War, unless actually invaded, or in such imminent Danger as will not admit of delay.

ARTICLE II.

Section 1. The executive Power shall be vested in a President of the United States of America. He shall hold his Office during the term of four Years, and, together with the Vice President, chosen for the same Term, be elected, as follows

Each State shall appoint, in such Manner as the Legislature thereof may direct, a Number of Electors, equal to the whole Number of Senators and Representatives to which the State may be entitled in the Congress: but no Senator or Representative, or Person holding an Office of Trust or Profit under the United States, shall be appointed an Elector.

The Electors shall meet in their respective States, and vote by Ballot for two Persons, of whom one at least shall not be an Inhabitant of the same State with themselves. and they shall make a List of all the Persons voted for, and of the Number of Votes for each; which List they shall sign and certify, and transmit sealed to the Seat of the Government of the United States, directed to the President of the Senate. The President of the Senate shall, in the Presence of the Senate and House of Representatives, open all the Certificates, and the Votes shall then be counted. The Person having the greatest Number of Votes shall be the President, if such Number be a Majority of the whole Number of electors appointed; and if there be more than one who have such Majority, and have an equal Number of Votes, then the House of Representatives shall immediately chuse by Ballot one of them for President; and if no Person have a Majority, then for the five highest on the List the said House shall in like Manner chuse the President. But in chusing the President, the Votes shall be taken by States, the Representation from each State having one Vote; A quorum for this Purpose shall consist of a Member or Members from two thirds of the States, and a Majority all the States shall be necessary to a Choice. In every Case, after the Choice of the President, the Person having the greatest Number of Votes of the Electors shall be the Vice President. But if there should remain two or more who have equal Votes, the Senate shall chuse from them by Ballot the Vice President.

The Congress may determine the Time of chusing the Electors, and the Day on which they shall give their Votes; which Day shall be the same throughout the United States.

No Person except a natural born Citizen, or a Citizen of the United States, at the time of the Adoption of this Constitution, shall be eligible to the Office of President, neither shall any Person be eligible to that Office who shall not have attained to the Age of thirty five Years, and been fourteen Years a Resident within the United States.

In Case of the Removal of the President from Office, or of his Death, Resignation, or Inability to discharge the Powers and Duties of the said Office, the Same shall devolve on the Vice President, and the Congress may by Law provide for the Case of Removal, Death, Resignation or Inability, both of the President and Vice President, declaring what Officer shall then act as President, and such Officer shall act accordingly, until the Disibility be removed, or a President shall be elected.

The President shall, at stated Times, receive for his Services, a Compensation, which shall neither be encreased or diminished during the Period for which he shall have been elected, and he shall not receive within that Period any other Emolument from the United States, or any of them.

Before he enters on the Execution of his Office, he shall take the following Oath or Affirmation:—"I do solemnly swear (or affirm) that I will faithfully execute the Office of President of the United States, and will to the best of my Ability, preserve, protect and defend the Constitution of the United States."

Section 2. The President shall be Commander in Chief of the Army and Navy of the United States, and of the Militia of the several States, when called into the actual Service of the United States; he may require the Opinion, in writing, of the principal Officer in each of the executive Departments, upon any Subject relating to the Duties of their respective Offices, and he shall have Power to grant Reprieves and Pardons for Offences against the United States, except in Cases of Impeachment.

He shall have Power, by and with the Advice and Consent of the Senate, to make Treaties, provided two thirds of the Senators present concur; and he shall nominate, and by and with the Advice and Consent of the Senate, shall appoint Ambassadors, other public Ministers and Consuls, Judges of the supreme Court, and all other officers of the United States, whose Appointments are not herein otherwise provided for, and which shall be established by Law; but the Congress may by Law vest the Appointment of such inferior Officers, as they think proper, in the President alone, in the Courts of Law, or in the Heads of Departments.

The President shall have Power to fill up all Vacancies that may happen during the Recess of the Senate, by granting Commissions which shall expire at the End of their next Session.

Section 3. He shall from time to time give to the Congress Information of the State of the Union, and recommend to their Consideration such Measures as he shall judge necessary and expedient; he may, on extraordinary Occasions, convene both Houses, or either of them, and in Case of Disagreement between them, with Respect to the Time of Adjournment, he may adjourn them to such Time as he shall think proper; he shall receive Ambassadors and other public Ministers; he shall take Care that the Laws be faithfully executed, and shall Commission all the Officers of the United States.

Section 4. The President, Vice President and all civil Officers of the United States, shall be removed from Office on Impeachment for, and Conviction of, Treason, Bribery, or other high Crimes and Misdemeanors.

ARTICLE III.

Section 1. The judicial Power of the United States, shall be vested in one supreme Court, and in such inferior Courts as the Congress may from time to time ordain and establish. The Judges, both of the supreme and inferior Courts, shall hold their Offices during good Behaviour, and shall, at stated Times, receive for their Services, a Compensation, which shall not be diminished during their Continuance in Office.

Section 2. The judicial Power shall extend to all Cases, in Law and Equity, arising under this Constitution, the Laws of the United States, and Treaties made, or which shall be made, under their Authority;—to all Cases affecting Ambassadors, other public Ministers and Consuls;—to all Cases of admiralty and maritime Jurisdiction;—to Controversies to which the United States shall be a Party;—to Controversies between two or more States;—between a State and Citizens of another State;—between Citizens of different States,—between Citizens of the same State claiming Lands under Grants of different States, and between a State, or the Citizens thereof, and foreign States, Citizens or Subjects.

In all cases affecting Ambassadors, other public Ministers and Consuls, and those in which a State shall be Party, the supreme Court shall have original Jurisdiction. In all the other Cases before mentioned, the supreme Court shall have appellate Jurisdiction, both as to Law and Fact, with such Exceptions, and under such Regulations as the Congress shall make.

The Trial of all Crimes, except in Cases of Impeachment, shall be by Jury; and such Trial shall be held in the State where the said Crimes shall have been committed; but when not committed within any State, the Trial shall be at such Place or Places as the Congress may by Law have directed.

Section 3. Treason against the United States, shall consist only in levying War against them, or in adhering to their Enemies, giving them Aid and Comfort. No Person shall be convicted of Treason unless on the Testimony of two Witnesses to the same overt Act, or on Confession in open Court.

The Congress shall have Power to declare the Punishment of Treason, but no Attainder of Treason shall work Corruption of Blood, or Forfeiture except during the Life of the Person attainted.

ARTICLE IV.

Section 1. Full Faith and Credit shall be given in each State to the public Acts, Records, and judicial Proceedings of every other State. And the Congess may by general Laws prescribe the Manner in which such Acts, Records and Proceedings shall be proved, and the Effect thereof.

Section 2. The Citizens of each State shall be entitled to all Privileges and Immunities of Citizens in the several States.

A Person charged in any State with Treason, Felony, or other Crime, who shall flee from Justice, and be found in another State, shall on Demand of the executive Authority of the State from which he fled, be delivered up, to be removed to the State having Jurisdiction of the Crime.

No Person held to Service or Labour in one State, under the Laws thereof, escaping into another, shall, in Consequence of any Law or Regulation therein, be discharged from such Service or Labour, but shall be delivered up on Claim of the Party to whom such Service or Labour may be due.

Section 3. New States may be admitted by the Congress into this Union; but no new State shall be formed or erected within the Jurisdiction of any other State; nor any State be formed by the Junction of two or more States, or Parts of States, without the consent of the Legislatures of the States concerned as well as of the Congress.

The Congress shall have Power to dispose of and make all needful Rules and Regulations respecting the Territory or other Property belonging to the United States; and nothing in this Constitution shall be so construed as to Prejudice any Claims of the United States, or of any particular States.

Section 4. The United States shall guarantee to every State in this Union a Republican Form of Government, and shall protect each of them against Invasion; and on Application of the Legislature, or of the Executive (when the Legislature cannot be convened) against domestic Violence.

ARTICLE V.

The Congress, whenever two thirds of both Houses shall deem it necessary, shall propose Amendments to this Constitution, or, on the Application of the Legislatures of two thirds of the several States shall call a Convention for proposing Amendments, which, in either Case, shall be valid to all Intents and Purposes, as Part of this Constitution, when ratified by the Legislatures of three fourths of the several States, or by Conventions in three fourths thereof, as the one or the other Mode of Ratification may be proposed by the Congress; Provided that no Amendment which may be made prior to the Year One thousand eight hundred and eight shall in any Manner affect the first and fourth Clauses in the Ninth Section of the first Article; and that no State, without its Consent, shall be deprived of it's equal Suffrage in the Senate.

ARTICLE VI.

All Debts contracted and Engagements entered into, before the Adoption of this Constitution, shall be as valid against the United States under this Constitution, as under the Confederation.

This Constitution, and the Laws of the United States which shall be made in Pursuance thereof; and all Treaties made, or which shall be made, under the Authority of the United States, shall be the supreme Law of the Land; and the Judges in every State shall be bound thereby, any Thing in the Constitution or Laws of any State to the Contrary notwithstanding.

The Senators and Representatives before mentioned, and the Members of the several State Legislatures, and all executive and judicial Officers, both of the United States and of the several States, shall be bound by Oath or Affirmation, to support this Constitution; but no religious Test shall ever be required as a Qualification to any Office or public Trust under the United States.

ARTICLE VII.

The Ratification of the Conventions of nine States, shall be sufficient for the Establishment of this Constitution between the States so ratifying the Same.

Done in Convention by the Unanimous Consent of the States present the Seventeenth Day of September in the Year of our Lord one thousand seven hundred and Eighty seven and of the Independence of the United States of America the Twelfth. In witness thereof We have hereunto subscribed our Names,

G⁰: WASHINGTON—Presidᵗ and deputy from Virginia

New Hampshire { John Langdon
Nicholas Gilman

Massachusetts { Nathaniel Gorham
Rufus King

Connecticut { Wᵐ Samˡ Johnson
Roger Sherman

New York { Alexander Hamilton

New Jersey { Wil: Livingston
David A. Brearley.
Wᵐ Paterson.
Jona: Dayton

Pennsylvania { B. Franklin
Thomas Mifflin
Robᵗ Morris
Geo. Clymer
Thoˢ. FitzSimons
Jared Ingersoll
James Wilson
Gouv Morris

Delaware { Geo: Read
Gunning Bedford jun
John Dickinson
Richard Bassett
Jaco: Broom

Maryland { James McHenry
Dan of Sᵗ Thoˢ
Jenifer
Danˡ Carroll

Virginia { John Blair—
James Madison Jr.

North Carolina { Wᵐ. Blount
Richᵈ Dobbs
Spaight.
Hu Williamson

South Carolina { J. Rutledge
Charles Cotesworth Pinckney
Charles Pinckney
Pierce Butler.

Georgia { William Few
Abr Baldwin

Amendments to the Constitution

Articles in addition to, and Amendment of the Constitution of the United States of America, proposed by Congress, and ratified by the Legislatures of the several States, pursuant to the fifth Article of the original Constitution.

AMENDMENT 1.

Congress shall make no law respecting an establishment of religion, or prohibiting the free exercise thereof; or abridging the freedom of speech, or of the press; or the right of the people peaceably to assemble, and to petition the Government for a redress of grievances.

AMENDMENT 2.

A well regulated Militia, being necessary to the security of a free State, the right of the people to keep and bear Arms, shall not be infringed.

AMENDMENT 3.

No Soldier shall, in time of peace be quartered in any house, without the consent of the Owner, nor in time of war, but in a manner to be prescribed by law.

AMENDMENT 4.

The right of the people to be secure in their persons, houses, papers, and effects, against unreasonable searches and seizures, shall not be violated, and no Warrants shall issue, but upon probable cause, supported by Oath or affirmation, and particularly describing the place to be searched, and the persons or things to be seized.

AMENDMENT 5.

No person shall be held to answer for a capital, or otherwise infamous crime, unless on a presentment or indictment of a Grand Jury, except in cases arising in the land or naval forces, or in the Militia, when in actual service in time of War or public danger; nor shall any person be subject for the same offence to be twice put in jeopardy of life or limb; nor shall be compelled in any criminal case to be a witness against himself, nor be deprived of life, liberty, or property, without due process of law; nor shall private property be taken for public use, without just compensation.

AMENDMENT 6.

In all criminal prosecutions, the accused shall enjoy the right to a speedy and public trial, by an impartial jury of the State and district wherein the crime shall have been committed, which district shall have been previously ascertained by law, and to be informed of the nature and cause of the accusation; to be confronted with the witnesses against him; to have compulsory process for obtaining witnesses in his favor, and to have the Assistance of Counsel for his defence.

AMENDMENT 7.

In Suits at common law, where the value in controversy shall exceed twenty dollars, the right of trial by jury shall be preserved, and no fact tried by a jury, shall be otherwise re-examined in any Court of the United States, than according to the rules of the common law.

AMENDMENT 8.

Excessive bail shall not be required, nor excessive fines imposed, nor cruel and unusual punishments inflicted.

AMENDMENT 9.

The enumeration in the Constitution, of certain rights, shall not be construed to deny or disparage others retained by the people.

AMENDMENT 10.

The powers not delegated to the United States by the Constitution, nor prohibited by it to the States, are reserved to the States respectively, or to the people. [Amendments 1–10 **(The Bill of Rights)** ratified, 1791]

AMENDMENT 11.

The Judicial power of the United States shall not be construed to extend to any suit in law or equity, commenced or prosecuted against one of the United States by Citizens of another State, or by Citizens or Subjects of any Foreign State. [ratified, 1795]

AMENDMENT 12.

The Electors shall meet in their respective states, and vote by ballot for President and Vice-President, one of whom, at least, shall not be an inhabitant of the same state with themselves; they shall name in their ballots the person voted for as President, and in distinct ballots the person voted for as Vice-President, and they shall make distinct lists of all persons voted for as President, and of all persons voted for as Vice-President, and of the number of votes for each, which lists they shall sign and certify, and transmit sealed to the seat of the government of the United States, directed to the President of the Senate;—The President of the Senate shall, in the presence of the Senate and House of Representatives, open all the certificates and the votes shall then be counted;—The person having the greatest number of votes for President, shall be the President, if such number be a majority of the whole number of Electors appointed; and if no person have such majority, then from the persons having the highest numbers not exceeding three on the list of those voted for as President, the House of Representatives shall choose immediately, by ballot, the President. But in choosing the President, the votes shall be taken by states, the representation from each state having one vote: a quorum for this purpose shall consist of a member or members from two-thirds of the states, and a majority of all the states shall be necessary to a choice. And if the House of of Representatives shall not choose a President whenever the right of choice shall devolve upon them, before the fourth day of March next following, then the Vice-President shall act as President, as in the case of the death or other constitutional disability of the President.—The person having the greatest number of votes as Vice-President, shall be the Vice-President, if such number be a majority of the whole number of Electors appointed, and if no person have a majority, then from the two highest numbers on the list, the Senate shall choose the Vice-President; a quorum for the purpose shall consist of two-thirds of the whole number of Senators, and a majority of the whole number shall be necessary to a choice. But no person constitutionally ineligible to the office of President shall be eligible to that of Vice-President of the United States. [ratified, 1804]

AMENDMENT 13.

Section 1. Neither slavery not involuntary servitude, except as a punishment for crime whereof the party shall have been duly convicted, shall exist within the United States, or any place subject to their jurisdiction.

Section 2. Congress shall have power to enforce this article by appropriate legislation. [ratified, 1865]

AMENDMENT 14.

Section 1. All persons born or naturalized in the United States, and subject to the jurisdiction thereof, are citizens of the United States and of the State wherein they reside. No State shall make or enforce any law which shall abridge the privileges or immunities of citizens of the United States; nor shall any State deprive any person of life, liberty, or property, without due process of law; not deny to any person within its jurisdiction the equal protection of the laws.

Section 2. Representatives shall be apportioned among the several States according to their respective numbers, counting the whole number of persons in each State, excluding Indians not taxed. But when the right to vote at any election for the choice of electors for President and Vice President of the United States, Representatives in Congress, the Executive and Judicial officers of a State, or the members of the Legislature thereof, is denied to any of the male inhabitants of such State, being twenty-one years of age, and citizens of the United States, or in any way abridged, except for participation in rebellion, or other crime, the basis of representation therein shall be reduced in the proportion which the number of such male citizens shall bear to the whole number of male citizens twenty-one years of age in such State.

Section 3. No person shall be a Senator or Representative in Congress, or elector of President and Vice President, or hold any office, civil or military, under the United States, or under any State, who, having previously taken an oath, as a member of Congress, or as an officer of the United States, or as a member of any State legislature, or as an executive or judicial officer of any State, to support the Constitution of the United States, shall have engaged in insurrection or rebellion against the same, or given aid or comfort to the enemies thereof. But Congress may by a vote of two-thirds of each House, remove such disability.

Section 4. The validity of the public debt of the United States, authorized by law, including debts incurred for payment of pensions and bounties for services in suppressing insurrection or rebellion, shall not be questioned. But neither the United States nor any State shall assume or pay any debt or obligation incurred in aid of insurrection or rebellion against the United States, or any claim for the loss or emancipation of any slave; but all such debts, obligations and claims shall be held illegal and void.

Section 5. The Congress shall have power to enforce, by appropriate legislation, the provisions of this article. [ratified, 1868]

AMENDMENT 15.

Section 1. The right of citizens of the United States to vote shall not be denied or abridged by the United States or by any State on account of race, color, or previous condition of servitude.

Section 2. The Congress shall have power to enforce this article by appropriate legislation. [ratified, 1870]

AMENDMENT 16.

The Congress shall have power to lay and collect taxes on incomes, from whatever source derived, without apportionment among the several States, and without regard to any census or enumeration. [ratified, 1913]

AMENDMENT 17.

The Senate of the United States shall be composed of two senators from each State, elected by the people thereof, for six years; and each Senator shall have one vote. The electors in each State shall have the qualifications requisite for electors of the most numerous branch of the State legislature.

When vacancies happen in the representation of any State in the Senate, the executive authority of such State shall issue writs of election to fill such vacancies: *Provided,* That the legislature of any State may empower the executive thereof to make temporary appointments until the people fill the vacancies by election as the legislature may direct.

This amendment shall not be so construed as to affect the election or term of any senator chosen before it becomes valid as part of the Constitution. [ratified, 1913]

AMENDMENT 18.

After one year from the ratification of this article, the manufacture, sale, or transportation of intoxicating liquors within, the importation thereof into, or the exportation thereof from the United States and all territory subject to the jurisdiction thereof for beverage purposes is hereby prohibited.

The Congress and the several States shall have concurrent power to enforce this article by appropriate legislation.

This article shall be inoperative unless it shall have been ratified as an amendment to the Constitution by the legislatures of the several States, as provided in the Constitution, within seven years from the date of the submission thereof to the States by Congress. [ratified, 1919]

AMENDMENT 19.

The right of citizens of the United States to vote shall not be denied or abridged by the United States or by any State on account of sex.

The Congress shall have power by appropriate legislation to enforce the provisions of this article. [ratified, 1920]

AMENDMENT 20.

Section 1. The terms of the President and Vice-President shall end at noon on the twentieth day of January, and the terms of Senators and Representatives at noon on the third day of January, of the years in which such terms would have ended if this article had not been ratified; and the terms of their successors shall then begin.

Section 2. The Congress shall assemble at least once in every year, and such meeting shall begin at noon on the third day of January, unless they shall by law appoint a different day.

Section 3. If, at the time fixed for the beginning of the term of the President, the President-elect shall have died, the Vice-President-elect shall become President. If a President shall not have been chosen before the time fixed for the beginning of his term, or if the President-elect shall have failed to qualify, then the Vice-President-elect shall act as President until a President shall have qualified; and the Congress may by law provide for the case wherein neither a President-elect nor a Vice-President-elect shall have qualified, declaring who shall then act as President, or the manner in which one who is to act shall be selected, and such person shall act accordingly until a President or Vice-President shall have qualified.

Section 4. The Congress may by law provide for the case of the death of any of the persons from whom the House of Representatives may choose a President whenever the right of choice shall have devolved upon them, and for the case of the death of any of the persons from whom the Senate may choose a Vice-President whenever the right of choice shall have devolved upon them.

Section 5. Sections 1 and 2 shall take effect on the 15th day of October following the ratification of this article.

Section 6. This article shall be inoperative unless it shall have been ratified as an amendment to the Constitution by the legislatures of three-fourths of the several States within seven years from the date of its submission. [ratified, 1933]

AMENDMENT 21.

Section 1. The eighteenth article of amendment to the Constitution of the United States is hereby repealed.

Section 2. The transportation or importation into any State, Territory or possession of the United States for delivery or use therein of intoxicating liquors, in violation of the laws thereof, is hereby prohibited.

Section 3. This article shall be inoperative unless it shall have been ratified as an amendment to the Constitution by convention in the several States, as provided in the Constitution, within seven years from the date of the submission thereof to the States by the Congress. [ratified, 1933]

AMENDMENT 22.

Section 1. No person shall be elected to the office of the President more than twice, and no person who has held the office of President, or acted as President, for more than two years of a term to which some other person was elected President shall be elected to the office of the President more than once. But this Article shall not apply to any person holding the office of President when this Article was proposed by the Congress, and shall not prevent any person who may be holding the office of President, or acting as President, during the term within which this Article becomes operative from holding the office of President or acting as President during the remainder of such term.

Section 2. This article shall be inoperative unless it shall have been ratified as an amendment to the Constitution by the legislatures of three-fourths of the several States within seven years from the date of its submission to the States by the Congress. [ratified, 1951]

AMENDMENT 23.

Section 1. The District constituting the seat of government of the United States shall appoint in such manner as the Congress may direct:

A number of electors of President and Vice-President equal to the whole number of Senators and Representatives in Congress to which the District would be entitled if it were a State, but in no event more than the least populous State; they shall be in addition to those appointed by the States, but they shall be considered, for the purposes of the election of President and Vice-President, to be electors appointed by a State; and they shall meet in the District and perform such duties as provided by the twelfth article of amendment.

Section 2. The Congress shall have the power to enforce this article by appropriate legislation. [ratified, 1961]

AMENDMENT 24.

Section 1. The right of citizens of the United States to vote in any primary or other election for President or Vice President, for electors for President or Vice President, or for Senator or Representative in Congress, shall not be denied or abridged by the United States or any State by reason of failure to pay any poll tax or other tax.

Section 2. The Congress shall have power to enforce this article by appropriate legislation. [ratified, 1964]

AMENDMENT 25.

Section 1. In case of the removal of the President from office or of his death or resignation, the Vice President shall become President.

Section 2. Whenever there is a vacancy in the office of Vice President, the President shall nominate a Vice President who shall take office upon confirmation by a majority vote of both Houses of Congress.

Section 3. Whenever the President transmits to the President pro tempore of the Senate and the Speaker of the House of Representatives his written declaration that he is unable to discharge the powers and duties of his office, and until he transmits to them a written declaration to the contrary, such powers and duties shall be discharged by the Vice President as Acting President.

Section 4. Whenever the Vice President and a majority of either the principal officers of the executive departments or of such other body as Congress may by law provide, transmit to the President pro tempore of the Senate and the Speaker of the House of Representatives their written declaration that the President is unable to discharge the powers and duties of his office, the Vice President shall immediately assume the powers and duties of the office as Acting President.

Thereafter, when the President transmits to the President pro tempore of the Senate and the Speaker of the House of Representatives his written declaration that no inability exists, he shall resume the powers and duties of his office unless the Vice President and a majority of either the principal officers of the executive departments or of such other body as Congress may by law provide, transmit within four days to the President pro tempore of the Senate and the Speaker of the House of Representatives their written declaration that the President is unable to discharge the powers and duties of his office. Thereupon Congress shall decide the issue, assembling within forty-eight hours for that purpose if not in session. If the Congress, within twenty-one days after receipt of the latter written declaration, or, if Congress is not in session, within twenty-one days after Congress is required to assemble, determines by two-thirds vote of both Houses that the President is unable to discharge the powers and duties of his office, the Vice President shall continue to discharge the same as Acting President; otherwise, the President shall resume the powers and duties of his office. [ratified, 1967]

AMENDMENT 26.

Section 1. The right of citizens of the United States, who are eighteen years of age or older, to vote shall not be denied or abridged by the United States or by any State on account of age.

Section 2. The Congress shall have power to enforce this article by appropriate legislation. [ratified, 1971]

Appendix 3

Federalist Papers #10 and #51

NO. 10: MADISON

Among the numerous advantages promised by a well-constructed Union, none deserves to be more accurately developed than its tendency to break and control the violence of faction. The friend of popular governments never finds himself so much alarmed for their character and fate as when he contemplates their propensity to this dangerous vice. He will not fail, therefore, to set a due value on any plan which, without violating the principles to which he is attached, provides a proper cure for it. The instability, injustice, and confusion introduced into the public councils have, in truth, been the mortal diseases under which popular governments have everywhere perished, as they continue to be the favorite and fruitful topics from which the adversaries to liberty derive their most specious declamations. The valuable improvements made by the American constitutions on the popular models, both ancient and modern, cannot certainly be too much admired; but it would be an unwarrantable partiality to contend that they have as effectually obviated the danger on this side, as was wished and expected. Complaints are everywhere heard from our most considerate and virtuous citizens, equally the friends of public and private faith and of public and personal liberty, that our governments are too unstable, that the public good is disregarded in the conflicts of rival parties, and that measures are too often decided, not according to the rules of justice and the rights of the minor party, but by the superior force of an interested and overbearing majority. However anxiously we may wish that these complaints had no foundation, the evidence of known facts will not permit us to deny that they are in some degree true. It will be found, indeed, on a candid review of our situation, that some of the distresses under which we labor have been erroneously charged on the operation of our governments; but it will be found, at the same time, that other causes will not alone account for many of our heaviest misfortunes; and, particularly, for that prevailing and increasing distrust of public engagements and alarm for private rights which are echoed from one end of the continent to the other. These must be chiefly, if not wholly, effects of the unsteadiness and injustice with which a factious spirit has tainted our public administration.

By a faction I understand a number of citizens, whether amounting to a majority or minority of the whole, who are united and actuated by some common impulse of passion, or of interest, adverse to the rights of other citizens, or to the permanent and aggregate interests of the community.

There are two methods of curing the mischiefs of faction: the one, by removing its causes; the other, by controlling its effects.

There are again two methods of removing the causes of faction: the one, by destroying the liberty which is essential to its existence; the other, by giving to every citizen the same opinions, the same passions, and the same interests.

It could never be more truly said than of the first remedy that it was worse than the disease. Liberty is to faction what air is to fire, an aliment without which it instantly expires. But it could not be a less folly to abolish liberty, which is essential to political life, because it nourishes faction than it would be to wish the annihilation of air, which is essential to animal life, because it imparts to fire its destructive agency.

The second expedient is as impracticable as the first would be unwise. As long as the reason of man continues fallible, and he is at liberty to exercise it, different opinions will be formed. As long as the connection subsists between his reason and his self-love, his opinions and his passions will have a reciprocal influence on each other; and the former will be objects to which the latter will attach themselves. The diversity in the faculties of men, from which the rights of property originate, is not less an insuperable obstacle to a uniformity of interests. The protection of these faculties is the first object of government. From the protection of different and unequal faculties of acquiring property, the possession of different degrees and kinds of property immediately results; and from the influence of these on the sentiments and views of the respective proprietors ensues a division of the society into different interests and parties.

The latent causes of faction are thus sown in the nature of man; and we see them everywhere brought into different degrees of activity, according to the different circumstances of civil society. A zeal for different opinions concerning religion, concerning government, and many other points, as well of speculation as of practice; an attachment to different leaders ambitiously contending for pre-eminence and power; or to persons of other descriptions whose fortunes have been interesting to the human passions, have, in turn, divided mankind into parties, inflamed them with mutual animosity, and rendered them much more disposed to vex and oppress each other than to co-operate for their common good. So strong is this propensity of mankind to fall into mutual animosities that where no substantial occasion presents itself the most frivolous and fanciful distinctions have been sufficient to kindle their unfriendly passions and excite their most violent conflicts. But the most common and durable source of factions has been the various and unequal distribution of property. Those who hold and those who are without property have ever formed distinct interests in society. Those who are creditors, and those who are debtors, fall under a like discrimination. A landed interest, a manufacturing interest, a mercantile interest, a moneyed interest, with many lesser interests, grow up of necessity in civilized nations, and divide them into different classes, actuated by different sentiments and views. The regulation of these various and interfering interests forms the principal task of modern legislation and involves the spirit of party and faction in the necessary and ordinary operations of government.

No man is allowed to be a judge in his own cause, because his interest would certainly bias his judgment, and, not improbably, corrupt his integrity. With equal, nay with greater reason, a body of men are unfit to be both judges and parties at the same time; yet what are many of the most important acts of legislation but so many judicial determinations, not indeed concerning the rights of single persons, but concerning the rights of large bodies of citizens? And what are the different classes of legislators but advocates and parties to the causes which they determine? Is a law proposed concerning private debts? It is a question to which the creditors are parties on one side and the debtors on the other. Justice ought to hold the balance between them. Yet the parties are, and must be, themselves the judges; and the most numerous party, or in other words, the most powerful faction must be expected to prevail. Shall domestic manufacturers be encouraged, and in what degree, by restrictions on foreign manufacturers? are questions which would be differently decided by the landed and the manufacturing classes, and probably by neither with a whole regard to justice and the public good. The apportionment of taxes on the various descriptions of property is an act which seems to require the most exact impartiality; yet there is, perhaps, no legislative act in which greater opportunity and temptation are given to a predominant party to trample on the rules of justice. Every shilling with which they overburden the inferior number is a shilling saved to their own pockets.

It is in vain to say that enlightened statesmen will be able to adjust these clashing interests and render them all subservient to the public good. Enlightened statesmen will not always be at the helm. Nor, in many cases, can such an adjustment be made at all without taking into view indirect and remote considerations, which will rarely prevail over the immediate interest which one party may find in disregarding the rights of another or the good of the whole.

The inference to which we are brought is that the *causes* of faction cannot be removed and that relief is only to be sought in the means of controlling its *effects*.

If a faction consists of less than a majority, relief is supplied by the republican principle, which enables the majority to defeat its sinister views by regular vote. It may clog the administration, it may convulse the society; but it will be unable to execute and mask its violence under the forms of the Constitution. When a majority is included in a faction, the form of popular government, on the other hand, enables it to sacrifice to its ruling passion or interst both the public good and the rights of other citizens. To secure the public good and private rights against the danger of such a faction, and at the same time to preserve the spirit and the form of popular government, is then the great object to which our inquiries are directed. Let me add that it is the great desideratum by which alone this form of government can be rescued from the opprobrium under which it has so long labored and be recommended to the esteem and adoption of mankind.

By what means is this object attainable? Evidently by one of two only. Either the existence of the same passion or interest in a majority at the same time must be prevented, or the majority, having such coexistent passion or interest, must be rendered, by their number and local situation, unable to concert and carry into effect schemes of oppression. If the impulse and the opportunity be suffered to coincide, we well know that neither moral nor religious motives can be relied on as an adequate control. They are not found to be such on the injustice and violence of individuals, and lose their efficacy in proportion to the number combined together, that is, in proportion as their efficacy becomes needful.

From this view of the subject it may be concluded that a pure democracy, by which I mean a society consisting of a small number of citizens, who assemble and administer the government in person, can admit of no cure for the mischiefs of faction. A common passion or interest will, in almost every case, be felt by a majority of the whole; a communication and concert results from the form of government itself; and there is nothing to check the inducements to sacrifice the weaker party or an obnoxious individual. Hence it is that such democracies have ever been spectacles of turbulence and contention; have ever been found incompatible with personal security or the rights of property; and have in general been as short in their lives as they have been violent in their deaths. Theoretic politicians, who have patronized their species of government, have erroneously supposed that by reducing mankind to a perfect equality in their political rights, they would at the same time be perfectly equalized and assimilated in their possessions, their opinions, and their passions.

A republic, by which I mean a government in which the scheme of representation takes place, opens a different prospect and promises the cure for which we are seeking. Let us examine the points in which it varies from pure democracy, and we shall comprehend both the nature of the cure and the efficacy which it must derive from the Union.

The two great points of difference between a democracy and a republic are: first the delegation of the government, in the latter, to a small number of citizens elected by the rest; secondly, the great number of citizens and greater sphere of country over which the latter may be extended.

The effect of the first difference is, on the one hand, to refine and enlarge the public views by passing them through the medium of a chosen body of citizens, whose wisdom may best discern the true interest of their country and whose patriotism and love of justice will be least likely to sacrifice it to temporary or partial considerations. Under such a regulation it may well happen that the public voice, pronounced by the representatives of the people, will be more consonant to the public good than if pronounced by the people themselves, convened for the purpose. On the other hand, the effect may be inverted. Men of factious tempers, of local prejudices, or of sinister designs, may, by intrigue, by corruption, or by other means, first obtain the suffrages, and then betray the interests of the people. The question resulting is, whether small or extensive republics are most favorable to the election of proper guardians of the public weal; and it is clearly decided in favor of the latter by two obvious considerations.

In the first place it is to be remarked that however small the republic may be the representatives must be raised to a certain number in order to guard against the cabals of a few; and that however large it may be they must be limited to a certain number in order to guard against the confusion of a multitude. Hence, the number of representatives in the two cases not being in proportion to that of the constituents, and being proportionally greatest in the small republic, it follows that if the proportion of fit characters be not less in the large than in the small republic, the former will present a greater option, and consequently a greater probability of a fit choice.

In the next place, as each representative will be chosen by a greater number of citizens in the large than in the small republic, it will be more difficult for unworthy candidates to practise with success the vicious arts by which elections are too often carried; and the suffrages of the people being more free, will be more likely to center on men who possess the most attractive merit and the most diffusive and established characters.

It must be confessed that in this, as in most other cases, there is a mean, on both sides of which inconveniencies will be found to lie. By enlarging too much the number of electors, you render the representative too little acquainted with all their local circumstances and lesser interests; as by reducing it too much, you render him unduly attached to these, and too little fit to comprehend and pursue great and national objects. The federal Constitution forms a happy combination in this respect; the great and aggregate interests being referred to the national, the local and particular to the State legislatures.

The other point of difference is the greater number of citizens and extent of territory which may be brought within the compass of republican than of democratic government; and it is this circumstance principally which renders factious combinations less to be dreaded in the former than in the latter. The smaller the society, the fewer probably will be the distinct parties and interests composing it; the fewer the distinct parties and interests, the more frequently will a majority be found of the same party; and the smaller the number of individuals composing a majority, and the smaller the compass within which they are placed, the more easily will they concert and execute their plans of oppression. Extend the sphere and you take in a greater variety of parties and interests; you make it less probable that a majority of the whole will have a common motive to invade the rights of other citizens; or if such a common motive exists, it will be more difficult for all who feel it to discover their own strength and to act in unison with each other. Besides other impediments, it may be remarked that, where there is a consciousness of unjust or dishonorable purposes, communication is always checked by distrust in proportion to the number whose concurrence is necessary.

Hence, it clearly appers that the same advantage which a republic has over a democracy in controlling the effects of faction is enjoyed by a large over a small republic—is enjoyed by the Union over the States composing it. Does this advantage consist in the substitution of representatives whose enlightened views and virtuous sentiments render them superior to local prejudices and to schemes of injustice? It will not be denied that the representation of the Union will be most likely to possess these requisite endowments. Does it consist in the greater security afforded by a greater variety of parties, against the event of any one party being able to outnumber and oppress the rest? In an equal degree does the increased variety of parties comprised within the Union increase this security? Does it, in fine, consist in the greater obstacles opposed to the concert and accomplishment of the secret wishes of an unjust and interested majority? Here again the extent of the Union gives it the most palpable advantage.

The influence of factious leaders may kindle a flame within their particular States but will be unable to spread a general conflagration through the other States. A religious sect may degenerate into a political faction in a part of the Confederacy; but the variety of sects dispersed over the entire face of it must secure the national councils against any danger from that source. A rage for paper money, for an abolition of debts, for an equal division of property, or for any other improper or wicked project, will be less apt to pervade the whole body of the Union than a particular member of it, in the same proportion as such a malady is more likely to taint a particular county or district than an entire State.

In the extent and proper structure of the Union, therefore, we behold a republican remedy for the diseases most incident to republican government. And according to the degree of pleasure and pride we feel in being republicans ought to be our zeal in cherishing the spirit and supporting the character of federalists.   PUBLIUS

NO. 51: MADISON

To what expedient, then, shall we finally resort, for maintaining in practice the necessary partition of power among the several departments as laid down in the Constitution? The only answer that can be given is that as all these exterior provisions are found to be inadequate the defect must be supplied, by so contriving the interior structure of the government as that its several constituent parts may, by their mutual relations, be the means of keeping each other in their proper places. Without presuming to undertake a full development of this important idea I will hazard a few general observations which may perhaps place it in a clear light, and enable us to form a more correct judgment of the principles and structure of the government planned by the convention.

In order to lay a due foundation for that separate and distinct exercise of the different powers of government, which to a certain extent is admitted on all hands to be essential to the preservation of liberty, it is evident that each department should have a will of its own; and consequently should be so constituted that the members of each should have as little agency as possible in the appointment of the members of the others. Were this principle rigorously adhered to, it would require that all the appointments for the supreme executive, legislative, and judiciary magistracies should be drawn from the same fountain of authority, the people, through channels having no communication whatever with one another. Perhaps such a plan of constructing the several departments would be less difficult in practice than it may in contemplation appear. Some difficulties, however, and some additional expense would attend the execution of it. Some deviations, therefore, from the principle must be admitted. In the constitution of the judiciary department in particular, it might be inexpedient to insist rigorously on the principle: first, because peculiar qualifications being essential in the members, the primary consideration ought to be to select that mode of choice which best secures these qualifications; second, because the permanent tenure by which the appointments are held in that department must soon destroy all sense of dependence on the authority conferring them.

It is equally evident that the members of each department should be as little dependent as possible on those of the others for the emoluments annexed to their offices. Were the executive magistrate, or the judges, not independent of the legislature in this particular, their independence in every other would be merely nominal.

But the great security against a gradual concentration of the several powers in the same department consists in giving to those who administer each department the necessary constitutional means and personal motives to resist encroachments of the others. The provision for defense must in this, as in all other cases, be made commensurate to the danger of attack. Ambition must be made to counteract ambition. The interest of the man must be connected with the constitutional rights of the place. It may be a reflection on human nature that such devices should be necessary to control the abuses of government. But what is government itself but the greatest of all reflections on human nature? If men were angels, no government would be necessary. If angels were to govern men, neither external nor internal controls on government would be necessary. In framing a government which is to be administered by men over men, the great difficulty lies in this: you must first enable the government to control the governed; and in the next place oblige it to control itself. A dependence on the people is, no doubt, the primary control on the government; but experience has taught mankind the necessity of auxiliary precautions.

This policy of supplying, by opposite and rival interests, the defect of better motives, might be traced through the whole system of human affairs, private as well as public. We see it particularly displayed in all the subordinate distributions of power, where the constant aim is to divide and arrange the several offices in such a manner as that each may be a check on the other— that the private interest of every individual may be a sentinel over the public rights. These inventions of prudence cannot be less requisite in the distribution of the supreme powers of the State.

But it is not possible to give to each department an equal power of self-defense. In republican government, the legislative authority necessarily predominates. The remedy for this inconveniency is to divide the legislature into different branches; and to render them, by different modes of election and different principles of action, as little connected with each other as the nature of their common functions and their common dependence on the society will admit. It may even be necessary to guard against dangerous encroachments by still further precautions. As the weight of the legislative authority requires that it should be thus divided, the weakness of the executive may require, on the other hand, that it should be fortified. An absolute negative on the legislature appears, at first view, to be the natural defense with which the executive magistrate should be armed. But perhaps it would be neither altogether safe nor alone sufficient. On ordinary occasions it might not be exerted with the requisite firmness, and on extraordinary occasions it might be perfidiously abused. May not this defect of an absolute negative be supplied by some qualified connection between this weaker department and the weaker branch of the stronger department, by which the latter may be led to support the constitutional rights of the former, without being too much detached from the rights of its own department?

If the principles on which these observations are founded be just, as I persuade myself they are, and they be applied as a criterion to the several State constitutions, and to the federal Constitution, it will be found that if the latter does not perfectly correspond with them, the former are infinitely less able to bear such a test.

There are, moreover, two considerations particularly applicable to the federal system of America, which place that system in a very interesting point of view.

First. In a single republic, all the power surrendered by the people is submitted to the administration of a single government; and the usurpations are guarded against by a division of the government into distinct and separate departments. In the compound republic of America, the power surrendered by the people is first divided between two distinct governments, and then the portion allotted to each subdivided among distinct and separate departments. Hence a double security arises to the rights of the people. The different governments will control each other, at the same time that each will be controlled by itself.

Second. It is of great importance in a republic not only to guard the society against the oppression of its rulers, but to guard one part of the society against the injustice of the other part. Different interests necessarily exist in different classes of citizens. If a majority be united by a common interest, the rights of the minority will be insecure. There are but two methods of providing against this evil: the one by creating a will in the community independent of the majority—that is, of the society itself; the other, by comprehending in the society so many separate descriptions of citizens as will render an unjust combination of a majority of the whole very improbable, if not impracticable. The first method prevails in all governments possessing an hereditary or self-appointed authority. This, at best, is but a precarious security; because a power independent of the society may as well espouse the unjust views of the major as the rightful interests of the minor party, and may possibly be turned against both parties. The second method will be exemplified in the federal republic of the United States. Whilst all authority in it will be derived from and dependent on the society, the society itself will be broken into so many parts, interests and classes of citizens, that the rights of individuals, or of the minority, will be in little danger from interested combinations of the majority. In a free government the security for civil rights must be the same as that for religious rights. It consists in the one case in the multiplicity of interests, and in the other in the multiplicity of sects. The degree of security in both cases will depend on the number of interests and sects; and this may be presumed to depend on the extent of country and number of people comprehended under the same government. This view of the subject must particularly recommend a proper federal system to all the sincere and considerate friends of republican government, since it shows that in exact proportion as the territory of the Union may be formed into more circumscribed Confederacies, or States, oppressive combinations of a majority will be facilitated; the best security, under the republican forms, for the rights of every class of citizen, will be diminished; and consequently the stability and independence of some member of the government, the only other security, must be proportionally increased. Justice is the end of government. It is the end of civil society. It ever has been and ever will be pursued until it be obtained, or until liberty be lost in the pursuit. In a society under the forms of which the stronger faction can readily unite and oppress the weaker, anarchy may as truly be said to reign as in a state of nature, where the weaker individual is not secured against the violence of the stronger; and as, in the latter state, even the stronger individuals are prompted, by the uncertainty of their condition, to submit to a government which may protect the weak as well as themselves; so, in the former state, will the more powerful factions or parties be gradually induced, by a like motive, to wish for a government which will protect all parties, the weaker as well as the more powerful. It can be little doubted that if the State of Rhode Island was separated from the Confederacy and left to itself, the insecurity of rights under the popular form of government within such narrow limits would be displayed by such reiterated oppressions of factious majorities that some power altogether independent of the people would soon be called for by the voice of the very factions whose misrule had proved the necessity of it. In the extended republic of the United States, and among the great variety of interests, parties, and sects which it embraces, a coalition of a majority of the whole society could seldom take place on any other principles than those of justice and the general good; whilst there being thus less danger to a minor from the will of a majority party, there must be less pretext, also, to provide for the security of the former, by introducing into the government a will not dependent on the latter, or, in other words, a will independent of the society itself. It is no less certain than it is important, notwithstanding the contrary opinions which have been entertained, that the larger the society, provided it lie within a practicable sphere, the more duly capable it will be of self-government. And happily for the *republican cause*, the practicable sphere may be carried to a very great extent by a judicious modification and mixture of the *federal principle*.

PUBLIUS

Appendix 4

The Transition and First Hundred Days of the Bush Administration

On January 20, 1989, George Bush was sworn in by Chief Justice William Rehnquist as the forty-first president of the United States.

AP/Wide World

As you are examining this textbook, I am writing this chapter, The Transition and First Hundred Days of the Bush Administration. This special chapter will be bound into every student copy of the text for fall 1989 and beyond. The publisher will send an advanced copy of the chapter to you later this spring.

Glossary

This glossary is intended to serve as a learning aid. Short definitions are given for all **boldface terms** in the text and other terms common to discussions of American government and politics. These may help you focus on particular terms, but for a full explanation, it is best to consult the text discussion. Some listings in the glossary reflect ideas in the text, though are not necessarily named as such. Text chapter and page references accompany each entry in the glossary.

activists Persons highly involved in politics, for example, by running for public office, working in campaigns, contributing time and money to political causes, etc. *[Ch. 4, pp. 97–99; Ch. 11, p. 379]*

affirmative action A plan or program involving active efforts to overcome past discrimination based on race, ethnicity, or sex, through recruiting more students from the groups that have been discriminated against in the past or by extending employment opportunities to members of these groups. *[Ch. 15, p. 540]*

affluent society A society where national wealth is such that most people are decisively removed from concerns over having enough food, or adequate clothing and shelter. The economic advances in the United States after World War II left much of the country's population clearly beyond subsistence concerns. *[Ch. 2, p. 27]*

amendment Formal changes made in the language of a constitution, or a piece of legislation. The Constitution of the United States has been amended 26 times since the basic document was ratified in 1789. *[Ch. 4, p. 92; Ch. 5, p. 129]*

American exceptionalism The idea, shared by many Americans since the eighteenth century, that their country possessed unique resources, opportunity, and promise. Sociologist Daniel Bell describes the idea: "Having a common political faith from the start, [America] would escape the ideological vicissitudes and divisive passions of the European polity, and, being entirely a middle-class society . . . it would not become 'decadent' as had every other society in history." *[Ch. 4, pp. 69–71]*

amicus curiae (briefs) This Latin term means literally "friend of the court." Individuals or groups, not direct parties to a law suit, sometimes seek to influence the court's judgment by filing a brief—a written argument—setting forth the issues in the case as the group sees them. *[Ch. 11, p. 400]*

anti-federalists Americans who were against adoption of the new Constitution in 1787 and 1788, on the grounds that it established too strong a central government, one which would threaten individual and states' rights. Among the leading anti-federalists were George Mason, Richard Henry Lee, and Patrick Henry of Virginia, and George Clinton and Robert Yates of New York. *[Ch. 4, pp. 80–81]*

appeal A formal legal proceeding in which a party losing a case in a lower court requests a higher court to review aspects of the decision. More specifically, the term refers to cases that may be brought to the U.S. Supreme Court—the country's highest court of appeals—as a matter of right; this includes cases where legislation is declared unconstitutional. Such cases must be heard by the Supreme Court "on appeal." *[Ch. 9, p. 319]*

appellate jurisdiction Judicial authority to review lower court decisions. The Supreme Court and the federal circuit courts of appeal have appellate jurisdiction, and all states have appeals courts to review decisions of lower state courts. *[Ch. 9, p. 318]*

appropriations bills Measures enacted by legislatures granting funds for governmental programs and agencies. Appropriations committees of the House and Senate of the U.S. Congress have the responsibility of drafting appropriations bills for the federal government. *[Ch. 6, p. 192]*

aristocracy The hereditary ruling class in societies built on the premise of ascribing or determining social position by birth. *[Ch. 3, pp. 58–59; Ch. 4, pp. 78–79]*

Articles of Confederation The first constitution of the United States, agreed to by the thirteen original states as the basis for their joint government. Drafted in 1776, the Articles were not ratified by all the states until 1781; they were replaced in 1789 by the United States Constitution. *[Ch. 4, p. 72]*

balance of power In international relations, a relationship where opposing alliances of countries are sufficiently equal that no nation or bloc is able to impose itself on the others. Countries have sometimes sought to maintain an international balance or equilibrium—as Great Britain did in the nineteenth and early twentieth centuries. *[Ch. 19, p. 683]*

bicameralism Refers to a two-house legislature, in contrast to unicameralism, where there is only one house to a legislature. The United States Congress is bicameral, composed of the Senate and House of Representatives, and every American state legislature is bicameral with the exception of Nebraska, which is unicameral. *[Ch. 4, pp. 78–79; Ch. 6, pp. 160–61]*

bilateral aid Foreign economic or military assistance given directly by one government to another. In contrast, multilateral assistance is contributed by a number of countries to some international body, like the United Nations or the World Bank, which then distributes the assistance to less developed nations. *[Ch. 19, p. 684]*

bill of attainder An act of a legislature declaring the guilt of an individual or a group and prescribing punishment without judicial proceeding. Sections 9 and 10 of Article I of the U.S. Constitution forbid Congress and the state legislatures from enacting bills of attainder. *[Ch. 5, p. 131]*

Bill of Rights The first ten amendments to the U.S. Constitution, ratified in 1791, guaranteeing freedom of speech, assembly, religion, and specifying rights of persons accused of crimes. *[Ch. 4, p. 84]*

bipartism A party system where competition for elective office is largely between two contending parties. The United States, where the Democrats and the Republicans dominate government at all levels, is a prime case of bipartism. *[Ch. 11, pp. 393–94]*

"Boll Weevils" Term ascribed in the 1890s to conservative southern Democrats who crossed over party lines to vote with Republicans on various pieces of legislation. *[Ch. 5, p. 114]*

boycott An organized effort to achieve a social, economic, or political objective by refusing to deal with a person, organization, or nation seen as the offending party. Civil rights groups have urged their supporters to boycott products of corporations they consider unsupportive of civil rights objectives, such as equal employment opportunity. *[Ch. 15, p. 553]*

bureaucracy Literally, rule by bureaus or by groups of appointed officials. The term now connotes an administrative system—governmental or private—that carries out policy through standardized procedures and is based on a specialization of duties. This term also sometimes connotes excessive growth and red tape in administrative agencies. *[Ch. 2, pp. 26–27; Ch. 8, p. 258]*

bureaus The major working units of governmental departments or agencies. Bureaus like the Public Health Service of the federal Department of Health and Human Services and the Bureau of Indian Affairs of the Department of the Interior have primary program responsibilities in their respective areas. *[Ch. 8, p. 258]*

cabinet The heads (secretaries) of the thirteen executive departments granted senior status for the breadth and importance of their program responsibilities form an informal group known as the president's cabinet. In parliamentary systems, cabinets have formal statutory responsibilities: the cabinet is collectively the government. *[Ch. 5, p. 119; Ch. 8, pp. 253–55]*

calendar In a legislature, a schedule containing all bills to be considered. In the House of Representatives, when a committee reports out a bill, it is placed on one of five calendars: *union*, for appropriations and revenue legislation; *House*, for nonfiscal public bills; *consent*, for noncontroversial measures; *private*, for legislative measures dealing with specific individuals or groups; and *discharge*, for petitions to remove committees from their jurisdiction over a legislative measure. *[Ch. 6, pp. 165–66]*

capitalism An economic philosophy or type of economy based on private property, in which prices are set in the market place on the basis of supply and demand. *[Ch. 3, pp. 54–56]*

caucus A legislative caucus is the meeting of all members of a political party in a legislature to pick party leaders or decide the party's position on proposed legislation. A nominating caucus, on the other hand, is a meeting of party officials or members to select candidates for an upcoming election. *[Ch. 6, pp. 183–84; Ch. 12, p. 434]*

censorship Governmental restraint on speech or other forms of expression. Supreme Court rulings have distinguished between censorship in the case of political speech (justified in only the most extreme circumstances) and that of certain forms of nonpolitical expression, such as material that might be deemed pornographic (where some forms of censorship can be more readily defended). *[Ch. 15, pp. 574–75]*

certiorari, writ of An order issued by an appeals court to a lower court to transmit the records of a case for review. Most of the cases heard by the U.S. Supreme Court reach it through *writs of certiorari*, authorized by the Judiciary Act of 1925. When at least four of the nine justices conclude a case should be reviewed, *certiorari* is granted. *[Ch. 9, pp. 318–19]*

checks and balances In the American system, the constitutional grant of authority to the executive, legislative, and judicial branches such that each can limit actions of the others. Examples include the president's authority to veto legislation passed by Congress and the Supreme Court's power to invalidate acts of both the executive and legislative branches on grounds of their unconstitutionality. *[Ch. 4, p. 78]*

civil liberties The rights of individuals to the freedoms of expression specified in the First Amendment, and to protection when they are accused of crimes. Civil liberties problems typically involve persons made unpopular by their individual beliefs or actions—rather than by attributes of birth like race or sex. *[Ch. 15, pp. 546–48]*

civil rights For a long time synonymous with the claims of black Americans for nondiscrimination and equal treatment under the laws, civil rights is now seen to encompass all groups in the population that have encountered categoric discrimination, such as other ethnic minorities and women. Membership in groups subject to this kind of discrimination is something over which individuals have no control. *[Ch. 15, pp. 546–48]*

civil service Civilian employees of government who gain their employment through the nonpolitical standards and tests of a merit system. A civil service took shape in the United States following legislative reforms of the late nineteenth century that were designed to end the "spoils system," under which most government workers were political appointees. *[Ch. 8, pp. 273–75]*

class-action suits A lawsuit brought by an individual or group on behalf of all individuals who share a similar grievance. The famous school desegregation case, *Brown v. Board of Education of Topeka, Kansas* (1954), is an example; it was brought not just on behalf of Linda Brown but for all black students in the Topeka public schools. *[Ch. 9, p. 320]*

class conflict Political conflict organized around the contending interests of social classes—such as "capitalists," or business class, and "proletariats," or working class. The term connotes strong tensions or fundamental disagreements among the main economic groups making up the society. *[Ch. 2, p. 32]*

classical liberalism A broad political ideology that developed in Europe in the seventeenth and eighteenth centuries, brought to the United States by the early settlers, and still the dominant cluster of underlying American political beliefs. A strong individualism is central to classical liberalism, including an emphasis on individual rights, political liberty, private property, and a minimum of restraint by government. *[Ch. 3, pp. 57–58]*

"clear and present danger" First propounded by Supreme Court Justice Oliver Wendell Holmes, Jr. in *Schenck v. United States* (1919), this test has been variously applied by the Court to determine the permissible boundaries under which speech may be restricted: "The question in every case is whether the words used are used in such circumstances and are of such a nature as to create a clear and present danger that they bring about the substantive evils that Congress has a right to prevent." *[Ch. 15, pp. 573–74]*

closed primaries Elections in which rank-and-file party members choose the party's nominees, with the requirement that party adherence must be avowed before they can participate. For example, only declared Democrats can vote in a closed Democratic primary. *[Ch. 12, p. 432]*

cloture A parliamentary procedure used to end debate in a legislative body which, like the U.S. Senate, provides in its general rules for unlimited debate. Senate Rule 22 provides that if a petition to end debate on a measure is approved by three-fifths of the Senate (60 senators), no senator may thereafter speak on it for more than one hour. Cloture is necessary because the right to extended debate is sometimes used by legislative minorities to "talk a bill to death." See filibuster. *[Ch. 6, pp. 164–65]*

coalition The coming together of various parties, groups, or political interests to advance shared political objectives. Each of the two major political parties in the United States is a heterogeneous coalition of political interests united to win governmental power. *[Ch. 11, pp. 390–93]*

coattails The capacity of a popular candidate at the head of a party's slate to draw votes for other party candidates on the same ballot. For example, the strong backing for Ronald Reagan in his run for reelection as president in 1984 brought some votes to Republican candidates for Congress and for state and local office that they otherwise would not have had. Many observers think the "coattails effect" is generally weaker now than in the past, because more voters are inclined to split their tickets. *[Ch. 13, pp. 497–98]*

COLAs Acronym for cost-of-living adjustments. Used to describe annual increments in program benefits or wages that adjust for annual rise in cost of living. *[Ch. 5, pp. 116–18; Ch. 8, p. 271]*

cold war The prolonged rivalry and conflict in the years since World War II between the Western democracies and the Communist countries; it is called "cold" because the conflict typically has not extended to the battlefield, has not involved open or "hot" warfare. *[Ch. 19, p. 687]*

commerce clause Article I, Section 8 of the Constitution gives Congress the power "to regulate commerce with foreign nations, and among the several states, and with Indian tribes." Historically, much federal government intervention in domestic economic affairs has been justified on the grounds that the regulation of some facet of interstate commerce was involved. *[Ch. 4, p. 73]*

"Committees of Correspondence" When political parties took shape in the United States in the 1790s, one of the first steps was the establishment of "Corresponding Committees" in support of candidates. These committees were usually appointed for the purpose of helping to elect a favored candidate. Through them, likeminded people in various communities around a state kept in contact and formed a political network. *[Ch. 13, p. 488]*

comparable worth A doctrine or policy perspective advanced with the support of women's groups and some trade unions to remedy inequities in the compensation levels for jobs held disproportionately by women. The doctrine of comparable worth holds that employers should be forbidden from paying employees of one sex at a rate less than that paid employees of the opposite sex for work of "comparable character" on jobs which require "comparable skills." It thus differs significantly from the idea of *"equal* pay for *equal* work," which holds only that men and women must not be paid differently for performing the same job. *[Ch. 15, pp. 576–79]*

concurrent jurisdiction Authority granted to two or more courts to adjudicate cases involving the same subject matter. The term commonly refers to areas where federal and state courts may hear the same kind of case. *[Ch. 9, p. 318]*

confederation An association of independent states, in which the latter agree to confer certain limited authority upon a central government while retaining their full individual sovereignty. The first Constitution of the United States, the Articles of Confederation, provided for such a system; the thirteen states possessed virtually all governmental power, having simply joined together in what the Articles called a "firm league of friendship." *[Ch. 4, pp. 72–73]*

conference committees Special joint committees of the U.S. Congress formed to resolve conflicts in the form of legislation passed by the House and Senate. Since a bill must be passed by both houses in exactly the same form for it to become law, conference committees are essential elements in the legislative process. *[Ch. 6, pp. 167–68]*

consensus General agreement; like views held on certain issues; solidarity of belief. *[Ch. 5, p. 126]*

conservative As used in the contemporary United States, a political philosophy that seeks to limit the role of government in domestic affairs and/or to encourage traditional social values and relationships. In foreign affairs, the term connotes an inclination to favor high levels of defense spending and a "hard-line" foreign policy toward the Soviet Union, *[Ch. 3, p. 57; Ch. 19, p. 693]*

constant dollars The price of goods and services expressed in dollars adjusted to account for the effects of inflation—that is, dollars of constant purchasing power. Unless constant dollar adjustments are made, comparisons of expenditures at one point in time to those at another may be very deceiving. *[Ch. 19, p. 696]*

Constitution A fundamental law that prescribes the framework of government and the nature and extent of governmental authority. The American Constitution treats only the most basic institutional arrangements and powers, and the basic rights of citizenship, leaving it to simple legislation to specify the program details. *[Ch. 4, p. 67]*

containment policy American foreign policy since World War II, aimed at maintaining an international balance of power and curbing the Soviet or Communist expansion. *[Ch. 19, pp. 684–85]*

Court-packing plan The famous attempt by President Franklin Roosevelt in 1937 to secure congressional approval of legislation permitting the president to nominate a new Supreme Court justice for every sitting justice on the Court who, upon reaching 70 years of age, did not retire. Congress rejected Roosevelt's proposal. *[Ch. 5, pp. 124–25]*

dealignment The weakening of voter's loyalties to the political parties, expressed in larger proportions of the electorate calling themselves independents and alternating in their support of one party's candidates and the other's. *[Ch. 13, pp. 485–86]*

***de facto* segregation** Racial segregation in schools resulting not from public policy or design but from the fact of racial concentrations in residence. Thus, if pupils attend schools in their neighborhoods, and the neighborhoods are virtually all black, or all white, school segregation will in fact occur. *[Ch. 15, p. 569]*

deficit The amount by which governmental expenditures exceed revenues. *[Ch. 16, p. 596]*

deflation An economic condition in which the price of goods and services falls—as opposed to *inflation*, which is a rise in the price level. In the 1920s and the 1930s in the United States, there was a dramatic decline in prices, which discouraged investment in new factories and other productive facilities, as businessmen saw the prospect of falling returns on their investment. *[Ch. 16, pp. 592–93]*

***de jure* segregation** Racial segregation based on the law or the formal policies of governmental agencies. Up until the school desegregation decisions of the 1950s, laws throughout the South provided for separate school systems for black and white pupils. *[Ch. 15, pp. 557, 569]*

democracy Derived from the Greek word *demos* (the people) and *kratos* (authority), democracy is a system of government in which ultimate political power rests with the public at large. The American idea of democracy blends rule by the people with an emphasis on the recognition of basic rights of minorities which even strong popular majorities may not infringe. *[Ch. 4, p. 86]*

depression A severe economic slump including high unemployment, a reduced production of goods and services, and a falling national income. The worst of these economic crises in the U.S., known as the Great Depression, began with the stock market crash in 1929 and persisted throughout the 1930s. *[Ch. 16, pp. 592–94]*

deregulation The political movement in the United States in the 1970s and 1980s to reduce the level of governmental regulation, especially of prices and the entry of firms into various markets. Deregulation has proceeded furthest in such industries as trucking, airlines, and banking. *[Ch. 16, pp. 604–7]*

détente A description of efforts to reduce tensions between countries whose contending interests and philosophies leave them antagonistic; specifically, the emphasis on limited cooperation between the United States and the Soviet Union in an effort to reduce the likelihood of overt conflict between the superpowers. *[Ch. 19, p. 690]*

direct-action protests Civil rights marches, sit-ins, boycotts, and other nonviolent actions aimed at overturning segregation and gross discrimination, especially in the American South in the 1950s and 1960s. *[Ch. 15, pp. 553–54]*

direct primary An election in which rank-and-file members of a political party vote to determine who the party's nominees will be. Direct primaries were advanced by the Progressives in the early nineteenth century to weaken the hold of party "bosses" on nominee selection. *[Ch. 4, pp. 94–95]*

discharge petition A legislative procedure, used in the House of Representatives, whereby a committee with jurisdiction over a bill may be relieved of its jurisdiction by majority vote of the entire House. The procedure is used when a committee is seeking to kill a bill by holding on to it and not reporting it out for House action. *[Ch. 6, p. 166]*

discount rate The rate of interest Federal Reserve Banks charge commercial banks for the money the latter borrow from the Fed; the higher the discount rate, the higher the rate of interest commercial banks must in turn charge their customers. *[Ch. 16, p. 615]*

dissenting opinion When judges of appeals courts disagree with a decision of their court's majority, they may express their formal written disagreement. Strong, cogent dissenting opinions by Supreme Court justices have often had lasting influence in helping to reshape thinking on an issue. *[Ch. 9, p. 302]*

district courts (federal) The courts where most cases originating in the federal system are first tried. Federal district courts have "original jurisdiction," as the workhorse trial courts. *[Ch. 9, p. 315]*

double jeopardy The Fifth Amendment to the U.S. Constitution provides that no person shall be "subject for the same offense to be twice put in jeopardy of life or limb"; that is, a person tried for a crime and found innocent shall not be again put on trial for that same offense. The Fifth Amendment originally applied just to cases in federal court, but in 1969 the Supreme Court held the protection against double jeopardy binding on the states through the due process clause of the Fourteenth Amendment. *[Ch. 4, p. 84]*

due process The Fifth and Fourteenth Amendments to the Constitution provide that the national and state governments, respectively, shall not arbitrarily deny any person his life, liberty, or property. The idea of due process has always connoted adherence to proper procedures of action established in law, and at times the Supreme Court has additionally interpreted the term as requiring both the reasonableness of governmental actions and limits on the scope of those actions. *[Ch. 5, p. 131]*

egalitarianism A political-philosophic position that stresses the value of social equality. The "egalitarian revolution" which began in the West in the seventeenth and eighteenth centuries rejected the rigid social hierarchy and inequality inherent in the then-existing aristocratic societies. *[Ch. 3, pp. 62–64]*

electoral college Americans do not vote directly for the candidates for president and vice-president, but rather for slates of electors in each state pledged to one candidate or the other. Each state has a number of electoral votes equal to the number of representatives it has in Congress—its two senators plus however many members of the House of Representatives it has. The candidates receiving a majority of the electoral votes (at least 270) are declared elected president and vice-president. *[Ch. 7, p. 207]*

electronic press Refers to the fact that the electronic media of communication—radio and television—have become primary sources of political information for many Americans. The press is no longer confined to newspapers and news magazines. *[Ch. 14, p. 502]*

elites Groups of persons who possess disproportionately large amounts of some scarce value—money, social prestige, political power, etc. Political elites exert extensive influence over political decision-making. *[Ch. 4, p. 99]*

entitlement programs Government programs requiring the payment of benefits to all individuals who meet the established eligibility requirements set forth in the legislation. Thus expenditures for an entitlement program such as Social Security are determined not by annual appropriations limits established by Congress, but rather by what is required to give all those eligible for benefits the level of monetary payments the law prescribes. *[Ch. 17, pp. 634–35]*

equal employment opportunity The policy that racial, religious, sex, and age discrimination must be barred in hiring and firing employees and setting other conditions of their employment. At the federal level, the Equal Employment Opportunity

Commission is charged with enforcing relevant federal statutes. *[Ch. 15, p. 539]*

equal time rule A provision of Section 315 of the Federal Communications Act of 1934 that requires that broadcasters who permit one candidate for public office to campaign on their stations must give equal opportunity to every other candidate for that office. They cannot sell airtime to a Democratic candidate for the House of Representatives, for example, and deny the same type of time at the same rates to a Republican candidate. *[Ch. 14, p. 512]*

equality of opportunity The political-philosophic position that insists a society should take all reasonable steps to assure its citizens an equal chance to pursue successfully life, liberty, and happiness, but that it should recognize the legitimacy of different levels of actual attainment. *[Ch. 15, p. 542]*

equality of result The position that a society should seek to achieve a condition where each citizen has approximately equal resources—where, for example, salaries are relatively equal. The varieties of socialism seek some measure of equality of result. *[Ch. 17, pp. 625–26]*

establishment clause The First Amendment to the U.S. Constitution provides that "Congress shall make no law respecting an establishment of religion. . . ." It was enacted initially to prevent the creation of an official church or religion in the United States. *[Ch. 4, pp. 90–93]*

exclusionary rule A legal position developed by the Supreme Court requiring that evidence or statements unlawfully obtained may not be used in court proceedings against individuals accused of crimes. *[Ch. 15, pp. 563, 566–68]*

exclusive jurisdiction The assignment to one court only of jurisdiction over a certain category of cases. For example, cases arising from alleged violation of state criminal statutes originate exclusively in the designated trial courts of the state. *[Ch. 9, p. 318]*

ex post facto law Article I, sections 9 and 10 of the Constitution forbid the national and state governments from enacting any subsequent legislation that makes illegal an act that was legal at the time it was committed or that changes the penalty for a crime after its commission. The Latin words mean simply "after the fact." *[Ch. 5, p. 131]*

factions A term used variously in the eighteenth century to refer to what we would now call interest groups, or to loosely organized cliques of like-minded political leaders—in the sense of a "faction" in a state legislature. *[Ch. 4, p. 79; Ch. 11, p. 371]*

fairness doctrine Section 315 of the Federal Communications Act of 1934 requires radio and television broadcasters who air material on controversial issues to provide reasonable time for the expression of opposing viewpoints. *[Ch. 14, p. 511]*

Federal Reserve System The central bank of the United States, including the Board of Governors and the Federal Reserve Banks located throughout the United States, with broad powers to regulate the money supply and interest rates. *[Ch. 16, pp. 614–15]*

federalism A system of government, found in the United States and a number of other countries including Canada, Switzerland, and India, in which power is constitutionally divided between a central government and governments of the constituent states or provinces. *[Ch. 5, pp. 127–49]*

Federalist Papers Eighty-five essays authored by John Jay, James Madison, and Alexander Hamilton, published in New York newspapers in later 1787 and early 1788, defending the newly proposed U.S. Constitution and urging its ratification. *[Ch. 5, p. 89]*

federalists Initially, those who favored ratification of the U.S. Constitution establishing a federal system of government in place of the previous confederal form. Later, a political party whose most prominent leaders were Alexander Hamilton and John Adams, which had its principal supporters among mercantile and other business interests in the Northeast. The Federalist party disappeared early in the nineteenth century. *[Ch. 4, pp. 80–81]*

filibuster An attempt in the U.S. Senate to defeat a bill by taking advantage of the unlimited debate provisions of Senate rules and talking indefinitely on it, preventing action on other legislative business. *[Ch. 6, p. 164]*

fiscal policy Governmental efforts to maintain a prospering economy by varying taxation and expenditure levels. For example, if government increases expenditures well beyond tax revenues, its fiscal policy is providing economic stimulus. *[Ch. 16, 597, 604]*

fiscal year (FY) The twelve-month span in which financial accounting is made. The accounting year of the federal government runs from October 1 to September 30. "FY '88" refers to the fiscal year ending September 30, 1988. *[Ch. 16, p. 596]*

"fourth branch of government" Refers to the prominent position of the press in government and politics in democracies like the United States—such that the press is seen figuratively as a branch of the government itself. *[Ch. 14, p. 525]*

franchise The right to vote. *[Ch. 12, pp. 411–15]*

Frostbelt Refers to the older industrial states of the Northeast and Midwest that have experienced at times painful adjustments with the movement of people and jobs to more newly industrializing (and warmer) states South and West. *[Ch. 2, p. 41]*

full faith and credit Article IV, Section 1 of the U.S. Constitution requires that "full faith and credit shall be given in each state to the public acts, records, and judicial proceedings of every other state." *[Ch. 5, p. 132]*

gender gap A term expressing the differing outlooks and attitudes held by women and men as revealed in voting patterns and aggregate responses to public policy questions. In 1988, men gave Republican George Bush a significantly higher margin of support than did women. *[Ch. 13, p. 484]*

gerrymandering Drawing legislative district lines to obtain partisan political advantage. Some legislative districts have truly bizarre shapes, reflecting a party's efforts to carve the constituency to its advantage. *[Ch. 6, p. 161]*

grants-in-aid Funds appropriated by Congress to state and local governments for various programs administered by state agencies under federal standards: health, welfare, and highway construction programs are important ones built on federal grants-in-aid. *[Ch. 5, p. 141]*

gross national product (GNP) A statistical measure of the total value of goods and services produced in a country in a particular period. Changes in the gross national product of the United States from one year to another are primary indicators of the rate of economic growth. *[Ch. 16, pp. 586–87]*

habeas corpus (writ of) An order of a court requiring officials who have custody of a prisoner to bring the prisoner to court and justify his detention. *[Ch. 4, p. 84]*

ideology A set of political beliefs and values that are constrained or linked together. Political ideologies prescribe answers to such questions as how government should be organized, what roles it should play, how a nation's economy should be managed, the distribution of resources among groups making up the populace, etc. *[Ch. 3, p. 56]*

impeachment The bringing of formal charges of misconduct in office against a public official; the president of the United States and other federal officers may be impeached for "high crimes and misdemeanors" by the House of Representatives, following which a trial on the impeachment charges is held in the Senate. *[Ch. p. 7, 210]*

impoundment The president's holding back funds which Congress appropriated for various stated purposes. Richard Nixon's ambitious use of impoundment in the late 1960s and early 1970s provoked a major confrontation with Congress and led to the passage of important new legislation restricting the president's use of this tool. *[Ch. 6, p. 191]*

incumbency The condition of holding public office. The term has acquired particular significance in recent congressional elections where the extraordinary resources available to incumbents seeking re-election—especially in House races—have given them great advantage over challengers. *[Ch. 13, p. 485]*

independent regulatory commissions Agencies charged with regulation of American economic life, including interstate commerce, banking, and financial affairs, communications, and labor relations. The independent regulatory commissions were set up with the idea that they should be insulated from regular presidential leadership and political direction; commissioners are appointed for long (five years or more), staggered terms, and may be dismissed by the president only for "inefficiency, neglect of duty, or malfeasance in office." *[Ch. 8, pp. 257–58]*

individualism A political and social philosophy that places special emphasis on the rights of individuals and on individual freedom and initiative as the basis for social action. *[Ch. 3, p. 57; Ch. 11, pp. 401–2]*

industrial policy An approach to economic policy in the contemporary United States which blends an emphasis on stimulating economic growth with an enlarged role for government, especially in promoting the conditions for growth. Advocates of industrial policy look to Japan for ideas of a new government-business partnership to stimulate growth industries. *[Ch. 16, pp. 611–12]*

inflation Increases in the price of goods and services. Bouts of "double-digit inflation"—annual increases in consumer prices of 10% or more—in the United States in the 1970s prompted a strong public demand for corrective actions by government. *[Ch. 16, p. 597]*

initiative An electoral procedure through which citizens may propose legislation or constitutional amendments by petitions signed by a requisite number of voters—usually in the range of 5–15% of the total in a state. Propositions receiving the requisite number of signatures are placed on the ballot for decision by majority vote in the next election. *[Ch. 4, pp. 95–96]*

in-kind benefits Benefits in the form of goods and services, rather than cash. For example, welfare programs in the United States often provide beneficiaries with hospital and doctor's care, subsidized housing, food stamps, and other noncash assistance. *[Ch. 17, p. 627]*

interest group A body of people acting in an organized fashion to advance shared political interests. *[Ch. 11]*

iron triangle Refers to the close interaction that often occurs in policy formation in the United States among the executive branch bureau with immediate responsibility for a policy area, the legislative subcommittee that supervises the agency and policy, and the interest groups with immediate stakes in the area. It is the relatively closed nature of these bureau-subcommittee-interest group relationships that led to their depiction as iron-hard. *[Ch. 8, p. 64; Ch. 11, p. 405]*

isolationism A description often given, somewhat erroneously, to American foreign policy prior to World War II, suggesting that the U.S. somehow sought to isolate itself from the rest of the world. In fact, American foreign policy was typically based on the premise that the country should intervene in world afairs as its interests dictate, but that its intervention should *not* be through an established system of alliances. *[Ch. 19, p. 683]*

"Jim Crow" laws The name applied to a body of laws enacted in southern states for a century after the Civil War providing for the segregation of blacks and their exclusion from full participation in social, economic, and political life. *[Ch. 15, p. 552]*

joint committees Legislative committees composed of members of both houses in bicameral legislatures. *[Ch. 6, pp. 67–68]*

joint resolution A resolution voted by both houses of Congress that expresses the sense of Congress but that does not carry the force of law. *[Ch. 6, p. 198]*

judicial activism The broadening intervention of higher courts, especially the federal courts, in policy formation and execution. Advocates of judicial activism endorse this expanded role, arguing that greater juridical protection of individual rights is needed. *[Ch. 9, pp. 312–14]*

judicial review The power of courts, such as the U.S. Supreme Court, to review acts of the legislative and executive branches and, ultimately, to invalidate them if they are held to be in violation of constitutional requirements. *[Ch. 9, pp. 297–301]*

jurisdiction The authority of a court to hear and decide a category of cases. *[Ch. 9, p. 314]*

justiciability The issue of whether courts are institutionally suited to providing remedies in a particular type of case. Is there something that a court can do for a plaintiff if the plaintiff is in the legal right? Does the subject lend itself to resolution by a court of law? *[Ch. 9, pp. 320–21]*

Keynesian economics Economic perspectives and understanding that owe an intellectual debt to the pioneering work of British economist John Maynard Keynes (1883–1946). Present-day Keynesians remain committed to the use of fiscal policy to promote economic growth, and to an expanding welfare state. *[Ch. 16, pp. 589–91]*

laboratories of democracy An allusion to the states as desirable places to test different approaches to solving public policy problems. The concept was elaborated by Justice Brandeis in a famous dissent in *New State Ice Co.* v. *Liebmann* (1932). *[Ch. 5, p. 148]*

"lame duck" Reference to the supposedly weakened political position of a president in his second term, who is barred by the 22nd Amendment from running again. *[Ch. 7, p. 234]*

legislative apportionment The distribution of legislative seats among the states or, more generally, among any set of constituent governmental units. *[Ch. 9, pp. 306–8]*

legislative oversight The attempt by Congress (or by a state legislature) to supervise the executive branch as it administers the laws the legislature has enacted. *[Ch. 6, pp. 191, 195–96]*

legislative veto The president or some executive branch agency is granted authority to act in a given policy or administrative area, but with the stipulation that the subsequent resolution of one or both houses of Congress may overturn the executive action. The constitutionality of the legislative veto under the American system of separation of powers is now under challenge. *[Ch. 6, pp. 196–99]*

libel Publication of a story harmful to the reputation of an individual that can be demonstrated to be untrue. In the United States, before libel may be established in the case of a public official against some news medium, not only defamatory inaccuracy but also malicious intent must be demonstrated. *[Ch. 14, pp. 512–13]*

liberal In contemporary American usage, a position which favors a more expansive use of government in economic management and the promotion of public welfare. Historically, the term refers to classical liberalism—a doctrine developed in Europe in the seventeenth and eighteenth centuries and brought to the U.S. by early settlers, emphasizing individual rights, private property, and limited government. *[Ch. 3, p. 57]*

the "L" word A sometimes whimsical, sometimes sarcastic reference to the term "liberal," coined by Republican campaign strategists in the 1988 presidential elections to criticize the political philosophy of the national Democratic party. *[Ch. 13, p. 484]*

libertarian A political doctrine emphasizing individual liberty as the primary value society should promote and insisting that governmental restraints on individual action be kept to a minimum. *[Ch. 4, p. 103]*

lobbying Refers to the various efforts by interest group officials to influence governmental decisions, especially legislative votes. The term "lobby" was first used in seventeenth-century England, when a large anteroom near the House of Commons was referred to as "the lobby," and those who approached members of Parliament trying to influence them were lobbying. *[Ch. 11]*

machine The American aversion to strong party organizations has led to the use of a number of pejorative terms to refer to them. Strong organizations are "machines," and their efforts at political influence are "machine politics." The nefarious chaps who head these political machines are the party "bosses." *[Ch. 13, pp. 495–96]*

majority leader Usually, the chief spokesman and ranking official of the majority party in a legislature. In the American House of Representatives, however, the Speaker is in fact the leader of the majority party, and the person designated majority leader is in fact his principal deputy and floor lieutenant. *[Ch. 6, pp. 174–75]*

mandamus, writ of A court order requiring an individual corporation, or government official to perform a specified act—fulfilling a contract, meeting his or her clear ministerial responsibilities, etc. *[Ch. 9, pp. 298–99]*

manifest destiny The idea, widely shared by eighteenth- and nineteenth-century Americans, that the country was justified in expanding territorially, because of a special virtue and mission of the American people different from anything known previously. *[Ch. 4, pp. 69–74]*

Marxism An economic and political philosophy derived from the writings of the nineteenth-century German theorist Karl Marx, proclaimed by modern-day Communist countries and movements as their theoretical underpinnings. *[Ch. 4, p. 99]*

the melting pot The idea of America as a land where people of diverse backgrounds come together to form one nation; the achievement of strong American national unity out of diverse backgrounds. *[Ch. 3, pp. 61–62]*

merit system Often used interchangeably with "civil service," a merit system is, specifically, a set of procedures for hiring, promoting, and dismissing government employees on the basis of their professional or technical performance, rather than political preference. *[Ch. 8, p. 273]*

military-industrial complex A term first used by President Dwight Eisenhower, referring to the growth in post–World War II America of a big permanent defense establishment and a large array of business corporations heavily dependent upon defense contracts. *[Ch. 19, pp. 707–8]*

minority leader The leader of the minority party in a legislative body. *[Ch. 6, pp. 174–75]*

"Miranda Rules" A specific set of procedures that the Supreme Court has required law enforcement officials to follow in questioning persons accused of crimes—including the explicit warning to the accused that he has a right to remain silent, that any statement he may make may be used as evidence against him, and that he has the right to the presence of an attorney during any interrogation. *[Ch. 15, pp. 563–65]*

"molecular government" A description of the policy process in the United States as one broken down into a series of relatively small, separate and distinct environments where policies affecting a particular collection of groups or interests are worked out. *[Ch. 11, p. 406]*

monetarism A school in economic thought which places strong emphasis on controlling the money supply and the price of money (the interest rate) to secure a growing and inflation-free economy. *[Ch. 16, p. 609]*

monetary policy Encompasses issues of management of the country's money supply: decisions on how much it should be expanded at any time, and such related matters as interest rates and the ease of borrowing capital. *[Ch. 16, pp. 608–12]*

national interest A concern of paramount importance to a nation's security or well-being. *[Ch. 19, pp. 676–77]*

"necessary and proper" clause The final clause of Article I, Section 8 of the U.S. Constitution gives Congress the authority to enact all laws "necessary and proper" to the carrying out of the specific powers and responsibilities previously enumerated. Because it is so expansive a grant of authority, it is sometimes known as the "elastic" clause. *[Ch. 5, pp. 134–35]*

neutral competence The ideal that civil servants would be seen by their political superiors, and would so see their roles, as sources of policy expertise and administrative skills serving any lawfully constituted government, whatever its political leanings. *[Ch. 8, p. 279]*

the New Deal The administration in the 1930s of Democratic president

Franklin D. Roosevelt and the new programs of economic management and public welfare that his administration developed. [Ch. 3, p. 455]

New Deal realignment The pronounced shift in the standing of the political parties, in which the Democrats replaced the Republicans as the new majority party, on the basis of new policy commitments that secured broad approval. [Ch. 13, p. 455]

North Atlantic Treaty Organization (NATO) An alliance of the United States, Canada, and a number of European nations, established under the North Atlantic Treaty of 1949, as a collective defense to balance the Soviet Union and its East European satellites. [Ch. 19, p. 686]

nullification The extreme States Rights doctrine, espoused by various political leaders including John C. Calhoun, holding that the states retain the right to review actions and laws of the central government and, if need be, to declare them "null and void." [Ch. 5, pp. 133–35]

oligarchy A system of government in which political power is held and exercised by a small elite group, whose position is based on military power, wealth, and/or social position. [Ch. 4, p. 86]

open primary A system of primary elections for choosing party nominees which permits voters to decide on election day which party primary they will participate in without expressing any affiliation with that party. [Ch. 12, p. 432; Ch. 13, pp. 494, 499–500]

opinion of the court The majority opinion handed down by a court of law in a particular case. [Ch. 9, p. 302]

original jurisdiction Authority to adjudicate a case at its inception. The federal district courts are the primary courts of original jurisdiction in the federal system; trial courts in every state have this same responsibility. [Ch. 9, p. 318]

parliamentary government A system of government where authority is vested in the legislature and in a cabinet elected by and responsible to that legislature. At present, the British, Canadian, West German, and Italian governments are examples of the parliamentary form. [Ch. 6, p. 160]

participatory democracy An ideal of democratic government which emphasizes the importance of maximum direct participation in governmental affairs and decision-making by individual citizens. [Ch. 4, pp. 93–94]

party identification Voters' feelings of attachment to or loyalty for a political party. In the United States, where few people hold any formal party membership, the Republican and Democratic parties are seen to be composed of people who simply think of themselves as Republicans or Democrats. [Ch. 13, pp. 457–58]

party platforms Statements of values and programs developed by Democratic and Republican party leaders and delegates at their national nominating conventions. [Ch. 13, pp. 479–80]

party press Early in American history, most newspapers had avowed ties to one political party or the other and, indeed, depended on subsidies from the parties—printing contracts and the like. Far from espousing the ideal of objectivity or neutrality, newspapers saw themselves as spokesmen for the contending parties. [Ch. 14, p. 513]

patronage The granting of jobs, contracts, and other political favors by the party in power. [Ch. 8, pp. 266, 273–75]

Pentagon The huge five-sided office building in Arlington, Virginia, across the Potomac River from Washington, D.C., which is the headquarters of the Department of Defense. *[Ch. 19, p. 708]*

per capita GNP The total dollar value of the country's production of goods and services in a given period of time, divided by the number of people in the country; that is, the level of national economic output expressed on a per-person basis. *[Ch. 16, pp. 586–87]*

plaintiff The person who initiates a law suit in civil law; in criminal law, it is the government that formally brings charges and is known as the prosecution. *[Ch. 9, p. 304]*

pluralism The concept referring to a society as composed of diverse interests and groups which compete to achieve their social and political objectives and share in the exercise of political power—as opposed to a condition of society where one group or set of interests possesses disproportionate political power, to the exclusion of other groups' interests. *[Ch. 4, pp. 101–2]*

plural-member district A legislative district from which two or more representatives are elected; in the United States, the preponderance of legislative districts are of the *single-member* variety. *[Ch. 12, p. 429]*

political action committees (PACs) Organizations formed by business corporations, labor unions, trade associations, ideological groups, and the like to raise and disperse funds for political objectives—including making contributions to candidates for electoral office. The activities of PACs are formally sanctioned and tightly regulated in federal campaign finance legislation. *[Ch. 11, p. 385; Ch. 12, p. 444]*

political culture The general attitudes and values of a people which bear on the conduct of government and politics. *[Ch. 1, p. 4]*

political socialization The introduction of young people to a country's political norms and values—through the family, the press, the schools, etc. *[Ch. 3, p. 56]*

polity Generally, a term meaning "political system"; specifically, a term meaning a type of democratic government with constitutional protection of minority rights. *[Preface; Ch. 4, p. 86]*

poll tax A tax that must be paid in order to vote. Widely used earlier in American history, poll taxes are now held to be unconstitutional. *[Ch. 12, p. 413]*

popular sovereignty The concept which holds that ultimate political authority resides with the general public; synonymous with "government by the people," the idea of popular sovereignty is at the core of democracy. *[Ch. 4, p. 90]*

postindustrial Term referring to socioeconomic conditions which have recently appeared in the United States and a few other economically advanced countries, where the dominant occupational center has moved from manufacturing to the service sector, and where high levels of education and advanced technology contribute to new clusters of political interests as well as to a new dynamic for further economic development. *[Ch. 1, p. 16; Ch. 2]*

power elite A group or cluster of political interests held to exercise disproportionate power; a term introduced by sociologist C. Wright Mills. *[Ch. 4, pp. 99–100]*

power of the purse The historic authority of democratic legislatures to control governmental finance by the requirement that no monies may be expanded without explicit legislative appropriation; Article I, Section 9 of the U.S. Constitution grants the Congress the power of the purse. *[Ch. 6, p. 191]*

president pro tempore The presiding officer of the U.S. Senate in the absence of the vice-president; position conferred on the senator from the majority party who has the greatest seniority in the Senate. *[Ch. 6, pp. 174–75]*

presidential primary Election held for choosing delegates to the Republican or Democratic party's national presidential nominating convention; developed early in the nineteenth century to open up delegate selection to the rank and file of party adherents. *[Ch. 12, pp. 432–33]*

primary election An election held before the general election, in which rank-and-file voters select candidates for the Democratic and Republican party slates; primaries began replacing party organizational bodies—such as state central committees and state conventions—as the instruments of nominee selection early in the twentieth century. *[Ch. 12, p. 432]*

probability sampling Public opinion polls now rely on select respondents through statistical approaches designed to give every individual an equal or known chance of being included in the sample. *[Ch. 10, p. 357]*

progressive taxation Based on the principle that the tax rate should increase as the amount of income increases; the federal income tax is a progressive tax, whereas state sales taxes typically provide for the same rate or percentage of taxation regardless of income. *[Ch. 17, pp. 584–85]*

progressivism A political movement that developed in the United States early in the twentieth century, especially strong in the urban, professional middle classes, which sought governmental reforms to weaken "party bosses" and special interests and to reduce corruption. *[Ch. 4, p. 94; Ch. 11, pp. 403–4]*

proportional representation (PR) Electoral systems based on multi-member districts, where seats are divided among the contending parties in proportion to their percentages of the votes cast. *[Ch. 12, p. 430]*

public-interest group An interest group that seeks collective goods, the achievement of which will not materially benefit the group's members or activists; contrasts with more conventional interest groups based on immediate economic interests; includes groups with environmental objectives, civil liberties goals, etc. *[Ch. 11, p. 379]*

quota sampling A means of selecting respondents in public opinion polls in which quotas of respondents are drawn to match known group distributions in the population—so many men and women, so many young people, so many manual workers, etc. In the U.S., quota sampling has largely been replaced by probability sampling. *[Ch. 10, p. 356]*

quotas The setting of numerical targets for admitting minority-group students or hiring minority employees, with the intent of increasing the representation of groups historically subject to discrimination. *[Ch. 15, p. 542]*

random-digit dialing A means of selecting respondents in telephone surveys that applies the theory of probability sampling. *[Ch. 10, p. 357]*

ranking member The legislator with the greatest seniority on a particular committee of any member of his political party; in Congress the ranking majority party member on a committee typically becomes the committee chairman. *[Ch. 6, pp. 169–73]*

ratification The formal approval of a constitution or compact or amendments thereto. Amendments to the U.S. Constitution require ratification by extraordinary majorities, including three-fourths of all the states. *[Ch. 4, pp. 80–81]*

realignment A major shift in the partisan support of the social groups making up a society and in the lines of conflict over public policy. *[Ch. 13, pp. 455–56]*

reapportionment The redrawing of legislative district lines to reflect changed conditions, typically, in the U.S., to reflect population shifts following each decennial census. *[Ch. 9, pp. 306–8]*

reconciliation A legislative procedure in the U.S. Congress through which a resolution passed by both houses reconciles the specific appropriations for individual programs and agencies with an overall budget ceiling that Congress has set. *[Ch. 6, p. 194]*

referendum An electoral procedure widely used in American state and local governments where rank-and-file voters may approve or disapprove a legislative act; the legislature refers a policy matter or constitutional amendment to the electorate for final action. *[Ch. 4, p. 95]*

regressive taxation Forms of taxation where the tax burden falls disporportionately on low-income persons; the application of sales taxes to food and other necessities, which is done in a few states, is an example of highly regressive taxation. *[Ch. 17, pp. 584–85]*

representative democracy A democratic system in which the public chooses representatives, including legislators, who are charged with working out the details of legislation and policy—as opposed to direct democracy in which the public expresses itself directly on specific policy questions. *[Ch. 4, pp. 89–90]*

republicanism A philosophy of government which holds that institutions and policies should reflect popular wishes, rather than being the province of some elite such as a hereditary aristocracy. *[Ch. 4, p. 89]*

research and development (R&D) Expenditures for scientific research and technological development required for the development of new products, weaponry, medical advances, etc. *[Ch. 2, pp. 21–22]*

revenue-sharing A form of federal grants-in-aid in which federal funds are made available to state and local governments to be used largely at the latter's discretion—subject only to the requirement that they may not be used for programs which discriminate on the basis of race, national origin, sex, age, religion, or physical handicap. *[Ch. 5, pp. 141–42]*

right of rebuttal A provision of Section 315 of the Federal Communications Act of 1934 which involves the right of individuals to respond to personal attacks made on them over radio or television which might be held to damage their reputations. *[Ch. 14, p. 512]*

roll-call vote (or record vote) The vote by a legislature in which the roll of all members of the body is called, or now in which the vote of each member is recorded electronically. *[Ch. 6, p. 174]*

rule A set of provisions issued by the Rules Committee of the House of Representatives which stipulate the conditions under which a bill is debated on the House floor—whether and how subsequent amendments may be introduced, the time limit for debate, etc. *[Ch. 6, p. 164]*

sampling error Refers to the extent to which the results in a sample of respondents in a public opinion survey can be expected to differ from the results that would be obtained if everyone in the population had been interviewed. *[Ch. 10, p. 357]*

secession The extreme states' rights position which argued that the American states retained sovereignty and could leave the government established by the Constitution if they so chose; finally rejected at Appomattox Court House in 1865. *[Ch. 5, p. 134]*

segregation The separation of whites and blacks in public facilities; established by law throughout the states of the American South after the Civil War and survived largely intact up until the 1950s and 1960s. *[Ch. 15, pp. 548–49]*

select and special committees In Congress, committees established to investigate special problems and to report on them to the parent chamber—e.g., the House Select Committee on Aging—and those established to perform special functions for one party or the other in Congress, such as the Republican Senatorial Campaign Committee. *[Ch. 6, p. 168]*

selective incorporation A series of rulings by the U.S. Supreme Court that the various specific guarantees of the first ten amendments to the Constitution, which applied initially only to the federal government, be applied as well against state infringement through the due process clause of the Fourteenth Amendment—that no state may deny any person "life, liberty, or property, without due process of law." *[Ch. 15, p. 561]*

senatorial courtesy The unwritten agreement among senators whereby they will not agree to a president's appointment of various officials, especially federal district court judges, if these nominations are not acceptable to the senator or senators of the president's party from the state where the office is located. *[Ch. 9, p. 323]*

senior executive service (SES) Established by the 1978 Civil Service Reform Act, the SES includes about 8500 executives in the three highest General Service (GS) grades of federal employment and in the top levels of the Executive Schedule; an effort to develop in the U.S. a cadre of skilled, experienced career officials trusted and relied upon by succeeding administrations with contrasting political goals. *[Ch. 8, p. 279]*

seniority Custom long observed in the U.S. Congress whereby many leadership positions, especially committee and subcommittee chairmanships, are assigned on the basis of length of service in Congress or on a particular committee. *[Ch. 6, p. 169]*

separate but equal doctrine A doctrine proclaimed by the Supreme Court in *Plessy v. Ferguson* (1896), permitting segregated facilities for blacks in various states on the pretense that these facilities are equal to those available to whites. "Separate but equal" was overturned by the Supreme Court in a series of decisions in the 1940s and 1950s, especially *Brown v. Board of Education of Topeka* (1954). *[Ch. 9, pp. 303–4]*

separation of powers A central principle of American government whereby governmental power is constitutionally divided among the executive legislative, and judicial branches. *[Ch. 4, p. 79; Ch. 6, p. 160]*

single-member districts Legislative districts from which only a single legislator is chosen, typically by plurality vote. Seats in the U.S. Congress, and in state legislatures, are apportioned on the single-member district basis. *[Ch. 12, p. 429]*

"smokestack chasing" Efforts by states to persuade industries to relocate within their borders by offering incentives, such as tax abatements. *[Ch. 18, p. 669]*

sociopolitical periods Refers to the persistence of underlying social and economic relationships, and their accompanying demands on government, over a span of time. The United States had seen four great sociopolitical periods or settings over the last two centuries: the first running from the 1780s to the 1860s, characterized by rural and agricultural society; the second from the 1870s to the 1920s, distinguished by industrial development; the third from the 1930s to the 1960s, involving a mature industrial base; and the fourth from the 1960s to the present, built around advanced technology, electronic communications, high levels of education and a service economy, known as postindustrialism. *[Ch. 1, pp. 10–11]*

sound bite The condensation of news, views, or issues into a short (e.g., 30 to 60 seconds) TV spot—a style of delivery highly valued by much of the electronic media today. *[Ch. 12, p. 410]*

Speaker The chief presiding officer of the U.S. House of Representatives, who is also the leader of the majority party in the House and elected by that majority; second in line of presidential succession, after the vice-president. *[Ch. 4, pp. 74–75; Ch. 6, pp. 182–83]*

spin A televised interpretation by news analysts of the significance of just-concluded telecasts of public addresses or debates by prominent personages. Public perceptions of "who won" a given presidential campaign debate, are, for example, often colored by such interpretations. *[Ch. 12, p. 449]*

split-ticket voting Ballots cast in which voters support candidates of one party for certain offices while backing the other party's candidates in other contests on the same ballot; split-ticket voting has become increasingly common over the last quarter-century. *[Ch. 15, p. 510]*

spoils system Awarding government jobs to political supporters of the winning party; widely followed in the U.S. until the development of merit civil service systems in the late nineteenth and early twentieth centuries. *[Ch. 8, p. 273]*

"spreading the action" A series of steps taken in the U.S. Congress in the late 1960s and 1970s to strengthen the position of individual representatives—increasing their staffs, enlarging the number of subcommittees, extending subcommittee independence, etc. *[Ch. 6, p. 169]*

standing To bring suit, an individual must show that he has sustained or been threatened with real injury; merely having an interest in a matter is not sufficient to establish standing to sue. *[Ch. 9, p. 320]*

standing committees The permanently established committees responsible for legislation in the various major substantive areas—such as the foreign relations, judiciary, and appropriations committees in the U.S. Congress. *[Ch. 6, p. 167]*

states' rights In the most general sense, those rights and powers reserved to the states in the American federal system; more specifically, the various arguments made historically which emphasize the claims of states against various federal actions. *[Ch. 5, p. 133]*

straight-ticket voting Casting a ballot in which one supports a party's nominees for all of the offices being voted upon. *[Ch. 13, p. 485]*

suffrage The right to vote; gradually extended in the United States in the nineteenth and twentieth centuries, so that now the suffrage extends to virtually all citizens 18 years of age and older. *[Ch. 9, p. 308; Ch. 12, p. 411]*

Sunbelt Refers to the warm-weather states of the South and West that have received substantial in-migrations and economic development over the last quarter-century. *[Ch. 2, p. 41]*

supply-side economics An approach to questions of political economy in the United States which emphasizes the importance of tax cuts and other measures designed to encourage greater individual initiative, investment, and overall economic growth, especially by reducing high marginal tax rates. *[Ch. 16, pp. 609–10]*

supremacy doctrine Article VI of the U.S. Constitution provides that the Constitution and laws enacted by the national government under it are the supreme law of the land, to which state legislation and actions must submit. *[Ch. 5, p. 131; Ch. 9, pp. 283–84]*

third parties In the United States, where two parties have historically dominated electoral contests, all other minor parties. *[Ch. 12, p. 431; Ch. 13, p. 492]*

three-fifths compromise Refers to an agreement reached by delegates to the Constitutional Convention in 1787 over how slaves should be counted in determining how many House of Representatives seats states would get. In general, southerners favored a full inclusion of slaves in the population totals on which representation would be based; northerners argued for a complete exclusion, on the grounds that the southern states had denied slaves their basic rights. In the end the convention compromised, counting toward the total for determining representation a number equal to three-fifths of the slave population. *[Ch. 4, p. 78]*

"Tweedledum and Tweedledee" Refers to the argument that the two major political parties in the U.S. are pretty much alike in their policy commitments; a literary illusion to creations of Lewis Carroll in his *Through the Looking Glass:*

Some say compared to Bonocini
That Mynheer Handel's but a ninny;
Others aver that he to Handel
Is scarcely fit to hold a candle.
Strange all this difference should be
'Twixt tweedle-dum and tweedle-dee.
[Ch. 4, p. 103; Ch. 13, p. 492]

unanimous consent A time-saving procedure used in Congress and other legislative bodies in the adoption of noncontroversial legislation, motions, etc.; "without objection," regular procedures, including roll-call votes, are dispensed with when such noncontroversial measures are being considered. *[Ch. 6, p. 165]*

unemployment compensation Benefits for unemployed workers, first established in the United States at the national level by the Social Security Act of 1936. *[Ch. 17, p. 637]*

unilateralism The dominant approach in U.S. foreign policy until World War II, in which the United States elected to "go it alone" in the sense of avoiding a system of regular alliances with foreign countries. *[Ch. 19, p. 683]*

veto The power of a political executive, such as the president, to kill a piece of legislation by refusing to sign it; the president's veto of bills may be overridden by Congress by a two-thirds vote. *[Ch. 4, p. 79]*

vote of "no confidence" A vote by a parliament declaring lack of support for the government in office, thus forcing the resignation of that government. *[Ch. 5, p. 124]*

welfare state A concept referring to the role of government as a basic provider of individual economic security and well-being; the complex array of social programs developed in many modern societies, in the case of the United States beginning with the New Deal. *[Ch. 17, pp. 621–32]*

whip An assistant floor leader in a legislature, whose responsibilities include trying to persuade his party's legislators to hold to the position the leadership has determined. *[Ch. 6, pp. 174–75]*

white primary To continue to exclude blacks from meaningful electoral participation, even following passage of the Fifteenth Amendment, which forbids states from denying the right to vote on the grounds of race, southern states took the position that primaries were not in fact Fifteenth Amendment covered elections but rather the instruments of parties as private organizations. The "private" Democratic parties of the South then forbade black participation. The white primary was declared unconstitutional by the Supreme Court in *Smith v. Allright* (1944. *[Ch. 12, pp. 413–14]*

yellow journalism Refers to the sensationalism which came to flourish in the American press in the late nineteenth century as publishers such as William Randolph Hearst sought to expand greatly their readership with a stream of color and titillation. *[Ch. 14, pp. 517–18]*

PHOTOGRAPH CREDITS

Index